THE

IMPENDING CRISIS

OF

THE SOUTH:

HOW TO MEET IT.

BY

HINTON ROWAN HELPER,

OF NORTH CAROLINA.

COUNTRYMEN! I sue for simple justice at your hands,
Naught else I ask, nor less will have,
Act right, therefore, and yield my claim,
Or, by the great God that made all things,
I'll fight, till from my bones my flesh be hack'd!—*Shakspeare.*

The liberal deviseth liberal things,
And by liberal things shall he stand.—*Isaiah.*

FIFTIETH THOUSAND.

NEW-YORK:
A. B. BURDICK, No. 145 NASSAU STREET.
1860.

To

HENRY M. WILLIS,

OF CALIFORNIA,

FORMERLY OF MARYLAND.,

WOODFORD C. HOLMAN,

OF OREGON,

FORMERLY OF KENTUCKY,

MATTHEW K. SMITH,

OF WASHINGTON TERRITORY,

FORMERLY OF VIRGINIA,

AND TO THE

NON-SLAVEHOLDING WHITES OF THE SOUTH

GENERALLY,

WHETHER AT HOME OR ABROAD

THIS WORK IS MOST CORDIALLY

DEDICATED

BY THEIR

SINCERE FRIEND AND FELLOW-CITIZEN,

THE AUTHOR.

PREFACE.

If my countrymen, particularly my countrymen of the South, s ill more particularly those of them who are non-slaveholders, shall peruse this work, they will learn that no narrow and partial doctrines of political or social economy, no prejudices of early education have induced me to write it. If, in any part of it, I have actually deflected from the tone of true patriotism and nationality, I am unable to perceive the fault. What I have committed to paper is but a fair reflex of the honest and long-settled convictions of my heart.

In writing this book, it has been no part of my purpose to cast unmerited opprobrium upon slaveholders, or to display any special friendliness or sympathy for the blacks. I have considered my subject more particularly with reference to its economic aspects as regards the whites—not with reference, except in a very slight degree, to its humanitarian or religious aspects. To the latter side of the question, Northern writers have already done full and timely justice. The genius of the North has also most ably and eloquently discussed the subject in the form of novels. Yankee wives have written the most popular anti-slavery literature of the day. Against this I have nothing to say; it is all well enough for women to give the fictions of slavery; men should give the facts.

I trust that my friends and fellow-citizens of the South will read this book—nay, proud as any Southerner though I am, I entreat, I beg of them to do so. And as the work, considered with reference to its author's nativity, is a novelty—the South being my birth-place and my home, and my ancestry having resided there for more than a century—so I indulge the hope that its reception by my fellow-Southrons will also be novel; that is to say, that they will receive it, as it is offered, in a reasonable and friendly spirit, and that they will read it and reflect upon it as an honest and faithful endeavor to treat a subject of enormous import, without rancor or prejudice, by one who naturally comes within the pale of their own sympathies.

An irrepressibly active desire to do something to elevate the South to an honorable and powerful position among the enlightened quarters of the globe, has been the great leading principle that has actuated me in the preparation of the present volume; and so well convinced am I that the plan which I have proposed is the only really practical one for achieving the desired end, that I earnestly hope to see it prosecuted with energy and zeal, until the Flag of Freedom shall wave triumphantly alike over the valleys of Virginia and the mounds of Mississippi.

H. R. H.

June, 1857.

CONTENTS.

CHAPTER I.

CHAPTER II.

CHAPTER III.

CHAPTER VII.

CHAPTER VIII.

CHAPTER IX.

CHAPTER X.

CHAPTER XI.

CHAPTER I

COMPARISON BETWEEN THE FREE AND THE SLAVE STATES.

It is not our intention in this chapter to enter into an elaborate ethnographical essay, to establish peculiarities of difference, mental, moral, and physical, in the great family of man. Neither is it our design to launch into a philosophical disquisition on the laws and principles of light and darkness, with a view of educing any additional evidence of the fact, that as a general rule, the rays of the sun are more fructifying and congenial than the shades of night. Nor yet is it our purpose, by writing a formal treatise on ethics, to draw a broad line of distinction between right and wrong, to point out the propriety of morality and its advantages over immorality, nor to waste time in pressing a universally admitted truism—that virtue is preferable to vice. Self-evident truths require no argumentative demonstration.

What we mean to do is simply this: to take a survey of the relative position and importance of the several states of this confederacy, from the adoption of the national compact; and when, of two sections of the country starting under the same auspices, and with equal natural advantages, we find the one rising to a degree of almost unexampled power and eminence, and the other sinking into a state of comparative imbecility and obscurity, it is our determination to trace out the causes which have led to the elevation of the former, and the depression of the latter, and to use our most earnest and honest endeavors to utterly extirpate whatever opposes the progress and prosperity of any portion of the union.

This survey we have already made; we have also instituted an impartial comparison between the cardinal sections of the country, north, south, east, and west; and as a true hearted southerner, whose ancestors have resided in North Carolina between one and two hundred years, and as one who would rather have his native clime excel than be excelled, we feel constrained to confess that we are deeply abashed and chagrined at the disclosures of the comparison thus instituted. At the time of the adoption of the Constitution, in 1789, we commenced an even race with the North. All things considered, if either the North or the South had the advantage, it was the latter. In proof of this, let us introduce a few statistics, beginning with the states of

NEW YORK AND VIRGINIA.

In 1790, when the first census was taken, New York contained 340,120 inhabitants; at the same time the population of Virginia was 748,308, being more than twice the number of New York. Just sixty years afterward, as we learn from the census of 1850, New York had a population of 3,097,394; while that of Virginia was only 1,421,661, being less than half the number of New York!

In 1791, the exports of New York amounted to $2,505,-465 ; the exports of Virginia amounted to $3,130,865. In 1852, the exports of New York amounted to $87,484,456 ; the exports of Virginia, during the same year, amounted to only $2,724,657. In 1790, the imports of New York and Virginia were about equal ; in 1853, the imports of New York amounted to the enormous sum of $178,270,-999 ; while those of Virginia, for the same period, amounted to the pitiful sum of only $399,004. In 1850, the products of manufactures, mining and the mechanic arts in New York amounted to $237,597,249 ; those of Virginia amounted to only $29,705,387. At the taking of the last census, the value of real and personal property in Virginia, including negroes, was $391,646,438 ; that of New York, exclusive of any monetary valuation of human beings, was $1,080,309,216.

In August, 1856, the real and personal estate assessed in the City of New-York amounted in valuation to $511,-740,491, showing that New-York City alone is worth far more than the whole State of Virginia.

What says one of Virginia's own sons ? He still lives ; hear him speak. Says Gov. Wise :

" It may be painful, but nevertheless, profitable, to recur occasionally to the history of the past ; to listen to the admonitions of experience, and learn lessons of wisdom from the efforts and actions of those who have preceded us in the drama of human life The records of former days show that at a period not very remote, Virginia stood preeminently the first commercial State in the Union ; when her commerce exceeded in amount that of all the New

England States combined; when the City of Norfolk owned more than one hundred trading ships, and her direct foreign trade exceeded that of the City of New-York, now the centre of trade and the great emporium of North America. At the period of the war of independence, the commerce of Virginia was four times larger than that of New-York."

The cash value of all the farms, farming implements and machinery in Virginia, in 1850, was $223,423,315; the value of the same in New-York, in the same year, was $576,631,568. In about the same ratio does the value of the agricultural products and live stock of New-York exceed the value of the agricultural products and live stock of Virginia. But we will pursue this humiliating comparison no further. With feelings mingled with indignation and disgust, we turn from the picture, and will now pay our respects to

MASSACHUSETTS AND NORTH CAROLINA.

In 1790, Massachusetts contained 378,717 inhabitants; in the same year North Carolina contained 393,751; in 1850, the population of Massachusetts was 994,514, all freemen; while that of North Carolina was only 869,039, of whom 288,548 were slaves. Massachusetts has an area of only 7,800 square miles; the area of North Carolina is 50,704 square miles, which, though less than Virginia, is considerably larger than the State of New-York. Massachusetts and North Carolina each have a harbor, Boston and Beaufort, which harbors, with the States that back them, are, by nature, possessed of about equal capacities and advantages for commercial and manufacturing enterprise. Boston has grown to be the second commercial city in the Union ; her ships, freighted with the useful and unique inventions and manufactures of her ingenious artisans and mechanics, and bearing upon their stalwart arms the majestic flag of our country, glide triumphantly through the winds and over the waves of every ocean. She has done, and is now doing, great honor to herself, her State and the nation, and her name and fame are spoken with reverence in the remotest regions of the earth.

How is it with Beaufort, in North Carolina, whose harbor is said to be the safest and most commodious anywhere to be found on the Atlantic coast south of the harbor of New-York, and but little inferior to that? Has anybody ever heard of her? Do the masts of her ships ever cast a shadow on foreign waters? Upon what distant or benighted shore have her merchants and mariners ever hoisted our national ensign, or spread the arts of civilization and peaceful industry? What changes worthy of note have taken place in the physical features of her superficies since "the evening and the morning were the third day?" But we will make no further attempt to draw a comparison between the populous, wealthy, and renowned city of Boston and the obscure, despicable little village of Beaufort, which, notwithstanding "the placid bosom of its deep and well-protected harbor," has no place in the annals or records of the country, and has scarcely ever been heard of fifty miles from home.

In 1853, the exports of Massachusetts amounted to

$16,895,304, and her imports to $41,367,956; during the same time, and indeed during all the time, from the period of the formation of the government up to the year 1853, inclusive, the exports and imports of North Carolina were so utterly insignificant that we are ashamed to record them. In 1850, the products of manufactures, mining and the mechanic arts in Massachusetts, amounted to $151,-137,145; those of North Carolina, to only $9,111,245. In 1856, the products of these industrial pursuits in Massachusetts had increased to something over $288,000,000, a sum more than twice the value of the entire cotton crop of all the Southern States! In 1850, the cash value of all the farms, farming implements and machinery in Massachusetts, was $112,285,931; the value of the same in North Carolina, in the same year, was only $71,823,298. In 1850, the value of all the real and personal estate in Massachusetts, without recognizing property in man, or setting a monetary price on the head of a single citizen, white or black, amounted to $573,342,286; the value of the same in North Carolina, including negroes, amounted to only $226,800,472. In 1856, the real and personal estate assessed in the City of Boston amounted in valuation to within a fraction of $250,000,000, showing conclusively that so far as dollars and cents are concerned, that single city could buy the whole State of North Carolina, and by right of purchase, if sanctioned by the Constitution of the United States, and by State Constitutions, hold her as a province. In 1850, there were in Massachusetts 1,861 native white and free colored persons over twenty years of age who could not read and write; in the same year, the same class of persons in North Carolina numbered 80,083; while her 288,548 slaves were, by legislative enactments, kept in a state of absolute ignorance and unconditional subordination.

Hoping, however, and believing, that a large majority of the most respectable and patriotic citizens of North Carolina have resolved, or will soon resolve, with unyielding purpose, to cast aside the great obstacle that impedes their progress, and bring into action a new policy which will lead them from poverty and ignorance to wealth and intellectual greatness, and which will shield them not only from the rebukes of their own consciences, but also from the just reproaches of the civilized world, we will, for the present, in deference to their feelings, forbear the further enumeration of these degrading disparities, and turn our attention to

PENNSYLVANIA AND SOUTH CAROLINA.

An old gentleman, now residing in Charleston, told us, but a few months since, that he had a distinct recollection of the time when Charleston imported foreign fabrics for the Philadelphia trade, and when, on a certain occasion, his mother went into a store on Market-street to select a silk dress for herself, the merchant, unable to please her fancy, persuaded her to postpone the selection for a few days, or until the arrival of a new stock of superb styles and fashions which he had recently purchased in the metropolis of South Carolina. This was all very proper Charleston had a spacious harbor, a central position, and a mild climate ; and from priority of settlement and business connections, to say nothing of other advantages, she enjoyed greater facilities for commercial transactions than Philadelphia. She had a right to get custom wherever she could find it, and in securing so valuable a customer as the Quaker City, she exhibited no small degree of laudable enterprise. But why did she not maintain her supremacy? If the answer to this query is not already in the reader's mind, it will suggest itself before he peruses the whole of this work. For the present, suffice it to say, that the cause of her shameful insignificance and decline is essentially the same that has thrown every other Southern city and State in the rear of progress, and rendered them tributary, in a commercial and manufacturing point of view, almost entirely tributary, to the more sagacious and enterprising States and cities of the North.

A most unfortunate day was that for the Palmetto State, and indeed for the whole South, when the course of trade was changed, and she found herself the retailer of foreign and domestic goods, imported and vended by wholesale merchants at the North. Philadelphia ladies no longer look to the South for late fashions, and fine silks and satins ; no Quaker dame now wears drab apparel of Charleston importation. Like all other *niggervilles* in our disreputable part of the confederacy, the commercial emporium of South Carolina is sick and impoverished ; her silver cord has been loosed ; her golden bowl has been broken ; and her unhappy people, without proper or profitable employment, poor in pocket, and few in number, go mourning or loafing about the streets. Her annual importations are actually less now than they were a century ago, when South Carolina was the second commercial province on the continent, Virginia being the first.

In 1760, as we learn from Mr. Benton's "Thirty Years' View," the foreign imports into Charleston were $2,662,000; in 1855, they amounted to only $1,750,000! In 1854, the imports into Philadelphia, which, in foreign trade, ranks at present but fourth among the commercial cities of the union, were $21,963,021. In 1850, the products of manufactures, mining, and the mechanic arts, in Pennsylvania, amounted to $155,044,910; the products of the same in South Carolina, amounted to only $7,063,513.

As shown by the census report of 1850, which was prepared under the superintendence of a native of South Carolina, who certainly will not be suspected of injustice to his own section of the country, the Southern states, the cash value of all the farms, farming implements, and machinery in Pennsylvania, was $422,598,640; the value of the same in South Carolina, in the same year, was only $86,518,038. From a compendium of the same census, we learn that the value of all the real and personal property in Pennsylvania, actual property, no slaves, amounted to $729,144,998; the value of the same in South Carolina, including the estimated—we were about to say fictitious—value of 384,925 negroes, amounted to only $288,257,694. We have not been able to obtain the figures necessary to show the exact value of the real and personal estate in Philadelphia, but the amount is estimated to be not less than $300,000,000; and as, in 1850, there were 408,762 free inhabitants in the single city of Philadelphia, against 283,544 of the same class, in the whole state of South Carolina, it is quite evident that the former is more powerful than the latter, and far ahead of her in all the elements of genuine and permanent superiority. In Pennsylvania, in 1850, the annual income of public schools amounted to $1,348,249 ; the same in South Carolina, in the same year, amounted to only $200,600 ; in the former state there were 393 libraries other than private, in the latter only 26 ; in Pennsylvania 310 newspapers and periodicals were published, circulating 84,898,672 copies annually ; in South Carolina only 46 newspapers and periodicals were published, circulating but 7,145,930 copies per annum.

The incontrovertible facts we have thus far presented are, we think, amply sufficient, both in number and magnitude, to bring conviction to the mind of every candid reader, that there is something wrong, socially, politically and morally wrong, in the policy under which the South has so long loitered and languished. Else, how is it that the North, under the operations of a policy directly the opposite of ours, has surpassed us in almost everything great and good, and left us standing before the world, an object of merited reprehension and derision?

For one, we are heartily ashamed of the inexcusable weakness, inertia and dilapidation everywhere so manifest throughout our native section ; but the blame properly attaches itself to an usurping minority of the people, and we are determined that it shall rest where it belongs. More on this subject, however, after a brief but general survey of the inequalities and disparities that exist between those two grand divisions of the country, which, without reference to the situation that any part of their territory bears to the cardinal points, are every day becoming more familiarly known by the appropriate appellation of

THE FREE AND THE SLAVE STATES.

It is a fact well known to every intelligent Southerner that we are compelled to go to the North for almost every article of utility and adornment, from matches, shoepegs and paintings up to cotton-mills, steamships and statuary; that we have no foreign trade, no princely merchants, nor respectable artists; that, in comparison with the free states, we contribute nothing to the literature, polite arts and inventions of the age; that, for want of profitable employment at home, large numbers of our native population find themselves necessitated to emigrate to the West, whilst the free states retain not only the larger proportion of those born within their own limits, but induce, annually, hundreds of thousands of foreigners to settle and remain amongst them; that almost everything produced at the North meets with ready sale, while, at the same time, there is no demand, even among our own citizens, for the productions of Southern industry; that, owing to the absence of a proper system of business amongst us, the North becomes, in one way or another, the proprietor and dispenser of all our floating wealth, and that we are dependent on Northern capitalists for the means necessary to build our railroads, canals and other public improvements; that if we want to visit a foreign country, even though it may lie directly South of us, we find no convenient way of getting there except by taking passage through a Northern port; and that nearly all the profits arising from the exchange of commodities, from insurance and shipping offices, and from the thousand and one industrial pursuits of the country, accrue to the North, and are there invested in the erection of those magnificent cities and stupendous works of art which dazzle the eyes of the South, and attest the superiority of free institutions!

The North is the Mecca of our merchants, and to it they must and do make two pilgrimages per annum—one in the spring and one in the fall. All our commercial, mechanical, manufactural, and literary supplies come from there. We want Bibles, brooms, buckets and books, and we go to the North; we want pens, ink, paper, wafers and envelopes, and we go to the North; we want shoes, hats, handkerchiefs, umbrellas and pocket knives, and we go to the North; we want furniture, crockery, glassware and pianos, and we go to the North; we want toys, primers, school books, fashionable apparel, machinery, medicines, tombstones, and a thousand other things, and we go to the North for them all. Instead of keeping our money in circulation at home, by patronizing our own mechanics, manufacturers, and laborers, we send it all away to the North, and there it remains; it never falls into our hands again.

In one way or another we are more or less subservient to the North every day of our lives. In infancy we are swaddled in Northern muslin; in childhood we are humored with Northern gewgaws; in youth we are instructed out of Northern books; at the age of maturity we sow our "wild oats" on Northern soil; in middle-life we exhaust our wealth, energies and talents in the dishonorable vocation of entailing our dependence on our children and on our children's children, and, to the neglect of our own interests and the interests of those around us, in giving aid and succor to every department of Northern power; in the decline of life we remedy our eye-sight with Northren spectacles, and support our infirmities with Northern canes; in old age we are drugged with Northern physic; and, finally, when we die, our inanimate bodies, shrouded in Northern cambric, are stretched upon the bier, borne to the grave in a Northern carriage, entombed with a Northern spade, and memorized with a Northern slab!

But it can hardly be necessary to say more in illustration of this unmanly and unnational dependence, which is so glaring that it cannot fail to be apparent to even the most careless and superficial observer. All the world sees, or ought to see, that in a commercial, mechanical, manufactural, financial, and literary point of view, we are as helpless as babes; that, in comparison with the Free States, our agricultural resources have been greatly exaggerated, misunderstood and mismanaged; and that, instead of cultivating among ourselves a wise policy of mutual assistance and co-operation with respect to individuals, and of self-reliance with respect to the South at large, instead of giving countenance and encouragement to the industrial enterprises projected in our midst, and instead of building up, aggrandizing and beautifying our own States, cities and towns, we have been spending our substance at the North, and are daily augmenting and strengthening the very power which now has us so completely under its thumb.

It thus appears, in view of the preceding statistical facts and arguments, that the South, at one time the superior of the North in almost all the ennobling pursuits and conditions of life, has fallen far behind her competitor, and now ranks more as the dependency of a mother country than as the equal confederate of free and independent States. Following the order of our task, the next duty that devolves upon us is to trace out the causes which have conspired to bring about this important change, and to place on record the reasons, as we understand them,

WHY THE NORTH HAS SURPASSED THE SOUTH.

And now that we have come to the very heart and soul of our subject, we feel no disposition to mince matters, but mean to speak plainly, and to the point, without any equivocation, mental reservation, or secret evasion whatever. The son of a venerated parent, who, while he lived, was a considerate and merciful slaveholder, a native of the South, born and bred in North Carolina, of a family whose home has been in the valley of the Yadkin for nearly a century and a half, a Southerner by instinct and by all the influences of thought, habits, and kindred, and with the desire and fixed purpose to reside permanently within the limits of the South, and with the expectation of dying there also—we feel that we have the right to express our opinion, however humble or unimportant it may be, on any and every question that affects the public good; and, so help us God, "sink or swim, live or die, survive or perish," we are determined to exercise that right with manly firmness, and without fear, favor or affection.

And now to the point. In our opinion, an opinion which has been formed from data obtained by assiduous researches, and comparisons, from laborious investigation, logical reasoning, and earnest reflection, the causes which have impeded the progress and prosperity of the South, which have dwindled our commerce, and other similar pursuits, into the most contemptible insignificance; sunk a large majority of our people in galling poverty and ignorance, rendered a small minority conceited and tyrannical, and driven the rest away from their homes; entailed upon us a humiliating dependence on the Free States; disgraced us in the recesses of our own souls, and brought us under reproach in the eyes of all civilized and enlightened nations—may all be traced to one common source, and there find solution in the most hateful and horrible word, that was ever incorporated into the vocabulary of human economy—*Slavery!*

Reared amidst the institution of slavery, believing it to be wrong both in principle and in practice, and having seen and felt its evil influences upon individuals, communities and states, we deem it a duty, no less than a privilege, to enter our protest against it, and to use our most strenuous efforts to overturn and abolish it! Then we are an abolitionist? Yes! not merely a freesoiler, but an abolitionist, in the fullest sense of the term. We are not only in favor of keeping slavery out of the territories, but, carrying our opposition to the institution a step further, we here unhesitatingly declare ourself in favor of its immediate and unconditional abolition, in every state in this confederacy, where it now exists! Patriotism makes us a freesoiler; state pride makes us an emancipationist; a profound sense of duty to the South makes us an abolitionits; a reasonable degree of fellow feeling for the negro, makes us a colonizationist. With the free state men in Kanzas and Nebraska, we sympathize with all our heart We love the whole country, the great family of states and territories, one and inseparable, and would have the word Liberty engraved as an appropriate and truthful motto, on the escutcheon of every member of the confederacy. We love freedom, we hate slavery, and rather than give up the one or submit to the other, we will forfeit the pound of flesh nearest our heart. Is this sufficiently explicit and categorical? If not, we hold ourself in readiness at all times, to return a prompt reply to any proper question that may be propounded.

Our repugnance to the institution of slavery, springs from no one-sided idea, or sickly sentimentality. We have not been hasty in making up our mind on the subject; we have jumped at no conclusions; we have acted with perfect calmness and deliberation; we have carefully considered, and examined the reasons for and against the institution, and have also taken into account the propable consequences of our decision. The more we investigate the matter, the deeper becomes the conviction that we are right; and with this to impel and sustain us, we pursue our labor with love, with hope, and with constantly renewing vigor

That we shall encounter opposition we consider as certain; perhaps we may even be subjected to insult and violence. From the conceited and cruel oligarchy of the South, we could look for nothing less. But we shall shrink from no responsibility, and do nothing unbecoming a man; we know how to repel indignity, and if assaulted, shall not fail to make the blow recoil upon the aggressor's head. The road we have to travel may be a rough one, but no impediment shall cause us to falter in our course. The line of our duty is clearly defined, and it is our intention to follow it faithfully, or die in the attempt.

But, thanks to heaven, we have no ominous forebodings of the result of the contest now pending between Liberty and Slavery in this confederacy. Though neither a prophet nor the son of a prophet, our vision is sufficiently penetrative to divine the future so far as to be able to see that the "peculiar institution" has but a short, and, as heretofore, inglorious existence before it. Time, the righter of every wrong, is ripening events for the desired consummation of our labors and the fulfillment of our cherished hopes. Each revolving year brings nearer the inevitable crisis. The sooner it comes the better; may heaven, through our humble efforts, hasten its advent.

The first and most sacred duty of every Southerner, who has the honor and the interest of his country at heart, is to declare himself an unqualified and uncompromising abolitionist. No conditional or half-way declaration will avail; no mere threatening demonstration will succeed. With those who desire to be instrumental in bringing about the triumph of liberty over slavery, there should be neither evasion vacillation, nor equivocation. We should listen to no modifying terms or compromises that may be proposed by the proprietors of the unprofitable and ungodly institution. Nothing short of the complete abolition of slavery can save the South from falling into the vortex of utter ruin. Too long have we yielded a submissive obedience to the tyrannical domination of an inflated oligarchy; too long have we tolerated their arrogance and self-conceit; too long have we submitted to their unjust and savage exactions. Let us now wrest from them the sceptre of power, establish liberty and equal rights throughout the land, and henceforth and forever guard our legislative halls from the pollutions and usurpations of pro-slavery demagogues.

We have stated, in a cursory manner, the reasons, as we understand them, why the North has surpassed the South, and have endeavored to show, we think successfully, that the political salvation of the South depends upon the speedy and unconditional abolition of slavery. We will not, however, rest the case exclusively on our own arguments, but will again appeal to incontrovertible facts and statistics to sustain us in our conclusions. But before we do so, we desire to fortify ourself against a charge that is too frequently made by careless and superficial readers. We allude to the objections so often urged against the use of tabular statements and statistical facts It is worthy of note, however, that those objections never come from thorough scholars or profound thinkers. Among the majority of mankind, the science of statistics is only beginning to be appreciated; when well understood, it will be recognized as one of the most important branches of knowledge, and, as a matter of course, be introduced and taught as an indispensable element of practical education in all our principal institutions of learning. One of the most vigorous and popular transatlantic writers of the day, Wm. C. Taylor, LL.D., of Dublin, says :

"The cultivation of statistics must be the source of all future improvement in the science of political economy, because it is to the table of the statistician that the economist must look for his facts ; and all speculations not founded upon facts, though they may be admired and applauded when first propounded, will, in the end, assuredly be forgotten. Statistical science may almost be regarded as the creation of this age. The word statistics was invented in the middle of the last century by a German professor,* to express a summary view of the physical, moral, and social conditions of States ; he justly remarked, that a numerical statement of the extent, density of population, imports, exports, revenues, etc., of a country, more perfectly explained its social condition than general statements, however graphic or however accurate. When such statements began to be collected, and exhibited in a popular form, it was soon discovered that the political and economical sciences were likely to gain the position of physical sciences ; that is to say, they were about to obtain records of observation, which would test the accuracy of recognized principles, and lead to the discovery of new modes of action. But the great object of this new science is to lead to the knowledge of human nature ; that

* Achenwall, a native of Elbing, Prussia. Born 1719, died 1792

is, to ascertain the general course of operation of man's mental and moral faculties, and to furnish us with a correct standard of judgment, by enabling us to determine the average amount of the past as a guide to the average probabilities of the future. This science is yet in its infancy, but has already produced the most beneficial effects. The accuracy of the tables of life have rendered the calculations of rates of insurance a matter of much greater certainty than they were heretofore; the system of keeping the public accounts has been simplified and improved; and finally, the experimental sciences of medicine and political economy, have been fixed on a firmer foundation than could be anticipated in the last century. Even in private life this science is likely to prove of immense advantage, by directing attention to the collection and registration of facts, and thus preventing the formation of hasty judgments and erroneous conclusions."

The compiler, or rather the superintendent of the seventh United States census, Prof. De Bow, a gentleman of more than ordinary industry and practical learning, who, in his excellent Review, has, from time to time, displayed much commendable zeal in his efforts to develop the industrial resources of the Southern and South-western states, and who is, perhaps, the greatest statistician in the country, says:—

"Statistics are far from being the barren array of figures ingeniously and laboriously combined into columns and tables, which many persons are apt to suppose them. They constitute rather the ledger of a nation, in which, like the merchant in his books, the citizen can read, at one view, all of the results of a year or of a period of years, as compared with other periods, and deduce the profit or the loss which has been made, in morals, education, wealth or power."

Impressed with a sense of the propriety of introducing, in this as well as in the succeeding chapters of our work, a number of tabular statements exhibiting the comparative growth and prosperity of the free and slave states, we have deemed it eminently proper to adduce the testimony of these distinguished authors in support of the claims which official facts and accurate statistics lay to our consideration. And here we may remark that the statistics which we propose to offer, like those already given, have been obtained from official sources, and may, therefore, be relied on as correct. The object we have in view in making a free use of facts and figures, if not already apparent, will soon be understood. It is not so much in its moral and religious aspects that we propose to discuss the question of slavery, as in its social and political character and influences. To say nothing of the sin and the shame of slavery, we believe it is a most expensive and unprofitable institution; and if our brethren of the South will but throw aside their unfounded prejudices and preconceived opinions, and give us a fair and patient hearing, we feel confident that we can bring them to the same conclusion. Indeed, we believe we shall be enabled—not alone by our own contributions, but with the aid of incontestable facts and arguments which we shall introduce from other sources—to convince all true-hearted, candid and intelligent Southerners, who may chance to read our book, (and we hope their name may be legion) that slavery, and nothing but slavery, has retarded the progress and prosperity of our portion of the Union ; depopulated and impoverished our cities by forcing the more industrious and enterprising natives of the soil to emigrate to the free states ; brought our domain under a sparse and inert population by preventing foreign immigration ; made us tributary to the North, and reduced us to the humiliating condition of mere provincial subjects in fact, though not in name. We believe, moreover, that every patriotic Southerner thus convinced will feel it a duty he owes to himself, to his country, and to his God, to become a thorough, inflexible, practical abolitionist. So mote it be !

Now to our figures. Few persons have an adequate idea of the important part the cardinal numbers are now playing in the cause of Liberty. They are working wonders in the South. Intelligent, business men, from the Chesapeake to the Rio Grande, are beginning to see that slavery, even in a mercenary point of view, is impolitic, because it is unprofitable. Those unique, mysterious little Arabic sentinels on the watch-towers of political economy, 1, 2, 3, 4, 5, 6, 7, 8, 9, 0, have joined forces, allied themselves to the powers of freedom, and are hemming in and combatting the institution with the most signal success. If let alone, we have no doubt the digits themselves would soon terminate the existence of slavery ; but we do not mean to let them alone ; they must not have all the honor of annihilating the monstrous iniquity. We want to become an auxiliary in the good work, and facilitate it. The liberation of five millions of "poor white trash" from the second degree of slavery, and of three millions of miserable kidnapped negroes from the first degree, cannot be accomplished too soon. That it was not accomplished many years ago is our misfortune. It now behooves us to take a bold and determined stand in defence of the inalienable rights of ourselves and of our fellow men, and to avenge the multiplicity of wrongs, social and political, which we have suffered at the hands of a villainous oligarchy. It is madness to delay. We cannot be too hasty in carrying out our designs. Precipitance in this matter is an utter impossibility. If to-day we could emancipate all the slaves in the Union, we would do it, and the country and everybody in it would be vastly better off to-morrow. Now is the time for action ; let us work.

By taking a sort of inventory of the agricultural products of the free and slave States in 1850, we now propose to correct a most extraordinary and mischievous error into which the people of the South have unconsciously fallen. Agriculture, it is well known, is the sole boast of the South ; and, strange to say, many pro-slavery Southerners, who, in our latitude, pass for intelligent men, are so puffed up with the idea of our importance in this respect, that they speak of the North as a sterile region, unfit for cultivation, and quite dependent on the South for the necessaries of life ! Such rampant ignorance ought to be knocked in the head ! We can prove that the North produces greater quantities of bread-stuffs than the South ! Figures shall show the facts. Properly, the South has nothing left to boast of ; the North has surpassed her in everything, and is going farther and farther ahead of her every day.

We ask the reader's careful attention to the following tables, which we have prepared at no little cost of time and trouble, and which, when duly considered in connection with the foregoing and subsequent portions of our work, will, we believe, carry conviction to the mind that the downward tendency of the South can be arrested only by the abolition of slavery.

TABLE NO. I.

AGRICULTURAL PRODUCTS OF THE FREE STATES—1850.

States.	Wheat, bushels.	Oats, bushels.	Indian Corn, bushels.
California	17,228		12,236
Connecticut	41,762	1,258,738	1,935,043
Illinois	9,414,575	10,087,241	57,646,984
Indiana	6,214,458	5,655,014	52,964,363
Iowa	1,530,581	1,524,345	8,656,799
Maine	296,259	2,181,037	1,750,056
Massachusetts	31,211	1,165,146	2,345,490
Michigan	4,925,889	2,866,056	5,641,420
New Hampshire	185,658	973,381	1,573,670
New Jersey	1,601,190	3,378,063	8,759,704
New York	13,121,498	26,552,814	17,858,400
Ohio	14,487,351	13,472,742	59,078,695
Pennsylvania	15,367,691	21,538,156	19,835,214
Rhode Island	49	215,232	539,201
Vermont	535,955	2,307,734	2,032,396
Wisconsin	4,286,131	3,414,672	1,988,979
	72,157,486	96,590,371	242,618,650

TABLE NO. II.

AGRICULTURAL PRODUCTS OF THE SLAVE STATES—1850.

States.	Wheat, bushels.	Oats, bushels.	Indian Corn, bushels.
Alabama	294,044	2,965,696	28,754,048
Arkansas	199,639	656,183	8,893,939
Delaware	482,511	604,518	3,145,542
Florida	1,027	66,586	1,996,809
Georgia	1,088,534	3,820,044	30,080,099
Kentucky	2,142,822	8,201,311	58,672,591
Louisiana	417	89,637	10,266,373
Maryland	4,494,680	2,242,151	10,749,858
Mississippi	137,990	1,503,288	22,446,552
Missouri	2,981,652	5,278,079	36,214,537
North Carolina	2,130,102	4,052,078	27,941,051
South Carolina	1,066,277	2,322,155	16,271,454
Tennessee	1,619,386	7,703,086	52,276,223
Texas	41,729	199,017	6,028,876
Virginia	11,212,616	10,179,144	35,254,319
	27,904,476	49,882,979	348,992,282

TABLE NO. III.

AGRICULTURAL PRODUCTS OF THE FREE STATES—1850.

States.	Potatoes, (I. & S.) bush.	Rye, bushels.	Barley, bushels.
California	10,292		9,712
Connecticut	2,689,805	600,893	19,099
Illinois	2,672,294	83,364	110,795
Indiana	2,285,048	78,792	45,483
Iowa	282,363	19,916	25,093
Maine	3,436,040	102,916	151,731
Massachusetts	3,585,384	481,021	112,385
Michigan	2,361,074	105,871	75,249
New Hampshire	4,307,919	183,117	70,256
New Jersey	3,715,251	1,255,578	6,492
New York	15,403,997	4,148,182	3,585,059
Ohio	5,245,760	425,918	354,358
Pennsylvania	6,032,904	4,805,160	165,584
Rhode Island	651,029	26,409	18,875
Vermont	4,951,014	176,233	42,150
Wisconsin	1,402,956	81,253	209,692
	59,033,170	12,574,623	5,002,013

TABLE NO. IV.

AGRICULTURAL PRODUCTS OF THE SLAVE STATES—1850.

States.	Potatoes, (I. & S.) bush.	Rye, bushels.	Barley, bushels.
Alabama	5,721,205	17,261	3,958
Arkansas	981,981	8,047	177
Delaware	305,985	8,066	56
Florida	765,054	1,152	
Georgia	7,213,807	53,750	11,501
Kentucky	2,490,666	415,073	95,343
Louisiana	1,524,085	475	
Maryland	973,932	226,014	745
Mississippi	5,003,277	9,606	228
Missouri	1,274,511	44,268	9,631
North Carolina	5,716,027	229,563	2,735
South Carolina	4,473,960	43,790	4,583
Tennessee	3,845,560	89,137	2,737
Texas	1,426,803	3,108	4,776
Virginia	3,130,567	458,930	25,437
	44,847,420	1 608,240	161,907

TABLE NO. V.

AGRICULTURAL PRODUCTS OF THE FREE STATES—1850.

States.	Buckwheat, bushels.	Beans & Peas, bushels.	Clov. & Grass seeds, bush.
California		2,292	
Connecticut	229,297	19,090	30,469
Illinois	184,509	82,814	17,807
Indiana	149,740	35,773	30,271
Iowa	52,516	4,475	2,438
Maine	104,523	205,541	18,311
Massachusetts	105,895	43,709	6,087
Michigan	472,917	74,254	26,274
New Hampshire	65,265	70,856	8,900
New Jersey	878,934	14,174	91,331
New York	3,183,955	741,546	184,715
Ohio	638,060	60,168	140,501
Pennsylvania	2,193,692	55,231	178,943
Rhode Island	1,245	6,846	5,036
Vermont	209,819	104,649	15,696
Wisconsin	79,878	20,657	5,486
	8,550,245	1 542,295	762,265

TABLE NO. VI.

AGRICULTURAL PRODUCTS OF THE SLAVE STATES—1850.

States.	Buckwheat, bushels.	Beans & Peas, bushels.	Clov. & Grass seeds, bush.
Alabama	348	892,701	685
Arkansas	175	285,738	526
Delaware	8,615	4,120	3,928
Florida	55	135,359	2
Georgia	250	1,142,011	560
Kentucky	16,097	202,574	24,711
Louisiana	3	161,732	99
Maryland	103,671	12,816	17,778
Mississippi	1,121	1,072,757	617
Missouri	23,641	46,017	4,965
North Carolina	16,704	1,584,252	1,851
South Carolina	283	1,026,900	406
Tennessee	19,427	369,321	14,214
Texas	59	179,351	10
Virginia	214,898	521,579	53,155
	405,357	7,637,227	123,517

TABLE NO. VII.

AGRICULTURAL PRODUCTS OF THE FREE STATES—1850.

States.	Flaxseed, bushels.	Val. of Garden products.	Val. of Orchard prod'ts
California		$75,275	$17,700
Connecticut	703	196,874	175,118
Illinois	10,787	127,494	446,049
Indiana	36,888	72,864	324,940
Iowa	1,959	8,848	8,434
Maine	580	122,387	342,865
Massachusetts	72	600,020	463,995
Michigan	519	14,738	132,650
New Hampshire	189	56,810	248,560
New Jersey	16,525	475,242	607,268
New York	57,963	912,047	1,761,950
Ohio	188,880	214,004	695,921
Pennsylvania	41,728	688,714	723,389
Rhode Island		98,298	63,994
Vermont	939	18,853	315,255
Wisconsin	1,191	32,142	4,823
	358,923	$3,714,605	$6,332,914

TABLE NO. VIII.

AGRICULTURAL PRODUCTS OF THE SLAVE STATES—1850.

States.	Flaxseed, bushels.	Val. of Garden products.	Val. of Orchard prod'ts.
Alabama	69	$84,821	$15,408
Arkansas	321	17,150	40.141
Delaware	904	12,714	46,574
Florida		8,721	1,280
Georgia	622	76,500	92,776
Kentucky	75,801	303,120	106.230
Louisiana		148,329	22.259
Maryland	2,446	200,869	164,051
Mississippi	26	46,250	50,405
Missouri	13,696	99,454	514.711
North Carolina	38,196	39,462	34.348
South Carolina	55	47,286	35.108
Tennessee	18,904	97,183	52 894
Texas	26	12,354	12.505
Virginia	52,318	183,047	177,137
	203,484	$1,377,260	$1,355,827

RECAPITULATION—FREE STATES.

Wheat............	72,157,486	bush.	@	1.50......	$108,236,229
Oats.............	96,590,371	"	"	40.......	38,636,148
Indian Corn.......	242,618,650	"	"	60.......	145,571,190
Potatoes (I. & S.).	59,033,170	"	"	38.......	22,432,604
Rye..............	12,574,623	"	"	1.00.......	12,574,623
Barley...........	5,002,013	"	"	90.......	4,501,811
Buckwheat.......	8,550,245	"	"	50.......	4,275,122
Beans & Peas.....	1,542,295	"	"	1.75.......	2,699,015
Clov. & Grass seeds	762,265	"	"	3.00.......	2,286,795
Flax Seeds.......	358,923	"	"	1.25.......	448,647
Garden Products..				....	3,714,605
Orchard Products.				....	6,332,914
Total,......	499,190,041	bushels, valued as above, at			$351,709,703

RECAPITULATION—SLAVE STATES.

Wheat............	27,904,476	bush.	@	1.50......	$ 41,856,714
Oats.............	49,882,799	"	"	40.......	19,953,191
Indian Corn.......	348,992,282	"	"	60.......	209,395,369
Potatoes (I. & S.).	44,847,420	"	"	38.......	17,042,019
Rye..............	1,608,240	"	"	1.00.......	1,608,240
Barley...........	161,907	"	"	90.......	145,716
Buckwheat.......	405,357	"	"	50.......	202,678
Beans & Peas.....	7,637,227	"	"	1.75.......	13,365,147
Clov. & Grass seeds	123,517	"	"	3.00.......	370,551
Flax Seeds.......	203,484	"	"	1.25.......	254,355
Garden Products..				....	1,377,260
Orchard Products.				....	1,355,827
Total.......	481,766,889	bushels, valued as above, at			$306,927,067

TOTAL DIFFERENCE—BUSHEL-MEASURE PRODUCTS.

	Bushels.		Value.
Free States.........	499,190,041	....	$351,709,703
Slave States........	481,766,889	....	306,927,067
Balance in bushels	17,423,152	Difference in value...	$44,782,636

So much for the boasted agricultural superiority of the South! Mark well the balance in bushels, and the difference in value! Is either in favor of the South? No! Are both in favor of the North? Yes! Here we have unquestionable proof that of all the bushel-measure products of the nation, the free states produce far more than one-half; and it is worthy of particular mention, that *the excess of Northern products is of the most valuable kind.* The account shows a balance against the South, in favor of the North, of *seventeen million four hundred and twenty-three thousand one hundred and fifty-two bushels,* and a difference in value of *forty-four million seven hundred and eighty-two thousand six hundred and thirty-six dollars.* Please bear these facts in mind, for, in order to show positively how the free and slave States do stand upon the great and important subject of rural economy, we intend to take an account of all the other products of the soil, of the live-stock upon farms, of the animals slaughtered, and, in fact, of every item of husbandry of the two sections; and if, in bringing our tabular exercises to a close, we find slavery gaining upon freedom—a thing it has never yet been known to do—we shall, as a matter of course, see that the above amount is transferred to the credit of the side to which it of right belongs.

In making up these tables we have two objects in view; the first is to open the eyes of the non-slaveholders of the South, to the system of deception, that has so long been practiced upon them, and the second is to show slaveholders themselves—we have reference only to those who are not too perverse, or ignorant, to perceive naked truths

—that free labor is far more respectable, profitable, and productive, than slave labor. In the South, unfortunately, no kind of labor is either free or respectable. Every white man who is under the necessity of earning his bread, by the sweat of his brow, or by manual labor, in any capacity, no matter how unassuming in deportment, or exemplary in morals, is treated as if he was a loathsome beast, and shunned with the utmost disdain. His soul may be the very seat of honor and integrity, yet without slaves—himself a slave—he is accounted as nobody, and would be deemed intolerably presumptuous, if he dared to open his mouth, even so wide as to give faint utterance to a three-lettered monosyllable, like yea or nay, in the presence of an august knight of the whip and the lash.

There are few Southerners who will not be astonished at the disclosures of these statistical comparisons, between the free and the slave States. That the astonishment of the more intelligent and patriotic non-slaveholders will be mingled with indignation, is no more than we anticipate. We confess our own surprise, and deep chagrin, at the result of our investigations. Until we examined into the matter, we thought and hoped the South was really ahead of the North in *one* particular, that of agriculture; but our thoughts have been changed, and our hopes frustrated, for instead of finding ourselves the possessors of a single advantage, we behold our dear native South stripped of every laurel, and sinking deeper and deeper in the depths of poverty and shame; while, at the same time, we see the North, our successful rival, extracting and absorbing the few elements of wealth yet remaining amongst us, and rising higher and higher in the scale of fame, fortune, and invulnerable power. Thus our disappointment gives way to a feeling of intense mortification, and our soul involuntarily, but justly, we believe, cries out for retribution against the treacherous, slave-driving legislators, who have so basely and unpatriotically neglected the interests of their poor white constituents and bargained away the rights of posterity. Notwithstanding the fact that the white non-slaveholders of the South, are in the majority, as five to one, they have never yet had any part or lot in framing the laws under which they live. There is no legislation except for the benefit of slavery, and slaveholders. As a general rule, poor white persons are regarded with less esteem and attention than negroes, and though the condition of the latter is wretched beyond description, vast numbers of the former are infinitely worse off. A cunningly devised mockery of freedom is guarantied to them, and that is all. To all intents and purposes they are disfranchised, and outlawed, and the only privilege extended to them, is a shallow and circumscribed participation in the political movements that usher slaveholders into office.

We have not breathed away seven and twenty years in the South, without becoming acquainted with the demagogical manœuverings of the oligarchy. Their intrigues and tricks of legerdemain are as familiar to us as household words; in vain might the world be ransacked for a more precious junto of flatterers and cajolers It is amusing to ignorance, amazing to credulity, and insulting to intelligence, to hear them in their blattering efforts to mystify and pervert the sacred principles of liberty, and turn the curse of slavery into a blessing. To the illiterate poor whites—made poor and ignorant by the system of slavery—they hold out the idea that slavery is the very bulwark of our liberties, and the foundation of American independence! For hours at a time, day after day, will they expatiate upon the inexpressible beauties and excellencies of this great, *free* and *independent* nation; and finally, with the most extravagant gesticulations and rhetorical flourishes, conclude their nonsensical ravings, by attributing all the glory and prosperity of the country, from Maine to Texas, and from Georgia to California, to the "invaluable institutions of the South!" With what patience we could command, we have frequently listened to the incoherent and truth-murdering declamations of these champions of slavery, and, in the absence of a more politic method of giving vent to our disgust and indignation, have involuntarily bit our lips into blisters.

The lords of the lash are not only absolute masters of the blacks, who are bought and sold, and driven about like so many cattle, but they are also the oracles and arbiters of all non-slaveholding whites, whose freedom is merely nominal, and whose unparalleled illiteracy and degradation is purposely and fiendishly perpetuated. How little the "poor white trash," the great majority of the Southern people, know of the real condition of the country is, indeed, sadly astonishing. The truth is, they know nothing of public measures, and little of private affairs, except what their imperious masters, the slave-drivers, condescend to tell, and that is but precious little, and even that little, always garbled and one-sided, is never told except in public harangues; for the haughty cavaliers of shackles and handcuffs will not degrade themselves by holding private converse with those who have neither dimes nor hereditary rights in human flesh.

Whenever it pleases, and to the extent it pleases, a slaveholder to become communicative, poor whites may hear with fear and trembling, but not speak. They must be as mum as dumb brutes, and stand in awe of their august superiors, or be crushed with stern rebukes, cruel oppressions, or downright violence. If they dare to think for themselves, their thoughts must be forever concealed. The expression of any sentiment at all conflicting with the gospel of slavery, dooms them at once in the community in which they live, and then, whether willing or unwilling, they are obliged to become heroes, martyrs, or exiles. They may thirst for knowledge, but there is no Moses among them to smite it out of the rocks of Horeb. The black veil, through whose almost impenetrable meshes light seldom gleams, has long been pendent over their eyes, and there, with fiendish jealousy, the slave-driving ruffians sedulously guard it. Non-slaveholders are not only kept in ignorance of what is transpiring at the North, but they are continually misinformed of what is going on even in the South. Never were the poorer classes of a people, and those classes so largely in the majority, and all inhabiting the same country, so basely duped, so adroitly swindled, or so damnably outraged.

It is expected that the stupid and sequacious masses, the white victims of slavery, will believe, and, as a general thing, they do believe, whatever the slaveholders tell them ; and thus it is that they are cajoled into the notion that they are the freest, happiest and most intelligent people in the world, and are taught to look with prejudice and disapprobation upon every new principle or progressive movement. Thus it is that the South, woefully inert and inventionless, has lagged behind the North, and is now weltering in the cesspool of ignorance and degradation.

We have already intimated that the opinion is prevalent throughout the South that the free States are quite sterile and unproductive, and that they are mainly dependent on us for breadstuffs and other provisions. So far as the cereals, fruits, garden vegetables and esculent roots are concerned, we have, in the preceding tables, shown the utter falsity of this opinion ; and we now propose to show that it is equally erroneous in other particulars, and very far from the truth in the general reckoning. We can prove, and we intend to prove, from facts in our possession, that the hay crop of the free States is worth considerably more in dollars and cents than all the cotton, tobacco, rice, hay and hemp produced in the fifteen slave States. This statement may strike some of our readers with amazement, and others may, for the moment, regard it as quite incredible ; but it is true, nevertheless, and we shall soon proceed to confirm it. The single free State of New-York produces more than *three times* the quantity of hay that is produced in all the slave States. Ohio produces a larger number of tons than all the Southern and Southwestern States, and so does Pennsylvania. Vermont, little and unpretending as she is, does the same thing, with the exception of Virginia. Look at the facts as presented in the tables, and let your own eyes, physical and intellectual, confirm you in the truth.

And yet, forsooth, the slave-driving oligarchy would whip us into the belief that agriculture is not one of the leading and lucrative pursuits of the free States, that the soil there is an uninterrupted barren waste, and that our Northern brethren, having the advantage in nothing except wealth, population, inland and foreign commerce, manufactures, mechanism, inventions, literature, the arts and sciences, and their concomitant branches of profitable industry,—miserable objects of charity—are dependent on us for the necessaries of life.

Next to Virginia, Maryland is the greatest Southern hay-producing State; and yet, it is the opinion of several of the most extensive hay and grain dealers in Baltimore, with whom we have conversed on the subject, that the domestic crop is scarcely equal to one-third the demand, and that the balance required for home consumption, about two-thirds, is chiefly brought from New-York, Pennsylvania and Massachusetts. At this rate, Maryland receives and consumes not less than three hundred and fifteen thousand tons of Northern hay every year; and this, as we are informed by the dealers above-mentioned, at an average cost to the last purchaser, by the time it is stowed in the mow, of at least twenty-five dollars per ton; it would thus appear that this most popular and valuable provender, one of the staple commodities of the North, commands a market in a single slave State, to the amount of seven million eight hundred and seventy-five thousand dollars per annum.

In this same State of Maryland, less than one million of dollar's worth of cotton finds a market, the whole number of bales sold here in 1850 amounting to only twenty-three thousand three hundred and twenty-five, valued at seven hundred and forty-six thousand four hundred dollars. Briefly, then, and in round numbers, we may state the case thus Maryland buys annually seven millions of dollars worth of hay from the North, and one million of dollars worth of cotton from the South. Let slaveholders and their fawning defenders read, ponder and compare.

The exact quantities of Northern hay, rye, and buckwheat flour, Irish potatoes, fruits, clover and grass seeds, and other products of the soil, received and consumed in all the slaveholding States, we have no means of ascertaining; but for all practical purposes, we can arrive sufficiently near to the amount by inference from the above data, and from what we see with our eyes and hear with our ears wherever we go. Food from the North for man or for beast, or for both, is for sale in every market in the South. Even in the most insignificant little villages in the interior of the slave States, where books, newspapers and other mediums of intelligence are unknown, where the poor whites and the negroes are alike bowed down in heathenish ignorance and barbarism, and where the news is received but once a week, and then only in a Northern-built stage-coach, drawn by horses in Northern harness, in charge of a driver dressed *cap-a-pie* in Northern habiliments, and with a Northern whip in his hand,—the agricultural products of the North, either crude, prepared, pickled or preserved, are ever to be found.

Mortifying as the acknowledgment of the fact is to us, it is our unbiased opinion—an opinion which will, we believe, be endorsed by every intelligent person who goes into a careful examination and comparison of all the facts in the case—that the profits arising to the North from the sale of provender and provisions to the South, are far greater than those arising to the South from the sale of cotton, tobacco and breadstuffs to the North. It follows, then, that the agricultural interests of the North being not only equal but actually superior to those of the South, the hundreds of millions of dollars which the commerce and manufactures of the former annually yield, is just so much clear and independent gain over the latter. It follows, also, from a corresponding train or system of deduction, and with all the foregoing facts in view, that the difference between freedom and slavery is simply the difference between sense and nonsense, wisdom and folly, good and evil, right and wrong.

Any observant American, from whatever point of the compass he may hail, who will take the trouble to pass through the Southern markets, both great and small, as we have done, and inquire where this article, that and the other came from, will be utterly astonished at the variety and quantity of Northern agricultural productions kept for sale. And this state of things is growing worse and worse every year. Exclusively agricultural as the South is in her industrial pursuits, she is barely able to support her sparse and degenerate population. Her men and her domestic animals, both dwarfed into shabby objects of commiseration under the blighting effects of slavery, are constantly feeding on the multifarious products of Northern soil. And if the whole truth must be told, we may here add, that these products, like all other articles of merchandize purchased at the North, are generally bought on a credit, and, in a great number of instances, by far too many, never paid for—not, as a general rule, because the purchasers are dishonest or unwilling to pay, but because they are impoverished and depressed by the retrogressive and deadening operations of slavery, that most unprofitable and pernicious institution under which they live.

To show how well we are sustained in our remarks upon hay and other special products of the soil, as well as to give circulation to other facts of equal significance, we quote a single passage from an address by Paul C. Cameron, before the Agricultural Society of Orange County, North Carolina. This production is, in the main, so powerfully conceived, so correct and plausible in its statements and conclusions, and so well calculated, though, perhaps, not intended, to arouse the old North State to a sense of her natural greatness and acquired shame, that we could wish to see it published in pamphlet form, and circulated throughout the length and breadth of that unfortunate and degraded heritage of slavery. Mr. Cameron says:

"I know not when I have been more humiliated, as a North Carolina farmer, than when, a few weeks ago, at a railroad depot at the very doors of our State capital, I saw wagons drawn by Kentucky mules, loading with Northern hay, for the supply not only of the town, but to be taken to the country. Such a sight at the capital of a State whose population is almost exclusively devoted to agriculture, is a most humiliating exhibition. Let us cease to use every thing, as far as it is practicable, that is not the product of our own soil and workshops—not an axe, or a broom, or bucket, from Connecticut. By every consideration of self-preservation, we are called to make better efforts to expel the Northern grocer from the State with his butter, and the Ohio and Kentucky horse, mule and hog driver, from our county at least. It is a reproach on us as farmers, and no little deduction from our wealth, that we suffer the population of our towns and villages to supply themselves with butter from another Orange County in New-York."

We have promised to prove that the hay crop of the free states is worth considerably more than all the cotton, tobacco, rice, hay and hemp produced in the fifteen slave States. The compilers of the last census, as we learn from Prof. De Bow, the able and courteous superintendent, in making up the hay-tables, allowed two thousand two hundred and forty pounds to the ton. The price per ton at which we should estimate its value has puzzled us to some extent. Dealers in the article in Baltimore think it will average twenty-five dollars, in their market. Four or five months ago they sold it at thirty dollars per ton. At the very time we write, though there is less activity in the article than usual, we learn, from an examination of sundry prices-current and commercial journals, that hay is selling in Savannah at $33 per ton ; in Mobile and New Orleans at $26 ; in Charleston at $25 ; in Louisville at $24 ; and in Cincinnati at $23. The average of these prices is *twenty-six dollars sixteen and two-third cents ;* and we suppose it would be fair to employ the figures which would indicate this amount, the net value of a single ton, in calculating the total market value of the entire crop. Were we to do this—and, with the foregoing facts in view, we submit to intelligent men whether we would not be justifiable in doing it,—the hay crop of the free states, 12,690,982 tons, in 1850, would amount in valuation to the enormous sum of $331,081,695—more than four times the value of all the cotton produced in the United States during the same period !

But we shall not make the calculation at what we have found to be the average value per ton throughout the country. What rate, then, shall be agreed upon as a basis of comparison between the value of the hay crop of the North and that of the South, and as a means of testing the truth of our declaration—that the former exceeds the aggregate value of all the cotton, tobacco, rice, hay and hemp produced in the fifteen slave States ? Suppose we take $13,08⅓—just half the average value—as the multiplier in this arithmetical exercise. This we can well afford to do ; indeed, we might reduce the amount per ton to much less than half the average value, and still have a large margin left for triumphant demonstration. It is not our purpose, however, to make an overwhelming display of the incomparable greatness of the free States.

In estimating the value of the various agricultural products of the two great sections of the country, we have been guided by prices emanating from the Bureau of Agriculture in Washington; and in a catalogue of those prices now before us, we perceive that the average value of hay throughout the nation is supposed to be not more than half a cent per pound—$11.20 per ton—which, as we have seen above, is considerably less than half the present market value;—and this, too, in the face of the fact that prices generally rule higher than they do just now. It will be admitted on all sides, however, that the prices fixed upon by the Bureau of Agriculture, taken as a whole, are as fair for one section of the country as for the other, and that we cannot blamelessly deviate from them in one particular without deviating from them in another. Eleven dollars and twenty cents ($11.20) per ton shall therefore be the price; and, notwithstanding these greatly reduced figures, we now renew, with an addendum, our declaration and promise, that—*We can prove, and we shall now proceed to prove, that the annual hay crop of the free States is worth considerably more in dollars and cents than all the cotton, tobacco, rice, hay, hemp and cane sugar annually produced in the fifteen slave States.*

HAY CROP OF THE FREE STATES—1850.

12,690 982 tons *a* 11,20........................... $142,138,998

SUNDRY PRODUCTS OF THE SLAVE STATES—1850.

Cotton	2,445,779 bales	*a*	32,00	$78,264,928
Tobacco,	185,023,906 lbs.	"	10	18,502,390
Rice (rough)	215,313 497 lbs.	"	4	8,612,539
Hay	1,137,784 tons	"	11,20	12,743,180
Hemp	34,673 tons	"	112,00	3,883,376
Cane Sugar	237,133,000 lbs.	"	7	16,599,310
				$138,605,723

RECAPITULATION.

Hay crop of the free States	$142,138,998
Sundry products of the slave States	138,605,723
Balance in favor of the free States	$3,533,275

There is the account; look at it, and let it stand in attestation of the exalted virtues and surpassing powers of freedom. Scan it well, Messieurs lords of the lash, and learn from it new lessons of the utter inefficiency, and despicable imbecility of slavery. Examine it minutely, liberty-loving patriots of the North, and behold in it additional evidences of the beauty, grandeur, and super-excellence of free institutions. Treasure it up in your minds, outraged friends and non-slaveholders of the South, and let the recollection of it arouse you to an inflexible determination to extirpate the monstrous enemy that stalks abroad in your land, and to recover the inalienable rights and liberties, which have been filched from you by an unprincipled oligarchy.

In deference to truth, decency and good sense, it is to

be hoped that negro-driving politicians will never more have the effrontery to open their mouths in extolling the agricultural achievements of slave labor. Especially is it desirable, that, as a simple act of justice to a basely deceived populace, they may cease their stale and senseless harangues on the importance of cotton. The value of cotton to the South, to the North, to the nation, and to the world, has been so grossly exaggerated, and so extensive have been the evils which have resulted in consequence of the extraordinary misrepresentations concerning it, that we should feel constrained to reproach ourself for remissness of duty, if we failed to make an attempt to explode the popular error. The figures above show what it is, and what it is not. Recur to them, and learn the facts.

So hyperbolically has the importance of cotton been magnified by certain pro-slavery politicians of the South, that the person who would give credence to all their fustian and bombast, would be under the necessity of believing that the very existence of almost everything, in the heaven above, in the earth beneath, and in the water under the earth, depended on it. The truth is, however, that the cotton crop is of but little value to the South. New England and Old England, by their superior enterprise and sagacity, turn it chiefly to their own advantage. It is carried in their ships, spun in their factories, woven in their looms, insured in their offices, returned again in their own vessels, and, with double freight and cost of manufacturing added, purchased by the South at a high premium. Of all the parties engaged or interested in its transportation and manufacture, the South is the only one that does not make a profit. Nor does she, as a general thing, make a profit by producing it.

We are credibly informed that many of the farmers in the immediate vicinity of Baltimore, where we now write, have turned their attention exclusively to hay, and that from one acre they frequently gather two tons, for which they receive fifty dollars. Let us now inquire how many dollars may be expected from an acre planted in cotton. Mr. Cameron, from whose able address before the Agricultural Society of Orange County, North Carolina, we have already gleaned some interesting particulars, informs us, that the cotton planters in his part of the country, "have contented themselves with a crop yielding only *ten or twelve dollars per acre*," and that "the summing up of a large surface gives but a living result." An intelligent resident of the Palmetto State, writing in De Bow's Review, not long since, advances the opinion that the cotton planters of South Carolina are not realizing more than one per cent. on the amount of capital they have invested. While in Virginia, very recently, an elderly slaveholder, whose religious walk and conversation had recommended and promoted him to an eldership in the Presbyterian church, and who supports himself and family by raising niggers and tobacco, told us that, for the last eight or ten years, aside from the increase of his human chattels, he felt quite confident he had not cleared as much even as one per cent. per annum on the amount of his investment. The real and personal property of this aged *Christian* consists chiefly in a large tract of land and about thirty negroes, most of whom, according to his own confession, are more expensive than profitable. The proceeds arising from the sale of the tobacco they produce, are all absorbed in the purchase of meat and bread for home consumption, and when the crop is stunted by drought, frost, or otherwise cut short, one of the negroes must be sold to raise funds for the support of the others. Such are the agricultural achievements of slave labor; such are the results of "the sum of all villainies." The diabolical institution subsists on its own flesh. At one time children are sold to procure food for the parents, at another, parents are sold to procure food for the children. Within its pestilential atmosphere, nothing succeeds; progress and prosperity are unknown; inanition and slothfulness ensue; everything becomes dull, dismal and unprofitable; wretchedness and desolation run riot throughout the land; an aspect of most melancholy inactivity and dilapidation broods over every city and town; ignorance and prejudice sit enthroned over the minds of the people; usurping despots wield the sceptre of power; everywhere, and in everything, between Delaware Bay and the Gulf of Mexico, are the multitudinous evils of slavery apparent.

The soil itself soon sickens and dies beneath the unnatural tread of the slave. Hear what the Hon. C. C. Clay, of Alabama, has to say upon the subject. His testimony is eminently suggestive, well-timed, and truthful; and we heartily commend it to the careful consideration of every spirited Southron who loves his country, and desires to see it rescued from the fatal grasp of "the mother of harlots:" Says he:

"I can show you, with sorrow, in the older portions of

Alabama, and in my native county of Madison, the sad memorials of the artless and exhausting culture of cotton. Our small planters, after taking the cream off their lands, unable to restore them by rest, manures, or otherwise, are going further West and South, in search of other virgin lands, which they may and will despoil and impoverish in like manner. Our wealthier planters, with greater means and no more skill, are buying out their poorer neighbors, extending their plantations, and adding to their slave force. The wealthy few, who are able to live on smaller profits, and to give their blasted fields some rest, are thus pushing off the many who are merely independent. Of the $20,000,000 annually realized from the sales of the cotton crop of Alabama, nearly all not expended in supporting the producers, is re-invested in land and negroes. Thus the white population has decreased and the slave increased almost *pari passu* in several counties of our State. In 1825, Madison county cast about 3,000 votes; now, she cannot cast exceeding 2,300. In traversing that county, one will discover numerous farm-houses, once the abode of industrious and intelligent freemen, now occupied by slaves, or tenantless, deserted and dilapidated; he will observe fields, once fertile, now unfenced, abandoned, and covered with those evil harbingers, fox-tail and broom-sedge; he will see the moss growing on the mouldering walls of once thrifty villages, and will find 'one only master grasps the whole domain,' that once furnished happy homes for a dozen white families. Indeed, a country in its infancy, where fifty years ago scarce a forest tree had been felled by the axe of the pioneer, is already exhibiting the painful signs of senility and decay, apparent in Virginia and the Carolinas."

Some one has said that "an honest confession is good for the soul," and if the adage be true, as we have no doubt it is, we think Mr. C. C. Clay is entitled to a quiet conscience on one score at least. In the extract quoted above, he gives us a graphic description of the ruinous operations and influences of slavery in the Southwest; and we, as a native of Carolina, and a traveler through Virginia, are ready to bear testimony to the fitness of his remarks when he referred to those States as examples of senility and decay. With equal propriety, however, he might have stopped nearer home for a subject of comparison. Either of the States bordering upon Alabama, or, indeed, any other slave States, would have answered his purpose quite as well as Virginia and the Carolinas. Wherever slavery exists there he may find parallels to the destruction that is sweeping with such deadly influence over his own unfortunate State.

As for examples of vigorous, industrious and thrifty communities, they can be found anywhere beyond the Upas-shadow of slavery—nowhere else. New-York and Massachusetts, which, by nature, are confessedly far inferior to Virginia and the Carolinas, have, by the more liberal and equitable policy which they have pursued, in substituting liberty for slavery, attained a degree of eminence and prosperity altogether unknown in the slave States.

Amidst all the hyperbole and cajolery of slave-driving politicians, who, as we have already seen, are 'the books, the arts, the academies, that show, contain, and govern all the South,' we are rejoiced to see that Mr. Clay, Mr. Cameron, and a few others, have had the boldness and honesty to step forward and proclaim the truth. All such frank admissions are to be hailed as good omens for the South. Nothing good can come from any attempt to conceal the unconcealable evidences of poverty and desolation everywhere trailing in the wake of slavery. Let the truth be told on all occasions, of the North as well as of the South, and the people will soon begin to discover the egregiousness of their errors, to draw just comparisons, to inquire into cause and effect, and to adopt the more utile measures, manners and customs of their wiser cotemporaries.

In wilfully traducing and decrying everything North of Mason and Dixon's line, and in excessively magnifying the importance of everything South of it, the oligarchy have, in the eyes of all liberal and intelligent men, only made an exhibition of their uncommon folly and dishonesty. For a long time, it is true, they have succeeded in deceiving the people, in keeping them humbled in the murky sloughs of poverty and ignorance, and in instilling into their untutored minds passions and prejudices expressly calculated to strengthen and protect the accursèd institution of slavery; but, thanks to heaven, their inglorious reign is fast drawing to a close; with irresistible brilliancy, and in spite of the interdict of tyrants, light from the pure fountain of knowledge is now streaming over the dark places of our land, and, ere long—mark our words—there will ascend from Delaware, and from Texas, and from all the intermediate States, a huzza for Freedom and for Equal Rights, that will utterly confound the friends of despotism, set at defiance the authority of usurpers, and carry consternation to the heart of every slavery-propagandist.

To undeceive the people of the South, to bring them to a knowledge of the inferior and disreputable position which they occupy as a component part of the Union, and to give prominence and popularity to those plans which, if adopted, will elevate us to an equality, socially, morally, intellectually, industrially, politically, and financially, with the most flourishing and refined nation in the world, and, if possible, to place us in the van of even that, is the object of this work. Slaveholders, either from ignorance or from a wilful disposition to propagate error, contend that the South has nothing to be ashamed of, that slavery has proved a blessing to her, and that her superiority over the North in an agricultural point of view makes amends for all her shortcomings in other respects. On the other hand, we contend that many years of continual blushing and severe penance would not suffice to cancel or annul the shame and disgrace that justly attaches to the South in consequence of slavery —the direst evil that e'er befell the land—that the South bears nothing like even a respectable approximation to the North in navigation, commerce, or manufactures, and that, contrary to the opinion entertained by ninety-nine hundredths of her people, she is far behind the free States in the only thing of which she has ever dared to boast—agriculture. We submit the question to the arbitration of figures, which, it is said, do not lie. With regard to the bushel-measure products of the soil, of which we have already taken an inventory, we have seen that there is a balance against the South in favor of the North of *seventeen million four hundred and twenty-three thousand one hundred and fifty-two bushels*, and a difference in the value of the same, also in favor of the North, of *forty-four million seven hundred and eighty-two thousand six hundred and thirty-six dollars.* It is certainly a most novel kind of agricultural superiority that the South claims on that score!

Our attention shall now be directed to the twelve principal pound-measure products of the free and of the slave States—hay, cotton, butter and cheese, tobacco, cane, sugar, wool, rice, hemp, maple sugar, beeswax and honey, flax, and hops—and in taking an account of them, we shall, in order to show the exact quantity produced in each State, and for the convenience of future reference, pursue the same plan as that adopted in the preceding tables. Whether slavery will appear to better advantage on the scales than it did in the half-bushel, remains to be seen. It is possible that the rickety monster may make a better show on a new track; if it makes a more ridiculous display, we shall not be surprised. A careful examination of its precedents, has taught us the folly of expecting anything good to issue from it in any manner whatever. It has no disposition to emulate the magnanimity of its betters, and as for a laudable ambition to excel, that is a characteristic altogether foreign to its nature. Languor and inertia are the insalutary viands upon which it delights to satiate its morbid appetite; and "from bad to worse" is the ill-omened motto under which, in all its feeble efforts and achievements, it ekes out a most miserable and deleterious existence

TABLE NO. IX.

AGRICULTURAL PRODUCTS OF THE FREE STATES—1850.

States.	Hay, tons.	Hemp, tons.	Hops, lbs.
California	2,038		
Connecticut	516,131		554
Illinois	601,952		3,551
Indiana	403,230		92,796
Iowa	89,055		8,242
Maine	755,889		40,120
Massachusetts	651,807		121,595
Michigan	404,934		10,663
New Hampshire	598,854		257,174
New Jersey	435,950		2,133
New York	3,728,797	4	2,536,299
Ohio	1,443,142	150	63,731
Pennsylvania	1,842,970	44	22,088
Rhode Island	74,418		277
Vermont	866,153		288,023
Wisconsin	275,662		15,930
	12,690,982	198	3,463,176

TABLE NO. X.

AGRICULTURAL PRODUCTS OF THE SLAVE STATES—1850.

States.	Hay, tons.	Hemp, tons.	Hops, lbs.
Alabama	32,685		276
Arkansas	3,976	15	157
Delaware	30,159		348
Florida	2,510		14
Georgia	23,449		261
Kentucky	113,747	17,787	4,309
Louisiana	25,752		125
Maryland	157,956	63	1,870
Mississippi	12,504	7	473
Missouri	116,925	16,028	4,130
North Carolina	145,653	39	9,246
South Carolina	20,925		26
Tennessee	74,091	595	1,032
Texas	8,354		7
Virginia	369,098	139	11,506
	1,137,784	34,673	33,780

TABLE NO. XI.

AGRICULTURAL PRODUCTS OF THE FREE STATES—1850.

States.	Flax, lbs.	Maple Sugar, lbs.	Tobacco, lbs.
California			1,000
Connecticut	17,928	50,796	1,267,624
Illinois	160,063	248,904	841,394
Indiana	584,469	2,921,192	1,044,620
Iowa	62,660	78,407	6,041
Maine	17,081	93,542	
Massachusetts	1,162	795,525	138,246
Michigan	7,152	2,439,794	1,245
New Hampshire	7,652	1,298,863	50
New Jersey	182,965	2,197	310
New York	940,577	10,357,484	83,189
Ohio	446,932	4,588,209	10,454,449
Pennsylvania	530,307	2,326,525	912,651
Rhode Island	85	28	
Vermont	20,852	6,349,357	
Wisconsin	68,393	610,976	1,268
	3,048,278	32,161,799	14,752,087

TABLE NO. XII.

AGRICULTURAL PRODUCTS OF THE SLAVE STATES—1850.

States.	Flax, lbs.	Maple Sugar, lbs.	Tobacco, lbs.
Alabama	3,921	643	164,990
Arkansas	12,291	9,330	218,936
Delaware	17,174		
Florida	50		998,614
Georgia	5,387	50	423,924
Kentucky	2,100,116	437,405	55,501,196
Louisiana		255	26,878
Maryland	35,686	47,740	21,407,497
Mississippi	665		49,960
Missouri	627,160	178,910	17,113,784
North Carolina	593,796	27,932	11,984,786
South Carolina	333	200	74,285
Tennessee	368,131	158,557	20,148,932
Texas	1,048		66,897
Virginia	1,000,450	1,227,665	56,803,227
	4,76[illegible],198	2,088,6[illegible]	185,023,906

TABLE NO. XIII.

ANIMAL PRODUCTS OF THE FREE STATES—1850.

States.	Wool, lbs.	Butter and Cheese, lbs.	Beeswax and Honey, lbs.
California	5,520	855	
Connecticut	497,454	11,861,396	93,304
Illinois	2,150.113	13,804,768	869,444
Indiana	2,610,287	13,506,099	935,329
Iowa	373,898	2,381,028	321,711
Maine	1,364,034	11,678,265	189,618
Massachusetts	585,136	15,159,512	59,508
Michigan	2,043,283	8,077,390	359,232
New Hampshire	1,108,476	10,173,619	117,140
New Jersey	375,396	9,852,966	156,694
New York	10,071,301	129,507,507	1,755,830
Ohio	10,196,371	55,268,921	804,275
Pennsylvania	4,481,570	42,383,452	839,509
Rhode Island	129,692	1,312,178	6,347
Vermont	3,400,717	20,858,814	249,422
Wisconsin	253,963	4,034,033	131,005
	39,647,211	349,860,783	6,888,368

TABLE NO. XVI.

ANIMAL PRODUCTS OF THE SLAVE STATES—1850.

States.	Wool, lbs.	Butter and Cheese, lbs.	Beeswax and Honey, lbs.
Alabama	657,118	4,040,223	897,021
Arkansas	182,595	1,884,327	192,338
Delaware	57,768	1,058,495	41,248
Florida	23,247	389,513	18,971
Georgia	990,019	4,687,535	732,514
Kentucky	2,297,433	10,161,477	1,158,019
Louisiana	109,897	685,026	96,701
Maryland	477,438	3,810,135	74,802
Mississippi	559,619	4,367,425	397,460
Missouri	1,627,164	8,037,931	1,328,972
North Carolina	970,738	4,242,211	512,289
South Carolina	487,233	2,986,820	216,281
Tennessee	1,364,378	8,317,266	1,036,572
Texas	131,917	2,440,199	380,825
Virginia	2,860,765	11,525,651	880,767
	12,797,329	68,634,224	7,964,760

TABLE NO. XV.

AGRICULTURAL PRODUCTS OF THE SLAVE STATES—1850.

States.	Cotton, bales of 400 lbs.	Cane Sugar, hhds. 1000 lbs.	Rough Rice, lbs.
Alabama	564,429	87	2,312,252
Arkansas	65,344		63,179
Delaware			
Florida	45,131	2,750	1,075,090
Georgia	499,091	846	38,950,691
Kentucky	758	10	5,688
Louisiana	178,737	226,001	4,425,349
Maryland			
Mississippi	484,292	8	2,719,856
Missouri			700
North Carolina	50,545		5,465,868
South Carolina	300,901	77	159,930,613
Tennessee	194,532	3	258,854
Texas	58,072	7,351	88,203
Virginia	3,947		17,154
	2,445,779	237,133	215,313,497

RECAPITULATION—FREE STATES.

Hay	28,427,799,680	lbs.	@	1-2 c.	$142,138,998
Hemp	443,520	"	"	5 "	22,176
Hops	3,463,176	"	"	15 "	519,476
Flax	3,048,278	"	"	10 "	304,827
Maple Sugar	32,161,799	"	"	8 "	2,572,943
Tobacco	14,752,087	"	"	10 "	1,475,208
Wool	39,647,211	"	"	35 "	13,876,523
Butter and Cheese	349,860,783	"	"	15 "	52,479,117
Beeswax and Honey	6,888,368	"	"	15 "	1,033,255
Total,	28,878,064,902	lbs., valued as above,			$214,422,523

RECAPITULATION —SLAVE STATES.

Hay	2,548,636,160	lbs.	@	1-2	c.	$12,743,180
Hemp	77,667,520	"	"	5	"	3,883,376
Hops	33,780	"	"	15	"	5,067
Flax	4,766,198	"	"	10	"	476,619
Maple Sugar	2,088,687	"	"	8	"	167,094
Tobacco	185,023,906	"	"	10	"	18,502,390
Wool	12,797,329	"	"	35	"	4,479,065
Butter and Cheese	68,634,224	"	"	15	"	10,295,133
Beeswax and Honey	7,964,760	"	"	15	"	1,194,714
Cotton	978,311,600	"	"	8	"	78,264,928
Cane Sugar	237,133,000	"	"	7	"	16,599,310
Rice (rough)	215,313,497	"	"	4	"	8,612,539
Total	4,338,370,661	lbs. valued as above, at				$155,223,415

TOTAL DIFFERENCE—POUND-MEASURE PRODUCTS.

	Pounds.	*Value.*
Free States	28,878,064,902	$214,422,523
Slave States	4,338,370,661	155,223,415
Balance in pounds,	24,539,694,241	Difference in value, $59,199,108

Both quantity and value again in favor of the North! Behold also the enormousness of the difference! In this comparison with the South, neither hundreds, thousands, nor millions, according to the regular method of computation, are sufficient to exhibit the excess of the pound-measure products of the North. Recourse must be had to an almost inconceivable number; billions must be called into play; and there are the figures telling us, with unmistakable emphasis and distinctness, that, in this department of agriculture, as in every other, the North is vastly the superior of the South—the figures showing a total balance in favor of the former of *twenty-four billion five hun-*

dred and thirty-nine million six hundred and ninety-four thousand two hundred and forty-one pounds, valued at *fifty-nine million one hundred and ninety-nine thousand one hundred and eight dollars.* And yet, the North is a poor, God-forsaken country, bleak, inhospitable, and unproductive!

What next? Is it necessary to adduce other facts in order to prove that the rural wealth of the free States is far greater than that of the slave States? Shall we make a further demonstration of the fertility of northern soil, or bring forward new evidences of the inefficient and desolating system of terra-culture in the South? Will nothing less than "confirmations strong as proofs of holy writ," suffice to convince the South that she is standing in her own light, and ruining both body and soul by the retention of slavery? Whatever duty and expedience require to be done, we are willing to do. Additional proofs are at hand. Slaveholders and slave-breeders shall be convinced, confuted, convicted, and converted. They shall, in their hearts and consciences, if not with their tongues and pens, bear testimony to the triumphant achievements of free labor. In the two tables which immediately follow these remarks, they shall see how much more vigorous and fruitful the soil is when under the prudent management of free white husbandmen, than it is when under the rude and nature-murdering tillage of enslaved negroes; and in two subsequent tables they shall find that the live stock, slaughtered animals, farms, and farming implements and machinery, in the free States, are worth at least *one thousand million of dollars* more than the market value of the same in the slave States! In the face, however, of all these most significant and incontrovertible facts, the oligarchy have the unparalleled audacity to tell us that the South is the greatest agricultural country in the world, and that the North is a dreary waste, unfit for cultivation, and quite dependent on us for the necessaries of life. How preposterously false all such babble is, the following tables will show:—

TABLE NO. XVI.

ACTUAL CROPS PER ACRE ON THE AVERAGE IN THE FREE STATES—1850.

States.	Wheat, bushels.	Oats, bushels.	Rye. bushels.	Ind. Corn, bushels.	Irish Potatoes, bush.
Connecticut........		21		40	85
Illinois.	11	29	14	33	115
Indiana	12	20	18	33	100
Iowa....	14	36		32	100
Maine............	10			27	120
Massachusetts....	16	26	13	31	170
Michigan.........	10	26		32	140
New Hampshire...	11	30		30	220
New Jersey.......	11	26		33	
New York........	12	25	17	27	100
Ohio....	12	21	25	36	
Pennsylvania.....	15			20	75
Rhode Island.....		30			100
Vermont.........	13		20	32	178
Wisconsin........	14	35		30	
	161	325	107	436	1,503

TABLE NO. XVII.

ACTUAL CROPS PER ACRE ON THE AVERAGE IN THE SLAVE STATES—1850.

States.	Wheat, bushels.	Oats, bushels.	Rye, bushels.	Ind. Corn, bushels.	Irish Potatoes, bush.
Alabama.........	5	12		15	60
Arkansas.........		18		22	
Delaware.........	11	20		20	
Florida	15				175
Georgia..........	5	18	7	16	125
Kentucky........	8	18	11	24	130
Louisiana.				16	
Maryland.........	13	21	18	23	75
Mississippi.......	9	12		18	105
Missouri.........	11	26		34	110
North Carolina....	7	10	15	17	65
South Carolina....	8	12		11	70
Tennessee....	7	19	7	21	120
Texas......	15			20	250
Virginia..	7	13	5	18	75
	121	199	63	275	1,360

RECAPITULATION OF ACTUAL CROPS PER ACRE ON THE AVERAGE — 1850.

FREE STATES.		SLAVE STATES.	
Wheat 12	bushels per acre.	Wheat 9	bushels per acre.
Oats........27	" "	Oats........17	" "
Rye 18	" "	Rye 11	" "
Indian Corn 31	" "	Indian Corn .20	" "
Irish Potatoes 125	" "	Irish Potatoes 113	" "

What an obvious contrast between the vigor of Liberty and the impotence of Slavery! What an unanswerable argument in favor of free labor! Add up the two columns of figures above, and what is the result? Two hundred and thirteen bushels as the products of five acres in the North, and only one hundred and seventy bushels as the products of five acres in the South. Look at each item separately, and you will find that the average crop per acre of every article enumerated is greater in the free States than it is in the slave States. Examine the table at large, and you will perceive that while Massachusetts produces sixteen bushels of wheat to the acre, Virginia produces only seven; that Pennsylvania produces fifteen and Georgia only five: that while Iowa produces thirty-six bushels of oats to the acre, Mississippi produces only twelve; that Rhode Island produces thirty, and North Carolina only ten: that while Ohio produces twenty-five bushels of rye to the acre, Kentucky produces only eleven; that Vermont produces twenty, and Tennessee only seven: that while Connecticut produces forty bushels of Indian corn to the acre, Texas produces only twenty; that New Jersey produces thirty-three, and South Carolina only eleven: that while New Hampshire produces two hundred and twenty bushels of Irish potatoes to the acre, Maryland produces only seventy-five; that Michigan produces one hundred and forty, and Alabama only sixty. Now for other beauties of slavery in another table.

TABLE NO. XVIII.

VALUE OF FARMS AND DOMESTIC ANIMALS IN THE FREE STATES —1850.

States.	Value of Live Stock.	Val. of Animals Slaughtered.	Cash Val. of Farms, Farm. Imp. & Mac.
California	$3,351,058	$107,173	$3,977,524
Connecticut	7,467,490	2,202,266	74,618,963
Illinois..........	24,209,258	4,972,286	102,538,851
Indiana.	22,478,555	6,567,935	143,089,617
Iowa...........	3,689,275	821,164	17,830,436
Maine..	9,705,726	1,646,773	57,146,305
Massachusetts...	9,647,710	2,500,924	112,285,931
Michigan........	8,008,734	1,328,327	54,763,817
New Hampshire..	8,871,901	1,522,873	57,560,122
New Jersey..	10,679,291	2,638,552	124,663,014
New York.......	73,570,499	13,573,883	576,631,568
Ohio....	44.121.741	7,439,243	371.509,188
Pennsylvania....	41,500,053	8,219,848	422,598,640
Rhode Island...	1,532,637	667,486	17,568,003
Vermont....	12,643,228	1,861,336	66,106,509
Wisconsin.	4,897,385	920.178	30,170,131
	$286,376,541	$56,990,237	$2,233 058 619

TABLE NO. XIX.

VALUE OF FARMS AND DOMESTIC ANIMALS IN THE SLAVE STATES —1850.

States.	Value of Live Stock.	Val. of Animals Slaughtered.	Cash Val. of Farms, Farm. Imp. & Mac.
Alabama........	$21.690,112	$4,823,485	$69,448,887
Arkansas........	6,647,969	1,163,313	16,866,541
Delaware........	1,849,281	373,665	19,390,310
Florida	2.880,058	514,685	6,981,904
Georgia........	25,728,416	6,339.762	101,647,595
Kentucky.......	29,661.436	6,462.598	160,190.299
Louisiana.	11,152,275	1,458,990	87,391,336
Maryland........	7,997,634	1,954,800	89,641,988
Mississippi......	19,403,662	3,636.582	60,501,561
Missouri........	19,887,580	3,367,106	67,207,068
North Carolina...	17,717,647	5,767,866	71,823,298
South Carolina...	15,060,015	3,502.637	86,568,038
Tennessee.......	29,978,016	6,401,765	103,211,422
Texas....	10,412,927	1,116,137	18,701,712
Virginia.... ...	33,656,659	7,502,986	223,423,315
	$253,723.687	$54,388,377	$1,183,995,274

RECAPITULATION—FREE STATES.

Value of live Stock	$286,376,541
Value of Animals slaughtered,	56,990,237
Value of Farms, Farming-Implements and Machinery,	2,233,058,619
	$2,576,425,397

RECAPITULATION—SLAVE STATES.

Value of Live Stock	$253,723,687
Value of Animals slaughtered	54,388,377
Value of Farms, Farming Implements and Machinery,	1,183,995,274
	$1,492,107,338

DIFFERENCE IN VALUE—FARMS AND DOMESTIC ANIMALS.

Free States,	$2,576,425,397
Slave States	1,492,107,338
Balance in favor of the Free States	$1,084,318,059

By adding to this last balance in favor of the free States the differences in value which we found in their favor in our account of the bushel-and-pound-measure products, we shall have a very correct idea of the extent to which the undivided agricultural interests of the free States preponderate over those of the slave States. Let us add the differences together, and see what will be the result.

BALANCES—ALL IN FAVOR OF THE NORTH.

Difference in the value of bushel-measure products..	$44,782,636
Difference in the value of pound-measure products..	59,199,108
Difference in the value of farms and domestic animals	1,084,318,059
Total	$1,188,299,803

No figures of rhetoric can add emphasis or significance to these figures of arithmetic. They demonstrate conclusively the great moral triumph of Liberty over Slavery. They show unequivocally, in spite of all the blarney and boasting of slave-driving politicians, that the entire value of all the agricultural interests of the free States is very nearly twice as great as the entire value of all the agricultural interests of the slave States—the value of those interests in the former being twenty-five hundred million of dollars, that of those in the latter only fourteen hundred million, leaving a balance in favor of the free States of *one billion one hundred and eighty-eight million two hundred and ninety-nine thousand eight hundred and three dollars!* That is what we call a full, fair and complete vindication of Free Labor. Would we not be correct in calling it a total eclipse of the Black Orb? Can it be possible that the slavocracy will ever have the hardihood to open their mouths again on the subject of terra-culture in the South? Dare they ever think of cotton again? Ought they not, as a befitting confession of their crimes and misdemeanors, and as a reasonable expiation for the countless evils which they have inflicted on society, to clothe themselves in sackcloth, and, after a suitable season of contrition and severe penance, follow the example of one Judas Iscariot, and go and hang themselves?

It will be observed that we have omitted the Territories and the District of Columbia in all the preceding tables. We did this purposely. Our object was to draw an equitable comparison between the value of free and slave labor in the thirty-one sovereign States, where the two systems, comparatively unaffected by the wrangling of politicians, and, as a matter of course, free from the interference of the general government, have had the fullest opportunities to exert their influence, to exhibit their virtues, and to commend themselves to the sober judgments of enlightened and discriminating minds. Had we counted the Territories on the side of the North, and the District of Columbia on the side of the South, the result would have been still greater in behalf of free labor. Though "the sum of all villanies" has but a mere nominal existence in Delaware and Maryland, we have invariably counted those States on the side of the South; and the consequence is, that, in many particulars, the hopeless fortunes of slavery have been propped up and sustained by an imposing array of figures which of right ought to be regarded as the property of freedom. But we like to be generous to an unfortunate foe, and would utterly disdain the use of any unfair means of attack or defence.

We shall take no undue advantage of slavery. It shall have a fair trial, and be judged according to its deserts. Already has it been weighed in the balance, and found wanting; it has been measured in the half-bushel, and found wanting; it has been apprized in the field, and found wanting. Whatever redeeming traits or qualities it may possess, if any, shall be brought to light by subjecting it to other tests.

It was our desire and intention to furnish a correct table of the gallon-measure products of the several States of the Union; but we have not been successful in our attempt to procure the necessary statistics. Enough is known, however, to satisfy us that the value of the milk, wine, ardent spirits, malt liquors, fluids, oils, and molasses, annually produced and sold in the free States, is at east fifty millions of dollars greater than the value of the same articles annually produced and sold in the slave States. Of sweet milk alone, it is estimated that the monthly sales in three Northern cities, New York, Philadelphia and Boston, amount to a larger sum than the marketable value of all the rosin, tar, pitch, and turpentine, annually produced in the Southern States.

Our efforts to obtain reliable information respecting another very important branch of profitable industry, the lumber business, have also proved unavailing ; and we are left to conjecture as to the amount of revenue annually derived from it in the two grand divisions of our country. The person whose curiosity prompts him to take an account of the immense piles of Northern lumber now lying on the wharves and houseless lots in Baltimore, Richmond, and other slaveholding cities, will not, we imagine, form a very flattering opinion of the products of Southern forests. Let it be remembered that nearly all the clippers, steamers, and small craft, are built at the North ; that large cargoes of Eastern lumber are exported to foreign countries ; that nine-tenths of the wooden-ware used in the Southern States is manufactured in New England ; that, in outrageous disregard of the natural rights and claims of Southern mechanics, the markets of the South are forever filled with Northern furniture, vehicles, ax helves, walking canes, yard-sticks, clothes-pins and pen-holders that the extraordinary number of factories, steam-engines, forges and machine-shops in the free States, require an extraordinary quantity of cord-wood ; that a large majority of the magnificent edifices and other structures, both private and public, in which timber, in its various forms, is extensively used, are to be found in the free States—we say, let all these things be remembered, and the truth will at once flash across the mind that the forests of the North are a source of far greater income than those of the South. The difference is simply this: At the North everything is turned to advantage. When a tree is cut down, the main body is sold or used for lumber, railing or paling, the stump for matches and shoepegs, the knees for shipbuilding, and the branches for fuel. At the South everything is either neglected or mismanaged. Whole forests are felled by the ruthless hand of slavery, the trees are cut into logs, rolled into heaps, covered with the limbs and brush, and then burned on the identical soil that gave them birth. The land itself next falls a prey to the fell destroyer, and that which was once a beautiful, fertile and luxuriant woodland, is soon despoiled of all its treasures, and converted into an eye-offending desert.

Were we to go beneath the soil and collect all the mineral and lapidarious wealth of the free States, we should find it so much greater than the corresponding wealth of the slave States, that no ordinary combination of figures would suffice to express the difference. To say nothing of the gold and quicksilver of California, the iron and coal of Pennsylvania, the copper of Michigan, the lead of Illinois, or the salt of New-York, *the marble and free-stone quarries of New England are, incredible as it may seem to those unacquainted with the facts, far more important sources of revenue than all the subterranean deposits in the slave States.* From the most reliable statictics within our reach, we are led to the inference that the total value of all the precious metals, rocks, minerals, and medicinal waters, annually extracted from the bowels of the free States, is not less than eighty-five million of dollars ; the whole value of the same substances annually brought up from beneath the surface of the slave States does not exceed twelve millions. In this respect to what is our poverty ascribable ? To the same cause that has impoverished and dishonored us in all other respects—the thriftless and degrading institution of slavery.

Nature has been kind to us in all things. The strata and substrata of the South are profusely enriched with gold and silver, and precious stones, and from the natural orifices and aqueducts in Virgina and North Carolina, flow the purest healing waters in the world. But of what avail is all this latent wealth ? Of what avail will it ever be, so long as slavery is permitted to play the dog in the manger ? To these queries there can be but one reply. Slavery must be suppressed ; the South, so great and so glorious by nature, must be reclaimed from her infamy and degradation ; our cities, fields and forests, must be kept intact from the unsparing monster ; the various and ample resources of our vast domain, subterraneous as well as superficial, must be developed, and made to contribute to our pleasures and to the necessities of the world.

A very significant chapter, and one particularly pertinent to many of the preceding pages, might be written on the Decline of Agriculture in the Slave States ; but as the press of other subjects admonishes us to be concise upon this point, we shall present only a few of the more striking instances. In the first place, let us compare the crops of wheat and rye in Kentucky, in 1850, with the corresponding crops in the same State in 1840—after which, we will apply a similar rule of comparison to two or three other slaveholding states.

KENTUCKY.

	Wheat, bus.		Rye, bus.
Crop of 1840	4,803,152		1,321,373
" " 1850	2,142,822		415,073
Decrease	2,660,330 bus.	Decrease	906,300 bus.

TENNESSEE.

	Wheat, bus.		Tobacco, lbs.
Crop of 1840	4,569,692		29,550,432
" " 1850	1,619,386		20,148,932
Decrease	2,950,306 bus.	Decrease	9,401,500 lbs.

VIRGINIA.

	Rye, bus.		Tobacco, lbs.
Crop of 1840	1,482,799		75,347,106
" " 1850	458,930		56,803,227
Decrease	1,023,869 bus.	Decrease	18,543,879 lbs.

ALABAMA.

	Wheat, bus.		Rye, bus.
Crop of 1840	838,052		51,000
" " 1850	294,044		17,261
Decrease	544,008 bus.	Decrease	33,739 bus

The story of these figures is too intelligible to require words of explanation; we shall, therefore, drop this part of our subject, and proceed to compile a couple of tables that will exhibit on a single page the wealth, revenue and expenditure, of the several states of the confederacy. Let it be distinctly understood, however, that, in the compilation of these tables, three million two hundred and four thousand three hundred and thirteen negroes are valued as personal property, and credited to the Southern States as if they were so many horses and asses, or bridles and blankets—and that no monetary valuation whatever is placed on any creature, of any age, color, sex or condition, that bears the upright form of man in the free States.

TABLE NO. XX.

WEALTH, REVENUE AND EXPENDITURE OF THE FREE STATES—1850.

States.	Real and Personal property.	Revenue.	Expenditure.
California	$22,161,872	$366,825	$925,625
Connecticut	155,707,980	150,189	137,326
Illinois	156,265,006	736,030	192.940
Indiana	202,650,264	1,283,064	1,061,605
Iowa	23,714,638	139,681	131,631
Maine	122,777,571	744,879	624,101
Massachusetts	573,342,286	598,170	674,622
Michigan	59,787,255	548,326	431,918
New Hampshire	103,652,835	141,686	149,890
New Jersey	153,151,619	139,166	180,614
New York	1,080,309,216	2,698,310	2,520,932
Ohio	504,726,120	3,016,403	2,736.060
Pennsylvania	729,144,998	7,716,552	6,876,480
Rhode Island	80,508,794	124,944	115.835
Vermont	92,205,049	185,830	183,058
Wisconsin	42,056,595	135,155	136,096
	$4,102,172,108	$18,725,211	$17,076,733

TABLE NO. XXI.

WEALTH, REVENUE AND EXPENDITURE OF THE SLAVE STATES—1850.

States.	Real and Personal property.	Revenue.	Expenditure.
Alabama	$228,204,332	$658 976	$513,559
Arkansas	39,841,025	68,412	74,076
Delaware	18,855,863		
Florida	23,198.734	60,619	55,234
Georgia	335,425,714	1,142,405	597,882
Kentucky	301,628,456	779,293	674,697
Louisiana	233,998,764	1,146,568	1,098.911
Maryland	219,217,364	1,279,953	1,360,458
Mississippi	228,951,130	221,200	223,637
Missouri	137,247,707	326,579	207,656
North Carolina	226,800,472	219,000	228,173
South Carolina	288,257,694	532,152	463.021
Tennessee	207,454,704	502.126	623,625
Texas	55,362,340	140,688	156,622
Virginia	391,646,438	1,265,744	1,272,382
	$2,936,090,737	$8,343,715	$7,549,933

Entire Wealth of the Free States,................	$4,102,172,108
Entire Wealth of the Slave States, including Slaves,	2,936,090,737
Balance in favor of the Free States,..........	$1,166,081,371

What a towering monument to the beauty and glory of Free Labor! What irrefragable evidence of the unequaled efficacy and grandeur of free institutions! These figures are, indeed, too full of meaning to be passed by without comment. The two tables from which they are borrowed are at least a volume within themselves; and, after all the pains we have taken to compile them, we shall, perhaps, feel somewhat disappointed if the reader fails to avail himself of the important information they impart.

Human life, in all ages, has been made up of a series of adventures and experiments, and even at this stage of the world's existence, we are almost as destitute of a perfect rule of action, secular or religious, as were the erratic cotemporaries of Noah. It is true, however, that we have made some progress in the right direction; and as it seems to be the tendency of the world to correct itself, we may suppose that future generations will be enabled, by intuition, to discriminate between the true and the false, the good and the bad, and that with the development of this faculty of the mind, error and discord will begin to wane, and finally cease to exist. Of all the experiments that have been tried by the people in America, slavery has proved the most fatal; and the sooner it is abolished the better it will be for us, for posterity, and for the world. One of the evils resulting from it, and that not the least, is apparent in the figures above. Indeed, the *unprofitableness* of

4*

slavery is a monstrous evil, when considered in all its bearings; it makes us poor; poverty makes us ignorant; ignorance makes us wretched; wretchedness makes us wicked, and wickedness leads to the devil!

> "Ignorance is the curse of God,
> Knowledge the wing wherewith we fly to heaven."

Facts truly astounding are disclosed in the two last tables, and we could heartily wish that every intelligent American would commit them to memory. The total value of all the real and personal property of the free States, with an area of only 612,597 square miles, is one billion one hundred and sixty-six million eighty-one thousand three hundred and seventy-one dollars greater than the total value of all the real and personal property, including the price of 3,204,313 negroes, of the slave States, which have an area of 851,508 square miles! But extraordinary as this difference is in favor of the North, it is much less than the true amount. *On the authority of Southrons themselves, it is demonstrable beyond the possibility of refutation that the intrinsic value of all the property in the free States is more than three times greater than the intrinsic value of all the property in the slave States.*

James Madison, a Southern man, fourth President of the United States, a most correct thinker, and one of the greatest statesmen the country has produced, "thought it wrong to admit the idea that there could be property in man," and we indorse, to the fullest extent, this opinion of the profound editor of the *Federalist.* We shall not recognize property in man; the slaves of the South are not worth a groat in any civilized community; no man of genuine decency and refinement would hold them as property on any terms; in the eyes of all enlightened nations and individuals, they are men, not merchandize. Southern pro-slavery politicians, some of whom have not hesitated to buy and sell their own sons and daughters, boast that the slaves of the South are worth sixteen hundred million of dollars, and we have seen the amount estimated as high as two thousand million. Mr. De Bow, the Southern superintendent of the seventh census, informs us that the value of all the property in the slave States, real and personal, including slaves, was, in 1850, only $2,936,090,737; while, according to the same authority, the value of all the real and personal property in the free States, genuine property, property that is everywhere recognized as property, was, at the same time, $4,102,172,108. Now all we have to do in order to ascertain the real value of all the property of the South, independent of negroes, whose value, if valuable at all, is of a local and precarious character, is to subtract from the sum total of Mr. De Bow's return of the entire wealth of the slave States the estimated value of the slaves themselves; and then, by deducting the difference from the intrinsic value of all the property in the free States, we shall have the exact amount of the overplus of wealth in the glorious land of free soil, free labor, free speech, free presses, and free schools. And now to the task.

Entire Wealth of the Slave States, including Slaves	$2,936,090,737
Estimated Value of the Slaves,....................	1,600,000,000
True Wealth of the Slave States,.............	$1,336,090,737

True Wealth of the Free States,....................	$4,102,172,108
True Wealth of the Slave States,..................	1,336,090,737
Balance in favor of the Free States,...........	$2,766,081,371

There, friends of the South and of the North, you have the conclusion of the whole matter. Liberty and slavery are before you; choose which you will have; as for us, in the memorable language of the immortal Henry, we say, "give us liberty, or give us death!" In the great struggle for wealth that has been going on between the two rival systems of free and slave labor, the balance above exhibits the net profits of the former. The struggle on the one side has been calm, laudable, and eminently successful; on the other, it has been attended by tumult, unutterable cruelties and disgraceful failure. We have given the slave drivers every conceivable opportunity to vindicate their domestic policy, but for them to do it is a moral impossibility.

Less than three-quarters of a century ago—say in 1789, for that was about the average time of the abolition of slavery in the Northern States—the South, with advantages in soil, climate, rivers, harbors, minerals, forests, and, indeed, almost every other natural resource, began an even race with the North in all the important pursuits of life; and now, in the brief space of scarce three score years and ten, we find her completely distanced, enervated, dejected and dishonored. Slave-drivers are the sole authors of her disgrace; as they have sown so let them reap.

As we have seen above, a careful and correct inventory of all the real and personal *property* in the two grand divisions of the country, discloses the astounding fact that, in 1850 the free States were worth precisely *two thousand seven hundred and sixty-six million eighty-one thousand three hundred and seventy-one dollars* more than the slave States! Twenty-seven hundred and sixty-six million of dollars!—Think of it! What a vast and desirable sum, and how much better off the South would be with it than without it! Such is the enormous amount out of which slavery has defrauded us during the space of sixty-one years—from 1789 to 1850—being an average of about forty-five million three hundred and fifty thousand dollars per annum. During the last twenty-five or thirty years, however, our annual losses have been far greater than they were formerly. There has been a gradual increase every year, and now the ratio of increase is almost incredible. No patriotic Southerner can become conversant with the facts without experiencing a feeling of alarm and indignation. Until the North abolished slavery, she had no advantage of us whatever; the South was more than her equal in every respect. But no sooner had she got rid of that hampering and pernicious institution than she began to absorb our wealth, and now it is confidently believed that the merchants and negro-driving pleasure-seekers of the South annually pour one hundred and twenty million of dollars into her coffers! Taking into account, then, the probable amount of money that has been drawn from the South and invested in the North within the last six years, and adding it to the grand balance above—the net profits of the North up to 1850—it may be safely assumed that, in the present year of grace, 1857, *the free States are worth at least thirty-four hundred million of dollars more than the slave States!* Let him who dares, gainsay these remarks and calculations; no truthful tongue will deny them; no honorable pen can controvert them.

One more word now as to the valuation of negroes. Were our nature so degraded, or our conscience so elastic as to permit us to set a price upon men, as we would set a price upon cattle and corn, we should be content to abide by the appraisement of the slaves of the South, and would then enter into a calculation to ascertain the value of foreigners to the North. Not long since, it was declared in the South that "one free laborer is equal to five slaves," and as there are two million five hundred thousand Europeans in the free States, all of whom are free laborers, we might bring Southern authority to back us in estimating their value at *sixty-two hundred million of dollars*—a handsome sum wherewithal to offset the account of *sixteen hundred million of dollars*, brought forward as the value of Southern slaves! It is obvious, therefore, that if we were disposed to follow the barbarian example of the traffickers in human flesh, we could prove the North vastly richer than the South in bone and sinew—to say nothing of mind and morals, which shall receive our attention hereafter. The North has just as good a right to appraise the Irish immigrant, as the South has to set a price on the African slave. But as it would be wrong to do either, we shall do neither. It is not our business to think of man as a merchantable commodity; and we will not, even by implication, admit "the wild and guilty fantasy," that the condition of chattelhood may rightfully attach to sentient and immortal beings.

In this connection, we would direct the special attention of the reader to the following eloquent passage, exhibiting the philosophy of free and slave labor, from the facile pen of the editor of the *North American and United States Gazette*:

"In the very nature of things, the freeman must produce more than the slave. There is no conclusion of science more certain. Under a system which gives to a laboring man the fruit of his toil, there is every motive to render him diligent and assiduous. If he relies on being employed by others, his wages rise with his reputation for industry, skill, and faithfulness. And as owner of the soil, there is every assurance that he will do what he can to cultivate it to the best advantage, and develope its latent wealth. Self-interest will call forth what powers of intellect and of invention he has to aid him in his work, and employ his physical strength to the greatest possible advantage. Free labor receives an immediate reward, which cheers and invigorates it; and above all, it has that chief spring of exertion, hope, whose bow always spans the heaven before it. It has an inviolate hearth; it has a home. But it looks forward to a still better condition, to brighter prospects in the future, to which its efforts all contribute. The children in such a household are chief inducements to nerve the arm of labor, that they may be properly cared for, fed, clothed, educated, accomplished, instructed in some useful and honorable calling, and provided for when they shall go out upon the world. All its sentiments, religious and otherwise, all its affections for parents and kindred, all its tastes are so many impelling and stimulating forces. It is disposed to read, to ornament its home, to travel, to enjoy social intercourse, and to attain these ends, it rises to higher exertions and a stricter economy of time ; it explores every path of employment, and is, therefore, in the highest degree productive.

"How different is it with slave labor ! The slave toils for another, and not for himself. Whether he does little or much, whether his work is well or ill performed, he has a subsistence, nothing less, nothing more ; and why should he toil beyond necessity ? He cannot accumulate any property for the decline of his years, or to leave to his children when he is departed. Nay, he cannot toil to better the present condition of his children. They belong to another, and not to him. He cannot supply his hut with comforts, or embellish it with the adornments of taste. He does not read. He does not journey for pleasure. Inducements to exertion, he has none. That he may adapt himself to his condition, and enjoy the present hour, he deadens those aspirations that must always be baffled in his case, and sinks down into ease and sensuality. His mind is unlighted and untutored ; dark with ignorance. Among those who value him most, he is proverbially indolent, thievish, and neglectful of his master's interests. It is common for even the advocates of slavery to declare that one freeman is worth half a dozen slaves. With every cord to exertion thus sundered, the mind benighted, the man nearly lost in the animal, it requires no deep philosophy to see why labor cannot be near as productive as it would be were these conditions all reversed. Though ever so well directed by the superior skill, and urged forward by the strong arm of the master, slave labor is necessarily a blight to the soil—sterility follows in its steps, and not afar off.

"What a difference, plain and heaven-wide, between the outward and interior life of a slave and of a free community, resulting directly and palpably from this difference in its labor. The cottage-home, amid trees and shrubbery, its apartments well adorned and furnished, books on its shelves, and the passing literature of the day scattered around; the few, perhaps, but well-tilled acres, belonging to the man who tills them; the happy children with sunny prospects; the frequent school; the church arrayed with beauty; the thriving, handsome village; the flourishing cities and prosperous marts of trade; the busy factories; railroads, traffic, travel—where free labor tills the ground, how beautiful it all is in contrast to the forlorn and dreary aspect of a country tilled by slaves. The villages of such a country are mainly groups of miserable huts. Its comparatively few churches are too often dilapidated and unsightly. The common school-house, the poor man's college, is hardly known, showing how little interest is felt in the chief treasures of the State, the immortal minds of the multitude who are not born to wealth. The signs of premature old age are visibly impressed upon everything that meets the eye. The fields present a dread monotony. Everywhere you see lands that are worn out, barren and deserted, in consequence of slave tillage, left for more fertile lands in newer regions, which are also, in their turn, to be smitten with sterility and forsaken. The free community may increase its population almost without limit.

The capacity of slave countries to sustain a population is soon at an end, and then it diminishes. In all the elements of essential prosperity, in all that elevates man, how striking the contrast between the region that is tilled by slave, and the region that is tilled by free labor."

For the purpose of showing what Virginia, once the richest, most populous, and most powerful of the States, has become under the blight of slavery, we shall now introduce an extract from one of the speeches delivered by Henry A. Wise, during the last gubernatorial campaign in that degraded commonwealth. Addressing a Virginia audience, in language as graphic as it is truthful, he says :—

"Commerce has long ago spread her sails, and sailed away from you. You have not, as yet, dug more than coal enough to warm yourselves at your own hearths; you have set no tilt-hammer of Vulcan to strike blows worthy of gods in your own iron-foundries ; you have not yet spun more than coarse cotton enough, in the way of manufacture, to clothe your own slaves. You have no commerce, no mining, no manufactures. You have relied alone on the single power of agriculture, and *such agriculture!* Your sedge-patches outshine the sun. Your inattention to your only source of wealth, has seared the very bosom of mother earth. Instead of having to feed cattle on a thousand hills, you have had to chase the stump-tailed steer through the sedge-patches to procure a tough beef-steak. The present condition of things has existed too long in Virginia The landlord has skinned the tenant, and the tenant has skinned the land, until all have grown poor together."

With tears in its eyes, and truth on its lips, for the first time after an interval of twenty years, the *Richmond Enquirer* helps to paint the melancholy picture. In 1852, that journal thus bewailed the condition of Virginia :—

"We have cause to feel deeply for our situation. Philadelphia herself contains a population far greater than the whole free population of Eastern Virginia. The little State of Massachusetts has an aggregate wealth exceeding that of Virginia by more than $126,000,000."

Just a score of years before these words were penned, the same paper, then edited by the elder Ritchie, made a most earnest appeal to the intelligence and patriotism of Virginia, to adopt an effectual measure for the speedy overthrow of the damnable institution of human bondage Here is an extract from an article which appeared in its editorial column under date of January 7th, 1832 :

"Something must be done, and it is the part of no honest man to deny it—of no free press to affect to conceal it. When this dark population is growing upon us ; when every new census is but gathering its appalling numbers upon us ; when, within a period equal to that in which this Federal Constitution has been in existence, these numbers will increase to more than two millions within Virginia ; when our sister States are closing their doors upon our blacks for sale, and when our whites are moving westwardly in greater numbers than we like to hear of when this, the fairest land on all this continent, for soil, and climate and situation, combined, might become a sort of garden spot, if it were worked by the hands of white men alone, can we, ought we, to sit quietly down, fold our arms, and say to each other, 'Well, well; this thing will not come to the worst in our days; we will leave it to our children, and our grandchildren, and great-grandchildren, to take care of themselves, and to brave the storm!' Is this to act like wise men? Means, sure but gradual, systematic but discreet, ought to be adopted for reducing the mass of evil which is pressing upon the South, and will still more press upon her, the longer it is put off. We say now, in the utmost sincerity of our hearts, that our wisest men cannot give too much of their attention to this subject, nor can they give it too soon."

Better abolition doctrine than this is seldom heard. Why did not the *Enquirer* continue to preach it? What potent influence hushed its clarion voice, just as it began to be lifted in behalf of a liberal policy and an enlightened humanity? Had Mr. Ritchie continued to press the truth home to the hearts of the people, as he should have done, Virginia, instead of being worth only $392,000,000 in 1850—negroes and all—would have been worth at least $800,000,000 in genuine property; and if the State had emancipated her slaves at the time of the adoption of the Constitution, the last census would no doubt have reported her wealth, and correctly, at a sum exceeding a thousand millions of dollars.

Listen now to the statement of a momentous fact. The value of all the property, real and personal, including slaves, in seven slave States, Virginia, North Carolina, Tennessee, Missouri, Arkansas, Florida and Texas, is less than the real and personal estate, which is unquestionable property, in the single State of New-York. Nay, worse; if eight entire slave States, Arkansas, Delaware, Florida, Maryland, Missouri, Mississippi, Tennessee and Texas, and the District of Columbia—with all their hordes of human merchandize—were put up at auction, New-York could buy them all, and then have one hundred and thirty-three millions of dollars left in her pocket! Such is the amazing contrast between freedom and slavery, even in a pecuniary point of view. When we come to compare the North with the South in regard to literature, general intelligence, inventive genius, moral and religious enterprises, the discoveries in medicine, and the progress in the arts and sciences, we shall, in every instance, find the contrast equally great on the side of Liberty.

It gives us no pleasure to say hard things of the Old Dominion, the mother of Washington, Jefferson, Henry, and other illustrious patriots, who, as we shall prove hereafter, were genuine abolitionists; but the policy which she has pursued has been so utterly inexcusable, so unjust to the non-slaveholding whites, so cruel to the negroes, and so disregardful of the rights of humanity at large, that it becomes the duty of every one who makes allusion to her history, to expose her follies, her crimes, and her poverty, and to publish every fact, of whatever nature, that would be instrumental in determining others to eschew her bad example. She has wilfully departed from the faith of the founders of this Republic. She has not only turned a deaf ear to the counsel of wise men from other States in the Union, but she has, in like manner, ignored the teachings of the great warriors and statesmen who have sprung from her own soil. In a subsequent chapter, we expect to show that all, or nearly all, the distinguished Virginians, whose bodies have been consigned to the grave, but whose names have been given to history, and whose memoirs have a place in the hearts of their countrymen, were the friends and advocates of universal freedom—that they were inflexibly opposed to the extension of slavery into the Territories, devised measures for its restriction, and, with hopeful anxiety, looked forward to the time when it should be eradicated from the States themselves. With them, the rescue of our country from British domination, and the establishment of the General Government upon a firm basis, were considerations of paramount importance; they supposed, and no doubt earnestly desired, that the States, in their sovereign capacities, would soon abolish an institution which was so palpably in conflict with the principles enunciated in the Declaration of Independence. Indeed, it would seem that, among the framers of that immortal instrument and its equally immortal sequel, the Constitution of the United States, there was a tacit understanding to this effect; and the Northern States, true to their implied faith, abolished it within a short period after our national independence had been secured. Not so with the South. She has pertinaciously refused to perform her duty. She has apostatized from the faith of her greatest men, and even at this very moment repudiates the sacred principle that "all men are endowed by their Creator with certain unalienable rights," among which "are life, liberty, and the pursuit of happiness" It is evident, therefore, that the free States are the only members of this confederacy that have established republican forms of government based upon the theories of Washington, Jefferson, Madison, Henry, and other eminent statesmen of Virginia.

The great revolutionary movement which was set on foot in Charlotte, Mecklenburg county, North Carolina, on the 20th day of May, 1775, has not yet been terminated, nor will it be, until every slave in the United States is freed from the tyranny of his master. Every victim of the vile institution, whether white or black, must be reinvested with the sacred rights and privileges of which he has been deprived by an inhuman oligarchy. What our noble sires of the revolution left unfinished it is our duty to complete. They did all that true valor and patriotism could accomplish. Not one iota did they swerve from their plighted faith; the self-sacrificing spirit which they evinced will command the applause of every succeeding age. Not in vindication of their own personal rights merely, but of the rights of humanity; not for their own generation and age simply, but for all ages to the end of time, they gave their toil, their treasure and their blood, nor deemed them all too great a price to pay for the establishment of so comprehensive and beneficent a principle. Let their posterity emulate their courage, their disinterestedness, and their zeal, and especially remember that it is the duty of every existing generation so to provide for its individual interests, as to confer superior advantages on that which is to follow. To this principle the North has adhered with the strictest fidelity. How has it been with the South? Has she imitated the praiseworthy example of our illustrious ancestors? No! She has treated it with the utmost contempt; she has been extremely selfish—so selfish, indeed, that she has robbed posterity of its natural rights. From the period of the formation of the government down to the present moment, her policy has been downright suicidal, and, as a matter of course, wholly indefensible. She has hugged a viper to her breast; her whole system has been paralyzed, her conscience is seared, and she is becoming callous to every principle of justice and magnanimity. Except among the non-slaveholders, who, besides being kept in the grossest ignorance, are under the restraint of all manner of iniquitous laws, patriotism has ceased to exist within her borders. And here we desire to be distinctly understood, for we shall have occasion to refer to this matter again. We repeat, therefore, the substance of our averment, that, at this day, there is not a grain of patriotism in the South, except among the non-slaveholders. Subsequent pages shall testify to the truth of this assertion. Here and there, it is true, a slaveholder, disgusted with the institution, becomes ashamed of himself, emancipates his negroes, and enters upon the walks of honorable life; but these cases are exceedingly rare, and do not, in any manner, disprove the general correctness of our remark. All persons who do voluntarily manumit their slaves, as mentioned above, are undeniably actuated by principles of pure patriotism, justice and humanity; and so believing, we delight to do them honor.

Once more to the Old Dominion. At her door we lay the bulk of the evils of slavery. The first African sold in America was sold on James River, in that State, on the

20th of August, 1620; and although the institution was fastened upon her and the other colonies by the mother country, she was the first to perceive its blighting and degrading influences, her wise men were the first to denounce it, and, after the British power was overthrown at York Town, she should have been the first to abolish it. Fifty-seven years ago she was the Empire State; now, with half a dozen other slaveholding states thrown into the scale with her, she is far inferior to New-York, which, at the time Cornwallis surrendered his sword to Washington, was less than half her equal. Had she obeyed the counsels of the good, the great and the wise men of our nation—especially of her own incomparable sons, the extendible element of slavery would have been promptly arrested, and the virgin soil of nine Southern States, Kentucky, Tennessee, Louisiana, Mississippi, Alabama, Missouri, Arkansas, Florida, and Texas, would have been saved from its horrid pollutions. Confined to the original states in which it existed, the institution would soon have been disposed of by legislative enactments, and long before the present day, by a gradual process that could have shocked no interest and alarmed no prejudice, we should have rid ourselves not only of African slavery, which is an abomination and a curse, but also of the negroes themselves, who, in our judgment, whether viewed in relation to their actual characteristics and condition, or through the strong antipathies of the whites, are, to say the least, an undesirable population.

This, then, is the ground of our expostulation with Virginia: that, in stubborn disregard of the advice and friendly warnings of Washington, Jefferson, Madison, Henry, and a host of other distinguished patriots who sprang from her soil—patriots whose voices shall be heard before we finish our task—and in utter violation of every principle of justice and humanity, *she still persists in* fostering an institution which is so manifestly detrimental to her vital interests. Every Virginian, whether living or dead, whose name is an honor to his country, has placed on record his abhorrence of slavery, and in doing so, has borne testimony to the blight and degradation that everywhere follow in its course. One of the best abolition speeches we have ever read was delivered in the Virginia House of Delegates, January 20th, 1832, by Charles James Faulkner, who still lives, and who has, we understand, generously emancipated several of his slaves, and sent them to Liberia. Here follows an extract from his speech; let Southern politicians read it attentively, and imbibe a moiety of the spirit of patriotism which it breathes:—

"Sir, I am gratified to perceive that no gentleman has yet risen in this Hall, the avowed advocate of slavery. *The day has gone by when such a voice could be listened to with patience, or even with forbearance.* I even regret, Sir, that we should find those amongst us who enter the lists of discussion as its *apologists*, except alone upon the ground of uncontrollable necessity. And yet, who could have listened to the very eloquent remarks of the gentleman from Brunswick, without being forced to conclude that he at least considered slavery, however *not to be defended upon principle*, yet as being divested of much of its enormity, as you approach it in practice.

"Sir, if there be one who concurs with that gentleman in the harmless character of this institution, let me request him to compare the condition of the slaveholding portion of this commonwealth—*barren, desolate, and seared as it were by the avenging hand of Heaven*—with the descriptions which we have of this country from those who first broke its virgin soil. To what is this change ascribable? *Alone to the withering and blasting effects of slavery.* If this does not satisfy him, let me request him to extend his travels to the *Northern States of this Union*, and beg him to contrast the happiness and contentment which prevail throughout that country, the busy and cheerful sound of industry, the rapid and swelling growth of their population, their means and institutions of education, their skill and proficiency in the useful arts, their enterprise and public spirit, the monuments of their commercial and manufacturing industry; and, above all, their devoted attachment to the government from which they derive their protection, *with the derision, discontent, indolence, and poverty of the Southern country.* To what, Sir, is all this ascribable? *To that vice in the organization of society, by which one-half of its inhabitants are arrayed in interest and feeling against the other half*—to that unfortunate state of society in which freemen regard labor as disgraceful, and slaves shrink from it as a burden tyrannically imposed upon them—to that condition of things in which half a million of your population can feel no sympathy with the society in the prosperity of which they are forbidden to participate, and no attachment to a government at whose hands they receive nothing but injustice.

"If this should not be sufficient, and the curious and incredulous inquirer should suggest that the contrast which has been adverted to, and which is so manifest, might be traced to a difference of climate, or other causes distinct from slavery itself, permit me to refer him to the two States of Kentucky and Ohio. No difference of soil, no diversity of climate, no diversity in the original settlement of those two States, can account for the remarkable disproportion in their natural advancement. Separated by a river alone, *they seem to have been purposely and providentially designed to exhibit in their future histories the difference which necessarily results from a country free from, and a country afflicted with, the curse of slavery.*

"Vain and idle is every effort to strangle this inquiry. As well might you attempt to chain the ocean, or stay the avenging thunderbolts of Heaven, as to drive the people from any inquiry which may result in their better condition. This is too deep, too engrossing a subject of consideration. It addresses itself too strongly to our interests, to our passions, and to our feelings. I shall advocate no scheme that does not respect the right of property, *so far as it is entitled to be respected,* with a just regard to the safety and resources of the State. I would approach the subject as one of great magnitude and delicacy, as one whose varied and momentous consequences demand the calmest and most deliberate investigation. But still, Sir, I would approach it—aye, delicate as it may be, encompassed as it may be with difficulties and hazards, I would still approach it. The people demand it. Their security requires it. In the language of the wise and prophetic Jefferson, 'You mus approach it—you must bear it—you must adopt some plan of emancipation, or worse will follow.'"

Mr Curtis, in a speech in the Virginia Legislature in 1832, said:

"There is a malaria in the atmosphere of these regions, which the new comer shuns, as being deleterious to his views and habits. See the wide-spreading ruin which the avarice of our ancestral government has produced in the South, as witnessed in a sparse population of freemen, deserted habitations, and fields without culture! Strange to tell, even the wolf, driven back long since by the approach of man, now returns, after the lapse of a hundred years, to howl over the desolations of slavery."

Mr. Moore, also a member of the Legislature of Virginia, in speaking of the evils of slavery, said:

"The first I shall mention is the irresistible tendency which it has to undermine and destroy everything like virtue and morality in the community. If we look back through the long course of time which has elapsed since the creation to the present moment, we shall scarcely be able to point out a people whose situation was not, in many respects, preferable to our own, and that of the other States, in which negro slavery exists.

"In that part of the State below tide-water, the whole face of the country wears an appearance of almost utter desolation, distressing to the beholder. The very spot on which our ancestors landed, a little more than two hundred years ago, appears to be on the eve of again becoming the haunt of wild beasts."

Mr. Rives, of Campbell county, said:

"On the multiplied and desolating evils of slavery, he was not disposed to say much. The curse and deteriorating consequence were within the observation and experience of the members of the House and the people of Virginia, and it did not seem to him that there could be two opinions about it."

Mr. Powell said:

"I can scarcely persuade myself that there is a solitary gentleman in this House who will not readily admit that slavery is an evil, and that its removal, if practicable, is a consummation most devoutly to be wished. I have not heard, nor do I expect to hear, a voice raised in this Hall to the contrary."

In the language of another, "we might multiply extracts almost indefinitely from Virginia authorities—testifying to the blight and degradation that have overtaken the Old Dominion, in every department of her affairs. Her commerce gone, her agriculture decaying, her land falling in value, her mining and manufactures nothing, her schools dying out,—she presents, according to the testimony of her own sons, the saddest of all pictures—that of a sinking and dying State." Every year leaves her in a worse condition than it found her; and as it is with Virginia, so it is with the entire South. In the terse language of Governor Wise, "all have grown poor together." The black god of slavery, which the South has worshipped for two hundred and thirty-seven years, is but a devil in disguise; and if we would save ourselves from being engulphed in utter ruin we must repudiate this foul god, for a purer deity, and abandon his altars for a holier shrine. No time is to be lost; his fanatical adorers, the despotic adversaries of human liberty, are concocting schemes for the enslavement of all the laboring classes' irrespective of race or color. The issue is before us; we cannot evade it; we must meet it with firmness, and with unflinching valor.

What it was that paralyzed the tongues of all those members of the Virgina Legislature, who, at the session of 1831–'32, distinguished themselves by advocating a system of emancipation, is a mystery that has never yet been solved. Whether any or all of them shared a division of spoils with a certain newspaper editor, we have no means of knowing; but if all accounts be true, there was consummated in Richmond, in the latter part of the year 1832, one of the blackest schemes of bribery and corruption that was ever perpetrated in this or any other country. We are assured, however, that one thing is certain, and it is this: that the negro population of Virginia was very considerably and suddenly decreased by forcible emigration—that a large gang was driven further South, sold, and the proceeds divided among certain renegades and traitors, who, Judas-like, had agreed to serve the devil for a price.

We would fain avoid all personalities and uncomplimentary allusions to the dead, but when men, from love of lucre, from mere selfish motives, or from sheer turpitude of heart, inflict great injuries and outrages on the public, their villainy ought to be exposed, so that others may be deterred from following in their footsteps. As a general rule, man's moral nature is, we believe, so strong that it invariably prompts him to eschew vice and practice virtue—in other words, to do right; but this rule, like all others, has its exceptions, as might be most strikingly illustrated in the character of ——— ———, and some half-dozen or more of his pro-slavery coadjutors. From whose hands did this man receive fifty thousand dollars—improperly, if not illegally, taken from the public funds in Washington? When did he receive it?—and for what purpose?—and who was the arch-demagogue through whose agency the transfer was made? He was an oligarchical member of the Cabinet under Mr. Polk's administration in 1845,—and the money was *used*,—and who can doubt *intended*?—for the express purpose of establishing another negro-driving journal to support the tottering fortunes of slavery. From the second volume of a valuable political work, "by a Senator of thirty years," we make the following pertinent extract:—

"The *Globe* was sold, and was paid for, and how? becomes a question of public concern to answer; for it was paid for out of public money—those same $50,000 which were removed to the village bank in the interior of Pennsylvania by a Treasury order on the fourth of November, 1844. Three annual installments made the payment, and the Treasury did not reclaim the money for these three years; and, though traveling through tortuous channels, the sharpsighted Mr. Rives traced the money back to its starting point from that deposit. Besides, Mr. Cameron, who had control of the village bank, admitted before a committee of Congress, that he had furnished money for the payments--an admission which the obliging Committee, on request, left out of their report. Mr. Robert J. Walker was Secretary of the Treasury during these three years, and the conviction was absolute, among the close observers of the course of things, that he was the prime contriver and zealous manager of the arrangements which displaced Mr. Blair and installed Mr. Ritchie."

Thus, if we are to believe Mr. Benton, in his "Thirty Year's View," and we are disposed to regard him as good authority, the Washington *Union* was brought into existence under the peculiar auspices of the ostensible editor of the Richmond *Enquirer;* and the two papers, fathered by the same individual, have gone hand in hand for the last dozen or thirteen years, the shameless advocates and defenders of human bondage. To suppose that either has been sustained by fairer means than it was commenced with, would be wasting imagination on a great improbability. Both have uniformly and pertinaciously opposed every laudable enterprise that the white non-slaveholder has projected; indeed, so unmitigated has been their hostility to all manual pursuits in which their stupid and vulgar slaves can not be employed to advantage—and if there is any occupation under the sun in which they can be employed to good advantage, we known not what it is—that it is an extremely difficult matter to find a respectable merchant, mechanic, manufacturer, or business man of any calling whatever, within the bounds of their circulation.

We have been credibly informed by a gentleman from Powhattan county, in Virginia, that in the year 1836 or

'37, or about that time, the Hon. Abbott Lawrence, of Boston, backed by his brother Amos and other millionaires of New England, went down to Richmond with the sole view of reconnoitering the manufacturing facilities of that place—fully determined, if pleased with the water-power, to erect a large number of cotton-mills and machine-shops. He had been in the capital of Virginia only a day or two before he discovered, much to his gratification, that nature had shaped everything to his liking; and as he was a business man who transacted business in a business-like manner, he lost no time in making preliminary arrangements for the consummation of his noble purpose. His mission was one of peace and promise; others were to share the benefits of his laudable and concerted scheme; thousands of poor boys and girls in Virginia, instead of growing up in extreme poverty and ignorance, or of having to emigrate to the free States of the West, were to have avenues of profitable employment opened to them at home; thus they would be enabled to earn an honest and reputable living, to establish and sustain free schools, free libraries, free lectures, and free presses, to become useful and exemplary members of society, and to die fit candidates for heaven. The magnanimous New Englander was in ecstasies with the prospect that opened before him. Individually, so far as mere money was concerned, he was perfectly independent; his industry and economy in early life had secured to him the ownership and control of an ample fortune. With the aid of eleven other men, each equal to himself, he could have bought the whole city of Richmond—negroes and all—though it is not to be presumed that he would have disgraced his name by becoming a trader in human flesh. But he was not selfish; unlike the arrogant and illiberal slaveholder, he did not regard himself as the centre around whom everybody else should revolve. On the contrary, he was a genuine philanthropist. While, with a shrewdness that will command the admiration of every practical business man, he engaged in nothing that did not swell the dimensions of his own purse, he was yet always solicitous to invest his capital in a manner calculated to promote the interest of those around him. Nor was he satisfied with simply furnishing the means whereby his less fortunate neighbors were to become prosperous, intelligent and contented. With his generous heart and sagacious mind, he delighted to aid them in making a judicious application of his wealth to their own use. Moreover, as a member of society, he felt that the community had some reasonable claims upon him, and he made it obligatory on himself constantly to devise plans and exert his personal efforts for the public good. Such was the character of the distinguished manufacturer who honored Richmond with his presence nineteen or twenty years ago; such was the character of the men whom he represented, and such were the grand designs which they sought to accomplish.

To the enterprising and moneyed descendant of the Pilgrim Fathers it was a matter of no little astonishment, that the immense water-power of Richmond had been so long neglected. He expressed his surprise to a number of Virginians, and was at a loss to know why they had not, long prior to the period of his visit amongst them, availed themselves of the powerful element that is eternally gushing and foaming over the falls of James River. Innocent man! He was utterly unconscious of the fact that he was "interfering with the beloved institutions of the South," and little was he prepared to withstand the terrible denunciations that were immediately showered on his head through the columns of the Richmond *Enquirer*. Few words will suffice to tell the sequel. That negro-worshipping sheet, whose hireling policy, for the last four and twenty years, has been to support the worthless black slave and his tyrannical master at the expense of the free white laborer, wrote down the enterprise! and the noble son of New England, abused, insulted and disgusted, quietly returned to Massachusetts, and there employed his capital in building up the cities of Lowell and Lawrence, either of which, in all those elements of material and social prosperity that make up the greatness of States, is already far in advance of the most important of all the seedy and squalid niggervilles in the Old Dominion. Such is an inkling of the infamous means that have been resorted to, from time to time, for the purpose of upholding and perpetuating in America the accursed institution of slavery.

Having in view all the foregoing facts, we were not in the least surprised when, while walking through Hollywood Cemetery, in the western suburbs of Richmond, not long since, our companion, a Virginian of the true school, directed our attention to a monument of some pretentions, and exclaimed, "There lie the remains of a man upon whose monument should be inscribed in everlasting prominence the finger of scorn pointing downward." The reader scarcely needs to be told that we were standing at the tomb of ——— ———, who in the opinion of our friend, had, by concentrating within himself the views and purposes of all the evil spirits in Virginia, greatly retarded the abolition of slavery; so greatly, indeed, as, thereby, to throw the State at least fifty years behind her free competitors of the North, of the East, and of the West It is to be hoped that Virginia may never give birth to another man whose evil influence will so justly entitle him to the reprobation of posterity.

How any rational man in this or any other country, with the astounding contrasts between Freedom and Slavery ever looming in his view, can offer an apology for the existing statism of the South, is to us a most inexplicable mystery. Indeed, we cannot conceive it possible that the conscience of any man, who is really sane, would permit him to become the victim of such an egregious and diabolical absurdity. Therefore, at this period of our history, with the light of the past, the reality of the present, and the prospect of the future, all so prominent and so palpable, we infer that every person who sets up an unequivocal defence of the institution of slavery, must, of necessity, be either a fool, a knave, or a madman.

It is much to be regretted that the slavocrats look at but one side of the question. Of all the fanatics in the country, they have, of late, become the most unreasonable and ridiculous. Let them deliberately view the subject of slavery in all its aspects and bearings, and if they are possessed of honest hearts and convincible minds, they will readily perceive the grossness of their past errors, renounce their allegiance to a cause so unjust and disgraceful, and at once enroll themselves among the hosts of Freedom and the friends of universal Liberty. There are thirty-one States in the Union; let them drop California, or any other new free State, and then institute fifteen comparisons, first comparing New-York with Virginia, Pennsylvania with Carolina, Massachusetts with Georgia, and so on, until they have exhausted the catalogue. Then, for once, let them be bold enough to listen to the admonitions of their own souls, and if they do not soon start to their feet *demanding* the abolition of slavery, it will only be because they have reasons for suppressing their inmost sentiments. Whether we compare the old free States with the old slave States, or the new free States with the new slave States, the difference, unmistakable and astounding, is substantially the same. All the free States are alike, and all the slave States are alike. In the former, wealth, intelligence, power, progress, and prosperity, are the prominent characteristics; in the latter, poverty, ignorance, embecility, inertia, and extravagance, are the distinguishing features. To be convinced, it is only necessary for us to open our eyes and look at facts —to examine the *statistics* of the country, to free ourselves from obstinacy and prejudice, and to unbar our minds to convictions of truth. Let figures be the umpire. Close attention to the preceding and subsequent tables is all we ask; so soon as they shall be duly considered and understood, the primary object of this work will have been accomplished.

Not content with eating out the vitals of the South, slavery, true to the character which it has acquired for insatiety and rapine, is beginning to make rapid encroachments on new territory; and as a basis for a few remarks on the blasting influence which it is shedding over the broad and fertile domains of the West, which in accordance with the views and resolutions offered by the immortal Jefferson, should have been irrevocably dedicated to freedom, we beg leave to call the attention of the reader to another presentation of the philosophy of free and slave labor. Says the *North American and United States Gazette:*

"We have but to compare the States, possessing equal natural advantages, in which the two kinds of labor are employed, in order to decide with entire confidence as to which kind is the more profitable. At the origin of the government, Virginia, with a much larger extent of territory than New-York, contained a population of seven hundred and fifty thousand, and sent ten representatives to Congress; while New-York contained a population of three hundred and forty thousand, and sent six representatives to Congress. Behold how the figures are reversed. The population of New-York is three and a half millions, represented by thirty-three members in Congress; while the population of Virginia is but little more than one and a half millions, represented by thirteen members in Congress. It is the vital sap of free labor that makes the one tree so thrifty and vigorous, so capable of bearing with all ease the fruit of such a population. And it is slave labor which strikes a decadence through the other, drying up many of its branches with a fearful sterility, and rendering the rest but scantily fruitful; really incapable of sustaining more. Look at Ohio, teeming with inhabitants, its soil loaded with every kind of agricultural wealth, its people engaged in every kind of freedom's diversified employments, abounding with numberless happy homes, and with all the trophies of civilization, and it exhibits the magic effect of free labor, waking a wilderness into life and beauty; while Kentucky, with equal or superior natural advantages, nature's very garden in this Western world, which commenced its career at a much earlier date, and was in a measure populous when Ohio was but a slumbering forest, but which in all the elements of progress, is now left far, very far, behind its young rival, shows how slave labor hinders the development of wealth among a people, and brings a blight on their prosperity. The one is a grand and beautiful poem in honor of free labor. The other is an humble confession to the world of the inferiority of slave labor."

Equally significant is the testimony of Daniel R. Goodloe, of North Carolina, who says:—

"The history of the United States shows, that while the slave States increase in population less rapidly than the free, there is a tendency in slave society to diffusion, greater than is exhibited by free society. In fact, diffusion, or extension of area, is one of the necessities of slavery; the prevention of which is regarded as directly and immediately menacing to the existence of the institution. This arises from the almost exclusive application of slave labor to the one occupation of agriculture, and the difficulty, if not impossibility, of diversifying employments. Free society, on the contrary, has indefinite resources of development within a restricted area. It will far excel slave society in the cultivation of the ground—first, on account of the superior intelligence of the laborers; and secondly, in consequence of the greater and more various demands upon the earth's products, where commerce, manufactures, and the arts, abound. Then, these arts of life, by bringing men together in cities and towns, and employing them in the manufacture or transportation of the raw materials of the farmer, give rise to an indefinite increase of wealth and population. The confinement of a free people within narrow limits seems only to develop new resources of wealth, comfort and happiness; while slave society, pent up, withers and dies. It must continually be fed by new fields and forests, to be wasted and wilted under the poisonous tread of the slave."

Were we simply a freesoiler, or anything else less than a thorough and uncompromising abolitionist, we should certainly tax our ability to the utmost to get up a cogent argument against the extension of slavery over any part of our domain where it does not now exist; but as our principles are hostile to the institution even where it does exist, and, therefore, by implication and in fact, more hostile still to its introduction into new territory, we forbear the preparation of any special remarks on this particular subject.

With regard to the unnational and demoralizing institution of slavery, we believe the majority of Northern people are too scrupulous. They seem to think that it is enough for them to be mere freesoilers, to keep in check the diffusive element of slavery, and to prevent it from crossing over the bounds within which it is now regulated by municipal law. Remiss in their *national* duties, as we contend, they make no positive attack upon the institution in the Southern States. Only a short while since, one of their ablest journals—the *North American and United States Gazette*, published in Philadelphia—made use of the following language :—

"With slavery in the States, we make no pretence of having anything politically to do. For better or for worse, the system belongs solely to the people of those States ; and is separated by an impassable gulf of State sovereignty from any legal intervention of ours. We cannot vote it down any more than we can vote down the institution of caste in Hindostan, or abolish polygamy in the Sultan's dominions. Thus, precluded from all political action in reference to it, prevented from touching one stone of the edifice, not the slightest responsibility attaches to us as citizens for its continued existence. But on the question of extending slavery over the free Territories of the United States, it is our right, it is our imperative duty to think, to feel, to speak and to vote. We cannot interfere to cover the shadows of slavery with the sunshine of freedom, but we can interfere to prevent the sunshine of freedom from being eclipsed by the shadows of slavery. We can interpose to stay the progress of that institution, which aims to drive free labor from its own heritage. Kansas should be divided up into countless homes for the ownership of men who have a right to the fruit of their own labors. Free labor would make it bud and blossom like the rose ;

would cover it with beauty, and draw from it boundless wealth; would throng it with population; would make States, nations, empires out of it, prosperous, powerful, intelligent and free, illustrating on a wide theatre the beneficent ends of Providence in the formation of our government, to advance and elevate the millions of our race, and, like the heart in the body, from its central position, sending out on every side, far and near, the vital influences of freedom and civilization. May that region, therefore, be secured to free labor."

Now we fully and heartily indorse every line of the latter part of this extract; but, with all due deference to our sage cotemporary, we do most emphatically dissent from the sentiments embodied in the first part. Pray, permit us to ask—have the people of the North no interest in the United States as a *nation*, and do they not see that slavery is a great injury and disgrace to the *whole country*? Did they not, in "the days that tried men's souls," strike as hard blows to secure the independence of Georgia as they did in defending the liberties of Massachusetts, and is it not notoriously true that the Toryism of South Carolina prolonged the war two years at least? Is it not, moreover, equally true that the oligarchs of South Carolina have been unmitigated pests and bores to the General Government ever since it was organized, and that the free and conscientious people of the North are virtually excluded from her soil, in consequence of slavery? It is a well-known and incontestible fact, that the Northern States furnished about two-thirds of all the American troops engaged in the Revolutionary War; and, though they were neither more nor less brave or patriotic than their fellow-soldiers of the South, yet, inasmuch as the independence of our country was mainly secured by virtue of their numerical strength, we think they ought to consider it not only their right but their *duty* to make a firm and decisive effort to save the States which they fought to free, from falling under the yoke of a worse tyranny than that which overshadowed them under the reign of King George the Third. Freemen of the North! we earnestly entreat you to think of these things. Hitherto, as mere freesoilers, you have approached but half-way to the line of your duty; now, for your own sakes and for ours, and for the purpose of perpetuating this glorious Republic, which your fathers and our fathers founded in septennial streams of blood, we ask you, in all seriousness, to organize yourselves as *one man* under the banners of Liberty, and to aid us in *exterminating* slavery, which is the only thing that militates against our complete aggrandizement as a nation.

In this extraordinary crisis of affairs, no man can be a true patriot without first becoming an abolitionist. (A freesoiler is only a tadpole in an advanced state of transformation; an abolitionist is the full and perfectly developed frog.) And here, perhaps, we may be pardoned for the digression necessary to show the exact definition of the terms *abolish*, *abolition* and *abolitionist*. We have looked in vain for an explanation of the signification of these words in any Southern publication; for no dictionary has ever yet been published in the South, nor is there the least probability that one ever will be published within her bor ders, until slavery is *abolished;* but, thanks to Heaven, a portion of this continent is what our Revolutionary Fathers and the Fathers of the Constitution fought and labored and prayed to make it—a land of freedom, of power, of progress, of prosperity, of intelligence, of religion, of literature, of commerce, of science, of arts, of agriculture, of manufactures, of ingenuity, of enterprise, of wealth, of renown, of goodness, and of grandeur. From that glorious part of our confederacy—from the North, whence, on account of slavery in the South, we are under the humiliating necessity of procuring almost everything that is useful or ornamental, from primers to Bibles, from wafers to printing-presses, from ladles to locomotives, and from portfolios to portraits and pianos—comes to us a huge volume bearing the honored name of Webster—Noah Webster, who, after thirty-five years of unremitting toil, completed a work which is, we believe, throughout Great Britain and the United States, justly regarded as the standard vocabulary of the English language—and in it the terms *abolish, abolition,* and *abolitionist,* are defined as follows:—

"Abolish, *v. t.* To make void; to annul; to abrogate; applied chiefly and appropriately to establish laws, contracts, rites, customs and institutions; as to *abolish* laws by a repeal, actual or virtual. To destroy or put an end to; as to *abolish* idols."

"Abolition, *n.* The act of abolishing; or the state of being abolished; an annulling; abrogation; utter destruction; as the *abolition* of laws, decrees, or ordinances, rites, customs, &c. The putting an end to slavery; emancipation."

"Abolitionist, *n.* A person who favors abolition, or the immediate emancipation of slaves."

There, gentlemen of the South, you have the definitions of the transitive verb *abolish* and its two derivative nouns, *abolition* and *abolitionist;* can you, with the keenest possible penetration of vision, detect in either of these words even a tittle of the opprobrium which the oligarchs, in their wily and inhuman efforts to enslave all working classes irrespective of race or color, have endeavored to attach to them? We know you cannot; abolition is but another name for patriotism, and its other special synonyms are generosity, magnanimity, reason, prudence, wisdom, religion, progress, justice, and humanity.

And here, by the way, we may as well explain whom we refer to when we speak of gentlemen of the South. We say, therefore, that, deeply impressed with the conviction that slavery is a great social and political evil, a *sin and a crime*, in the fullest sense, whenever we speak of gentlemen of the South, or of gentlemen anywhere, or at whatever time, or in whatever connection we may speak of gentlemen, we seldom allude to slaveholders, for the simple reason that, with few exceptions, we cannot conscientiously recognize *them* as gentlemen. It is only in those rare instances where the crime is mitigated by circumstances over which the slaveholder has had no control, or where he himself, convinced of the impropriety, the folly and the wickedness of the institution, is anxious to abolish it, that we can sincerely apply to him the sacred appellation in question—an appellation which we would no sooner think of applying to a *pro-slavery* slaveholder, or any other pro-slavery man, than we would think of applying it to a border-ruffian, a thief or a murderer. Let it be understood, however, that the rare instances of which we speak are less rare than many persons may suppose. We are personally acquainted with several slaveholders in North Carolina, South Carolina, Maryland and Virginia, who have unreservedly assured us that they were disgusted with the institution, and some of them went so far as to say they would be glad to acquiesce in the provision of a statute which would make it obligatory on them all to manumit their slaves, without the smallest shadow or substance of compensation. These, we believe, are the sentiments of all the respectable and patriotic slaveholders, who have eyes to see, and see—ears to hear, and hear; who, perceiving the impoverishing and degrading effects of slavery, are unwilling to entail it on their children, and who, on account of their undeviating adherence to truth and justice, are, like the more intelligent non-slaveholders, worthy of being regarded as gentlemen in every sense of the term. Such slaveholders were Washington, Jefferson, Madison, and other illustrious Virginians, who, in the language of the great chief himself, declared it among their "*first wishes* to see some plan adopted by which slavery, in this country, may be abolished by law." The words embraced within this quotation were used by Washington, in a letter to John F. Mercer, dated September 9th, 1786—a letter from which we shall quote more freely hereafter; and we think his emphatic use of the participle *abolished*, at that early day, is proof positive that the glorious "Father of his Country" is entitled to the first place in the calendar of primitive American abolitionists.

It is against slavery on the whole, and against slaveholders as a body, that we wage an exterminating war. Those persons who, under the infamous slave-laws of the South—laws which have been correctly spoken of as a "disgrace to civilization," and which must be annulled simultaneously with the abolition of slavery—have had the vile institution entailed on them contrary to their wills, are virtually on our side ; we may, therefore, very properly strike them off from the black list of three hundred and forty-seven thousand slaveholders, who, as a body, have shocked the civilized world with their barbarous conduct, and from whose conceited and presumptuous ranks are selected the officers who do all the legislation, town, county, state and national, for (against) five millions of poor outraged whites, and three millions of enslaved negroes.

Non-slaveholders of the South ! farmers, mechanics and workingmen, we take this occasion to assure you that the slaveholders, the arrogant demagogues whom you have elected to offices of honor and profit, have hoodwinked you, trifled with you, and used you as mere tools for the consummation of their wicked designs. They have purposely kept you in ignorance, and have, by moulding your passions and prejudices to suit themselves, induced you to act in direct opposition to your dearest rights and interests. By a system of the grossest subterfuge and misrepresentation, and in order to avert, for a season, the vengeance that will most assuredly overtake them ere long, they have taught you to hate the abolitionists, who are your best and only true friends. Now, as one of your own number, we appeal to you to join us in our patriotic endeavors to rescue the generous soil of the South from the usurped and desolating control of these political vampires. Once and forever, at least so far as this country is concerned, the infernal question of slavery must be disposed of; a speedy and perfect abolishment of the whole institution is the true policy of the South—and this is the policy which we propose to pursue. Will you aid us, will you assist us, will you be freemen, or will you be slaves? These are questions of vital importance; weigh them well in your minds; come to a prudent and firm decision, and hold yourselves in readiness to act in accordance therewith. You must either be for us or against us—anti-slavery or pro-slavery; it is impossible for you to occupy a neutral ground; it is as certain as fate itself, that if you do not voluntarily oppose the usurpations and outrages of the slavocrats, they will force you into involuntary compliance with their infamous measures. Consider well the aggressive, fraudulent and despotic power which they have exercised in the affairs of Kanzas; and remember that, if, by adhering to erroneous principles of neutrality or non-resistance, you allow them to force the curse of slavery on that vast and fertile field, the broad area of all the surrounding States and Territories—the whole nation, in fact—will soon fall a prey to their diabolical intrigues and machinations. Thus, if you are not vigilant, will they take advantage of your neutrality, and make you and others the victims of their inhuman despotism. Do not reserve the strength of your arms until you shall have been rendered powerless to strike; the present is the

6

proper time for action; under all the circumstances, apathy or indifference is a crime. First ascertain, as nearly as you can, the precise nature and extent of your duty, and then, without a moment's delay, perform it in good faith. To facilitate you in determining what considerations of right, justice and humanity require at your hands, is one of the primary objects of this work; and we shall certainly fail in our desire if we do not accomplish our task in a manner acceptable to God and advantageous to man.

But we are carrying this chapter beyond all ordinary bounds; and yet, there are many important particulars in which we have drawn no comparison between the free and the slave States. The more weighty remarks which we intended to offer in relation to the new States of the West and Southwest, free and slave, shall appear in the succeeding chapter. With regard to agriculture, and all the multifarious interests of husbandry, we deem it quite unnecessary to say more. Cotton has been shorn of its magic power, and is no longer King; *dried grass*, commonly called hay, is, it seems, the rightful heir to the throne. Commerce, Manufactures, Literature, and other important subjects, shall be considered as we progress.

CHAPTER II.

HOW SLAVERY CAN BE ABOLISHED.

Preliminary to our elucidation of what we conceive to be the most discreet, fair and feasible plan for the abolition of slavery, we propose to offer a few additional reasons why it should be abolished Among the thousand and one arguments that present themselves in support of our position—which, before we part with the reader, we shall endeavor to define so clearly, that it shall be regarded as ultra only by those who imperfectly understand it.—is the influence which slavery invariably exercises in depressing the value of real estate ; and as this is a matter in which the non-slaveholders of the South, of the West, and of the Southwest, are most deeply interested, we shall discuss it in a sort of preamble of some length.

The oligarchs say we cannot abolish slavery without infringing on the right of property. Again we tell them we do not recognize property in man ; but even if we did, and if we were to inventory the negroes at quadruple, the value of their last assessment, still, impelled by a sense of duty to others, and as a matter of simple justice to ourselves, we, the non-slaveholders of the South, would be fully warranted in emancipating all the slaves at once, and that, too, without any compensation whatever to those who claim to be their absolute masters and owners We will explain. In 1850, the average value per acre, of land in the Northern States was $28,07; in the Northwestern $11,39; in the Southern $5,34; and in the Southwestern $6,26. Now, in consequence of numerous natural advantages, among which may be enumerated the greater mildness of climate, richness of soil, deposits of precious metals, abundance and spaciousness of harbors, and superexcellence of water-power, we contend that, had it not been for slavery, the average value of land in all the Southern and Southwestern States, would have been *at least* equal to the average value of the same in the Northern States. We conclude, therefore, and we think the conclusion is founded on principles of equity, that you, the slaveholders, are indebted to us, the non-slaveholders, in the sum of $22,73, which is the difference between $28,07 and $5,34, on every acre of Southern soil in our possession. This claim we bring against you, because slavery, which has inured exclusively to your own benefit, if, indeed, it has been beneficial at all, has shed a blighting influence over our lands, thereby keeping them out of market, and damaging every acre to the amount specified. Sirs! are you ready to settle the account? Let us see how much it is. There are in the fifteen slave States, 346,048 slaveholders, and 544,926,720 acres of land. Now the object is to ascertain how many acres are owned by slaveholders, and now many by non-slaveholders. Suppose we estimate five hundred acres as the average landed property of each slaveholder; will that be fair? We think it will, taking into consideration the fact that 174,503 of the whole number of slaveholders hold less than five slaves each—68,820 holding only one each. According to this hypothesis, the slaveholders own 173,024,000 acres, and the non-slaveholders the balance, with the exception of about 40,000,000 of acres, which belong to the General Government. The case may be stated thus:

Area of the Slave States 544,926,720 acres.

Estimates	Acres owned by slaveholders..	173,024,000	
	Acres owned by the government	40,000,000—	213,024,000
	Acres owned by non-slaveholders............		331,902,720

Now, chevaliers of the lash, and worshippers of slavery, the total value of three hundred and thirty-one million nine hundred and two thousand seven hundred and twenty acres, at twenty-two dollars and seventy-three cents per acre, is *seven billion five hundred and forty-four million one hundred and forty-eight thousand eight hundred and twenty-five dollars*; and this is our account against you on a single score. Considering how your villainous institution has retarded the development of our commercial and manufacturing interests, how it has stifled the aspirations of inventive genius; and, above all, how it has barred from us the heaven-born sweets of literature and religion—concernments too sacred to be estimated in a pecuniary point of view—might we not, with perfect justice and propriety, duplicate the amount, and still be accounted modest in our demands? Fully advised, however, of your indigent circumstances, we feel it would be utterly useless to call on you for the whole amount that is due us; we shall, therefore, in your behalf, make another draft on the fund of non-slaveholding generosity, and let the account, meagre as it is, stand as above. Though we have given you all the offices, and you have given us none of the benefits of legislation ; though we have fought the battles of the South, while you were either lolling in your piazzas, or playing the tory, and endeavoring to filch from us our birthright of freedom ; though you have absorbed the wealth of our communities in sending your own children to Northern seminaries and colleges, or in employing Yankee teachers to officiate exclusively in your own families, and have refused to us the limited privilege of common schools ; though you have scorned to patronize our mechanics and industrial enterprises, and have passed to the North for every article of apparel, utility, and adornment ; and though you have maltreated, outraged and defrauded us in every relation of life, civil, social, and political, yet we are willing to forgive and *forget* you, if you will but do us justice on a single count. Of you, the introducers, aiders and abettors of slavery, we demand indemnification for the damage our lands have sustained on account thereof ; the amount of that damage is $7,544,148,825 ; and now, Sirs, we are ready to receive the money, and if it is perfectly convenient to you, we would be glad to have you pay it in specie ! It will not avail you, Sirs, to parley or prevaricate. We must have a settlement. Our claim is just and overdue. We have already indulged you too long. Your criminal extravagance has almost ruined us. We are determined that you shall no longer play the profligate, and fair sumptuously every day at our expense. How do you propose to settle ? Do you offer us your negroes in part payment ? We do not want your negroes. We would not have all of them, nor any number of them, even as a gift. We hold ourselves above the disreputable and iniquitous practices of buying, selling, and owning slaves. What we demand is damages in money, or other absolute property, as an equivalent for the pecuniary losses we have suffered at your hands. You value your negroes at sixteen hundred millions of dollars, and propose to sell them to us for that sum; we should consider ourselves badly cheated, and disgraced for all time, here and hereafter, if we were to take them off your hands at sixteen farthings! We tell you emphatically, we are firmly resolved never to degrade ourselves by becoming the mercenary purchasers or proprietors of human beings. Except for the purpose of liberating them, we would not give a handkerchief or a tooth-pick for all the slaves in the world. But, in order to show how brazenly absurd are the howls and groans which you invariably set up for compensation, whenever we speak of the abolition of slavery, we will suppose your negroes are worth all you ask for them, and that we are bound to secure to you every cent of the sum before they can become free—in which case, our accounts would stand thus:

Non-slaveholder's account against Slaveholders......	$7,544,148,825
Slaveholder's account against Non-slaveholders.......	1,600,000,000
Balance due Non-slaveholders.............	$5,944,148,825

Now, Sirs, we ask you in all seriousness, Is it not true that you have filched from us nearly five times the amount of the assessed value of your slaves? Why, then, do you still clamor for more? Is it your purpose to make the game perpetual? Think you that we will ever continue to bow at the wave of your wand, that we will bring humanity into everlasting disgrace by licking the hand that smites us, and that with us there is no point beyond which forbearance ceases to be a virtue? Sirs, if these be your thoughts, you are laboring under a most fatal delusion. You can goad us no further; you shall oppress us no longer; heretofore, earnestly but submissively, we have asked you to redress the more atrocious outrages which you have perpetrated against us; but what has been the invariable fate of our petitions? With scarcely a perusal, with a degree of contempt that added insult to injury, you have laid them on the table, and from thence they have been swept into the furnance of oblivion. Henceforth, Sirs, we are demandants, not suppliants. We demand our rights, nothing more, nothing less. It is for you to decide whether we are to have justice peaceably or by violence, for whatever consequences may follow, we are determined to have it one way or the other. Do you aspire to become the victims of white non-slaveholding vengeance by day, and of barbarous massacre by the negroes at night? Would you be instrumental in bringing upon yourselves, your wives, and your children, a fate too horrible to contemplate? shall history cease to cite, as an instance of unexampled cruelty, the Massacre of St. Bartholomew, because the world—the South—shall have furnished a more direful scene of atrocity and carnage? Sirs, we would not wantonly pluck a single hair from your heads; but we have endured long, we have endured much; slaves only of the most despicable class would endure more. An enumeration or classification of all the abuses, insults, wrongs, injuries, usurpations, and oppressions, to which you have subjected us, would fill a larger volume than this ; it is our purpose, therefore, to speak only of those that affect us most deeply. Out of our effects your have long since overpaid yourselves for your negroes ; and now, Sirs, you *must* emancipate them—speedily emancipate them, or we will emancipate them for you! Every non-slaveholder in the South is, or ought to be, and will be, against you. You yourselves ought to join us at once in our laudable crusade against "the mother of harlots" Slavery has polluted and impoverished your lands ; freedom will restore them to their virgin purity, and add from twenty to thirty dollars to the value of every acre. Correctly speaking, emancipation will cost you nothing ; the moment you abolish slavery, that very moment will the putative value of the slave become actual value in the soil. Though there are ten millions of people in the South, and though you, the slaveholders, are only three hundred and forty-seven thousand in number, you have within a fraction of one-third of all the territory belonging to the fifteen slave States. You have a landed estate of 173,-024,000 acres, the present average market value of which is only $5,34 per acre ; emancipate your slaves on Wednesday morning, and on the Thursday following the value of your lands, and ours too, will have increased to an average of at least $28,07 per acre. Let us see, therefore, even in this one particular, whether the abolition of slavery will not be a real pecuniary advantage to you The present total market value of all your landed property, at $5,34 per acre, is only $923,248,160! With the beauty and sunlight of freedom beaming on the same estate, it would be worth, at $28,07 per acre, $4,856,873,680 The former sum, deducted from the latter, leaves a balance of $3,933,535,520, and to the full extent of this amount will *your* lands be increased in value whenever you abolish slavery; that is, provided you abolish it before it completely "dries up all the organs of increase." Here is a more manifest and distinct statement of the case:—

Estimated value of slaveholders' lands after slavery shall have been abolished..................	$4,856,783,680
Present value of slaveholders' lands...............	923,248,160
Probable aggregate enhancement of value........	$3,933,535,520

Now, Sirs, this last sum is considerably more than twice as great as the estimated value of your negroes; and those of you, if any there be, who are yet heirs to sane minds and honest hearts, must, it seems to us, admit that the bright prospect which freedom presents for a wonderful increase in the value of real estate, ours as well as yours, to say nothing of the thousand other kindred considerations, ought to be quite sufficient to induce all the Southern States, in their sovereign capacities, to abolish slavery at the earliest practical period. You yourselves, instead of losing anything by the emancipation of your negroes—even though we suppose them to be worth every dime of $1,600,000,000—would, in this one particular, the increased value of land, realize a ***net profit*** of over *twenty three hundred millions of dollars!* Here are the exact figures:—

Net increment of value which it is estimated will accrue to slaveholders' lands in consequence of the abolition of slavery....................	$3,933,535,520
Putative value of the slaves........................	1,600,000,000
Slaveholders' estimated net landed profits of eman.	$2,333,535,520

What is the import of these figures? They are full of meaning. They proclaim themselves the financial intercessors for freedom, and, with that open-hearted liberality which is so characteristic of the sacred cause in whose behalf they plead, they propose to pay you upward of three thousand nine hundred millions of dollars for the very "property" which you, in all the reckless extravagance of your inhuman avarice, could not find a heart to price at more than one thousand six hundred millions. In other words, your own lands, groaning and languishing under the monstrous burden of slavery, announce their willingness to pay you all you ask for the negroes, and offer you, besides, a bonus of more than twenty-three hundred millions of dollars, if you will but convert those lands into free soil! *Our* lands, also, cry aloud to be spared from the further pollutions and desolations of slavery; and now, Sirs, we want to know explicitly whether, or not, it is your intention to heed these lamentations of the ground? We want to know whether you are men or devils—whether you are entirely selfish and cruelly dishonest, or whether you have any respect for the rights of others. We, the non-slaveholders of the South, have many very important interests at stake—interests which, heretofore, you have steadily despised and trampled under foot, but which, henceforth, we shall foster and defend in utter defiance of all the unhallowed influences which it is possible for you, or any other class of slaveholders or slavebreeders to bring against us. Not the least among these interests is our landed property, which, to command a decent price, only needs to be disencumbered of slavery.

In his present condition, we believe man exercises one of the noblest virtues with which heaven has endowed him, when, without taking any undue advantage of his fellow-men, and with a firm, unwavering purpose to confine his expenditures to the legitimate pursuits and pleasures of life, he covets money and strives to accumulate it. Entertaining this view, and having no disposition to make an improper use of money, we are free to confess that we have a greater penchant for twenty-eight dollars than for five; for ninety than for fifteen; for a thousand than for one hundred. South of Mason and Dixon's line we, the non-slaveholders, have 331,902,720 acres of land, the present average market value of which, as previously stated, is only $5,34 per acre; by abolishing slavery we expect to enhance the value to an average of at least $28,07 per acre, and thus realize an average net increase of wealth of more than *seventy-five hundred millions of dollars.* The hope of realizing smaller sums has frequently induced men to perpetrate acts of injustice; we can see no reason why the certainty of becoming immensely rich in real estate, or other property, should make us falter in the performance of a *sacred duty.*

As illustrative of our theme, a bit of personal history may not be out of place in this connection. Only a few months have elapsed since we sold to an elder brother an interest we held in an old homestead which was willed to us many years ago by our dear departed father. The tract of land, containing two hundred acres, or thereabouts, is situated two and a half miles west of Mocksville, the capital of Davie County, North Carolina, and is very nearly equally divided by Bear Creek, a small tributary of the South Yadkin. More than one-third of this tract—on which we have plowed, and hoed, and harrowed, many a long summer without ever suffering from the effects of *coup de soleil*—is under cultivation; the remaining portion is a well-timbered forest, in which, without being very particular, we counted, while hunting through it not long since, sixty-three different kinds of indigenous trees—to say nothing of either coppice, shrubs or plants—among which the hickory, oak, ash, beech, birch, and black walnut, were most abundant. No turpentine or rosin is produced in our part of the State; but there are, on the place of which we speak, several species of the genus Pinus, by the light of whose flammable knots, as radiated on the contents of some half-dozen old books, which, by hook or by crook, had found their way into the neighborhood, we have been enabled to turn the long winter evenings to our advantage, and have thus *partially* escaped from the prison-grounds of those loathsome dungeons of illiteracy in which it has been the constant policy of the oligarchy to keep the masses, the non-slaveholding whites and the negroes, forever confined. The fertility of the soil may be inferred from the quality and variety of its natural productions; the meadow and the bottom, comprising, perhaps, an area of forty acres, are hardly surpassed by the best lands in the valley of the Yadkin. A thorough examination of the orchard will disclose the fact that considerable attention has been paid to the selection of fruits; the buildings are tolerable; the water is good. Altogether, to be frank, and nothing more, it is, for its size, one of the most desirable farms in the county, and will, at any time, command the maximum price of land in Western Carolina. Our brother, anxious to become the sole proprietor, readily agreed to give us the highest market price, which we shall publish by-and-bye. While reading the Baltimore *Sun*, the morning after we had made the sale, our attention was allured to a paragraph headed "Sales of Real Estate," from which, among other significant items, we learned that a tract of land containing exactly two hundred acres, and occupying a portion of one of the rural districts in the southeastern part of Pennsylvania, near the Maryland line, had been sold the week before, at *one hundred and five dollars and fifty cents* per acre. Judging from the succinct account given in the *Sun*, we are of the opinion that, with regard to fertility of soil, the Pennsylvania tract always has been, is now, and perhaps always will be, rather inferior to the one under special consideration. One is of the same size as the other; both are used for agricultural purposes; in all probability the only *essential* difference between them is this: one is blessed with the pure air of freedom, the other is cursed with the malaria of slavery. For our interest in the old homestead we received a nominal sum, amounting to an average of precisely *five dollars and sixty cents* per acre. No one but our brother, who was keen for the purchase, would have given us quite so much.

And, now, pray let us ask, what does this narrative teach? We shall use few words in explanation; there is an extensive void, but it can be better filled with reflection. The aggregate value of the one tract is $21,100; that of the other is only $1,120; the difference is $19,980. We contend, therefore, in view of all the circumstances detailed, that the advocates and retainers of slavery, have, to all intents and purposes, defrauded our family out of this last-mentioned sum. In like manner, and on the same basis of deduction, we contend that almost every non-slaveholder, who either is or has been the owner of real estate in the South, would, in a court of strict justice, be entitled to damages—the amount in all cases to be determined with reference to the quality of the land in question. We say this because, in violation of every principle of expediency, justice, and humanity, and in direct opposition to our solemn protests, slavery was foisted upon us, and has been thus far perpetuated, by and through the diabolical intrigues of the oligarchs, and by them alone and furthermore, because the very best agricultural lands in the Northern States being worth from one hundred to one hundred and seventy-five dollars per acre, there is no possible reason, except slavery, why the more fertile and congenial soil of the South should not be worth at least as much. If, on this principle, we could ascertain, in the matter of real estate, the total indebtedness of the slaveholders to the non-slaveholders, we should doubtless find the sum quite equivalent to the amount estimated on a preceding page—$7,544,148,825.

We have recently conversed with two gentlemen who to save themselves from the poverty and disgrace of slavery, left North Carolina six or seven years ago, and who are now residing in the territory of Minnesota, where they have accumulated handsome fortunes. One of them had traveled extensively in Kentucky, Missouri, Ohio,

Indiana, and other adjoining States ; and, according to his account, and we know him to be a man of veracity, it is almost impossible for persons at a distance, to form a proper conception of the magnitude of the difference between the current value of lands in the Free and the Slave States of the West. On one occasion, embarking at Wheeling, he sailed down the Ohio ; Virgina and Kentucky on the one side, Ohio and Indiana on the other. He stopped at several places along the river, first on the right bank, then on the left, and so on, until he arrived at Evansville ; continuing his trip, he sailed down to Cairo, thence up the Mississippi to the mouth of the Des Moines ; having tarried at different points along the route, sometimes in Missouri, sometimes in Illinois. Wherever he landed on free soil, he found it from one to two hundred per cent. more valuable than the slave soil on the opposite bank. If, for instance, the maximum price of land was eight dollars in Kentucky, the minimum price was sixteen in Ohio ; if it was seven dollars in Missouri, it was fourteen in Illinois. Furthermore, he assured us, that, so far as he could learn, two years ago, when he traveled through the States of which we speak, the range of prices of agricultural lands, in Kentucky, was from three to eight dollars per acre ; in Ohio, from sixteen to forty ; in Missouri, from two to seven ; in Illinois, from fourteen to thirty ; in Arkansas, from one to four ; in Iowa, from six to fifteen.

In all the old slave States, as is well known, there are vast bodies of land that can be bought for the merest trifle. We know an enterprising capitalist in Philadelphia, who owns in his individual name, in the State of

Virginia, *one hundred and thirty thousand acres*, for which he paid only *thirty-seven and a half cents* per acre! Some years ago, in certain parts of North Carolina, several large tracts were purchased at the rate of *twenty-five cents* per acre!

Hiram Berdan, the distinguished inventor, who has frequently seen freedom and slavery side by side, and who is, therefore, well qualified to form an opinion of their relative influence upon society, says:

"Many comparisons might be drawn between the free and the slave States, either of which should be sufficient to satisfy any man that slavery is not only ruinous to free labor and enterprise, but injurious to morals, and blighting to the soil where it exists The comparison between the States of Michigan and Arkansas, which were admitted into the Union at the same time, will fairly illustrate the difference and value of free and slave labor, as well as the difference of moral and intellectual progress in a free and in a slave State.

In 1836 these young Stars were admitted into the constellation of the Union. Michigan, with one-half the extent of territory of Arkansas, challenged her sister State for a twenty years' race, and named as her rider, 'Neither slavery, nor involuntary servitude, unless for the punishment of crime, shall ever be tolerated in this State.' Arkansas accepted the challenge, and named as her rider, 'The General Assembly shall have no power to pass laws for the emancipation of slaves without the consent of the owners.' Thus mounted, these two States, the one free and the other slave, started together twenty years ago, and now, having arrived at the end of the proposed race, let us review and mark the progress of each. Michigan comes out in 1856 with three times the population of slave Arkansas, with five times the assessed value of farms, farming implements and machinery and with eight times the number of public schools."

In the foregoing part of our work, we have drawn comparisons between the old free States and the old slave States, and between the new free States and the new slave States; had we sufficient time and space, we might with the most significant results, change this method of comparison, by contrasting the new free States with the old slave States. Can the slavocrats compare Ohio with Virginia, Illinois with Georgia, or Indiana with South Carolina, without experiencing the agony of inexpressible shame? If they can, then indeed has slavery debased them to a lower deep than we care to contemplate. Herewith we present a brief contrast, as drawn by a Maryland abolitionist, between the most important old slave State and the most important new free State:

"Virginia was a State, wealthy and prosperous, when Ohio was a wilderness belonging to her. She gave that territory away, and what is the result? Ohio supports a population of two million souls, and the mother contains but one and a half millions; yet Virginia is one-third larger than the Buckeye State. Virginia contains 61,000 square miles, Ohio but 40.000. The latter sustains 50 persons to the square mile, while Virginia gives employment to but 25 to the square mile. Notwithstanding Virginia's superiority in years and in soil—for she grows tobacco, as well as corn and wheat—notwithstanding her immense coal-fields, and her splendid Atlantic ports, Ohio, the infant State, had 21 representatives in Congress in 1850, while Virginia had but 13—the latter having *commenced* in the Union with 10 Congressmen. Compare the progress of these States, and then say, what is it but Free Labor that has advanced Ohio? and to what, except slavery, can we attribute the non-progression of the Old Dominion?"

As a striking illustration of the selfish and debasing influences which slavery exercises over the hearts and minds of slaveholders themselves, we will here state the fact that, when we, the non-slaveholders, remonstrate against the continuance of such a manifest wrong and inhumanity—a system of usurpation and outrage so obviously detrimental to *our* interests—they fly into a terrible passion, exclaiming, among all sorts of horrible threats, which are not unfrequently executed, "It's none of your business!"—meaning to say thereby that their slaves do not annoy us, that slavery affects no one except the masters and their chattels personal, and that *we* should give ourselves no concern about it, whatever! To every man of common sense and honesty of purpose the preposterousness of this assumption is so evident, that any studied attempt to refute it would be a positive insult. Would it be none of our business, if they were to bring the small-pox into the neighborhood, and, with premeditated design, let "foul contagion spread?" Or, if they were to throw a pound of strychnine into a public spring, would that be none of our business? Were they to turn a pack of mad dogs loose on the community, would we be performing the part of good citizens by closing ourselves within doors for the space of nine days, saying nothing to anybody? Small-pox is a nuisance; strychnine is a nuisance; mad dogs are a nuisance; slavery is a nuisance; slaveholders are a nuisance, and so are slave-breeders; it is our business, nay, it is our imperative duty, to abate nuisances; we propose, therefore, with the exception of strychnine, which is the least of all these nuisances, to exterminate this catalogue from beginning to end.

We mean precisely what our words express, when we say we believe thieves are, as a general rule, less amenable to the moral law than slaveholders ; and here is the basis of our opinion : Ordinarily, thieves wait until we acquire a considerable amount of property, and then they steal a dispensable part of it ; but they deprive no one of physical liberty, nor do they fetter the mind ; slaveholders, on the contrary, by clinging to the most barbarous relic of the most barbarous age, bring disgrace on themselves, their neighbors, and their country, depreciate the value of their own and others' lands, degrade labor, discourage energy and progress, prevent non-slaveholders from accumulating wealth, curtail their natural rights and privileges, doom their children to ignorance, and all its attendant evils, rob the negroes of their freedom, throw a damper on every species of manual and intellectual enterprise, that is not projected under their own roofs and for their own advantage, and, by other means equally at variance with the principles of justice, though but an insignificant fractional part of the population, they constitute themselves the sole arbiters and legislators for the entire South. Not merely so ; the thief rarely steals from more than one man out of an hundred ; the slaveholder defrauds ninety and nine, and the hundredth does not escape him. Again, thieves steal trifles from rich men ; slaveholders oppress poor men, and enact laws for the perpetuation of their poverty. Thieves practice deceit on the wise ; slaveholders take advantage of the ignorant.

We contend, moreover, that slaveholders are more criminal than common murderers. We know all slaveholders would not wilfully imbue their hands in the blood of their fellow-men ; but it is a fact, nevertheless, that all slaveholders are under the shield of a perpetual license to murder. This license they have issued to themselves. According to their own infamous statutes, if the slave raises his hand to ward off an unmerited blow, they are permitted to take his life with impunity. We are personally acquainted with three ruffians who have become actual murderers under circumstances of this nature. One of them killed two negroes on one occasion; the other two have murdered but one each. Neither of them has ever been subjected to even the preliminaries of a trial; not one of them has ever been arrested; their own private explanations of the homicides exculpated them from all manner of blame in the premises. They had done nothing wrong in the eyes of the community. The negroes made an effort to shield themselves from the tortures of a merciless flagellation, and were shot dead on the spot. Their murderers still live, and are treated as honorable members of society! No matter how many slaves or free negroes may witness the perpetration of these atrocious homicides, not one of them is ever allowed to lift up his voice in behalf of his murdered brother. In the South, negroes, whether bond or free, are never, under any circumstances, permitted to utter a syllable under oath, except for or against persons of their own color; their testimony against white persons is of no more consequence than the idle zephyr of the summer.

We shall now introduce four tables of valuable and interesting statistics, to which philosophic and discriminating readers will doubtless have frequent occasions to refer. Tables 22 and 23 will show the area of the several

States, in square miles and in acres, and the number of inhabitants to the square mile in each State; also the grand total, or the average, of every statistical column; tables 24 and 25 will exhibit the total number of inhabitants residing in each State, according to the census of 1850, the number of whites, the number of free colored, and the number of slaves. The recapitulations of these tables will be followed by a complete list of the number of slaveholders in the United States, showing the exact number in each Southern State, and in the District of Columbia. Most warmly do we commend all these statistics to the *studious* attention of the reader. Their language is more eloquent than any possible combination of Roman vowels and consonants. We have spared no pains in arranging them so as to express at a single glance the great truths of which they are composed; and we doubt not that the plan we have adopted will meet with general approbation. Numerically considered, it will be perceived that the slaveholders are, in reality, a very insignificant class. Of them, however, we shall have more to say hereafter.

TABLE NO. XXII.

AREA OF THE FREE STATES.

States.	Square Miles.	Acres.	Inhabit'nts to square mile.
California..............	155,980	99,827,200	.59
Connecticut..............	4,674	2,991,360	79.33
Illinois..............	55,405	35,359,200	15.37
Indiana..............	33,809	21,637,760	29.24
Iowa..............	50,914	32,584,960	3.78
Maine..............	31,766	20,330,240	18.36
Massachusetts..............	7,800	4,992,000	127.50
Michigan..............	56,243	35,995,520	7.07
New Hampshire..............	9,280	5,939,200	34.26
New Jersey..............	8,320	5,324,800	58.84
New York..............	47,000	30,080,000	65.90
Ohio..............	39,964	26,576,960	49.55
Pennsylvania..............	46,000	29,440,000	50.26
Rhode Island..............	1,306	835,840	112.97
Vermont..............	10,212	6,535,680	30.76
Wisconsin..............	53,924	34,511,360	5.66
	612,597	392,062,082	21,91

TABLE NO. XXIII.

AREA OF THE SLAVE STATES.

States.	Square Miles.	Acres.	Inhabit'nts to square mile.
Alabama..............	50,722	32,027,490	15 21
Arkansas..............	52,198	33,406,720	4.02
Delaware..............	2,120	1,356,800	43.18
Florida..............	59,268	37,931,520	1.48
Georgia..............	58,000	37,120,000	15.62
Kentucky..............	37,680	24,115,200	26.07
Louisiana..............	41,255	26,403,200	12.55
Maryland..............	11,124	7,119,360	52.41
Mississippi..............	47,156	30,179,840	12.86
Missouri..............	67,380	43,123,200	10.12
North Carolina..............	50,704	32,450,560	17.14
South Carolina..............	29,385	18,805,400	22.75
Tennessee..............	45,600	29,184,000	21.99
Texas..............	237,504	152,002,560	.89
Virginia..............	61,352	39,165,280	23.17
	851,448	544,926,720	11.29

TABLE NO. XXIV.

POPULATION OF THE FREE STATES—1850.

States.	Whites.	Free Colored.	Total.
California	91,635	962	92,597
Connecticut	363,099	7,693	370,792
Illinois	846,034	5,436	851,470
Indiana	977,154	11,262	988,416
Iowa	191,881	333	192,214
Maine	581,813	1,356	583,169
Massachusetts	985,450	9,064	994,514
Michigan	395,071	2,583	397,654
New Hampshire	317,456	520	317,976
New Jersey	465,509	23,810	489,555
New York	3,048,325	49,069	3,097,394
Ohio	1,955,050	25,279	1,980,329
Pennsylvania	2,258,160	53,626	2,311,786
Rhode Island	143,875	3,670	147,545
Vermont	313,402	718	314,120
Wisconsin	304,756	635	305,391
	13,233.670	196,116	13,434,922

TABLE NO. XXV.

POPULATION OF THE SLAVE STATES—1850.

States.	Whites.	Free Colored.	Slaves.	Total.
Alabama	426,514	2,265	342,844	771,623
Arkansas	162,189	608	47,100	209,897
Delaware	71,169	18,073	2,290	91,532
Florida	47,203	932	39,310	87,445
Georgia	521,572	2,931	381,622	906,185
Kentucky	761,413	10,011	210,981	982,405
Louisiana	255,491	17,462	244,809	517,762
Maryland	417,943	74,723	90,368	583,034
Mississippi	295,718	930	309,878	606,326
Missouri	592,004	2,618	87,422	682,044
North Carolina	553,028	27,463	288,548	869,039
South Carolina	274,563	8,960	384,984	668.507
Tennessee	756,836	6,422	239,459	1,002,717
Texas	154,034	397	58,161	212,592
Virginia	894,800	54,333	472,528	1,421,661
	6,184,477	228,138	3,200,364	9,612,979

RECAPITULATION—AREA.

	Square Miles.	Acres.
Area of the Slave States	851,448	544,926,720
Area of the Free States	612,597	392,062,032
Balances in favor of Slave States	238,851	152,864,638

RECAPITULATION—POPULATION—1850.

	Whites.	Total.
Population of the Free States	13,233,670	13,434,922
Population of the Slave States	6,184,477	9,612,976
Balances in favor of the Free States	7,049,193	3,821,946

FREE COLORED AND SLAVE—1850.

Free Negroes in the Slave States	228,138
Free Negroes in the Free States	196,116
Excess of Free Negroes in the Slave States	32,022

Slaves in the Slave States	3,200,364
Free Negroes in the Slave States	228,138
Aggregate Negro Population of the Slave States in 1850	3,428,502

THE TERRITORIES AND THE DISTRICT OF COLUMBIA.

	Area in Square Miles.	Population.
Indian Territory	71,127	
Kansas "	114,798	
Minnesota "	166,025	6,077
Nebraska "	335,882	
N. Mexico "	207,007	61,547
Oregon "	185,030	13,294
Utah "	269,170	11,380
Washington "	123,022	
Columbia, Dist. of	60	*51,687
Aggregate of Area and Population,	1,472,121	143,985

* Of the 51,687 inhabitants in the District of Columbia, in 1850, 10,057 were Free Colored, and 3,687 were slaves

NUMBER OF SLAVEHOLDERS IN THE UNITED STATES—1850.

Alabama	29,295
Arkansas	5,999
Columbia, District of,	1,477
Delaware	809
Florida	3,520
Georgia	38,456
Kentucky	38,385
Louisiana	20,670
Maryland	16,040
Mississippi	23,116
Missouri	19,185
North Carolina	28,303
South Carolina	25,596
Tennessee	33,864
Texas	7,747
Virginia	55,063
Total Number of Slaveholders in the United States	347,525

CLASSIFICATION OF THE SLAVEHOLDERS—1850.

Holders of 1 slave	68,820
Holders of 1 and under 5	105,683
Holders of 5 and under 10	80,765
Holders of 10 and under 20	54,595
Holders of 20 and under 50	29,733
Holders of 50 and under 100	6,196
Holders of 100 and under 200	1,479
Holders of 200 and under 300	187
Holders of 300 and under 500	56
Holders of 500 and under 1,000	9
Holders of 1,000 and over	2
Aggregate Number of Slaveholders in the United States	347,525

It thus appears that there are in the United States, three hundred and forty-seven thousand five hundred and twenty-five slaveholders. But this appearance is deceptive The actual number is certainly less than two hundred thousand. Professor De Bow, the Superintendent of the Census, informs us that "the number includes slave-hirers," and furthermore, that "where the party owns slaves in different counties, or in different States, he will be entered more than once." Now every Southerner, who has any practical knowledge of affairs, must know, and does know, that every New Year's day, like almost every other day, is desecrated in the South, by publicly hiring out slaves to large numbers of non-slaveholders. The slave-owners, who are the exclusive manufacturers of public sentiment, have popularized the dictum that white servants, decency, virtue, and justice, are unfashionable; and there are, we are sorry to say, nearly one hundred and sixty thousand non-slaveholding sycophants, who have subscribed to this false philosophy, and who are giving constant encouragement to the infamous practices of slaveholding and slave-breeding, by hiring at least one slave every year.

In the Southern States, as in all other slave countries, there are three odious classes of mankind; the slaves themselves, who are cowards; the slaveholders, who are tyrants; and the non-slaveholding slave-hirers, who are lickspittles. Whether either class is really entitled to the regards of a gentleman is a matter of grave doubt. The slaves are pitiable; the slaveholders are detestable; the slave-hirers are contemptible.

With the statistics at our command, it is impossible for us to ascertain the exact numbers of slaveholders and non-slaveholding slave-hirers in the slave States; but we have data which will enable us to approach very near to the facts. The town from which we hail, Salisbury, the capital of Rowan county, North Carolina, contains about twenty-three hundred inhabitants, including three hundred and seventy-two slaves, fifty-one slaveholders, and forty-three non-slaveholding slave-hirers. Taking it for granted that this town furnishes a fair relative proportion of all the slaveholders, and non-slaveholding slave-hirers in the slave States, the whole number of the former, including those who have been "entered more than once," is one hundred and eighty-eight thousand five hundred and fifty-one; of the latter, one hundred and fifty-eight thousand nine hundred and seventy-four; and, now, estimating that there are in Maryland, Virginia, and other grain-growing States, an aggregate of two thousand slave-owners, who have cotton plantations *stocked* with negroes in the far South, and who have been "entered more than once," we find, as the result of our calculations, that the total number of actual slaveholders in the Union, is precisely one hundred and eighty-six thousand five hundred and fifty-one—as follows:

Number of actual slaveholders in the United States......	186,551
Number "entered more than once"......................	2,000
Number of non-slaveholding slave-hirers................	158,974
Aggregate number, according to De Bow........	347,525

The greater number of non-slaveholding slave-hirers, are

a kind of third-rate aristocrats—persons who formerly owned slaves, but whom slavery, as is its custom, has dragged down to poverty, leaving them, in their false and shiftless pride, to eke out a miserable existence over the hapless chattels personal of other men.

So it seems that the total number of actual slave-owners, including their entire crew of cringing lickspittles against whom we have to contend, is but three hundred and forty-seven thousand five hundred and twenty-five. Against this army for the defense and propagation of slavery, we think it will be an easy matter—independent of the negroes, who, in nine cases out of ten, would be delighted with an opportunity to cut their masters' throats, and without accepting of a single recruit from either of the free States, England, France or Germany—to muster one at least three times as large, and far more respectable for its utter extinction. We hope, however, and believe, that the matter in dispute may be adjusted without arraying these armies against each other in hostile attitude. We desire peace, not war—justice, not blood. Give us fair-play, secure to us the right of discussion, the freedom of speech, and we will settle the difficulty at the ballot box, not on the battle-ground—by force of reason, not by force of arms. But we are wedded to one purpose from which no earthly power can ever divorce us. We are determined to abolish slavery at all hazards—in defiance of all the opposition, of whatever nature, which it is possible for the slavocrats to bring against us. Of this they may take due notice, and govern themselves accordingly.

Before we proceed further, it may be necessary to call

attention to the fact that, though the ostensible proprietorship of the slaves is vested in fewer individuals than we have usually counted in our calculations concerning them, the force and drift of our statistics remain unimpaired. In the main, all our figures are correct. The tables which we have prepared, especially, and the recapitulations of those tables, may be relied on with all the confidence that is due to American official integrity; for, as we have substantially remarked on a previous occasion, the particulars of which they are composed have been obtained from the returns of competent census agents, who, with Prof. De Bow as principal, were expressly employed to collect them. As for our minor labors in the science of numbers, we cheerfully submit them to the candid scrutiny of the impartial critic.

A majority of the slaveholders with whom we are acquainted—and we happen to know a few dozen more than we care to know—own, or pretend to own, at least fifteen negroes each; some of them are the masters of more than fifty each; and we have had the *honor (!)* of an introduction to one man who is represented as the owner of sixteen hundred! It is said that if all the lands of this latter worthy were in one tract, they might be formed into two counties of more than ordinary size; he owns plantations and woodlands in three cotton-growing States.

The quantity of land owned by the slaveholder is generally in proportion to the number of negroes at his "quarter;" the master of only one or two slaves, if engaged in agriculture, seldom owns less than three hundred acres; the holder of eight or ten slaves usually owns from a thousand to fifteen hundred acres ; five thousand acres are not unfrequently found in the possession of the master of fifty slaves ; while in Columbia, South Carolina, about twelve months ago, a certain noted slaveholder was pointed out to us, and reported as the owner of nearly two hundred thousand acres in the State of Mississippi. How the great mass of illiterate poor whites, a majority of whom are the indescribably wretched tenants of these slavocratic land-sharks, are specially imposed upon and socially outlawed, we shall, if we have time and space, take occasion to explain in a subsequent chapter.

Thus far, in giving expression to our sincere and settled opinions, we have endeavored to show, in the first place, that slavery is a great moral, social, civil, and political evil—a dire enemy to true wealth and national greatness, and an atrocious crime against both God and man ; and, in the second place, that it is a paramount duty which we owe to heaven, to the earth, to America, to humanity, to our posterity, to our consciences, and to our pockets, to adopt effectual and judicious measures for its immediate abolition. The questions now arise, How can the evil be averted ? What are the most prudent and practical means that can be devised for the abolition of slavery ? In the solution of these problems it becomes necessary to deal with a multiplicity of stubborn realities. And yet, we can see no reason why North Carolina, in her sovereign capacity, may not, with equal ease and success, do what forty-five other States of the world have done within the last forty-five years. Nor do we believe any good reason exists why Virginia should not perform as great a deed in 1859 as did New-York in 1799. Massachusetts abolished slavery in 1780; would it not be a masterly stroke of policy in Tennessee, and every other slave State, to abolish it in or before 1860?

Not long since, a slavocrat, writing on this subject, said, apologetically, "we frankly admit that slavery is a monstrous evil; but what are we to do with an institution which has baffled the wisdom of our greatest statesmen?" Unfortunately for the South, since the days of Washington, Jefferson, Madison, and their illustrious compatriots, she has never had more than half a dozen statesmen, all told; of mere politicians, wire-pullers, and slave-driving demagogues, she has had enough, and to spare; but of statesmen, in the true sense of the term, she has had, and now has, but precious few—fewer just at this time, perhaps, than ever before. It is far from a matter of surprise to us that slavery has, for such a long period, baffled the "wisdom" of the oligarchy; but our surprise is destined to culminate in amazement, if the wisdom of the non-slaveholders does not soon baffle slavery.

From the eleventh year previous to the close of the eighteenth century down to the present moment, slaveholders and slave-breeders, who, to speak naked truth, are, as a general thing, unfit to occupy any honorable station in life, have, by chicanery and usurpation, wielded all the official power of the South; and, excepting the patriotic services of the noble abolitionists above-mentioned, the sole aim and drift of their legislation has been to aggrandize themselves, to strengthen slavery, and to keep the poor whites, the constitutional majority, bowed down in the deepest depths of degradation. We propose to subvert this entire system of oligarchal despotism. We think there should be *some* legislation for decent white men, not alone for negroes and slaveholders. Slavery lies at the root of all the shame, poverty, ignorance, tyranny and imbecility of the South; slavery must be thoroughly eradicated; let this be done, and a glorious future will await us.

The statesmen who are to abolish slavery in Kentucky, must be mainly and independently constituted by the non-slaveholders of Kentucky; so in every other slave State. Past experience has taught us the sheer folly of ever expecting voluntary justice from the slaveholders. Their illicit intercourse with "the mother of harlots" has been kept up so long, and their whole natures have, in consequence, become so depraved, that there is scarcely a spark of honor or magnanimity to be found amongst them As well might one expect to hear highwaymen clamoring for a universal interdict against traveling, as to expect slaveholders to pass laws for the abolition of slavery. Under all the circumstances, it is the duty of the non-slaveholders to mark out an independent course for themselves, to steer entirely clear of the oligarchy, and to utterly contemn and ignore the many vile imstruments of power, animate and inanimate, which have been so freely and so effectually used for their enslavement. Now is the time for them to assert their rights and liberties; never before was there such an appropriate period to strike for Freedom in the South.

Had it not been for the better sense, the purer patriotism, and the more practical justice of the non-slaveholders, the Middle States and New England would still be groaning and groveling under the ponderous burden of slavery; New-York would never have risen above the dishonorable level of Virginia; Pennsylvania, trampled beneath the iron-heel of the black code, would have remained the unprogressive parallel of Georgia; Massachusetts would have continued till the present time, and Heaven only knows how much longer, the contemptible coequal of South Carolina

Succeeded by the happiest moral effects and the grandest physical results, we have seen slavery crushed beneath the wisdon of the non-slaveholding statesmen of the North; followed by corresponding influences and achievements, many of us who have not yet passed the meridian of life, are destined to see it equally crushed beneath the wisdom of the non-slaveholding Statesmen of the South. With righteous indignation, we enter our disclaimer against the base yet baseless admission that Louisiana and Texas are incapable of producing as great statesmen as Rhode Island and Connecticut. What has been done for New Jersey by the statesmen of New Jersey, can be done for North Carolina by the statesmen of North Carolina; the wisdom of the former State has abolished slavery; as sure as the earth revolves on its axis, the wisdom of the latter will not do less.

That our plan for the abolition of slavery, is the best that can be devised, we have not the vanity to contend; but that it is a good one, and will do to act upon until a better shall have been suggested, we do firmly and conscientiously believe. Though but little skilled in the delicate art of surgery, we have pretty thoroughly probed slavery, the frightful tumor on the body politic, and have, we think, ascertained the precise remedies requisite for a speedy and perfect cure. Possibly the less ardent friends of freedom may object to our prescription, on the ground that some of its ingredients are too griping, and that it will cost the patient a deal of most excruciating pain. But let them remember that the patient is exceedingly refractory, that the case is a desperate one, and that drastic remedies are indispensably necessary. When they shall have invented milder yet equally efficacious ones, it will be time enough to discontinue the use of ours—then no one will be readier than we to discard the infallible strong recipe for the infallible mild. Not at the persecution of a few thousand slaveholders, but at the restitution of natural rights and prerogatives to several millions of non-slaveholders, do we aim.

Inscribed on the banner, which we herewith unfurl to the world, with the full and fixed determination to stand by it or die by it, unless one of more virtuous efficacy shall be presented, are the mottoes which, in substance, embody the principles, as we conceive, that should govern us in our patriotic warfare against the most subtle and insidious foe that ever menaced the inalienable rights and liberties and dearest interests of America :

1st. Thorough Organization and Independent Political Action on the part of the Non-Slaveholding whites of the South.

2nd. Ineligibility of Slaveholders—Never another vote to the Trafficker in Human Flesh.

3rd. No Co-operation with Slaveholders in Politics—No Fellowship with them in Religion—No Affiliation with them in Society.

4th. No Patronage to Slaveholding Merchants—No Guestship in Slave-waiting Hotels—No Fees to Slaveholding Lawyers—No Employment of Slaveholding Physicians—No Audience to Slaveholding Parsons.

5th. No Recognition of Pro-slavery Men, except as Ruffians, Outlaws, and Criminals.

6th. Abrupt Discontinuance of Subscription to Pro-slavery Newspapers.

7th. The Greatest Possible Encouragement to Free White Labor.

8. No more Hiring of Slaves by Non-slaveholders.

9th. Immediate Death to Slavery, or if not immediate, unqualified Proscription of its Advocates during the Period of its Existence.

10th. A Tax of Sixty Dollars on every Slaveholder for each and every Negro in his Possession at the present time, or at any intermediate time between now and the 4th of July, 1863—said Money to be Applied to the transportation of the Blacks to Liberia, to their Colonization in Central or South America, or to their Comfortable Settlement within the Boundaries of the United States.

11th. An additional Tax of Forty Dollars per annum to be levied annually, on every Slaveholder for each and every Negro found in his possession after the 4th of July, 1863—said Money to be paid into the hands of the Negroes so held in Slavery, or, in cases of death, to their next of kin, and to be used by them at their own option

This, then, is the outline of our scheme for the abolition of slavery in the Southern States. Let it be acted upon with due promptitude, and, as certain as truth is mightier than error, fifteen years will not elapse before every foot of territory, from the mouth of the Delaware to the emboguing of the Rio Grande, will glitter with the jewels of freedom. Some time during this year, next, or the year following, let there be a general convention of non-slaveholders from every slave State in the Union, to deliberate on the momentous issues now pending. First, let them adopt measures for holding in restraint the diabolical excesses of the oligarchy; secondly, in order to cast off the thraldom which the infamous slave-power has fastened upon them, and, as the first step necessary to be taken to regain the inalienable rights and liberties with which they were invested by Nature, but of which they have been divested by the accursed dealers in human flesh, let them devise ways and means for the complete annihilation of slavery; thirdly, let them put forth an equitable and comprehensive platform, fully defining their position, and inviting the active sympathy and co-operation of the millions of down-trodden non-slaveholders throughout the Southern and Southwestern States. Let all these things be done, not too hastily, but with calmness, deliberation, prudence, and circumspection; if need be, let the delegates to the convention continue in session one or two weeks; only let their labors be wisely and thoroughly performed; let them, on Wednesday morning, present to the poor whites of the South, a well-digested scheme for the reclamation of their ancient rights and prerogatives, and, on the Thursday following, slavery in the United States will be worth absolutely less than nothing ; for then, besides being so vile and precarious that nobody will want it, it will be a lasting reproach to those in whose hands it is lodged.

Were it not that other phases of the subject admonish us to be economical of space, we could suggest more than a dozen different plans, either of which, if scrupulously carried out, would lead to a wholesome, speedy, and perfect termination of slavery. Under all the circumstances, however, it might be difficult for us—perhaps it would not be the easiest thing in the world for any body else—to suggest a better plan than the one above. Let it, or one embodying its principal features, be adopted forthwith, and the last wail of slavery will soon be heard, growing fainter and fainter, till it dies utterly away, to be succeeded by the jubilant shouts of emancipated millions.

Henceforth, let it be distinctly understood that ownership in slaves constitutes ineligibility—that it is a crime, as we verily believe it is, to vote for a slavocrat for any office whatever. Indeed, it is our honest conviction that all the pro-slavery slaveholders, who are alone responsible for the continuance of the baneful institution among us, deserve to be at once reduced to a parallel with the basest criminals that lie fettered within the cells of our public prisons. Beyond the power of computation is the extent of the moral, social, civil, and political evils which they have brought, and are still bringing, on the country. Were it possible that the whole number could be gathered together and transformed into four equal gangs of licensed robbers, ruffians, thieves, and murderers, society, we feel assured, would suffer less from their atrocities then than it does now. Let the wholesome public sentiment of the non-slaveholders be vigilant and persevering in bringing them down to their proper level. Long since, and in the most unjust and cruel manner, have they socially outlawed the non-slaveholders ; now security against further oppression, and indemnity for past grievances, make it incumbent on the non-slaveholders to cast them into the identical pit that they dug for their betters—thus teaching them how to catch a Tartar !

At the very moment we write, as has been the case ever since the United States have had a distinct national existence, and as will always continue to be the case, unless right triumphs over wrong, all the civil, political, and other offices, within the gift of the South, are filled with negro-nursed incumbents from the ranks of that execrable band of misanthropes—three hundred and forty-seven thousand in number—who, for the most part, obtain their living by breeding, buying and selling slaves. The magistrates in the villages, the constables in the districts, the commissioners of the towns, the mayors of the cities, the sheriffs of the counties, the judges of the various courts, the members of the legislatures, the governors of the States, the representatives and senators in Congress—are all slaveholders. Nor does the catalogue of their usurpations end here. Through the most heart-sickening arrogance and bribery, they have obtained control of the General Government, and all the consuls, ambassadors, envoys extraordinary and ministers plenipotentiary, who are chosen from the South, and commissioned to foreign countries, are selected with special reference to the purity of their pro slavery antecedents. If credentials have ever been issued to a single non-slaveholder of the South, we are ignorant of both the fact and the hearsay; indeed, it would be very strange if this much abused class of persons were permitted to hold important offices abroad, when they are not allowed to hold unimportant ones at home.

And, then, there is the Presidency of the United States, which office has been held *forty-eight* years by slaveholders from the South, and only *twenty* years by non-slaveholders from the North. Nor is this the full record of oligarchal obtrusion. On an average, the offices of Secretary of State, Secretary of the Treasury, Secretary of the Interior, Secretary of the Navy, Secretary of War, Postmaster-General and Attorney-General, have been under the control of slave-drivers nearly two-thirds of the time. The Chief Justices and the Associate Justices of the Supreme Court of the United States, the Presidents pro tem. of the Senate, and the Speakers of the House of Representatives, have, in a large majority of instances, been slave-breeders from the Southern side of the Potomac. Five slaveholding Presidents have been reëlected to the chief magistracy of the Republic, while no non-slaveholder has ever held the office more than a single term. Thus we see plainly that even the non-slaveholders of the North, to whose freedom, energy, enterprise, intelligence, wealth, population, power, progress, and prosperity, our country is almost exclusively indebted for its high position among the nations of the earth, have been arrogantly denied a due participation in the honors of federal office. When "the sum of all villainies" shall have ceased to exist, then the rights of the non slaveholders of the North, of the South, of the East, and of the West, will be duly recognized and respected; not before.

With all our heart, we hope and believe it is the full and fixed determination of a majority of the more intelligent and patriotic citizens of this Republic, that the Presidential chair shall never again be filled by a slavocrat. Safely may we conclude that the doom of the oligarchy is already sealed with respect to that important and dignified station; it now behooves us to resolve, with equal firmness and effect, that, after a certain period during the next decade of years, no slaveholder shall occupy any position in the Cabinet, that no slave-breeder shall be sent as a diplomatist to any foreign country, that no slave-driver shall be permitted to bring further disgrace on either the Senate or the House of Representatives, that the chief justices, associate justices, and judges of the several courts, the governors of the States, the members of the legislatures, and all the minor functionaries of the land, shall be free from the heinous crime of ownership in man.

For the last sixty-eight years, slaveholders have been the sole and constant representatives of the South, and what have they accomplished? It requires but little time and few words, to tell the story of their indiscreet and unhallowed performances. In fact, with what we have already said, gestures alone would suffice to answer the inquiry. We can make neither a more truthful nor emphatic reply than to point to our thinly inhabited States, to our fields despoiled of their virgin soil, to the despicable price of lands, to our unvisited cities and towns, to our vacant harbors and idle water-power, to the dreary absence of shipping and manufactories, to our unpensioned soldiers of the revolution, to the millions of living monuments of ignorance, to the poverty of the whites, and to the wretchedness of the blacks.

Either directly or indirectly, are slave-driving demagogues, who have ostentatiously set up pretensions to statesmanship, responsible for every dishonorable weakness and inequality that exists between the North and the South. Let them shirk the responsibility if they can ; but it is morally impossible for them to do so. We know how ready they have always been to cite the numerical strength of the North, as a valid excuse for their inability to procure appropriations from the General Government, for purposes of internal improvement, for the establishment of lines of ocean steamers to South American and European ports, and for the accomplishment of other objects. Before that apology ever escapes from their lips again, let them remember that the numerical weakness of the South is wholly attributable to their own villainous statism. Had the Southern States, in accordance with the principles enunciated in the Declaration of Independence, abolished slavery at the same time the Northern States abolished it, there would have been, long since, and most assuredly at this moment, a larger, wealthier, wiser, and more powerful population, south of Mason and Dixon's line, than there now is north of it. This fact being so well established that no reasonable man denies it, it is evident that the oligarchy will have to devise another subterfuge for even temporary relief.

Until slavery and slaveholders cease to be the only favored objects of legislation in the South, the North will continue to maintain the ascendency in every important particular. With those loathsome objects out of the way, it would not take the non-slaveholders of the South more than a quarter of a century to bring her up, in all respects, to a glorious equality with the North ; nor would it take them much longer to surpass the latter, which is the most vigorous and honorable rival that they have in the world. Three quarters of a century hence, if slavery is abolished within the next ten years, as it ought to be, the South will, we believe, be as much greater than the North, as the North is now greater than the South. Three quarters of a century hence, if the South retains slavery, which God forbid! she will be to the North much the same that Poland is to Russia, that Cuba is to Spain, or that Ireland is to England.

What we want and must have, as the only sure means of attaining to a position worthy of Sovereign States in this eminently progressive and utilitarian age, is an energetic, intelligent, enterprising, virtuous, and unshackled population ; an untrammeled press, and the Freedom of Speech. For ourselves, as white people, and for the negroes and other persons of whatever color or condition, we demand all the rights, interests and prerogatives, that are guarantied to corresponding classes of mankind in the North, in England, in France, in Germany, or in any other civilized and enlightened country. Any proposition that may be offered conceding less than this demand, will be promptly and disdainfully rejected.

Speaking of the non-slaveholders of the South, George M. Weston, a zealous co-laborer in the cause of Freedom, says:—

"The non-slaveholding whites of the South, being not less than seven-tenths of the whole number of whites, would seem to be entitled to some enquiry into their actual condition; and especially, as they have no real political weight or consideration in the country, and little opportunity to speak for themselves. I have been for twenty years a reader of Southern newspapers, and a reader and hearer of Congressional debates; but, in all that time, I do not recollect ever to have seen or heard these non-slaveholding whites referred to by Southern 'gentlemen,' as constituting any part of what they call '*the South*.' When the rights of the South, or its wrongs, or its policy, or its interests, or its institutions, are spoken of, reference is always intended to the rights, wrongs, policy, interests, and institutions of the three hundred and forty-seven thousand slaveholders. Nobody gets into Congress from the South but by their direction; nobody speaks at Washington for any Southern interest except theirs. Yet there is, at the South, quite another interest than theirs; embracing from two to three times as many white people; and, as we shall presently see, entitled to the deepest sympathy and commiseration, in view of the material, intellectual, and moral privations to which it has been subjected, the degradation to which it has already been reduced, and the still more fearful degradation with which it is threatened by the inevitable operation of existing causes and influences."

The following extract, from a paper on "Domestic Manufactures in the South and West," published by M. Tarver, of Missouri, may be appropriately introduced in this connection:—

"The non-slaveholders possess, generally, but very small means, and the land which they possess is almost universally poor, and so sterile that a scanty subsistence is all that can be derived from its cultivation; and the more fertile soil, being in the possession of the slaveholders, must ever remain out of the power of those who have none. This state of things is a great drawback, and bears heavily upon and depresses the moral energies of the poorer classes. The acquisition of a respectable position in the scale of wealth appears so difficult, that they decline the hopeless pursuit, and many of them settle down into habits of idleness, and become the almost passive subjects of all its consequences. And I lament to say that I have observed of late years, that an evident deterioration is taking place in this part of the population, the younger portion of it being less educated, less industrious, and in every point of view less respectable than their ancestors."

Equally worthy of attention is the testimony of Gov. Hammond, of South Carolina, who says:—

"According to the best calculation, which, in the absence of statistic facts, can be made, it is believed, that of the three hundred thousand white inhabitants of South Carolina, there are not less than fifty thousand whose industry, such as it is, and compensated as it is, is not, in the present condition of things, and does not promise to be hereafter, adequate to procure them, honestly, such a support as every white person is, and feels himself entitled to. And this, next to emigration, is, perhaps, the heaviest of the weights that press upon the springs of our prosperity. Most of these now follow agricultural pursuits, in feeble, yet injurious competition with slave labor. Some, perhaps, not more from inclination, than from the want of due encouragement, can scarcely be said to work at all. They obtain a precarious subsistence, by occasional jobs, by hunting, by fishing, sometimes by plundering fields or folds, and too often by what is, in its effects, far worse—trading with slaves, and seducing them to plunder for their benefit."

Conjoined with the sundry plain straightforward facts which have issued from our own pen, these extracts show conclusively that immediate and independent political action on the part of the non-slaveholding whites of the South, is, with them, a matter, not only of positive duty, but also of the utmost importance. As yet, it is in their power to rescue the South from the gulf of shame and guilt, into which slavery has plunged her; but if they do not soon arouse themselves from their apathy, this power will be wrenched from them, and then, unable to resist the strong arm of the oppressor, they will be completely degraded to a social and political level with the negroes, whose condition of servitude will, in the meantime, become far more abject and forlorn than it is now.

In addition to the reasons which we have already assigned why no slavocrat should, in the future, be elected to any office whatever, there are others that deserve to be carefully considered. Among these may be mentioned the illbreeding and the ruffianism of slaveholding officials. Tedious indeed would be the task to enumerate all the homicides, duels, assaults and batteries, and other crimes, of which they are the authors in the course of a single year. To the general reader their career at the seat of government is well known; there, on frequent occasions, choking with rage at seeing their wretched sophistries scattered to the winds by the sound, logical reasoning of the champions of Freedom, they have overstepped the bounds of common decency, vacated the chair of honorable controversy, and, in the most brutal and cowardly manner, assailed their unarmed opponents with bludgeons, bowie knives and pistols. Compared with some of their barbarisms at home, however, their frenzied onslaughts at the national Capital have been but the simplest breaches of civil deportment; and it is only for the purpose of avoiding personalities that we now refrain from divulging a few instances of the unparalleled atrocities which they have perpetrated in legislative halls South of the Potomac. Nor is it alone in the national and State legislatures that they substitute brute force for genteel behavior and acuteness of intellect. Neither court-houses nor public streets, hotels nor private dwellings, rum-holes nor law-offices, are held sacred from their murderous conflicts. About certain silly abstractions that no practical business man ever allows to occupy his time or attention, they are eternally wrangling; and thus it is that rencounters, duels, homicides, and other demonstrations of personal violence, have become so popular in all slaveholding communities. A few years of entire freedom from the cares and perplexities of public life, would, we have no doubt, greatly improve both their manners and their morals; and we suggest that it is a Christian duty, which devolves on the non-slaveholders of the South, to disrobe them of the mantle of office, which they have so long worn with disgrace to themselves, injustice to their constituents, and ruin to their country.

But what shall we say of such men as Botts, Stuart, and Macfarland of Virginia; of Raynor, Morehead, Miller, Stanly, Graves, and Graham of North Carolina; of Davis and Hoffman of Maryland; of Blair and Benton of Missouri; of the Marshalls of Kentucky; and of Etheridge of Tennessee? All these gentlemen, and many others of the same school, entertain, we believe, sentiments similar to those that were entertained by the immortal Fathers of the

Republic—that slavery is a great moral, social, civil, and political evil, to be got rid of at the earliest practical period—and if they do, in order to secure our votes, it is only necessary for them to "have the courage of their opinions," to renounce slavery, and to come out frankly, fairly and squarely, in favor of freedom. To neither of these patriotic sons of the South, nor to any one of the class to which they belong, would we give any offence whatever. In our strictures on the criminality of pro-slavery demagogues we have had heretofore, and shall have hereafter, no sort of reference to any respectable slaveholder—by which we mean, any slaveholder who admits the injustice and inhumanity of slavery, and who is not averse to the discussion of measures for its speedy and total extinction. Such slaveholders are virtually on our side, that is, on the side of the non-slaveholding whites, with whom they may very properly be classified. On this point, once for all, we desire to be distinctly understood; for it would be manifestly unjust not to discriminate between the anti-slavery proprietor who owns slaves by the law of entailment, and the pro-slavery proprietor who engages in the traffic and becomes an aider and abettor of the institution from sheer turpitude of heart; hence the propriety of this special disclaimer.

If we have a correct understanding of the positions which they assumed, some of the gentlemen whose names are written above, gave, during the last presidential campaign, ample evidence of their unswerving devotion to the interests of the great majority of the people, the non-slaveholding whites; and it is our unbiassed opinion that a more positive truth is no where recorded in Holy Writ, than Kenneth Raynor uttered, when he said, in substance, that the greatest good that could happen to this country would be the complete overthrow of slave-driving democracy, *alias* the nigger party, which has for its head and front the Ritchies and Wises of Virginia, and for its caudal termination the Butlers and Quatlebums of South Carolina.

And this, by the way, is a fit occasion to call attention to the fact, that slave-driving Democrats have been the perpetrators of almost every brutal outrage that ever disgraced our halls of legislation. Of countless instances of assault and battery, affrays, and fatal rencounters, that have occurred in the court-houses, capitols, and other public buildings in the Southern States, we feel safe in saying that the aggressor, in at least nine cases out of ten, has been a negro-nursed adherent of modern, miscalled democracy. So, too, the challenger to almost every duel has been an abandoned wretch, who, on many occasions during infancy, sucked in the corrupt milk of slavery from the breasts of his father's sable concubines, and who has never been known to become weary of boasting of a fact that invariably impressed itself on the minds of his auditors or observers, the very first moment they laid their eyes upon him, namely, that *he* was a member of the Democratic party. Brute violence, however, can hardly be said to be the worst characteristic of the slave-driving Democrat; his ignorance and squalidity are proverbial; his senseless enthusiasm is disgusting.

Peculiarly illustrative of the material of which sham democracy is composed was the vote polled at the Five Points precinct, in the city of New-York, on the 4th of November,

1856, when James Buchanan was chosen President by a *minority* of the people. We will produce the figures :

Five Points Precinct, New-York City, 1856.

Votes cast for James Buchanan	574
" " " John C. Fremont	16
" " " Millard Fillmore	9

It will be recollected that Col. Fremont's majority over Buchanan, in the State of New-York, was between seventy-eight and seventy-nine thousand, and that he ran ahead of the Fillmore ticket to the number of nearly one hundred and fifty-one thousand. We have not the shadow of a doubt that he is perfectly satisfied with Mr. Buchanan's triumph at the Five Points, which, with the exception of the slave-pens in Southern cities, is, perhaps, the most vile and heart-sickening locality in the United States.

One of the most noticeable and commendable features of the last general election is this : almost every State, whose inhabitants have enjoyed the advantages of free soil, free labor, free speech, free presses, and free schools, and who have, in consequence, become great in numbers, in virtue, in wealth, and in wisdom, voted for Fremont, the Republican candidate, who was pledged to use his influence for the extension of like advantages to other parts of the country. On the other hand, with a single honorable exception, all the States which "have got to hating everything with the prefix Free, from free negroes down and up through the whole catalogue—free farms, free labor, free society, free will, free thinking, free children, and free schools," and which have exposed their citizens to all the perils of numerical weakness, absolute ig norance, and hopeless poverty, voted for Buchanan, the Democratic candidate, who, in reply to the overtures of his slave-driving partisans, had signified his willingness to pursue a policy that would perpetuate and disseminate, without limit, the multitudinous evils of human bondage

Led on by a huckstering politician, whose chief vocation, at all times, is the rallying of ragamuffins, shoulder strikers, and liquor-house vagabonds, into the ranks of his party, and who, it is well known, receives from the agents of the slave power, regular installments of money for this infamous purpose, a Democratic procession, exceedingly motley and unrefined, marched through the streets of one of the great cities of the North, little less than a fortnight previous to the election of Mr. Buchanan to the Presidency; and the occasion gave rise, on the following day, to a communication in one of the morning papers, from which we make the following pertinent extract:

"While the Democratic procession was passing through the streets of this city, a few days since, I could not but think how significant the exultation of that ignorant multitude was of the ferocious triumphs which would be displayed if ever false Democracy should succeed in throwing the whole power of the country into the hands of the Slave Oligarchy. It is melancholy to think that every individual in that multitude, ignorant and depraved though he may bè, foreign perhaps in his birth, and utterly unacquainted with the principles upon which the welfare of the country depends, and hostile it may be to those principles, if he does understand them, is equal in the power which he may exercise by his vote to the most intelligent and upright man in the community.

"Of this, indeed, it is useless to complain. We enjoy our freedom with the contingency of its loss by the acts of a numerical majority. I behooves all men, therefore, who have a regard to the common good, to look carefully at the influences which may pervert the popular mind; and this, I think can only be done by guarding against the corruption of individual character. A man who has nothing but political business to attend to—I mean the management of elections—ought to be shunned by all honest men. If it were possible, he should have the mark of Cain put upon him, that he might be known as a plotter against the welfare of his country."

That less than *three* per cent. of those who voted for Col. Fremont, that only about *five* per cent. of those who gave their suffrages to Mr. Fillmore, and that more than *eighteen* per cent. of those who supported Mr. Buchanan, were persons over one and twenty years of age who could not read and write, are estimates which we have no doubt are not far from the truth, and which, in the absence of reliable statistics, we venture to give, hoping, by their publicity, to draw closer attention to the fact, that the illiterate foreigners of the North, and the unlettered natives of the South, were cordially united in their suicidal adherence to the Nigger party. With few exceptions, all the intelligent non-slaveholders of the South, in concert with the more respectable slaveholders, voted for Mr. Fillmore; certain rigidly patriotic persons of the former class, whose hearts were so entirely with the gallant Fremont that they refused to vote at all—simply because they did not dare to express their preference for him—form the exceptions to which we allude.

Though the Whig, Democratic, and Know-Nothing newspapers, in all the States, free and slave, denounced Col. Fremont as an intolerant Catholic, it is now generally conceded that he was nowhere supported by the peculiar friends of Pope Pius IX. The votes polled at the Five Points precinct, which is almost exclusively inhabited by low Irish Catholics, show how powerfully the Jesuitical influence was brought to bear against him. At that delectable locality, as we have already shown, the timid Sage of Wheatland received five hundred and seventy-four votes; whereas the dauntless Finder of Empire received only sixteen.

True to their instincts for Freedom, the Germans, generally, voted the right ticket, and they will do it again, and continue to do it. With the intelligent Protestant element of the Fatherland on our side, we can well afford to dispense with the ignorant Catholic element of the Emerald Isle. In the influences which they exert on society, there is so little difference between Slavery, Popery, and Negro-driving Democracy, that we are not at all surprised to see them going hand in hand in their diabolical works of inhumanity and desolation.

There is, indeed, no lack of evidence to show that the Democratic party of to-day is simply and unreservedly a sectional Nigger party. On the 15th of December, 1856, but a few weeks subsequent to the appearance of a scandalous message from an infamous governor of South Carolina, recommending the reöpening of the African slave trade, Emerson Etheridge of Tennessee—honor to his name!—submitted, in the House of Representatives, the following timely resolution:—

"Resolved, That this House regard all suggestions or propositions of every kind, by whomsoever made, for a revival of the slave trade, as shocking to the moral sentiments of the enlightened portion of mankind, and that any act on the part of Congress, legislating for, conniving at, or legalizing that horrid and inhuman traffic, would justly subject the United States to the reproach and execration of all civilized and Christian people throughout the world."

Who voted *for* this resolution? and who voted *against* it? Let the yeas and nays answer; they are on record, and he who takes the trouble to examine them will find that the resolution encountered no opposition worth mentioning, except from members of the Democratic party. Scrutinize the yeas and nays on any other motion or resolution affecting the question of slavery, and the fact that a majority of the members of this party have uniformly voted for the retention and extension of the "sum of all villanies," will at once be apparent.

For many years the slave-driving Democrats of the South have labored most strenuously, both by day and by night —we regret to say how unsuccessfully—to point out abolition proclivities in the Whig and Know-Nothing parties, the latter of which is now buried, and deservedly, so deep in the depths of the dead, that it is quite preposterous to suppose it will ever see the light of resurrection.

For its truckling concessions to the slave power, the Whig party merited defeat, and defeated it was, and that, too, in the most decisive and overwhelming manner. But there is yet in this party much vitality, and if its friends will reorganize, detach themselves from the burden of slavery, espouse the cause of the white man, and hoist the fair flag of freedom, the time may come, at a day by no means remote, when their hearts will exult in triumph over the ruins of miscalled Democracy.

It is not too late, however, for the Democratic party to secure to itself a pure renown and an almost certain perpetuation of its power. Let it at once discard the worship of slavery, and do earnest battle for the principles of freedom, and it will live victoriously to a period far in the future. On the other hand, if it does not soon repudiate the fatal heresies which it has incorporated into its creed, its doom will be inevitable. Until the black flag entirely disappears from its array, we warn the non-slaveholders of the South to repulse and keep it at a distance, as they would the emblazoned skull and cross-bones that flout them from the flag of the pirate.

With regard to the sophistical reasoning which teaches that abolitionists, before abolishing slavery, should compensate the slaveholders for all or any number of the negroes in their possession, we have, perhaps, said quite enough; but wishing to brace our arguments, in every important particular, with unequivocal testimony from men whom we are accustomed to regard as models of political sagacity and integrity—from Southern men as far as possible—we herewith present an extract from a speech delivered in the Virginia House of Delegates, January 20, 1832, by Charles James Faulkner, whose sentiments, as then and there expressed, can hardly fail to find a response in the heart of every intelligent, upright man:—

"But, Sir, it is said that society having conferred this property on the slaveholder, it cannot *now* take it from him without an adequate compensation, by which is meant full value. I may be singular in the opinion, but I defy the legal research of the House to point me to a principle recognized by the law, even in the ordinary course of its adjudications, where the community pays for property which is removed or destroyed because it is a nuisance, and found injurious to that society. There is, I humbly apprehend, no such principle. There is no obligation upon society to continue your right one moment after it becomes injurious to the best interests of society; nor to compensate you for the loss of that, the deprivation of which is demanded by the safety of the State, and in which general benefit you participate as members of the community. Sir, there is to my mind a manifest distinction between condemning private property to be applied to some beneficial public purpose, and condemning or removing private property which is ascertained to be a positive wrong to society. It is a distinction which pervades the whole genius of the law; and is founded upon the idea, that any man who holds property injurious to the peace of that society of which he is a member, thereby violates the condition upon the observance of which his right to the property is alone guarantied. For property of the first class condemned, there ought to be compensation; but for property of the latter class, none can be demanded upon principle, none accorded as matter of right.

"It is conceded that, at this precise moment of our legislation, slaves are injurious to the interests and threaten the subversion and ruin of this Commonwealth. Their present number, their increasing number, all admonish us of this. In different terms, and in more measured language, the same fact has been conceded by all who have yet addressed this House. '*Something must be done,*' emphatically exclaimed the gentleman from Dinwiddie; and I thought I could perceive a response to that declaration, in the countenance of a large majority of this body. And why must something be done? Because if not, says the gentleman from Campbell, the throats of all the *white* people of Virginia will be cut. No, says the gentleman from Dinwiddie—'The whites cannot be conquered—the throats of the *blacks* will be cut.' It is a trifling difference, to be sure, Sir, and matters not to the argument. For the fact is conceded, that one race or the other must be exterminated.

"Sir, such being the actual condition of this Commonwealth, I ask if we would not be justified *now*, supposing all considerations of policy and humanity concurred without even a moment's delay, in staving off this appalling and overwhelming calamity? Sir, if this immense negro population were now in arms, gathering into black and formidable masses of attack, would that man be listened to, who spoke about property, who prayed you not to direct your artillery to such or such a point, for you would destroy some of *his* property? Sir, to the eye of the Statesman, as to the eye of Omniscience, dangers pressing, and dangers that must *necessarily* press, are alike present. With a single glance he embraces Virginia now, with the elements of destruction reposing quietly upon her bosom, and Virginia is lighted from one extremity to the other with the torch of servile insurrection and massacre. It is not sufficient for him that the match is not yet applied. It is enough that the magazine is open, and the match will shortly be applied.

"Sir, it is true in national as it is in private contracts, that loss and injury to one party may constitute as fair a consideration as gain to the other. Does the slaveholder, while he is enjoying his slaves, reflect upon the deep injury and incalculable loss which the possession of that property inflicts upon the true interests of the country? Slavery, it is admitted, is an evil—it is an institution which presses heavily against the best interests of the State. It banishes free white labor, it exterminates the mechanic, the artisan, the manufacturer. It deprives them of occupation. It deprives them of bread. It converts the energy of a community into indolence, its power into imbecility, its efficiency into weakness. Sir, being thus injurious, have we not a right to demand its extermination? shall society suffer, that the slaveholder may continue to gather his *crop* of human flesh? What is his mere pecuniary claim, compared with the great interests of the common weal? Must the country languish, droop, die, that the slaveholder may flourish? Shall all interests be subservient to one—all rights subordinate to those of the slaveholder? Has not the mechanic, have not the middle classes their rights—rights incompatible with the existence of slavery?

"Sir, so great and overshadowing are the evils of slavery—so sensibly are they felt by those who have traced the causes of our national decline—so perceptible is the poisonous operation of its principles in the va ed and diversified interests of this Commonwealth, that all, whose minds are not warped by prejudice or interest, must admit that the disease has now assumed that mortal tendency, as to justify the application of any remedy which, under the great law of State necessity, we might consider advisable."

From the abstract of our plan for the abolition of slavery, it will be perceived that, so far from allowing slaveholders any compensation for their slaves, we are, and we think justly, in favor of imposing on them a tax of sixty dollars for each and every negro now in their possession, as also for each and every one that shall be born to them between now and the 4th of July, 1863; after which time, we propose that they shall be taxed forty dollars per annum, annually, for every person by them held in slavery, without regard to age, sex, color, or condition —the money, in both instances, to be used for the sole advantage of the slaves. As an addendum to this proposition, we would say that, in our opinion, if slavery is not totally abolished by the year 1869, the annual tax ought to be increased from forty to one hundred dollars; and furthermore, that if the institution does not then almost immediately disappear under the onus of this increased taxation, the tax ought in the course of one or two years thereafter, to be augmented to such a degree as will, in harmony with other measures, prove an infallible deathblow to slavery on or before the 4th of July, 1876.

At once let the good and true men of this country, the patriot sons of the patriot fathers, determine that the sun which rises to celebrate the centennial anniversary of our national independence, shall not set on the head of any slave within the limits of our Republic. Will not the non-slaveholders of the North, of the South, of the East, and of the West, heartily, unanimously sanction this proposition? Will it not be cheerfully indorsed by many of the slaveholders themselves? Will any *respectable* man enter a protest against it? On the 4th of July, 1876—sooner, if we can—let us make good, at least so far as we are concerned, the Declaration of Independence, which was proclaimed in Philadelphia on the 4th of July, 1776—that "all men are endowed by their Creator with certain inalienable rights; that among these, are life, liberty, and the pursuit of happiness; that to secure these rights, governments are instituted among men, deriving their just powers from the consent of the governed; that whenever any form of government becomes destructive of these ends, it is the right of the people to alter or to abolish it, and to institute a new government, laying its foundation on such principles, and organizing its powers in such form, as to them shall seem most likely to effect their safety and happiness." In purging our land of the iniquity of negro slavery, we will only be carrying on the great work that was so successfully commenced by our noble sires of the Revolution; some future generation may possibly complete the work by annulling the last and least form of oppression.

To turn the slaves away from their present homes—away from all the property and means of support which their labor has mainly produced, would be unpardonably cruel—exceedingly unjust. Still more cruel and unjust would it be, however, to the non-slaveholding whites no less than to the negroes, to grant further toleration to the existence of slavery. In any event, come what will, transpire what may, the institution must be abolished. The evils, if any, which are to result from its abolition, cannot, by any manner of means, be half as great as the evils which are certain to overtake us in case of its continuance. The perpetuation of slavery is the climax of iniquity.

Two hundred and thirty-seven years have the negroes in America been held in inhuman bondage. During the whole of this long period they have toiled unceasingly from the gray of dawn till the dusk of eve, for their cruel task-masters, who have rewarded them with scanty allowances of the most inferior qualities of victuals and clothes, with heartless separations of the tenderest ties of kindred, with epithets, with scoldings, with execrations, and with the lash—and, not unfrequently, with the fatal bludgeon or the more deadly weapon. From the labor of their hands, and from the fruit of their loins, the human-mongers of the South have become wealthy, insolent, corrupt, and tyrannical. In reason and in conscience the slaves might claim from their masters a much larger sum than we have proposed to allow them. If they were to demand an equal share of all the property, real and personal, which has been accumulated or produced through their efforts, Heaven, we believe, would recognize them as honest claimants.

Elsewhere we have shown, by just and liberal estimates, that, on the single score of damages to lands, the slaveholders are, at this moment, indebted to the non-slaveholding whites in the extraordinary sum of $7,544,148,825

Considered in connection with the righteous claim of wages for services which the negroes might bring against their masters, these figures are the heralds of the significant fact that, if strict justice could be meted out to all parties in the South, the slaveholders would not only be stripped of every dollar, but they would become in law as they are in reality, the hopeless debtors of the myriads of unfortunate slaves, white and black, who are now cringing, and fawning, and festering around them. In this matter, however, so far has wrong triumphed over right, that the slaveholders—a mere handful of tyrants, whose manual exercises are wholly comprised in the use they make of instruments of torture, such as whips, clubs, bowie-knives and pistols —have, as the result of a series of acts of their own villainous legislation, become the sole and niggardly proprietors of almost every important item of Southern wealth; not only do they own all the slaves—none of whom any really respectable person cares to own—but they are also in possession of the more valuable tracts of land and the appurtenances thereto belonging; while the non-slaveholding whites and the negroes, who compose at least nine-tenths of the entire population, and who are the actual producers of every article of merchandize, animal, vegetable, and mineral, that is sold from the South, are most wickedly despoiled of the fruits of their labors, and cast into the dismal abodes of extreme ignorance, destitution and misery..

For the services of the blacks from the 20th of August, 1620, up to the 4th of July, 1863—an interval of precisely two hund ed and forty-two years ten months and fourteen days—their masters, if unwilling, ought, in our judgment, to be compelled to grant them their freedom, and to pay each and every one of them at least sixty dollars cash in hand. The aggregate sum thus raised would amount to about two hundred and forty-five millions of dollars, which is less than the total market value of two entire crops of cotton—one-half of which sum would be amply sufficient to land every negro in this country on the coast of Liberia, whither, if we had the power, we would ship them all within the next six months. As a means of protection against the exigencies which might arise from a sudden transition from their present homes in America to their future homes in Africa, and for the purpose of enabling them there to take the initiatory step in the walks of civilized life, the remainder of the sum—say about one hundred and twenty-two millions of dollars—might, very properly, be equally distributed amongst them after their arrival in the land of their fathers.

Dr. James Hall, the Secretary of the Maryland Colonization Society, informs us that the average cost of sending negroes to Liberia does not exceed thirty dollars each; and it is his opinion that arrangements might be made on an extensive plan for conveying them thither at an average expense of not more than twenty-five dollars each.

The American colonization movement, as now systematized and conducted, is simply an American humane farce. At present the slaves are increasing in this country at the rate of nearly one hundred thousand per annum; within the last ten years, as will appear below, the American Colonization Society has sent to Liberia less than five thousand negroes.

Emigrants sent to Liberia by the American Colonization Society, during the ten years ending January 1st, 1857.

In 1847	39	Emigrants.
In 1848	213	
In 1849	474	
In 1850	590	
In 1851	279	
In 1852	568	
In 1853	583	
In 1854	783	
In 1855	207	
In 1856	544	
Total	4280	

The average of this total is precisely four hundred and twenty-eight, which may be said to be the number of negroes annually colonized by the society; while the yearly increase of slaves, as previously stated, is little less than one hundred thousand! Fiddlesticks for such colonization! Once for all, within a reasonably short period, let us make the slaveholders do something like justice to their negroes by giving each and every one of them his freedom, and sixty dollars in current money; then let us charter all the ocean steamers, packets and clipper ships that can be had on liberal terms, and keep them constantly plying between the ports of America and Africa, until all slaves shall enjoy freedom in the land of their fathers. Under a well-devised and properly conducted system of operations, but a few years would be required to redeem the United States from the monstrous curse of negro slavery

Some few years ago, when certain ethnographical oligarchs proved to their own satisfaction that the negro was an inferior "type of mankind," they chuckled wonderfully, and avowed, in substance, that it was right for the stronger race to kidnap and enslave the weaker—that because Nature had been pleased to do a trifle more for the Caucasian race than for the African, the former, by virtue of its superiority, was perfectly justifiable in holding the latter in absolute and perpetual bondage! No system of logic could be more antagonistic to the spirit of true democracy. It is probable that the world does not contain two persons who are exactly alike in all respects; yet "*all* men are endowed by their Creator with certain *inalienable* rights, among which are life, *liberty*, and the pursuit of happiness." All mankind may or may not be the descendants of Adam and Eve. In our own humble way of thinking, we are frank to confess, we do not believe in the unity of the races. This is a matter, however, which has little or nothing to do with the great question at issue. Aside from any theory concerning the original parentage of the different races of men, facts, material and immaterial, palpable and impalpable—facts of the eyes and facts of the conscience—crowd around us on every hand, heaping proof upon proof, that slavery is a shame, a crime, and a curse—a great moral, social, civil, and political evil—an oppressive burden to the blacks, and an incalculable injury to the whites—a stumbling-block to the nation, an impediment to progress, a damper on all the nobler instincts, principles, aspirations and enterprises of man, and a dire enemy to every true interest.

Waiving all other counts, we have, we think, shown to the satisfaction of every impartial reader, that, as elsewhere stated, on the single score of damages to lands, the slaveholders are, at this moment, indebted to us, the non-slaveholding whites, in the enormous sum of nearly seventy-six hundred millions of dollars. What shall be done with this amount? It is just; shall payment be demanded? No; all the slaveholders in the country could not pay it; nor shall we ever ask them for even a moiety of the amount—no, not even for a dime, nor yet for a cent; we are willing to forfeit every farthing for the sake of freedom; for ourselves we ask no indemnification for the past: we only demand justice for the future.

But, Sirs, knights of bludgeons, chevaliers of bowie-knives and pistols, and lords of the lash, we are unwilling to allow you to swindle the slaves out of all the rights and claims to which, as human beings, they are most sacredly entitled. Not alone for ourself as an individual, but for others also—particularly for five or six millions of Southern non-slaveholding whites, whom your iniquitous statism has debarred from almost all the mental and material comforts of life—do we speak, when we say, you *must* emancipate your slaves, and pay each and every one of them at least sixty dollars cash in hand. By doing this, you will be restoring to them their natural rights, and remunerating them at the rate of less than twenty-six cents per annum for the long and cheerless period of their servitude, from the 20th of August, 1620, when, on James River, in Virginia, they became the unhappy slaves of heartless masters. Moreover, by doing this you will be performing but a simple act of justice to the non-slave holding whites, upon whom the institution of slavery has weighed scarcely less heavily than upon the negroes themselves. You will also be applying a saving balm to your own outraged hearts and consciences, and your children—yourselves in fact—freed from the accursed stain of slavery, will become respectable, useful, and honorable members of society.

And now, Sirs, we have thus laid down our ultimatum. What are you going to do about it? Something dreadful, as a matter of course! Perhaps you will dissolve the Union *again*. Do it, if you dare! Our motto, and we would have you to understand it, is *the abolition of slavery, and the perpetuation of the American Union.* If, by any means, you do succeed in your treasonable attempts to take the South out of the Union to-day, we will bring her back to-morrow—if she goes away with you, she will return without you.

Do not mistake the meaning of the last clause of the last sentence; we could elucidate it so thoroughly that no intelligent person could fail to comprehend it; but, for reasons which may hereafter appear, we forego the task.

Henceforth there are other interests to be consulted in the South, aside from the interests of negroes and slaveholders. A profound sense of duty incites us to make the greatest possible efforts for the abolition of slavery; an equally profound sense of duty calls for a continuation of those efforts until the very last foe to freedom shall have been utterly vanquished. To the summons of the righteous monitor within, we shall endeavor to prove faithful;

no opportunity for inflicting a mortal wound in the side of slavery shall be permitted to pass us unimproved. Thus, terror-engenderers of the South, have we fully and frankly defined our position; we have no modifications to propose, no compromises to offer, nothing to retract Frown, Sirs, fret, foam, prepare your weapons, threat, strike, shoot, stab, bring on civil war, dissolve the Union, nay annihilate the solar system if you will—do all this, more, less, better, worse, anything—do what you will, Sirs, you can neither foil nor intimidate us; our purpose is as firmly fixed as the eternal pillars of Heaven; we have determined to abolish slavery, and, so help us God, abolish it we will! Take this to bed with you to-night, Sirs. and think about it, dream over it, and let us know how you feel to-morrow morning.

CHAPTER III.

SOUTHERN TESTIMONY AGAINST SLAVERY.

If it please the reader, let him forget all that we have written on the subject of slavery; if it accord with his inclination, let him ignore all that we may write hereafter. We seek not to give currency to our peculiar opinions; our greatest ambition, in these pages, is to popularize the sayings and admonitions of wiser and better men. Miracles, we believe, are no longer wrought in this bedeviled world; but if, by any conceivable or possible supernatural event, the great Founders of the Republic, Washington, Jefferson, Henry, and others, could be reinvested with corporeal life, and returned to the South, there is scarcely a slaveholder between the Potomac and the mouth of the Mississippi, that would not burn to pounce upon them with bludgeons, bowie-knives and pistols! Yes, without adding another word, Washington would be *mobbed* for what he has already said. Were Jefferson now employed as a professor in a Southern college, he would be dismissed and driven from the State, perhaps murdered before he reached the border. If Patrick Henry were a bookseller in Alabama, though it might be demonstrated beyond the shadow of a doubt that he had never bought, sold, received, or presented, any kind of literature except Bibles and Testaments, he would first be subjected to the ignominy of a coat of tar and feathers, and then limited to the option of unceremonious expatriation or death. How seemingly impossible are these statements, and yet how true! Where do we stand? What is our faith? Are we a flock without a shepherd? a people without a prophet? a nation without a government?

Has the past, with all its glittering monuments of genius and patriotism, furnished no beacon by which we may direct our footsteps in the future? If we but prove true to ourselves, and worthy of our ancestry, we have nothing to fear; our Revolutionary sires have devised and bequeathed to us an almost perfect national policy. Let us cherish, and defend, and build upon, the fundamental principles of that polity, and we shall most assuredly reap the golden fruits of unparalleled power, virtue and prosperity. Heaven forbid that a desperate faction of slaveholding criminals should succeed in their infamous endeavors to quench the spirit of liberty, which our forefathers infused into those two sacred charts of our political faith, the Declaration of Independence, and the Constitution of the United States. Oligarchal politicians are alone responsible for the continuance of African slavery in the South. For purposes of self-aggrandizement, they have kept learning and civilization from the people; they have wilfully misinterpreted the national compacts, and have outraged their own consciences by declaring to their illiterate constituents, that the Founders of the Republic were not abolitionists. When the dark clouds of slavery, error and ignorance shall have passed away,—and we believe the time is near at hand when they are to be dissipated,—the freemen of the South, like those of other sections, will learn the glorious truth, that inflexible opposition to Human Bondage has formed one of the distinguishing characteristics of every really good or great man that our country has produced.

The principles, aims and objects that actuated the framers of the Constitution, are most graphicallly and eloquently set forth, in the following extract from a speech recently delivered by the Hon. A. H. Cragin, of New Hampshire, in the House of Representatives :

"When our forefathers reared the magnificent structure of a free Republic in this Western land, they laid its foundations broad and deep in the eternal principles of right. Its materials were all quarried from the mountain of truth; and, as it rose majestically before an astonished world, it rejoiced the hearts and hopes of mankind. Tyrants only cursed the workmen and their workmanship. Its architecture was new. It had no model in Grecian or Roman history. It seemed a paragon, let down from Heaven to inspire the hopes of men, and to demonstrate the favor of God to the people of a new world. The builders recognized the rights of human nature as universal. Liberty, the great first right of man, they claimed for 'all men,' and claimed it from 'God himself.' Upon this foundation they erected the temple, and dedicated it to Liberty, Humanity, Justice, and Equality. Washington was crowned its patron saint."

"The work completed was the noblest effort of human wisdom. But it was not perfect. It had one blemish—a little spot—the black stain of slavery. The workmen—the friends of freedom everywhere—deplored this. They labored long and prayerfully to remove this deformity. They applied all the skill of their art; but they labored in vain. Self-interest was too strong for patriotism and love of liberty. The work stood still, and for a time it was doubtful whether the experiment would succeed. The blot must remain, or the whole must fail. The workmen revarnished their work, to conceal and cover up the stain. Slavery was recognized, but not sanctioned. The word slave or slavery must not mar the Constitution. So great an inconsistency must not be proclaimed to the world."

"All agreed, at that time, that the anomaly should not increase, and all concurred in the hope and belief that the blemish would gradually disappear. Those noble men looked forward to the time when slavery would be abolished in this land of ours. They believed that the principles of liberty were so dear to the people, that they would not long deny to others what they claimed for themselves. They never dreamed that slavery would be extended but firmly believed it would be wholly blotted out. *I challenge any man to show me a single patriot of the Revolution who was in favor of slavery, or who advocated its extension.* So universal was the sentiment of liberty then, that no man, North or South, could be found to justify it. Some palliated the evil, and desired that it might be gradually extinguished; but none contemplated it as a permanent institution."

"Liberty was then the national goddess, worshiped by all the people. They sang of liberty, they harangued for liberty, they prayed for liberty, and they sacrificed for liberty Slavery was then hateful. It was denounced by all. The British king was condemned for foisting it upon the Colonies. Southern men were foremost in entering their protest against it. It was then everywhere regarded as an evil, and a crime against humanity."

The fact is too palpable to be disguised, that slavery and slaveholders have always been a clog and a dead-weight upon the government—a disgrace and a curse to humanity. The slaveholding Tories of the South, particularly of South Carolina, in their atrocious hostility to freedom, prolonged the arduous war of the Revolution from two to three years; and since the termination of that momentous struggle, in which, thank Heaven, they were most signally defeated, it has been their constant aim and effort to subvert the dear-bought liberties which were achieved by the non-slaveholding patriots.

Non-slaveholders of the South! up to the present period, neither as a body, nor as individuals, have you ever had an independent existence; but, if true to yourselves and to the memory of your fathers, you, in equal copartnership with the non-slaveholders of the North, will soon become the honored rulers and proprietors of the most powerful, prosperous, virtuous, free, and peaceful nation, on which the sun has ever shone. Already has the time arrived for you to decide upon what basis you will erect your political superstructure. Upon whom will you depend for an equitable and judicious form of constitutional government? Whom will you designate as models for your future statesmen? Your choice lies between the dead and the living—between the Washingtons, the Jeffersons and the Madisons of the past, and the Quattlebums, the Quitmans and the Butlers of the present. We have chosen; choose ye, remembering that freedom or slavery is to be the issue of your option.

As the result of much reading and research, and at the expenditure of no inconsiderable amount of time, labor and money, we now proceed to make known the anti-slavery sentiments of those noble abolitionists, the Fathers of the Republic, whose liberal measures of public policy have been so criminally perverted by the treacherous advocates of slavery

Let us listen, in the first place, to the voice of him who

was "first in war, first in peace, and first in the hearts of his countrymen," to

THE VOICE OF WASHINGTON.

In a letter to John F. Mercer, dated September 9th, 1786, General Washington says:—

"I never mean, unless some particular circumstances should compel me to it, to possess another slave by purchase, it being among my *first wishes* to see some plan adopted by which slavery, in this country, may be abolished by law."

In a letter to Robert Morris, dated Mount Vernon, April 12, 1786, he says:—

"I can only say that there is not a man living who wishes more sincerely than I do to see a plan adopted for the abolition of it. But there is only one proper and effectual mode by which it can be accomplished, and that is by legislative authority; and this, as far as my suffrage will go, shall never be wanting."

He says, in a letter

"To the MARQUIS DE LAFAYETTE—April 5th, 1783:—
The scheme, my dear Marquis, which you propose as a precedent, to encourage the emancipation of the black people in this country from the state of bondage in which they are held, is a striking evidence of the benevolence of your heart. I shall be happy to join you in so laudable a work; but will defer going into a detail of the business till I have the pleasure of seeing you."

In another letter to Lafayette, he says:—

"The benevolence of your heart, my dear Marquis, is so conspicuous on all occasions, that I never wonder at any fresh proofs of it; but your late purchase of an estate in the Colony of Cayenne, with the view of emancipating the slaves on it, is a generous and noble proof of your humanity. Would to God a like spirit might diffuse itself generally into the minds of the people of this country."

In a letter to Sir John Sinclair, he further said :—

"There are in Pennsylvania laws for the gradual abolition of slavery, which neither Virginia nor Maryland have at present, but which nothing is more certain than they must have, and at a period *not remote.*"

From his last will and testament we make the following extract :

"Upon the decease of my wife, it is my will and desire that all the slaves which I hold in my own right shall receive their freedom. To emancipate them during her life would, though earnestly wished by me, be attended with such insuperable difficulties, on account of their intermixture by marriage with the dower negroes, as to excite the most painful sensation, if not disagreeable consequences, from the latter, while both descriptions are in the occupancy of the same proprietor, it not being in my power, under the tenure by which the dower negroes are held, to manumit them."

It is said that, "when Mrs. Washington learned, from the will of her deceased husband, that the only obstacle to the immediate perfection of this provision was her right of dower, she at once gave it up, and the slaves were made free." A man might possibly concentrate within himself more real virtue and influence than ever Washington possessed, and yet he would not be too good for such a wife.

From the Father of his Country, we now turn to the author of the Declaration of Independence. We will listen to

THE VOICE OF JEFFERSON.

On the 39th and 40th pages of his Notes on Virginia, Jefferson says :—

"There must doubtless be an unhappy influence on the manners of our people, produced by the existence of slavery among us. The whole commerce between master and slave is a perpetual exercise of the most boisterous passions—the most unremitting despotism on the one part, and degrading submissions on the other. Our children see this, and learn to imitate it; for man is an imitative animal. This quality is the germ of all education in him. From his cradle to his grave, he is learning to do what he sees others do. If a parent could find no motive, either in his philanthropy or his self-love, for restraining the intemperance of passion towards his slave, it should always be a sufficient one that his child is present. But generally it is not sufficient. The parent storms, the child looks on, catches the lineaments of wrath, puts on the same airs in the circle of smaller slaves, gives a loose rein to the worst of passions; and, thus nursed, educated, and daily exercised in tyranny, cannot but be stamped by it with odious peculiarities. The man must be a prodigy who can retain his manners and morals undepraved by such circumstances. And with what execration should the Statesman be loaded, who, permitting one half the citizens thus to trample on the rights of the other, transforms those into despots and these into enemies, destroys the morals of the one part and the *amor patriae* of the other; for if a slave can have a country in this world, it must be any other in preference to that in which he is born to live and labor for another; in which he must look up the faculties of his nature, contribute, as far as depends on his individual endeavors, to the evanishment of the human race, or entail his own miserable condition on the endless generations proceeding from him. With the morals of the people, their industry also is destroyed; for, in a warm climate, no man will labor for himself who can make another labor for him. This is so true, that of the proprietors of slaves a very small proportion, indeed, are ever seen to labor. And can the liberties of a nation be thought secure, when we have removed their only firm basis—a conviction in the minds of the people that these liberties are of the gift of God? that they are not to be violated but with his wrath? Indeed, I tremble for my country when I reflect that God is just; that his justice cannot sleep forever; that considering numbers, nature, and natural means only, a revolution of the wheel of fortune, an exchange of situation is among possible events; that it may become probable by supernatural interference! The Almighty has no attribute which can take side with us in such a contest."

While Virginia was yet a Colony, in 1774, she held a Convention to appoint delegates to attend the first general Congress, which was to assemble, and did assemble, in Philadelphia, in September of the same year. Before that Convention, Mr. Jefferson made an exposition of the rights of British America, in which he said:—

"The abolition of domestic slavery is the greatest object of desire in these Colonies, where it was unhappily introduced in their infant State. But previous to the enfranchisement of the slaves, it is necessary to exclude further importations from Africa. Yet our repeated attempts to effect this by prohibitions, and by imposing duties which might amount to prohibition, have been hitherto defeated by his Majesty's negative; thus preferring the immediate advantage of a few African corsairs to the lasting interests of the American States, and the rights of human nature, deeply wounded by this infamous practice."

In the original draft of the Declaration of Independence, of which it is well known he was the author, we find this charge against the King of Great Britain:—

"He has waged cruel war against human nature itself, violating its most sacred rights of life and liberty, in the persons of a distant people who never offended him, captivating and carrying them into slavery in another hemisphere, or to incur miserable death in their transportation thither. This piratical warfare, the opprobrium of infidel powers, is the warfare of the Christian King of Great Britain. Determined to keep a market where men should be bought and sold, he has at length prostituted his negative for suppressing any legislative attempt to prohibit and restrain this execrable commerce."

Hear him further; he says:—

"We hold these truths to be self-evident, that all men are created equal; that they are endowed by their Creator with certain unalienable rights; that among these are life, liberty, and the pursuit of happiness; that to secure these rights, governments are instituted among men, deriving their just powers from the consent of the governed."

Under date of August 7th, 1785, in a letter to Dr. Price of London, he says:—

"Northward of the Chesapeake you may find, here and there an opponent of your doctrine, as you may find, here and there, a robber and murderer; but in no great number. Emancipation is put into such a train, that in a few years there will be no slaves northward of Maryland. In Maryland I do not find such a disposition to begin the redress of this enormity, as in Virginia. This is the next State to which we may turn our eyes for the interesting spectacle of justice in conflict with avarice and oppression; a conflict wherein the sacred side is gaining daily recruits from the influx into office of young men grown up, and growing up. These have sucked in the principles of liberty, as it were, with their mother's milk; and it is to them I look with anxiety to turn the fate of the question."

In another letter, written to a friend in 1814, he made use of the following emphatic language:—

"Your favor of July 31st was duly received, and read with peculiar pleasure. The sentiments do honor to the head and heart of the writer. Mine on the subject of the slavery of negroes have long since been in the possession of the public, and time has only served to give them stronger root. The love of justice and the love of country plead equally the cause of these people, and it is a reproach to us that they should have pleaded it so long in vain."

Again, he says:—

"What an incomprehensible machine is man! who can endure toil, famine, stripes, imprisonment, and death itself, in vindication of his own liberty; and the next moment be deaf to all those motives whose power supported him through his trial, and inflict on his fellow man a bondage, one hour of which is fraught with more misery than ages of that which he rose in rebellion to oppose."

Throughout the South, at the present day, especially among slaveholders, negroes are almost invariably spoken of as "goods and chattels," "property," "human cattle." In our first quotation from Jefferson's works, we have seen that he spoke of the blacks as *citizens*. We shall now hear him speak of them as *brethren*. He says:—

"We must wait with patience the workings of an overruling Providence, and hope that that is preparing the deliverance of these our brethren. When the measure of their tears shall be full, when their groans shall have involved Heaven itself in darkness, doubtless a God of justice will awaken to their distress. Nothing is more certainly written in the Book of Fate, than that this people shall be free."

In a letter to James Heaton, on this same subject, dated May 20, 1826, only six weeks before his death, he says:—

"My sentiments have been forty years before the public. Had

I repeated them forty times, they would have only become the more stale and threadbare. Although I shall not live to see them consummated, they will not die with me."

From the Father of the Declaration of Independence, we now turn to the Father of the Constitution. We will listen to

THE VOICE OF MADISON.

Advocating the abolition of the slave-trade, Mr. Madison said :—

"The dictates of humanity, the principles of the people, the national safety and happiness, and prudent policy, require it of us. It is to be hoped, that by expressing a national disapprobation of the trade, we may *destroy* it, and save our country from reproaches, and our posterity from the imbecility ever attendant on a country filled with slaves."

Again, he says :—

"It is wrong to admit into the Constitution the idea that there can be property in man."

In the 39th No. of "The Federalist," he says :—

"The first question that offers itself is, whether the general form and aspect of the government be strictly Republican. It is evident that no other form would be reconcilable with the genius of the people of America, and with the fundamental principles of the Revolution, or with that honorable determination which animates every votary of freedom, to rest all our political experiments on the capacity of mankind for self-government."

In the Federal Convention, he said —

"And in the third place, where slavery exists, the Republican theory becomes still more fallacious."

On another occasion, he says :—

"We have seen the mere distinction of color made, in the most enlightened period of time, a ground of the most oppressive dominion ever exercised by man over man."

THE VOICE OF MONROE.

In a speech in the Virginia Convention, Mr. Monroe said :—

"We have found that this evil has preyed upon the very vitals of the Union, and has been prejudicial to all the States, in which it has existed."

THE VOICE OF HENRY.

The eloquent Patrick Henry says, in a letter dated January 18, 1773 :—

"Is it not a little surprising that the professors of Christianity, whose chief excellence consists in softening the human heart, in cherishing and improving its finer feelings, should encourage a practice so totally repugnant to the first impressions of right and wrong? What adds to the wonder is, that this abominable practice has been introduced in the most enlightened ages. Times that seem to have pretensions to boast of high improvements in the arts and sciences, and refined morality, have brought into general use, and guarded by many laws, a species of violence and tyranny which our more rude and barbarous, but more honest ancestors detested. Is it not amazing that at a time when the rights of humanity are defined and understood with precision, in a country above all others fond of liberty—that in such an age and in such a country, we find men professing a religion the most mild, humane, gentle, and generous, adopting such a principle, as repugnant to humanity as it is inconsistent with the Bible, and destructive to liberty? Every thinking, honest man rejects it in speculation. How free in practice from conscientious motives! Would any one believe that I am master of slaves of my own purchase? I am drawn along by the general inconvenience of living here without them. I will not, I cannot justify it. However culpable my conduct, I will so far pay my devoir to virtue as to own the excellence and rectitude of her precepts, and lament my want of conformity to them. I believe a time will come when an opportunity will be offered to abolish this lamentable evil. Everything we can do is to improve it, if it happens in our day; if not, let us transmit to our descendants, together with our slaves, a pity for their unhappy lot, and an abhorrence for slavery. If we cannot reduce this wished-for reformation to practice, let us treat the unhappy victims with lenity. It is the furthest advance we can make towards justice. It is a debt we owe to the purity of our religion, to show that it is at variance with that law which warrants slavery."

Again, this great orator says:—

"It would rejoice my very soul, that every one of my fellow-beings was emancipated. We ought to lament and deplore the necessity of holding our fellow-men in bondage. Believe me, I shall honor the Quakers for their noble efforts to abolish slavery."

THE VOICE OF RANDOLPH.

That excentric genius, John Randolph, of Roanoke, in a letter to William Gibbons, in 1820, says:—

"With unfeigned respect and regard, and as sincere a deprecation on the extension of slavery and its horrors, as any other man, be him whom he may, I am your friend, in the literal sense of that much abused word. I say much abused, because it is applied to the leagues of vice and avarice and ambition, instead of good will toward man from love of him who is the Prince of Peace."

While in Congress, he said:

"Sir, I envy neither the heart nor the head of that man from the North who rises here to defend slavery on principle."

It is well known that he emancipated all his negroes. The following lines from his will are well worth perusing and preserving:—

"I give to my slaves their freedom, to which my conscience tells me they are justly entitled. It has a long time been a matter of the deepest regret to me that the circumstances under which I inherited them, and the obstacles thrown in the way by the laws of the land, have prevented my emancipating them in my life-time, which it is my full intention to do in case I can accomplish it."

THOMAS M. RANDOLPH.

In an address to the Virginia Legislature, in 1820, Gov. Randolph said:—

"We have been far outstripped by States to whom nature has been far less bountiful. It is painful to consider what might have been, under other circumstances, the amount of general wealth in Virginia."

THOMAS JEFFERSON RANDOLPH.

In 1832, Mr. Randolph, of Albemarle, in the Legislature of Virginia, used the following most graphic and emphatic language:—

"I agree with gentlemen in the necessity of arming the State for internal defence. I will unite with them in any effort to restore confidence to the public mind, and to conduce to the sense of the safety of our wives and our children. Yet, Sir, I must ask upon whom is to fall the burden of this defence? Not upon the lordly masters of their hundred slaves, who will never turn out except to retire with their families when danger threatens. No, Sir! it is to fall upon the less wealthy class of our citizens chiefly upon the non-slaveholder. I have known patrols turned out when there was not a slaveholder among them; and this is the practice of the country. I have slept in times of alarm quiet in bed, without having a thought of care, while these individuals, owning none of this property themselves, were patrolling under a compulsory process, for a pittance of seventy-five cents per twelve hours, the very curtilage of my house, and guarding that property which was alike dangerous to them and myself. After all, this is but an expedient. As this population becomes more numerous, it becomes less productive. Your guard must be increased, until finally its profits will not pay for the expense of its subjection. Slavery has the effect of lessening the free population of a country.

"The gentleman has spoken of the increase of the female slaves being a part of the profit. It is admitted; but no great evil can be averted, no good attained, without some inconvenience. It may be questioned how far it is desirable to foster and encourage this branch of profit. It is a practice, and an increasing practice, in parts of Virginia, to rear slaves for market. How can an honorable mind, a patriot, and a lover of his country, bear to see this Ancient Dominion, rendered illustrious by the noble devotion and patriotism of her sons in the cause of liberty, converted into one grand menagerie, where men are to be reared for the market, like oxen for the shambles? Is it better, is it not worse, than the slave trade—that trade which enlisted the labor of the good and wise of every creed, and every clime, to abolish it? The trader receives the slave, a stranger in language, aspect, and manners, from the merchant who has brought him from the interior. The ties of father, mother, husband, and child, have all been rent in twain; before he receives him, his soul has become callous. But here, Sir, individuals whom the master has known from infancy, whom he has seen sporting in the innocent gambols of childhood, who have been accustomed to look to him for protection, he tears from the mother's arms and sells into a strange country among strange people, subject to cruel taskmasters.

"He has attempted to justify slavery here, because it exists in Africa, and has stated that it exists all over the world. Upon the same principle, he could justify Mahometanism, with its plurality of wives, petty wars for plunder, robbery, and murder, or any other of the abominations and enormities of savage tribes. Does slavery exist in any part of civilized Europe? No, Sir, in no part of it."

PEYTON RANDOLPH.

On the 20th of October, 1774, while Congress was in session in Philadelphia, Peyton Randolph, President, the following resolution, among others, was unanimously adopted :—

"That we will neither import nor purchase any slave imported after the first day of December next; after which time we will wholly discontinue the slave-trade, and will neither be concerned in it ourselves, nor will we hire our vessels, nor sell our commodities or manufactures, to those who are concerned in it."

EDMUND RANDOLPH.

The Constitution of the United States contains the following provision :—

"No person held to service or labor in another State, under the laws thereof, escaping to another, shall, in consequence of any law or regulation therein, be discharged from such service or labor, but shall be delivered up on claim of the party to whom such service or labor may be due."

To the studious attention of those vandals who contend that the above provision requires the rendition of fugitive *slaves*, we respectfully commend the following resolution, which, it will be observed, was *unanimously* adopted :—

"On motion of Mr. Randolph, the word *servitude'* was struck out, and '*service*' unanimously inserted—the former being thought to express the condition of *slaves*, and the latter the obligation of *free* persons."—*Madison Papers, vol.* III., *p.* 1569.

Well done for the Randolphs!

THE VOICE OF CLAY.

Henry Clay, whom everybody loved, and at the mention of whose name the American heart always throbs with emotions of grateful remembrance, said, in an address before the Kentucky Colonization Society, in 1829:—

"It is believed that nowhere in the *farming* portion of the United States would slave-labor be generally employed, if the proprietor were not tempted to raise slaves by the high price of the Southern market, which keeps it up in his own."

In the United States Senate, in 1850, he used the following memorable words:—

"I am extremely sorry to hear the Senator from Mississippi say that he requires, first the extension of the Missouri Compromise line to the Pacific, and also that he is not satisfied with that, but requires, if I understand him correctly, a positive provision for the admission of slavery South of that line. And now, Sir, coming from a slave State, as I do, I owe it to myself, I owe it to truth, I owe it to the subject to say that no earthly power could induce me to vote for a specific measure for the introduction of slavery where it had not before existed, either South or North of that line. Coming as I do from a slave State, it is my solemn, deliberate and well-matured determination that no power, no earthly power, shall compel me to vote for the positive introduction of slavery either South or North of that line. Sir while you reproach, and justly too, our British ancestors for the introduction of this institution upon the continent of America I am, for one, unwilling that the posterity of the present inhabitants of California and of New Mexico, shall reproach us for doing just what we reproach Great Britain for doing to us. If the citizens of those territories choose to establish slavery, and if they come here with Constitutions establishing slavery, I am for admitting them with such provisions in their Constitutions; but then it will be their own work, and not ours, and their posterity will have to reproach them, and not us, for forming Constitutions allowing the institution of slavery to exist among them. These are my views, Sir, and I choose to express them; and I care not how extensively or universally they are known."

Hear him further; he says:—

"So long as God allows the vital current to flow through my veins, I will never, never, never, by word, or thought, by mind or will, aid in admitting one rood of free territory to the everlasting curse of human bondage."

A bumper to the memory of noble Harry of the West!

CASSIUS M. CLAY

Of the great number of good speeches made by members of the Republican party during the late Presidential campaign, it is, we believe, pretty generally admitted that the best one was made by Cassius M. Clay, of Kentucky, at the Tabernacle, in New-York City, on the 24th of October, 1856. From the speech of that noble champion of freedom, then and there delivered, we make the following graphic extract:—

"If there are no manufactures, there is no commerce. In vain do the slaveholders go to Knoxville, to Nashville, to Memphis and to Charleston, and resolve that they will have nothing to do with these abolition eighteen millions of Northern people; that they will build their own vessels, manufacture their own goods ship their own products to foreign countries, and break down

New-York, Philadelphia and Boston! Again they resolve and reresolve, and yet there is not a single ton more shipped and not a single article added to the wealth of the South. But, gentlemen, they never invite such men as I am to attend their Conventions. They know that I would tell them that slavery is the cause of their poverty, and that I will tell them that what they are aiming at is the dissolution of the Union—that they may be prepared to strike for that whenever the nation rises. They well know that by slave labor the very propositions which they make can never be realized; yet when we show these things, they cry out, 'Oh, Cotton is King!' But when we look at the statistics, we find that so far from Cotton being King, Grass is King. There are nine articles of staple productions which are larger than that of cotton in this country."

"I suppose it does not follow because slavery is endeavoring to modify the great dicta of our fathers, that cotton and free labor are incompatible. In the extreme South, at New Orleans, the laboring men—the stevedores and hackmen on the levee, where the heat is intensified by the proximity of the red brick buildings, are all white men, and they are in the full enjoyment of health. But how about cotton? I am informed by a friend of mine—himself a slaveholder, and therefore good authority—that in Northwestern Texas, among the German settlements, who. true to their national instincts, will not employ the labor of a slave—they produce more cotton to the acre, and of a better quality, and selling at prices from a cent to a cent and a half a pound higher than that produced by slave labor. This is an experiment that illustrates what I have always held, that whatever is right is expedient."

THE VOICE OF BENTON.

In his "Thirty Years' View," Thomas H. Benton says:—

"My opposition to the extension of slavery dates further back than 1844—forty years further back; and as this is a suitable time for a general declaration, and a sort of general conscience delivery, I will say that my opposition to it dates from 1804, when

I was a student at law in the State of Tennessee, and studied the subject of African slavery in an American book—a Virginia book—Tucker's edition of Blackstone's Commentaries."

Again, in a speech delivered in St. Louis, on the 3rd of November, 1856, he says :—

"I look at white people, and not at black ones; I look to the peace and reputation of the race to which I belong. I look to the peace of this land—the world's last hope for a free government on the earth. One of the occasions on which I saw Henry Clay rise higher than I thought I ever saw him before, was when in the debate on the admission of California, a dissolution was apprehended if slavery was not carried into this Territory, where it never was. Then Mr. Clay, rising, loomed colossally in the Senate of the United States, as he rose declaring that for no earthly purpose, no earthly object, could he carry slavery into places where it did not exist before. It was a great and proud day for Mr. Clay, towards the latter days of his life, and if an artist could have been there to catch his expression as he uttered that sentiment, with its reflex on his face, and his countenance beaming with firmness of purpose, it would have been a glorious moment in which to transmit him to posterity—his countenance all alive and luminous with the ideas that beat in his bosom. That was a proud day. I could have wished that I had spoken the same words. I speak them now, telling you they were his, and adopting them as my own."

THE VOICE OF MASON.

Colonel Mason, a leading and distinguished member of the Convention that formed the Constitution, from Virginia, when the provision for prohibiting the mportation of slaves was under consideration, said :—

"The present question concerns not the importing States alone, but the whole Union. Slavery discourages arts and manufactures. The poor despise labor when performed by slaves. They prevent the emigration of whites who really enrich and strengthen a country. They produce the most pernicious effect on manners. Every master of slaves is born a petty tyrant. They bring the judgment of Heaven on a country. As nations cannot be rewarded or punished in the next world, they must be in this. By an inevitable chain of causes and effects, Providence punishes national sins by national calamities. He lamented that some of our Eastern brethren had, from a lust of gain, embarked in this nefarious traffic. As to the States being in possession of the right to import, this was the case with many other rights, now to be properly given up. He held it essential, in every point of view, that the General Government should have power to prevent the increase of slavery."

THE VOICE OF MCDOWELL.

In 1832, Gov. McDowell used this language in the Virginia Legislature:—

"Who that looks to this unhappy bondage of an unhappy people, in the midst of our society, and thinks of its incidents or issues, but weeps over it as a curse as great upon him who inflicts as upon him who suffers it? Sir, you may place the slave where you please—you may dry up, to your uttermost, the fountains of his feelings, the springs of his thought—you may close upon his mind every avenue of knowledge, and cloud it over with artificial night—you may yoke him to your labors, as the ox, which liveth only to work and worketh only to live—you may put him under any process which, without destroying his value as a slave, will debase and crush him as a rational being—you may do this, and the idea that he was born to be free will survive t all. It is allied to his hope of immortality—it is the etherial part of his nature which oppression cannot rend. It is a torch lit up in his soul by the hand of Deity, and never meant to be extinguished by the hand of man."

THE VOICE OF IREDELL.

In the debates of the North Carolina Convention, Mr. Iredell, afterwards a Judge of the United States Supreme Court, said :—

"When the entire abolition of slavery takes place, it will be an event which must be pleasing to every generous mind and every friend of human nature."

THE VOICE OF PINKNEY.

William Pinkney, of Maryland, in the House of Delegates in that State, in 1789, made several powerful arguments in favor of the abolition of slavery. Here follows a brief extract from one of his speeches :—

"Iniquitous and most dishonorable to Maryland, is that dreary system of partial bondage which her laws have hitherto supported with a solicitude worthy of a better object, and her citizens by their practice, countenanced. Founded in a disgraceful traffic, to which the parent country lent its fostering aid, from motives of interest, but which even she would have disdained to encourage, had England been the destined mart of such inhuman merchandize, its continuance is as shameful as its origin.

I have no hope that the stream of general liberty will forever flow unpolluted through the mire of partial bondage, or that they who have been habituated to lord it over others, will not, in time, become base enough to let others lord it over them. If they resist, it will be the struggle of pride and selfishness, not of principle."

THE VOICE OF LEIGH.

In the Legislature of Virginia, in 1832, Mr. Leigh said :—

"I thought, till very lately that it was known to every body that, during the Revolution, and for many years after, the abolition of slavery was a favorite topic with many of our ablest Statesmen, who entertained with respect all the schemes which wisdom or ingenuity could suggest for its accomplishment."

THE VOICE OF MARSHALL.

Thomas Marshall, of Fauquier, said, in the Virginia Legislature, in 1832 :—

"Wherefore, then, object to slavery? Because it is ruinous to the whites—retards improvements, roots out an industrious population, banishes the yeomanry of the country—deprives the spinner, the weaver, the smith, the shoemaker, the carpenter, of employment and support."

THE VOICE OF BOLLING.

Philip A. Bolling, of Buckingham, a member of the Legislature of Virginia in 1832, said :—

"The time will come—and it may be sooner than many are willing to believe—when this oppressed and degraded race cannot be held as they now are—when a change will be effected, abhorrent, Mr. Speaker, to you, and to the feelings of every good man.

The wounded adder will recoil, and sting the foot that tramples upon it. The day is fast approaching, when those who oppose all action upon this subject, and, instead of aiding in devising some feasible plan for freeing their country from an acknowledged curse, cry '*impossible*,' to every plan suggested, will curse their perverseness, and lament their folly."

THE VOICE OF CHANDLER.

Mr. Chandler, of Norfolk, member of the Virginia Legislature, in 1832, took occasion to say :—

"It is admitted, by all who have addressed this House, that

slavery is a curse, and an increasing one. That it has been destructive to the lives of our citizens, history, with unerring truth, will record. That its future increase will create commotion, cannot be doubted."

THE VOICE OF SUMMERS.

Mr. Summers, of Kanawha, member of the Legislature of Virginia, in 1832, said :—

"The evils of this system cannot be enumerated. It were unnecessary to attempt it. They glare upon us at every step. When the owner looks to his wasted estate, he knows and feels them."

THE VOICE OF PRESTON.

In the Legislature of Virginia, in 1832, Mr. Preston said :—

"Sir, Mr. Jefferson, whose hand drew the preamble to the Bill of Rights, has eloquently remarked that we had invoked for ourselves the benefit of a principle which we had denied to others. He saw and felt that slaves, as men, were embraced within this principle."

THE VOICE OF FREMONT.

John Charles Fremont, one of the noblest sons of the South, says :—

"I heartily concur in all movements which have for their object to repair the mischiefs arising from the violation of good faith in the repeal of the Missouri Compromise. I am opposed to slavery in the abstract, and upon principles sustained and made habitual by long settled convictions. I am inflexibly opposed to its extension on this continent beyond its present limits."

"The great body of non-slaveholding Freemen, including those of the South, upon whose welfare slavery is an oppression, will discover that the power of the General Government over the Public Lands may be beneficially exerted to advance their interests, and secure their independence, knowing this, their suffrages will not be wanting to maintain that authority in the Union, which is absolutely essential to the maintenance of their own liberties, and which has more than once indicated the purpose of disposing of the Public Lands in such a way as would make every settler upon them a freeholder."

THE VOICE OF BLAIR.

In an Address to the Republicans of Maryland, in 1856, Francis P. Blair says :—

"In every aspect in which slavery among us can be considered, it is pregnant with difficulty. Its continuance in the States in which it has taken root has resulted in the monopoly of the soil, to a great extent, in the hands of the slaveholders, and the entire control of all departments of the State Government; and yet a majority of people in the slave States are not slave-owners. This produces an anomaly in the principle of our free institutions, which threatens in time to bring into subjugation to slave-owners the great body of the free white population."

THE VOICE OF MAURY.

Lieut. Maury, to whom has been awarded so much well-merited praise in the world of science, says :—

"The fact must be obvious to the far-reaching minds of our Statesmen, that unless some means of relief be devised, some channel afforded, by which the South can, when the time comes, get rid of the excess of her slave population, she will be ultimately found with regard to this institution, in the predicament of the man with the wolf by the ears; too dangerous to hold on any longer, and equally dangerous to let go. To our mind, the event is as certain to happen as any event which depends on the contingencies of the future, viz.: that unless means be devised for gradually relieving the slave States from the undue pressure of this class upon them—unless some way be opened by which they may be rid of their surplus black population—the time will come—it may not be in the next nor in the succeeding generation—but, sooner or later, come it will, and come it must—when the two races will join in the death struggle for the mastery."

THE VOICE OF BIRNEY.

James G. Birney, of Kentucky, under whom the Abolitionists first became a National Party, and for whom they voted for President in 1844, giving him 66,304 votes, says:

"We have so long practiced injustice, adding to it hypocrisy, in the treatment of the colored race, both negroes and Indians, that we begin to regard injustice as an element—a chief element—the chief element of our government. But no government which admits injustice as an element can be a harmonious one or a permanent one. Harmony is the antagonist of injustice, ever has been, and ever will be; that is, so long as injustice lasts, which cannot always be, for it is a lie, a semblance, therefore, perishable. True, from the imperfection of man, his ambition and selfishness, injustice often finds its way incidentally into the administration of public affairs, and maintains its footing a long time before it is cast out by the legitimate elements of government."

"Our slave States, especially the more southern of them, in which the number of slaves is greater, and in which, of course the sentiment of injustice is stronger than in the more northern ones, are to be placed on the list of decaying communities. To a philosophic observer, they seem to be falling back on the scale of civilization. Even at the present point of retrogression, the cause of civilization and human improvement would lose nothing by their annihilation."

THE VOICE OF DELAWARE.

Strong anti-slavery sentiment had become popular in

Delaware as early as 1785. With Maryland and Missouri, it may now be ranked as a semi-slave State. Mr. McLane, a member of Congress from this State in 1825, said:—

"I shall not imitate the example of other gentlemen by making professions of my love of liberty and abhorrence of slavery, not, however, because I do not entertain them. I am an enemy to slavery."

THE VOICE OF MARYLAND.

Slavery has little vitality in Maryland. Baltimore, the greatest city of the South—greatest because freest—has a population of more than two hundred thousand souls, and yet less than three thousand of these are slaves. In spite of all the unjust and oppressive statutes enacted by the oligarchy, the non-slaveholders, who with the exception of a small number of slaveholding emancipationists, may in truth be said to be the only class of respectable and patriotic citizens in the South, have wisely determined that their noble State shall be freed from the sin and the shame, the crime and the curse of slavery; and in accordance with this determination, long since formed, they are giving every possible encouragement to free white labor, thereby, very properly, rendering the labor of slaves both unprofitable and disgraceful. The formation of an Abolition Society in this State, in 1789, was the result of the influence of the masterly speeches delivered in the House of Delegates, by the Hon. William Pinkney whose undying testimony we have already placed on record. Nearly seventy years ago, this eminent lawyer and Statesman declared to the people of America, that if they did not mark out the bounds of slavery, and adopt measures for its total extinction, it would finally " work a decay of the spirit of liberty in the free States." Further, he said that, " by the eternal principles of natural justice, no master in the State has a right to hold his slave in bondage a single hour." In 1787, Luther Martin, of this State, said :—

"Slavery is inconsistent with the genius of republicanism, and has a tendency to destroy those principles on which it is supported, as it lessens the sense of the equal rights of mankind, and habituates us to tyranny and oppression."

THE VOICE OF VIRGINIA.

After introducing the unreserved and immortal testimony of Washington, Jefferson, Madison, Henry, and the other great men of the Old Dominion, against the institution of slavery, it may to some, seem quite superfluous to back the cause of Freedom by arguments from other Virginia abolitionists ; but this State, notwithstanding all her more modern manners and inhumanity, has been so prolific of just views and noble sentiments, that we deem it eminently fit and proper to blazon many of them to the world as the redeeming features of her history. An Abolition Society was formed in this State in 1791. In a memorial which the members of this Society presented to Congress, they pronounced slavery "not only an odious degradation, but an outrageous violation of one of the most essential rights of human nature, and utterly repugnant to the precepts of the Gospel." A Bill of Rights, unanimously agreed upon by the Virginia Convention of June 12, 1776, holds—

"That all men are, by nature, equally free and independent;

That Government is, or ought to be, instituted for the common benefit, protection, and security, of the People, Nation, or Community;

That elections of members to serve as representatives of the people in assembly ought to be free;

That all men having sufficient evidence of permanent common interest with, and attachment to, the community, have the right of suffrage, and cannot be taxed or deprived of their property, for public uses, without their own consent or that of their representatives so elected, nor bound by any law to which they have not in like manner assented, for the public good;

That the freedom of the Press is one of the greatest bulwarks of Liberty, and can never be restrained but by despotic Governments;

That no free Government or the blessing of Liberty can be preserved to any people, but by a firm adherence to justice, moderation, temperance, frugality, and virtue, and by a frequent recurrence to fundamental principles."

The "Virginia Society for the Abolition of Slavery," organized in 1791, addressed Congress in these words:—

"Your memorialists, fully aware that righteousness exalteth a nation, and that slavery is not only an odious degradation, but an outrageous violation of one of the most essential rights of human nature, and utterly repugnant to the precepts of the gospel, which breathes 'peace on earth and good will to men,' lament that a practice so inconsistent with true policy and the inalienable rights of men, should subsist in so enlightened an age, and among a people professing that all mankind are, by nature equally entitled to freedom."

THE VOICE OF NORTH CAROLINA.

If the question, *slavery* or *no slavery*, could be fairly presented for the decision of the legal voters of North Carolina at the next popular election, we believe at least two-thirds of them would deposite the *no slavery* ticket. Perhaps one-fourth of the slaveholders themselves would vote it, for the slaveholders in this State are more moderate, decent, sensible, and honorable, than the slaveholders in either of the adjoining States, or the States further South; and we know that many of them are heartily ashamed of the vile occupations of slaveholding and slave-breeding in which they are engaged, for we have the assurance from their own lips. As a matter of course, all the non-slaveholders, who are so greatly in the majority, would vote to suppress the degrading institution which has kept them so long in poverty and ignorance, with the exception of those who are complete automatons to the beck and call of their imperious lords and masters, the major-generals of the oligarchy

How long shall it be before the citizens of North Carolina shall have the privilege of expressing, at the ballot-box, their true sentiments with regard to this vexed question? Why not decide it at the next general election? Sooner or later, it must and will be decided—decided correctly, too—and the sooner the better. The first Southern State that abolishes slavery will do herself an immortal honor. God grant that North Carolina may be that State, and soon! There is at least one plausible reason why this good old State should be the first to move in this important matter, and we will state it. On the 20th of May, 1775, just one year one month and fourteen days prior to the adoption of the Jeffersonian Declaration of Independence, by the Continental Congress in Philadelphia, July 4, 1776, the Mecklenburg Declaration of Independence, the authorship of which is generally attributed to Ephrain Brevard, was proclaimed in Charlotte, Mecklenburg county North Carolina, and fully ratified in a second Conventior of the people of said county, held on the 31st of the same month. And here, by the way, we may remark, that it is supposed Mr. Jefferson made use of this last-mentioned document as the basis of his draft of the indestructible title-deed of our liberties. There is certainly an identicalness of language between the two papers that is well calculated to strengthen this hypothesis. This, however, is a controversy about which we are but little concerned. For present purposes, it is, perhaps, enough for us to know, that on the 20th of May, 1775, when transatlantic tyranny and oppression could no longer be endured, North Carolina set her sister colonies a most valorous and praiseworthy example, and that they followed it. To her infamous slaveholding sisters of the South, it is now meet that she should set another noble example of decency, virtue, and independence. Let her at once inaugurate a policy of common justice and humanity—enact a system of equitable laws, having due regard to the rights and interests of all classes of persons, poor whites, negroes, and nabobs, and the surrounding States will ere long applaud her measures, and adopt similar ones for the governance f themselves.

Another reason, and a cogent one, why North Carolina should aspire to become the first free State of the South is this: The first slave State that makes herself respectable by casting out "the mother of harlots," and by rendering enterprise and industry honorable, will immediately receive a large accession of most worthy citizens from other States in the Union, and thus lay a broad foundation of permanent political power and prosperity. Intelligent white farmers from the Middle and New England States will flock to our more congenial clime, eager to give thirty dollars per acre for the same lands that are now a drug in the market because nobody wants them at the rate of five dollars per acre; an immediate and powerful impetus will be given to commerce, manufactures, and all the industrial arts; science and literature will be revived, and every part of the State will reverberate with the triumphs of manual and intellectual labor.

At this present time, we of North Carolina are worth less than either of the four adjoining States; let us abolish slavery at the beginning of the next regular decade of years, and if our example is not speedily followed, we shall, on or before the first day of January, 1870, be enabled to purchase the whole of Virginia and South Carolina, including, perhaps, the greater part of Georgia. An exclusive lease of liberty for ten years would unquestionably make us the Empire State of the South. But we have no disposition to debar others from the enjoyment of liberty or any other inalienable right; we ask no special favors; what we demand for ourselves we are willing to concede to our neighbors. Hereby we make application for a lease of freedom for ten years; shall we have it? May God enable us to secure it, as we believe He will. We give fair notice, however, that if we get it for ten years, we shall, with the approbation of Heaven, keep it twenty—forty—a thousand—forever!

We transcribe the Mecklenburg Resolutions, which, it will be observed, acknowledge the "inherent and inalienable rights of man," and "declare ourselves a free and independent people, are, and of right ought to be, a sovereign and self-governing association, under the control of no power other than that of our God, and the general government of the Congress."

MECKLENBURG DECLARATION OF INDEPENDENCE,

As proclaimed in the town of Charlotte, North Carolina, May 20th, 1775, and ratified by the County of Mecklenburg, in Convention, May 31st, 1775.

"I. *Resolved*—That whosoever, directly or indirectly, abetted, or in any way, form or manner, countenanced the unchartered and dangerous invasion of our rights as claimed by Great Britain, is an enemy to this country, to America, and to the inherent and inalienable rights of man.

"II. *Resolved*—That we the citizens of Mecklenburg County, do hereby dissolve the political bands which have connected us to the mother country, and hereby absolve ourselves from all allegiance to the British Crown, and abjure all political connection, contract or association with that nation, who have wantonly trampled on our rights and liberties, and inhumanly shed the blood of American patriots at Lexington.

"III. *Resolved*—That we do hereby declare ourselves a free and independent people, are, and of right ought to be, a sovereign and self-governing association, under the control of no power other than that of our God, and the general government of the Congress; to the maintenance of which independence, we solemnly pledge to each other our mutual co-operation, our lives, our fortunes, and our most sacred honor.

"IV. *Resolved*—That as we now acknowledge the existence and control of no law or legal officer, civil or military, within this county, we do hereby ordain and adopt, as a rule of life, all, each, and every of our former laws—wherein, nevertheless, the crown of Great Britain never can be considered as holding rights, privileges, immunities or authority therein."

Had it not been for slavery, which, with all its other blighting and degrading influences, stifles and subdues every noble impulse of the heart, this consecrated spot would long since have been marked by an enduring monument, whose grand proportions should bear witness that the virtues of a noble ancestry are gratefully remembered by an emulous and appreciative posterity. Yet, even as things are, we are not without genuine consolation. The star of hope and promise is beginning to beam brightly over the long-obscured horizon of the South; and we are firm in the belief, that freedom, wealth, and magnanimity, will soon do justice to the memory of those fearless patriots, whose fair fame has been suffered to moulder amidst the multifarious abominations of slavery, poverty, ignorance and grovelling selfishness.

Judge Iredell's testimony, which will be found on a preceding page, and to which we request the reader to recur, might have been appropriately introduced under our present heading.

In the Provincial Convention held in North Carolina, in August, 1774, in which there were sixty-nine delegates, representing nearly every county in the province, it was—

"*Resolved*—That we will not import any slave or slaves, or purchase any slave or slaves imported or brought into the Province by others, from any part of the world, after the first day of November next."

In Iredell's Statutes, revised by Martin, it is stated that,

'In North Carolina, no general law at all was passed, prior to the revolution, declaring who might be slaves."

That there is no *legal* slavery in the Southern States, and that slavery no where can be legalized, any more than theft, arson or murder can be legalized, has been virtually admitted by some of the most profound Southern jurists themselves; and we will here digress so far as to furnish the testimony of one or two eminent lawyers, not of North Carolina, upon this point.

In the debate in the United States Senate, in 1850, on the Fugitive Slave Bill, Mr. Mason, of Virginia, objected to Mr. Dayton's amendment, providing for a trial by jury, because, said he:—

"A trial by jury necessarily carries with it a trial of the whole right, and a trial of the right to service will be gone into, according to all the forms of the Court, in determining upon any other fact. Then, again, it is proposed, as a part of the proof to be adduced at the hearing, after the fugitive has been re-captured, that evidence shall be brought by the claimant to show that slavery is established in the State from which the fugitive has absconded. Now this very thing, in a recent case in the city of New-York, was required by one of the judges of that State, which case attracted the attention of the authorities of Maryland, and against which they protested. In that case the State judge went so far as to say that the only mode of proving it was by reference to the Statute book. Such proof is required in the Senator's amendment; and if he means by this that proof shall be brought that slavery is established by existing laws, it is impossible to comply with the requisition, for no such law can be produced, I apprehend, in any of the slave States. I am not aware that there is a single State in which the institution is established by positive law."

Judge Clarke, of Mississippi, says:—

"In this State the legislature have considered slaves as reasonable and accountable beings; and it would be a stigma upon the character of the State, and a reproach to the administration of justice, if the life of a slave could be taken with impunity, or if he could be murdered in cold blood, without subjecting the offender to the highest penalty known to the criminal jurisprudence of the country. Has the slave no rights, because he is deprived of his freedom? He is still a human being, and possesses all those rights of which he is not deprived by the positive provisions of the law. The right of the master exists not by force of the law of nature or nations, but by virtue only of the positive law of the State."

The Hon. Judge Ruffin, of North Carolina, says:—

"Arguments drawn from the well-established principles, which confer and restrain the authority of the parent over the child, the tutor over the pupil, the master over the apprentice, have been pressed on us. The Court does not recognize their application; there is no likeness between the cases; they are in opposition to each other, and there is an impassable gulf between them. The difference is that which exists between freedom and slavery and a greater cannot be imagined. In the one, the end in view is the happiness of the youth, born to equal rights with that governor on whom the duty devolves of training the young to usefulness, in a station which he is afterwards to assume among freemen. To such an end, and with such a subject, moral and intellectual instruction seem the natural means, and, for the most part, they are found to suffice. Moderate force is superadded only to make the others effectual. If that fail, it is better to leave the party to his own headstrong passions, and the ultimate correction of the law, than to allow it to be immoderately inflicted by a private person. With slavery it is far otherwise. The end is the profit of the master, his security, and the public safety; the subject, one doomed, in his own person and his posterity, to live without knowledge, and without the capacity to make anything his own, and to toil that another may reap the fruits. What moral considerations shall be addressed to such a being to convince him, what it is impossible but that the most stupid must feel and know can never be true, that he is thus to labor upon a principle of natural duty, or for the sake of his own personal happiness? Such services can only be expected from one who has no will of his own; who surrenders his will in implicit obedience to that of another. Such obedience is the consequence only of uncontrolled authority over the body. There is nothing else which can operate to produce the effect. The power of the master must be absolute to render the submission of the slave perfect. I most freely confess my sense of the harshness of this proposition. I feel it as deeply as any man can; and as a principle of moral right, every person in his retirement must repudiate it."

An esteemed friend, a physician, who was born and bred in Rowan county, North Carolina, and who now resides there, informs us that Judge Gaston, who was one of the half dozen Statesmen whom the South has produced since the days of the venerable fathers of the Republic, was an avowed abolitionist, and that he published an address to the people of North Carolina, delineating, in a masterly manner, the material, moral, and social disadvantages of slavery. Where is that address? Has it been suppressed by the oligarchy? The fact that slaveholders have, from time to time, made strenuous efforts to expunge the sentiments of freedom which now adorn the works of nobler men than the noble Gaston, may, perhaps, fully account for the oblivious state into which his patriotic address seems to have fallen.

THE VOICE OF SOUTH CAROLINA.

Poor South Carolina! Folly is her nightcap; fanaticism is her day-dream; fire-eating is her pastime. She has lost her better judgment; the dictates of reason and philosophy have no influence upon her actions. Like the wife who is pitiably infatuated with a drunken, worthless husband, she still clings, with unabated love, to the cause of her shame, her misery, and her degradation.

A Kentuckian has recently expressed his opinion of this State in the following language:—

"South Carolina is bringing herself irrecoverably in the public contempt. It is impossible for any impartial lover of his country, for any just thinking man, to witness her senseless and quenchless malignancy against the Union without the most immeasurable disgust and scorn. She is one vast hot-bed of disunion. Her people think and talk of nothing else. She is a festering mass of treason."

In 1854, there were assessed for taxation in

SOUTH CAROLINA,

Acres of Land	17,289,359
Valued at	$22,836,374
Average value per acre	$1,32

At the same time there were in

NEW JERSEY,

Acres of Land	5,324,800
Valued at	$153,161,619
Average value per acre	$28,76

We hope the Slavocrats will look, first on that picture, and then on this; from one or the other, or both, they may glean a ray or two of wisdom, which, if duly applied, will be of incalculable advantage to them and their posterity We trust, also, that the non-slaveholding whites will view, with discriminating minds, the different lights and shades of these two pictures ; they are the parties most deeply interested ; and it is to them we look for the glorious revolution that is to substitute Freedom for Slavery. They have the power to retrieve the fallen fortunes of South Carolina, to raise her up from the loathsome sink of iniquity into which slavery has plunged her, and to make her one of the most brilliant stars in the great constellation of States. While their minds are occupied with other considerations, let them not forget the difference between *twenty-eight dollars and seventy-six cents*, the value of land per acre in New Jersey, which is a second-rate free State, and *one dollar and thirty-two cents*, the value of land per acre in South Carolina, which is, *par excellence*, the model slave State. The difference between the two sums is twenty-seven dollars and forty-four cents, which would amount to precisely two thousand seven hundred and forty-four dollars on every hundred acres. To present the subject in another form, the South Carolina tract of land, containing two hundred acres, is worth now only two hundred and sixty-four dollars, and is depreciating every day. Let slavery be abolished, and in the course of a few years, the same tract will be worth five thousand seven hundred and fifty-two dollars, with an upward tendency. At this rate, the increment of value on the total area of the State will amount to more than three times as much as the present estimated value of the slaves !

South Carolina has not always been, nor will she always continue to be, on the wrong side. From Ramsay's History of the State, we learn that, in 1774, she—

"*Resolved*—That His Majesty's subjects in North America (without respect to color or other accidents) are entitled to all the inherent rights and liberties of his natural born subjects within the Kingdom of Great Britain; that it is their fundamental right, that no man should suffer in his person or property without a fair trial, and judgment given by his peers, or by the law of the land."

One of her early writers, under the *non de plume* of Philodemus, in a political pamphlet published in Charleston in 1784, declares that—

"Such is the fatal influence of slavery on the human mind, that it almost wholly effaces from it even the boasted characteristic of rationality."

This same writer, speaking of the particular interests of South Carolina, says:—

"It has been too common with us to search the records of other nations, to find precedents that may give sanction to our own errors, and lead us unwarily into confusion and ruin. It is our business to consult their histories, not with a view to tread right or wrong in their steps, but in order to investigate the real sources of the mischiefs that have befallen them, and to endeavor to escape the rocks which they have all unfortunately split upon. It is paying ourselves but a poor compliment, to say that we are incapable of profiting by others, and that, with all the information which is to be derived from their fatal experience, it is in vain for us to attempt to excel them. If, with all the peculiar advantages of our present situation, we are incapable of surpassing our predecessors, we must be a degenerate race indeed, and quite unworthy of those singular bounties of Heaven, which we are so unskilled or undesirous to turn to our benefit."

A recent number of Frazer's Magazine contains a well-timed and well written article from the pen of Wm. Henry

Hurlbut, of this State ; and from it we make the following extract :—

"As all sagacious observers of the operation of the system of slavery have demonstrated, the profitable employment of slave-labor is inconsistent with the development of agricultural science, and demands a continual supply of new and unexhausted soil. The slaveholder, investing his capital in the purchase of the laborers themselves, and not merely in soil and machines paying his free laborers out of the profit, must depend for his continued and progressive prosperity upon the cheapness and facility with which he can transfer his slaves to fresh and fertile lands. An enormous additional item, namely, the price of slaves, being added to the cost of production, all other elements of that cost require to be proportionably smaller, or profits fail."

In an address delivered before the South Carolina Institute, in Charleston, Nov. 20th, 1856, Mr. B. F. Perry, of Greenville, truthfully says :—

"It has been South Carolina's misfortune, in this utilitarian age, to have her greatest talents and most powerful energies directed to pursuits, which avail her nothing, in the way of wealth and prosperity. In the first settlement of a new country, agricultural industry necessarily absorbs all the time and occupation of its inhabitants. They must clear the forests and cultivate the earth, in order to make their bread. This is their first consideration. Then the mechanical arts, and manufactures, and commerce, must follow in the footsteps of agriculture, to insure either individual or national prosperity. No people can be highly prosperous without them. No people ever have been. Agriculture, alone, will not make or sustain a great people. The true policy of every people is to cultivate the earth, manufacture its products, and send them abroad, in exchange for those comforts and luxuries, and necessaries, which their own country and their own industry cannot give or make. The dependence of South Carolina on Europe and the Northern States for all the necessaries, comforts and luxuries, which the mechanic arts afford, has, in fact, drained her of her wealth, and made her positively poor, when compared with her sister States of the Confederacy. It is at once mortifying and alarming, to see and reflect on our own dependence in the mechanic arts and manufactures, on strangers and foreigners. In the Northern States their highest talents and energy have been diversified, and more profitably employed in developing the resources of the country, in making new inventions in the mechanic arts, and enriching the community with science and literature, commerce and manufactures."

THE VOICE OF GEORGIA.

Of the States strictly Southern, Georgia is, perhaps, the most thrifty. This prosperous condition of the State is mainly ascribable to her hundred thousand free white laborers—more than eighty-three thousand of whom are engaged in agricultural pursuits. In few other slave States are the non-slaveholders so little under the domination of the oligarchy. At best, however, even in the most liberal slave States, the social position of the non-slaveholding whites is but one short step in advance of that of the negroes; and as there is, on the part of the oligarchy, a constantly increasing desire and effort to usurp greater power, the more we investigate the subject the more fully are we convinced that nothing but the speedy and utter annihilation of slavery from the entire nation, can save the masses of white people in the Southern States from ultimately falling to a political level with the blacks—both occupying the most abject and galling condition of servitude of which it is possible for the human mind to conceive.

Gen. Oglethorpe, under whose management the Colony

f Georgia was settled, in 1733, was bitterly opposed to the institution of slavery. In a letter to Granville Sharp, dated Oct. 13th, 1776, he says :—

"My friends and I settled the Colony of Georgia, and by charter were established trustees, to make laws, &c. We determined not to suffer slavery there. But the slave merchants and their adherents occasioned us not only much trouble, but at last got the then government to favor them. We would not suffer slavery, (which is against the Gospel, as well as the fundamental law of England,) to be authorized under our authority ; we refused, as trustees, to make a law permitting such a horrid crime. The government, finding the trustees resolved firmly not to concur with what they believed unjust, took away the charter by which no law could be passed without our consent."

On the 12th of January, 1775, in indorsing the proceedings of the first American Congress, among other resolutions, "the Representatives of the extensive District of Darien, in the Colony of Georgia" adopted the following :—

"5. To show the world that we are not influenced by any contracted or interested motives, but a general philanthropy for all mankind, of whatever climate, language, or complexion, we hereby declare our disapprobation and abhorrence of the unnatural practice of slavery in America, (however the uncultivated state of our country or other specious arguments may plead for it,) a practice founded in injustice and cruelty, and highly dangerous to our liberties, (as well as lives,) debasing part of our fellow creatures below men, and corrupting the virtue and morals of the rest; and is laying the basis of that liberty we contend for, (and which we pray the Almighty to continue to the latest posterity,) upon a very wrong foundation. We therefore resolve, at all times, to use our utmost endeavors for the manumission of our slaves in this Colony upon the most safe and equitable footing for the masters and themselves

The Hon. Mr. Reid, of this State, in a speech delivered in Congress, Feb. 1, 1820, says :—

"I am not the panegyrist of slavery. It is an unnatural state, a dark cloud, which obscures half the lustre of our free institutions. For my own part, though surrounded by slavery from my cradle to the present moment, yet—

'I hate the touch of servile hands,
I loathe the slaves who cringe around.'"

As an accompaniment to those lines, he might have uttered these :—

"I would not have a slave to till my ground ;
To carry me, to fan me while I sleep
And tremble when I wake, for all the wealth
That sinews bought and sold have ever earned."

Thus have we presented a comprehensive summary of the most unequivocal and irrefragable testimony of the South against the iniquitous institution of human slavery What more can we say? What more can we do? We might fill a folio volume with similar extracts ; but we must forego the task ; the remainder of our space must be occupied with other arguments. In the foregoing excerpts is revealed to us, in language too plain to be misunderstood, the important fact that every truly great and good man the South has ever produced, has, with hopeful confidence, looked forward to the time when this entire continent shall be redeemed from the crime and the curse of slavery. Our noble self-sacrificing forefathers have performed their part, and performed it well. They have laid us a foundation as enduring as the earth itself ; in their dying moments they admonished us to carry out their designs in the up building and completion of the superstructure. Let us obey their patriotic injunctions.

From each of the six original Southern States we have introduced the most ardent aspirations for liberty—the most positive condemnations of slavery. From each of the nine slave States which have been admitted into the Union since the organization of the General Government, we could introduce, from several of their wisest and best citizens, anti-slavery sentiments equally as strong and convincing as those that emanated from the great founders of our movement—Washington, Jefferson, Madison, Patrick Henry and the Randolphs. As we have already remarked, however, the limits of this chapter will not admit of the introduction of additional testimony from either of the old or of the new slave States.

The reader will not fail to observe that, in presenting these solid abolition doctrines of the South, we have been careful to make such quotations as triumphantly refute, in every particular, the more specious sophistries of the oligarchy.

The mention of the illustrious names above, reminds us of the fact, that the party newspapers, whose venal columns are eternally teeming with vituperation and slander, have long assured us that the Whig ship was to be steered by the Washington rudder, that the Democratic barque was to sail with the Jefferson compass, and that the Know-Nothing brig was to carry the Madison chart. Imposed upon by these monstrous falsehoods, we have, from time to time, been induced to engage passage on each of these corrupt and rickety old hulks; but, in every instance, we have been basely swamped in the sea of slavery, and are alone indebted for our lives to the kindness of Heaven and the art of swimming. Washington the founder of the Whig party! Jefferson the founder of the Democratic party! Voltaire the founder of Christianity! God forbid that man's heart should always continue to be the citadel of deception—that he should ever be to others the antipode of what he is to himself.

There is now in this country but one party that promises, in good faith, to put in practice the principles of Washington, Jefferson, Madison, and the other venerable Fathers of the Republic—the Republican party. To this party we pledge unswerving allegiance, so long as it shall continue to pursue the statism advocated by the great political prototypes above-mentioned, but no longer. We believe it is, as it ought to be, the desire, the determination, and the destiny of this party, to give the death-blow to slavery; should future developments prove the party at variance with this belief—a belief, by the bye, which it has recently inspired in the breasts of little less than one and a half millions of the most intelligent and patriotic voters in America—we shall shake off the dust of our feet against it, and join one that will, in a summary manner, extirpate the intolerable grievance.

CHAPTER IV.

NORTHERN TESTIMONY.

THE best evidence that can be given of the enlightened patriotism and love of liberty in the Free States, is the fact that, at the Presidential election in 1856, they polled thirteen hundred thousand votes for the Republican candidate, JOHN C. FREMONT. This fact of itself seems to preclude the necessity of strengthening our cause with the individual testimony of even their greatest men. Having, however, adduced the most cogent and conclusive anti-slavery arguments from the Washingtons, the Jeffersons, the Madisons, the Randolphs, and the Clays of the South, we shall now proceed to enrich our pages with gems of Liberty from the Franklins, the Hamiltons, the Jays, the Adamses, and the Websters of the North. Too close attention cannot be paid to the words of wisdom which we have extracted from the works of these truly eminent and philosophic Statesmen. We will first listen to

THE VOICE OF FRANKLIN.

Dr. Franklin was the first president of "The Pennsylvania Society for promoting the Abolition of Slavery;"

and it is now generally conceded that this was the first regularly organized American abolition Society—it having been formed as early as 1774, while we were yet subjects of the British government. In 1790, in the name and on behalf of this Society, Dr. Franklin, who was then within a few months of the close of his life, drafted a memorial "to the Senate and House of Representatives of the United States," in which he said:—

"Your memorialists, particularly engaged in attending to the distresses arising from slavery, believe it to be their indispensable duty to present this subject to your notice. They have observed, with real satisfaction, that many important and salutary powers are vested in you, for 'promoting the welfare and securing the blessings of liberty to the people of the United States; and as they conceive that these blessings ought rightfully to be administered, without distinction of color, to all descriptions of people, so they indulge themselves in the pleasing expectation that nothing which can be done for the relief of the unhappy objects of their care, will be either omitted or delayed.

From a persuasion that equal liberty was originally the portion, and is still the birthright of all men, and influenced by the strong ties of humanity and the principles of their institution, your memorialists conceive themselves bound to use all justifiable endeavors to loosen the bonds of slavery, and promote a general enjoyment of the blessings of freedom. Under these impressions, they earnestly entreat your attention to the subject of slavery; that you will be pleased to countenance the restoration to liberty of those unhappy men, who, alone, in this land of freedom, are degraded into perpetual bondage, and who, amid the general joy of surrounding freemen, are groaning in servile subjection; that you will devise means for removing this inconsistency of character from the American people; that you will promote mercy and justice towards this distressed race; and that you will step t: the very verge of the power vested in you for discouraging every species of traffic in the persons of our fellow-men."

On another occasion, he says:—"Slavery is an atrocious debasement of human nature."

THE VOICE OF HAMILTON.

Alexander Hamilton, the brilliant Statesman and financier, tells us that—

"The sacred rights of mankind are not to be rummaged for among old parchments or musty records. They are written as with a sunbeam, in the whole volume of human nature, by the hand of the Divinity itself, and can never be erased or obscured by mortal power."

Again, in 1774, addressing himself to an American Tory, he says:—

"The fundamental source of all your errors, sophisms, and false reasonings, is a total ignorance of the natural rights of mankind. Were you once to become acquainted with these, you could never entertain a thought, that all men are not, by nature, entitled to equal privileges. You would be convinced that natural liberty is the gift of the beneficent Creator to the whole human race; and that civil liberty is founded on that."

THE VOICE OF JAY.

John Jay, first Chief Justice of the United States under the Constitution of 1789, in a letter to the Hon. Elias Boudinot, dated Nov. 17, 1819, says:—

"Little can be added to what has been said and written on the subject of slavery. I concur in the opinion that it ought not to be introduced nor permitted in any of the new States, and that it ought to be gradually diminished and finally abolished in all of them

"To me, the constitutional authority of the Congress to prohibit the migration and importation of slaves into any of the States does not appear questionable.

"The first article of the Constitution specifies the legislative powers committed to the Congress. The 9th section of that article has these words: 'The *migration* or *importation* of such persons as any of the *now-existing* States shall think proper to admit, shall not be prohibited by the Congress prior to the year 1808, but a tax or duty may be imposed on such importation, not exceeding ten dollars for each person.'

"I understand the sense and meaning of this clause to be, that the power of the congress, although competent to prohibit such migration and importation, was to be exercised with respect to the *then* existing States, and them only, until the year 1808, but the Congress were at liberty to make such prohibitions as to any *new* State, which might in the *mean* time be established. And further, that from and after *that* period, they were authorized to make such prohibitions as to *all* the States, whether *new* or *old*.

"It will, I presume, be admitted, that slaves were the persons intended. The word slaves was avoided, probably on account of the existing toleration of slavery, and its discordancy with the principles of the Revolution, and from a consciousness of its being repugnant to the following positions in the Declaration of Independence: 'We hold these truths to be self-evident: that all men are created equal; that they are endowed by their Creator with certain inalienable rights; that among these are life, liberty, and the pursuit of happiness.'"

In a previous letter, written from Spain, whither he had been appointed as minister plenipotentiary, he says, speaking of the abolition of slavery:—

"Till America comes into this measure, her prayers to Heaven will be impious. This is a strong expression, but it is just. I believe that God governs the world, and I believe it to be a maxim in His, as in our Courts, tha those who ask for equity ought to d) it."

WILLIAM JAY.

The Hon. Wm. Jay, a noble son of Chief Justice John Jay, says :—

" A crisis has arrived in which we must maintain our rights, or surrender them for ever. I speak not to abolitionists alone, but to all who value the liberty our fathers achieved. Do you ask what we have to do with slavery? Let our muzzled presses answer—let the mobs excited against us by the merchants and politicians answer—let the gag laws threatened by our governors and legislatures answer, let the conduct of the National Government answer."

THE VOICE OF ADAMS.

From the Diary of John Quincy Adams, "the old man eloquent," we make the following extract :—

" It is among the evils of slavery, that it taints the very sources of moral principle. It establishes false estimates of virtue and vice; for what can be more false and more heartless than this doctrine, which makes the first and holiest rights of humanity to depend upon the color of the skin? It perverts human reason and induces men endowed with logical powers to maintain that slavery is sanctioned by the Christian religion; that slaves are happy and contented in their condition; that between master and slave there are ties of mutual attachment and affection; that the virtues of the master are refined and exalted by the degradation of the slave, while at the same time they vent execrations upon the slave-trade, curse Britain for having given them slaves, burn at the stake negroes convicted of crimes, for the terror of the example, and writhe in agonies of fear at the very mention of human rights as applicable to men of color."

THE VOICE OF WEBSTER.

In a speech which he delivered at Niblo's Garden, in

the city of New-York, on the 15th of March, 1847, Daniel Webster, the great Expounder of the Constitution, said :—

"On the general question of slavery, a great part of the community is already strongly excited. The subject has not only attracted attention as a question of politics, but it has struck a far deeper one ahead. It has arrested the religious feeling of the country, it has taken strong hold on the consciences of men. He is a rash man, indeed, and little conversant with human nature, and especially has he an erroneous estimate of the character of the people of this country, who supposes that a feeling of this kind is to be trifled with or despised. It will assuredly cause itself to be respected. But to endeavor to coin it into silver, or retain its free expression, to seek to compress and confine it, warm as it is, and more heated as such endeavors would inevitably render it—should this be attempted, I know nothing, even in the Constitution or Union itself, which might not be endangered by the explosion which might follow."

When discussing the Oregon Bill in 1848, he said :—

"I have made up my mind, for one, that under no circumstances will I consent to the further extension of the area of slavery in the United States, or to the further increase of slave representation in the House of Representatives."

Under date of February 15th, 1850, in a letter to the Rev. Mr. Furness, he says :—

"From my earliest youth I have regarded slavery as a great moral and political evil. I think it unjust, repugnant to the natural equality of mankind, founded only in superior power; a standing and permanent conquest by the stronger over the weaker. All pretense of defending it on the ground of different races, I have ever condemned. I have even said that if the black race is weaker, that is a reason against, not for, its subjection and oppression. In a religious point of view I have ever regarded it, and even spoken of it, not as subject to any express denunciation, either in the Old Testament or the New, but is opposed to the whole spirit of the Gospel and to the teachings of Jesus Christ. The religion of Jesus Christ is a religion of kindness, justice, and brotherly love. But slavery is not kindly affectionate, it does not seek anothers, and not its own; it does not let the oppressed go free. It is, as I have said, but a continual act of oppression. But then, such is the influence of a habit of thinking among men, and such is the influence of what has been long established, that even minds, religious and tenderly conscientious, such as would be shocked by any single act of oppression, in any single exercise of violence and unjust power, are not always moved by the reflection that slavery is a continual and permanent violation of human rights."

While delivering a speech at Buffalo, in the State of New York, in the summer of 1851, only about twelve months prior to his decease, he made use of the following emphatic words :—

"I never would consent, and never have consented, that there should be one foot of slave territory beyond what the old thirteen States had at the formation of the Union. Never, never."

NOAH WEBSTER.

Noah Webster, the great American vocabulist, says :—

"That freedom is the sacred right of every man, whatever be his color, who has not forfeited it by some violation of municipal law, is a truth established by God himself, in the very creation of human beings. No time, no circumstance, no human power or policy can change the nature of this truth, nor repeal the fundamental laws of society, by which every man's right to liberty is guarantied. The act of enslaving men is always a violation of those great primary laws of society, by which alone, the master himself holds every particle of his own freedom."

THE VOICE OF CLINTON.

DeWitt Clinton, the father of the great system of internal improvements in the State of New York, speaking of despotism in Europe, and of slavery in America, asks:—

"Have not prescription and precedent—patriarchal dominion—divine right of kings and masters, been alternately called in to sanction the slavery of nations? And would not all the despotisms of the ancient and modern world have vanished into air, if the natural equality of mankind had been properly understood and practiced? * * * This declares that the same measure of justice ought to be measured out to all men, without regard to adventitious inequalities, and the intellectual and physical disparities which proceed from inexplicable causes."

THE VOICE OF WARREN.

Major General Joseph Warren, one of the truest patriots of the Revolution, and the first American officer of rank that fell in our contest with Great Britain, says:—

"That personal freedom is the natural right of every man, and that property, or an exclusive right to dispose of what he has honestly acquired by his own labor, necessarily arises therefrom, are truths that common sense has placed beyond the reach of contradiction. And no man, or body of men, can, without being guilty of flagrant injustice, claim a right to dispose of the persons or acquisitions of any other man or body of men, unless it can be proved that such a right has arisen from some compact between the parties in which it has been explicitly and freely granted."

Otis, Hancock, Ames, and others, should be heard, but for the want of space. Volumes upon volumes might be filled with extracts similar to the above, from the works of the deceased Statesmen and sages of the North, who, while living, proved themselves equal to the task of exterminating from their own States the matchless curse of human slavery. Such are the men who, though no longer with us in the flesh, "still live." A living principle—an immortal interest—have they, invested in every great and good work that distinguishes the free States. The railroads, the canals, the telegraphs, the factories, the fleets of merchant vessels, the magnificent cities, the scientific modes of agriculture, the unrivaled institutions of learning, and other striking evidences of progress and improvement at the North, are, either directly or indirectly, the offspring of their gigantic intellects. When, if ever, commerce, and manufactures, and agriculture, and great enterprises, and truth, and liberty, and justice, and magnanimity, shall have become obsolete terms, then their names may possibly be forgotten, but not tell then.

An army of brave and worthy successors—champions of Freedom now living, have the illustrious forefathers of the North, in the persons of Garrison, Greeley, Giddings, Goodell, Grow, and Gerrit Smith; in Seward, Sumner, Stowe, Raymond, Parker, and Phillips; in Beecher, Banks, Burlingame, Bryant, Hale, and Hildreth; in Emerson, Dayton, Thompson, Tappan, King and Cheever; in Whittier, Wilson, Wade, Wayland, Weed, and Burleigh. These are the men whom, in connection with their learned and eloquent compatriots, the Everetts, the Bancrofts, the Prescotts, the Chapins, the Longfellows, and the Danas, future historians, if faithful to their calling, will place on record as America's true statesmen, literati, preachers, philosophers, and philanthropists, of the present age

In this connection, however, it may not be amiss to remark that the Homers, the Platos, the Bacons, the Newtons, the Shakspeares, the Miltons, the Blackstones, the Cuviers, the Humboldts, and the Macaulays of Amercia, have not yet been produced; nor, in our humble judgment, will they be, until slavery shall have been overthrown and freedom established in the States of Virginia, Kentucky, and Tennessee. Upon the soil of those States, when free, or on other free soil crossed by about the same degrees of latitude, and not distant from the Appalachian chain of mountains, will, we believe, be nurtured into manhood, in the course of one or two centuries, perhaps, as great men as those mentioned above—greater, possibly, than any that have ever yet lived. Whence their ancestors may come, whether from Europe, from Asia, from Africa, from Oceanica, from North or South America, or from the islands of the sea, or whatever honorable vocation they may now be engaged in, matters nothing at all. For ought we know, their great-grandfathers are now humble artisans in Maine, or moneyed merchants in Massachusetts; illiterate poor whites in Mississippi, or slave-driving lordlings in South Carolina; frugal farmers in Michigan, or millionaires in Illinois; daring hunters in the Rocky Mountains, or metal-diggers in California; peasants in France, or princes in Germany—no matter where, or what, the scope of country above-mentioned is, in our opinion, destined to be the birth-place of their illustrious offspring—the great savans of the New World, concerning whom we should console ourselves with the hope that they are not buried deeply in the matrix of the future.

CHAPTER V.

TESTIMONY OF THE NATIONS.

To the true friends of freedom throughout the world, it is a pleasing thought, and one which, by being communicated to others, is well calculated to universalize the principles of liberty, that the great heroes, statesmen, and sages, of all ages and nations, ancient and modern, who have ever had occasion to speak of the institution of human slavery, have entered their most unequivocal and positive protests against it. To say that they disapproved of the system would not be sufficiently expressive of the utter detestation with which they uniformly regarded it. That they abhorred it as the vilest invention that the Evil-One has ever assisted bad men to concoct, is quite evident from the very tone and construction of their language.

Having, with much pleasure and profit, heard the testimony of America, through her representative men, we will now hear that of other nations, through their representative men—doubting not that we shall be more than remunerated for our time and trouble. We will first listen to

THE VOICE OF ENGLAND.

In the case of James Somerset, a negro who had been kidnapped in Africa, transported to Virginia, there sold into slavery, thence carried to England, as a waiting-boy, and there induced to institute proceedings against his master for the recovery of his freedom,

MANSFIELD says :—

"The state of slavery is of such a nature that it is incapable of being introduced on any reasons, moral or political, but only by positive law, which preserves its force long after the reasons, occasion, and time itself whence it was created, is erased from the memory. It is so odious that nothing can be sufficient to support it but positive law. Whatever inconveniences, therefore, may follow from the decision, I cannot say this case is allowed or approved by the law of England, and therefore the black must be discharged."

LOCKE says :—

"Slavery is so vile, so miserable a state of man, and so directly opposite to the generous temper and courage of our nation, that it is hard to be convinced that an Englishman, much less a gentleman, should plead for it."

Again, he says :—

"Though the earth, and all inferior creatures be common to all men, yet every man has a property in his own person; this nobody has any right to but himself."

PITT says :—

"It is injustice to permit slavery to remain for a single hour."

FOX says :—

"With regard to a regulation of slavery, my detestation of its existence induces me to know no such thing as a regulation of robbery, and a restriction of murder. Personal freedom is a right of which he who deprives a fellow-creature is criminal in so depriving him, and he who withholds is no less criminal in withholding."

SHAKSPEARE says :—

"A man is master of his liberty."

Again, he says :—

"It is the curse of Kings, to be attended
By slaves, that take their humors for a warrant
To break within the bloody house of life,
And, on the winking of authority,
To understand a law; to know the meaning
Of dangerous majesty, when, perchance, it frowns
More upon humor than advised respect."

Again :—

"Heaven will one day free us from this slavery."

Again :—

"Liberty! Freedom! Tyranny is dead!—
Run hence, proclaim, cry it about the streets;
Some to the common pulpits, and cry out,
Liberty, freedom, and enfranchisement"

COWPER says :—

"Slaves cannot breathe in England; if their lungs
Receive our air, that moment they are free.
They touch our country and their shackles fall.
That's noble, and bespeaks a nation proud
And jealous of the blessing. Spread it then,
And let it circulate through every vein
Of all your Empire, that where Britain's power
Is felt, mankind may feel her mercy too!"

MILTON asks :—

"Where is the beauty to see,
Like the sun-brilliant brow of a nation when free?"

Again, he says :—

"If our fathers promised for themselves, to make themselves slaves, they could make no such promise for us."

Again :—

"Since, therefore, the law is chiefly right reason, if we are bound to obey a magistrate as a minister of God, by the very same reason and the very same law, we ought to resist a tyrant, and minister of the devil."

DR. JOHNSON says :—

"No man is by nature the property of another. The rights of nature must be some way forfeited before they can justly be taken away."

DR. PRICE says :—

"If you have a right to make another man a slave, he has a right to make you a slave."

BLACKSTONE says :—

"If neither captivity nor contract can, by the plain law of nature and reason, reduce the parent to a state of slavery, much less can they reduce the offspring."

Again, he says :—

"The primary aim of society is to protect individuals in the enjoyment of those absolute rights which were vested in them by the immutable laws of nature. Hence it follows that the first and primary end of human laws is to maintain those absolute rights o individuals.

Again :—

"If any human law shall allow or require us to commit crime, we are bound to transgress that human law, or else we must offend both the natural and divine."

COKE says :—

"What the Parliament doth, shall be holden for naught, whenever it shall enact that which is contrary to the rights of nature."

HAMPDEN says :—

"The essence of all law is justice. What is not justice is not law; and what is not law, ought not to be obeyed."

HARRINGTON says :—

"All men naturally, are equal; for though nature with a noble variety has made different features and lineaments of men, yet as to freedom, she has made every one alike, and given them the same desires."

FORTESCUE says :—

"Those rights which God and nature have established, and which are therefore called natural rights, such as life and liberty, need not the aid of human laws to be more effectually invested in every man than they are; neither do they receive any additional strength when declared by the municipal laws to be inviolable. On the contrary, no human power has any authority to abridge or destroy them, unless the owner himself shall commit some act that amounts to a forfeiture."

Again, he says :—

'The law, therefore, which supports slavery and opposes liberty, must necessarily be condemned as cruel, for every feeling of human nature advocates liberty. Slavery is introduced by human wickedness, but God advocates liberty, by the nature which he has given to man.'

BROUGHAM says :—

"Tell me not of rights—talk not of the property of the planter in his slaves. I deny the right; I acknowledge not the property. In vain you tell me of laws that sanction such a claim. There is a law above all the enactments of human codes, the same throughout the world, the same in all times; it is the law written by the finger of God on the hearts of men; and by that law, unchangeable and eternal, while men despise fraud, and loathe rapine, and abhor blood, they shall reject with indignation the wild and guilty phantasy that man can hold property in man."

THE VOICE OF IRELAND.

BURKE says :—

"Slavery is a state so improper, so degrading, and so ruinous to the feelings and capacities of human nature, that it ought not to be suffered to exist."

CURRAN says :—

"I speak in the spirit of British law, which makes liberty commensurate with and inseparable from British soil; which proclaims even to the stranger and the sojourner, the moment he sets his foot upon British earth, that the ground on which he treads is holy and consecrated by the genius of Universal Emancipation. No matter in what language his doom may have been pronounced; no matter what complexion, incompatible with freedom, an Indian or African sun may have burnt upon him; no matter in what disastrous battle his liberty may have been cloven down; no matter with what solemnities he may have been devoted upon the altar of slavery, the moment he touches the sacred soil of Britain, the altar and the god sink together in the dust; his soul walks abroad in her own majesty; and he stands redeemed, regenerated and disenthralled by the irresistible genius of Universal Emancipation."

The Dublin University Magazine for December, 1856, says :—

"The United States must learn, from the example of Rome, that Christianity and the pagan institution of slavery cannot co-exist together. The Republic must take her side and choose her favorite child ; for if she love the one, she must hate the other."

THE VOICE OF SCOTLAND.

BEATTIE says :—

"Slavery is inconsistent with the dearest and most essential rights of man's nature ; it is detrimental to virtue and industry ; it hardens the heart to those tender sympathies which form the most lovely part of human character ; it involves the innocent in hopeless misery, in order to procure wealth and pleasure for the authors of that misery ; it seeks to degrade into brutes beings whom the Lord of Heaven and Earth endowed with rational souls, and created for immortality ; in short, it is utterly repugnant to every principle of reason, religion, humanity, and conscience. It is impossible for a considerate and unprejudiced mind, to think of slavery without horror."

MILLER says :—

"The human mind revolts at a serious discussion of the subject of slavery. Every individual, whatever be his country or complexion, is entitled to freedom."

MACKNIGHT says :—

Men-stealers are inserted among the daring criminals against whom the law of God directed its awful curses. These were persons who kidnapped men to sell them for slaves ; and this practice seems inseparable from the other iniquities and oppressions of slavery ; nor can a slave dealer easily keep free from this criminality, i indeed the receiver is as bad as the thief."

THE VOICE OF FRANCE.

LAFAYETTE says :—

"I would never have drawn my sword in the cause o America, if I could have conceived that thereby I was founding a land of slavery."

Again, while in the prison of Magdeburg, he says :—

"I know not what disposition has been made of my plantation at Cayenne ; but I hope Madame de Lafayette will take care that the negroes who cultivate it shall preserve their liberty."

O. LAFAYETTE, grandson of General Lafayette, in a letter under date of April 26th, 1851, says :—

"This great question of the Abolition of Negro Slavery, which has my entire sympathy, appears to me to have established its importance throughout the world. At the present time, the States of the Peninsula, if I do not deceive myself, are the only European powers who still continue to possess slaves ; and America, while continuing to uphold slavery, feels daily, more and more how heavily it weighs upon her destinies."

MONTESQUIEU asks :—

"What civil law can restrain a slave from running away, since he is not a member of society?"

Again, he says :—

"Slavery is contrary to the fundamental principles of all societies."

Again :—

"In democracies, where they are all upon an equality, slavery is contrary to the principles of the Constitution."

Again :—

"Nothing puts one nearer the condition of a brute than always to see freemen and not be free."

Again :—

"Even the earth itself, which teems with profusion under the cultivating hand of the free born laborer, shrinks into barrenness from the contaminating sweat of a slave."

LOUIS X. issued the following edict :—

"As all men are by nature free born, and as this Kingdom is called the Kingdom of Franks, (freemen) it shall be so in reality. It is therefore decreed that enfranchisement shall be granted throughout the whole Kingdom upon just and reasonable terms."

BUFFON says :—

"It is apparent that the unfortunate negroes are endowed with excellent hearts, and possess the seeds of every human virtue. I cannot write their history without lamenting their miserable condition." "Humanity revolts at those odious oppressions that result from avarice."

ROUSSEAU says :—

"The terms *slavery* and *right*, contradict and exclude each other."

BRISSOT says :—

"Slavery, in all its forms, in all its degrees, is a violation of divine law and a degradation of human nature."

THE VOICE OF GERMANY.

GROTIUS says :—

"Those are men-stealers who abduct, keep, sell or buy slaves or free men. To steal a man is the highest kind of theft."

GOETHE says :—

Such busy multitudes I fain would see
Stand upon free soil with a people free."

LUTHER says :—

"Unjust violence is, by no means, the ordinance of God, and therefore can bind no one in conscience and right, to obey, whether the command comes from pope, emperor, king or master."

An able German writer of the present day, says, in a recent letter to his friends in this country :—

"Consider that the cause of American liberty is the cause of universal liberty; its failure, a triumph of despotism everywhere. Remember that while American liberty is the great argument of European Democracy, American slavery is the greater argument of its despotism. Remember that all our actions should be governed by the golden rule, whether individual, social, or political; and no government, and, above all, no republican government, is safe in the hands of men that practically deny that rule. Will you support by your vote a system that recognizes property of man in man? A system which sanctions the sale of the child by its own father, regardless of the purpose of the buyer? What need is there to present to you the unmitigated wrong of slavery? It is the shame of our age that argument is needed against slavery.

"Liberty is no exclusive property; it is the property of mankind of all ages. She is immortal, though crushed, can never die; though banished, she will return; though fettered, she will yet be free."

THE VOICE OF ITALY.

CICERO says :—

"By the grand laws of nature, all men are born free, and this law is universally binding upon all men."

Again, he says :—

"Eternal justice is the basis of all human laws."

Again :—

"Law is not something wrought out by man's ingenuity, nor is it a decree of the people, but it is something eternal, governing the world by the wisdom of its commands and prohibitions."

Again :—

"Whatever is just is also the true law, nor can this true law be abrogated by any written enactments."

Again :—

"If there be such a power in the decrees and commands of fools, that the nature of things is changed by their votes, why do they not decree that what is bad and pernicious shall be regarded as good and wholesome, or why, if the law can make wrong right, can it not make bad good?"

Again :—

"Those who have made pernicious and unjust decrees, have made anything rather than laws."

Again :—

"The law of all nations forbids one man to pursue his advantage at the expense of another."

LACTANTIUS says :—

"Justice teaches men to know God and to love men, to love and assist one another, being all equally the children of God."

LEO X. says :—

"Not only does the Christian religion, but nature herself cry out against the state of slavery."

THE VOICE OF GREECE.

SOCRATES says :—

"Slavery is a system of outrage and robbery."

ARISTOTLE says :—

"It is neither for the good, nor is it just, seeing all men are by nature alike, and equal, that one should be lord and master over others."

POLYBIUS says :—

'None but unprincipled and beastly men in society assume the mastery over their fellows, as it is among bulls, bears, and cocks."

PLATO says :—

"Slavery is a system of the most complete injustice."

From each of the above, and from other nations, additional testimony is at hand; but, for reasons already assigned, we forbear to introduce it. Corroborative of the correctness of the position which we have assumed, even Persia has a voice, which may be easily recognized in the tones of her immortal Cyrus, who says :

"To fight, in order not to be made a slave, is noble."

Than Great Britain no nation has more heartily or honorably repented of the crime of slavery—no nation, on the perception of its error, has ever acted with more prompt magnanimity to its outraged and unhappy bondsmen. Entered to her credit, many precious jewels of liberty remain in our possession, ready to be delivered when called for; of their value some idea may be formed, when we state that they are filigreed with such names as Wilberforce, Buxton, Granville, Grattan, Camden, Clarkson, Sharp, Sheridan, Sidney, Martin, and Macaulay.

Virginia, the Carolinas, and other Southern States, which are provided with *republican (!)* forms of government, and which have abolished freedom, should learn, from the history of the monarchal governments of the Old World, if not from the example of the more liberal and enlightened portions of the New, how to abolish slavery. The lesson is before them in a variety of exceedingly interesting forms, and, sooner or later, they must learn it, either voluntarily or by compulsion. Virginia, in particular, is a spoilt child, having been the pet of the General Government for the last sixty-eight years; and like most other spoilt children, she has become froward, peevish, perverse, sulky and irreverent—not caring to know her duties, and failing to perform even those which she does know. Her superiors perceive that the abolition of slavery would be a blessing to her; she is, however, either too ignorant to understand the truth, or else, as is the more probable, her false pride and obstinacy restrain her from acknowledging it. What is to be done? Shall ignorance, or prejudice, or obduracy, or willful meanness, triumph over knowledge, and liberality, and guilelessness, and laudable enterprise? No, never! Assured that Virginia and all the other slaveholding States are doing wrong every day, it is our duty to make them do right, if we have the power; and we believe we have the power now resident within their own borders. What are the opinions, generally, of the non-slaveholding whites? Let them speak.

CHAPTER VI.

TESTIMONY OF THE CHURCHES.

"Run hence, proclaim, cry it about the streets,
Some to the common pulpits, and cry out,
Liberty, freedom, and enfranchisement!"

In quest of arguments against slavery, we have perused the works of several eminent Christian writers of different denominations, and we now proceed to lay before the reader the result of a portion of our labor. As it is the special object of this chapter to operate on, to correct and cleanse the consciences of slaveholding professors of religion, we shall adduce testimony only from the five churches to which they, in their satanic piety, mostly belong—the Presbyterian, the Episcopal, the Baptist, the Methodist, and the Roman Catholic—all of which, thank Heaven, are destined, at no distant day, to become thoroughly abolitionized. With few exceptions, all the other Christian sects are, as they should be, avowedly and inflexibly opposed to the inhuman institution of slavery. The Congregational, the Quaker, the Lutheran, the Dutch and German Reformed, the Unitarian, and the Universalist, especially, are all honorable, able, and eloquent defenders of the natural rights of man. We will begin by introducing a mass of

PRESBYTERIAN TESTIMONY.

The Rev. Albert Barnes, of Philadelphia, one of the most learned Presbyterian preachers and commentators of the day, says :—

"There is a deep and growing conviction in the minds of the mass of mankind, that slavery violates the great laws of our nature; that it is contrary to the dictates of humanity; that it is essentially unjust, oppressive, and cruel; that it invades the rights of liberty with which the Author of our being has endowed all human beings; and that, in all the forms in which it has ever existed, it has been impossible to guard it from what its friends and advocates would call '*abuses* of the system.' It is a violation of the first sentiments expressed in our Declaration of Independence, and on which our fathers founded the vindication of their own conduct in an appeal to arms. It is at war with all that a man claims for himself and for his own children; and it is opposed to all the struggles of mankind, in all ages, for freedom. The claims of humanity plead against it. The struggles for freedom everywhere in our world condemn it. The instinctive feeling in every man's own bosom in regard to himself is a condemnation of it. The noblest deeds of valor, and of patriotism in our own land, and in all lands where men have struggled for freedom, are a condemnation of the system. All that is noble in man is opposed to it; all that is base, oppressive, and cruel pleads for it.

"The spirit of the New Testament is against slavery, and the principles of the New Testament, if fairly applied, would abolish it. In the New Testament no man is commanded to purchase and own a slave; no man is commended as adding anything to the evidences of his Christian character, or as performing the appropriate duty of a Christian, for owning one. No where in the New Testament is the institution referred to as a good one, or as a desirable one. It is commonly—indeed, it is almost universally—conceded that the proper application of the principles of the New Testament would abolish slavery everywhere, or that. the state of things which will exist when the Gospel shall be fairly applied to all the relations of life, slavery will not be found among those relations.

"Let slavery be removed from the church, and let the voice of the church, with one accord, be lifted up in favor of freedom; let the church be wholly detached from the institution, and let there be adopted by all its ministers and members an interpretation of the Bible—as I believe there may be and ought to be—that shall be in accordance with the deep-seated principles of our nature in favor of freedom, and with our own aspirations for liberty, and with the sentiments of the world in its onward progress in regard to human rights, and not only would a very material objection against the Bible be taken away—and one which would be fatal if it were well founded—but the establishment of a very strong argument *in favor* of the Bible, as a revelation from God, would be the direct result of such a position."

Thomas Scott, the celebrated English Presbyterian Commentator, says:—

"To number the persons of men with beasts, sheep, and horses as the stock of a farm, or with bales of goods, as the cargo of a ship, is, no doubt, a most detestable and anti-Christian practice."

From a resolution denunciatory of slavery, unanimously adopted by the General Assembly of the Presbyterian Church, in 1818, we make the following extract:—

"We consider the voluntary enslaving of one part of the human race by another as a gross violation of the most precious and sacred rights of human nature, as utterly inconsistent with the law of God, which requires us to love our neighbor as ourselves, and as totally irreconcilable with the spirit and principles of the Gospel of Christ, which enjoins that 'all things whatsoever ye would that men should do to you, do ye even so to them.' * * * We rejoic that the church to which we belong commenced, as early as any other in this country, the good work of endeavoring to put an end to slavery, and that in the same work many of its members have ever since been, and now are, among the most active, vigorous, and efficient laborers. * * * We earnestly exhort them to continue, and, if possible, to increase, their exertions to effect a total abolition of slavery."

A Committee of the Synod of Kentucky, in an address to the Presbyterians of that State, says :—

"That our negroes will be worse off, if emancipated, is, we feel, but a specious pretext for lulling our own pangs of conscience, and answering the argument of the philanthropist. None of us believe that God has so created a whole race that it is better for them to remain in perpetual bondage."

EPISCOPAL TESTIMONY.

BISHOP HORSLEY says :—

"Slavery is injustice, which no consideration of policy can extenuate."

BISHOP BUTLER says :—

"Despicable as the negroes may appear in our eyes, they are the creatures of God, and of the race of mankind, for whom Christ died, and it is inexcusable to keep them in ignorance of the end for which they were made, and of the means whereby they may become partakers of the general redemption."

BISHOP PORTEUS says :—

"The Bible classes men-stealers or slave-traders among the murderers of fathers and mothers, and the most profane criminals on earth."

John Jay, Esq., of the City of New-York—a most exemplary Episcopalian—in a pamphlet entitled, "Thoughts on the Duty of the Episcopal Church, in Relation to Slavery," says :—

"Alas! for the expectation that she would conform to the spirit of her ancient mother! She has not merely remained a mute and careless spectator of this great conflict of truth and justice with hypocrisy and cruelty, but her very priests and deacons may be seen ministering at the altar of slavery, offering their talents and influence at its unholy shrine, and openly repeating the awful blasphemy, that the precepts of our Saviour sanction the system of American slavery. Her Northern clergy, with rare exceptions, whatever they may feel on the subject, rebuke it neither in public nor in private, and her periodicals, far from advancing the progress of abolition, at times oppose our societies, impliedly defending slavery, as not incompatible with Christianity, and occasionally withholding information useful to the cause of freedom."

A writer in a late number of "The Anti-Slavery Churchman," published in Geneva, Wisconsin, speaking of a certain portion of the New Testament, says :—

"This passage of Paul places necessary work in the hands of Gospel ministers. If they preach the whole Gospel, they must preach what this passage enjoins—and if they do this, they must preach against American slavery. Its being connected with politics does not shield them. Political connections cannot place sin under protection. They cannot throw around it guards that the public teachers of morals may not pass. Sin is a violation of God's law—and God's law must be proclaimed and enforced at all hazards. This is the business of the messenger of God, and if anything stands in its way, it is his right, rather it is his solemn commission, to go forward—straightway to overpass the lines that would shut him out, and utter his warnings. Many sins there are, that, in like manner, might be shielded. Fashion, and rank, and business, are doing their part to keep much sin in respectability, and excuse it from the attacks of God's ministers. But what are these, that they should seal a minister's lips—what more are the w hes of politicians?"

For further testimony from this branch of the Christian system, if desired, we refer the reader to the Rev. Dudley A. Tyng, the Rev. Evan M. Johnson, and the Rev. J. McNamara,—all Broad Church Episcopalians, whose magic eloquence and irresistible arguments bid fair, at an early day, to win over to the paths of progressive freedom, truth, justice and humanity, the greater number of their High and Low Church brethren.

BAPTIST TESTIMONY.

Concerning a certain text, the Rev. Mr. Brisbane, once a slaveholding Baptist in South Carolina, says:—

"Paul was speaking of the law as having been made for men-stealers. Where is the record of that law? It is in Exodus xxi. 16, and in these words: 'He that stealeth a man, and selleth him, or if he be found in his possession, he shall surely be put to death.' Here it will be perceived that it was a crime to sell the man, for which the seller must suffer death. But it was no less a crime to hold him as a slave, for this also was punishable with death. A man may be kidnapped out of slavery into freedom. There was no law against that. And why? Because kidnapping a slave and placing him in a condition of freedom, was only to restore him to his lost rights. But if the man who takes him becomes a slaveholder, or a slave seller, then he is a criminal, liable to the penalty of death, because he robs the man of liberty. Perhaps some will say this law was only applicable to the first holder of the slave, that is, the original kidnapper, but not to his successors who might have purchased or inherited him. But what is kidnapping? Suppose I propose to a neighbor to give him a certain sum of money if he will steal a white child in Carolina and deliver him to me. He steals him; I pay him the money upon his delivering the child to me. Is it not my act as fully as his? Am I not also the thief? But does it alter the case whether I agree before hand or not, to pay him for the child? He steals him, and then sells him to me. He is found by his parents in my hands. Will it avail me to say I purchased him and paid my money for him? Will it not be asked, Do you not know that a white person is not merchantable? And shall I not have to pay the damage for detaining that child in my service as a slave? Assuredly, not only in the eyes of the law, but in the judgment of the whole community, I would be regarded a criminal. So when one man steals another and offers him for sale, no one, in view of the Divine law, can buy him, for the reason that the Divine law forbids that man shall in the first place be made a merchantable article. The inquiry must be, if I buy, I buy in violation of the Divine law, and it will not do for me to plead that I bought him. I have him in possession, and that is enough, God condemns me for it as a man-stealer. My having him in possession is evidence against me, and the Mosaic law says, if he be found in my hands, I must die. Now, when Paul said the law was made for men-stealers, was it not also saying the law was made for slaveholders? I am not intending to apply this term in harsh spirit. But I am bound, as I fear God to speak what I am satisfied is the true meaning of the apostle."

In his "Elements of Moral Science," the Rev. Francis Wayland, D.D., one of the most erudite and distinguished Baptists now living, says:—

"Domestic slavery proceeds upon the principle that the master has a right to control the actions, physical and intellectual, of the slave, for his own, that is, the master's individual benefit; and, of course, that the happiness of the master, when it comes in competition with the happiness of the slave, extinguishes in the latter the right to pursue it. It supposes, at best, that the relation between master and slave, is not that which exists between man and man, but is a modification, at least, of that which exists between man and the brutes.

"Now, this manifestly supposes that the two classes of beings are created with dissimilar rights: that the master posseses rights which have never been conceded by the slave; and that the slave has no rights at all over the means of happiness which God has given him, whenever these means of happiness can be rendered available to the service of his master. It supposes that the Creator intended one human being to govern the physical, intellectual and moral actions of as many other human beings as by purchase he can bring within his physical power; and that one human being may thus acquire a right to sacrifice the happiness of any number of other human beings, for the purpose of promoting his own. Slavery thus violates the personal liberty of man as a physical, intellectual, and moral being.

"It purports to give to the master a right to control the physical labor of the slave, not for the sake of the happiness of the slave, but for the sake of the happiness of the master. It subjects the amount of labor, and the kind of labor, and the remuneration for labor, entirely to the will of the one party, to the entire exclusion of the will of the other party.

"But if this right in the master over the slave be conceded there are of course conceded all other rights necessary to insure its possession. Hence, inasmuch as the slave can be held in this condition only while he remains in the lowest state of mental imbecility, it supposes the master to have the right to control his intellectual development, just as far as may be necessary to secure entire subjection. Thus, it supposes the slave to have no right to use his intellect for the production of his own happiness; but, only to use it in such manner as may conduce to his master's profit.

And, moreover, inasmuch as the acquisition of the knowledge of his duty to God could not be freely made without the acquisition of other knowledge, which might, if universally diffused, endanger the control of the master, slavery supposes the master to have the right to determine how much knowledge of his duty a slave shall obtain, the manner in which he shall obtain it, and the manner in which he shall discharge that duty after he shall have obtained a knowledge of it. It thus subjects the duty of man to God entirely to the will of man; and this for the sake of pecuniary profit. It renders the eternal happiness of the one party subservient to the temporal happiness of the other. And this principle is commonly carried into effect in slaveholding countries.

If argument were necessary to show that such a system as this must be at variance with the ordinance of God, it might be easily drawn from the effects which it produces both upon *morals* and *national wealth.*

Its effects must be disastrous upon the *morals* of both parties. By presenting objects on whom passion may be satiated without resistance and without redress, it cultivates in the master, pride, anger, cruelty, selfishness and licentiousness. By accustoming the slave to subject his moral principles to the will of another, it tends to abolish in him all moral distinction; and thus fosters in him lying, deceit, hypocrisy, dishonesty, and a willingness to yield himself up to minister to the appetites of his master.

The effects of slavery on *national wealth*, may be easily seen from the following considerations:—

Instead of imposing upon all the necessity of labor, it restricts the number of laborers, that is of producers, within the smallest possible limit, by rendering labor disgraceful.

It takes from the laborers the natural stimulus to labor, namely the desire in the individual of improving his condition; and substitutes, in the place of it, that motive which is the least operative and the least constant, namely, the fear of punishment without the consciousness of moral delinquency.

It removes, as far as possible, from both parties, the disposition and the motives to frugality. Neither the master learns frugality from the necessity of labor, nor the slave from the benefits which it confers. And here, while the one party wastes from ignorance of the laws of acquisition, and the other because he can have no motive to economy, capital must accumulate but slowly, if indeed it accumulate at all.

No country, not of great fertility, can long sustain a large slave population. Soils of more than ordinary fertility can not sustain it long, after the richness of the soil has been exhausted. Hence, slavery in this country is acknowledged to have impoverished many of our most valuable districts; and, hence, it is continually migrating from the older settlements, to those new and untilled regions, where the accumulated manure of centuries of vegetation has formed a soil, whose productiveness may, for a wh le, sustain a system at variance with the laws of nature. Many of our free and of our slaveholding States were peopled at about the same time. The slaveholding States had every advantage, both in soil and climate, over their neighbors. And yet the accumulation of capital has been greatly in favor of the latter. If any one doubts whether this difference be owing to the use of slave labor, let him ask himself what would have been the condition of the slave-holding States, at this moment, if they had been inhabited, from the beginning, by an industrious yeomanry; each one holding his own land, and each one tilling it with the labor of his own hands.

The moral precepts of the Bible are diametrically opposed to slavery. They are, Thou shalt love thy *neighbor* as *thyself*, and *all things whatsoever* ye would that men should do unto you, do ye even so unto them.

The application of these precepts is universal. Our neighbor is *every one whom we may benefit*. The obligation respects *all things whatsoever*. The precept, then, manifestly, extends to *men, as men*, or *men in every condition;* and if to all things whatsoever, certainly to a thing so important as the right to personal liberty.

Again. By this precept, it is made our duty to cherish as tender and delicate a respect for the right which the meanest individual posseses over the means of happiness bestowed upon him by God, as we cherish for our own right over our own means of happiness, or as we desire any other individual to cherish for it. Now, were this precept obeyed, it is manifest that slavery could not in fact exist for a single instant. The principle of the precept is absolutely subversive of the principle of slavery. That of the one is the entire equality of right; that of the other, the entire absorption of the rights of one in the rights of the other.

If any one doubts respecting the bearing of the Scripture precept upon this case, a few plain questions may throw additional light upon the subject. For instance,—

"Do the precepts and the spirit of the Gospel allow me to derive my support from a system which extorts labor from my fellow-men, without allowing them any voice in the equivalent which they shal receive; and which can only be sustained by keeping them in a state of mental degradation, and by shutting them out, in a great degree, from the means of salvation?

"Would the master be willing that another person should subject him to slavery, for the same reasons, and on the same grounds, that he holds his slave in bondage?

"Would the Gospel allow us, if it were in our power, to reduce our fellow-citizens of our own color to slavery? If the gospel be diametrically opposed to the *principle* of slavery, it must be opposed to the *practice* of slavery; and therefore, were the principles of the gospel fully adopted, slavery could not exist.

"The very course which the gospel takes on this subject, seems to have been the only one that could have been taken, in order to effect the universal abolition of slavery. The gospel was designed, not for one race, or for one time, but for all races, and for all times. It looked not at the abolition of this form of evil for that age alone, but for its universal abolition. Hence, the important object of its Author was, to gain it a lodgment in every part of the known world; so that, by its universal diffusion among all classes of society, it might quietly and peacefully modify and subdue the evil passions of men; and thus, without violence, work a revolution in the whole mass of mankind.

"If the system be wrong, as we have endeavored to show, if it be at variance with our duty both to God and to man, it must be abandoned. If it be asked when, I ask again, when shall a man begin to cease doing wrong? Is not the answer, *immediately?* If a man is injuring *us*, do we ever doubt as to the time when *he* ought to cease? There is then no doubt in respect to the time when we ought to cease inflicting injury upon others."

Abraham Booth, an eminent theological writer of the Baptist persuasion, says:—

"I have not a stronger conviction of scarcely anything, than that slaveholding (except when the slave has forfeited his liberty by crimes against society) is wicked and inconsistent with Christian character. To me it is evident, that whoever would purchase an innocent black man to make him a slave, would with equal readiness purchase a white one for the same purpose could he do it with equal impunity, and no more disgrace."

At a meeting of the General Committee of the Baptists of Virginia, in 1789, the following resolution was offered by Eld. John Leland, and adopted :—

"*Resolved*, That slavery is a violent deprivation of the rights of nature, and inconsistent with republican government, and therefore we recommend it to our brethren to make use of every measure to extirpate this horrid evil from the land; and pray Almighty God that our honorable legislature may have it in their power to proclaim the great jubilee, consistent with the principles of good policy."

METHODIST TESTIMONY.

John Wesley, the celebrated founder of Methodism, says :—

"Men buyers are exactly on a level with men stealers."

Again, he says :—

"American Slavery is the vilest that ever saw the sun; it constitutes the sum of all villanies."

The learned Dr. Adam Clarke, author of a voluminous commentary on the Scriptures, says :—

"Slave-dealers, whether those who carry on the traffic in human flesh and blood; or those who steal a person in order to sell him into bondage; or those who buy such stolen men or women, no matter of what color, or what country; or the nations who legalize or connive at such traffic; all these are men-stealers, and God classes them with the most flagitious of mortals."

One of the rules laid down in the Methodist Discipline as amended in 1784, was as follows :—

"Every member of our Society who has slaves in his possession, shall, within twelve months after notice given to him by the assistant, legally execute and record an instrument, whereby he emancipates and sets free every slave in his possession."

Another rule was in these words :—

"No person holding slaves shall in future be admitted into Society, or to the Lord's Supper, till he previously complies with these rules concerning slavery."

The answer to the question—"What shall be done with those who buy or sell slaves, or give them away"—is couched in the following language :—

"They are immediately to be expelled, unless they buy tnem on purpose to free them."

In 1785, the voice of this church was heard as follows :—

"We do hold in the deepest abhorrence the practice of slavery, and shall not cease to seek its destruction, by all wise and prudent means."

In 1797, the Discipline contained the following wholesome paragraph :—

"The preachers and other members of our Society are requested to consider the subject of negro slavery, with deep attention, and that they impart to the General Conference, through the medium of the Yearly Conferences, or otherwise, any important thoughts on the subject, that the Conference may have full light, in order to take further steps towards eradicating this enormous evil from that part of the Church of God with which they are connected. The Annual Conferences are directed to draw up addresses for the gradual emancipation of the slaves, to the legislatures of those States in which no general laws have been passed for that purpose. These addresses shall urge, in the most respectful but pointed manner. the necessity of a law for the gradual emancipation of slaves. Proper committees shall be appointed by the Annual Conferences, out of the most respectable of our friends, for conducting the business; and presiding elders, elders, deacons, and traveling preachers, shall procure as many proper signatures as possible to the addresses, and give all the assistance in their power, in every respect, to aid the committees, and to forward the blessed undertaking. Let this be continued from year to year, till the desired end be accomplished."

CATHOLIC TESTIMONY.

It has been only about twenty years since Pope Gregory XVI. immortalized himself by issuing the famous Bull against slavery, from which the following is an extract:—

"Placed as we are on the Supreme seat of the apostles, and acting, though by no merits of our own, as the vicegerent of Jesus Christ, the Son of God, who, through his great mercy, condescended to make himself man, and to die for the redemption of the world, we regard as a duty devolving on our pastoral functions, that we endeavor to turn aside our faithful flocks entirely from the inhuman traffic in negroes, or any other human beings whatever. * * * In progress of time, as the clouds of heathen superstition became gradually dispersed, circumstances reached that point, that during several centuries there were no slaves allowed amongst the great majority of the Christian nations; but with grief we are compelled to add, that there afterwards arose, even among the faithful, a race of men, who, basely blinded by the appetite and desire of sordid lucre, did not hesitate to reduce, in remote regions of the earth, Indians, negroes, and other wretched beings, to the misery of slavery; or, finding the trade established and augmented, to assist the shameful crime of others. Nor did many of the most glorious of the Roman Pontiffs omit severely to reprove their conduct, as injurious to their souls' health, and disgraceful to the Christian name. Among these may be especially quoted the bull of Paul III which bears the date of the 29th of May, 1537 addressed to the Cardinal Archbishop of Toledc, and another still more comprehensive, by Urban VIII., dated the 22d of April, 1636, to the collector Jurius of the Apostolic chamber in Portugal, most severely castigating by name those who presumed to subject either East or West Indians to slavery, to sell, buy, exchange, or give them away, to separate them from their wives and children, despoil them of their goods and property, to bring or transmit them to other places, or by any means to deprive them of liberty, or retain them in slavery; also most severely castigating those who should presume or dare to afford council, aid, favor or assistance, under any pretext, or borrowed color, to those doing the aforesaid; or should preach or teach that it is lawful, or should otherwise presume or dare to co-operate, by any possible means, with the aforesaid. * * * Wherefore, we, desiring to divert this disgrace from the whole confines of Christianity, having summoned several of our venerable brothers, their Eminences the Cardinals, of the H. R. Church, to our council, and, having maturely deliberated on the whole matter, pursuing the footsteps of our predecessors, admonished by our apostolical authority, and urgently invoke in the Lord, all Christians, of whatever condition, that none henceforth dare to subject to slavery, unjustly persecute, or despoil of their goods, Indians, negroes, or other classes of men, or be accessories to others, or furnish them aid or assistance in so doing; and on no account henceforth to exercise that inhuman traffic by which negroes are reduced to slavery, as if they were not men, but automata or chattels, and are sold in defiance of all the laws of justice and humanity, and devoted to severe and intolerable labors. We further reprobate, by our apostolical authority, all the above-described offences as utterly unworthy of the Christian name; and by the same authority we rigidly prohibit and interdict all and every individual, whether ecclesiastical or laical, from presuming to defend that commerce in negro slaves under pretence or borrowed color, or to teach or publish in any manner, publicly or privately, things contrary to the admonitions which we have given in these letters.

"And, lnally, that these, our letters, may be rendered more apparent to all, and that no person may allege any ignorance thereof we decree and order that it shall be published according to custom, and copies thereof be properly affixed to the gates of St. Peter and of the Apostolic Chancel, every and in like manner to the General Court of Mount Citatorio, and in the field of the Campus Florae and also through the city, by one of our heralds, according to aforesaid custom.

"Given at Rome, at the Palace of Santa Maria Major, under the seal of the fisherman, on the 3d day of December, 1837, and in the ninth year of our pontificate.

"Countersigned by Cardinal A. Lambruschini."

We have already quoted the language of Pope Leo X., who says :—

"Not only does the Christian religion, but nature herself cry out against the State of slavery."

The Abbe Raynal says :—

"He who supports slavery is the enemy of the human race. He divides it into two societies of legal assassins, the oppressors and the oppressed. I shall not be afraid to cite to the tribunal of reason and justice those governments which tolerate this cruelty, or which even are not ashamed to make it the basis of their power."

From the proceedings of a Massachusetts Anti-slavery Convention in 1855, we make the following extract :—

"Henry Kemp, a Roman Catholic, came forward to defend the Romish Church in reply to Mr. Foster. He claimed that the Catholic Church is thoroughly anti-slavery—as thoroughly as even his friend Foster."

Thus manfully do men of pure hearts and noble minds, whether in Church or State, and without regard to sect or party, lift up their voices against the wicked and pernicious institution of human slavery. Thus they speak, and thus they are obliged to speak, if they speak at all; it is only the voice of Nature, Justice, Truth, and Love, that issues from them. The divine principle in man prompts him to speak and strike for Freedom; the diabolical principle within him prompts him to speak and strike for slavery.

From those churches which are now—as all churches ought to be, and will be, ere the world becomes Christianized—thoroughly imbued with the principles of freedom, we do not, as already intimated, deem it particularly necessary to bring forward new arguments in opposition to slavery. If, however, the reader would be pleased to hear from the churches to which we chiefly allude—and, by the bye, he might hear from them with much profit to himself—we respectfully refer him to Henry Ward Beecher, George B. Cheever, Joseph P. Thompson, Theodore Parker, E. H. Chapin, and H. W. Bellows, of the North, and to M D. Conway, John G. Fee, James S. Davis, Daniel Wilson, and W. E. Lincoln, of the South. All these reverend gentlemen, ministers of different denominations, feel it their duty to preach against slavery, and, to their honor be it said, they do preach against it with unabated zeal and success. Our earnest prayer is, that Heaven may enable them, their cotemporaries and successors, to preach against it with such energy and effect, as will cause it to disappear forever from the soil of our Republic.

CHAPTER VII.

BIBLE TESTIMONY.

Every person who has read the Bible, and who has a proper understanding of its leading moral precepts, feels, in his own conscience, that it is the only original and complete anti-slavery text-book. In a crude state of society—in a barbarous age—when men were in a manner destitute of wholesome laws, either human or divine, it is possible that a mild form of slavery may have been tolerated, and even regulated, as an institution clothed with the importance of temporary recognition; but the Deity never approved it, and, for the very reason that it is impossible for him to do wrong, he never will, never can approve it. The worst system of servitude of which we have any account in the Bible—and, by the way, it furnishes no account of anything so bad as slavery (the evil-one and his hot home alone excepted)—was far less rigorous and atrocious than that now established in the Southern States of this Confederacy. Even that system, however, the worst, which seems to have been practiced to a considerable extent by those venerable old fogies, Abraham, Isaac, and Jacob, was one of the monstrous inventions of Satan that God "winked" at; and, to the mind of the biblical scholar, nothing can be more evident than that He determined of old, that it should, in due time, be abolished. To say that the Bible sanctions slavery is to say that the sun loves darkness; to say that one man was created to domineer over another is to call in question the justice, mercy, and goodness of God.

We will now listen to a limited number of the

PRECEPTS AND SAYINGS OF THE OLD TESTAMENT.

"Proclaim liberty throughout all the land, unto all the inhabitants thereof."

"Let the oppressed go free."

"Thou shalt love thy neighbor as thyself."

"Thou shalt not respect the person of the poor, nor honor the person of the mighty; but in righteousness shalt thou judge thy neighbor."

"The wages of him that is hired shall not abide with thee all night until the morning."

"Envy thou not the oppressor, and choose none of his ways."

"Do justice to the afflicted and needy; rid them out of the hand of the wicked."

"Execute judgment and justice; take away your exactions from my people, saith the Lord God."

"Therefore thus saith the Lord; ye have not hearkened unto me, in proclaiming liberty, every one to his brother, and every man to his neighbor: behold, I proclaim a liberty for you, saith the Lord, to the sword, to the pestilence, and to the famine; and I will make you to be removed into all the kingdoms of the earth"

"He that stealeth a man, and selleth him, or if he be found in his hand, he shall surely be put to death."

"Whoso stoppeth his ears at the cry of the poor, he also shall cry, but shall not be heard."

"He that oppresseth the poor reproacheth his Maker."

"I will be a swift witness against the sorcerers, and against the adulterers, and against false swearers, and against those that oppress the hireling in his wages, the widow, and the fatherless, and that turn aside the stranger from his right, and fear not me, saith the Lord of Hosts."

"As the partridge setteth on eggs, and hatcheth them not; so he that getteth riches, and not by right, shall leave them in the midst of his days, and at his end shall be a fool."

And now we will listen to a few selected

PRECEPTS AND SAYINGS OF THE NEW TESTAMENT.

"Call no man master, neither be ye called masters."

"All things whatsoever ye would that men should do to you do ye even so to them."

"Be kindly affectionate one to another with brotherly love; in honor preferring one another."

"Do good to all men, as ye have opportunity."

"Stand fast therefore in the liberty wherewith Christ hath made you free, and be not entangled again with the yoke of bondage."

"If thou mayest be made free, use it rather."

"The laborer is worthy of his hire."

"Where the Spirit of the Lord is, there is liberty."

Some years ago a clerical lickspittle of the slave power

had the temerity to publish a book or pamphlet entitled "Bible Defence of Slavery," which the Baltimore *Sun*, in the course of a caustic criticism, handled in the following manner:—

"Bible defence of slavery! There is no such thing as a Bible defence of slavery at the present day. Slavery in the United States is a social institution, originating in the convenience and cupidity of our ancestors, existing by State laws, and recognized to a certain extent—for the recovery of slave property—by the Constitution. And nobody would pretend that, if it were inexpedient and unprofitable for any man or any State to continue to hold slaves, they would be bound to do so on the ground of a "Bible defence" of it. Slavery is recorded in the Bible, and approved, with many degrading characteristics. War is recorded in the Bible, and approved, under what seems to us the extreme of cruelty. But are slavery and war to *endure* for ever because we find them in the Bible? or are they to *cease* at once and for ever because the Bible inculcates peace and brotherhood?"

Thus, in the last five chapters inclusive, have we introduced a mass of anti-slavery arguments, human and divine, that will stand, irrefutable and convincing, as long as the earth itself shall continue to revolve in its orbit. Aside from unaffected truthfulness and candor, no merit is claimed for anything we have said on our own account. With the best of motives, and in the language of nature more than that of art, we have simply given utterance to the honest convictions of our heart—being impelled to it by a long-harbored and unmistakable sense of duty which grew stronger and deeper as the days passed away.

If half the time which has been spent in collecting and arranging these testimonies had been occupied in the composition of original matter, the weight of paper and binding and the number of pages would have been much greater, but the value and the effect of the contents would have been far less. From the first, our leading motive has been to convince our fellow-citizens of the South, non-slaveholders and slaveholders, that slavery, whether considered in all its bearings, or, setting aside the moral aspect of the question, and looking at it in only a pecuniary point of view, is impolitic, unprofitable, and degrading; how well, thus far, we have succeeded in our undertaking, time will, perhaps, fully disclose.

In the words of a contemporaneous German writer, whose language we readily and heartily endorse, "It is the shame of our age that argument is needed against slavery." Taking things as they are, however, argument being needed, we have offered it; and we have offered it from such sources as will, in our honest opinion, confound the devil and his incarnate confederates.

These testimonies, culled from the accumulated wisdom of nearly six thousand centuries, beginning with the great and good men of our own time, and running back through distant ages to Saint Paul, Saint John, and Saint Luke, to Cicero, Plato, and Socrates, to Solomon, David, and Moses, and even to the Deity himself, are the pillars of strength and beauty upon which the popularity of our work will, in all probability, be principally based. If the ablest writers of the Old Testament; if the eloquent prophets of old; if the renowned philosophers of Greece and Rome; if the heavenly-minded authors and compilers of the New Testament; if the illustrious poets and prose-writers, heroes, statesmen, sages of all nations, ancient and modern; if God himself and the hosts of learned ministers whom he has commissioned to proclaim his word—if all these are wrong, then we are wrong; on the other hand, however, if they are right, we are right; for, in effect, we only repeat and endeavor to enforce their precepts.

If we are in error, we desire to be corrected; and, if it is not asking too much, we respectfully request the advocates of slavery to favor us with an *exposé* of what they, in their one-sided view of things, conceive to be the advantages of their favorite and peculiar institution. Such an *exposé*, if skillfully executed, would doubtless be regarded as the funniest novel of the times—a fit production, if not too immoral in its tendencies, to be incorporated into the next edition of D'Israeli's curiosities of literature.

CHAPTER VIII.

FREE FIGURES AND SLAVE.

UNDER this heading we propose to introduce the remainder of the more important statistics of the Free and of the Slave States ;—especially those that relate to Commerce, Manufactures, Internal Improvements, Education and Religion. Originally it was our intention to devote a separate chapter to each of the industrial and moral interests above-named: but other considerations have so greatly encroached on our space, that we are compelled to modify our design. To the thoughtful and discriminating reader, however, the chief statistics which follow will be none the less interesting for not being the subjects of annotations.

At present, all we ask of pro-slavery men, no matter in what part of the world they may reside, is to look these figures fairly in the face. We wish them to do it, in the first instance, not on the platforms of public debate, where the exercise of eloquence is too often characterized by violent passion and subterfuge, but in their own private apartments, where no eye save that of the All-seeing One will rest upon them, and where, in considering the relations which they sustain to the past, the present, and the future, an opportunity will be afforded them of securing that most valuable of all possessions attainable on earth, a conscience void of offence toward God and man.

Each separate table or particular compilation of statistics will afford food for at least an hour's profitable reflection; indeed, the more these figures are studied, and the better they are understood, the sooner will the author's object be accomplished,—the sooner will the genius of Universal Liberty dispel the dark clouds of slavery.

TABLE NO. XXVI.

TONNAGE, EXPORTS AND IMPORTS OF THE FREE STATES—1855.

States.	Tonnage.	Exports.	Imports.
California	92,623	$8,224,066	$5,951,379
Connecticut	137,170	878,874	636,826
Illinois	53,797	547,053	54,509
Indiana	3,698		
Iowa			
Maine	806,587	4,851,207	2,927,443
Massachusetts	970,727	28,190,925	45,113,774
Michigan	69,490	568,091	281,379
New Hampshire	30,330	1,523	17,786
New Jersey	121,020	687	1,473
New York	1,404,221	113,731,238	164,776,511
Ohio	91,607	847,143	600,656
Pennsylvania	397,768	6,274,338	15,300,935
Rhode Island	51,038	336,023	536,387
Vermont	6,915	2,895,468	591,593
Wisconsin	15,624	174,057	48,159
	4,252,615	$167,520,693	$236,847,810

TABLE NO. XXVII.

TONNAGE, EXPORTS AND IMPORTS OF THE SLAVE STATES—1855.

States.	Tonnage.	Exports.	Imports.
Alabama	36,274	$14,270,585	$619,964
Arkansas			
Delaware	19,186	68,087	5,821
Florida	14,835	1,403,594	45,998
Georgia	29,505	7,543,519	273,716
Kentucky	22,680		
Louisiana	204,149	55,367,962	12,900,821
Maryland	234,805	10,395,984	7,788,949
Mississippi	2,475		1,661
Missouri	60,592		
North Carolina	60,077	433,818	243,083
South Carolina	60,935	12,700,250	1,588,542
Tennessee	8,404		
Texas	8,812	916,961	262,568
Virginia	92,788	4,379,928	855,405
	855,517	$107,480,688	$24,586,528

TABLE NO. XXVIII.

PRODUCT OF MANUFACTURES IN THE FREE STATES—1850.

States.	Val. of Annual products.	Capital invested.	Hands employed.
California	$12,862,522	$1,006,197	3,964
Connecticut	45,110,102	23,890,348	47,770
Illinois	17,236,073	6,385,387	12,065
Indiana	18,922,651	7,941,602	14,342
Iowa	3,551,783	1,292,875	1,707
Maine	24,664,135	14,700,452	28,078
Massachusetts	151,137,145	83,357,642	165,938
Michigan	10,976,894	6,534,250	9,290
New Hampshire	23,164,503	18,242,114	27,092
New Jersey	39,713,586	22,184,730	37,311
New York	237,597,249	99,904,405	199,349
Ohio	62,647,259	29,019,538	51,489
Pennsylvania	155,044,910	94,473,810	146,766
Rhode Island	22,093,258	12,923,176	20,881
Vermont	8,570,920	5,001,377	8,445
Wisconsin	9,293,068	3,382,148	6,089
	$842,586,058	$430,240,051	780,576

TABLE NO. XXIX.

PRODUCT OF MANUFACTURES IN THE SLAVE STATES—1850.

States.	Val. of Annual products.	Capital invested.	Hands employed.
Alabama	$4,538,878	$3,450,606	4,936
Arkansas	607,436	324,065	903
Delaware	4,649,296	2,978,945	3,888
Florida	668,338	547,060	991
Georgia	7,086,525	5,460,483	8,378
Kentucky	24,588,483	12,350,734	24,385
Louisiana	7,320,948	5,318,074	6,437
Maryland	32,477,702	14,753,143	30,124
Mississippi	2,972,038	1,833,420	3,173
Missouri	23,749,265	9,079,695	16,850
North Carolina	9,111,245	7,252,225	12,444
South Carolina	7,063,513	6,056,865	7,009
Tennesse	9,728,438	6,975,279	12,032
Texas	1,165,538	539,290	1,066
Virginia	29,705,387	18,109,993	29,109
	$165,413,027	$95,029,879	161,733

TABLE NO. XXX.

MILES OF CANALS AND RAILROADS IN THE FREE STATES—1854–1857.

States.	Canals, miles, 1854.	Railroads, miles, 1857.	Cost of Railroads, 1855.
California		22	
Connecticut	61	600	$25,224,191
Illinois	100	2,524	55,663,656
Indiana	367	1,806	29,585,923
Iowa		253	2,300,000
Maine	50	442	13,749,021
Massachusetts	100	1,285	59,167,781
Michigan		600	22,370,397
New Hampshire	11	645	15,860,949
New Jersey	147	472	13,840,030
New York	989	2,700	111,882,503
Ohio	921	2,869	67,798,202
Pennsylvania	936	2,407	94,657,675
Rhode Island		85	2,614,484
Vermont		515	17,998,835
Wisconsin		629	5,600,000
	3,682	17,855	$538,313,647

TABLE NO. XXXI.

MILES OF CANALS AND RAILROADS IN THE SLAVE STATES—1854–1857.

States.	Canals, miles, 1854.	Railroads, miles, 1857.	Cost of Railroads, 1855.
Alabama	51	484	$3,986,208
Arkansas			
Delaware	14	120	600,000
Florida		86	250,000
Georgia	28	1,062	17,034,802
Kentucky	486	306	6,179,072
Louisiana	101	263	1,731,000
Maryland	184	597	12,654,333
Mississippi		410	4,520,000
Missouri		189	1,000,000
North Carolina	13	612	6,847,213
South Carolina	50	706	13,547,093
Tennessee		508	10,436,610
Texas		57	16,466,250
Virginia	181	1,479	
	1,116	6,859	$95,252,581

TABLE NO. XXXII.

BANK CAPITAL IN THE FREE AND IN THE SLAVE STATES—1855.

Free States.		Slave States.	
California		Alabama........	$2,296,400
Connecticut........	$15,597,891	Arkansas........	
Illinois...........	2,513,790	Delaware........	1,393,175
Indiana...........	7,281,934	Florida..........	
Iowa..............		Georgia.........	13,413,100
Maine............	7,301,252	Kentucky........	10,369,717
Massachusetts...	54,492,660	Louisiana.......	20,179,107
Michigan.........	980,416	Maryland........	10,411,874
New Hampshire..	3,626,000	Mississippi......	240,165
New Jersey......	5,314,885	Missouri........	1,215,398
New York........	83,773,288	North Carolina...	5,205,073
Ohio.............	7,166,581	South Carolina...	16,603,253
Pennsylvania....	19,864,825	Tennessee........	6,717,848
Rhode Island....	17,511,162	Texas............	
Vermont.........	3,275,656	Virginia.........	14,033,838
Wisconsin.......	1,400,000		
Total.....	$230,100,340	Total.....	$102,078,940

TABLE NO. XXXIII.

MILITIA FORCE OF THE FREE AND THE SLAVE STATES—1852.

Free States.		Slave States.	
California		Alabama........	76,662
Connecticut......	51,649	Arkansas	17,137
Illinois..........	170,359	Delaware........	9,229
Indiana..........	53,918	Florida	12,122
Iowa.......... ..		Georgia.........	57,312
Maine...........	62,588	Kentucky.......	81,810
Massachusetts....	119,690	Louisiana.	43,823
Michigan........	63,938	Maryland	46,864
New Hampshire..	32,151	Mississippi......	36,084
New Jersey......	39,171	Missouri........	61,000
New York........	265,293	North Carolina...	79,448
Ohio............	176,455	South Carolina...	55,209
Pennsylvania.....	276,070	Tennessee.......	71,252
Rhode Island.....	14,443	Texas...........	19,766
Vermont........	23,915	Virginia.........	125,128
Wisconsin.......	32,203		
Total.....	**1,381,845**	**Total...**	**792,876**

TABLE NO. XXXIV.

POST OFFICE OPERATIONS IN THE FREE STATES—1855.

States.	Stamps sold.	Total Postage collected.	Cost of Trans. the mails.
California	$81,437	$234,591	$135,386
Connecticut	79,284	179,230	81,462
Illinois	105,252	279,887	280,038
Indiana	60,578	180,405	190,480
Iowa	28,198	82,420	84,428
Maine	60,165	151,358	82,218
Massachusetts	259,062	532,184	153,091
Michigan	49,763	142,188	148,204
New-Hampshire	38,387	95,609	46,631
New-Jersey	31,495	109,697	80,084
New-York	542,498	1,383,157	481,410
Ohio	167,958	452,643	421,870
Pennsylvania	217,293	583,013	251,833
Rhode Island	30,291	58,624	13,891
Vermont	36,314	92,816	64,437
Wisconsin	33,538	112,903	92,842
	$1,719,513	$4,670,725	$2,608,295

TABLE NO. XXXV.

POST OFFICE OPERATIONS IN THE SLAVE STATES—1855.

States.	Stamps sold.	Total Postage collected.	Cost of Trans. the mails.
Alabama	$44,514	$104,514	226,816
Arkansas	8,941	30,664	117,659
Delaware	7,298	19,644	9,243
Florida	8,764	19,275	77,553
Georgia	73,880	149,063	216,003
Kentucky	55,694	130,067	144,161
Louisiana	50,778	133,753	133,810
Maryland	77,743	191,485	192,743
Mississippi	31,182	78,739	170,785
Missouri	53,742	139,652	185,096
North Carolina	34,235	72,759	148,249
South Carolina	47,368	91,600	192,216
Tennessee	48,377	103,686	116,091
Texas	24,580	70,436	209,936
Virginia	96,799	217,861	245,592
	$666,845	$1,553,198	$2,885,958

TABLE NO. XXXVI.

PUBLIC SCHOOLS OF THE FREE STATES—1850.

States.	Number.	Teachers.	Pupils.
California	2	2	49
Connecticut	1,656	1,787	71,269
Illinois	4,052	4,248	125,725
Indiana	4,822	4,860	161,500
Iowa	740	828	29,556
Maine	4,042	5,540	192,815
Massachusetts	3,679	4,443	176,475
Michigan	2,714	3,231	110,455
New Hampshire	2,381	3,013	75,643
New Jersey	1,473	1,574	77,930
New York	11,580	13,965	675,221
Ohio	11,661	12,886	484,153
Pennsylvania	9,061	10,024	413,706
Rhode Island	416	518	23,130
Vermont	2,731	4,173	93,457
Wisconsin	1,423	1,529	58,817
	62,433	72,621	2,769,901

TABLE NO. XXXVII.

PUBLIC SCHOOLS IN THE SLAVE STATES—1850.

States.	Number.	Teachers.	Pupils.
Alabama	1,152	1,195	28,380
Arkansas	353	355	8,493
Delaware	194	214	8,970
Florida	69	73	1,878
Georgia	1,251	1,265	32,705
Kentucky	2,234	2,306	71,429
Louisiana	664	822	25,046
Maryland	898	986	33,111
Mississippi	782	826	18,746
Missouri	1,570	1,620	51,754
North Carolina	2,657	2,730	104,095
South Carolina	724	739	17,838
Tennessee	2,680	2,819	104,117
Texas	349	360	7,946
Virginia	2,930	2,997	67,353
	18,507	19,807	581,861

TABLE NO. XXXVIII.

LIBRARIES OTHER THAN PRIVATE IN THE FREE STATES—1850.

States.	Number.	Volumes.
California		
Connecticut	164	165,318
Illinois	152	62,486
Indiana	151	68,403
Iowa	32	5,790
Maine	236	121,969
Massachusetts	1,462	684,015
Michigan	417	107,943
New Hampshire	129	85,759
New Jersey	128	80,885
New York	11,013	1,760,820
Ohio	352	186,826
Pennsylvania	393	363,400
Rhode Island	96	104,342
Vermont	96	64,641
Wisconsin	72	21,020
	14,911	3,888,234

TABLE NO. XXXIX.

LIBRARIES OTHER THAN PRIVATE IN THE SLAVE STATES—1850.

States.	Number.	Volumes.
Alabama	56	20,623
Arkansas	3	420
Delaware	17	17,950
Florida	7	2,660
Georgia	38	31,788
Kentucky	80	79,466
Louisiana	10	26,800
Maryland	124	125,042
Mississippi	117	21,737
Missouri	97	75,056
North Carolina	38	29,592
South Carolina	26	107,472
Tennessee	34	22,896
Texas	12	4,230
Virginia	54	88,462
	695	649,577

TABLE NO. XL.

NEWSPAPERS AND PERIODICALS PUBLISHED IN THE FREE STATES—1850.

States.	Number.	Copies Printed annually.
California	7	761,200
Connecticut	46	4,267,932
Illinois	107	5,102,276
Indiana	107	4,316,828
Iowa	29	1,512,800
Maine	49	4,203,064
Massachusetts	202	64,820,564
Michigan	58	3,247,736
New Hampshire	38	3,067,552
New Jersey	51	4,098,678
New York	428	115,385,473
Ohio	261	30,473,407
Pennsylvania	309	84,898,672
Rhode Island	19	2,756,950
Vermont	35	2,567,662
Wisconsin	46	2,665,487
	1,790	334,146,281

TABLE NO. XLI.

NEWSPAPERS AND PERIODICALS PUBLISHED IN THE SLAVE STATES—1850.

States.	Number.	Copies Printed annually.
Alabama	60	2,662,741
Arkansas	9	377,000
Delaware	10	421,200
Florida	10	319,800
Georgia	51	4,070,868
Kentucky	62	6,582,838
Louisiana	55	12,416,224
Maryland	68	19,612,724
Mississippi	50	1,752,504
Missouri	61	6,195,560
North Carolina	51	2,020,564
South Carolina	46	7,145,930
Tennessee	50	6,940,750
Texas	34	1,296,924
Virginia	87	9,223,068
	704	81,038,693

TABLE NO. XLII.

ILLITERATE WHITE ADULTS IN THE FREE STATES—1850.

States.	Native.	Foreign.	Total.
California	2,201	2,917	5,118
Connecticut	826	4,013	4,739
Illinois	34,107	5,947	40,054
Indiana	67,275	3,265	70,540
Iowa	7,043	1,077	8,120
Maine	1,999	4,148	6,147
Massachusetts	1,055	26,484	27,539
Michigan	4,903	3,009	7,912
New Hampshire	893	2,064	2,957
New Jersey	8,370	5,878	14,248
New York	23,241	68,052	91,293
Ohio	51,968	9,062	61,030
Pennsylvania	41,944	24,989	66,928
Rhode Island	981	2,359	3,340
Vermont	565	5,624	6,189
Wisconsin	1,459	4,902	6,361
	248,725	173,790	422,515

TABLE NO. XLIII.

ILLITERATE WHITE ADULTS IN THE SLAVE STATES—1850.

States.	Native.	Foreign.	Total.
Alabama	33,618	139	33,757
Arkansas	16,792	27	16,819
Delaware	4,132	404	4,536
Florida	3,564	295	3,859
Georgia	40,794	406	41,200
Kentucky	64,340	2,347	66,687
Louisiana	14,950	6,271	21,221
Maryland	17,364	3,451	20,815
Mississippi	13,324	81	13,405
Missouri	34,420	1,861	36,281
North Carolina	73,226	340	73,566
South Carolina	15,580	104	15,684
Tennessee	77,017	505	77,522
Texas	8,037	2,488	10,525
Virginia	75,868	1,137	77,005
	493,026	19,856	512,882

TABLE NO. XLVI.

POPULAR VOTE FOR PRESIDENT BY THE FREE STATES —1856.

States.	*Republican.* Fremont.	*American.* Fillmore.	*Democratic.* Buchanan.	Total.
California	20,339	35,113	51,925	107,377
Connecticut......	42,715	2,615	34,995	80,325
Illinois..........	96,189	37,444	105,348	238,981
Indiana.........	94,375	22,386	118,670	235,431
Iowa............	43,954	9,180	36,170	89,304
Maine...........	67,379	3,325	39,080	109,784
Massachusetts...	108,190	19,626	39,240	167,056
Michigan........	71,762	1,660	52,136	125,558
New Hampshire..	38,345	422	32,789	71,556
New Jersey......	28,338	24,115	46,943	99,396
New York.......	276,907	124,604	195,878	597,389
Ohio............	187,497	28,126	170,874	386,497
Pennsylvania....	147,510	82,175	230,710	460,395
Rhode Island....	11,467	1,675	6,580	19,722
Vermont........	39,561	545	10,569	50,675
Wisconsin.......	66,090	579	52,843	119,512
	1,340,618	393,590	1,224,750	2,958,958

TABLE NO. XLVII.

POPULAR VOTE FOR PRESIDENT BY THE SLAVE STATES—1856.

States.	*Republican.* Fremont.	*American.* Fillmore.	*Democratic.* Buchanan.	Total.
Alabama........		28,552	46,739	75,291
Arkansas		10,787	21,910	32,697
Delaware........	308	6,175	8,004	14,487
Florida		4,833	6,358	11,191
Georgia.........		42,228	56,578	98,806
Kentucky.......	314	67,416	74,642	142,372
Louisiana.......		20,709	22,164	42,873
Maryland	281	47,460	39,115	86,856
Mississippi......		24,195	35,446	59,641
Missouri........		48,524	58,164	106 688
North Carolina ..		36,886	48,246	85,132
South Carolina*..				
Tennessee.......		66,178	73,638	139,816
Texas...........		15,244	28,757	44,001
Virginia.........	291	60,278	89,826	150,395
	1,194	479,465	609,587	1,090,2[illegible]6

* No popular vote.

TABLE NO. XLVIII.

VALUE OF CHURCHES IN THE FREE AND IN THE SLAVE STATES—1850.

Free States.		Slave States.	
California	$288,400	Alabama	$1,244,741
Connecticut	3,599,330	Arkansas	149,686
Illinois	1,532,305	Delaware	340,345
Indiana	1,568,906	Florida	192,600
Iowa	235,412	Georgia	1,327,112
Maine	1,794,209	Kentucky	2,295,353
Massachusetts	10,504,888	Louisiana	1,940,495
Michigan	793,180	Maryland	3,974,116
New Hampshire	1,433,266	Mississippi	832,622
New Jersey	3,712,863	Missouri	1,730,135
New York	21,539,561	North Carolina	907,785
Ohio	5,860,059	South Carolina	2,181,476
Pennsylvania	11,853,291	Tennessee	1,246,951
Rhode Island	1,293,600	Texas	408,944
Vermont	1,251,655	Virginia	2,902,220
Wisconsin	512,552		
Total	$67,773,477	Total	$21,674,581

TABLE NO. XLIX

PATENTS ISSUED ON NEW INVENTIONS IN THE FREE AND IN THE SLAVE STATES—1856.

Free States.		Slave States.	
California	13	Alabama	11
Connecticut	142	Arkansas	
Illinois	93	Delaware	8
Indiana	67	Florida	3
Iowa	14	Georgia	13
Maine	42	Kentucky	26
Massachusetts	331	Louisiana	30
Michigan	22	Maryland	49
New Hampshire	43	Mississippi	8
New Jersey	78	Missouri	32
New York	592	North Carolina	9
Ohio	139	South Carolina	10
Pennsylvania	267	Tennessee	23
Rhode Island	18	Texas	4
Vermont	35	Virginia	42
Wisconsin	33		
Total	1,929	Total	268

TABLE NO. L.

BIBLE CAUSE AND TRACT CAUSE IN THE FREE STATES—1855.

States.	Contribu. for the Bible Cause.	Contribu. for the Tract Cause.
California	$1,900	$ 5
Connecticut	24,528	15,872
Illinois	28,403	3,786
Indiana	6,755	1,491
Iowa	4,216	2,005
Maine	5,449	2,981
Massachusetts	43,444	11,492
Michigan	5,554	1,114
New-Hampshire	6,271	1,288
New-Jersey	15,475	8,546
New-York	123,386	61,233
Ohio	25,758	9,576
Pennsylvania	25,360	12,121
Rhode Island	2,669	2,121
Vermont	5,709	2,867
Wisconsin	4,790	474
	$319,667	$131,972

TABLE NO. LI.

BIBLE CAUSE AND TRACT CAUSE IN THE SLAVE STATES—1855.

States.	Contribu. for the Bible Cause.	Contribu. for the Tract Cause.
Alabama	$3,351	4,77
Arkansas	2,950	110
Delaware	1,037	163
Florida	1,957	5
Georgia	4,532	1,468
Kentucky	5,956	1,366
Louisiana	1.810	1,099
Maryland	8,909	5,365
Mississippi	1,067	267
Missouri	4,711	936
North Carolina	6,197	1.419
South Carolina	3,984	3 222
Tennessee	8,383	1,807
Texas	3,985	127
Virginia	9,296	6,894
	$68,125	$24,725

TABLE NO. L.

BIBLE CAUSE AND TRACT CAUSE IN THE FREE STATES—1855.

States.	Contribu. for the Bible Cause.	Contribu. for the Tract Cause.
California	$1,900	$ 5
Connecticut	24,528	15,872
Illinois	28,403	3,786
Indiana	6,755	1,491
Iowa	4,216	2,005
Maine	5,449	2,981
Massachusetts	43,444	11,492
Michigan	5,554	1,114
New-Hampshire	6,271	1,288
New-Jersey	15,475	3,546
New-York	123,386	61,233
Ohio	25,758	9,576
Pennsylvania	25,360	12,121
Rhode Island	2,669	2,121
Vermont	5,709	2,867
Wisconsin	4,790	474
	$319,667	$131,972

TABLE NO. LI.

BIBLE CAUSE AND TRACT CAUSE IN THE SLAVE STATES—1855.

States.	Contribu. for the Bible Cause.	Contribu. for the Tract Cause.
Alabama	$3,351	4,77
Arkansas	2,950	110
Delaware	1,037	163
Florida	1,957	5
Georgia	4,532	1,468
Kentucky	5,956	1,366
Louisiana	1.810	1,009
Maryland	8,909	5,365
Mississippi	1,067	267
Missouri	4,711	936
North Carolina	6,197	1.419
South Carolina	3,984	3 222
Tennessee	8,383	1,807
Texas	3,985	127
Virginia	9,296	6,894
	$68,125	$24,725

TABLE NO. LII.

MISSIONARY CAUSE AND COLONIZATION* CAUSE IN THE FREE STATES—1855–1856.

States.	Contributions for Miss'y purposes, 1855.	Contributions for Coloniza. pur., 1856
California	$ 192	$ 1
Connecticut	48,044	9,233
Illinois	10,040	543
Indiana	4,705	34
Iowa	1,750	3
Maine	13,929	1,719
Massachusetts	128,505	1,422
Michigan	4,935	4
New Hampshire	11,963	1,130
New Jersey	19,946	3,261
New York	172,115	24,371
Ohio	19,890	2,687
Pennsylvania	43,412	4,287
Rhode Island	9,440	2,125
Vermont	11,094	304
Wisconsin	2,216	806
	$502,174	$51,930

TABLE NO. LIII.

MISSIONARY CAUSE AND COLONIZATION* CAUSE IN THE SLAVE STATES—1855–1856.

States.	Contributions for Miss'y purposes, 1855.	Contributions for Coloniza. pur., 1856.
Alabama	$5,963	$1,113
Arkansas	455	1
Delaware	1,003	250
Florida	340	13
Georgia	9,846	5,323
Kentucky	6,953	4,436
Louisiana	334	871
Maryland	20,677	406
Mississippi	4,957	2,177
Missouri	2,712	813
North Carolina	6,010	969
South Carolina	15,248	129
Tennessee	4,971	1,611
Texas	349	6
Virginia	22,106	10,000
	$101,934	$27,618

* For colonizing free blacks in Liberia.

TABLE NO. LIV.

DEATHS IN THE FREE STATES—1850.*

States.	Number of deaths.	Ratio to the Number living.
California		
Connecticut	5,781	64.13
Illinois	11,619	73.28
Indiana	12,728	77.65
Iowa	2,044	94.03
Maine	7,545	77.29
Massachusetts	19,414	51.23
Michigan	4,520	88.19
New Hampshire	4,268	74.49
New Jersey	6,467	75.70
New York	44,339	69.85
Ohio	28,949	68.41
Pennsylvania	28,318	81.63
Rhode Island	2,241	65.83
Vermont	3,132	100.13
Wisconsin	2,884	105.82
	184,249	72.91

TABLE NO. LV.

DEATHS IN THE SLAVE STATES—1850.*

States.	Number of deaths.	Ratio to the Number living.
Alabama	9,084	84.94
Arkansas	2,987	70.18
Delaware	1,209	75.71
Florida	933	93.67
Georgia	9,920	91.93
Kentucky	15,206	64.60
Louisiana	11,948	42.85
Maryland	9,594	60.77
Mississippi	8,711	69.93
Missouri	12,211	55.81
North Carolina	10,207	85.12
South Carolina	7,997	83.59
Tennessee	11,759	85.34
Texas	3,046	69.79
Virginia	19,053	74.61
	133,865	71.82

* For an explanation of this Table see the next six pages.

TABLE NO. LVI.

FREE WHITE MALE PERSONS OVER FIFTEEN YEARS OF AGE ENGAGED IN AGRICULTURAL AND OTHER OUT-DOOR LABOR IN THE SLAVE-STATES—1850.

States.	No. engaged in Agriculture.	No. engaged in other out-door labor.	Total.
Alabama	67,742	7,229	74,971
Arkansas	28,436	5,596	34,032
Delaware	6,225	4,184	10,409
Florida	5,472	2,598	8,070
Georgia	82,107	11,054	93,161
Kentucky	110,119	26,308	136,427
Louisiana	11,524	13,827	25,351
Maryland	24,672	17,146	41,818
Mississippi	50,028	5,823	55,851
Missouri	64,292	19,900	84,192
North Carolina	76,338	21,876	98,214
South Carolina	37,612	6,991	44,603
Tennessee	115,844	16,795	132,[illegible]39
Texas	24,987	22,713	47,700
Virginia	97,654	33,928	131,582
	803,052	215,968	1,019,020

Too hot in the South, and too unhealthy there—white men "can't stand it"—negroes only can endure the heat of Southern climes! How often are our ears insulted with such wickedly false assertions as these! In what degree of latitude—pray tell us—in what degree of latitude do the rays of the sun become too calorific for white men? Certainly in no part of the United States, for in the extreme South we find a very large number of non-slaveholding whites over the age of fifteen, who derive their entire support from manual labor in the open fields. The sun, that bugbear of slaveholding demagogues, shone on more than one million of free white laborers—mostly agriculturists—in the slave States in 1850, exclusive of those engaged in commerce, trade, manufactures, the mechanic arts, and mining. Yet, notwithstanding all these instances of exposure to his wrath, we have had no intelligence whatever of a single case of *coup de so-leil*. Alabama is not too hot; sixty-seven thousand white sons of toil till her soil. Mississippi is not too hot; fifty-five thousand free white laborers are hopeful devotees of her outdoor pursuits. Texas is not too hot; forty-seven thousand free white persons, males, over the age of fifteen, daily perform their rural vocations amidst her unsheltered air.

It is stated on good authority that, in January, 1856, native ice, three inches thick, was found in Galveston Bay; we have seen it ten inches thick in North Carolina, with the mercury in the thermometer at two degrees below zero. In January, 1857, while the snow was from three to five feet deep in many parts of North Carolina, the thermometer indicated a degree of coldness seldom exceeded in any State in the Union—thirteen degrees below zero. The truth is, instead of its being too hot in the South for white men, it is too cold for negroes; and we long to see the day arrive when the latter shall have entirely receded from their uncongenial homes in America, and given full and undivided place to the former.

Too hot in the South for white men! It is not too hot for white women. Time and again, in different counties in North Carolina, have we seen the poor white wife of the poor white husband, following him in the harvest-field from morning till night, binding up the grain as it fell from his cradle. In the immediate neighborhood from which we hail, there are not less than thirty young women, non-slaveholding whites, between the ages of fifteen and twenty-five—some of whom are so well known to us that we could call them by name—who labor in the fields every summer; two of them in particular, near neighbors to our mother, are in the habit of hiring themselves out during harvest-time, the very hottest season of the year, to bind wheat and oats—each of them keeping up with the reaper; and this for the paltry consideration of twenty-five cents per day.

That any respectable man—any man with a heart or a soul in his composition—can look upon these poor toiling white women without feeling indignant at that accursed system of slavery which has entailed on them the miseries of poverty, ignorance, and degradation, we shall not do ourself the violence to believe. If they and their husbands, and their sons and daughters, and brothers and sisters, are not righted in some of the more important particulars in which they have been wronged, the fault shall lie at other doors than our own. In their behalf, chiefly, have we written and compiled this work; and until our object shall have been accomplished, or until life shall have been extinguished, there shall be no abatement in our efforts to aid them in regaining the natural and inalienable prerogatives out of which they have been so infamously swindled. We want to see no more plowing, or hoeing, or raking, or grain-binding, by white women in the Southern States; employment in cotton-mills and other factories would be far more profitable and congenial to them, and this they shall have within a short period after slavery shall have been abolished.

Too hot in the South for white men! What is the testimony of reliable Southrons themselves? Says Cassius M. Clay, of Kentucky :—

"In the extreme South, at New Orleans, the laboring men—the stevedores and hackmen on the levee, where the heat is intensified by the proximity of the red brick buildings, are all white men, and they are in the full enjoyment of health. But how about Cotton? I am informed by a friend of mine—himself a slaveholder, and therefore good authority—that in Northwestern Texas, among the German settlements, who true to their national instincts, will not employ the labor of a slave—they produce more cotton to the acre, and of a better quality, and selling at prices from a cent to a cent and a half a pound higher than that produced by slave labor."

Says Gov. Hammond, of South Carolina:—

"The steady heat of our summers is not so prostrating as the short, but frequent and sudden, bursts of Northern summers."

In an extract which may be found in our second chapter, and to which we respectfully refer the reader, it will be seen that this same South Carolinian, speaking of "not less than fifty thousand" non-slaveholding whites, says—"most of these now follow agricultural pursuits."

Says Dr. Cartwright of New Orleans :—

"Here in New Orleans, the larger part of the drudgery—work requiring exposure to the sun, as railroad-making, street-paving, dray-driving, ditching and building, is performed by white people."

To the statistical tables which show the number of deaths in the free and in the slave States in 1850, we would direct special attention. Those persons, particularly the propogandists of negro slavery, who, heretofore, have been so dreadfully exercised on account of what they have been pleased to term "the insalubrity of Southern climes," will there find something to allay their fearful apprehensions. A critical examination of said tables will disclose the fact that, in proportion to population, deaths occur more frequently in Massachusetts than in any Southern State except Louisiana; more frequently in New York than in any of the Southern States, except Maryland, Missouri, Kentucky, Louisiana, and Texas; more frequently in New Jersey, in Pennsylvania, and in Ohio, than in either Georgia, Florida, or Alabama. Leaving Wisconsin and Louisiana out of the account, and then comparing the bills of mortality in the remaining Northern States, with those in the remaining Southern States, we find the difference decidedly in favor of the latter; for, according to this calculation, while the ratio of deaths is as only one to 74.60 of the living population in the Southern States, it is as one to 72.39 in the Northern.

Says Dr. J. C. Nott, of Mobile:—

"Heat, moisture, animal and vegetable matter are said to be the elements which produce the diseases of the South, and yet the testimony in proof of the health of the banks of the lower portion of the Mississippi River, is too strong to be doubted,—not only the river itself but also the numerous bayous which meander through Louisiana. Here is a perfectly flat alluvial country, covering several hundred miles, interspersed with interminable lakes, lagunes and jungles, and still we are informed by Dr. Cartwright, one of the most acute observers of the day, that this country is exempt from miasmatic disorders, and is extremely healthy. His assertion has been confirmed to me by hundreds of witnesses, and we know from our own observation, that the population present a robust and healthy appearance."

But the best part is yet to come. In spite of all the blatant assertions of the oligarchy, that the climate of the South was arranged expressly for the negroes, and that the negroes were created expressly to inhabit it as the healthful servitors of other men, a carefully kept register of all the deaths that occurred in Charleston, South Carolina, for the space of six years, shows that, even in that locality which is generally regarded as so unhealthy, the annual mortality was much greater among the blacks, in proportion to population, than among the whites. Dr. Nott himself shall state the facts. He says :—

"The average mortality for the last six years in Charleston for all ages is 1 in 51, including all classes. Blacks alone 1 in 44; whites alone, 1 in 58—a very remarkable result, certainly. This mortality is perhaps not an unfair test, as the population during the last six years has been undisturbed by emigration and acclimated in a greater proportion than at any former period."

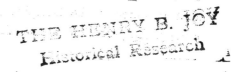

Numerous other authorities might be cited in proof of the general healthiness of the climate south of Mason and Dixon's line. Of 127 remarkable cases of American longevity, published in a recent edition of Blake's Biographical Dictionary, 68 deceased centenarians are credited to the Southern States, and 59 to the Northern—the list being headed with Betsey Trantham, of Tennessee—a white woman, who died in 1834, at the extraordinarily advanced age of 154 years

TABLE NO. LVII.

NATIVES OF THE SLAVE STATES IN THE FREE STATES, AND NATIVES OF THE FREE STATES IN THE SLAVE STATES.—1850.

States.	Natives of the Slave States.	States.	Natives of the Free States.
California..........	24,055	Alabama..........	4,947
Connecticut..........	1,390	Arkansas..........	7,965
Illinois..........	144,809	Delaware..........	6,996
Indiana..........	176,581	Florida..........	1,718
Iowa..........	31,392	Georgia..........	4,249
Maine..........	458	Kentucky..........	31,340
Massachusetts.....	2,980	Louisiana..........	14,567
Michigan..........	3,634	Maryland..........	23,815
New-Hampshire.....	215	Mississippi..........	4,517
New-Jersey..........	4,110	Missouri..........	55,664
New-York..........	12,625	North Carolina.....	2,167
Ohio..........	152,319	South Carolina.....	2,427
Pennsylvania..........	47,180	Tennesee..........	6,571
Rhode Island......	982	Texas..........	9,982
Vermont..........	140	Virginia..........	28,999
Wisconsin..........	6,353		
	609,223		205,924

This last table, compiled from the 116th page of the Compendium of the Seventh Census, shows, in a most lucid and startling manner, how negroes, slavery and slaveholders are driving the native non-slaveholding whites away from their homes, and keeping at a distance other decent people. From the South the tide of emigration still flows in a westerly and north-westerly direction, and it will continue to do so until slavery is abolished. The following remarks, which we extract from an editorial article that appeared in the Memphis (Tenn.) *Bulletin* near the close of the year 1856, are worth considering in this connection :—

" We have never before observed so large a number of immigrants going westward as are crossing the river at this point daily, the two ferry boats—sometimes three—going crowded from early morn until the boats cease making their trips at night. It is no uncommon sight to see from twenty to forty wagons encamped on the bluff for the night, notwithstanding there has been a steady stream going across the river all day, and yet the cry is, still they come."

About the same time the Cassville (Geo.) *Standard* spoke with surprise of the multitude of emigrants crowding the streets of that town bound for the far West.

Prof. B. S. Hedrick, late of Chapel Hill, North Carolina, says:—

"Of my neighbors, friends and kindred, nearly one-half have left the State since I was old enough to remember. Many is the time I have stood by the loaded emigrant wagon, and given the parting hand to those whose faces I was never to look upon again. They were going to seek homes in the free West, knowing, as they did, that free and slave labor could not both exist and prosper in the same community. If any one thinks that I speak without knowledge, let him refer to the last census. He will there find that in 1850 there were fifty-eight thousand native North Carolinians living in the free States of the West—thirty-three-thousand in Indiana alone. There were, at the same time, one hundred and eighty thousand Virginians living in the free States. Now, if these people were so much in love with the 'institution,' why did they not remain where they could enjoy its blessings?

"From my knowledge of the people of North Carolina, I believe that the majority of them who will go to Kansas during the next five years, would prefer that it should be a free State. I am sure that if I were to go there I should vote to exclude slavery."

For daring to have political opinions of his own, and because he did not deem it his duty to conceal the fact that he loved liberty better than slavery, the gallant author of the extract above quoted was peremptorily dismissed from his post of analytical and agricultural chemist in the University of North Carolina, ignominiously subjected to the indignities of a mob, and then savagely driven beyond the borders of his native State. His villainous persecutors, if not called to settle their accounts in another world within the next ten years, will probably survive to repent of the enormity of their pro-slavery folly.

TABLE NO. LVIII.

VALUE OF THE SLAVES AT $400 PER HEAD.—1850.*

States.	Value of the Slaves at $400 per head.	Val. of Real and Per. Estate, less the val. of slaves at $400 p. head.
Alabama	$137,137.600	$81,066,732
Arkansas	18,840,000	21,001,025
Delaware	916,000	17,939,863
Florida	15,724.000	7,474,734
Georgia	152.672.800	182,752,914
Kentucky	84,392,400	217,236.056
Louisiana	97,923,600	136,075,164
Maryland	36,147,200	183.070.164
Mississippi	123,951,200	105,000,000
Missouri	34,968,800	102 278,907
North Carolina	115,419,200	111,381.272
South Carolina	153,993,600	134,264.094
Tennessee	95,783.600	111,671,104
Texas	23.264,400	32.097,940
Virginia	189,011.200	202,634,638
	$1,280,145,600	$1,655,945,137

TABLES 34 and 35 show that, on account of the pitiable poverty and ignorance of slavery, the mails were transported throughout the Southern States, during the year

* It is intended that this Table shall be considered in connection with Tables XX and XXI, on page 80.

1855, at an extra cost to the General Government of more than six hundred thousand dollars! In the free States, postages were received to the amount of more than two millions of dollars over and above the cost of transportation.

To Dr. G. Bailey, editor of the *National Era*, Washington city, D. C., we are indebted for the following useful and interesting statistics, to which some of our readers will doubtless have frequent occasion to refer :–

PRESIDENTS OF THE UNITED STATES.

Appointed.	
March 4, 1789 " 3, 1797	George Washington, *Virginia.*
March 4, 1797 " 3, 1801	John Adams, *Massachusetts.*
March 4, 1801 " 3, 1809	Thomas Jefferson, *Virginia.*
March 4, 1809 " 3, 1817	James Madison, *Virginia.*
March 4, 1817 " 3, 1825	James Monroe, *Virginia.*
March 4, 1825 " 3, 1829	John Q. Adams, *Massachusetts.*
March 4, 1829 " 3, 1837	Andrew Jackson, *Tennessee.*
March 4, 1837 " 3, 1841	Martin Van Buren, *New York.*
March 4, 1841 " 3, 1845	William H. Harrison, *Ohio.*
March 4, 1845 " 3, 1849	James K. Polk, *Tennessee.*
March 4, 1849 " 3, 1853	Zachary Taylor, *Louisiana.*
March 4, 1853 " 3, 1857	Franklin Pierce, *New Hampshire.*
March 4, 1857 " 3, 1861	James Buchanan, *Pennsylvania.*

At the close of the term for which Mr. Buchanan is elected,

it will have been seventy-two years since the organization of the present Government.

In that period, there have been eighteen elections for President, the candidates chosen in twelve of them being Southern men and slaveholders, in six of them Northern men and non-slaveholders.

No Northern man has ever been re-elected, but five Southern men have been thus honored.

Gen. Harrison, of Ohio, died one month after his inauguration, Gen. Taylor, of Louisiana, about four months after his inauguration. In the former case, John Tyler, of Virginia, became acting President, in the latter, Millard Fillmore, of New York.

Of the seventy-two years, closing with Mr. Buchanan's term, should he live it out, Southern men and slaveholders have occupied the Presidential chair forty-eight years and three months, or a little more than two-thirds of the time.

THE SUPREME COURT.

The judicial districts are organized so as to give five judges to the slave States, and four to the free, although the population, wealth, and business of the latter are far in advance of those of the former. The arrangement affords, however, an excuse for constituting the Supreme Court, with a majority of judges from the slaveholding States.

MEMBERS.

Chief Justice—R. B. Taney, *Maryland.*
Associate Justice—J. M. Wayne, *Georgia.*
" " John Catron, *Tennessee.*
" " P. V. Daniel, *Virginia.*
" " John A. Campbell. *Alabama.*
" " John McLean, *Ohio.*
" " S. Nelson, *New York.*
" " R. C. Grier, *Pennsylvania.*
" " B. R. Curtis, *Massachusetts.*
Reporter—B. C. Howard, *Maryland.*
Clerk—W T. Carroll, *D. C.*

SECRETARIES OF STATE.

The highest office in the Cabinet is that of Secretary of State, who has under his charge the foreign relations of the country. Since the year 1789, there have been twenty-two appointments to the office—fourteen from slave States, eight from free. Or, counting by years, the post has been filled by Southern men and slaveholders very nearly forty years out of sixty-seven, as follows:

Appointed.

Sept. 26, 1789, Thomas Jefferson, *Virginia.*
Jan. 2, 1794, E. Randolph. *Virginia.*
Dec. 10, 1795, T. Pickering, *Massachusetts.*
May 13, 1800, J. Marshall, *Virginia.*
March 5, 1801, James Madison, *Virginia.*
March 6, 1809, R. Smith, *Maryland.*
April 2, 1811, James Monroe, *Virginia.*
Feb. 28, 1815, " " "
March 5, 1815, J. Q. Adams, *Massachusetts.*
March 7, 1825, Henry Clay, *Kentucky.*
March 6, 1829, Martin Van Buren, *New York.*
May 24, 1831, E. Livingston, *Louisiana.*
May 29, 1833, Louis McLane, *Delaware.*
June 27, 1834, J. Forsyth, *Georgia.*
March 5, 1841, Daniel Webster, *Massachusetts.*
July 24, 1843, A. P. Upshur, *Virginia.*
March 6, 1844, J. C. Calhoun, *South Carolina.*
March 5, 1845, James Buchanan, *Pennsylvania.*
March 7, 1849, J. M. Clayton, *Delaware.*
July 20, 1850, Daniel Webster, *Massachusetts.*
Dec. 9, 1851, E. Everett, *Massachusetts.*
March 5, 1853 W. L. Marcy, *New York.*

PRESIDENTS PRO TEM. OF THE SENATE.

Since the year 1809, every President *pro tem.* of the Senate of the United States has been a Southern man and slaveholder, with the exception of Samuel L. Southard, of New Jersey, who held the office for a very short time, and Mr. Bright, of Indiana, who has held it for one or two sessions, we believe, having been elected, however, as a known adherent of the slave interest, be. eved to be interested in slave "property."

SPEAKERS OF THE HOUSE OF REPRESENTATIVES.

April, 1789 March 3, 1791	F. A. Muhlenberg, *Penn.*
Oct. 24. 1791 March 2, 1793	J. Trumbull, *Connecticut.*
Dec. 2, 1793 March 3. 1795	F. A. Muhlenberg, *Penn.*
Dec. 7, 1795 March 3, 1797	Jonathan Dayton, *New Jersey.*
May 15, 1797 March 3, 1799	" " "
Dec. 2, 1799 March 3, 1801	Theodore Sedgwick, *Mass.*
Dec. 7, 1801 March 3, 1807	Nathaniel Macon, *N. Car.*
Oct. 26, 1807 March 3, 1811	J. B. Varnum, *Massachusetts.*
March 4, 1811 Jan. 19, 1814	Henry Clay, *Kentucky.*
Jan. 19, 1814 March 2, 1815	Langdon Cheves, *S. Car.*
Dec. 4, 1815 Nov. 13, 1820	Henry Clay, *Kentucky.*
Nov. 15, 1820 March 3, 1821	J. W. Taylor, *New-York.*
Dec. 3, 1821 March 3, 1823	P. B. Barbour, *Virginia.*
Dec. 1, 1823 March 3, 1825	Henry Clay, *Kentucky.*
Dec. 5, 1825 March 3, 1827	J. W. Taylor, *New-York.*
Dec. 3, 1827 June 2, 1834	A. Stevenson, *Virginia.*
June 2, 1834 March 3, 1835	John Bell, *Tennessee.*
Dec. 7, 1835 March 3, 1839	James K. Polk, *Tennessee.*
Dec. 16, 1839 March 3, 1841	R. M. T. Hunter, *Virginia.*
May 31, 1841 March 3, 1843	John White. *Tennessee.*

Dec. 4, 1843 March 3, 1845	J. W. Jones, *Virginia.*
Dec. 1, 1845 March 3, 1847	J. W. Davis, *Indiana.*
Dec. 6, 1847 March 3, 1849	R. C. Winthrop, *Mass.*
Dec. 22, 1849 March 3, 1851	Howell Cobb, *Georgia.*
Dec. 1, 1851 March 3, 1853	Linn Boyd, *Kentucky.*
Dec. 1, 1853 March 3, 1855	" " "
Feb. 28, 1856 March 3, 1857	Nathaniel P. Banks, *Mass.*

POSTMASTERS-GENERAL.

Appointed—

Sept. 26, 1789, S. Osgood, *Massachusetts.*
Aug. 12, 1791, T. Pickering, *Massachusetts.*
Feb. 25, 1795, J. Habersham, *Georgia.*
Nov. 28, 1801, G. Granger, *Connecticut.*
March 17, 1814, R. J. Meigs, *Ohio.*
June 25, 1823, John McLean, *Ohio.*
March 9, 1829, W. T. Barry, *Kentucky.*
May 1, 1835, A. Kendall, *Kentucky.*
May 18, 1840, J. M. Niles, *Connecticut.*
March 6, 1841, F. Granger, *New York.*
Sept. 13, 1841, C. A. Wickliffe, *Kentucky.*
March 5, 1845, C. Johnson, *Tennessee.*
March 7, 1849, J. Collamer, *Vermont.*
July 20, 1850, N. K. Hall, *New York.*
Aug. 31, 1852, S. D. Hubbard, *Connecticut.*
March 5, 1853, J. Campbell, *Pennsylvania.*

Sectionalism does not seem to have had much to do with this Department or with that of the Interior, created in 1848-'49.

SECRETARIES OF THE INTERIOR.

Appointed—

March 7, 1849, T. Ewing, *Ohio.*
July 20, 1850, J. A. Pearce, *Maryland.*
Aug. 15, 1850, T. M. T. McKennon, *Pennsylvania.*
Sept. 12, 1850, A. H. H. Stuart, *Virginia.*
March 5, 1853, R. McClelland, *Michigan.*

ATTORNEYS-GENERAL.

Appointed—

Sept. 26, 1789, E. Randolph, *Virginia.*
June 27, 1794, W. Bradford, *Pennsylvania.*
Dec. 10, 1795, C. Lee, *Virginia.*
Feb. 20, 1801, T. Parsons, *Massachusetts.*
March 5, 1800, L. Lincoln, *Massachusetts.*
March 2, 1805, R. Smith, *Maryland.*
Dec. 23, 1805, J. Breckinridge, *Kentucky.*
Jan. 20, 1807, C. A. Rodney, *Pennsylvania.*
Dec. 11, 1811, W. Pinkney, *Maryland.*
Feb. 10, 1814, R. Rush, *Pennsylvania.*
Nov. 13, 1817, W. Wirt, *Virginia.*
March 9, 1829, J. McPherson Berrien, *Georgia.*
July 20, 1831, Roger B. Taney, *Maryland.*
Nov. 15, 1833, B. F. Butler, *New York.*
July 7, 1838, F. Grundy, *Tennessee.*
Jan. 10, 1840, H. D. Gilpin, *Pennsylvania.*
March 5, 1841, J. J. Crittenden, *Kentucky.*
Sept. 13, 1841, H. S. Legare, *South Carolina.*
July 1, 1843, John Nelson, *Maryland.*
March 5, 1845, J. Y. Mason, *Virginia.*
Oct. 17, 1846, N. Clifford, *Maine.*
June 21, 1848, Isaac Toucey, *Connecticut.*
March 7, 1849, R. Johnson, *Maryland.*
July 20, 1850, J. J. Crittenden, *Kentucky.*
March 5 1853, C. Cushing, *Massachusetts.*

SECRETARIES OF THE TREASURY.

The post of Secretary of the Treasury, although one of great importance, requires financial abilities of a high order, which are more frequently found in the North than in the South, and affords little opportunity for influencing general politics, or the questions springing out of Slavery. We need not therefore be surprised to learn that Northern men have been allowed to discharge its duties some forty-eight years out of sixty-seven, as follows:

Appointed—

Sept. 11, 1789, A. Hamilton, *New York.*
Feb. 3, 1795, O. Wolcott, *Connecticut.*
Dec. 31, 1800, S. Dexter, *Massachusetts.*
May 14, 1801, A. Gallatin, *Pennsylvania.*
Feb. 9, 1814, G. W. Campbell, *Tennessee.*
Oct. 6, 1814, A. J. Dallas, *Pennsylvvania.*
Oct. 22, 1816, W. H. Crawford, *Georgia.*
March 7, 1825, R. Rush, *Pennsylvania.*
March 6, 1829, S. D. Ingham, *Pennsylvania.*
Aug. 8, 1831, L. McLane, *Delaware.*
May 29, 1833, W. J. Duane, *Pennsylvania.*
Sept. 23, 1833, Roger B. Taney, *Maryland.*
June 27, 1834, L. Woodbury, *New Hampshire.*
March 5, 1841, Thomas Ewing, *Ohio.*
Sept. 13, 1841, W. Forward, *Pennsylvania.*
March 3, 1843, J. C. Spencer, *New York.*
June 15, 1844, G. M. Bibb, *Kentucky.*
March 5, 1845, R. J. Walker, *Mississippi.*
March 7, 1849, W. M. Meredith, *Pennsylvania.*
June 20, 1850, Thomas Corwin, *Ohio.*
March 5, 1843, James Guthrie, *Kentucky.*

SECRETARIES OF WAR AND THE NAVY.

The Slaveholders since March 8th, 1841, a period of nearly sixteen years, have taken almost exclusive supervision of the Navy, Northern men having occupied the Secretaryship only two years. Nor has any Northern man been Secretary of War since 1849. Considering that nearly all the shipping belongs to the free States, which also supply the seamen, it does seem remarkable that Slaveholders should have monopolized for the last sixteen years the control of the Navy.

SECRETARIES OF WAR.

Appointed—

Sept. 12, 1789, Henry Knox, *Massachusetts.*
Jan. 2, 1795, T. Pickering, *Massachusetts.*
Jan. 27, 1796, J. McHenry, *Maryland.*
May 7, 1800, J. Marshall, *Virginia.*
May 13, 1800, S. Dexter, *Massachusetts.*
Feb. 3, 1801, R. Griswold, *Connecticut.*
March 5, 1801, H. Dearborn, *Massachusetts.*
March 7, 1802, W. Eustis, *Massachusetts.*
Jan. 13, 1813, J. Armstrong, *New York.*
Sept. 27, 1814, James Monroe, *Virginia.*
March 3, 1815, W. H. Crawford, *Georgia.*
April 7, 1817, G. Graham, *Virginia.*
March 5, 1817, J. Shelby, *Kentucky.*
Oct. 8, 1817, J. C. Calhoun, *South Carolina*
March 7, 1825, J. Barbour, *Virginia.*
May 26, 1828, P. B. Porter, *Pennsylvania.*
March 9, 1829, J. H. Eaton, *Tennessee.*
Aug. 1, 1831, Lewis Cass, *Ohio.*
March 3, 1837, B. F. Butler, *New York.*
March 7, 1837, J. R. Poinsett, *South Carolina*
March 5, 1841, James Bell, *Tennessee.*
Sept. 13, 1841, John McLean, *Ohio.*
Oct. 12, 1841, J. C. Spencer, *New York.*
March 8, 1843, J. W. Porter, *Pennsylvania.*
Feb. 15, 1844, W. Wilkins, *Pennsylvania.*
March 5, 1845, William L. Marcy, *New York*
March 7, 1849, G. W. Crawford, *Georgia.*
July 20, 1850, E. Bates, *Missouri.*
Aug. 15, 1850, C. M. Conrad, *Louisiana.*
March 5, '853, Jefferson Davis *Mississippi.*

SECRETARIES OF THE NAVY.

Appointed—

May 3, 1798, G. Cabot, *Massachusetts.*
May 21, 1798, B. Stoddart, *Massachusetts.*
July 15, 1801, R. Smith, *Maryland.*
May 3, 1805, J. Crowninshield, *Massachusetts.*
March 7, 1809, P. Hamilton, *South Carolina.*
Jan. 12, 1813, W. Jones, *Pennsylvania.*
Dec. 17, 1814, B. W. Crowninshield, *Massachusetts.*
Nov. 9, 1818, Smith Thompson, *New York.*
Sept. 1, 1823, John Rogers, *Massachusetts.*
Sept. 16, 1823, S. L. Southard, *New Jersey.*
March 9, 1819, John Branch, *North Carolina.*
May 23, 1831, L. Woodbury, *New Hampshire.*
June 30, 1834, M. Dickerson, *New Jersey.*
June 20, 1838, J. K. Paulding, *New York.*
March 5, 1841, G. F. Badger, *North Carolina.*
Sept. 13, 1841, A. P. Upshur, *Virginia.*
July 24, 1843, D. Henshaw, *Massachusetts.*
Feb. 12, 1844, T. W. Gilmer, *Virginia.*
March 14, 1844, James Y. Mason, *Virginia.*
March 10, 1845, G. Bancroft, *Massachusetts.*
Sept. 9, 1846, James Y. Mason, *Virginia.*
March 7, 1849, W. B. Preston, *Virginia.*
July 20, 1850, W. A. Graham, *N. Carolina.*
July 22, 1852, J. P. Kennedy, *Maryland.*
March 3, 1853, J. C. Dobbin, *N. Carolina.*

RECAPITULATION.

Presidency.—Southern men and Slaveholders, 48 years 3 months; Northern men, 23 years 9 months.

Pro. Tem. Presidency of the Senate.—Since 1809, held by Southern men and Slaveholders, except for three or four sessions by Northern men.

Speakership of the House.—Filled by Southern men and Slaveholders forty-three years, Northern men, twenty-five.

Supreme Court.—A majority of the Judges, including Chief Justice, Southern men and Slaveholders.

Secretaryship of State.—Filled by Southern men and Slaveholders forty years, Northern, twenty-seven.

Attorney Generalship.—Filled by Southern men and Slaveholders forty-two years, Northern men, twenty-five.

War and Navy.—Secretaryship of the Navy, Southern men and Slaveholders, the last sixteen years, with an interval of two years.

William Henry Hurlbut, of South Carolina, a gentleman of enviable literary attainments, and one from whom we may expect a continuation of good service in the eminently holy crusade now going on against slavery and the devil, furnished not long since, to the *Edinburgh Review*, in the course of a long and highly interesting article, the following summary of oligarchal usurpations—showing that shaveholders have occupied the principal posts of the Government nearly two-thirds of the time :—

Presidents - - - - - -	11 out of 16
Judges of the Supreme Court - -	17 out of 28
Attorneys-General - - - - -	14 out of 19
Presidents of the Senate - - -	61 out of 77
Speakers of the House - - -	21 out of 33
Foreign Ministers - - - -	80 out of 134

As a matter of general interest, and as showing that, while there have been but 11 non-slaveholders directly before the people as candidates for the Presidency, there have been *at least* 16 slaveholders who were willing to serve their country in the capacity of chief magistrate, the following table may be here introduced :—

RESULT OF THE PRESIDENTIAL ELECTIONS IN THE UNITED STATES FROM 7796 TO 1856.

Year.	Name of Candidate.	Elect'l vote.
1796	John Adams	71
	Thomas Jefferson	68
1800	Thomas Jefferson	73
	John Adams	64
1804	Thomas Jefferson	162
	Charles C. Pinckney	14
1808	James Madison	128
	Charles C. Pinckney	45
1812	James Madison	122
	De Witt Clinton	89
1816	James Monroe	183
	Rufus King	34
1820	James Monroe	218
	No opposition but one vote	
1824	Andrew Jackson*	99
	John Q. Adams	84
	W. H. Crawford	41
	Henry Clay	37
1828	Andrew Jackson	178
	John Q. Adams	83
1832	Andrew Jackson	219
	Henry Clay	49
	John Floyd	11
	William Wirt	7
1836	Martin Van Buren	170
	William H. Harrison	73
	Hugh L. White	26
	Willie P. Mangum	11
	Daniel Webster	14
1840	William H. Harrison	234
	Martin Van Buren	60
1844	James K. Polk	170
	Henry Clay	105
1848	Zachary Taylor	163
	Lewis Cass	127
1852	Franklin Pierce	254
	General Winfield Scott	42
1856	James Buchanan	174
	John C. Fremont	114
	Millard Fillmore	8

* No choice by the people; John Q. Adams elected by the House of Representatives.

AID FOR KANSAS.

As a sort of accompaniment to tables, 50, 51, 52 and 53, we will here introduce a few items which will more fully illustrate the liberality of Freedom and the niggardliness of Slavery.

From an editorial article that appeared in the Richmond (Va.,) *Dispatch,* in July, 1856, bewailing the close-fistedness of slavery, we make the following extract :—

"Gerrit Smith, the Abolitionist, has just pledged himself to give $1,500 a month for the next twelve months to aid in establishing Freedom in Kansas. He gave, but a short time since, at the Kansas relief meeting in Albany, $3,000. Prior to that, he had sent about $1,000 to the Boston Emigrant Committee. Out of his own funds, he subsequently equipped a Madison county company, of one hundred picked men, and paid their expenses to Kansas. At Syracuse he subscribed $10,000 for Abolition purposes, so that his entire contributions amount to at least $40,000."

An Eastern paper says :—

"The sum of $500 was contributed at a meeting at New Bedford on Monday evening, to make Kansas free. The following sums have been contributed for the same purpose: $2,000 in Taunton: $600 in Raynham: $800 in Clinton: $300 in Danbury, Ct. In Wisconsin, $2,500 at Janesville: $500 at Dalton: $500 at the Women's Aid Meeting in Chicago: $2,000 in Rockford, Ill."

A telegraphic dispatch, dated Boston, January 2, 1857, informs us that—

"The Secretary of the Kansas Aid Committee acknowledges the receipt of $42,678."

Exclusive of the amounts above, the readers of the New-

York *Tribune* have contributed about $30,000 for the purpose of securing Kansas to Freedom; and, with the same object in view, other individuals and societies have, from time to time, made large contributions, of which we have failed to keep a memorandum. The legislature of Vermont has appropriated $20,000; and other free State legislatures are prepared to appropriate millions, if necessary. Free men have determined that Kansas shall be free, and free it soon shall be, and ever so remain. Harmoniously the work proceeds.

Now let us see how slavery has rewarded the poor, ignorant, deluded, and degraded mortals—swaggering lickspittles—who have labored so hard to gain for it "a local habitation and a name" in the disputed territory. One D. B. Atchison, Chairman of the Executive Committee of Border Ruffians, shall tell us all about it. Over date of October 13th, 1856, he says:

"Up to this moment, from all the States except Missouri, we have only received the following sums, and through the following persons:—

A. W. Jones, Houston, Miss., ...	$152
H. D. Clayton, Eufala, Ala., ...	500
Capt. Deedrick, South Carolina, ...	500
	$1,152."

On this subject, further comment is unnecessary.

Numerous other contrasts, equally disproportionate, might be drawn between the vigor and munificence of freedom and the impotence and stinginess of slavery. We will, however, in addition to the above, advert to only a single instance. During the latter part of the summer of

1855, the citizens of the niggervilles of Norfolk and Portsmouth, in Virginia, were sorely plagued with yellow fever. Many of them fell victims to the disease, and most of those who survived, and who were not too unwell to travel, left their homes, horror-stricken and dejected. To the horror of mankind in general, and to the glory of freemen in particular, contributions in money, provisions, clothing, and other valuable supplies, poured in from all parts of the country, for the relief of the sufferers. Portsmouth alone, according to the report of her relief association, received $42,547 in cash from the free States, and only $12,182 in cash from all the slave States, exclusive of Virginia, within whose borders the malady prevailed. Including Virginia, the sum total of all the slave State contributions amounted to only $33,398. Well did the Richmond *Examiner* remark at the time—"we fear that generosity of Virginians is but a figure of speech." Slavery! thy name is shame!

IN CONNECTION with tables 44 and 45 on page 292, it will be well to examine the following statistics of Congressional representation, which we transcribe from Reynold's Political Map of the United States:—

UNITED STATES SENATE.

16 free States, with a white population of 13,238,670, have 32 Senators.

15 slave States, with a white population of 6,186,477, have 30 Senators.

So that 413,708 free men of the North enjoy but the same political privileges in the U. S. Senate as is given to 206,215 slave propagandists.

HOUSE OF REPRESENTATIVES.

The free States have a total of 144 members.

The slave States have a total of 90 members.

One free State Representative represents 91,935 white men and women.

One slave State Representative represents 68,725 white men and women.

Slave Representation gives to slavery an advantage over freedom of 30 votes in the House of Representatives.

CUSTOM-HOUSE RECEIPTS.—1854.

Free States,..	$60,010,489
Slave States,..	5,136,969
Balance in favor of the Free States,....................	$54,873,520

A contrast quite distinguishable !

THAT THE apologists of slavery cannot excuse the shame and the shabbiness of themselves and their country, as we have frequently heard them attempt to do, by falsely asserting that the North has enjoyed over the South the advantages of priority of settlement, will fully appear from the following table :—

FREE STATES.

1614. New-York first settled by the Dutch.
1620. Massachusetts settled by the Puritans.
1623. New-Hampshire settled by the Puritans.
1624. New-Jersey settled by the Dutch.
1635. Connecticut settled by the Puritans.
1636. Rhode Island settled by Roger Williams.
1682. Pennsylvania settled by William Penn.
1791. Vermont admitted into the Union.
1802. Ohio admitted into the Union.
1816. Indiana admitted into the Union.

1818. Illinois admitted into the Union.
1820. Maine admitted into the Union.
1836. Michigan admitted into the Union.
1846. Iowa admitted into the Union.
1848. Wisconsin admitted into the Union.
1850. California admitted into the Union.

SLAVE STATES.

1607. Virginia first settled by the English.
1627. Delaware settled by the Swedes and Fins.
1635. Maryland settled by Irish Catholics.
1650. North Carolina settled by the English.
1670. South Carolina settled by the Huguenots.
1733. Georgia settled by Gen. Oglethorpe.
1782. Kentucky admitted into the Union.
1796. Tennessee admitted into the Union.
1811. Louisiana admitted into the Union.
1817. Mississippi admitted into the Union.
1819. Alabama admitted into the Union.
1821. Missouri admitted into the Union.
1836. Arkansas admitted into the Union.
1845. Florida admitted into the Union.
1846. Texas admitted into the Union.

In the course of an exceedingly interesting article on the early settlements in America, R. K. Browne, formerly editor and proprietor of the San Francisco *Evening Journal*, says :—

"Many people seem to think that the Pilgrim Fathers were the first who settled upon our shores, and therefore that they ought to be entitled, in a particular manner, to our remembrance and esteem.

This is not the case, and we herewith present to our readers a list of settlements made in the present United States, prior to that of Plymouth :

1564. A Colony of French Protestants under Ribaul. settled in Florida.

1565. St. Augustine* founded by Pedro Melendez.

1584. Sir Walter Raleigh obtains a patent and sends two vessels to the American coast, which receives the name of Virginia.

1607. The first effectual settlement made at Jamestown, Va., by the London Company.

1614. A fort erected by the Dutch upon the site of New-York.

1615. Fort Orange built near the site of Albany, N. Y.

1619. The first General Assembly called in Virginia.

1620. The Pilgrims land on Plymouth Rock."

FREEDOM AND SLAVERY AT THE FAIR.

WHAT FREEDOM DID.

At an Agricultural Fair held at Watertown, in the State of New-York, on the 2d day of October, 1856, two hundred and twenty premiums, ranging from three to fifty dollars each, were awarded to successful competitors—the aggregate amount of said premiums being $2,396, or an average of $10.89 each. From the proceedings of the Awarding Committee we make the following extracts :—

	Best Horse Colt,	George Parish, -	$25.00
	Best Filly,	J. Staplin, - - -	20.00
	Best Brood Mare,	A. Blunt, - - -	25.00
	Best Bull,	Wm. Johnson, -	25.00
	Best Heifer,	A. M. Rogers, -	20.00
	Best Cow,	C. Baker, - - -	25.00
	Best Stall-fed Beef,	J. W. Taylor, -	10.00
	Best sample Wheat,	Wm. Ottley, - -	5.00
	Best sample Flaxseed,	H. Weir, - - -	3.00
	Best sample Timothy Seed,	E. S. Hayward -	3.00
(Highest)	Best Team of Oxen,	Hiram Converse,	50.00
(Lowest)	Best sample Sweet Corn,	L. Marshall, - -	3.00

Aggregate amount of twelve premiums, - - - - $214.00

An average of $17.83 each.

* The oldest town in the United States.

WHAT SLAVERY DID.

At the Rowan County Agricultural Fair, held at Mineral Springs, in North Carolina, on the 13th day of November, 1856, thirty premiums, ranging from twenty-five cents to two dollars each, were awarded to successful competitors —the aggregate amount of said premiums being $42, or an average of $1.40 each. From the proceedings of the Awarding Committee we make the following extracts :—

	Best Horse Colt,	T. A. Burke, - -	$2.0C
	Best Filly,	James Cowan, - -	2.00
	Best Brood Mare	M. W. Goodman, -	2.00
	Best Bull,	J. F. McCorkle, - -	2.00
	Best Heifer,	J. F. McCorkle, -	2.00
	Best Cow,	T. A. Burke, - -	2.00
	Best Stall-fed Beef,	S. D. Rankin, - -	1.00
	Best Sample Wheat,	M. W. Goodman, -	50
	Best lot Beets,	J. J. Summerell, -	25
	Best lot Turnips,	Thomas Barber, - -	25
(Highest)	Best pair Match Horses,	R. W. Griffith, - -	2.00
(Lowest)	Best lot Cabbage,	Thomas Hyde - -	25
	Aggregate amount of twelve premiums,		$16.25
	An average of $1.36 each.		

Besides the two hundred and twenty premiums, amounting in the aggregate to $2,396, freedom granted several diplomas and silver medals ; besides the thirty premiums amounting in the aggregate to $42, slavery granted none —nothing. While examining these figures, it should be recollected that agriculture is the peculiar province of the slave States. If commerce or manufactures had been the subject of the fair, the result might have shown even a greater disproportion in favor of freedom, and yet there would have been some excuse for slavery, for it makes no pretensions to either the one or the other; but as agriculture was the subject, slavery can have no excuse whatever, but must bear all the shame of its niggardly and revolting impotence; this it must do for the reason that agriculture is its special and almost only pursuit.

THE REPORTS of the Comptrollers of the States of New York and North Carolina, for the year 1856, are now before us. From each report we have gleaned a single item, which, when compared, the one with the other, speaks volumes in favor of freedom and against slavery. We refer to the average value per acre of lands in the two States; let slavocrats read, reflect, and repent.

In 1856, there were assessed for taxation in the State of

NEW YORK,

Acres of land	30,080,000
Valued at	$1,112,133,136
Average value per acre . .	$36.97

In 1856, there were assessed for taxation in the State of

NORTH CAROLINA,

Acres of land	32,450,560
Valued at	$98,800,636
Average value per acre . .	$3.06

It is difficult for us to make any remarks on the official facts above. Our indignation is struck almost dumb at this astounding and revolting display of the awful wreck that slavery is leaving behind it in the South. We will however, go into a calculation for the purpose of ascer taining as nearly as possible, in this one particular, how much North Carolina has lost by the retention of slavery. As we have already seen, the average value per acre of land in the State of New York is $36.97 ; in North Carolina it is only $3.06 ; why is it so much less, or even any less, in the latter than in the former? The answer is, *slavery.* In soil, in climate, in minerals, in water-power for manufactural purposes, and in area of territory, North Carolina has the advantage of New York, and, with the exception of slavery, no plausible reason can possibly be assigned why land should not be *at least* as valuable in the valley of the Yadkin as it is along the banks of the Genesee.

The difference between $36.97 and $3.06 is $33.91, which, multiplied by the whole number of acres of land in North Carolina, will show, in this one particular, the enormous loss that Freedom has sustained on account of Slavery in the Old North State. Thus :—

32,450,560 acres *a* $33,91....$1,100,398,489.

Let it be indelibly impressed on the mind, however, that this amount, large as it is, is only a moity of the sum that it has cost to maintain slavery in North Carolina. From time to time, hundreds upon hundreds of millions of dollars have left the State, either in search of profitable, permanent investment abroad, or in the shape of profits to Northern merchants and manufactures, who have become the moneyed aristocracy of the country by supplying to the South such articles of necessity, utility, and adornment, as would have been produced at home but for the pernicious presence of the peculiar institution.

A reward of Eleven Hundred Millions of Dollars is offered for the conversion of the lands of North Carolina into free soil. The lands themselves, desolate and impoverished under the fatal foot of slavery, offer the reward. How, then, can it be made to appear that the abolition of slavery in North Carolina, and, indeed, throughout all the Southern States—for slavery is exceedingly inimical to them all—is not demanded by every consideration of justice, prudence, and good sense? In 1850, the total value of all the slaves of the State, at the rate of four hundred dollars per head, amounted to less than one hundred and sixteen millions of dollars. Is the sum of one hundred and sixteen millions of dollars more desirable than the sum of eleven hundred millions of dollars? When a man has land for sale, does he reject thirty-six dollars per acre and take three? Non-slaveholding whites! look well to your interests! Many of you have lands; comparatively speaking, you have nothing else. Abolish slavery, and you will enhance the value of every league, your own and your neighbors', from three to thirty-six dollars per acre. Your little tract containing two hundred acres, now valued at the pitiful sum of only six hundred dollars, will then be worth seven thousand. Your children, now deprived of even the meagre advantages of common schools, will then reap the benefits of a collegiate education. Your rivers and smaller streams, now wasting their waters in idleness, will then turn the wheels of multitudinous mills. Your bays and harbors, now unknown to commerce, will then swarm with ships from every enlightened quarter of the globe. Non-slaveholding whites! look well to your interests!

Would the slaveholders of North Carolina lose anything by the abolition of slavery? Let us see. According to their own estimate, their slaves are worth, in round numbers, say, one hundred and twenty millions of dollars. There are in the State twenty-eight thousand slaveholders, owning, it may be safely assumed, an average of at least five hundred acres of land each—fourteen millions of acres in all. This number of acres, multiplied by thirty-three dollars and ninety-one cents, the difference in value between free soil and slave soil, makes the enormous sum of four hundred and seventy-four millions of dollars—showing that, by the abolition of slavery, the slaveholders themselves would realize a net profit of not less than three hundred and fifty-four millions of dollars!

Compensation to slaveholders for the negroes now in their possession! The idea is preposterous. The suggestion is criminal. The demand is unjust, wicked, monstrous, damnable. Shall we pat the bloodhounds of slavery for the sake of doing them a favor? Shall we fee the curs of slavery in order to make them rich at our expense? Shall we pay the whelps of slavery for the privilege of converting them into decent, honest, upright men? No, never! The non-slaveholders expect to gain, and will gain, something by the abolition of slavery; but slaveholders themselves will, by far, be the greater gainers; for, in proportion to population, they own much larger and more fertile tracts of land, and will, as a matter of course, receive the lion's share of the increase in the value of not only real estate, but also of other genuine property, of which they are likewise the principal owners. How ridiculously absurd, therefore, is the objection, that, if we liberate the slaves, we ruin the masters! Not long since, a gentleman in Baltimore, a native of Maryland, remarked in our presence that he was an abolitionist because he felt that it was right and proper to be one; "but," inquired he, "are there not, in some of the States, many widows and orphans who would be left in destitute circumstances, if their negroes were taken from them?" In answer to the question, we replied that slavery had already reduced thousands and tens of thousands of non-slaveholding widows and orphans to the lowest depths of poverty and ignorance, and that we did not believe one slaveholding widow and three orphans were of more, or even of as much consequence as five non-slaveholding widows and fifteen orphans. "You are right," exclaimed the gentleman, "I had not viewed the subject in that light before; I perceive you go in for the greatest good to the greatest number." Emancipate the negroes, and the ex-slaveholding widow would still retain her lands and tenements, which, in consequence of being surroundnd by the magic influences of liberty, would soon render her far more wealthy and infinitely more respectable, than she could possibly ever become while trafficking in human flesh.

The fact is, every slave in the South costs the State in which he resides at least three times as much as he, in the whole course of his life, is worth to his master. Slavery benefits no one but its immediate, individual owners, and them only in a pecuniary point of view, and at the sacrifice of the dearest rights and interests of the whole mass of non-slaveholders, white and black. Even the masters themselves, as we have already shown, would be far better off without it than with it. To all classes of society the institution is a curse; an especial curse is it to those who own it not. Non-slaveholding whites! look well to your interests!

CHAPTER IX.

COMMERCIAL CITIES—SOUTHERN COMMERCE.

Our theme is a city—a great Southern importing, exporting, and manufacturing city, to be located at some point or port on the coast of the Carolinas, Georgia or Virginia, where we can carry on active commerce, buy, sell, fabricate, receive the profits which accrue from the exchange of our own commodities, open facilities for direct communication with foreign countries, and establish all those collateral sources of wealth, utility, and adornment, which are the usual concomitants of a metropolis, and which add so very materially to the interest and importance of a nation. Without a city of this kind, the South can never develop her commercial resources nor attain to that eminent position to which those vast resources would otherwise exalt her. According to calculations based upon reasonable estimates, it is owing to the lack of a great commercial city in the South, that we are now *annually* drained of more than One Hundred and Twenty Millions of Dollars! We should, however, take into consideration the negative loss as well as the positive. Especially should we think of the influx of emigrants, of the visits of strangers and cosmopolites, of the patronage to hotels and public halls, of the profits of travel and transportation, of the emoluments of foreign and domestic trade, and of numerous other advantages which have their origin exclusively in wealthy, enterprising, and densely populated cities.

Nothing is more evident than the fact, that our people have never entertained a proper opinion of the importance of home cities. Blindly, and greatly to our own injury, we have contributed hundreds of millions of dollars towards the erection of mammoth cities at the North, while our own magnificent bays and harbors have been most shamefully disregarded and neglected. Now, instead of carrying all our money to New-York, Philadelphia, Boston, and Cincinnati, suppose we had kept it on the south side of Mason and Dixon's line—as we would have done, had it not been for slavery—and had disbursed it in the upbuilding of Norfolk, Beaufort, Charleston, or Savannah, how much richer, better, greater, would the South have been to-day! How much larger and more intelligent would have been our population. How many hundred thousand natives of the South would now be thriving at home, instead of adding to the wealth and political power of other parts of the Union. How much greater would be the number and length of our railroads, canals, turnpikes, and telegraphs. How much greater would be the extent and diversity of our manufactures. How much greater would be the grandeur, and how much larger would be the number of our churches, theatres, schools, colleges, lyceums, banks, hotels, stores, and private dwellings. How many more clippers and steamships would we have sailing on the ocean, how vastly more reputable would we be abroad, how infinitely more respectable, progressive, and happy, would we be at home.

That we may learn something of the importance of cities in general, let us look for a moment at the great capitals of the world. What would England be without London? What would France be without Paris? What would Turkey be without Constantinople? Or, to come nearer home, what would Maryland be without Baltimore? What would Louisiana be without New Orleans? What would South Carolina be without Charleston? Do we ever think of these countries or States without thinking of their cities also? If we want to learn the news of the country, do we not go to the city, or to the city papers? Every metropolis may be regarded as the nucleus or epitome of the country in which it is situated; and the more prominent features and characteristics of a country, particularly of the people of a country, are almost always to be seen within the limits of its capital city. Almost invariably do we find the bulk of the floating funds, the best talent, and the most vigorous energies of a nation concentrated in its chief cities; and does not this concentration of wealth, energy, and talent, conduce, in an extraordinary degree, to the growth and prosperity of the nation? Unquestionably. Wealth develops wealth, energy develops energy, talent develops talent. What, then, must be the condition of those countries which do not possess the means or facilities of centralizing their material forces, their energies, and their talents? Are they not destined to occupy an inferior rank among the nations of the earth? Let the South answer.

And now let us ask, and we would put the question particularly to Southern merchants, what do we so much need as a great Southern metropolis? Merchants of the South, slaveholders! you are the avaricious assassinators of your country! You are the channels through which more than one hundred and twenty millions of dollars—$120,000,000—are annually drained from the South and conveyed to the North. You are daily engaged in the unmanly and unpatriotic work of impoverishing the land of your birth. You are constantly enfeebling our resources and rendering us more and more tributary to distant parts of the nation. Your conduct is reprehensible, base, criminal.

Whether Southern merchants ever think of the numerous ways in which they contribute to the aggrandizement of the North, while, at the same time, they enervate and dishonor the South, has, for many years, with us, been a matter of more than ordinary conjecture. If, as it would seem, they have never yet thought of the subject, it is certainly desirable that they should exercise their minds upon it at once. Let them scrutinize the workings of Southern money after it passes north of Mason and Dixon's line. Let them consider how much they pay to Northern railroads and hotels, how much to Northern merchants and shop-keepers, how much to Northern shippers and insurers, how much to Northern theatres, newspapers, and periodicals. Let them also consider what disposition is made of it after it is lodged in the hands of the North.

Is not the greater part of it paid out to Northern manufacturers, mechanics, and laborers, for the very articles which are purchased at the North—and to the extent that this is done, are not Northern manufacturers, mechanics, and laborers directly countenanced and encouraged, while, at the same time, Southern manufacturers, mechanics, and laborers, are indirectly abased, depressed, and disabled? It is, however, a matter of impossibility, on these small pages, to notice or enumerate all the methods in which the money we deposit in the North is made to operate against us; suffice it to say that it is circulated and expended there, among all classes of the people, to the injury and impoverishment of almost every individual in the South. And yet, our cousins of the North are not, by any means, blameworthy for availing themselves of the advantages which we have voluntarily yielded to them. They have shown their wisdom in growing great at our expense, and we have shown our folly in allowing them to do so. Southern merchants, slaveholders, and slave-breeders, should be the objects of our censure; they have desolated and impoverished the South; they are now making merchandize of the vitals of their country; patriotism is a word nowhere recorded in their vocabulary; town, city, country—they care for neither; with them, self is always paramount to every other consideration.

Having already compared slavery with freedom in the States, we will now compare it with freedom in the cities. From every person as yet unconvinced of the despicableness of slavery, we respectfully ask attention to the following letters, which fully explain themselves :—

FINANCE DEPARTMENT COMPTROLLER'S OFFICE,
New-York, February 17th, 1857.

H. R. HELPER, ESQ.,

Dear Sir :—

Your letter to Mayor Wood has been handed to me for an answer, which I take pleasure in giving as follows:

The last assessment of property in this city was made in August, 1856.

The value of all the real and personal property in the city, according to that assessment, is $511,740,492.

A census of the city was taken in 1855, and the number of inhabitants at that time can be obtained only from the Secretary of State.

Very truly yours,

A. S. CADY.

STATE OF NEW-YORK, SECRETARY'S OFFICE,
Albany, February 24, 1857.

H. R. HELPER, ESQ.,

Dear Sir :—

Yours of the 17th February, in regard to the population of the city of New York, is before me. According to the census of

1855 the population was - - - - - - -	629,810
1850 " " " - - - - - - - -	515,547
1845 " " " - - - - - - - -	371,223
1840 " " " - - - - - - - -	312,710
1835 " " " - - - - - - - -	268,089
1830 " " " - - - - - - - -	197,112

As to the population now, you have the same facilities of judging that we have from the above table.

Very truly yours,

A. N. WAKEFIELD *Chief Clerk.*

MAYOR'S OFFICE, CITY HALL,
Baltimore, December 26, 1856.

H. R. HELPER, ESQ.,

Dear Sir —

His Honor the Mayor of this City has requested me to reply to your communication of the 24th inst.. addressed to him, requesting answers to certain questions.

In answer to your first interrogatory, I would state that the amount of direct taxation assessed January 1st, 1856, was $102,053,839 ; the amount of exempt taxation (i. e. property out of the limits of direct tax) assessed at that date was $6,054,733.

In reply to your second inquiry, I would state that no census of the city has been taken since 1850. The estimated population at this time is about 250,000. Respectfully Yours, &c., &c.,

D. H. BLANCHARD, *Secretary.*

OFFICE OF THE MAYOR OF THE CITY OF PHILADELPHIA,
December 30, 1856.

H. R. HELPER, ESQ.,

Dear Sir:

In reply to your note of the 25th inst., received to-day, I hasten to give you the estimates you ask.

Real Estate, 150 millions ; it is about one-half the real value. Its market price is at least 300 million dollars.

The Personal Estate is returned at 20 millions ; it is over 110 millions. There has been no census since 1850. The population now is 500,000.

Yours truly,

G. VAUX.

STATE OF LOUISIANA, MAYORALTY OF NEW ORLEANS,
City Hall, 3d day of Jan'y, 1857.

Mr. H. R. HELPER,

New-York:

Dear Sir :—

In answer to your note of the 24th December, I beg to refer you to the enclosed abstract for the value of real estate and slaves according to the last assessment.

15

There has heretofore been no assessment of personal property—there having been no tax authorized until this year. The assessment is now being made and will probably add about $5,000,000 to the assessment as stated in the abstract.

There has been no census since the U. S. census of 1850, except an informal census, made in 1852, for the purpose of dividing the city into wards anew.

The estimated population now is about 150 to 175,000 inhabitants—permanent population—including the floating population at this season, it would probably reach not less than 210,000 inhabitants. The U. S. census was taken in the summer months, and is very incorrect as to the absolute population of New Orleans.

Very respectfully,
Your obed't serv't,
J. B. WALTON,
Secretary.

By reference to the abstract of which Mr. Walton speaks, we find that the value of real and personal property is summed up as follows :—

Real Estate, - - - -	$67,460,115
Slaves, - - - - -	5,183,580
Capital, - - - -	18,544,300
Total, - - - -	$91,188,195

CITY HALL, BOSTON,
Dec. 31, 1856.

Dear Sir:—Yours of the 25th inst., addressed to the Mayor, has been handed to me for a reply—and I would accordingly state that the value of real and personal estate in this city, on the first day of May, A.D. 1856, was $249,162,500.

The census of the city of Boston, on the first day of May, A.D 1855, was 162,748 persons.

The estimated population of the city of Boston at this date—say January 1st, 1857—is 165,000.

Yours, very respectfully,
SAML. T. McCLEARY,
City Clerk.

ST. LOUIS,
Feb. 27, 1857.

H. R. HELPER, ESQ.,
New-York :

Dear Sir:—

In reply to yours of the 9th inst., I beg leave to state, that a census of our population was taken in the spring of 1856 by the Sheriff, and although it was inaccurate, yet the population as returned by him was then 125,500. That his census is too low there is no doubt. Our population at this time is at least 140,000.

Our last assessment was made in February, 1856. Value of real and personal estate, is, in round numbers, $63,000,000.

Trusting this information will be sufficient for your purpose, I remain,

Yours, &c.,
JOHN HOW,
Mayor.

MAYOR'S OFFICE, CITY HALL, BROOKLYN,
January 24th, 1857.

H. R. HELPER, ESQ.,

Sir:—

The answers to your inquiries are as follows:

The last assessment of property in this city was made in August, 1856.

The value of all the real and personal property in the city, according to that assessment, is $95,800,440.

A census of the city was taken in 1855, and the number of inhabitants, according to it, was 205,250.

The estimated population now is 225,000.

The last annual report of the Comptroller, together with a

communication of the Mayor to the Common Council, made on the 5th of Jan., 1857, have been transmitted by mail to your address, and from them you may be able to obtain any further information you may desire. Yours, respectfully,

S. S. POWELL,
Mayor.
By C. S. BRAINERD.

MAYOR'S OFFICE,
Charleston, Feb. 16, 1857.

H. R. HELPER, ESQ.,
(New York,)
Dear Sir:—

Yours of the 9th has just been received, I sent you, through the Clerk of Council, some time ago, the Annual Fiscal Statement of the Committee on Accounts made to the City Council, which would give some of the information which you desire. I will have another copy sent you.

No census has been taken since 1848. The population at present must be between fifty and sixty thousand.

Any information which it may be in my power to furnish you with, will always give me pleasure to supply.

Very respectfully,
WM. PORCHER MILES,
Mayor.

From a report of the "Annual accounts of the city of Charleston, for the fiscal year ending the 31st of August, 1856," it appears that the total value of real and personal property, including slaves—nearly half the population—was $36,127,751.

MAYOR'S OFFICE,
Cincinnati, Jan'y 2, 1857.

Dear Sir:—In reply to your note of the 25th ult., I beg leave to say that the value of all the real and personal property in this city, as assessed for taxation, amounts to $88.810,734. The realty being $60,701,267 ; the personalty $20,795,203, and the bank and brokers' capital $7,314,264. The assessment of the realty was made in 1853 ; that of the personalty is made in March of each year.

Our present population is estimated at 210,000. No complete census has been taken since 1850.

The total of taxes levied on the above assessment of $88,810,734, for city purposes, was $529,727,05.

Very respectfully,
Your ob'dt. serv't,

H. R. Helper, Esq.,
New-York.

Jas. J. Faran,
Mayor.

Mayor's Office,
Louisville, Ky., January 1st, 1857.

H. R. Helper, Esq.,
New-York City,
Dear Sir :—

Your favor 24th ult. is received—contents noted. I will remark in reply, that the taxes of this city are levied only on real estate, slaves, and merchandise, (exclusive of home manufactures.) which are taken at what is supposed to be their cash value, but is much less than the real value. Our last assessment was made the 10th January, 1856, and amounted to $31.500,000.

There has been no census of this city taken since 1850, our charter requiring that it shall be taken this year. I am now preparing to have it done. It is supposed Louisville at this time has a population of 65 or 70 thousand.

I send with this my last annual message to the Gen. Council and accompanying documents.

Respectfully yours,
John Barbee *Mayor.*

DAILY TRIBUNE OFFICE,
Chicago, May 21, 1857.

H. R. HELPER, ESQ.

Sir:—

In the May No. of Hunt's Merchants' Magazine you will find some of your questions answered. The actual cash value of property is not taken by the assessors. Citizens are not sworn as to the value of their personal effects, nor is real estate given in at twenty per cent. of its selling cash price. An elaborate estimate of the real value, in cash, of Chicago, which we have seen, puts the real estate at - - - - - - $125,000,000
Improvements on the same, - - - - - $24,000,000
Personal property, - - - - - - - - $22,000,000

In 1857 total value, - - - - - - $171,000,000

On half a dozen streets in this city lots sell readily at $1,000 to $1,200 per foot front, exclusive of improvements.

A census of the population of Chicago was taken in October, 1853, and in June, 1855, the latter by State authority. That of October '53 found 60,652; that of June '55 found 80,509. The best estimate at present makes the number, on May 1st, 1857, to be 112,000, which is rather under than over the truth. The amount of building, in the city, is immense, but as quickly as a tenement can be spiked together, it is taken at a high rent; and at no former period has there seemed so rapid an augmentation of population. Very truly yours,

RAY & MEDILL,
Eds. Ch. Trib.

RICHMOND, Va.
April 25th, '57.

H. R. HELPER, ESQ.,

Dear Sir:—

Yours of the 14th inst. has been received and should have been answered sooner, but it was impossible to get the information you desired earlier. The value of the real estate in the city of Richmond is $18,000,000. The value of the personal is $191,920. Total value $18,201,920. This does not include slaves, of whom there are 6,472 in the city. The State values each slave at $300 each—making $1,941,600, which, added to the total above, makes $20,143,520. The number of inhabitants—white and black, is 34,612 within the corporation limits. The assessment was made in 1855 throughout the whole State.

Yours, very respectfully,
B. W. Starke.

Mayor's Office,
Providence, Dec. 31st, 1856.

H. R. Helper, Esq.,
New York,
Dear Sir:—

Yours of 25th is this moment received. You will receive with this a communication from the Chairman of the Board of Assessors, giving the requisite information from that department. I send you this day a census report, taken 1855, which will give you the information asked. Our population at this time is between 50 and 60,000. Respectfully,

James Y. Smith,
Mayor.

Assessor's Office,
Providence, Dec. 31st, 1856.

H. R. Helper, Esq.,
Dear Sir:—

His Honor, the Mayor of this City, has requested me to answer your communication of the 25th inst., addressed to him, so far as relates to the valuation of this city, &c., which is herewi h presented.

The valuation of this City in 1856 is as follows:

Real Estate, - - - - - -	$36,487,116
Personal Estate, - - - - -	21,577,400
Total,	$58,064,516

Our last assessment was ordered in June last, and completed on the 1st day of September last.

Rates of taxation $7 75 per $1000.
Amount of tax raised $450,000.

Respectfully yours,
JOSEPH MARTIN,
Chairman of the Board of Assessors.

HERALD OFFICE,
Norfolk, Va., 28th April, 1857.

H. R. HELPER, ESQ.,
New-York,
Dear Sir:—

The value of all the real estate, as re-assessed about two months ago, is set down, say, in round numbers, at five and a half millions. The actual value would bring it somewhat above that mark. The assessment of the personal property will be completed in three or four weeks hence; but its *exact* value cannot be arrived at from the fact that a large portion of this description of property—including slaves—is taxed specifically without regard to its value. It is estimated by the assessors, however, that the *personal* exceeds the *real estate*, and may be safely set down at six and a half millions.

There has been no census taken since 1850. The State authorities assume the population to be 16,000, but I am informed by the assessors that 17,000 is a fairer estimate.

Hoping that the information given may answer the purpose for which you require it, I am, Respectfully yours,
R. G. BROUGHTON.

MAYOR'S OFFICE,
Buffalo, March 10, 1857.

Dear Sir:—Yours, of the 9th inst., was received this morning. The answers to your questions are as follows:

The last valuation of the property of our city was made in April, 1856.

Valuation of real estate, . . .	$38,114,040
" personal estate, . .	7,360.436
Total real and personal,	$45,474,476

The last census was the State census, taken in the summer of 1855. That showed a population of 74,214; a fair estimate now is 90,000.

Respectfully,

Your ob't serv't,

F. P. STEVENS.

MAYOR'S OFFICE,
Savannah, 9th January, 1856.

H. R. HELPER, ESQ.,
New-York,

Dear Sir:—

In reply to your first interrogatory, I send you the last Mayor's report. in which you will find the information you seek.

No census has been taken of the city since 1850.

The estimated population is 25,000.

Very respectfully yours,

J. P. SCREVEN,

Mayor.

From the Mayor's annual report, we learn that the "assessments or value of lands and improvements," for the year ending October 31st, 1856, amounted to $8,999,015. The value of the personal property is, perhaps, about $3,000,000—total value of real and personal estate $11,999,015.

CITY OF NEW-BEDFORD,
Mayor's Room, 1 mo., 6th, 1857.

H. R. HELPER:—

Yours of the 4th inst. came to hand this morning.

In reply to your inquiries, I will say that the amount assessed on the 1st day of May, 1856, was as follows:—

Real Estate, - - - - - -	$9,311,500
Personal, - - - - - - -	17,735,500
Total, - - - - - -	$27,047,000

The returns of a census taken the previous autumn gave 20,391 persons, from which there is not probably much change.

Respectfully,

GEO. HOWLAND, JR.

Mayor.

MAYOR'S OFFICE,
Wilmington, N. C., May 23d, 1857.

H. R HELPER, ESQ.,

New-York,

Dear Sir :—

I am in receipt of yours of 19th inst. The value of real estate as per last assessment, 1st April, 1856, was $3,350,000

We have no system by which to arrive at the value of personal property : I estimate the amount, however, exclusive of merchandize, at $4.509,000

There has been no census taken since 1850—the present number of inhabitants is estimated at 10,000.

I regret my inability to afford you more definite information.

Very respectfully, &c.,

O. G. PARSLEY,

Mayor.

From the foregoing communications, we make up the following summary of the more important particulars :—

NINE FREE CITIES.

Name.	Population.	Wealth.	Wealth per capita
New York...........	700,000	$511,740,492	$731
Philadelphia	500,000	325,000,000	650
Boston	165,000	249,162,500	1,510
Brooklyn............	225,000	95,800,440	425
Cincinnati...........	210,000	88,810,734	422
Chicago.............	112,000	171,000,000	1,527
Providence..........	60,000	58,064,516	967
Buffalo..............	90,000	45,474,476	505
New Bedford........	21,000	27,047,000	1,288
	2,083,000	$1,572,100,158	$754

NINE SLAVE CITIES.

Name.	Population.	Wealth.	Wealth per capita.
Baltimore...........	250,000	$102,053,839	$408
New Orleans.........	175,000	91,188,195	521
St. Louis............	140,000	63,000,000	450
Charleston..........	60,000	36,127,751	602
Louisville...........	70,000	31,500,000	450
Richmond...........	40,000	20,143,520	503
Norfolk.............	17,000	12,000,000	705
Savannah...........	25,000	11,999,015	480
Wilmington..........	10,000	7,850,000	785
	787,000	$375,862,320	$477

Let it not be forgotten that the slaves themselves are valued at so much per head, and counted as part of the wealth of slave cities ; and yet, though we assent, as we have done, to the inclusion of all this fictitious wealth, it will be observed that the residents of free cities are far wealthier, *per capita*, than the residents of slave cities. We trust the reader will not fail to examine the figures with great care

In this age of the world, commerce is an indispensable element of national greatness. Without commerce we can have no great cities, and without great cities we can have no reliable tenure of distinct nationality. Commerce is the forerunner of wealth and population; and it is mainly these that make invincible the power of undying States.

Speaking in general terms of the commerce of this country, and of the great cities through which that commerce is chiefly carried on, the Boston *Traveler* says:—

"The wealth concentrated at the great commercial points of the United States is truly astonishing. For instance, one-eighth part of the entire property of this country is owned by the cities of New-York and Boston. Boston alone, in its corporate limits, owns one-twentieth of the property of this entire Union, being an amount equal to the wealth of any three of the New-England States, except Massachusetts. In this city is found the richest community, *per capita*, of any in the United States. The next city in point of wealth, according to its population, is Providence, (R. I.,) which city is one of the richest in the Union, having a valuation of fifty-six millions, with a population of fifty thousand."

The same paper, in the course of an editorial article on the "Wealth of Boston and its Business," says:—

"The assessors' return of the wealth of Boston will probably show this year an aggregate property of nearly three hundred millions. This sum, divided among 160,000 people, would give nearly $2,000 to each inhabitant, and will show Boston to be much the wealthiest community in the United States, save New York alone, with four times its population. The value of the real estate in this city is increasing now with great rapidity, as at least four millions of dollars' worth of new houses and stores will be built this year. The personal estate in ships, cargoes.

stocks, &c., is greatly increasing with each succeeding year, notwithstanding the many disasters and losses constantly occurring in such kinds of property.

"It is impossible to get the exact earnings of the nearly six hundred thousand tons of shipping owned in this city. But perhaps it would not be much out of the way to set the total amount for 1855 at from fifteen to twenty millions of dollars. This sum has probably been earned by our fleet engaged in the domestic trade, and in commercial transactions with the East and West Indies, South America, the Pacific, Europe and Africa. The three sources from which the population of Boston is maintained, and its prosperity continued, are these: Commerce, trade, and manufactures. Its annual trade and sales of merchandise are said now, by competent judges, to amount to three hundred millions of goods per annum, and will soon greatly exceed that vast sum. The annual manufactures of this city are much more in amount than in many entire States in this Union. They amount, according to recent statistics, to nearly seventy-five millions of dollars."

Freeman Hunt, the accomplished editor of *Hunt's Merchants' Magazine,* writing on the "Progressive Growth of Cities," says :—

"London is now the greatest concentration of human power the world has ever known. Will its supremacy be permanent? or will it, like its predecessors, be eclipsed by western rivals? New-Yorkers do not doubt, and indeed have no reason to doubt, that their city, now numbering little more than one-third of the population of London, will, within the next fifty years, be greater than the metropolis of the British empire.

"New York, with her immediate dependencies, numbers about 900,000. Since 1790 she has established a law of growth which doubles her population once in fifteen years. If this law continues to operate, she may be expected to possess 1,800,000 in 1871, 3,600,000 in 1886, and 7,200,000 in 1901. If twenty years be allowed New York as her future period of duplication, she would overtake London by the end of fifty years; London may then have five millions; New-York will almost certainly have more than that number.

Will the star of empire become stationary at New-York? The interior plain of North America has within itself more means to sustain a dense population in civilized comfort than any other region of the world. The star of empire cannot be arrested in its western course before it reaches this plain. Its most promising city at present is Chicago. The law of its growth since 1840 seems o be a duplication within four years. In 1840 it numbered 4,379. In June of this year it will contain 88,000. At the same rate of increase carried forward, it would overtake New-York within twenty years. If six years be allowed for each future duplication, Chicago would overtake New-York in thirty-three years. If the growth of Chicago should in future be measured by a duplication of every seven years, it would contain 5,622,000 in forty-two years.

"In 1901, forty-five years from this time, the central plain, including the Canadas, will contain about eighty millions of people. Its chief city may be reasonably expected to contain about one-tenth of this population. Before the end of this century the towns and cities of the central plain will contain, with their suburbs, not less than half the entire population; that is to say, forty millions. How these millions shall be apportioned among the cities of that day, is a subject for curious speculation."

A FLEET OF MERCHANTMEN.

The Boston *Journal*, of a late date, says:—

"About one hundred sail of vessels, of various descriptions, entered this port yesterday, consisting of traders from Europe, South America, the West Indies, and from coastwise ports. The waters of the bay and harbor presented a beautiful appearance from the surrounding shores, as this fleet of white-winged messengers made their way towards the city, and crowds of people must have witnessed their advent with great delight. A more magnificent sight is seldom seen in our harbor."

Would to God that such sights could sometimes be seen

in Southern harbors! When slavery shall cease to paralyse the energies of our people, then ships, coming to us from the four quarters of the globe, will, with majestic grandeur, begin to loom in the distance; our bays will rejoice in the presence of "the white-winged messengers," and our levees resound as never before with the varied din of commerce.

COMMERCE OF NORFOLK.

The *Southern Argus* thus speaks of the ruined commerce of a most despicable niggerville:—

"We question if any other community, certainly no other in the United States of America, have made greater exertions to resuscitate the trade of Norfolk than the mercantile portion of the inhabitants; in proof of which nineteen-twentieths of those engaged in foreign commerce have terminated in their insolvency, the principal cause of which has been in the unrelenting hostility, to this day, from the commencement of the present century, of the Virginia Legislature, with the co-operation of at least the commercial portions of the citizens of Richmond, Petersburg and Portsmouth."

How it is, in this enlightened age, that men of ordinary intelligence can be so far led into error as to suppose that commerce, or any other noble enterprise, can be established and successfully prosecuted under the dominion of slavery, is, to us, one of the most inexplicable of mysteries. "Commercial" Conventions, composed of the self-titled lordlings of slavery—Generals, Colonels, Majors, Captains, etcætera—may act out their annual programmes of farcical nonsense from now until doomsday; but they will never add one iota to the material, moral, or mental interests of the

South,—never can, until their ebony idol shall have been utterly demolished.

BALTIMORE—PAST, PRESENT, AND FUTURE.

We are indebted to the Baltimore *Patriot* for the following interesting sketch of the Monumental City as it was, and as it is, and as it may be :—

"The population of Baltimore in 1790 was 13.503; in 1800, 15.514; in 1810, 35.583; in 1820, 62,738; in 1830, 80,625; in 1840, 110,313; in 1850, 169,054. The increase of inhabitants within two particular decades, will be found, by reference to the above table, to be remarkable. Between 1800 and 1810, the population nearly doubled itself; between 1840 and 1850, the increase was two-thirds; and for the past five years, the numerical extension of our population has been even more rapid than during the previous decade. We may safely assume that Baltimore contains at the present time not less than 250.000 inhabitants. But the increase in the manufactured products of the State, as shown by the report of the Secretary of the Treasury, is a matter of even greater astonishment. The statistical tables cf 1840 estimate the aggregate value of the manufactures of Maryland at $13,509,636—*thirteen million five hundred and nine thousand six hundred and thirty-six dollars.* In 1850, the value of the articles manufactured within the limits of the State amounted to $32.593,635—*thirty-two million five hundred and ninety-three thousand six hundred and thirty-five dollars!* A signal proof that the wealth of the State has increased with even far greater rapidity than its population. A quarter of a century ago, the sum of our manufactures did not much exceed five millions of dollars per annum. At this day it may be set down as falling but little short of fifty millions. These are facts taken from official sources, and therefore understated rather than exceeded. They are easily verified by any one who will take the necessary trouble to examine the reports for himself; and they justify us in the assertion that we are but fifteen years behind Philadelphia in population, and are only at the same relative distance from her in point of wealth.

A change has been going on for some time past in our commercial and industrial affairs which all may have noticed, but the extent of which is known to but few, and we hazard nothing in saying that this enormous progression must continue, because it is based upon a solid foundation, and therefore subject to no ordinary contingencies.

Occupying geographically the most central position on this Continent, with vast mines of coal lying within easy distance to the North and West of us, with a harbor easy of access, and with railroads penetrating by the shortest routes the most fertile sections of the Union, we need nothing but the judicious fostering of a proper spirit among our citizens to make Baltimore not only the commercial emporium of the South and West, but also the great coal mart of the Union. Our flour market is already the most extensive in the known world—we speak without exaggeration, for this also is proven by unquestionable facts. There is more guano annually brought into our port than into all the other ports of the United States put together, and the demand for this important article of commerce is steadily increasing. Our shipments of tobacco are immense, and as the improvement in the depth of the channel of the Patapsco increases, must inevitably become much greater.

Such, then, is our present condition as a commercial community, and when we add that our prosperity is as much owing to our admirable geographical position as to the energy of our merchants and manufacturers, we design to cast no imputation on these excellent citizens, but rather to stimulate them to renewed efforts in a field where enterprise cannot fail of reaping its due reward.

Take any common map of the United States and rule an air line across it from Baltimore to St. Louis, and midway between the two it will strike Cincinnati—the great inland centre of trade—traversing at the same time those wonderfully fertile valleys which lie between the latter point and the Mississippi river. Now let it be remembered that since the introduction of railways fluvial navigation has been, to a considerable extent, superseded by inland transport, because of the greater speed and certainty of the latter. Let it be remembered also that the migration westward is incessantly going on, and that with every farm opened within striking distance of a great arterial railway, or its anastomosing branches, a certain amount of freight must find its way to the seaboard markets, while the demand for manufactured products, and for domestic or foreign commodities, in exchange for breadstuffs or raw material, must necessarily increase; thereby adding greatly to the prosperity of the commercial centre towards which articles of export tend, and from which imports in return are drawn. It would be difficult to estimate the value of what this trade will be fifty years hence, or what the population of Baltimore, situated as she is, will by that time have become.

Reasoning from causes to effects, and presuming that ordinary perseverance will be used in promoting the interests of our city, industrially and commercially, we are justified in believing that its progress must be in an accelerated ratio, and that there are those now living who will look back with surprise and wonder at its growth and magnitude, as we have done while comparing its present aspect with that which it exhibited within our own memory."

It is a remarkable fact, but one not at all surprising to those whose philosophy leads them to think aright, that Baltimore and St. Louis, the two most prosperous cities in the slave States, have fewer slaves in proportion to the aggregate population than any other city or cities in the South. While the entire population of the former is now estimated at 250,000, and that of the latter at 140,000—making a grand total of 390,000 in the two cities, less than 6,000 of this latter number are slaves; indeed, neither city is cursed with half the number of 6,000.

In 1850, there were only 2,946 slaves in Baltimore, and 2,656 in St. Louis—total in the two cities 5,602; and in both places, thank Heaven, this heathenish class of the population was rapidly decreasing. The census of 1860 will, in all probability, show that the two cities are entirely exempt from slaves and slavery ; and that of 1870 will, we prayerfully hope, show that the United States at large, a. that time, will have been wholly redeemed from the unspeakable curse of human bondage.

What about Southern Commerce? Is it not almost entirely tributary to the commerce of the North? Are we not dependent on New-York, Philadelphia, Boston, and Cincinnati, for nearly every article of merchandise, whether foreign or domestic? Where are our ships, our mariners, our naval architects? Alas! echo answers, where?

Reader! would you understand how abjectly slaveholders themselves are enslaved to the products of Northern industry? If you would, fix your mind on a Southern "gentleman"—a slave-breeder and human-flesh monger, who professes to be a Christian! Observe the routine of his daily life. See him rise in the morning from a Northern bed, and clothe himself in Northern apparel ; see him walk across the floor on a Northern carpet, and perform his ablutions out of a Northern ewer and basin. See him uncover a box of Northern powders, and cleanse his teeth with a Northern brush ; see him reflecting his physiognomy in a Northern mirror, and arranging his hair with a Northern comb See him dosing himself with the mendicaments of Northern quacks, and perfuming his handkerchief with Northern cologne. See him referring to the time in a Northern watch, and glancing at tne news in a Northern gazette. See him and his family sitting in

Northern chairs, and singing and praying out of Northern books. See him at the breakfast table, saying grace over a Northern plate, eating with Northern cutlery, and drinking from Northern utensils. See him charmed with the melody of a Northern piano, or musing over the pages of a Northern novel. See him riding to his neighbor's in a Northern carriage, or furrowing his lands with a Northern plow. See him lighting his segar with a Northern match, and flogging his negroes with a Northern lash. See him with Northern pen and ink, writing letters on Northern paper, and sending them away in Northern envelopes, sealed with Northern wax, and impressed with a Northern stamp. Perhaps our Southern "gentleman" is a merchant; if so, see him at his store, making an unpatriotic use of his time in the miserable traffic of Northern gimcracks and haberdashery; see him when you will, where you will, he is ever surrounded with the industrial products of those whom, in the criminal inconsistency of his heart, he execrates as enemies, yet treats as friends His labors, his talents, his influence, are all for the North, and not for the South; for the stability of slavery, and for the sake of his own personal aggrandizement, he is willing to sacrifice the dearest interests of his country.

As we see our ruinous system of commerce exemplified in the family of our Southern "gentleman," so we may see it exemplified, to a greater or less degree, in almost every other family throughout the length and breadth of the slaveholding States. We are all constantly buying, and selling, and wearing, and using Northern merchandise, at a doul e expense to both ourselves and our neighbors. If we but look at ourselves attentively, we shall find that we are all clothed *cap a pie* in Northern habilaments. Our hats, our caps, our cravats, our coats, our vests, our pants, our gloves, our boots, our shoes, our under-garments—all come from the North; whence, too, Southern ladies procure all their bonnets, plumes, and flowers; dresses, shawls, and scarfs; frills, ribbons, and ruffles; cuffs, capes, and collars.

True it is that the South has wonderful powers of endurance and recuperation; but she cannot forever support the reckless prodigality of her sons. We are all spendthrifts; some of us should become financiers. We must learn to take care of our money; we should withhold it from the North, and open avenues for its circulation at home. We should not run to New-York, to Philadelphia, to Boston, to Cincinnati, or to any other Northern city, every time we want a shoe-string or a bedstead, a fish-hook or a handsaw, a tooth-pick or a cotton-gin. In ease and luxury we have been lolling long enough; we should now bestir ourselves, and keep pace with the progress of the age. We must expand our energies, and acquire habits of enterprise and industry; we should arouse ourselves from the couch of lassitude, and inure our minds to thought and our bodies to action. We must begin to feed on a more substantial diet than that of pro-slavery politics; we should leave off our siestas and post-meridian naps, and employ our time in profitable vocations. Before us there is a vast work to be accomplished—a work which has been accumulating on our hands for many years. It is no less a work than that of infusing the spirit of liberty into all our systems of commerce, agriculture, manufactures, government, literature, and religion. Oligarchal despotism must be overthrown ; slavery must be abolished.

For the purpose of showing how absolutely Southern "gentlemen," particularly slaveholding merchants, are lost to all sense of true honor and patriotism, we will here introduce an extract from an article which appeared more than three years ago in one of the editorial columns of the leading daily newspaper of the city of New-York. It is in these words :—

> "Southern merchants do indeed keep away from New-York for the reason that they can't pay their debts ; there is no doubt that if the jobbers of this city had not trusted Southern traders for the past three years, they would be a great deal better off than they are. * * * Already our trade with Canada is becoming as promising, sure, and profitable, as our trade with the South is uncertain, riskful, and annoying."

Now, by any body of men not utterly debased by the influences of slavery, this language would have been construed into an invitation to stay at home. But do Southern merchants stay at home ? Do they build up Southern commerce ? No ! off they post to the North as regularly as the seasons, spring and fall, come round, and there, like cringing sycophants, flatter, beg, and scheme, for favors which they have no money to command.

The better classes of merchants, and indeed of all other people, at the North, as elsewhere, have too much genuine respect for themselves to wish to have any dealings whatever with those who make merchandise of human beings. Limited as is our acquaintance in the city of New-York, we know one firm there, a large wholesale house, that makes it an invariable rule never to sell goods to a merchant from the slave States except for cash. Being well acquainted with the partners, we asked one of them, on one occasion, why he refused to trust slave-driving merchants. "Because," said he, "they are too long-winded and uncertain; when we credit them, they occasion us more loss and bother than their trade is worth." Non-slaveholders of the South! recollect that slavery is the only impediment to your progress and prosperity, that it stands diametrically opposed to all needful reforms, that it seeks to sacrifice you entirely for the benefit of others, and that it is the one great and only cause of dishonor to your country. Will you not abolish it? May Heaven help you to do your duty!

CHAPTER X.

FACTS AND ARGUMENTS BY THE WAYSIDE.

Finding that we shall have to leave unsaid a great many things which we intended to say, and that we shall have to omit much valuable matter, the product of other pens than our own, but which, having collected at considerable expense, we had hoped to be able to introduce, we have concluded to present, under the above heading, only a few of the more important particulars.

In the first place, we will give an explanation of the reason

WHY THIS WORK WAS NOT PUBLISHED IN BALTIMORE.

A considerable portion of this work was written in Baltimore; and the whole of it would have been written and published there, but for the following odious clause, which we extract from the Statutes of Maryland:—

"Be it enacted by the General Assembly of Maryland, That after the passage of his act, it shall not be lawful for any citizen of this State, knowingly to make, print or engrave, or aid in the making, printing or engraving, within this State, any pictorial representation, or to write or print, or to aid in the writing or printing any pamphlet, newspaper, handbill or other paper of an inflammatory character, and having a tendency to excite discontent or stir up insurrection amongst the people of color of this State, or of either of the other States or Territories of the United States, or knowingly to carry or send, or to aid in the carrying or sending the same for circulation amongst the inhabitants of either of the other States or Territories of the United States, and any person so offending shall be guilty of a felony, and shall on conviction be sentenced to confinement in the penitentiary of this State, for a period not less than ten nor more than twenty years, from the time of sentence pronounced on such person."—*Act passed Dec.* 1831. *See 2nd Dorsey, page* 1218.

Now so long as slaveholders are clothed with the mantle of office, so long will they continue to make laws, like the above, expressly calculated to bring the non-slaveholding whites under a system of vassalage little less onerous and debasing than that to which the negroes themselves are accustomed. What wonder is it that there is no native literature in the South? The South can never have a literature of her own until after slavery shall have been abolished. Slaveholders are too lazy and ignorant to write it, and the non-slaveholders—even the few whose minds are cultivated at all—are not permitted even to make the attempt. Down with the oligarchy! Ineligibility of slaveholders—never another vote to the trafficker in human flesh!

LEGISLATIVE ACTS AGAINST SLAVERY.

In his Compendium of the Seventh Census, Mr. DeBow has compiled the following useful and highly interesting facts:—

"The Continental Congress of 1774 resolved to discontinue the slave trade, in which resolution they were anticipated by the Conventions of Delegates of Virginia and North Carolina. In 1789 the Convention to frame the federal Constitution, looked to the abolition of the traffic in 1808. On the 2nd of March, 1807, Congress passed an act against importations of Africans into the United States after January 1st, 1808. An act in Great Britain in 1807 also made the slave trade unlawful. Denmark forbid the introduction of African slaves into her colonies after 1804. The Congress of Vienna, in 1815, pronounced for the abolition of the trade. France abolished it in 1817, and also Spain, but the acts were to take effect after 1820. Portugal abolished it in 1818.

"In Pennsylvania slavery was abolished in 1780. In New Jersey it was provisionally abolished in 1784; all children born of a slave after 1804 are made free in 1820. In Massachusetts, it was declared after the revolution, that slavery was virtually abolished by their Constitution, (1780). In 1784 and 1797, Connecticut provided for a gradual extinction of slavery. In Rhode Island, after 1784, no person could be *born* a slave. The Constitutions of Vermont and New Hampshire, respectively, abolished slavery. In New York it was provisionally abolished in 1799, twenty-eight years' ownership being allowed in slaves born after that date, and in 1817 it was enacted that slavery was not to exist after ten years, or 1827. The ordinance of 1787 forbid slavery in the territory northwest of the Ohio."

Besides the instances enumerated above, slavery has been abolished in more than forty different parts of the world within the last half century, and with good results everywhere, except two or three West India islands, where the negro population was greatly in excess of the whites; and even in these, the evils, if any, that have followed, are not justly attributable to abolition, but to the previous demoralization produced by slavery.

In this connection we may very properly introduce the testimony of a West India planter to the relative advantages of Free over Slave Labor. Listen to Charles Petty john, of Barbadoes, who, addressing himself to a citizen of our own country, says :—

"In 1834, I came in possession of 257 slaves, under the laws of England, which required the owner to feed, clothe, and furnish them with medical attendance. With this number I cultivated my sugar plantation until the Emancipation Act of August 1st, 1838, when they all became free. I now hire a portion of those slaves, the best and cheapest of course, as you hire men in the United States. The average number which I employ is 100, with which I cultivate more land at a cheaper rate, and make more produce than I did with 257 slaves. With my slaves I made from 100 to 180 tons of sugar yearly. With 100 free negroes I think I do badly if I do not annually produce 250 tons.

If, in the forty and more instances to which we have alluded, the abolition of slavery had proved injurious in a majority of cases, the attempt to abolish it elsewhere might, perhaps, be regarded as an ill-advised effort ; but, seeing that its abolition has worked well in at least fourteen-fifteenths of all the cases on record, the fact becomes obvious that it is our duty and our interest to continue to abolish it until the whole world shall be freed, or until we shall begin to see more evil than good result from our acts of emancipation.

THE TRUE FRIENDS OF THE SOUTH.

Freesoilers and abolitionists are the only true friends of the South ; slaveholders and slave-breeders are downright enemies of their own section. Anti-slavery men are working for the Union and for the good of the whole world ; proslavery men are working for the disunion of the States, and for the good of nothing except themselves. Than such men as Greeley, Seward, Sumner, Clay, and Birney, the South can have no truer friends—nor can slavery have more implacable foes.

For the purpose of showing that Horace Greeley is not, as he is generally represented by the oligarchy, an inveterate hater of the South, we will here introduce an extract from one of his editorial articles in a late number of the New York *Tribune*—a faithful advocate of freedom, whose circulation, we are happy to say, is greater than the aggregate circulation of more than twenty of the principal proslavery sheets published at the South:—

"Is it in vain that we pile fact upon fact, proof on proof, showing that slavery is a blight and a curse to the States which cherish it? These facts are multitudinous as the leaves of the forest; conclusive as the demonstrations of geometry. Nobody attempts to refute them, but the champions of slavery extension seem determined to persist in ignoring them. Let it be understood, then, once for all, that we do not hate the South, war on the South, nor seek to ruin the South, in resisting the extension of slavery. We most earnestly believe human bondage a curse to the South, and to all whom it affects; but we do not labor for its overthrow otherwise than through the conviction of the South of its injustice and mischief. Its extension into new Territories we determinedly resist, not by any means from ill will to the South, but under the impulse of good will to all mankind. We believe the establishment of slavery in Kansas or any other Western Territory would prolong its existence in Virginia and Maryland, by widening the market and increasing the price of slaves, and thereby increasing the profits of slave-breeding, and the consequent incitement thereto. Those who urge that slavery would not go into Kansas if permitted, wilfully shut their eyes to the fact that it *has gone* into Missouri, lying in exactly the same latitude, and is now strongest in that north-western angle of said State, which was covertly filched from what is now Kansas within th last twenty years. Even if the growth of hemp, corn and tobacco were not so profitable in Eastern Kansas, as it evidently must be, the growth of slaves for more Southern consumption would inevitably prove as lucrative there as in Virginia and Maryland, which lie in corresponding latitudes, and whose chief staple export to-day consists of negro bondmen destined for the plantations of Louisiana and Mississippi, which could be supplied more conveniently and cheaply from Kansas than from their present breeding-places this side of the Alleghanies.

Whenever we draw a parallel between Northern and Southern production, industry, thrift, wealth, the few who seek to parry the facts at all complain that the instances are unfairly selected—that the commercial ascendancy of the North, with the profits and facilities thence accruing, accounts for the striking preponderance of the North. In vain we insist that slavery is the cause of this very commercial ascendancy—that Norfolk and Richmond and Charleston might have been to this country what Boston, New-York and Philadelphia now are, had not slavery spread its pall over and paralyzed the energies of the South."

This may be regarded as a fair expression of the sentiments of a great majority of the people north of Mason and Dixon's line. Our Northern cousins "do not hate the South, war on the South, nor seek to ruin the South;" on the contrary, they love our particular part of the nation, and, like dutiful, sensible, upright men, they would promote its interests by facilitating the abolition of slavery. Success to their efforts!

SLAVERY THOUGHTFUL—SIGNS OF CONTRITION.

The real condition of the South is most graphically described in the following doleful admissions from the Charleston *Standard*:—

"In its every aspect our present condition is provincial. We have within our limits no solitary metropolis of interest or ideas

-no marts of exchange—no radiating centres of opinion. Whatever we have of genius and productive energy, goes freely in to swell the importance of the North. Possessing the material which constitutes two-thirds of the commerce of the whole country, it might have been supposed that we could have influence upon the councils of foreign States; but we are never taken into contemplation. It might have been supposed that England, bound to us by the cords upon which depend the existence of four millions of her subjects, would be considerate of our feelings; but receiving her cotton from the North, it is for them she has concern, and it is her interest and her pleasure to reproach us. It might have been supposed, that, producing the material which is sent abroad, to us would come the articles that are taken in exchange for it; but to the North they go for distribution, and to us are parcelled out the fabrics that are suited to so remote a section.

Instead, therefore, of New-York being tributary to Norfolk, Charleston, Savannah or New Orleans, these cities are tributary to New-York. Instead of the merchants of New-York standing cap in hand to the merchants of Charleston, the merchants of Charleston stand cap in hand to the merchants of New-York.—Instead of receiving foreign ships in Southern waters, and calling up the merchants of the country to a distribution of the cargo, the merchants of the South are hurried off to make a distribution elsewhere. In virtue of our relations to a greater system, we have little development of internal interests; receiving supplies from the great centre, we have made little effort to supply ourselves. We support the makers of boots, shoes, hats, coats, shirts, flannels, blankets, carpets, chairs, tables, mantels, mats, carriages, jewelry, cradles, couches, coffins, by the thousand and hundreds of thousands; but they scorn to live amongst us. They must have the gaieties and splendors of a great metropolis, and are not content to vegetate upon the dim verge of this remote frontier.

As it is in material interests, so it is in arts and letters—our pictures are painted at the North, our books are published at the North, our periodicals and papers are printed at the North. We are even fed on police reports and villany from the North. The papers published at the South which ignore the questions at issue between the sections are generally well sustained; the books which expose the evils of our institution are even read with avidity beyond our limits, but the ideas that are turned to the condition of the South are intensely provincial. If, as things now are, a man should rise with all the genius of Shakspeare, or Dickens, or Fielding, or of all the three combined, and speak from the South, he would not receive enough to pay the costs of publication. If published at the South, his book would never be seen or heard of, and published at the North it would not be read.—So perfect is our provincialism, therefore, that enterprise is forced to the North for a sphere—talent for a market—genius for the ideas upon which to work—indolence for ease, and the tourist for attractions."

This extract exhibits in bold relief, and in small space, a large number of the present evils of past errors. It is charmingly frank and truthful. DeQuincey's Confessions of an opium eater are nothing to it. A distinguished writer on medical jurisprudence informs us that "the knowledge of the disease is half the cure;" and if it be true, as perhaps it is, we think the *Standard* is in a fair way to be reclaimed from the enormous vices of proslavery statism.

PROGRESS OF FREEDOM IN THE SOUTH.

"Now, by St. Paul, the work goes bravely on."

As well might the oligarchy attempt to stay the flux and reflux of the tides, as to attempt to stay the progress of Freedom in the South. Approved of God, the edict of the genius of Universal Emancipation has been proclaimed to the world, and nothing, save Deity himself, can possibly reverse it. To connive at the perpetuation of slavery is to disobey the commands of Heaven. Not to be an abolitionist is to be a wilful and diabolical instrument of the devil. The South needs to be free, the South wants to be free, the South *shall* be free !

The following extracts from Southern journals will show that the glorious light of a better era has already begun to penetrate and dispel the portentous clouds of slavery. The Wellsburg (Va.) *Herald*, an independent paper, referring to the vote of thirteen Democrats from that section, refusing, in the Virginia Legislature, in 1856, "to appropriate money from the general treasury for the recapture of runaway slaves," says :—

"We presume these delegates in some degree represent their constituents, and we are thereby encouraged and built up in the confidence that there are other interests in Virginia to be seen to besides those pertaining to slavery."

A non-slaveholding Southron, in the course of a communication in a more recent number of the same journal, says :—

"We are taxed to support slavery. The clean cash goes out of our own pockets into the pockets of the slaveholder, and this in many ways. I will now allude to but two. If a slave, for crime, is put to death or transported, the owner is paid for him out of the public treasury, and under this law thousands are paid out every year. Again, a standing army is kept up in the city of Richmond for no other purpose than to be ready to quell insurrection among the slaves ; this is paid for out of the public treasury annually. This standing army is called the public guard, but it is no less a standing army always kept up. We will quote from the acts of 1856 the expense of these two items to the State, on the 23d and 24th pages of the acts :—'To pay for slaves executed and transported, $22,000 ;' 'to the public guard at Richmond, $24,000.' This, be it noticed, is only for one year, making near $50,000 for these two objects in one year; but it can be shown by the present unequal plan of taxation between slave property and other property, that this is but a small item of our cash pocketed by the slaveholders; and yet some will say we have no reason to complain."

The editor of the Wheeling *Gazette* publishes the following as his platform on the slavery question:—

"Allying ourself to neither North nor South, on our own hook we adopt the following platform as our platform on this question, from which we never have and never will recede. *We may* FALL *on it, but* WILL NEVER LEAVE IT.

The severance of the General Government from slavery.

The REPEAL *of the fugitive slave law.*

The REPEAL *of the Nebraska Kansas Bill.*

No more slave territories.

THE PURCHASE AND MANUMISSION OF SLAVES IN THE DISTRICT OF COLUMBIA, OR THE REMOVAL OF THE SEAT OF GOVERNMENT TO FREE TERRITORY."

Says the Baltimore *Clipper*:—

'The South is contending for, and the North against, the extension of slavery into the territories; but we do not think that either side would consent to dissolve the Union about the negro population—a population which we look upon as a curse to the nation, and should rejoice to see removed to their native clime of Africa."

The *National Era*, one of the best papers in the country, published in Washington City, D. C., says:—

"The tendency of slavery to diffuse itself, and to crowd out free labor, was early observed by American patriots, North and South; and Mr. Jefferson, the great apostle of Republicanism, made an effort, in 1784, to cut short the encroaching tide of barbaric despotism, by prohibiting slavery in all the territories of the Union, down to thirty-one degrees of latitude, which was then our Southern boundary. His beneficent purpose failed, not for want of a decisive majority of votes present in the Congress of the Confederation, but in consequence of the absence of the delegates from one or two States, which were necessary to the constitutional majority. When the subject again came up, in 1787, Mr. Jefferson was Minister to France, and the famous ordinance of that year was adopted, prohibiting slavery North and West of the Ohio river. Between 1784 and 1787, the strides of slavery westward, into Tennessee and Kentucky, had become too considerable to admit of the policy of exclusion; and besides those regions were then integral parts of Virginia and North Carolina, and of course they could not be touched without the consent of those States. In 1820, another effort was made to arrest the progress of slavery, which threatened to monopolize the whole territory west of the Mississippi. In the meantime the South had apostatized from the faith of Jefferson. It had ceased to love universal liberty, and the growing importance of the cotton culture had caused the people to look with indifference upon the moral deformity of slavery; and, as a matter of course, the politicians became its apologists and defenders. After a severe struggle a compromise was agreed upon, by which Missouri was to be admitted with slavery, which was the immediate point in controversy; and slavery was to be excluded from all the territory North and West of that State.

"We have shown, from the most incontestable evidence, that there is in slave society a much greater tendency to diffuse itself into new regions, than belongs to freedom, for the reason that it has no internal vitality. It cannot live if circumscribed, and must, like a consumptive, be continually roving for a change of air to recuperate its wasting energies."

In the Missouri Legislature, in January, 1857, Mr. Brown, of St. Louis, proved himself a hero, a patriot, and a statesman, in the following words:—

"I am a Free-Soiler and I don't deny it. No word or vote of mine shall ever inure to the benefit of such a monstrous doctrine as the extension of Slavery over the patrimony of the free white laborers of the country. I am for the greatest good of the greatest number, and against the system which monopolizes the free and fertile territory of our country for a few slaveholders, to the exclusion of thousands upon thousands of the sinewy sons of toil. The time will come, and perhaps very soon, when the people will rule for their own benefit *and not for that of a class which, numerically speaking, is insignificant.* I stand here in the midst of the assembled Legislature of Missouri to avow myself a Free-Soiler. Let those who are scared at names shrink from the position if they will. I shall take my stand in favor of the white man. Here in Missouri I shall support the rights, the dignity and the welfare of the 800,000 non-slaveholders in preference to upholding and perpetuating the dominancy of the 30,000 slaveholders who inhabit our State."

The St. Louis *Democrat*, in an editorial article, under date of January 28, 1857, entitled itself to the favorable regard of every true lover of liberty, by talking thus boldly on the subject of the "Emancipation of Slavery in Missouri":—

"Viewing the question as a subject of State policy, we will venture to say that it is the grandest ever propounded to the people. If it were affirmed in a constitutional convention, and thoroughly carried out without any violation of vested rights, Missouri, in a few years subsequent to its consummation, would be the foremost State on the American continent. Population would flow in from all sides were the barrier of negro slavery once removed, and in place of 80,000 slaves, we should have 800,000 white men, which, in addition to the population we would have at that time, would give us at once an aggregate of two millions.

Is Missouri ambitious of political power?—a power which is slipping away from the South. The mode of acquiring it is found. We are not rash enough to attempt a description of our condition if the element of free labor were introduced. The earth would give up its hidden treasures at its bidding as the sea will give up its dead; and the soil would bloom more luxuriantly than if it drank the dews of Hermon nightly; ten thousand keels would vex our rivers, towns along their banks would grow into cities, and St. Louis would soon unite in itself the attributes of the greatest commercial manufacturing and literary metropolis in the world. Let it be remembered that we have every inanimate element of wealth and power within our limits, and that we require only labor—free labor—for we need not say that servile labor is inadequate. * * *

There need be no pernicious agitation, and even if there should, it is the penalty which we cannot avoid paying at some time; and it is easier to pay it now, than in the future. Who that watches passing events and indications, is not sensible of the fact that great internal convulsions await the slave States? Better to grapple with the danger in time, if danger there be, and avert it, than wait until it becomes formidable. One thing is certain, or history is no guide: that is, that slavery cannot be perpetuated anywhere. An agitation now would be the effort of the social system to throw off a disease which had not touched its vitals; hereafter it would be the struggle for life with a mortal sickness. But we do not apprehend any agitation more violent than has been forced upon us for years by the pro-slavery politicians. Agitating the slavery question, has been their constant business, and nothing worse has resulted from it than their elevation to office—no very trifling evil, by the way—and the temporary subjugation of Kansas.

Besides, we know that all the free States emancipated their slaves, and England and France theirs suddenly; and we have yet to learn that a dangerous agitation arose in any instance."

In addition to all this, it is well known, and we thank Heaven for the fact and for the indication, that, at the election held for Mayor of St. Louis, in April, 1857, the Abolition candidate, himself a native of Virginia, was triumphantly elevated to the chief magistracy of the city. Three cheers for St. Louis! nine for Missouri! thirteen for the South

In reference to the late election in St. Louis, in which the Emancipation party triumphed, the Wheeling (Va.) *Intelligencer* says :—

"These elections do demonstrate this fact, beyond a cavil, that the sentiment of the great majority of the people of this Union is irrevocably opposed to the extension of slavery ; that they are determined, if overwhelming public sentiment can avail anything, another slave State shall not be admitted into the confederacy. And why are they so determined? Because they believe, and not only believe, but see and know, that slavery is an unmitigated curse to the soil that sustains it. They know this, because they see every free State outstripping every slave State in all the elements that make a people powerful and prosperous; because they see the people in the one educated and thrifty, and in the other ignorant and thriftless ; because they have before their eyes a State like our own, once the very Union itself almost in importance, to-day taking her rank as a fifth rate power."

Non-slaveholders of the South ! fail not to support the papers—the Southern papers—that support your interests. Chief amongst those papers are the St. Louis (Mo.) *Democrat*, the *National Era*, published in Washington City, D. C., the Baltimore *Clipper*, the Wheeling (Va.) *Intelligencer*, and the Wellsburg (Va.) *Herald*.

A RIGHT FEELING IN THE RIGHT QUARTER.

There is but one way for the oligarchy to perpetuate slavery in the Southern States, and that is by perpetuating absolute ignorance among the non-slaveholding whites. This it is quite impossible for them to do. God has scattered the seeds of knowledge throughout every portion of the South, and they are, as might have been expected, beginning to take roo in her fertile soil. The following extracts from letters which have been received since we commenced writing this work, will show how powerfully the spirit of freedom is operating upon the minds of intelligent, thinking men in the slave States.

A Baltimorean, writing to us awhile previous to the last Presidential election, says :—

"I see that the Trustees of the University of North Carolina have dismissed Prof. Hedrick for writing a letter in favor of Republican principles. Oh, what an inglorious source of reflection for an American citizen! To think, to know that our boasted liberty of speech is a myth, an abstraction. To see a poor professor crushed under the feet of the tyrannical magnates of slavery, for daring to speak the honest sentiments of his heart. Where is fanaticism now, North or South? Oh, my country, my country, whither art thou tending? Truly we have fallen upon degenerate days. God grant that they may not be like those of ancient Greece and Rome, the forerunners of our country's ruin."

In a letter under date of November 1, 1856, a friend who resides in the eastern part of North Carolina, says :—

"In the papers which reached me last week I notice that our own State has been disgraced by a junto of pro-slavery hot-spurs, who had the audacity to meet in Raleigh for the express purpose of concocting measures for a dissolution of the Union. It appears that the three leading spirits of this cabal were the present governors of three neighboring States—three treasonable disturbers of the public peace, who, under the circumstances, should, in my opinion, have been shot dead upon the spot! I have each of their names noted down in my memorandum, and I shall certainly die unsatisfied, if I do not live to hear of their being thoroughly tarred and feathered, and ridden on a rail, by the non-slaveholding whites, agains whose welfare their machinations have been chiefly leveled. Rely upon it, that, if they do not soon sneak away into their graves, a day of retributive justice will most assuredly overtake them."

A native and resident of one of the towns in western North Carolina, under date of March 19, 1857, writes to us as follows :—

"While patrolling a few nights ago I was forcibly struck with the truthfulness of the remarks contained in your last letter.—Here I am, a poor but sober and industrious man, with a family dependent on me for support, and after I have finished my day's labor, I am compelled to walk the streets from nine in the evening till three in the morning, to restrain the roving propensities of other people's 'property'—niggers. Why should I thus be deprived of sleep that the slaveholder may slumber? I frankly acknowledge my indebtedness to you for opening my eyes upon this subject. The more I think and see of slavery the more I detest it. * * * I am becoming restless, and have been debating within my own mind whether I had not better emigrate to a free State. * * * If I live, I am determined to oppose slavery somewhere—here or elsewhere. It will be impossible for me to keep my lips sealed much longer. Indeed, I sometimes feel that I have been remiss in my duty in not having opened them ere now. But for the unfathomable ignorance that pervades the mass of the poor, deluded, slavery-saddled whites around me, I would not suppress my sentiments another hour."

Again, under date of April 7, 1857, he says :—

"I thank God that slavery will, in my opinion, soon be abolished. I wish to Heaven I had the ability to raise my voice successfully in favor of a just system to abolish it. I would indeed be rejoiced to have an opportunity to do something to relieve the South of the awful curse. Fear not that you will meet with no sympathizers in the South. You will have hosts of friends on every side—even in this town, if I am not greatly mistaken, a large majority of the citizens will add an enthusiastic *Amen!* to your work."

We might furnish similar extracts from other letters, but these, we think, are quite sufficient to show that the millennium of freedom is rapidly dawning throughout the benighted regions of slavery. Coveted events are happening in charming succession. All we have to do is to wait and work a little longer.

THE ILLITERATE POOR WHITES OF THE SOUTH.

Had we the power to sketch a true picture of life among the non-slaveholding whites of the South, every intelligent man who has a spark of philanthropy in his breast, and who should happen to gaze upon the picture, would burn with unquenchable indignation at that system of African slavery which entails unutterable miseries on the superior race. It is quite impossible, however, to describe accurately the deplorable ignorance and squalid poverty of the class to which we refer. The serfs of Russia have reason to congratulate themselves that they are neither the negroes nor the non-slaveholding whites of the South. Than the latter there can be no people in Christendom more unhappily situated. Below will be found a few extracts which will throw some light on the subject now under consideration.

Says William Gregg, in an address delivered before the South Carolina Institute, in 1851:—

"From the best estimates that I have been able to make, I put down the white people who ought to work, and who do not, or who are so employed as to be wholly unproductive to the State, at one hundred and twenty-five thousand. Any man who is an observer of things could hardly pass through our country, without being struck with the fact that all the capital, enterprise, and intelligence, is employed in directing slave labor; and the consequence is, that a large portion of our poor white people are wholly neglected, and are suffered to while away an existence in a state but one step in advance of the Indian of the forest. It is an evil of vast magnitude, and nothing but a change in public sentiment will effect its cure. These people must be brought into daily contact with the rich and intelligent—they must be stimulated to mental action, and taught to appreciate education and the comforts of civilized life; and this, we believe, may be effected only by the introduction of manufactures. My experience at Graniteville has satisfied me that unless our poor people can be brought together in villages, and some means of employment afforded them, it will be an utterly hopeless effort to undertake to educate them. We have collected at that place about eight hundred people, and as likely looking a set of country girls as may be found—industrious and orderly people, but deplorably ignorant, three-fourths of the adults not being able to read or to write their own names.

"It is only necessary to build a manufacturing village of shanties, in a healthy location, in any part of the State, to have crowds of these people around you, seeking employment at half the compensation given to operatives at the North. It is indeed painful to be brought in contact with such ignorance and degradation."

Again he asks:—

"Shall we pass unnoticed the thousands of poor, ignorant, degraded white people among us, who, in this land of plenty, live in comparative nakedness and starvation? Many a one is reared in *proud* South Carolina, from birth to manhood, who has never passed a month in which he has not, some part of the time, been stinted for meat. Many a mother is there who will tell you that her children are but scantily provided with bread, and much more scantily with meat; and, if they be clad with comfortable raiment, it is at the expense of these scanty allowances of food. These may be startling statements, but they are nevertheless true; and if not believed in Charleston, the members of our legislature who have traversed the State in electioneering campaigns can attest the truth."

In an article on "*Manufactures in South Carolina*," published some time ago in *DeBow's Review*, J. H. Taylor, of Charleston (S. C.) says:—

"There is in some quarters, a natural jealousy of the slightest innovation upon established habits, and because an effort has been made to collect the poor and unemployed white population into our new factories, fears have arisen that some evil would grow out of the introduction of such establishments among us. * * * The poor man has a vote as well as the rich man, and in our State the number of the former will largely overbalance the latter. So long as these poor but industrious people can see no mode of living except by a degrading operation of work with the negro upon the plantation, they will be content to endure life in its most discouraging forms, satisfied that they are *above* the slave, though faring often worse than he."

Speaking in favor of manufactures, the Hon. J. H. Lumpkin, of Georgia, said in 1852:—

"It is objected that these manufacturing establishments will become the hot-beds of crime. But I am by no means ready to concede that our poor, degraded, half-fed, half-clothed, and ignorant population—without Sabbath Schools, or any other kind of instruction, mental or moral, or without any just appreciation of character—will be injured by giving them employment, which will bring them under the oversight of employers, who will inspire them with self-respect by taking an interest in their welfare.'

In a paper on the "*Extension of Cotton and Wool Factories at the South*," Mr. Steadman, of Tennessee, says :—

"In Lowell, labor is paid the fair compensation of 80 cents a day for men, and $2 a week for women, beside board, while in Tennessee the average compensation for labor does not exceed 50 cents per day for men, and $1,25 per week for women."

In the course of a speech which he delivered in Congress several years ago, Mr. T. L. Clingman, of North Carolina, said :—

"Our manufacturing establishments can obtain the raw material (cotton) at nearly two cents on the pound cheaper than the New-England establishments. Labor is likewise one hundred per cent. cheaper. In the upper parts of the State, the labor of either a free man or a slave, including board, clothing, &c., can be obtained for from $110 to $120 per annum. It will cost at least twice that sum in New-England. The difference in the cost of female labor, whether free or slave, is even greater."

The Richmond (Va.) *Dispatch* says :—

"We will only suppose that the ready-made shoes imported into this city from the North, and sold here, were manufactured in Richmond. What a great addition it would be to the means of employment! How many boys and females would find the means of earning their bread, who are now suffering for a regular supply of the necessaries of life."

A citizen of New-Orleans, writing in *DeBow's Review*, says :—

"At present the sources of employment open to females (save in menial offices) are very limited; and an inability to procure suitable occupation is an evil much to be deplored, as tending in its consequences to produce demoralization. The superior grades of female labor may be considered such as imply a necessity for education on the part of the employee, while the menial class is generally regarded as of the lowest; and in a slave State, this standard is 'in the lowest depths, a lower deep,' from the fact, that, by association, it is a reduction of the white servant to the level of their colored fellow-menials."

Black slave labor, though far less valuable, is almost invariably better paid than free white labor. The reason is this: The fiat of the oligarchy has made it *fashionable* to "have negroes around," and there are, we are grieved to say, many non-slaveholding whites, (lickspittles,) who, in order to retain on their premises a hired slave whom they falsely imagine secures to them not only the appearance of wealth, but also a position of high social standing in the community, keep themselves in a perpetual strait.

Last Spring we made it our special business to ascertain the ruling rates of wages paid for labor, free and slave, in North Carolina. We found sober, energetic white men, between twenty and forty years of age, engaged in agricultural pursuits at a salary of $84 per annum—including board only; negro men, slaves, who performed little more than half the amount of labor, and who were exceedingly sluggish, awkward, and careless in all their movements, were hired out on adjoining farms at an average of about $115 per annum, including board, clothing, and medical attendance. Free white men and slaves were in the employ of the North Carolina Railroad Company; the former, whose services, in our opinion, were at least twice as valuable as the services of the latter, received only $12 per month each; the masters of the latter received $16 per month for every slave so employed. Industrious, tidy white girls, from sixteen to twenty years of age, had much difficulty in hiring themselves out as domestics in private families for $10 per annum—board only included; negro wenches, slaves, of corresponding ages, so ungraceful, stupid and filthy that no decent man would ever permit one of them to cross the threshold of his dwelling, were in brisk demand at from $65 to $70 per annum, including victuals, clothes, and medical attendance. These are facts, and in considering them, the students of political and social economy will not fail to arrive at conclusions of their own.

Notwithstanding the greater density of population in the free States, labor of every kind is, on an average, about one hundred per cent. higher there than it is in the slave States. This is another important fact, and one that every non-slaveholding white should keep registered in his mind.

Poverty, ignorance, and superstition, are the three leading characteristics of the non-slaveholding whites of the South. Many of them grow up to the age of maturity, and pass through life without ever owning as much as five dollars at any one time. Thousands of them die at an advanced age, as ignorant of the common alphabet as if it had never been invented. All are more or less impressed with a belief in witches, ghosts, and supernatural signs. Few are exempt from habits of sensuality and intemperance. None have anything like adequate ideas of the duties which they owe either to their God, to themselves, or to their fellow-men. Pitiable, indeed, in the fullest sense of the term, is their condition.

It is the almost utter lack of an education that has reduced them to their present unenviable situation. In the whole South there is scarcely a publication of any kind devoted to their interests. They are now completely under the domination of the oligarchy, and it is madness to suppose that they will ever be able to rise to a position of true manhood, until after the slave power shall have been utterly overthrown.

CHAPTER XI.

SOUTHERN LITERATURE.

It is with some degree of hesitation that we add a chapter on Southern Literature—not that the theme is inappropriate to this work; still less, that it is an unfruitful one; but our hesitation results from our conscious inability, in the limited time and space at our command, to do the subject justice. Few, except those whose experience has taught them, have any adequate idea of the amount of preparatory labor requisite to the production of a work into which the statistical element largely enters; especially is this so, when the statistics desired are not readily accessible through public and official documents. The author who honestly aims at entire accuracy in his statements, may find himself baffled for weeks in his pursuit of a single item of information, not of much importance in itself perhaps, when separately considered, but necessary in its connection with others, to the completion of a harmonious whole. Not unfrequently, during the preparation of the preceding pages, have we been subjected to this delay and annoyance.

The following brief references to the protracted preparatory labors and inevitable delays to which authors are subjected, may interest our readers, and induce them to regard with charity any deficiencies, either in detail or in general arrangement, which, owing to the necessary haste of preparation, these concluding pages of our work may exhibit:

Goldsmith was engaged nine years in the preparation of "*The Traveller,*" and five years in gathering and arranging the incidents of his "*Deserted Village,*" and two years in their versification.

Bancroft, the American Historian, has been more than thirty years engaged upon his History of the United States, from his projection of the work to the present date; and that History is not yet completed.

Hildreth, a no less eminent historian, from the time he began to collect materials for his History of the United States to the date of its completion, devoted no less than twenty-five years to the work.

Webster, our great lexicographer, gave thirty-five years of his life in bringing his Unabridged Dictionary of the English Language to the degree of accuracy and completeness in which we now find it.

Dr. John W. Mason, after ten years' labor in the accumulation of materials for a Life of Alexander Hamilton, was compelled to relinquish the work on account of impaired health.

Mr. James Banks, of Fayetteville, North Carolina, who recently delivered a lecture upon the Life and Character of Flora McDonald, was eighteen years in the collection of his materials.

Oulibicheff, a distinguished Russian author, spent twenty-five years in writing the Life of Mozart.

Examples of this kind might be multiplied to an almost indefinite extent. Indeed, almost all the poets, prose-writers, painters, sculptors, composers, and other devotees of Art, who have won undying fame for themselves, have done so through long years of earnest and almost unremitted toil.

We are quite conscious that the fullness and accuracy of statement which are desirable in this chapter cannot be attained in the brief time allowed us for its completion; but, though much will necessarily be omitted that ought to be said, we shall endeavor to make no statement of facts which are not well authenticated, and no inferences from the same which are not logically true. We can only promise to do the best in our power, with the materials at our command, to exhibit the inevitable influence of slavery upon Southern Literature, and to demonstrate that the accursed institution so cherished by the oligarchy, is no less prejudicial to our advancement in letters, than it is destructive of our material prosperity.

What is the actual condition of Literature at the South? Our question includes more than simple authorship in the various departments of letters, from the compilation of a primary reader to the production of a Scientific or Theological Treatise. We comprehend in it all the activities engaged in the creation, publication, and sale of books and periodicals, from the penny primer to the heavy folio, and from the dingy, coarse-typed weekly paper, to the large, well-filled daily.

It were unjust to deny a degree of intellectua activity to the South. It has produced a few good authors—a few competent editors, and a moderately large number of clever magazinists, paragraphists, essayists and critics Absolutely, then, it must be conceded that the South has something that may be called a literature ; it is only when we speak of her in comparison with the North, that we say, with a pardonably strong expression, "The South has no literature." This was virtually admitted by more than one speaker at the late "Southern Convention" at Savannah. Said a South Carolina orator on that occasion : "It is important that the South *should have* a literature of her own, to defend her principles and her rights ;" a sufficiently plain concession that she has not, now, such a literature. But *facts* speak more significantly than the rounded periods of Convention orators. Let us look at facts, then.

First, turning our attention to the periodical literature of the South, we obtain these results : By the census of 1850, we ascertain that the entire number of periodicals, daily, semi-weekly, weekly, semi-monthly, monthly and quarterly, published in the slave States, including the District of Columbia, were seven hundred and twenty-two. These had an aggregate *yearly* circulation of ninety-two million one hundred and sixty-seven thousand one hundred and twenty-nine. (92,167,129). The number of periodicals, of every class, published in the non-slaveholding States (exclusive of California) was one thousand eight hundred and ninety-three, with an aggregate yearly circulation of three hundred and thirty-three million three hundred and eighty-six thousand and eighty-one. (333,386,081).

We are aware that there may be inaccuracies in the foregoing estimates; but the compilers of the census, not we, are responsible for them. Besides, the figures are unquestionably as fair for the South as for the North; we accept them, therefore, as a just basis of our comparisons. Nearly seven years have elapsed since these statistics were taken, and these seven years have wrought an immense change in the journalism of the North, without any corresponding change in that of the South. It is noteworthy that, as a general thing, the principal journals of the free States are more comprehensive in their scope, more complete in every department, and enlist, if not a higher order of talent, at least *more* talent, than they did seven years ago. This improvement extends not only to the metropolitan, but to the country papers also. In fact, the very highest literary ability, in finance, in political economy, in science, in statism, in law, in theology, in medicine, in the belles-lettres, is laid under contribution by the journals of the non-slaveholding States. This is true only to a very limited degree of Southern journals. Their position, with but few exceptions, is substantially the same that it was ten years ago. They are neither worse nor better—the imbecility and inertia which attaches to everything which slavery touches, clings to them now as tenaciously as it did when Henry A. Wise thanked God for the paucity of newspapers in the Old Dominion, and the platitudes of "Father" Ritchie were recognized as the political gospel of the South. They have not, so far as we can learn, increased materially in number, nor in the aggregate of their yearly circulation. In the free States no week passes that does not add to the number of their journals, and extend the circle of their readers and their influence. Since the census tables to which we have referred were prepared, two of the many excellent weekly journals of which the city of New-York can boast, have sprung into being, and attained an aggregate circulation more than twice as large as that of the entire newspaper press of Virginia in 1850—and exceeding, by some thousands, the aggregate circulation of the two hundred and fifty journals of which Alabama, Arkansas, Kentucky, Georgia, North Carolina and Florida, could boast at the time above-mentioned.

In this connection, we beg leave to introduce the following letter, kindly furnished us by the proprietors of the N. Y. Tribune, in answer to enquiries which we addressed to them :—

TRIBUNE OFFICE, NEW YORK,
30th May, 1857.

MR. H. R. HELPER,

Sir :—

In answer to your inquiry we inform you that we employ in our building one hundred and seventy-six persons regularly: this does not include our carriers and cartmen, nor does it include the men employed in the Job Office in our building. During the past year we have used in printing *The Tribune*, Forty-four thousand nine hundred and seventy nine (44,979) reams of paper weighing two million three hundred and ten thousand one hundred and thirty (2,310,130) pounds. We publish one hundred and seventy-six thousand copies of our weekly edition, which goes to press, the second form, at 7 1-2 o'clock, A. M. and is finished at 2 A. M. the next morning. Our mailers require eighteen to nineteen hours to mail our Weekly, which makes from thirty to thirty-two cart loads.

Very respectfully,
GREELEY & MCELRATH.

Throughout the non-slaveholding States, the newspaper or magazine that has *not* improved during the last decade of years, is an exception to the general rule. Throughout the entire slaveholding States, the newspaper or magazine that *has* improved during that time, is no less an exception to the general rule that there obtains. Outside of the larger cities of the South, there are not, probably, half a dozen newspapers in the whole slaveholding region that can safely challenge a comparison with the country-press of the North. What that country-press was twenty years ago, the country-press of the South is now.

We do not deny that the South has produced able journalists; and that some of the newspapers of her principal cities exhibit a degree of enterprise and talent that cannot fail to command for them the respect of all intelligent men. But these journals, we regret to say, are marked exceptions to the general condition of the Southern press; and even the best of these fall far below the standard of excellence attained by the leading journals of the North. In fact, whether our comparison embraces quantity only, or extends to both quantity and quality, it is found to be immeasurably in favor of the non-slaveholding States, which in journalism, as in all other industrial pursuits, leave their slavery-cursed competitors at an infinite distance behind them, and thus vindicate the superiority of free institutions, which, recognizing labor as honorable, secure its rewards for all.

The literary vassalage of the South to the North constitutes in itself a most significant commentary upon the diatribes of the former concerning "a purely Southern literature." To begin at the beginning—the Alphabetical Blocks and Educational tables from which our Southern abecedarian takes his initial lesson, were projected and manufactured in the North. Going forward a step, we find the youngling intent in spelling short sentences, or gratifying his juvenile fondness for the fine arts by copying the wood-cuts from his Northern primer. Yet another step, and we discover him with his Sanders' Reader, his Mitchell's Geography, his Emerson's Arithmetic, all produced by Northern mind and Northern enterprise. There is nothing *wrong* in this; it is only a little ridiculous in view of the fulminations of the Southern proslavery press against the North. Occasionally however we are amused by the efforts of the oligarchs to make their own school-books, or to root out of all educational text-books every reference to the pestilential heresy of freedom. A "gentleman" in Charleston, S. C. is devoting his energies to the preparation of a series of pro-slavery elementary works, consisting of primers, readers, &c.—and lo! they are all printed, stitched and bound north of Mason and Dixon's line! A single *fact* like this is sufficient to overturn whole folios of *theory* concerning the divinity of slavery. The truth is, that, not school-books alone, but works of almost every class produced by the South, depend upon Northern enterprise and skill for their introduction to the public Mr. DeBow, the eminent Statistician, publishes a Southern Review, purporting to be issued from New Orleans. It is printed and bound in the city of New York. We clip the following paragraph from a recent number of the Vicksburgh (Miss.) *Whig*:—

"SOUTHERN ENTERPRIZE.—Even the Mississippi Legislature, at its late session allowed its laws to go to Boston to be printed, and made an appropriation of $3,000 to pay one of its members to go there and read the proof sheets instead of having it done in the State. and thereby assisting in building up a Southern publishing house. What a commentary on the Yankee-haters!"

The Greensboro (N. C.) *Patriot* thus records a similar contribution, on the part of that State, to "the creation of a purely Southern Literature:"

"We have heard it said, that those who had the control of the printing of the revised Statutes of North Carolina, in order to save a few dimes, had the work executed in Boston, in preference to giving the job to a citizen of this State. We impugn not the motives of the agents in this matter; but it is a little humiliating that no work except the commonest labor, can be done in North Carolina; that everything which requires a little skill, capital, or ingenuity, must be sent North. In the case under consideration, we have heard it remarked, that when the whole bill of expenses connected with the printing of the Revised Statutes in Boston was footed up, it only amounted to a few thousand dollars more than the job would have cost in this State. But then we have the consolation of knowing that the book *came from the North*, and that it was printed among the *abolitionists* of Boston; the *peculiar friends* of North Carolina and the South generally.—Of course we ought to be willing to pay a few extra thousands in consideration of these important facts!"

Southern divines give us elaborate "Bible Arguments;" Southern statists heap treatise upon treatise through which the Federal Constitution is tortured into all monstrous shapes; Southern novelists bore us *ad infinitum* with pictures of the beatitudes of plantation life and the negro-quarters; Southern verse-wrights drone out their drowsy dactyls or grow ventricous with their turgid heroics all in defence of slavery,—priest, politician, novelist, bardling, severally ringing the changes upon "the Biblical institution," "the conservative institution," "the humanizing institution," "the patriarchal institution"—and then—have their books printed on Northern paper, with Northern types, by Northern artizans, stitched, bound and made ready for the market by Northern industry; and yet fail to see in all this, as a true philosophical mind *must* see, an overwhelming refutation of their miserable sophisms in behalf of a system against which humanity in all its impulses and aspirations, and civilization in all its activities and triumphs, utter their perpetual protest.

From a curious article in the "American Publishers Circular" on "Book Making in America," we give the following extracts:

"It is somewhat alarming to know that the number of houses now actually engaged in the publishing of books, not including periodicals, amounts to more than three hundred. About three-fourths of these are engaged in Boston, New-York, Philadelphia, and Baltimore—the balance being divided between Cincinnati, Buffalo, Auburn, Albany, Louisville, Chicago, St. Louis, and a few other places. There are more than three thousand booksellers who dispense the publications of these three hundred, besides six or seven thousand apothecaries, grocers, and hardware dealers, who connect literature with drugs, molasses, and nails.

"The best printing in America is probably now done in Cambridge; the best cloth binding in Boston, and the best calf and morocco in New-York and Philadelphia. In these two latter styles we are, as yet, a long distance from Heyday, the pride of London. His finish is supreme. There is nothing between it and perfection.

"Books have multiplied to such an extent in our country, that it now takes 750 paper mills, with 2,000 engines in constant operation, to supply the printers, who work day and night, endeavoring to keep their engagements with publishers. These tireless mills produced 270,000,000 pounds of paper the past year, which immense supply has sold for about $27,000,000. A pound and a quarter of rags were required for a pound of paper, and 400,000,000 pounds were therefore consumed in this way last year. The cost of manufacturing a twelve months' supply of paper for the United States, aside from labor and rags, is computed at $4,000,000. * * *

"The Harper establishment, the largest of our publishing houses, covers half an acre of ground. If old Mr. Caxton, who printed those stories of the Trojan war so long ago, could follow the Ex-Mayor of New-York in one of his morning rounds in Franklin Square, he would be, to say the least, a little surprised. He would see in one room the floor loaded with the weight of 150 tons of presses. The electrotyping process would puzzle him somewhat; the drying and pressing process would startle him; the bustle would make his head ache; and the stock-room would quite finish him. An edition of Harpers' Monthly Magazine alone consists of 175,000. Few persons have any idea how large a number this is as applied to the edition of a book. It is computed that if these magazines were to rain down, and one man should attempt to pick them up like chips, it would take him a fortnight to pick up the copies of one single number, supposing him to pick up one every second, and to work ten hours a day."

"The rapidity with which books are now manufactured is almost incredible. A complete copy of one of Bulwer's novels, published across the water in three volumes, and reproduced here in one, was swept through the press in New-York in fifty hours, and offered for sale smoking hot in the streets. The fabulous edifice proposed by a Yankee from Vermont, no longer seems an impossibility. 'Build the establishment according to my plan,' said he; 'drive a sheep in at one end, and he shall immediately come out at the other, four quarters of lamb, a felt hat, a leather apron, and a quarto Bible.'"

The business of the Messrs. Harper, whose establishment is referred to in the foregoing extract, is probably more generally diffused over every section of this country than that of any other publishing house. From enquiries recently made of them we learn that they issue, on an average, 3,000 bound volumes per day, throughout the year, and that each volume will average 500 pages—making a total of about one million of volumes, and not less than five hundred millions of pages per annum. This does not include the Magazine and books in pamphlet form, each of which contains as much matter as a bound volume.—Their bills for paper exceed $300,000 annually, and as the average cost is fifteen cents per pound, they consume more than two millions of pounds—say one thousand tons of white paper.

There are regularly employed in their own premises about 550 persons, including printers, binders, engravers, and clerks. These are all paid in full once a fortnight in bankable money. Besides these, there are numerous authors and artists in every section of the country, who furnish manuscripts and illustrations, on terms generally satisfactory to all the parties interested.

The Magazine has a monthly circulation of between 175,000 and 200,000, or about two millions of copies annually. Each number of the Magazine is closed up about the fifth of the month previous to its date. Three or four days thereafter the mailing begins, commencing with more distant subscribers, all of whom are supplied before any copies are sold for delivery in New-York. The intention of the publishers is, that it shall be delivered as nearly as possible on the same day in St. Louis, New-Orleans, Cincinnati, Philadelphia, Boston, and New-York. It takes from ten to twelve days to dispatch the whole edition, (which weighs between four and five tons,) by mail and express.

Their new periodical, "Harpers' Weekly," has, in a little more than four months, reached a sale of nearly 70,000 copies. The mailing of this commences on Tuesday night, and occupies about three days.

Ex-Mayor Harper, whom we have found to be one of the most affable and estimable gentlemen in the city of New-York, informed us, sometime ago, that, though he had no means of knowing positively, he was of the opinion that about eighty per cent. of all their publications find final purchasers in the free States—the remainder, about twenty per cent., in the slave States. Yet it is probable that, with one or two exceptions, no other publishing house in the country has so large a per centage of Southern trade.

Of the "more than three hundred houses engaged in the publication of books," to which the writer in the "American Publishers' Circular" refers, upwards of nine-tenths of the number are in the non-slaveholding States, and these represent not less than ninety-nine hundredths of the whole capital invested in the business. Baltimore has twice as many publishers as any other Southern city; and nearly as many as the whole South beside. The census returns of 1850 give but twenty-four publishers for the entire South, and ten of these were in Maryland. The relative disproportion which then existed in this branch of enterprise, between the North and the South, still exists; or, if it has been changed at all, that change is in favor of the North. So of all the capital, enterprise and industry involved in the manufacture of the *material* that enters into the composition of books. All the paper manufactories of the South do not produce enough to supply a single publishing house in the city of New-York.—Perhaps "a Southern Literature" does not necessarily involve the enterprises requisite to the *manufacture* of books; but experience has shown that there is a somewhat intimate relation between the author, printer, paper-maker and publisher; in other words, that the intellectual activity which expresses itself in books, is measurable by the mechanical activities engaged in their manufacture.—Thus a State that is fruitful in authors will almost necessarily be fruitful in publishers; and the number of both classes will be proportioned to the *reading* population. The poverty of Southern literature is legitimately shown, therefore, in the paucity of Southern publishers. We do not deny a high degree of cultivated talent to the South; we are familiar with the names of her sons whose genius has made them eminent; all that we insist upon is, that the same accursed influence which has smitten her industrial enterprises with paralysis, and retarded indefinitely her material advancement, has exerted a correspondiug influence upon her literature. How it has done this we shall more fully indicate before we close the chapter.

At the "Southern Convention" held some months since at Savannah, a good deal was said about "Southern literature," and many suggestions made in reference to the best means for its promotion. One speaker thought that "they could get text-books at home without going to either Old England or New England for them." Well—they can try. The effort will not harm them ; nor the North either. The orator was confident "that the South had talent enough to do anything that needs to be done, and independence enough to do it." The *talent* we shall not deny ; the *independence* we are ready to believe in when we see it. When she throws off the incubus of slavery under which she goes staggering like the Sailor of Bagdad under the weight of the Old Man of the Sea, she will prove her independence, and demonstrate her ability "to do anything that needs to be done." Till then she is but a fettered giant, whose vitals are torn by the dogs which her own folly has engendered.

Another speaker, on the occasion referred to, half-unconsciously it would seem, threw a gleam of light upon the subject under discussion, which, had not himself and his hearers been bat-blind, would have revealed the clue that conducts from the darkness in which they burrow to the day of redemption for the South. Said he :—

"Northern publishers employ the talent of the South and of the whole country to write for them, and pour out thousands annually for it ; but Southern men expect to get talent without paying for it. The *Southern Quarterly Review* and the *Literary Messenger* are literally struggling for existence, for want of material aid. * * * It is not the South that builds up Northern literature—*they do it themselves.* There is talent and mind and poetic genius enough in the South to build up a literature of a high order ; but Southern publishers cannot get money enough to assist them in their enterprises, and, therefore, the South has no literature.

Here are truths. "Southern men expect to get talent without paying for it." A very natural expectation, considering that they have been accustomed to have all their material wants supplied by the uncompensated toil of their slaves. In this instance it may seem an absurd one, but it results legitimately from the system of slavery. That system, in fact, operates in a two-fold way against the Southern publisher: first, by its practical repudiation of the scriptural axiom that the laborer is worthy of his hire; and secondly, by restricting the circle of readers through the ignorance which it inevitably engenders. How is it that the people of the North build up their literature?—Two words reveal the secret: *intelligence—compensation.* They are *a reading people*—the poorest artizan or day-laborer has his shelf of books, or his daily or weekly paper, whose contents he seldom fails to master before retiring at night; and *they are accustomed to pay for all the books and papers which they peruse.* Readers and payers—these are the men who insure the prosperity of publishers. Where a system of enforced servitude prevails, it is very apt to beget loose notions about the obligation of paying for anything; and many minds fail to see the distinction, morally, between compelling Sambo to pick cotton without paying him wages, or compelling Lippincott & Co. to manufacture books for the planter's pleasure or edification upon the same liberal terms. But more than this—where a system of enforced servitude prevails, a fearful degree of ignorance prevails also, as its necessary accompaniment. The enslaved masses are, of course, thrust back from the fountains of knowledge by the strong arm of law, while the poor non-slaveholding classes are almost as effectually excluded from the institutions of learning by their poverty—the sparse population of slaveholding districts being unfavorable to the maintenance of free schools, and the exigencies of their condition forbidding them to avail themselves of any more costly educational privileges.

Northern publishers can "employ the talent of the South and of the whole country to write for them, and pour out thousands annually for it," simply because a *reading* population, accustomed to *pay* for the service which it receives, enables them to do so. A similar population at the South would enable Southern publishers to do the same. Substitute free labor for slave labor, the institutions of freedom for those of slavery, and it would not long remain true that "Southern publishers cannot get money enough to assist them in their enterprises, and therefore the South has no literature." This is the discovery which the South Carolina orator from whom we quote, but narrowly escaped making, when he stood upon its very edge, and rounded his periods with the truths in whose unapprehended meanings was hidden this germ of redemption for a nation.

The self-stultification of folly, however, was never more evident than it is in the current gabble of the oligarchs about a "Southern literature." They do not mean by it a healthy, manly, normal utterance of unfettered minds, without which there can be no proper literature; but an emasculated substitute therefor, from which the element of freedom is eliminated; husks, from which the kernel has escaped—a body, from which the vitalizing spirit has fled—a literature which ignores manhood by confounding it with brutehood; or, at best, deals with all smiles of freedom as treason against the "peculiar institution." There is not a single great name in the literary annals of the old or new world that could drawf itself to the stature requisite to gain admission into the Pantheon erected by these devotees of the Inane for their Lilliputian deities. Thank God, a "Southern literature," in the sense intended by the champions of slavery, is a simple impossibility, rendered such by that exility of mind which they demand in its producers as a prerequisite to admission into the guild of Southern authorship. The tenuous thoughts of such authorlings could not survive a single breath of manly criticism. The history of the rise, progress, and decline of their literature could be easily written on a child's smooth palm, and leave space enough for its funeral oration and epitaph. The latter might appropriately be that which, in one of our rural districts, marks the grave of a still-born infant:—

"If so early I am done for,
I wonder what I was begun for!"

We desire to see the South bear its just proportion in the literary activities and achievements of our common country. It has never yet done so, and it never will until its own manhood is vindicated in the abolition of slavery. The impulse which such a measure would give to all industrial pursuits that deal with the elements of material prosperity, would be imparted also to the no less valuable but more intangible creations of the mind. Take from the intellect of the South the incubus which now oppresses it, and its rebound would be glorious; the era of its diviner inspirations would begin; and its triumphs would be a perpetual vindication of the superiority of free institutions over those of slavery.

To Duyckinck's "Cyclopedia of American Literature—a sort of *Omnium-gatherum* that reminds one of Jeremiah's figs—we are indebted for the following facts: The whole number of "American authors" whose place of nativity is given, is five hundred and sixty-nine. Of these seventy-nine were foreign born, eighty-seven were natives of the South, and four hundred and three—a vast majority of the whole, first breathed the vital air in the free North. Many of those who were born in the South, received their education in the North, quite a number of whom became permanent residents thereof. Still, for the purposes of this computation, we count them on the side of the South. Yet how significant the comparison which this computation furnishes! Throwing the foreign born (adopted citizens, mostly residents of the North) out of the reckoning, and the record stands,—Northern authors *four hundred and three;* Southern, *eighty-seven*—a difference of three hundred and sixteen in favor of the North! And this, probably, indicates very fairly the relative intellectual activity of the two sections.

We accept the facts gleaned from Duyckinck's work as a basis, simply, of our estimate: not as being absolutely accurate in themselves, though they are doubtless reliable in the main, and certainly as fair for the South as they are for the North. We might dissent from the judgment of the compiler in reference to the propriety of applying the term "literature" to much that his compilation contains; but as tastes have proverbially differed from the days of the venerable dame who kissed her cow —not to extend our researches into the condition of things anterior to that interesting event—we will not insist upon *our* view of the matter, but take it for granted that he has disentombed from forgotten reviews, newspapers, pamphlets, and posters, a fair relative proportion of "authors" for both North and South, for which "American Literature" is unquestionably under infinite obligations to him!

Griswold's "Poets and Poetry of America" and Thomas Buchanan Read's "Female Poets of America" furnish evidence, equally conclusive, of the benumbing influence of slavery upon the intellect of a country. Of course, these compilers say nothing about Slavery, and probably never thought of it in connection with their respective works, but none the less significant on that account is the testimony of the *facts* which they give. From the last edition of Griswold's compilation, (which contains the names of none of our female writers, he having included them in a separate volume) we find the names of one hundred and forty-one writers of verse: of these *one* was foreign-born, *seventeen* natives of the slaveholding, and *one hundred and twenty-three* of the non-slaveholding States. Of our female poets, whose nativity is given by Mr. Read, *eleven* are natives of the South; and *seventy-three* of the North! These simple arithmetical figures are God's eternal Scripture against the folly and madness of Slavery, and need no aid of rhetoric to give emphasis to the startling eloquence of their revelations.

But, after all, literature is not to be estimated by cubic

feet or pounds averdupois, nor measured by the bushel or the yardstick. Quality, rather than quantity, is the true standard of estimation. The fact, however, matters little for our present purpose ; for the South, we are sorry to say, is as much behind the North in the former as in the latter. We do not forget the names of Gayarre, Benton, Simms, and other eminent citizens of the Slave States, who have by their contributions to American letters conferred honor upon themselves and upon our common country, when we affirm, that those among our authors who enjoy a cosmopolitan reputation, are, with a few honorable exceptions, natives of the Free North ; and that the names which most brilliantly illustrate our literature, in its every department, are those which have grown into greatness under the nurturing influence of free institutions. "Comparisons are odious," it is said ; and we will not, unnecessarily, render them more so, in the present instance, by contrasting, name by name, the literary men of the South with the literary men of the North. We do not depreciate the former, nor overestimate the latter. But let us ask, whence come our geographers, our astronomers, our chemists, our meteorologists, our ethnologists, and others, who have made their names illustrious in the domain of the Natural Sciences? Not from the Slave States, certainly. In the Literature of Law, the South can furnish no name that can claim peership with those of Story and of Kent ; in History, none that tower up to the altitude of Bancroft, Prescott, Hildreth, Motley and Washington Irving ; in Theology, none that can challenge favorable comparison with those of Edwards, Dwight,

Channing, Taylor, Bushnell, Tyler and Wayland in Fiction, none that take rank with Cooper, and Mrs. Stowe; and but few that may do so with even the second class novelists of the North;* in Poetry, none that can command position with Bryant, Halleck, and Percival, with Whittier, Longfellow, and Lowell, with Willis, Stoddard and Taylor, with Holmes, Saxe, and Burleigh; and—we might add twenty other Northern names before we found their Southern peer, with the exception of poor Poe, who, within a narrow range of subjects, showed himself a poet of consummate art, and occupies a sort of debatable ground between our first and second-class writers.

We might extend this comparison to our writers in every department of letters, from the compiler of school-books to the author of the most profound ethical treatise, and with precisely the same result. But we forbear. The task is distasteful to our State pride, and would have been entirely avoided had not a higher principle urged us to its performance. It remains for us now to enquire,

WHAT HAS PRODUCED THIS LITERARY PAUPERISM OF THE SOUTH? One single word, most pregnant in its terrible meanings, answers the question. That word is—SLAVERY! But we have been so long accustomed to the ugly thing itself, and have become so familiar with its no less ugly fruits, that the common mind fails to apprehend the connection between the one, as cause, and the other as effect; and

* We Southrons all glory in the literary reputation of Mr. Simms; yet we must confess his inferiority to Cooper, and prejudice alone will refuse to admit, that, while in the *art* of the novelist he is the superior of Mrs. Stowe in genius he must take position below her.

it therefore becomes necessary to give a more detailed answer to our interrogatory.

Obviously, then, the conditions requisite to a flourishing literature are wanting at the South. These are—

I. Readers. The people of the South are not a reading people. Many of the adult population never learned to read ; still more, do not care to read. We have been impressed, during a temporary sojourn in the North, with the difference between the middle and laboring classes in the Free States, and the same classes in the Slave States, in this respect. Passing along the great routes of travel in the former, or taking our seat in the comfortable cars that pass up and down the avenues of our great commercial metropolis, we have not failed to contrast the employment of our fellow-passengers with that which occupies the attention of the corresponding classes on our various Southern routes of travel. In the one case, a large proportion of the passengers seem intent upon mastering the contents of the newspaper, or some recently published book. The merchant, the mechanic, the artizan, the professional man, and even the common laborer, going to or returning from their daily avocations, are busy with their morning or evening paper, or engaged in an intelligent discussion of some topic of public interest. This is their leisure hour, and it is given to the acquisition of such information as may be of immediate or ultimate use, or to the cultivation of a taste for elegant literature. In the other case, newspapers and books seem generally ignored, and noisy discussions of village and State politics, the tobacco and cotton crops, filibusterism in Cuba, Nicaragua, or Sonora, the price of negroes generally, and especially of "fine-looking wenches," the beauties of lynch-law, the delights of horse-racing, the excitement of street fights with bowie-knives and revolvers, the "manifest destiny" theory that justifies the stealing of all territory contiguous to our own, and kindred topics, constitute the warp and woof of conversation. All this is on a level with the general intelligence of the Slave States. It is true, these States have their educated men,—the majority of whom owe their literary culture to the colleges of the North. Not that there are no Southern colleges—for there are institutions, so called, in a majority of the Slave States.—Some of them, too, are not deficient in the appointments requisite to our higher educational institutions; but as a general thing, Southern colleges are colleges only in *name*, and will scarcely take rank with a third-rate Northern academy, while our academies, with a few exceptions, are immeasurably inferior to the public schools of New-York, Philadelphia, and Boston. The truth is, there is a vast inert mass of stupidity and ignorance, too dense for individual effort to enlighten or remove, in all communities cursed with the institution of slavery. Disguise the unwelcome truth as we may, slavery is the parent of ignorance, and ignorance begets a whole brood of follies and of vices, and every one of these is inevitably hostile to literary culture. The masses, if they think of literature at all, think of it only as a costly luxury, to be monopolized by the few.

The proportion of white adults over twenty years of age,

in each State, who cannot read and write, to the *whole* white population, is as follows:

Connecticut,	1	to every	568	Louisiana,	1	to every	38½
Vermont,	1	"	473	Maryland	1	"	27
N. Hampshire,	1	"	310	Mississippi,	1	"	20
Massachusetts,	1	"	166	Delaware,	1	"	18
Maine,	1	"	108	South Carolina,	1	"	17
Michigan,	1	"	97	Missouri,	1	"	16
Rhode Island,	1	"	67	Alabama,	1	"	15
New Jersey,	1	"	58	Kentucky,	1	"	13½
New York,	1	"	56	Georgia,	1	"	13
Pennsylvania,	1	"	50	Virginia,	1	"	12½
Ohio,	1	"	43	Arkansas,	1	"	11⅓
Indiana,	1	"	18	Tennessee,	1	"	11
Illinois,	1	"	17	North Carolina,	1	"	7

In this table, Illinois and Indiana are the only Free States which, in point of education, are surpassed by any of the Slave States; and this disgraceful fact is owing, principally, to the influx of foreigners, and to immigrants from the Slave States. New-York, Rhode Island, and Pennsylvania have also a large foreign element in their population, that swells very considerably this percentage of ignorance. For instance, New-York shows, by the last census, a population of 98,722 who cannot read and write, and of this number 68,052 are foreigners; Rhode Island, 3,607, of whom 2,359 are foreigners; Pennsylvania, 76,272, of whom 24,989 are foreigners. On the other hand, the ignorance of the Slave States is principally *native* ignorance, but comparatively few emigrants from Europe seeking a home upon a soil cursed with "the peculiar institution." North Carolina has a foreign population of only 340, South Carolina only 104, Arkansas only 27, Tennessee only 505, and Virginia only 1,137, who cannot read and write; while the aggregate of *native* ignorance in these five States (exclusive of the *slaves*, who are debarred all education by *law*) is 278,948! No longer ago than 1837, Governor Clarke, of Kentucky, in his message to the Legislature of that State, declared that "by the computation of those most familiar with the subject, *one-third of the adult population of the State are unable to write their names*;" and Governor Campbell, of Virginia, reported to the Legislature, that "from the returns of ninety-eight clerks, it appeared that of 4,614 applications for marriage licenses in 1837, no less than 1,047 were made by men unable to write."

In the Slave States the proportion of free white children between the ages of five and twenty, who are found at any school or college, is not quite *one-fifth* of the whole; in the Free States, the proportion is more than *three-fifths*.

We could fill our pages with facts like these to an almost indefinite extent, but it cannot be necessary. No truth is more demonstrable, nay, no truth has been more abundantly demonstrated, than this: that Slavery is hostile to general education; its strength, its very life, is in the ignorance and stolidity of the masses; it naturally and necessarily represses general literary culture. To talk, therefore, of the "creation of a purely Southern Literature," without *readers* to demand, or *writers* to produce it, is the mere babble of idiocy.

II. Another thing essential to the creation of a literature is Mental Freedom. How much of *that* is to be found in the region of Slavery? We will not say that there is *none;* but if it exists, it exists as the outlawed antagonist of human chattelhood. He who believes that the despotism of the accursed institution expends its malignant forces upon the *slave*, leaving intact the white and (so called) free population, is the victim of a most monstrous delusion. One end of the yoke that bows the African to the dust, presses heavily upon the neck of his Anglo-Saxon master. The entire mind of the South either stultifies itself into acquiescence with Slavery, succumbs to its authority, or chafes in indignant protest against its monstrous pretensions and outrageous usurpations. A free press is an institution almost unknown at the South. Free speech is considered as treason against slavery: and when people dare neither speak nor print their thoughts, free thought itself is well nigh extinguished. All that can be said in *defence* of human bondage, may be spoken freely; but question either its morality or its policy, and the terrors of lynch law are at once invoked to put down the pestilent heresy. The legislation of the Slave States for the suppression of the freedom of speech and the press, is disgraceful and cowardly to the last degree, and can find its parallel only in the meanest and bloodiest despotisms of the Old World. No institution that could bear the light would thus sneakingly seek to burrow itself in utter darkness. Look, too, at the mobbings, lynchings, robberies, social and political proscriptions, and all manner of nameless outrages, to which men in the South have been subjected, simply upon the suspicion that they were the enemies of Slavery. We could fill page after page of this volume with the record of such atrocities. But a simple reference to them is enough. Our countrymen have not yet forgotten why John C. Underwood was, but a few months since, banished from his home in Virginia, and the accomplished Hedreck driven from his College professorship in North Carolina. They believed Slavery inimical to the best interest of the South, and for daring to give expression to this belief in moderate yet manly language, they were ostracised by the despotic Slave Power, and compelled to seek a refuge from its vengeance in States where the principles of freedom are better understood. Pending the last Presidential election, there were thousands, nay, tens of thousands of voters in the Slave States, who desired to give their suffrages for the Republican nominee, John C. Fremont, himself a Southron, but a non-slaveholder. The Constitution of the United States guaranteed to these men an expression of their preference at the ballot-box. But were they permitted such an expression? Not at all. They were denounced, threatened, overawed, by the Slave Power—and it is not too much to say that there was really no *Constitutional election*,—that is, no such free expression of political preferences as the Constitution aims to secure—in a majority of the Slave States.

From a multiplicity of facts like these, the inference is unavoidable, that Slavery tolerates no freedom of the press—no freedom of speech—no freedom of opinion. To expect that a whole-souled, manly literature can flourish under such conditions, is as absurd as it would be to look for health amid the pestilential vapors of a dungeon, or for the continuance of animal life without the aid of oxygen.

III. Mental activity—force—enterprise—are requisite to the creation of literature. Slavery tends to sluggishness—imbecility—inertia. Where free thought is treason, the masses will not long take the trouble of thinking at all. Desuetude begets incompetence—the *dare-not* soon becomes the *cannot.* The mind thus enslaved, necessarily loses its interest in the processes of other minds ; and its tendency is to sink down into absolute stolidity or sottishness. Our remarks find melancholy confirmation in the abject servilism in which multitudes of the non-slaveholding whites of the South are involved. In them, ambition, pride, self-respect, hope, seem alike extinct. Their slaveholding fellows are, in some respects, in a still more unhappy condition—helpless, nerveless, ignorant, selfish ; yet vain-glorious, self-sufficient and brutal. Are these the chosen architects who are expected to build up "a purely Southern literature?"

The truth is, slavery destroys, or vitiates, or pollutes, whatever it touches. No interest of society escapes the influence of its clinging curse. It makes Southern religion a stench in the nostrils of Christendom—it makes Southern politics a libel upon all the principles of Republicanism—it makes Southern literature a travesty upon the honorable profession of letters. Than the better class of Southern authors themselves, none will feel more keenly the truth of our remarks. They write books, but can find for them neither publishers nor remunerative sales at the South The executors of Calhoun seek, for his works, a

Northern publisher. Benton writes history and prepares voluminous compilations, which are given to the world through a Northern publisher. Simms writes novels and poems, and they are scattered abroad from the presses of a Northern publisher. Eighty per cent. of all the copies sold are probably bought by Northern readers.

When will Southern authors understand their own interests? When will the South, as a whole, abandoning its present suicidal policy, enter upon that career of prosperity, greatness, and true renown, to which God by his word and his providences, is calling it? "If thou take away from the midst of thee the yoke, the putting forth of the finger and speaking vanity; and if thou draw out thy soul to the hungry and satisfy the afflicted soul; then shall thy light rise in obscurity and thy darkness be as the noonday: And the Lord shall guide thee continually and satisfy thy soul in drought, and make fat thy bones; and thou shalt be like a watered garden, and like a spring of water, whose waters fail not. And they that shall be of thee shall build the old waste places; thou shalt raise up the foundations of many generations; and thou shalt be called, The repairer of the breach, The restorer of paths to dwell in."

Our limits, not our materials, are exhausted. We would gladly say more, but can only, in conclusion, add as the result of our investigations in this department of our subject, that *Literature and Liberty are inseparable; the one can never have a vigorous existence without being wedded to the other.*

Our work is done. It is the voice of the non-slaveholding whites of the South, through one identified with them by interest, by feeling, by position. That voice, by whomsoever spoken, must yet be heard and heeded. The time hastens—the doom of slavery is written—the redemption of the South draws nigh.

In taking leave of our readers, we know not how we can give more forcible expression to our thoughts and intentions than by saying that, in concert with the intelligent free voters of the North, we, the non-slaveholding whites of the South, expect to elevate JOHN C. FREMONT, CASSIUS M. CLAY, JAMES G. BIRNEY, or some other Southern non-slaveholder, to the Presidency in 1860; and that the patriot thus elevated to that dignified station will, through our cordial co-operation, be succeeded by WILLIAM H. SEWARD, CHARLES SUMNER, JOHN McLEAN, or some other non-slaveholder of the North;—and furthermore, that if, in these or in any other similar cases, the oligarchs do not quietly submit to the will of a constitutional majority of the people, as expressed at the ballot-box, the first battle between freedom and slavery will be fought at home—and may God defend the right!

THE END.

GENERAL INDEX.

A Voice Still Heard . . .

The Sacred Songs of the Ashkenazic Jews

A Publication in

the Leo Baeck Institute Series

A Voice Still Heard . . .

The Sacred Songs of the Ashkenazic Jews

A Publication in

the Leo Baeck Institute Series

A Voice Still Heard . . .

The Sacred Songs of the Ashkenazic Jews

Eric Werner

The Pennsylvania State University Press

University Park and London

Frontispiece:
The Hazan praying in the synagogue. (Behind him are two ritually required "bystanders" wearing medieval Jew's hats.) A miniature from the fourteenth-century Machsor Lipsiae, in possession of the Leipzig University Library (annotated facsimile edition, edited by Elias Katz, Hanau-Main, 1964). By courtesy of the Edition Leipzig.

Library of Congress Cataloging in Publication Data

Werner, Eric.
A voice still heard.

Includes bibliographical references and index.
1. Music—Jews. 2. Synagogue music—History and criticism. I. Title.
ML3195.W43 783'.029'6 75-26522
ISBN 0-271-01167-X

Designed by Glenn Ruby

Printed in the United States of America

To the blessed memory of my friends and mentors

Isak HEINEMANN (*1876–1957*)

Curt SACHS (*1881–1959*)

Isaiah SONNE (*1887–1960*)

ספר זה מוקדש בהערצה

לזכרונם המבורך של מורי וידידי

יצחק היינמן

קורט זקס

ישעיה זונא

יצירותיהם תעמודנה לעד.

Note: A cassette recording of synagogal music selected by the author and chanted by Cantor Erwin Hirsch of Congregation Habonim, New York, is available from The Pennsylvania State University Press.

Contents

Abbreviations

Adler, *Pratique*	Israel Adler, *La Pratique Musicale Savante des Juifs*, vol. 1 (Paris, 1966)
AZJ	*Allgemeine Zeitung des Judentums* (Leipzig and Berlin, 1837–1921)
BAL	Franz Magnus Boehme, *Altdeutsches Liederbuch* (Leipzig, 1877)
Baron	Salo W. Baron, *A Social and Religious History of the Jews*, 2d ed. (New York, 1960–)
BT	Abraham Baer, *Baal Tefillah* or *Der practisches Vorbeter*, reprint (New York, 1921)
Consolo, *Libro*	Federico Consolo, *Libro dei Canti d'Israele* (Florence, 1892)
Eben Bohen	Kalonymos ben Kalonymos, *Eben Bohen*, ed. Joseph Cohen Zedek (Lemberg, 1865)
Elbogen	Ismar Elbogen, *Der Juedische Gottesdienst* (Berlin, 1913–1921)
Ginzberg	Louis Ginzberg, *Ginzei Schechter* (New York, 1929–1930)
Goldschmidt, *Mah'zor*	Eduard Daniel Goldschmidt, Introduction to *Mah'zor Ashkenazi, Tefillot ha-Keva* (Jerusalem, 1970)
HOM	Abraham Z. Idelsohn, *Hebrew Oriental Melodies*, 10 vols. (Leipzig, New York, and Jerusalem, 1914–1933)
HUCA	*Hebrew Union College Annual, Cincinnati*
Idelsohn, "Maqamen"	Abraham Z. Idelsohn, "Maqamen der arabischen Musik," *Sammelbaende der internationalen Musikgesellschaft* 15 (1913–1914)
———, *Music*	Abraham Z. Idelsohn, *Jewish Music in its Historical Development* (New York, 1929)
———, "Songs and Singers"	Abraham Z. Idelsohn, "Songs and Singers of the Eighteenth Century," *HUCA*, Jubilee vol. (1925)
———, "Traditional Songs"	Abraham Z. Idelsohn, "Traditional Songs of German Jews in Italy," *HUCA* 11 (1936)

JE	*Jewish Encyclopedia* (New York, 1905–1906)
JQR	*Jewish Quarterly Review*
Kirschner, *Poesien-Singweisen*	E. Kirschner, *Ueber mittelaltlicher Hebraeische Poesien- und ihre Singweisen* (Nuremberg, 1914)
Lachmann, "Musiksysteme"	Robert Lachmann, "Musiksysteme," *Zeitschrift fuer Vergleichende Musikwissenschaft* 3 (1935)
Loewe, *Minstrelsy*	Herbert M. J. Loewe, *Medieval Hebrew Minstrelsy* (London, 1926)
MGG	F. Blume, *Die Musik in Geschichte und Gegenwart* (Kassel-Basel-Paris-London-New York, 1949–)
MGWJ	*Monatschrift fuer die Geschichte und Wissenschaft des Judentums* (Breslau, 1851–1939)
REJ	*Révue des Études Juives* (Paris, 1881–1959)
Sachs, *Wellsprings*	Curt Sachs, *The Wellsprings of Music* (The Hague, 1962)
Steinschneider	Moritz Steinschneider, *Catalogus Librorum Hebraeorum in Biblioteca Bodleiana* (Berlin, 1852–1860)
Sulzer, *Denkschrift*	Salomon Sulzer, *Denkschrift* (Vienna, 1876)
———, *Schir Zion* I	Salomon Sulzer, *Schir Zion*, 1st ed. (Vienna, 1839)
———, *Schir Zion* II	Salomon Sulzer, *Schir Zion*, pt. 2 (Vienna, 1865)
Wagner, *Gregorianische Melodien*	Peter Wagner, *Einfuehrung in die Gregorianische Melodien*, vol. 1 (Leipzig, 1911), vol. 2 (Wiesbaden, 1921), vol. 3 (Wiesbaden, 1921)
———, *Jacobusliturgie*	Peter Wagner, *Die Gesaenge der Jacobusliturgie zu Santiago de Compostela* (Fribourg [Switzerland], 1931)
Werner, *Mendelssohn*	Eric Werner, *Mendelssohn, A New Image of the Composer and his Age* (New York, 1963)
Wise, *Reminiscences*	Isaac M. Wise, *Reminiscences* (Cincinnati, 1901)
WSB	Eric Werner, *The Sacred Bridge* (New York and London, 1959)
Zunz, *Poesie*	Leopold Zunz, *Synagogal Poesie des Mittelalters*, 2d ed. (Berlin, 1865–67)
———, *Ritus*	Leopold Zunz, *Die Ritus des synagogalen Gottesdienstes* (Berlin, 1859)

Preface

To explore in depth the genesis and essence of the sacred songs of Ashkenazic Jewry, to recapture that voice—faint but still audible—which reaches us over many centuries, that was the task entrusted to me by the Leo Baeck Institute of New York. I gratefully accepted this opportunity to pay my respects to the world of my forefathers and to examine thoroughly its songs, the sacred songs that they were ever ready to praise and never willing to abandon. Such an enterprise is surely timely now, since the geographical and historical centers of Ashkenazic Jewry—Germany, the lands of the former Austrian monarchy, Poland, and Russia—perished in an unspeakable tragedy. As a result, the continuity of the Ashkenazic tradition was and remains in danger of being altogether broken. While fully realizing the acute emotional apprehension besetting the subject, I still could not shirk the duty of presenting the musical corpus of *minhag ashkenaz* and its true genesis and growth, cleansed of the innumerable accretions that encumber it today.

Nor could I be satisfied with a plain and bald description of our musical tradition bereft of all critical evaluation. The term "tradition," of course, means many things to many people. The Jews are not alone in cherishing the belief that anything considered traditional is, ipso facto, beyond good and evil. In the twilight of mental inertia, of lovingly cultivated customs and superstitions, pseudo-traditions grow well and fast. It is the trend of our hypernationalistic times to deem as fine and noble everything Jewish, just because it is Jewish. This collective narcissism is as foolish as it is dangerous. If our prophets had thought this way, neither Judaism nor Israel would exist today.

It may be questioned whether an exclusively musical evaluation could do justice to *minhag ashkenaz* in its entirety. For this corpus of music is not a homogeneous entity, but a hybrid conglomeration of Jewish, German, Polish, and even Russian folklore, which has been further reshaped and stylized by many generations of singers, cantors, and folk musicians. Moreover, its liturgical significance is so strong and pronounced that our criteria cannot be solely musical. Psychological associations evoked by the Hebrew texts or by musical symbols anchored deep in ritual and the memories of synagogue worshipers transcend purely musical standards. Hence the question of style and stylization must be examined if one is to understand the forms and forces that have shaped the songs of *minhag ashkenaz*. All time-bound styles are but phenomena of interference in the free play of dialectically opposite forces: in our case the foundations of Jewish tradition stood against the influx of foreign elements that were both championed and resisted by different groups within the Jewish community.

There have been few comprehensive studies devoted to *minhag ashkenaz*, in sharp contrast to a veritable flood of what must be regarded as journalistic twaddle and indiscriminate causeries engendered or sponsored by well-meaning but ill-advised organizations. The works of only three scholars stand out as possessing true substance and stature: the numerous essays of Eduard Birnbaum (1855–1920), which first applied critical methods to our musical tradition; of Abraham Z. Idelsohn (1882–1938), who devoted two rich chapters and two important volumes to the traditional chants of *minhag ashkenaz*; and of Jacob Schoenberg (1900–1962), who, following Idelsohn's methods, published an analytical study on the songs of the German synagogue. Some valuable and reliable articles have been written by a number of young Israeli and American scholars, and I will refer to them in this volume.

For reasons of documentation I have placed the western Ashkenazic tradition in the foreground. Being considerably older than the eastern branch, its written sources would seem to be more authentic, better notated, and more copious. Another reason for this stance is the dearth of contemporary Russian literature on the subject. While Russian scholarship has contributed to Jewish music in a trickle of publications about secular Yiddish folklore, the once ample sources of eastern European Jewish religious song and its scholarly evaluation were officially repressed after 1920. It is to be regretted that Russian scholars were not afforded the opportunity to participate in the increasingly advanced exploration of Jewish liturgical music after the publication of Idelsohn's major works. The Polish sector is considered here at least in part, but the hasidic component is touched upon only cursorily in view of that sect's well-known antitraditional attitude toward liturgical music. It must also be remembered that the hasidic prayer book differs from the standard *siddur* and *maḥzor* of *minhag ashkenaz*.

The scope and framework of this volume were thus easily determined. However, one question still remained: should priority be given to the historical or the morphological aspect of these traditional songs of the synagogue? Since I view liturgy as the organic link between these two points at issue, I have generally stressed the liturgical data as determining factors in both history and morphology of the traditional songs of the synagogue. This approach may well fall short in certain instances, notably in the assessment of the mystical component of Jewish liturgy and its music. I have therefore had to find support in the principle that in a rational study based on rational procedures of thought, one is not free to lean on mystical concepts. Instead I have contented myself with stating their existence and influence. It was mainly this thought that induced me to refrain from an extended discussion of hasidic chant.

In the absence of a generally accepted system of transliteration of Hebrew words I have used the modified Sephardic pronunciation as a basis for the system used in this book:

The Hebrew ק is represented as *k*; כ by *kh*; ב generally as *b*; ז by *z*; צ by *Tz*; and ח as *ḥ*. For the purpose of this book comprehensibility of the text is considered more important than strict consistency. For the same reason some texts of the Passover *Haggadah* and others were left in the conventional Ashkenazic pronunciation and transliteration.

I owe a heavy debt of gratitude to those who encouraged me to undertake this task, which, to echo the words of the great Leopold Zunz, must be described as "thankless." My first acknowledgment goes to Dr. Max Gruenewald and Fred Grubel, of the Leo Baeck Institute in New York, who commissioned this book and gave me their unstinted help and support. Likewise I gratefully acknowledge a grant from the Alexander Kohut Memorial Foundation of the American Academy for Jewish Research in New York. My dear friend, Dr. Judith K. Eisenstein, was my indefatigable editor, completing a job that I could not consider enviable. I owe her a thousand thanks. I am indebted to my dear advisers and friends, the late Dr. Edward Kiev, Librarian of the Hebrew Union College-Jewish Institute of Religion in New York, and Dr. Paltiel Birnbaum, who often guided me in the intricacies of Judaic matters. I am also grateful to the authorities of the Hebrew Union College Library in Cincinnati, especially to its librarian, Dr. Herbert Zafren, for their kind cooperation and help. To Mr. Albert Weisser belongs my gratitude for some critical suggestions. I am deeply obliged to Dr. Friedrich Racek, Chief Librarian of the Vienna *Stadtbibliothek*, who by his helpfulness compensated me for the less cooperative attitude of the Vienna Jewish *Kultus Gemeinde*. My sincere thanks go also to the never-tiring ladies of the library of the Hebrew Union College-Jewish Institute of Religion in New York, Susan Tabor, Catherine Markush, and Lillian Weber. This book has kept them busy indeed.

E.W.

1

Historical and Liturgical Conditions

From the ends of the earth
We hear songs of praise,
Of glory to the Righteous One,
But I say: "I pine away,
I pine away! Woe is me!
For the treacherous
deal treacherously!"
(Isaiah 24:1)

Not far from Jerusalem, in the village of Abu Gosh, there stands an old Crusaders' cathedral. Its façade, hewn out of rude boulders, offers nothing to the hurried sightseer. Careful observers, however, will notice among the dark brown asymmetrical blocks a white rectangle, precisely cut as a modern tile, a relic from an ancient Roman hall dedicated to the famous tenth legion. Formed from this and other stones found among the rubble of Arabic, Greek, and Jewish houses, the strange façade of the French Crusaders' church could be symbolic of the treasure contained in the songs of the Ashkenazic Synagogue. That treasure, the musical tradition of the Jews from central Europe, we call *minhag ashkenaz*. It consists of fragments of forgotten songs of the Middle Ages, here and there a relic of antiquity, an old Italian dance, a German love song, a Polish air, all embedded in a Jewish foundation with an ancient mortar. In its essence, this *minhag ashkenaz* is somewhat older than the French cathedral.

Through the tides of time, through misery and deliverance, the Jews have carried with them their religion, its songs no less than its laws, with unswerving faithfulness. The songs of their religious institution, the Synagogue, do not necessarily comprise their entire musical repertory. These constitute only a part, albeit an important one, of the musical tradition familiar to the community of worshipers. The traditional religious music of a particular group is determined by theological, ethnic, geographic, and historical factors. In *minhag ashkenaz* the tradition is intrinsically linked to liturgical texts, in particular to the established prayer books, the Ashkenazic *siddur* and *maḥzor*. A recent scholar has correctly stressed the distinction between *minhag ashkenaz* and the Ashkenazim themselves.[1] The prayers and some of the Ashkenazic customs of rendering them are familiar to other Jewish groups as well, groups that do not consider themselves Ashkenazim. Hence the question of demographic and ethnic differences between the Ashkenazim and the Sephardic (Spanish-Mediterranean) group, though justified, is irrelevant for this study. Our

interest is exclusively focused on the liturgico-musical aspects of Ashkenazic tradition. The *minhag ashkenaz* is here understood as the sum total of the traditions that developed in the sphere of Jews who used either the German or the Yiddish vernacular as their mother tongue.

It is generally assumed that organized liturgies reflect the theological thoughts of the times of their origins. This apparently self-evident assumption cannot, at close examination, be applied to Jewish liturgy generally, without far-reaching modifications. Though many traditional prayers may reflect Jewish thinking of ancient times, mainly of the late Hellenistic period, neither Jewish theology nor Jewish songs, nor even their forms, have remained unchanged during subsequent centuries —this notwithstanding the naive assumptions of some uninstructed diehards. Yet these many, and often tragic changes did not always find adequate liturgical expression.

Even if one applies the conventional differentiation between principal prayers (*Stammgebete*, after I. Elbogen), called *tefillot keva*, and later poetic additions, called *piyutim*, one still cannot fill in the remaining gaps, if one is seeking evidence of a "current" liturgy, reflecting contemporary thoughts and events. Rarely can we single out prayers that mirror exactly the vicissitudes of Jewish political history later than the sixteenth century. Such a liturgy would have been topical when related to certain specific circumstances, but ephemeral or simply unintelligible at all other times; for example, even during the latest holocaust, its victims fell back, in their hour of agony and death, upon the medieval prayers of "blood and tears," *Ani ma'amin*, and the still older *Alenu le-shabe'aḥ*.

The tunes of the Ashkenazic Synagogue are by no means as old as their texts. Yet they constitute a more faithful and accurate reflection of the life, suffering, and even death of the Jewish communities during their eventful history than do the prayer texts themselves. There can be no mistaking the intensively expressive and emotional character of these tunes, however radically the style of the Ashkenazic chant may have changed in the course of a whole millennium. It will therefore be the task of this book to explore the genesis as well as the structure and form of those songs whose strains distinguished the Ashkenazic ritual. Some important questions arise at the outset of our study:

1. What is understood as Ashkenazic tradition, and what are its texts?
2. Is there a special or even a common type of Hebrew chant, commonly recognizable, in all Ashkenazic synagogues, be they located in Siberia, Munich, or San Francisco?
3. Is it possible to single out the distinctive elements of these tunes and trace their origin and history?
4. What are the main forms of Ashkenazic chant?
5. What influence did the non-Jewish, in particular the German, environment have on the songs?

The text of the Ashkenazic *siddur* has a long history. To avoid controversy, we will operate with geographical and chronological boundaries defined by Goldschmidt.[2] While the original eastern boundary was the Elbe river, the migrations

of German Jewry widened the realm of Ashkenaz after the fourteenth century, until not even the Ural mountains nor the Black Sea remained the ultimate frontier. What distinguishes the prayer book [*siddur*] of the Ashkenazim from that of the Sephardim and Yemenites are mainly the *piyutim* that had been written by Palestinian authors such as Yannai and Yose ben Yose. These the Babylonians (and the Sephardim) at first rejected.[3] Goldschmidt is fully aware of the complexity that besets the question of the origin of *minhag ashkenaz*. It seems that the migrations of the Palestinian Jews had brought their customs into close contact with the traditions of Italian, Babylonian, and Spanish Jews. Rashi was perhaps the first, but certainly not the last scholar to doubt the exclusively Palestinian origin of the Ashkenazic *siddur*.[4] Yet some of the oldest German-Jewish scholars opposed his opinion, perhaps because they felt offended by the Sephardic-Babylonian claim to Jerusalemitic nobility, as based upon Obadiah's prophecy.[5] Hence Kalonymos ben Kalonymos brusquely denied the validity of that claim.

The undeniable Italian-Jewish component was clearly seen by H. Vogelstein: "Whether or not the settlement of an Italian dynasty of scholars in Germany by a German king is only a legend . . . or a historical fact, it is the indisputable result of well-established . . . traditions, according to which one knew in Germany that the revival of talmudic studies there and in France was due to the efforts of . . . immigrant Italian talmudists (especially Rabbi Moshe ben Kalonymos). The decisive year of the migration from Rome was probably 787."[6] This connection with Italian scholars and their views remained characteristic of *minhag ashkenaz;* far into the sixteenth century the correspondence between, and exchange of, German and Italian rabbis and students continued as a normal procedure.[7]

During the first three centuries after Charlemagne, contact with the Provençal scholars was also alive, as we know from R. Gershom of Mayence, the "Light of the Diaspora" [*Ma'or ha-golah*], who studied in southern France and there absorbed the *minhag b'ney Babel* (Babylonian tradition). These contacts affected only a small portion of the daily prayer book. More traces of them are to be found in the *maḥzor*. However, there is no evidence of any musical influence. On the other hand, there are clear indications of Italian influence on *minhag ashkenaz*. Nevertheless, such peripheral influences were less important in the forming of the tradition than were indigenous liturgical and theological conceptions, which affected performance practice, and, in turn, the very form of the melodies. The following examples may illustrate this point.

The sabbatical *va-yekhulu* (and the framing *tefillah*) was supposed to be sung most clearly and attractively, because everyone who joined in the chanting of it would be protected on his way home by two ministering angels who would shield and bless him. The passage was lengthened in its musical performance, for the sake of latecoming worshipers who might otherwise miss it.[8] Other homiletical or Midrashic ideas helped to form the festive songs, as will be seen in chapter 3. Certain verses of the *hallel* (Psalms 113–118) were sung as refrains;[9] furthermore, the practice of famous cantors was often quoted and imitated, as we learn from instances given by Zunz, so that their personal mannerisms achieved the status of regional traditions. Hence the rabbis continually tried to fix the ritual so as to obviate the

spontaneous flourishes and innovations of these cantors.[10] This was, of course, possible only within the limits of the authorized prayer books, i.e., the *Siddur R. Amram* and the *Maḥzor Vitry*. The question of which texts should be singled out for musical performance is an old one, but it was never settled to the satisfaction of both rabbis and cantors. In general, the cantors had a free hand in selecting those prayers that best suited their fancies. The reason for this unusual latitude was essentially theological.

There was no established gradation of the various categories of prayer. Although tannaitic literature is replete with speculations on the matter, and although intensive reflections on the categories and their respective merits continued to the time of the *geonim*, no authoritative conclusions were reached. The early Christians (as we can read in the contemporaneous Epistles of the New Testament) did order their prayers, setting praise and laudation at the top of their scale, personal supplication at the bottom, and thanksgiving and the profession of faith somewhere between.[11] The rabbinic categorization is similar: *keriat shema* (declaration of faith), *shebaḥ* (praise, adoration), *hoda'ah* (acknowledgment, thanksgiving), *tefillot vehabdalot*, as in B. *Ber.* 33b (prayers of distinction—there is no Christian counterpart for this category), and finally *taḥanun, bakashah* (supplication) and *seliḥah* (penitential prayers).

With reference to Deut. 33, the rabbinic rule merely demanded that "prayer should begin with ascriptions of praise to God, go on to personal petitions for men's needs, and close, as it began, with praise"; on this scheme the "eighteen benedictions" [*shemoneh esreh*] are arranged. This prayer, also called *Amidah* (stand), to be recited while standing, combines the elements of hymnic praise [*berakhah*] with that of petition. It is therefore called *tefillah* (plea), an expression whose etymology reaches into Babylonian and perhaps Egyptian origins.[12] This prayer is always at the core of the service, before and after praises or hymns. Thus theological doctrine postulates the *order of succession* for the prayers but does not determine their respective ranks.

To be sure, one does encounter speculations on the rank of the various types of prayer. There is a talmudic parable that structuralizes the *Amidah* in three parts: the first three, the middle twelve, and the last three *berakhot*. The rabbis Judah and Ḥaninah likened it to the appearance of slaves before the king's presence. They start with eulogies and praises, then they offer their personal petitions and supplications, finally they pronounce their gratitude and humbly take their leave.[13] According to this parable petition forms the central, but not necessarily the most valuable part of the *tefillah*. This opinion appears to be the last word on the order and relative importance of prayers for at least a millennium.

Aside from the voiced repetition of the *Amidah* demanded in early decisions, cantors were generally free to choose the texts they would sing, with the stricture that the musical style be appropriate to the texts. This begins to approach the Christian practice of assigning fixed formulas in Gregorian tradition to a *Te Deum*, a *Credo*, a *Sanctus*, and so on, in the liturgy. Attempts at such musical categorization were undertaken also in *minhag ashkenaz* by way of the prayer modes [*steiger*] that correspond, at least in theory, to the various types of prayers listed above. Yet the character of Ashkenazic chant is affected as much by its tonal structure and the

cadence of the Hebrew text as by its contents. Ignorance of the Hebrew language, combined with a deeply felt urgency of petition, has caused many a cantor to break up the rhythm of a prayer text by senseless repetition of trivial words such as "*she-ne'emar*" (as it is said).

Some facts governing the relation between tone and word in *minhag ashkenaz* should be noted here. A metrical poem is not necessarily set to metrical music; conversely, a considerable number of prose texts are frequently forced into metrical tunes, especially if the tunes are borrowed from an alien source. Of all Jewish traditions, *minhag ashkenaz* contains the largest share of metrical melodies, and the more recent the tune, the stronger its propensity toward metrical structure. Analogous tendencies prevail also in the Sephardic tradition, where Spanish or Arabic tunes are applied to Ladino or Hebrew texts; in *minhag ashkenaz*, German, then Bohemian, and finally Polish and Russian folk songs were adopted. Sometimes old and familiar tunes were used for newer texts, a practice well known in all liturgical traditions; even the psalmists made use of it. Several cases are listed by Zunz in his *Synagogal Poetry*.[14] (An old melody that evokes associations linking it to the new text is a contrafact; thus the song "My Country, 'tis of Thee" is a contrafact of "God Save the King.") The opposite combinations of an old text set to a new tune occurs, of course, much more frequently, and is chiefly responsible for the introduction of foreign tunes into the Jewish tradition.

There were times in the history of Ashkenazic synagogue music when this influx of foreign elements was condemned (thirteenth and fourteenth centuries); at other times it was tolerated by the authorities (fifteenth and sixteenth centuries); and at still other periods opinion fluctuated toward and against the use of Gentile popular song (during and after the Reformation). Immediately after the Emancipation (end of the nineteenth century) a strong wave of German and Slavonic folklore inundated *minhag ashkenaz*.[15]

In general the history of *minhag ashkenaz* falls quite naturally into three epochs: the first extends from about 900 to 1427 (with the death of R. Jacob Levi Mollin, called Maharil, the Nestor and highly respected codifier of *minhag ashkenaz*), the second from 1430 until the Emancipation, and the third from 1800 to 1910, which marks the terminal point of this study.

During these many centuries the geographical area of *minhag ashkenaz* expanded considerably. Originally a tradition of the Rhineland and of eastern France, it spread farther east and north. Its medieval derivates were *minhag Bohemia*, then *minhag Austria*,[16] and after 1400 *minhag Poland-Russia* and finally *minhag Hungary*. North of the Rhine-Main line this tradition struck firm roots first in northwest Germany, and later in Holland, where it coexisted in a certain rivalry with the Sephardic-Portuguese tradition. More or less the same situation prevailed in England after the readmission of Jews during the time of Cromwell, when first Sephardim and then Ashkenazim immigrated. In Palestine *minhag ashkenaz* was introduced in the sixteenth century by German and Polish cabalistic rabbis. Later, Sephardic elements were introduced into it and still further new Aramaic passages, and it crystallized eventually as *minhag Ari* (after R. Isaac Luria). This formed the basis for the subsequent hasidic prayer book. During the eighteenth and nineteenth centuries the

minhag ashkenaz proper was introduced into Palestine and America by German and Austrian immigrants. The old French tradition [*minhag tzarfat*] did not survive the expulsions at the end of the fourteenth century, and has practically vanished.[17]

Musical Forms

The musical forms encountered in *minhag ashkenaz* are best classified with reference to their treatment of the Hebrew text, or to their performance practice. Only the main categories are listed here.

Plain psalmody. This term defines tunes satisfying three conditions: the text is rendered syllabically, one syllable to one tone; the bulk of the text is rendered on one or two recitation pitches called tenors; and the text and the chant fall into two corresponding halves, according to the principles of parallel structure, characteristic of all Semitic poetry. The end of each verse and also its caesura are marked grammatically by elongated forms of the respective words. In psalmodic chant, these pausal words are musically marked by "punctuating melismata." These are slight deviations from the syllabic principle, and they appear as little melodic flourishes. In Hebrew scriptures these points in the verse are indicated by certain Masoretic accents (the strong disjunctives), and they are called *pausae* in Latin terminology.[18] In table I, no. 1, there are some examples of plain psalmody: 1*a* is a bipartite Hebrew verse, 1*b* is a tripartite Hebrew verse. In 1*c* and 1*d* we have examples of Latin verses, bipartite and tripartite, respectively.

Ornate psalmody. Most of the tenor-recitation is resolved in ornamental patterns: however, the basic psalmodic structure is still easily identifiable. Parallelism and *pausae* are usually observed in the chant. Only a few words are chanted strictly syllabically. See table I, no. 2, *a* and *b*.

Plain response. A precentor renders a prayer, which customarily is answered by a congregational response; it may or may not be metrical. The form types of the responses depend on the parallelistic style of the text. The practice of response goes back to the Second Temple. The term "*le'anot*" and its derivatives occur early in the Bible, for example, in Exodus 15:21, 1 Samuel 21:12, 1 Samuel 18:7, Ezra 3:11, and Numbers 21:17; all signify the singing in alternation. The Latin *responsorium*, the Greek *ὑποψάλμα*, the Syriac *enyana*, and the Nestorian *unaya* all reveal extensive use of this form and practice. Of these the *hypopsalma* is the most extensively developed of the various traditions of Christian and Jewish chant.[19]

Refrain. This practice can be traced back to the times of the psalmists. There are a few well-known examples of refrains in the texts of the psalter, the Dead Sea Scrolls, and, later, the medieval *piyutim*.

Antiphony. The chanting by alternating choruses is called antiphony, or antiphonal rendition. Whereas it was frequently used in the Second Temple, it fell

into oblivion in the Synagogue, which did not employ the required professional choristers. Nonetheless, traces of antiphonal practice have remained among oriental Jewish communities.[20] The Gregorian *antiphon*, familiar to all students of plainchant, may have evolved from this sort of antiphonal singing, but it is quite different, being an inserted passage preceding and following a psalmody (resulting in a sort of ternary form).[21] Judaism did not develop this form, but it came very close to it, as we see in the Dead Sea Scrolls.[22]

Free melismatic recitative. The form types mentioned thus far are common to all Jewish (and most Christian) liturgies, but the free melismatic recitative is a typically Ashkenazic rendition of certain prose and a few poetic texts. It was established relatively late by the hazanim, who wished to have more leeway for displaying their voices. Elements of Slavonic and German folk song, of military band music, and of Italian opera were mixed without much sense of style. Characteristic of this form is its often senseless repetition of words or even syllables. In general it does not seem to have appeared before about 1730, and even at the end of the century it was not universally accepted in the West, as we learn from many antagonistic, even outright contemptuous remarks.[23] However, it is, to this day, a favorite form type of eastern European hazanim and their congregations, now chiefly located in the United States and Israel. Seen in historical perspective it must be considered a decline of true tradition and pure style, however emotionally effective it may be.

Missinai tunes and chants. This group of melodies and the style derived from them in subsequent centuries is the most distinctive element of *minhag ashkenaz*. No other Jewish *minhag* contain a set of tunes so ingeniously constructed and of so elevated a standard. They originated in the Rhineland during the twelfth to fifteenth centuries under sad and tragic circumstances. To their history, structural development, and stylistic significance chapter 3 is dedicated. In general, the *Missinai* tunes are applied to the prayers and rites of the High Holy Days and the Three Festivals; they have made hardly any inroads into the daily or Sabbath ritual.

Pure melismatic chant. Here we have long vocalises or meaningless syllables instead of texts to serve as bases for the melodies.[24] These are alien to traditional Ashkenazic chant, and the rabbis disliked and even forbade the practice early and repeatedly.[25] Yet in Ḥasidism it was revived and brought to bloom. There it is highly respected as the most "spiritualized" type of vocal music.[26] In most cases the tune [*niggun*] is the result of spirited improvisation by the *rebbe* or *tzaddik* and follows certain theological tenets that determine its structure.[27] Its history and musical significance are discussed briefly in chapter 8. The *niggun* was and is generally chanted upon meaningless syllables: *ba*, *boh*, *bam*, *oy*, *trei*, *dei*, and the like. Ecstatic in spirit, it is subterraneously related to the wordless hymns of early Christianity, the *jubili*, and also to the dirges and jubilations of primitive Moslem Bedouins (who use a trill on the syllables *li li*), to the *ululare* and *ελελίζω* of classical antiquity, and to similar phenomena known to musical anthropology.[28]

Cantillation of scriptural texts. In contradistinction to the form types just mentioned, cantillation is not a primarily *musical* form of practice but the rabbinically prescribed custom of chanting the scriptural texts according to certain signs or accents [*ta'amei ha-mikra*]. The resulting melodic line is not autonomous from the musical point of view; it depends on the ever-changing constellation of the Masoretic accents, which in turn mirror the structure of each verse. At least three traditions of scriptural cantillation are known in *minhag ashkenaz*: the Western standard chant, the eastern European popular chant, and the cantillation for the High Holy Days. To this important and highly characteristic constituent of Ashkenazic melos, whose fluctuations are of considerable interest, chapter 5 is devoted.

Cantorial fantasia. This term was coined by Dr. Hanoch Avenary to designate the latest form. It is a free potpourri of different thematic elaborations, the ghetto counterpart of the thematic development by the classical composers. This form was based on the concept of independent *ritornelli* that appeared and were or were not repeated according to the composer's whim.[29]

Liturgical Considerations

A few illustrations will exemplify the close link between the musical practice and the liturgical tradition of the fixed [*keva*] prayers. The *birkhot ha-shaḥar* (benedictions of the morning prayer) of weekday or Sabbath belong to the oldest rubrics of the *siddur*. They are recited every day of the year; in this case the traditional melodies that accompany them do indeed reflect the great age of the texts.[30]

Although all liturgical music usually draws from old sources, an old text is not necessarily set to an old melody. And yet, what a spirit breathes in these ancient psalmodies that were born in the last years of the Temple, during the first years of Judeo-Christianity, under the severe discipline of the militant Pharisees. Daily use during the subsequent two thousand years has whittled these down to their bare skeletons, but even so their intended austerity remains immensely impressive. The archetypes of their chants are psalmodies of a pre-modal, four-tone structure, closely akin to corresponding patterns of Gregorian and Byzantine plainchant. In table I, compare 1*a*, 1*b*, 4*a*, 4*c*, with 1*c*, 1*d*, and 4*b*.

Another example of the link between melody and liturgy stems from the inclusion of a Sabbath or festival motif in the *kiddush* (blessing over the wine) and in the *kedushat ha-yom* (sanctification of the day). This practice is likewise assumed to hark back to tannaitic times.[31] The ancient benediction over wine, the εὐλογία, sometimes the εὐχαριστία of the New Testament, had been part of the domestic Sabbath ritual even before the destruction of the Temple, and was later transplanted to the Synagogue. The *kedushat ha-yom* is the name of that benediction in the *Amidah* that immediately follows the three introductory benedictions on Sabbaths, High Holy Days, and festivals. The following diagram of the *Amidah* may clarify this:

Introductory Benedictions
abot, praise of God, shield of the patriarchs
geburot, praise of God's omnipotence and mercy
kedushat ha-shem, sanctification of his name

Intermediary Benedictions
on weekdays, thirteen
on Sabbaths and festivals, one, the *kedushat ha-yom*
on High Holy Days, *kedushat ha-yom* and two special benedictions

Concluding Benedictions
hoda'ah, thanksgiving
birkhat tziyon, prayer for the redemption of Zion (Israel)
birkhat shalom, prayer for peace[32]

The *kedushat ha-yom* is thus the fourth benediction of the *Amidah* on Sabbaths, High Holy Days, and festivals, and always refers to the specific occasion of its recitation. It derives from the tannaitic period (about C.E. 100), whereas the framework of the *Tefillah* (or *Amidah*) probably antedates Christianity.[33]

The text of the *Tefillah* is the same (with minor variations that are obviously necessary) in the morning and evening services. However, the modes of the chant are different for each in *minhag ashkenaz*, which customarily distinguishes between morningsong and evensong. On the other hand, the *kedushat ha-yom* has no distinctive melody, in spite of the age of its text. In the course of eighteen centuries many tunes from many cultures have been applied to it. Usually a leading motif representing the special season or occasion for reciting the benediction was applied to it. As it is sung today it is clearly in the style of the seventeenth or eighteenth century. Yet its basic lines (different on Sabbaths, High Holy Days, and festivals) can be traced to the thirteenth or early fourteenth century. From that time on, the motifs were adjusted to the changing tastes of the Jewish communities. Such changes of musical tastes—indeed such "fashions"—play a considerable part in our study. In most cases it was the cantor who championed new fashions, and in fact often engendered them himself.

The Hazan

In view of the important role that the cantor has played in such setting of fashions in *minhag ashkenaz*, it is necessary to pause for an examination of the history of the cantorate. If ever there was an issue to keep the spirits of the congregants eager and alive, it was the controversial matter of the office and, often enough, also the person of the cantor. From its inception to the present, the cantorate has been the center of debate, sometimes of communal strife, but also the source of exultation and of spiritual revival. In any study of the music of *minhag ashkenaz*, the function and the influence of the one singer of the Synagogue merit a complete and detailed study.[34] Here it will suffice to sketch briefly the origin and development of the institution.

The singing functionary of the community was known, during a long and eventful history, under two different names: *shaliaḥ tzibbur* and hazan. The title *shaliaḥ tzibbur* (the delegate of the congregation) originated in the most ancient Palestinian and Babylonian synagogues. During the period when the Mishnah was in the process of formation (ca. 70 B.C.E.–C.E. 200) a distinction was made between an occasional and a regular (elected) precentor. The former is described thus: "He who has read the prophetic lesson [*Haftarah*] is also to read the *Shema*, to lead in prayer, and, if he is of priestly descent [*Kohen*] to pronounce the priestly blessing. If he has not reached manhood, his father or teacher prays in his place."[35] One could volunteer as precentor or was invited to serve as such before the institution of a permanent precentor. As long as such a regular precentor was lacking, the recitation of the prescribed prayers sometimes got out of hand. Such men as R. Eliezer and his disciples allowed themselves almost excessive liberties.[36] Only after R. Simeon, the son of Gamaliel I, ordered the eighteen benedictions (the fundamental and obligatory prayer) and precluded excessive prayers was the path cleared for a regular and responsible precentor. To function as a *shaliaḥ tzibbur* one had to be a pious layman, fit to act as delegate of the community. The position was formally created by Rabban Gamaliel II (fl. C.E.90): "Rabban Gamaliel stated that the precentor relieved the multitude of their duties."[37] This means that the individual worshiper needed only listen carefully and attentively to the precentor, and by saying the prescribed responses, especially the "Amen" at the end of each benediction, he fulfilled all his obligations. This is easily understood, when one realizes that the writing down of prayers was not permitted until the eighth century. The *shaliaḥ tzibbur* was neither appointed nor paid but served as an elected honorary officer. Generally he was a retired "gentleman of leisure" [*batlan*] who had a good voice and a good memory. His position was not that of a singer or musician; it corresponded with that of the lector in a church.[38] In many small communities this kind of precentor can still be found, especially on weekdays or for the less demanding portions of the services for the High Holy Days.

The title of hazan, on the other hand, was given to a paid and appointed (not elected) professional singer and functionary of the community. The office of hazan came into being around C.E. 600 or a little earlier and was directly connected with the *piyut*. Since the text and the chant of the *piyut* were entrusted to the hazan, this position became important, powerful, indeed practically indispensable. For the *piyut*, being a metrical, rhymed hymn, required a smattering of musical knowledge for its proper musical representation, and was in itself the subject of heated rabbinic controversies through many centuries. Even during the early nineteenth century the old battle cries for and against the *piyut* were heard again. However, we still do not understand the conditions under which this type of liturgical poetry emerged and, after three or four centuries, dominated all prayer books. What follows is a brief outline of the present state of research and debate on the origins of *piyut* and *ḥazanut*.

Three main causes have been suggested for the rise of the *piyut* after biblical times:

1. The incessant oppression and persecution of Palestinian Jewry by the Byzantine empire, which lasted until 636, culminated in a decree by Emperor Justinian —the so-called Novella 146, which forbade any kind of oral tradition in the service of the synagogue. The law would, of course, have eliminated the study of Talmud and Midrash. To circumvent this pernicious law, poets created *piyutim* which incorporated parts of *Halakhah* and *Haggadah* in disguised form in the regular prayers. (Regular portions of the liturgy were not forbidden.) After the Arab conquest in 636, when freedom of worship was restored, the *piyutim* lost their legal *raison d'être*. Yet, through their melodies, their performance by able singers, and their emotive style, they had won the hearts of the worshipers. Furthermore, they acted as an antidote against the hymns and canticles of the Church. Nevertheless, the rabbinic opposition grew in strength and vehemence against the *piyutim* and their champions, the hazanim.[39]

2. Many scholars are convinced that the form of the *piyut*—and its Greek, Latin, and Syriac counterparts—was an inevitable development. It was "in the air," and reflected the *Zeitgeist* of the Near East during the fifth to eighth centuries. It cannot be denied that the churches of the area exerted considerable attraction, by virtue of their ceremonies, in which hymns played a weighty role. It is interesting to note that the introduction of artistic forms within the liturgy of Egyptian or Palestinian monasteries encountered stubborn opposition similar to that of the contemporary synagogue. Stern abbots, such as Sylvanus of Gaza and Pambo of Maiouma, condemned the hymns of the *Octoechos* (the eight modes of psalm tones and their poems) just as fervently as the rabbis of their time rejected the *piyut* and the hazan.[40]

3. The dispute between the talmudic academies of Sura and Pumbaditha is occasionally cited as a possible cause for the emerging *piyut*. Many intricacies of this controversy came to light only after the discovery of the rich material sheltered in the Cairo Genizah. The best and most extensive survey of that long-lasting dispute was given by the late Professor Louis Ginzberg in his monumental source work *Ginzei Schechter*.[41]

In his presentation of the dispute, Professor Ginzberg stresses that the academy of Sura took a more lenient attitude to the *piyutim*, while its rival Pumbaditha remained strict, and would have prohibited them altogether. Each school claimed the same Mishnaic authority for its position as the other,[42] but offered diametrically opposite interpretations. To the severe Babylonian legalists all forms of extralegal prayer constituted heretical practice, since they could not find sanction for them in the early strata of the Talmud. Saadyah Gaon, the most celebrated representative of Sura, held the opinion that the Mishnaic expression stated simply, "If one so desires, one may lengthen the prayer service, or, if one desires otherwise, shorten it."[43] This interpretation gave sufficient leeway and would justify the insertion of all kinds of poems surrounding the *Shema*. That was exactly what the poets (called *payetanim*) wanted. Yet the authorities of Pumbaditha understood the passage in question quite differently and claimed that there was no legal loophole that would

permit the insertion of such new prayers. It should be noted that the original text of the Mishnah can justifiably be interpreted both ways.

Some scholars believe that the *piyutim* were recited by the hazan exclusively; this sounds plausible, if one takes into consideration the generally prevailing ignorance of the Hebrew language. Another argument for this opinion is the identification of the term *ḥazanut* (or *ḥižana* in Arabic) with *piyutim* as generally used by the Jewish-Arabic renegade Samuel ben Yeḥiyah (Al-Marabi) in his anti-Jewish book, *The Silencing of the Jew*.[44] It is noteworthy that Leopold Zunz concurred in this opinion.[45] Yet the very same Al-Marabi stated: "The prayer is said by the hazan whereas the *piyutim* were recited by the *shaliaḥ tzibbur* and the congregation."[46] This may refer to poems with refrains, especially to those that use as refrains scriptural passages familiar to the worshipers. Without question, the diminishing knowledge of the Hebrew language made the role of the hazan more dominant. Once the cantor dared to arrogate to himself the role of the "model worshiper," he considered himself fit, as well as entitled to compose his own prayers, or *piyutim*, often neglecting both the needs and the customs of his congregation.[47] In this connection Ginzberg cites a *gaon*'s remark, which describes the situation rather picturesquely: "In the academies and in all places in which there are learned men, nothing is changed in the order of the prayers, as it was arranged by the sages; no *piyutim* are said and no hazan is introduced into the synagogue, who might indulge in *payetanut*. In a synagogue in which *piyutim* are recited, the members thereby testify to their own ignorance."[48]

When rabbinic opposition assumed unexpected strength, the existence of both hazan and *piyut* was seriously imperiled. Early in the eighth century the *gaon* of Sura, R. Yehudai, took it upon himself to shield both the hazan and *piyut* with his undeniably commanding authority. This sage had a fine judgment of music, as we know from some of his responsa. His words were respected and his actions acclaimed. He not only defended the hazanim but he instructed them in the musical tradition of prayers. It seems that he quite concretely taught them the musical tradition in which he himself had grown up.[49] And although he was not able to stem the flood of hostile rabbinical comments concerning the hazan, he deserves, for many reasons, the title of "father of all cantorial art."[50] Even the opinion of so respected an authority as Maimonides could not eliminate the scorned *piyutim* and their champions, the hazanim. The passage written ex cathedra, in his great work, the *Guide to the Perplexed*, reads: [1,59] ". . . unlike the fools who, in truth exaggerate their praises of God and lengthen and increase their words in prayer by composing parables by which they fancy to approach God. . . . This is particularly the custom with singers and homilists [i.e., preachers] who compose poems which sometimes become positively heretical and which, at other times, contain plain nonsense and which despoil right thinking. . . ." In *minhag ashkenaz* these controversies and hostilities, especially the antagonism between rabbi and cantor, seem not to have taken excessive form, at least not during the formative years, or before the thirteenth century. This is evident from the fact that such admired masters as Rashi, his grandson Solomon, even R. Meir of Rothenburg did not disdain to officiate as precentors.[51] Some of the early singer-preachers (the homilists of whom Mai-

monides spoke so contemptuously) were known to have composed *piyutim* to which they also set tunes—R. Meir Isaac of Worms, the singer (d. about 1096), is said to have written the Aramaic *Akdamut.* Yet the very same Meir of Rothenburg decided against *piyutim,* as may be seen by the following anecdote. He was asked whether the Reader of the Torah was permitted to recite the *piyut* called *debara* while reading the Ten Commandments. His reply was, "No, when reading the scroll the reader is not permitted to add any extraneous material, lest it should be confused with the [scriptural] text in the minds of the listeners." Zunz has correctly called this a severe reply, reflecting "*halachischen stabilismus und zuenftige Vornehmtuerei*" (halakhic conservatism and professional snobbism).[52]

Under relatively tranquil political circumstances the rabbis watched over the hazanim and did not permit them any extravagances in Germany and eastern France. Until the High Middle Ages the fact that the hazan was a paid functionary was resented by some rabbis. Rabbi Juda the Pious objected to it, but a certain R. Eliezer (of Bohemia) took issue with him and defended the meager income of the hazan.[53] Yet during the Crusades and the never-ending persecutions the cantors and their moving songs could give more comfort than the best halakhic decisions. Hence it is understandable that, despite the incessant rabbinic hostility, the hazanim and their *piyutim* won out in *minhag ashkenaz,* in both East and West. The resulting ebullience and self-assurance of the hazanim characterized the professional precentors of the Renaissance and Baroque periods. In fact their feeling of being indispensable harmed the cause of Jewish musical tradition much more than it helped it. All nostalgic memories of those "good old days" of *ḥazanut* are either pipe-dreams or documents of ignorance—and sometimes even combinations of both. The truly great and indeed historic epoch of the Ashkenazic hazan was that of the *Missinai* tunes, the period between 1200 and 1450.

Main Lines of Liturgical-Musical Development

To trace the main lines of the liturgical-musical development, the entire corpus of the musical *minhag ashkenaz* can be divided into five categories in order of their historical appearance in the music of the Synagogue: psalmody of biblical or prayer texts; *neginot,* the cantillation of Torah and *Haftarah*; chant of the original prayers especially on weekdays and Sabbaths, according to their traditional modes; *Missinai* tunes and recitatives; and metrical melodies of either metrical or nonmetrical texts.

Of these five categories, the first three forms are common to all Jewish traditions, although their melodies differ according to the geographic and cultural environments. The fourth and fifth, however, are characteristic of *minhag ashkenaz* and exist only there. These songs portray the entire Jewish life of the Middle Ages. The two song types concomitant with the liturgical *minhag ashkenaz* reveal two opposite tendencies: the *Missinai* tunes are introvert and centripetal, whereas the metrical melodies imitate the popular ditties of the Gentile environment and reveal a clearly centrifugal direction.

2

On Tradition and Its Transmitters

Rabbi Meir taught: "Whosoever studies Torah without teaching it, of him it is said: 'He has despised the words of the Lord.'"
(B. *Sanhedrin* 99b)

In the past, scholars have questioned the continuity of the musical tradition of Judaism, not only because of the many centuries of dispersion that at times endangered the ethnic identity of Jewry, nor because of the coexistence of three different main traditions, but chiefly because of the almost total lack of written sources until the seventeenth century.[1] We might not be amiss in remembering that, at least in Judaism, oral tradition is not considered inferior to documents. Quite the contrary! Priests and rabbis opposed the codification of both laws and prayers for many centuries, and only the growing ignorance of Hebrew forced them to give up their former obstinate opposition. There was no authentic prayer book in existence until well into the ninth century, when R. Amram Gaon sanctioned, with his name and authority, the first *siddur*, which underwent a great number of alterations in various regions and in subsequent centuries.[2]

The rabbinic theology of organized and canonized prayer is not free from occasional paradoxes. Although fixed prayer was made obligatory in Judaism, voices were heard expressing doubt about the value of such "fixed prayers." Indeed they doubted the value of all obligation to pray fixed texts at fixed times. Such heterodox opinions can be found even in the Mishnah, which otherwise represents the prevailing opinions among the rabbis. For example, in Mishnah Berakhot 29b we read, "R. Eliezer says, 'If a man makes his prayer a fixed task [*tefillat keva*], it is not a genuine supplication.'" And in the Gemara, which comments on this, "What is meant by a fixed task? R. Jacob ben Idi said in the name of R. Oshaiah, 'Anyone whose prayer is like a heavy burden to him.' The rabbis say, 'Whoever does not say it in the manner of supplication.' Rabbah and R. Joseph both say, 'Whoever is not able to insert something fresh into it.' R. Zeira said, 'I can insert something fresh, but I am afraid to do so for fear I should become confused (to forget where I stopped when making the insertion).'"[3]

We must remember that the entire discussion revolved around *memorized, not written* prayers, and that certain prayers were considered so canonical that any deviation from the accepted text was regarded as a grave sin. The reason for the rabbis' stubborn resistance to written compilations, as they themselves state it,

was their fear of mechanical prayer, a fear that was, as we know all too well, quite justified and generally vindicated in the centuries to follow. They preferred a flexible, *spontaneous* "outpouring of the heart" in spoken as well as in chanted prayer to any fixed and prescribed text. The people's ignorance of Hebrew eventually forced their hands, but they felt that at least melody and chant should be spontaneous and not bound to any particular text.

The Jewish authorities were not completely indifferent to the aesthetic nature of the chant of the regular prayers. However, their aims were determined not by aesthetic principles, but rather by theological and ethical concerns.[4]

The *spontaneity* of chanted prayer, its extemporal quality, was first demanded and logically postulated by the philosopher-poet Yehudah Ha-Levi in his celebrated book on the essence of Judaism, the *Kuzari*. The pertinent passage will be quoted and discussed in chapter 4. Many similar passages advocate the use of improvisation (in Arabic, *tartil*) for chanted prayer. Since Ha-Levi, himself a celebrated poet of artfully rhymed and structured poems, was opposed to them in worship, his words seem to apply to prayers of prose texts only. A few centuries later another Sephardic thinker, Profiat Duran (Ephodi), expressed himself in favor of clear and simple chant, for "if you listen to chanted poetry of other nations, you will find them in flux, until they almost lose the form of stanzas, and become hard to understand—there remains merely tone and syllable. For they were intended only for the sensual pleasure of hearing the constant change of the voice's volume between *piano* and *forte*, and they lose, in the melodies and tunes, the form of the [original] stanzas."[5]

If improvisation and spontaneity were the desired properties of chanted prayers, how could a musical tradition emerge without any notation and still retain its basic characteristics over the centuries? The answer is complex. The continuity of tradition was safeguarded by the art of modal improvisation. This was not free invention but was restricted to a finite number of prescribed and well-established melodic patterns, transmitted orally from master to disciple over the generations. This type of "tradition-bound improvisation" is known to us from antiquity. The cuneiform remarks about certain hymns to be performed at the ancient courts of Mesopotamia, especially in Sumer and Babylonia, indicate such a tradition.[6] Of the many references to this practice in biblical literature only one is quoted here, because of its far-reaching significance: "David lamented with this lamentation over Saul and over Jonathan his son, and he said, the children of Judah should be taught the bow [song]; behold it is written in the book *Yashar*" (2 Samuel 1:17–27). This verse means that both text and tune of that famous dirge were to be taught orally, and that certain variations were thus unavoidable.[7]

Skipping to a time (more than a thousand years later) shortly before musical notation began to fix the Christian tradition, we read in the writings of the monk Cassiodorus (fl. 570–585) that "the great treasury of Alleluia-chants is nothing but the result of an insatiable urge to vary and extemporize." These daily improvisations began to crystallize into tonal formulas, melodic patterns, modes, half-fixed ornaments—a process that was still not fully completed in the tenth century. Stylization was undertaken by the many *scholae cantorum* in western Europe that reached their zenith after the Carolingian period.

Stylization

The stylization of the oral tradition is a characteristic of *minhag ashkenaz*, but it changes with every fashion in Western music. It follows a path different from the general development of folk song. The tradition is not autonomous but is directed or guided in accordance with certain ideal postulates grounded in Jewish theology. In concrete musical terms this guidance, occasionally resembling coercion, led to the preference for certain modes, the strong approval of unison singing, with its concomitant denial or at least neglect of all harmony and polyphony for many centuries,[8] and the long-lasting reluctance to fix melodic lines by musical notation.

In rabbinic literature the preference for traditional tunes is nowhere expressed in precise terms, but quite frequent and fervent is the condemnation of those who sang or imitated "foreign" or non-Jewish tunes in the synagogue.[9] Such warnings occur in the literature of *minhag ashkenaz* again and again, especially in the *Sefer Ḥasidim*. This work, a moralistic book of prescriptions and warnings, written in the Rhineland, during the first Crusades, by R. Samuel the Pious and his son R. Judah, represents the vehement and bitter reaction to the pogroms and massacres to which the German Jews were exposed during the twelfth, thirteenth, and fourteenth centuries. Since the lower clergy (unlike the bishops) frequently took an active part in these persecutions, the hostile attitude of the book to every faint shade of Christian religion and, in particular, to everybody even suspected of acting for the Church, is understandable. A few passages referring to music illustrate that attitude: "It is forbidden to sing sacred songs in the presence of a priest or a Christian layman, or to quote to him songs of praise—this would be a sin and a betrayal.... Nobody should teach the letters of the [Hebrew] alphabet to a priest nor should he sing to him a pleasant song, lest the priest himself use that song for idolatry"; in addition, a Christian nurse was not to sing to a Jewish child any lullaby that might also be heard in church.[10]

Beyond this defensive attempt to eliminate foreign modes, there arose during the late Middle Ages a kind of half-intentional, half-instinctive feeling for the "inherent style" of synagogue chant. This sense of style, although often uncertain, might have been engendered by a kind of innate entelechy, which may be understood as built-in self-guidance.

The positive appraisal of unison singing as against harmonic and polyphonic singing had both theological and practical reasons. According to prophets and rabbis, Israel and the angels that surround the throne of God alternate with each other in His praise; and like the angels, so Israel is duty-bound to sing His praises "as if with one mouth," an idea that was absorbed by the Christian fathers and can be found in the works of Augustine and Jerome among others.[11] If the phrase "with one mouth" is taken literally, the result is the preference for unison singing to any other kind of performance, especially to polyphonic song.

Another reason for unison singing was the lack of musical notation, which is indispensable for harmony or polyphony. There were several reasons for the reluctance to write music. First, chanted prayers include not only praise of God, but also supplication, "outpouring of the soul," and penitence. This is usually done

by the individual himself without the hazan, and obviously cannot be done by a choir. At any rate, it would have to be improvised upon the inspiration of the moment. In the above-mentioned *Kuzari* the theological arguments in favor of improvisation and against "set" melodies are listed by Yehudah Ha-Levi.[12] This was one of the main reasons for rejecting the example of European music, which had systematically cleared all hurdles that stood in the way of the exact notation of melodies and harmonies. Even tõday most hazanim, although they all use notation to fix tunes they wish to remember, shy away from notation when they sing solo passages in the synagogue. There they practice improvisation that remains within the boundaries of the prescribed modes required by the tradition.

Some Jews of the Middle Ages and Renaissance were familiar with Western notation. For example, the oldest German songbook for chorus, the *Lochamer Liederbuch*, was written at least in part by the Jew Wolfflein von Locham, and its fifteenth-century notation was considerably more complex than our modern system.[13] This music, of course, had no relationship to the music of the synagogue. There are remnants of some medieval Hebrew manuscripts, but these were relegated to the dustbins of the genizah, which demonstrates that notation was not popular.[14] Nor did the group of Italian Jewish composers of the late Renaissance who mastered intricate polyphonic forms and their notation leave lasting traces in the Italian synagogue. Even the genius of Salomone de' Rossi could not overcome this suspicious regard of notated polyphonic music. Because of this wariness of notation, there are only two compendia of Italian synagogue music extant, of which one was compiled just before the twentieth century, the other even more recently.[15] Indeed, except for their Westernized musicians, the oriental Jews do not use notation to this very day. Perhaps one might associate the rejection of organized notation, "set tunes," harmony, and polyphony with the antipathy of most Semitic nations to painting and sculpture.

The insistence on "traditional" tunes for the synagogue without concomitant rejection of secular art music can be traced back to the ancient doctrine of *ethos* in music. In fact, all the theological and moral values attributed to various modes of music reflect this very system of thought. This complex of ideas, common to all ancient cultures, and important even today in Asiatic folklore, springs from one basic thesis: all music has the power to influence human behavior through emotions aroused by the performer, the innate character of the composition heard, and the corresponding sentiments stimulated in the listener's soul. In many civilizations the belief that music can "move" the soul within the body—hence the word "emotion"—entailed a vague and yet concrete correlation between certain modes, rhythms, instruments, and their moral qualities. The first detailed formulation of this widespread conviction appears in Plato's writings, especially in *Timaeus*, the *Laws*, and the *Republic*; today there is no doubt left that he received the doctrine from the Pythagorean fraternity. It is not germane to our subject to outline the various aspects of that doctrine; however, it was generally accepted as a valid explanation of musical power up to the Renaissance, and even later. Its vestigial ideas are still discernible in Mozart's *Magic Flute*, and also in the emotional rejection of early jazz for moral reasons.

In Jewish tradition the *ethos* doctrine is quite articulate, and often it is connected with the harmony of the spheres.[16] Curt Sachs, among others, successfully interpreted the *ethos* of the various instruments mentioned in Bible and Talmud;[17] the functional designation of the trumpets in the Dead Sea Scroll of "The War of the Sons of Light against the Children of Darkness" testifies concretely to the doctrine of *ethos*.[18] In the early Church the principle of *ethos* in music was deepened by the synthesis of Neoplatonism with Jewish and Christian mysticism.[19] The apostasy of a brilliant sage of the tannaitic era, R. Elisha ben Abuya, was attributed to the "frivolous Greek songs" that incessantly came from his mouth.[20]

Early synagogue music differed from music of the Temple in various specifics. Most important, the Temple music was in the hands of trained performers, professionals, the Levites, who enjoyed a hereditary privileged rank in the lower hierarchy. Synagogue singers, on the other hand, were laymen in every sense of the word. In addition, instrumental music—even simple accompaniment—was strictly prohibited by the rabbis. This prohibition, concocted from sources and principles that were neither fully authentic nor homogeneous, was the rabbis' safeguard against any evolution of artistic and professional music in the synagogue. Before the destruction of the Temple the rabbis had opposed the priests and their music. Afterward they glorified it in retrospect, yet forbade its emulation by the hazanim. This is a long and sad chapter in the history of Jewish music; its consequences have outlasted the tyrannical rule of the rabbis and can be felt to this day.[21]

The question arises, whether a musical tradition that has lived and developed in many countries in unbroken continuity and was transmitted both by honorary laymen and appointed hazanim can still be considered folklore. In order to judge, a careful and critical survey must be made of the entire corpus of the musical tradition. The musical tradition of *minhag ashkenaz* would most accurately be described (from the musicologist's point of view) as a stylization of Judeo-German folklore. The concrete criteria of "stylized folk song" were established as a result of empirical observations by students of comparative folklore during many years of studies in this field.[22] They were originally undertaken for each national group separately, after J. G. Herder had initiated and kindled the scientific interest in folk song. Only since 1900 have observations of specific ethnic groups been compared, coordinated, and to a certain extent generalized. In the following remarks some of these results, especially criteria of age and origin, will be applied to the repertory of *minhag ashkenaz*.

The raw material of that repertory was transmitted by bards, minstrels and joculators, until it finally reached the cantors of the European synagogues, derived from a wide variety of sources in location and period. Elements from the shores of the Mediterranean Sea, from Latin cities, Teutonic hamlets, and Slavonic settlements were absorbed during the period between 1000 and the middle of the nineteenth century. Like clay, the musical substance was not rigidly fixed when its transmitters heard, sang, and molded it. Nor did it lose its flexibility when finally adapted to Hebrew prayer texts, many centuries before notation. The oldest elements, of which today but a few short melodic formulas remain, seem to have come from the Holy Land well before the separation of the musical traditions (of Ashkenazim

and Sephardim) in the ninth century. They antedate any stylization according to the church modes of Western chant.[23]

Oriental, and, later, occidental writers described and listed certain types of melodic patterns, which in their oral traditions recur in an almost kaleidoscopic fashion. The systems of these patterns are called *makams* (Arabic), *ragas* (Hindu), or quite generally *modes*. Each of them serves as the matrix for many individual tunes, in which the skeletal tones of the basic mode occur in a certain order, handed down by oral tradition. Each of these oriental modes has characteristics of its own, expresses particular emotions, and corresponds to specific ideas of the doctrine of ethos.

During the eighteenth, nineteenth, and early twentieth centuries these modes were, for reasons of convenience and easy reference, forced into scales. In doing this, the theorists followed more or less the example of the medieval authors who had arranged—actually pressed—the modes of Gregorian, Byzantine, and Ambrosian plainchant into scales which were more or less willfully derived from ancient Greek scales. More than one error occurred in this transition from ancient Greek to European medieval theory. Yet the Catholic Church, of which all the medieval theorists were faithful adherents, sanctioned this categorization and the (erroneous) nomenclature of the various mode-scales. Today they are known under the terms church tones, octave species, ecclesiastical modes, and so on.[24] The weakness of this enforced connection between a melodic mode and its hypothetical scale may be seen in the first two examples in table II. In example 1*a* we have a chant, and in 1*b*, the extrapolation of its constituent tones. These clearly do not constitute a scale, for a scale is by definition the result of a rational division of the octave into equal or unequal parts. The mode is not connected with the concept of the octave, nor is this antiphon. Furthermore, a scale must repeat itself exactly in its upper and lower registers, whereas in a mode this is not necessary. In table II, no. 2*a*, we have the mode of *minhag ashkenaz* entitled *Adonai malakh* (to be discussed in more detail in chapter 4). The summary of its constituent tones in 2*b* shows clearly that there is an E-flat in the upper register, an E-natural in the lower.[25]

With these observations on stylization and modes in mind, we turn back to the question of transmission of tradition. Who, indeed, were the carriers of the melodies before the process of crystallization took place? Here our sources are scanty and we are obliged to rely on legendary material and on analogous situations in contemporary medieval literature.

At the courts of Navarre, Castile, and Aragon, Jewish *juglares* (Latin, *joculatores*, French, *jongleurs*) were familiar guests. The decision of the Council of Valladolid (1322) against them might even indicate that they were a little too familiar. Thanks to the late Monsignor Higinio Anglès, who found and published a vast number of sources pertaining to Jewish minstrels in Spain, we are fairly well informed about their musical abilities and their social status, which was lower than that of the *trobadors*.[26]

In German territories, the existence and activity of Jewish *Spielleute* is attested to by the "Gudrun" epic in Hebrew letters, and by an "Abraham" epic, which contains directions such as "in the tone of the Samuel book" [*be-nigun Shmuel-buch*].

The latter is a Judeo-German paraphrase of the biblical books of Samuel and Kings, couched in the meter and the stanza of the *Nibelungenlied.*[27] The existence of Jewish minnesingers seems to be undisputed, even if the case of the well-known Süsskind of Trimberg has recently become controversial.[28] Not controversial, however, is the fact that the *Lochamer Liederbuch* was at least partly written in mensural notation by a Jewish scribe and dedicated to his *gemaken* (wife) in Judeo-German script.[29]

The *Spielleute* and *Fahrenden* of other nationalities seemed to have transmitted their songs and melodies, wittingly or unwittingly, to their Jewish confreres, the *klezmorim* (musicians), the *badchanim* (jokesters), the *letzim* (mockers, clowns), etc. There were also so-called folksingers, who, being popular with Jews and Gentiles alike, heard a great many folk songs and brought them, however mutilated, into the walls of the ghetto. One of these singers was one Jacob Heilprunn (a name that is the precursor of all Heilperns, Halperns, Alpers, etc.), nicknamed the "tick Reb Jacob" (tick means gross), to whom the song "*Ich heb aber an ein alten Weis*" (I shall now intone an old song) is attributed.

Some of the old German *Weisen*, long forgotten today, were transmitted and preserved by these singers. A number of them were listed by Eduard Birnbaum: "*Niggun hurban Polin*" (tune of Poland's Destruction), "*Niggun galut*" (tune of the Jewish Exile), "*Niggun raḥmanut*" (tune of mercy), and others. Well known from old German folklore are tunes called "*Pavia*," "*Dietrich of Bern*," "*Herzog Ernst*," "*Pauern Lied*," "*Hoch rief der Waechter*" (The Watchman Called from the Tower).[30]

Yet as the *Spielleute* gradually vanished from the German scene, so did they disappear from Jewish life in central Europe, and the growing urbanization during the seventeenth century accelerated this process. The Jewish musicians and entertainers maintained their existence in the East (Poland, Russia, the Baltic countries) until the turn of this century. In America, of course, they became comedians and vaudevillians, but their direct ancestors were *klezmorim* and *badchanim*.

Rising and Descending Elements of Musical Tradition

We now know that the cantors of the Ashkenazic tradition were receivers of melodic substance, in an unrefined state, from the vagrant musicians described above. We know, too, that some of the texts were originally German or French when the cantors came upon them. Only later were the tunes subjected to a Judaizing stylization for the synagogue.

In modern folkloristic studies the transformations of a tune are traced in two directions. In some cases the process of change is described as *aufsteigend* (ascending). This occurs when a folk melody is taken up by a composer, stylized, and integrated into a work of art music. The opposite process, called *absinkend* (descending), is involved when a tune has its origin in a work of art and then becomes a folk song.

The first, or ascending, process was largely prevalent in the fourteenth and fifteenth centuries. Stylization of *musica composita* (art music) in France, Germany,

Italy, the Netherlands, Bohemia, and West Poland kept the melodies fairly close to their originals. The tunes of genuine folk songs, and of the *hofweisen* (tunes sung for the "courtly" epic or similar forms) related to them, such as the *chanson*, *canzona*, and *villanella*, were all but interchangeable. We find these elements often as *cantus firmi* of the art music of that time or in stylization and variations in arrangements for lutes or keyboard instruments. A good example is Benedetto Marcello's employment of traditional tunes of the Venetian Jews in his rather ambitious *Estro poetico-armonico*, which will be discussed later.

An example of the process of *aufsteigend* in the Jewish area is the parody motet *Cados, Cados* of the fifteenth century (formerly in the Columbine Library of Seville, at present in the Bibliothèque Nationale of Paris) in which the unknown composer used fragments of Sephardic chant in the upper two of three voices.[31] A later example is the music of A. Hirschmann. A *klezmer* in his youth, Hirschmann subsequently used a number of folk and popular tunes as the basis of thirty *Galanteries-Stuecke fuer Klavier* (1733). These remained in manuscript in the library of Darmstadt until they were destroyed in the bombing in World War II.

For examples of *absinkend* we have the case of the melody of "*Se vuol ballare*" from Mozart's *Marriage of Figaro*, which was corrupted into a trite synagogue chant for the period between Passover and Shabuoth. Also, we know instances of Italian courtly dances borrowed and reshaped by Jews. Unfortunately the elegance and symmetry of the dances were lost in transition.

This fluctuating interrelation between folk song and art music is certainly very old, but we can trace it back only to about the year 1000. What is remarkable is that in spite of these fluctuations, in spite of the changes—indeed, mutilations—of the basic traditions the *klezmorim* or *Spielleute* might have caused, the main archetypes of synagogue chant—i.e., psalmodic chant, scriptural cantillation, and prayer chant (from simple *parlando* to developed recitative)—were left intact. This is apparent from the fact that all traditions of the synagogue have preserved them to this day. The prayer modes will be discussed in chapter 4, and the scriptural cantillation in chapter 5.

The oldest remains of *minhag ashkenaz* are possibly of Palestinian origin. They are simple, almost primitive psalmodies, consisting of just a few tones. The daily benedictions of the morning prayer (*birkhot ha-shahar*) are the best examples. If we examine table II, no. 3, we observe the narrow tonal range and the equally limited number of tones used for the melody; both are regarded generally as criteria of great antiquity.

A second example (table II, no. 4) represents a more extended mode. This *v'hakohanim* (from the *musaf* service of Yom Kippur) comes from the Italian tradition. It is a primitive psalmody that is common to all ancient Christian and Jewish chant. In this case the parallelism is obvious: the caesura [*atnah*] occurs precisely where it emphasizes the dichotomy of the Hebrew text. This form type, which appears primitive to the untrained eye, is in fact a rather rigid stylization of a melodic pattern that was once fluid and facile. It is like what Robert Lach described as "frozen lava" after a volcanic eruption.[32] It contains three constitutive elements: a tone to which most of the verse is recited (tenor); two corresponding halves; and

the so-called punctuating melismas, the little flourishes in the middle [*atnah*] and end, or *punctus*, of the verse [*sof pasuk*]. Tunes patterned this way are very old, especially when the number of constituent tones is small and the range not larger than a fifth or sixth. Most of them belong to the category of psalmodies.

Such tunes form the oldest stratum of *minhag ashkenaz*; they are of oriental origin, but they were stylized and re-formed in Europe. The first stylization took place in Italy, and only later in Germany. Indeed, one may say that there are old Italian elements in *minhag ashkenaz*, just as German elements later infiltrated the Italian tradition. The Judeo-Italian elements consist of fragments of courtly or rural dances such as the *bergamasca* or the *villanella*, both of the fifteenth and sixteenth centuries. The German features, in turn, are either paraphrases of students' songs or ditties of Austrian military bands of the end of the eighteenth and early nineteenth century.

Italian Elements

The process in *minhag ashkenaz* of reshaping what were originally Italian melodies occurred without any clear direction. Idelsohn had a strong intuition about the close relationship between *minhag ashkenaz* of the post-Carolingian epoch and the Italian Jewish tradition.[33] He was unable to adduce truly convincing evidence because his studies were necessarily fragmentary. His one written source (in 1930) was Consolo, which was not a comprehensive work, and which left large areas of ritual chant unrecorded.[34] It was restricted to the pure Sephardic tradition of Leghorn, transcribed from oral performances by living persons. Idelsohn himself was working before the time of tape recording, so that he had no firsthand sources at his disposal.[35] Since his time a new compendium has appeared, the Piatelli volume mentioned earlier (see n. 15), recording the Roman repertoire. Piatelli admits in his introduction that his purpose was not to write a musicological study. His only reading in the field had been some of Idelsohn's studies, hence his work is not quite up to date. He also appears to be unaware of criteria for the determination of data and provenance of un-notated melodies, so that, deploring the lack of ancient manuscripts, he refuses to place his material in time and space, as if there were not sufficient criteria for age and provenance of an extended piece of music.

However, with the limitations of the Italian material in mind, it is still possible to draw some conclusions from a careful comparison of the Sephardic rite (Consolo), the Roman rite (Piatelli), and the *minhag ashkenaz*. The similarities in table II between nos. 5*a* and 5*b*,[36] between 6*a* and 6*b*, and between 7*a* and 7*c* are clearly discernible. However, the strong similarity between 7*c* and the two preceding excerpts from the Roman tradition is striking. The psalm-tone given here is found in the traditions of Yemen, Persia, *minhag ashkenaz*, and Gregorian psalmody. All of these illustrations reflect the influx of Italian and other older elements into *minhag ashkenaz*.

On the other hand, if we examine nos. 8*a*–8*d* we will quickly recognize that these tunes from the Roman rite (Piatelli) are directly influenced by German folk song of the eighteenth and nineteenth centuries. (No. 8*c* is an Austrian student song,

and 8*d* is the famous opening of the slow movement in Haydn's Surprise Symphony.) These examples demonstrate how difficult it sometimes is (especially in such cases as nos. 8*c* and 8*d*) to differentiate between descending art music and ascending folk song. Of the examples in table II, nos. 5 through 8, comprising sixteen tunes, six are metrical, the others are not, for a mode lends itself equally well to metrical and free rhythmical treatment (see nos. 6*a*, 6*b*). It was Idelsohn's fixed idea to distinguish categorically between metrical tunes, which he termed "melodies," and nonmetrical tunes, which he called "modes" [*Weisen*]. He claimed that only modes contained old traditions, whereas all "melodies" were of recent origin. This theory has proved to be untenable, as may be seen by the examples just quoted.[37] Thanks to the Piatelli volume, it is now possible to verify Idelsohn's guess of the close relationship between *minhag ashkenaz* and the musical traditions of Italian Jewry.

Evaluation of the Oral Tradition

While following methods of examining folklore as suggested by Bela Bartók, in evaluating *minhag ashkenaz* I must modify Bartók's categorical distinction of "rural" and "urban" transmission. (Jews did not have the exact equivalents.) Instead, I make the distinction between the honorary precentor, the *ba'al tefillah* of the smaller communities, the *landjuden* (strong defenders of *minhag ashkenaz*), and the appointed hazan of the larger communities, who remained in any given position only a few years and then moved on. (This characteristic of the hazan came into being particularly after the sixteenth century.) His task was much less the preservation of old traditions than the enticement of the masses, especially the drawing forth of tears of penitence and mourning, mainly during the High Holy Days.

In the view of the rabbis, this penitence was the most desirable effect the cantors could produce. At the same time, the rabbis were not willing to acknowledge their efforts and showed only contempt for them. For they well knew that the sources from which the cantors drew were not always pure and clear, and they suspected that the vagrant singers were their cantors' helpmates. For the rabbis these transmitters, Jewish or Gentile minstrels, were outcasts, their art sinful and frivolous. In this respect, as in many others, they were just as snobbish as their Christian contemporaries, who wrote the contemptuous lines:

Musicorum et cantorum magna est distantia	There is a great distance between musicians and singers
Isti dicunt, isti sciunt quae componit musica	The singers talk, the others know what music composes,
Nam qui facit, quod non sapit, definitur bestia.[38]	But he who performs what he does not understand is defined as beast.

The Jewish minstrels were often former Yeshiva students who found pleasure in the uninhibited life of the vagrants; knowing many ditties, they sold their songs and stories to the hazanim for a free meal. Some of them might have been the very

poets or musicians who compiled the Judeo-German epics of *Gudrun*, *Meister Hiltebrand*, and the *Book of Samuel* mentioned above, and who functioned as bards to Jewish audiences. Although many of them were talented, there were no great composers among them, to correspond to some of the *jongleurs* of their time who were men of noble birth and good education such as Adam de la Hâle or the legendary "Herr Volker" from Alzey, who was praised in the *Nibelungenlied*. Petrarch's comment that they were *non magni ingenii* was quite true in general. Yet there were significant exceptions, and even the celebrated Freidank seems to have been a *Spielmann*, since he sometimes bore the epithet *vagus*, or the vagrant.[39]

The *fahrenden jongleurs* left a number of poems or *chansons* that are identified by their names. But the names of the Jewish vagrants are unknown, although some of their writings have come down to us. Musical caricatures of their songs and dances were quite popular among the lutenists of the fifteenth and sixteenth centuries (see table II, no. 9).

It is hardly possible to form a true picture of the skill of Jewish minstrels from this satirical piece. The critical listener clearly senses the professional envy of musicians who either were unable to use chromaticism or were fearful of Jewish competition. A typical complaint about the Guild of Jewish musicians in Prague reads as follows: "They should be forbidden to play at Christian festivities, as they ruin and confound all music [*da sie die Musik confuse verstupfen, weder Tempo noch Tact fuehren*]."[40] To the professional or educated musician their music seemed ridiculous and meaningless, as it proceeded "*contra regulas Musicorum*" in every measure (M. Praetorius).

And yet we must remember that the hazanim who first shaped the *minhag ashkenaz* were not minstrels nor vagrants, nor were they educated musicians; they were appointed or honorary precentors whose duty it was to improvise the prayer chants according to certain unwritten laws *sui generis*. When they stylized borrowed tunes in order to assimilate them to the atmosphere of the synagogue, they observed certain fixed principles:

1. The selection of musical material. It was not to consist of Christian songs, either from Gregorian chant or from religious songs in the vernacular.[41] Notwithstanding all such laws, some ecclesiastical chants found their way into the repertoire of medieval Jewry—one even into the liturgy of the High Holy Days. (The resemblance between the *Barekhu* and *iste confessor* is discussed in chapter 3.) The hymn "*Alma Redemptoris Mater*," a famous poem in praise of the Virgin, seems also to have been a great favorite among German, English, and Spanish Jews (see chapter 6).[42]

2. The use of modes. Mixing the mode of the Torah lesson with that of the Prophetic lesson or of a lesson from the Hagiographa was not permitted.[43] This law concerns the prescribed manner in which the scriptural cantillation was to be performed; it had to remain in its supposedly pristine purity, as it was believed to have come directly from the revelation on Mount Sinai.[44] These *neginot* are not to be confused with the prayer modes. (Cantillation modes are discussed in chapter 5, prayer modes in chapter 4.)

3. Performance practice. The melodies were to be sung slowly, to move the

listeners to tears of penitence.[45] The requirement of slow and majestic tempi and the aim to evoke and instill contrition in the hearts of the worshipers are old. Rabbi Meir of Rothenburg, the greatest luminary of *minhag ashkenaz*, merely repeated it.[46]

4. *Zersingen* (expanding melodies far beyond their original scope) and variation. Both these techniques had to conform to the sense of the Hebrew text and to its liturgical function (see table II, no. 10*a* and *b*). The practices of *Zersingen* and variations, common to folk song of all nations, are noteworthy in the transition from folk song to art music (ascending culture) and even more so in the vulgarization of an art song (descending culture).[47] They appear either as pretexts for repetition of a melodic line or as occasions for coloratura flourishes. A favorite method of variation is the frequent use of sequences; they dominate entire sections of *minhag ashkenaz*, particularly in the eastern European versions. (See chapter 8 on the characteristics of the style typical of Polish Jewry.) Yet another technique, that of permutating sets of specific motifs, belongs to the sphere of art music.

Formulas that make up cadences are, like musical ornaments, characteristics of different stages in the development of folk song. In most cases they stress the rhyme or the refrain of a song. In *minhag ashkenaz*, even without taking into account the rhymed *piyutim*, the appearance of metrical cadences serves as a reliable criterion of the process of Germanization. The final clauses of psalmodies and recitatives that were fixed and came from an older stratum usually remained free of meter or rhyme and were not subjected to the fancies of improvising hazanim. Some of them originated in scriptural cantillation and were transplanted directly to the liturgy, carrying as they did an ample load of biblical allusions, full of meaning for the worshiper. Chronologically, these prayer chants are older than the *Missinai* tunes, and even some psalmodic cadences were attached to them to heighten their solemnity.[48] In *minhag ashkenaz* they stand at the end of a *berakhah* (benediction) as settings for the *ḥatimah* (seal and conclusion), or they heighten the solemnity of a chant, especially during the High Holy Days; at any rate, they are older than the chants that they conclude. None of these clauses belongs unequivocally to one tonality or mode—they are often interchangeable in their function of cadencing passages. In table II, nos. 11*a* through *g* belong to this category of concluding clauses. They occur in plainchant, in early minnesongs, and in some sequences and tropes of the tenth and eleventh centuries. We shall encounter some of them in the next chapter.

3

The *Missinai* Tunes

For the Law wills that
shrieks of anguish
death-rattle and the moan
of the maimed
Sound in your ears like
prayer, oath and paean.
(Karl Wolfskehl)

The music referred to as the *Missinai* melodies originated in a period whose history reads like an ominous prelude to the holocaust of our own century. A peaceful coexistence (rather than integration) of German and French Jews with their hosts was rudely interrupted by the Crusades and their concomitant mass hysteria. In Worms, Mayence, Speyer, Cologne, and Trier the first massacres took place. From 1096 well into the fourteenth century the Jews of western Europe were subjected to an ongoing series of atrocities, resulting in mass migration, and sometimes even mass suicides.[1]

The vow to avenge the blood of Jesus on the Jews had brought to the Rhineland Gottfried of Bouillon at the head of a horde of knights and rabble. It was only the payment of a large amount of "protection money" that forced Gottfried to mitigate his threats. One of the incidents that became typical of the next 250 years was the fate of Mar Isaak bar David of Mayence. After his wife was raped and he was forced to accept baptism, he killed his two children in the synagogue, set fire to it and to his house, and leaped into the flames. The second Crusade was favored by Pope Eugen III, who had exempted all participants from paying any interest to their creditors in the Church; his successor, Pope Innocenz III, preparing the fourth Crusade, demanded that the clergy force the Jews similarly to cancel all interest, if necessary by "secular powers." In spite of the humane intervention of Bernard of Clairvaux in favor of the Jews, they were not sure of their lives, unless they fled to the fortresses or castles where the nobles accepted and protected them. During the third Crusade the number of the victims increased, and in Mayence and Worms Jews were massacred.

While the Rhenish cities in their *Landfrieden* (1254) promised *pro forma* protection to the Jews, the first Hapsburg emperors, especially Rudolf I, used blackmail of the worst sort—he imprisoned the spiritual leader of the Ashkenazic community, R. Meir of Rothenburg (in Ensisheim, Alsace), and bargained even after the rabbi's

death for his body; finally, after fourteen years, a charitable Jew paid that shameful ransom. The Jews were impoverished, robbed by the rising burghers, and deprived of their privileges by the protagonists of the harsh anti-Jewish policy of the Holy See; its main representative during those years was a man of outstanding intellectual status—the philosopher and cardinal, Nicolaus Cusanus.

The bloody events and the realization that no law would protect them finally forced the Rhenish Jews to leave their old homes and to flee for their lives. They took their names, customs, language, and whatever "was not perishable" to the East, to Poland and Russia, where, at that time, they were accepted and even welcomed.[2] They left behind small, fear-ridden communities, whose state of mind hovered between the expectation of cruel death and a growing hope for the appearance of the Messiah. These extremes made themselves felt in poetry and music.[3]

Two kinds of poetry rose out of the atmosphere that reeked of blood and perdition, that vibrated in martyrdom, in hope against hope, fervent piety, and adoration. Laments of the martyrology, time-bound memorials, were created simultaneously, in the Rhineland, with hymns of God's unity and glory. Though the texts and most of the melodies of these *ad hoc piyutim* are forgotten, many of the tunes composed during the Crusades are still heard today as the settings for the great ancient *keva* prayers. They are called *Missinai* tunes and constitute not only the most original element of *minhag ashkenaz*, but also the one that is most valuable from the musical point of view. This is a fact typical of *minhag ashkenaz*: most of the lament texts are forgotten, while their tunes were absorbed by the regular prayers of the High Holy Days and the festivals.

The appellation *Missinai* (from Mount Sinai) is an indication of the veneration with which these melodies were regarded. It seems to go back to some remarks in the *Sefer Ḥasidim*, which assert that some of these songs were given to Moses at Mount Sinai. This is a formula indicating immemorial age.[4] The sources that give some information, however vague, on liturgical performance practice during the centuries of the Crusades are disparate and unequal in authenticity. The following are six of the most important:

Rashi (R. Shelomo ben Yitzhak), who lived in Troyes in the north of France, reported the visits of rabbis and precentors from Palestine and Yemen.[5]

Maharil (R. Jacob ha-Levi ben Moshe Mollin, 1358–1427), rabbi in Mayence, was the principal authority on *minhag ashkenaz* during the Middle Ages; he traveled frequently, as preacher and sometime marriage broker, and extended the hospitality of his house to many students from other cities.[6] His main works are descriptions and rules covering the synagogue worship of his time (they were edited and revised by his disciple, R. Zalman of St. Goar); like most rabbis of the Middle Ages, he was a strictly conservative lawmaker, and one of his most famous rules demanded the faithful preservation of those melodies that had become *minhagim* (tradition) in the community.[7]

Lebush (R. Mordecai Jaffa of Prague) was the author of a book wherein certain customs of the German and central European Jews are described and explained.[8]

Herz Treves (Herz Leb Dreyfus) was a rabbi and precentor in the Rhineland, and author of a commentary on the *siddur.*[9]

Ephraim ben Jacob of Bonn (1132–1197), a survivor of the second Crusade and a chronicler of the first Crusade, left a series of reports and poems [*kinot*] in memory of the Jewish martyrs.[10]

Samuel ben Simha, of Rashi's school in France, was the compiler of the important *Maḥzor Vitry*, a compilation of rules, historical and rabbinic texts, liturgical rubrics, and *takkanot* (statutes).[11]

Liturgical Place and Function

It would be futile to search for special prayer *texts* venerated by Ashkenazic tradition to a degree that would justify the epithet *Missinai.* Such reverence was felt only for certain melodies. Paradoxically, the texts of these melodies are generally far older than their chants. The latest prayer texts connected with *Missinai* tunes are the *seliḥot* and similar penitential poems of the fourteenth century, composed for the High Holy Days. Yet there are texts set to the same tunes that hark back to pre-Christian or early Christian centuries.[12] Some prayers, for example, the *Kaddish*, were ascribed to the "Men of the Great Assembly"; other daily prayers, to the tannaitic (before C.E. 200) or Amoraic (before C.E. 350) periods; the *Shema* with its surrounding benedictions, and all psalm verses, derive from biblical times.

At first inquiry it appears as if the texts of the *Missinai* tunes have nothing in common with each other. This assumption would be erroneous. Since it is easier to categorize the melodies than the texts, we must examine their inner relationship with each other in the context of the musical motifs. The melodies in this chapter are quoted from Abraham Baer, *Der Practische Vorbeter*, better known perhaps as *Ba'al Tefillah* (Gotenburg, 1873), and from two studies by Abraham Z. Idelsohn: "Der Missinai-gesang der deutschen Synagogue," in *Zeitschrift fuer Musikwissenschaft* 8 (1926), pp. 449 ff. and *HOM* vol. 7, introduction. The melodies are those that are sung to the following *keva* texts on Rosh Hashanah, Yom Kippur, and the Three Festivals: *Tefillah* (particularly of *musaf*), *Shema, Barekhu, Alenu, Kedushah, Kaddish.* They are also sung to the following special prayers: on the High Holy Days, *yotzer, abodah, u-netaneh tokef, ohila la'el, Kol Nidre, seliḥot, v'hakohanim, v'nislah, vidui*, and others; on the festivals, *geshem* (the prayer for rain) and *tal* (the prayer for dew).

Picked at random, the melodies show no conspicuous kinship to each other. For example, the *Kaddish* of the eve of Rosh Hashanah does not resemble the *Kol Nidre* tune, and the latter seems to have nothing in common with the Great *Alenu* of the High Holy Days. However, careful comparisons will reveal some striking similarities, indeed an organic relationship between apparently disparate elements: the melodies of the Rosh Hashanah morning prayers compared with the corresponding prayers of Yom Kippur; the melodies of Yom Kippur *musaf* juxtaposed with those of Yom Kippur eve.

That there are common motifs that migrate from prayer to prayer is demonstrable. In table IIIA we have sectional motifs that permeate the liturgy. Each of

these sectional motifs dominates a particular section of the liturgy. It is quite obvious that through the musical motifs the sections are characterized and set apart from each other. Aside from such tectonic motifs, there are others that bear more precise literary associations; i.e., certain melodies are set to individual words or sentences and will recur in the chant when some allusion to those words or sentences is intended.

These associations go beyond mere verbal resemblances; they touch upon theological-Midrashic thought and elements of ritual. This is illustrated in table IIIB. The acclamation "*Adonai melekh, Adonai malakh, Adonai Yimlokh*" (the Lord reigneth, the Lord has reigned, the Lord shall reign) occurs frequently in different prayers throughout the High Holy Days (no. 1, *a* and *b*).[12a] It occurs as part of the introduction to the Torah lesson, the *eyn kamokha.* It becomes the refrain for a *piyut.* In all such instances the same musical motif is used. But even where only an allusion to the verse is called for, as in the acclamation that follows the blowing of the shofar on the New Year, the melody recurs (table IIIB, no. 1*c*). The same is true and is most significant in the application of the motif to the passage *v'nislah* on the eve of Yom Kippur (IIIB, no. 1*d*), evincing the *associative* function of the *Missinai* tunes.

Another example of melodic linking is found in a series of *seliḥot* that lead up to the classic invocation of the thirteen attributes of God, quoted in the liturgy from Exodus 34:6–7. Table IIIB, no. 2*a* contains the invocation; 2*b* is an example of an introductory *seliḥah.*

A third clear example of association by musical motif may be found in table IIIB, no. 3: 3*a* is the motif from *Kol Nidre* for the words "*Sh'vikin, sh'vitin*" (abandoned, invalid) and occurs at many other significant points in the liturgy; 3*b* is the refrain of the *al ḥet*, the confessional of Yom Kippur, the words "*s'lah lanu, m'ḥal lanu, kaper lanu*" (forgive us, have mercy on us, pardon us); 3*c* is another humble plea for forgiveness for sins, "*s'laḥ na,*" from the *neilah* portion of the Day of Atonement.

Thus these migrating, or recurrent motifs containing literary or theological associations and allusions approach the function of leitmotifs, known to every music-lover from the program symphonies of Berlioz and Liszt, and even better from the operas of Richard Wagner. Many generations of faithful hazanim have created the liturgical structure by transmitting these motifs and their hermeneutic significance from generation to generation. It is because of the devotion of those hazanim that *minhag ashkenaz*, alone in Jewish tradition, stands as a living, developing, and creative musical structure, in contradistinction to the more or less petrified and stagnant Sephardic and Yemenite traditions. The latter may be of great historical interest, but musically they are far inferior to *minhag ashkenaz.*

Stylistic Features

The *Missinai* tunes were described by Idelsohn as being Jewish in tonality and motif development.[13] This observation is highly questionable, as we view it today. The tonalities of the *Missinai* tunes are those that were commonly employed in the Middle Ages in western Europe, in both secular and sacred song. It seems more

fruitful to examine the stylistic features of the melodies by the usual method of musical analysis: (1) tonality and modes; (2) tone-word relationships, rhythm and meter, types of melismatic passages; (3) comparison with similar non-Jewish tunes, or the question of influence and assimilation.

Tonality. The musical idiom of the *Missinai* tunes is determined by simple major or minor tonalities, or, to a lesser degree, by certain modally contrived passages. Of these, the mixolydian scale is most frequent (a major without a leading tone), and a few hypodorian patterns occur also, giving a simple melody a somewhat exotic flavor, as in the *Kaddish* of *neilah* (example 1). The pure Phrygian mode

Example 1

Example 2

occurs very rarely, but a mixture of natural minor with semicadences on the dominant is frequent among the older tunes of the High Holy Days, as seen in example 2. The augmented third of this example must not be considered as representing the *Ahabah Rabah* mode in this instance (see chapter 4).

Major-minor mode combinations are prominent and seem to indicate uncertainties of the musical transcribers; the older manuscripts contain fewer of these vacillations. Certain special cadences do occur in the older *minhag ashkenaz*, but they are not necessarily restricted to the *Missinai* tunes. They appear, although rarely, in older German folk songs as well, as in examples 3 and 4.

The prayer modes typical of *minhag ashkenaz* are not fully developed in the *Missinai* tunes, aside from modulations reminiscent of the so-called *Yishtabah-Steiger*, as in example 5.

Tone-word relationship, rhythm and meter, types of melismatic passages. Among the various patterns of melismatic chant one may discern two strata: the older one,

Example 3

Example 4

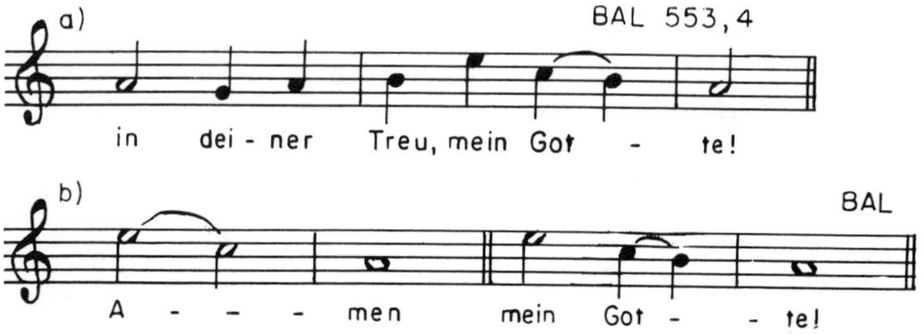

Example 5

whose melismata do not constitute an organic part of the melodic line but were probably added and inserted later by hazanim who wanted to exhibit the skill of their voices; and the more recent, whose melodies are elaborations of basic melismata. The latter originated during the Baroque age and sometimes carry elements reminiscent of similar passages in German art music of the seventeenth century. Compare example 2 above with the later chant in example 6.

Example 6

Few of the *Missinai* tunes are structured in strict meter. Most transcriptions of the nineteenth century used such fixed time signatures, but in doing so forced the tunes into a procrustean bed that distorts them badly (transcribers such as A. Baer, N. Deutsch, or M. Wodak). Sulzer usually notated them without time signature. In fact, the great majority of these melodies are free recitatives, embellished by melismata. Only a minority, mostly tunes originally set to metric poetry, are clearly composed metrically. During the time of their formation (before 1550) the struggle between metrical and mensural notation was still going on, and even German or French folk songs of the period frequently evade a metrical identification. Even melodies that open on a recurring metrical motif, such as the *Kol Nidre*, remain in meter for only a few measures and should not be pressed between bar lines.

Quotations from Scripture that occur frequently in the text of the prayers merit special consideration. Here much of the oral tradition depended on the erudition of the transmitter. If he was a learned man, he would either emphasize these biblical passages by allusion to cantillation motifs, or he would stress them in almost strictly syllabic, non-melismatic rendition, as in example 7. This form approaches a kind of solemn psalmody, a specialty of well-trained German cantors, that made listening to their chanted prayer an intellectual pleasure.

It can hardly be doubted that the compilers or, in rare cases, the composers of our *Missinai* tunes were learned men, versed at least in Scripture, and probably in Midrash as well. Their aim was to transmit the incipient *minhag ashkenaz*, stressing the full significance of each holy day and its prayers. Moreover, they were good

Example 7

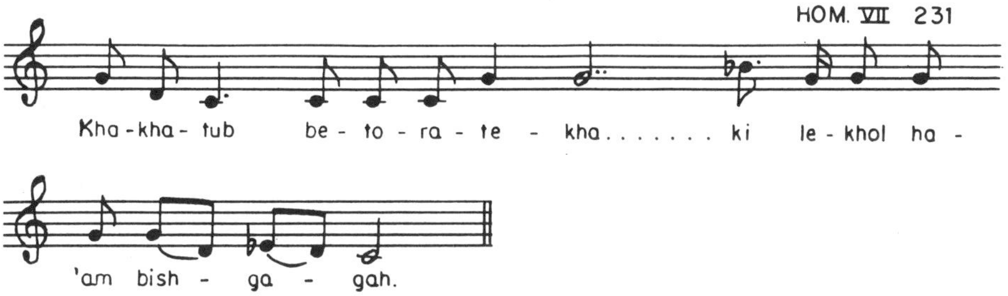

musicians with a highly developed sense for stylistic unity. Indeed, the *Missinai* tunes comprise the only stylistically uniform portion—musically speaking—of *minhag ashkenaz*.[14]

Comparison with similar non-Jewish tunes; the question of influence and assimilation. It is still difficult to isolate the original raw material of these melodies from the accretions and aftergrowths added by many subsequent generations of singers eager to embellish the original tunes. Yet one may safely say that the original material combined an old tradition with foreign elements, borrowed knowingly or unknowingly.

Before investigating the vast problem of "foreign elements" in *minhag ashkenaz* it will be useful to describe the method by which those elements will be singled out, and if possible traced back to their origins. For, unlike the scraps and shards of archaeological investigations, the musical fragments, at first glance, betray neither their age nor their origin. Often the microscopic methods of musical style analysis are needed to single out a motif as "special" or "foreign," and even then it is far from easy to trace back. The older method, which Idelsohn generally used, was to compare two melodies that have a few connected tones in common. This led to convincing results only in rare instances.[15] One example of Idelsohn's "typological" method is his comparison of the *Barekhu* motif (example 8a), which permeates the evening services of the High Holy Days, with a Gregorian hymn, "*Iste confessor*" (example 8b; text attributed to Paulus Diaconus who lived in the eighth century). It must be noted that Idelsohn altered two notes in his quotation of "*Iste confessor*," and they are of decisive importance.[16]

Example 8

A different approach is first to divide the chanted prayers into categories: the fixed prayers [*tefillot keva*], old *piyutim* (especially of the morning service), and *seliḥot* or *pizmonim*. The last category is seen to contain the largest number of foreign elements, which are invariably metrical and probably fit the strongly metrical texts of the *pizmonim*. This process leads to two general conclusions. First, the older the prayer text, the fewer the foreign elements to be found in its primary chant. Yet as the oldest prayers are those of the weekday and Sabbath services, we may assume that their musical tradition is, at least in essence, old and authentic. Second, the foreign elements may be ordered chronologically:

Nonmetrical tunes	to nonmetrical texts	before 1000
Nonmetrical tunes	to metrical texts	ca. 1100–1400
Metrical tunes	to nonmetrical texts	ca. 1450–1800
Metrical tunes	to metrical texts	ca. 1660 and after

There are, of course, exceptions and overlappings that are not entirely accounted for in this table. Many of these will emerge in later chapters.[17]

Nonmetrical tunes, too, show evidence of foreign elements, which are even harder to detect. Those instances represent a kind of natural intermingling of Jewish and Gentile raw material, grown together into an organic compound. The foreign elements were absorbed by the traditional in an "active assimilation," as opposed to a "passive assimilation"—to use a fine distinction made first by Hermann Cohen and elaborated upon by Benno Jacob. If we compare two English sentences with each other, e.g., "The lamp radiates light," where the first noun is a loan-word, the verb a foreign word, and the second noun has a genuine English root, the situation is well-balanced. Not so in "The *lied* emanates frivolity," which contains two foreign words and one loan-word. Thus the latter is a product of active, the foreign word one of passive assimilation. To demonstrate a case of active assimilation we shall revert to example 8 above, the *Barekhu* of the High Holy Day evening service. The nucleus of the melody goes back to a Gregorian hymn that was clearly metrically conceived. In example 9 it is interwoven with other motifs of Jewish tradition, but it is no longer metrical. In example 9a the nucleus is still easily recognizable; example 9b, the version found in a manuscript by M. Levy (from Esslingen, ca. 1845), is more difficult to identify. In this case the raw material came from Gregorian chant; this is actually rare in the *Missinai* tunes, and the warning words of the *Sefer Ḥasidim*—not to introduce songs of Christianity into the synagogue—were certainly disregarded. By and large, the foreign elements of

Example 9

the nonmetrical *Missinai* tunes, insofar as one can single them out, belong to French or German folk songs, or to strains from minnesingers, *trouvères*, and in exceptional cases to motifs of Burgundian art music.[18]

In the following pages some of the most characteristic *Missinai* tunes containing Gentile elements are examined. All of them are either free melodies set to non-metrical texts or semi-metrical tunes set to *piyutim*.

Kol Nidre. Text and melody of the famous prologue to Yom Kippur have memorable histories of their own, which mirror to a considerable degree the destiny of occidental Jewry. It is an amazing fact that many otherwise educated Jews connect this prayer and its well-known melody with the Spanish Inquisition. One may read this fable even in relatively recent books. The truth, however, is less romantic, for the Spanish Jews (Sephardim) do not chant the text but only recite it, sometimes once, sometimes three times. Idelsohn has stressed this fact time and again, yet to no avail; the Spanish "fable" has not vanished. And yet, with or without Spain, the text is sufficiently controversial to have elicited an entire literature in five or six languages. It has undergone a number of alterations for theological, legalistic, and also for apologetic reasons.[19]

The text and chant of the *Kol Nidre* was formally introduced by R. Yehudai Gaon (fl. 740) in his synagogue, more than 500 years before R. Meir of Rothenburg, yet it seems that at that time it had a different function, and certainly a different melody.[20] It was not repeated three times, nor did it contain the preamble:

> In the Academy on High and in the Academy on earth: in the sight of the Omnipotent and in the sight of the community, we permit to pray [together] with the transgressors.

The practice of repeating the *Kol Nidre* was given much consideration by all rabbinic responsa of *minhag ashkenaz*. The most important, by Maharil, states that the hazan is "to extend the chant of the *Kol Nidre* until nightfall."[21] He is obligated to chant the *Kol Nidre* three times, first "in an undertone," then with lifted voice, and voice lifted even more the third time, "for then we shall harken with awe and trembling."

Yet, as Idelsohn has rightly observed, Maharil does not refer to any specific tune for the text, but speaks only of "long drawn-out" melodies. It might be that the present melody was then in its formative stage, for it certainly would fit the description of being a long-extended tune. The first authoritative reference to the melody stems from R. Mordecai Jaffa of Prague, who was not satisfied with the version used by the hazanim. It seems they had corrupted and mixed the various versions of the text indiscriminately. He said that he had tried to substitute the "correct text for the [traditional] fixed melody."[22]

The first notation of the melody is to be found in the early eighteenth century.[23] If we reconstruct its pristine version by comparing the three oldest versions extant, we arrive at the rather simple melodic skeleton of example 10. Even in this highly simplified form, the motifs b1 and c seem to be too recent to belong to medieval melodic structures.

Example 10

Assuming that the "fixed melody" of R. Jaffa was this very current melody—which seems quite plausible after proper elimination of vocal embellishment added by generations of hazanim—the analysis of the reconstructed skeleton yields the following disposition:

a1 a2 b1 b2 a1 a2 c d coda

This can be reduced to the following:

A B A C coda

This form is almost identical with the medieval *Lais.*[24]

In later versions a more or less improvised "*entrata*," familiar to us from Baroque arias and concertos, prefaces the chanting of the text.[25] Two new motifs were added, which, like the older ones, serve as wandering melismata and connect the *Kol Nidre* with other significant texts.[26] These new motifs (referred to as n1 and n2) are seen in example 11.

The addition of these motifs blurs the old and clear *Lai* structure, and the melody of the *Kol Nidre* comes down to us, provided by hazanim with unending vocal coloraturas, as an amorphous rhapsodizing vocalise. Having lost its dignity, it becomes a rather senseless and tasteless exercise, instead of a solemn prologue to the greatest Jewish Holy Day. A sensible reform might do wonders!

The principal motifs, a2, b1, b2, c, d, and the two later additions, n1 and n2, permeate many prayers of Yom Kippur. The following tabulation lists some of the cross-references:

Utilization of the Kol Nidre Tune

Symbol of motif of the *Kol Nidre* tune	Incipit of prayer	Significant word or phrase	Source
a1			
a2	many prayers of the morning section of the High Holy Days	e.g., *adon ha-nifla'ot*	*BT* 1014
		Magen Avraham	1076
		Assumah	1170
b1	*B'rosh hashanah*	*mi vora'ash*	*HOM* 7, p. 73, no. 190b
	V'nislah	*bishgagah*	*HOM* 7, p. 80, no. 208b
	Alenu	*v'lo samanu*	*BT* 1227
b2	*B'rosh hashanah*	*beyom tzom kippur*	*HOM* 7, p. 163, no. 155
	Ki k'shimkha	*yesodo me'afar*	*HOM* 7, p. 164, no. 157
c, d	*Ein kitzvah*	*k'vodekha*	*BT* 1190, 1191
	B'rosh hashanah	*tzom kippur*	*HOM* 7, p. 72, no. 190a
n1	*Yareti*	*Kumi*	*BT* 1058
	Amidah	*Melekh oser*	*BT* 1067
n2	*Vidui*	*S'lah lanu*	*BT* 1357; *HOM* 7, p. 83, no. 211a, 220

Example 11

In artistically motivated collections, especially those of Sulzer and Lewandowski, many more "cross-references" can be found. Those rejuvenators of *minhag ashkenaz* recognized the structural force of the wandering motifs. From the table it is easy to see that the twin ideas of fear of God and of man's mortality, in contrast to God's transcendent power, are stressed by each recurrence of the motifs. This should result in the expression of humble penitence, represented by motif n2.

The morning prayers. In the category of *Missinai* are the following: *Ha-melekh*, and the subsequent *misod hakhamim, yareti, melekh elyon, temukhim badeshen*, and others. They all contain motif a2. It is noteworthy that Maharil mentions some of these chants. In particular, he asserts that a certain prayer is to be sung to the melody of *a'apid nezer*; [27] and the same tune was to be adapted to the *piyut* "*ein arokh elekha*," which occurs in the *musaf* of Yom Kippur.[28] Most interesting is the combination, which occurs in some New Year prayers, of a *shaḥarit* motif with one typical of *neilah* (example 12). This melody seems to be mentioned by Maharil, together with *ha'aderet veha'emunah*, as the perfect expression of the fear of God and of deep piety.

All of the morning motifs, including a2 from the *Kol Nidre*, are combined in the lovely tune of *oḥila la'el* (example 13). The form structure is again a three-stanza *Lai* with an *Abgesang* (coda), indicating the great age of the melody, in which the modal Dorian motif A1 struggles against the clear major-minor tonality of C1. This latter motif is identical with a passage in the *Alenu* of the High Holy Days, to be discussed later.

Example 12

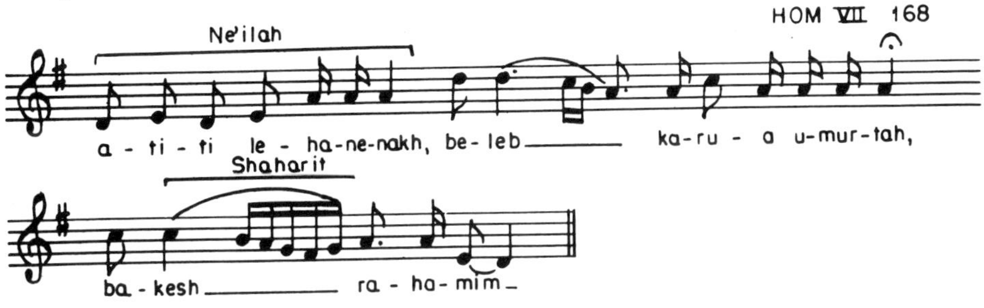

Example 13

Tunes of Abodah and Kedushah. These two are closely related. They are actually variants of the same melody. The preamble to the *Kedushah* (for *shaharit*, *musaf*, and *neilah*) contains the characteristic motif of example 14a. Especially unmistakable is the entwining of this *Kedushah* motif with the motif of the *Barekhu* in the versicle *mim'komo* of the *Kedushah*, as in example 14b. Here the sectional motif of the *musaf* service is borrowed from the *Barekhu* of the evening service, appropriately enough to the words "*l'eyney kol hai*" (to the eyes of all living), thus symbolizing the universalistic nature of the *Kedushah*. Its tune is of great solemnity; it is all but identical with the *Abodah* stressing the unity of "the Name." In the *Kedushah* the words "*hu abinu, malkhut'kha addir v'hazak*" use the same motif as the expression "*ha-shem ha-gadol*" in the *Abodah* (example 15).

The Kaddish of the Missinai stratum. The half-*Kaddish* alone among five *Kaddish* texts has retained its ancient function of concluding entire sections of the liturgy.[29] The chant of the half-*Kaddish* in the prayers of the High Holy Days fulfills yet another function: while it concludes one section, it introduces the next one by means of musical devices. As seen in example 16, in *minhag ashkenaz* there are no

Example 14

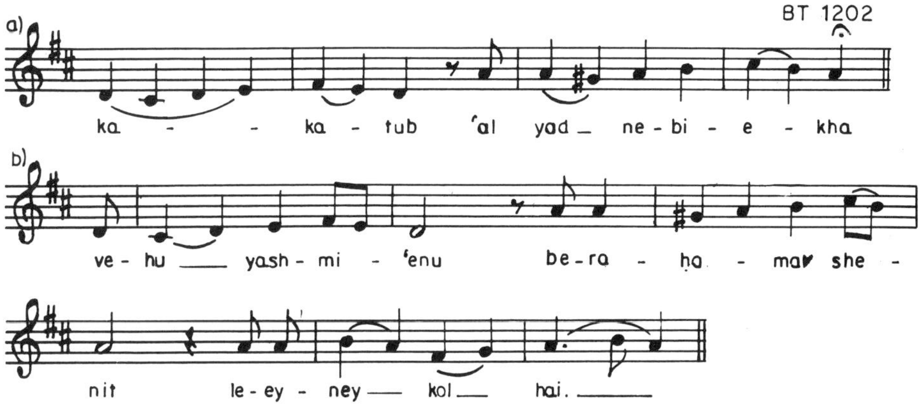

Example 15

less than five different types of *kaddish* melody for the High Holy Days: the types characterize the *ma'ariv*, the *shaharit*, the *musaf*, the Torah service, and the *neilah* of Yom Kippur. Yet in each case the tune of the *kaddish* anticipates, indeed, proclaims, the leading themes of the subsequent prayers. The rule is that the half-*Kaddish* intones subsequent motifs, thus familiarizing the praying community with the proper melodies. One exception is the *Kaddish* on the eve of the High Holy Days: its tune does not recur in the subsequent *Amidah*, which is not recited aloud. Here its function is simply that of concluding a section with the musical motif of the entire evening service.

Sometimes motifs of the *Kaddish* bear—intentionally or not—a theological symbolism. The *Kaddish* preceding the *musaf tefillah* of Yom Kippur contains musical elements that not only anticipate the chant of the subsequent *tefillah* itself but also refer back to the prayers of the previous evening, alluding to the *Kol Nidre*. It ends by quoting from the "Great *Alenu*," which is recited on both Rosh Hashanah and Yom Kippur. Thus the motifs of the *Kaddish* symbolize the theological unity of the "three awesome days." Probably a literary allusion is also intended at the end of the first *berakhah* of the *Amidah*, which repeats a motif of the preceding *Kaddish* (example 17). This is the coda motif of the *Kol Nidre*. The words of that

Example 16

Example 17

prayer refer to vows made in God's name, whereas the words of the line above state: "For the sake of His name, in love." Similar allusions through musical devices occur only in the *Missinai* melodies.

Consider one more example: in the Polish variant of the *shaḥarit* service the *berakhah* of the *yotzer* prayer introduces two motifs that clearly allude to the "Great *Alenu*" and the *Kol Nidre*, thus encompassing in one melody the opening morning service of the New Year, the *musaf* section of the same day, and the evening prayer of Yom Kippur (example 18).

This use of musical anticipation and cross-reference found only in *minhag ashkenaz* extends from the opening of the High Holy Days until their very end.

Example 18

As far as can be established today, all tunes of the half-*Kaddish* of the High Holy Days originated in Germany and have one motif in common, which connects all of them with the prayers for dew and rain on Passover and the eighth day of the Feast of Tabernacles, respectively (see also table IIIA, no. 5). This motif, seen in example 19, appears also in the art music of Burgundy in the fourteenth and fifteenth centuries.

Example 19

U-netaneh tokef. This text, like the subsequent "Great *Alenu*," is truly a prayer of "blood and tears" (Schechter) and has a long history. Legend has it that it was first uttered by R. Amnon of Mayence, when dying as a martyr. Goldschmidt dates the poem far back, earlier than the *piyutim* of Kallir.[30] The oldest written version (ca. 850) appears among genizah fragments[31] and begins with the words: "We shall accord the mighty holiness of this day according to the three [shofar] blasts of the day." This clearly indicates that the prayer was originally part of the New Year liturgy, and was only later inserted into the Yom Kippur service. The ideological basis of the poem is rooted in *Tosefta rosh ha-shanah*.[32]

In the chant of the *u-netaneh tokef* one may distinguish between a western and an eastern European tradition. The texts of the constitutive motifs in the western tradition are *u-v'shofar gadol*, *ke-vakorat ro'eh edro*, *be-rosh ha-shanah*, *emet ki atah*, and *ein kitzvah*. The eastern European tradition has only *be-rosh ha-shanah* and *emet ki atah* in common with the western. The western *minhag ashkenaz* also provides musical cross-references in the following passages: *be-rosh ha-shanah* to *lo sheririn* from the *Kol Nidre* and to *lo samanu* from the "Great *Alenu*."

Apparently the long-drawn-out tune was composed, or rather compounded, according to certain long-established rules, out of more or less fixed formulas that we already know from previous examples. This method of composition is widely used throughout the Near and Middle East, including Byzantium, whose church music contains many instances of this "composition by formulas."[33]

The "Great Alenu" (example 20). The text of this old prayer, known since the third century, has undergone some alterations in its long history.[34] The prayer is arranged in a kind of free meter, called homotony, wherein the number of stresses per verse remains constant (in the *Alenu* there are four) but the syllabic count varies. Long before the end of the first millennium it served as the martyr's *confessio Judaica.* Under most gruesome and bloody circumstances unique in Jewish history, the *Alenu* was chanted in Blois [France] in 1171. The entire community intoned it, as they died amid blazing flames. There are three reports extant that describe the event, most important among them a letter to R. Jacob of Orléans, from an eyewitness. The following passages are from that document: "When the flames blazed and licked the bodies of the victims, they raised their voices in a unison melody; at first it was a low chant and afterwards a high-sounding melody. The people [Gentiles] came and said: 'Which of your songs is this? For we have never heard such a melody from you before.' Yet we knew it very well, for it was the chant of the *Alenu.*"[35]

Example 20

Other reports add that the Gentiles bared their heads and "henceforth used that chant in their church."[36] Indeed, this is one *Missinai* tune whose path from the Synagogue into the Church can be traced not only through the above report, or through the earliest Gregorian source of that song, which dates the melody from France between the twelfth and thirteenth centuries; the melody is still heard in the Church as the *Sanctus* of the ninth mass of the Virgin. It has existed in this form, seen in example 21, since the Tridentine revision in the sixteenth century.

Example 21

Even more cogent than all reports, and than the parallel to the *Sanctus*, is a *Planctus Judei* (Jews' lament), an almost contemporaneous Christian ballad, of slightly macabre humor, discovered in a manuscript from the Library of Orléans, the city next to Blois. There is little reason to doubt the theory that this *Planctus* was the somewhat roughly stylized parody of a medieval Jewish *seliḥah* or *kinah* made by a Christian; it reflects the troubles and horrors of the outcast Jew. The document was discovered by Helen Wagenaar, and is quoted in example 22 with her permission.[37]

Example 22

As a focus of a strong lens unites different rays of light, so the melody of the *Alenu* (in its present form) integrates elements of many essential motifs of the High Holy Days. Thus we can see that at least part of the *Missinai* repertory was in a formative stage by the time the *Alenu* was sung, and that some of its characteristic motifs may antedate the year 1171. We have seen that the *Alenu* tune contains elements of other prayers, such as the *Kol Nidre* and *u-netaneh tokef.* However, neither the *Sanctus* nor the *Planctus* contains any of these cross-references. Hence we can assume that the interplay of characteristic motifs of the *Missinai* tunes was still in an inchoate state at the end of the twelfth century. Since the texts of *ha-melekh*, *Alenu*, and

others, were chanted to the same tunes in both the German and the Polish traditions, one may date the beginnings of *minhag ashkenaz* at about 1000–1050. This in turn confirms our assumption that the structure and composition of the *Missinai* tunes, based upon the devices of musical and textual cross-references, upon wandering motifs and permutation of themes, wrought by highly sophisticated techniques of composition such as the use of leitmotifs, took place during the period from the twelfth to the sixteenth centuries.

Summarizing the examination of the samples of *Missinai* tunes given above, we can define concisely the stylistic characteristics:

1. Tonality. The majority of these tunes tend to major or minor with small deviations. A lesser part preserves the octave-species of the Church-tones, with the mixolydian and the dorian prevalent.

2. Melodic contour. The melodies consist mainly of tetrachordal motifs and a few triadic motifs. To judge from the *Sanctus* and the *Planctus*, melismatic ornaments were not extravagant. Exceptions to this general rule are a few vocalises of long-drawn-out, almost wordless lines; they were said to obey certain rabbinical rules. The classic examples of this type are *ha-melekh* and the first *berakhah* of the *tefillah*. Most of the melodies are related to one another by a set of common motifs that often assume the character and function of leitmotifs.

3. Meter. In many cases a compound time prevails, combining duple and triple time. This is analogous to the contemporaneous art music of the Middle Ages. Some recitatives are completely nonmetrical, but they are the minority among *Missinai* tunes.

4. Form types. *Lais*, *Bar*-form, quasi-*Virelai*, and strophic song with choral refrain are the most frequent. In addition, there is a series of recitatives held together by the same type of cadence, corresponding to the formal close [*ḥatimah*] of each *berakhah*. The motifs are fraught with allusions to, or paraphrases of, German, Austrian, Bohemian, and French songs—and later of Polish songs and ditties. Yet these motley building-stones were cemented together by a mortar, strong and uniform, probably older than all the foreign elements: the ancient prayer modes of *minhag ashkenaz*. The next chapter investigates their origin, nature, and function.

4

The Musical Prayer Modes

Europe prefers fixed forms, and pre-established performance, whilst Asia prefers improvisation.
(B. Szabolcsi)

Beginning with the Middle Ages all Western nations used the same tonal system, based on the ecclesiastical modes, in their art music. The same cannot be said of their folk songs. The various languages affected both rhythm and mode, generating their distinctive, often irregular character, contributing specific charm to the songs.[1]

Although the tonal idiom of *minhag ashkenaz* after the seventeenth century more and more resembled that of Western art music, the rhythms of synagogal tunes, based on the Hebrew text, differed vastly from the conventional German or Polish cadences. Apart from its foreign rhythms what made the melodies of *minhag ashkenaz* sound so strange to Gentile ears? Strange they must have been, as is apparent from the musical caricatures of Jewish tunes, which occurred in the standard repertoire of seventeenth-century lutenists. Orazio Vecchi (1551–1605) even inserted a travesty of synagogue chant into his *Amfiparnasso*. Probably it was not just the ineptitude of poor Jewish musicians, but their peculiar, rhapsodical style, which irritated the Gentile listeners.

What were the characteristic elements, aside from rhythmic patterns, that set the music of *minhag ashkenaz* so clearly apart, in spite of the borrowings from German and Polish songs? It must have been a strain that permeated all of *minhag ashkenaz*—a continuous and nearly ubiquitous "connective tissue" in the body of Jewish musical tradition. In this tradition it is the prayer modes that serve such a connecting function. These flexible semi-improvised formulas provide easy transitions between tunes of different mode, character, or structure. Whereas in Western art music there are innumerable modulatory devices, known to every musician, there are only a handful of prayer modes that have remained alive in *minhag ashkenaz*. They differ from one another in tonality, and in their generating motifs, but they all serve the same functions: they operate as incipits (openings) of complexes of tunes, or as cadences (closings) of established traditional tunes, or as the junctions and separations of themes.

Such recurrent complexes of almost amorphous shape were known to Arabs and Jews as well as to Western theoreticians under various terms such as "*lahan*," "*usul*," "*differentia*," and "*res facienda*" (models for improvisation). These old terms are not really interchangeable or identical with each other, and their application to

minhag ashkenaz is quite recent.[2] When the prayer modes were first examined, the theoreticians were not interested in their distinctive melodic patterns. Rather, they studied the funds of constituent tones in each mode, and arranged them in scales. After an interesting, but half-hearted attempt by Samuel Naumbourg in the second half of the nineteenth century, in which he compared the hypothetical scales of *minhag ashkenaz* with the ecclesiastical modes of the Western theoreticians,[3] the matter rested until 1882. In that year the Vienna cantor Joseph Singer published a treatise, "*Die Tonarten des traditionellen Synagogen-Gesanges*" (The Tonalities of Traditional Synagogue Chant), in which he identified the "modal" character of three or four recurrent melodic patterns. Somewhat erroneously, he considered them keys and arranged them in scales of his own construction.

He should not be blamed too much for that error, however. His misconception was shared by all major scholars of Gregorian and Ambrosian chant, including the great Fétis, at that time. They were obsessed by the idea that every musical structure can be broken up into its constituent *scales*; neither the French, nor the German, nor the Italian schools of Gregorians knew any better. They based this idea upon the principle that all Gregorian tunes, even plain psalmodies, can be reduced to the eight *toni ecclesiae* (the eight octave-species or scales of the medieval theorists).[4]

Under the influence of the new "comparative musicology" [*vergleichende Musikwissenschaft*] at the end of the nineteenth century, and under the guidance of the French Benedictine masters Mocquereau and Potiron, the all-importance of the scalar octave-species was questioned, and the principle of "recurrent melodic motifs" began to replace it. Since Amédée Gastoué, and thanks to the great scholar Peter Wagner, old errors were eliminated at least in principle.[5] One of the pioneers of that generation of "explainers" was Abraham Z. Idelsohn, who, in his memorable study on the *Makamat* in Arabic music, laid the foundation for the proper understanding of the pattern-character of the *Makamat* and of the early modes.[6] Yet in spite of the concerted efforts of scholars and teachers, including researchers such as Curt Sachs, Erich von Hornbostel, and Jaap Kunst, the older misconceptions can still be found in many widely accepted textbooks.

Nevertheless, it will be useful to the reader to consult a conventional outline of the octave-species or "church modes."[7] A Gregorian chant can generally be analyzed according to this system, but it very often fails to apply to tunes from *minhag ashkenaz*. We have already seen in table II (nos. 1 and 2) how the constituent tones of some chants (even the Gregorian one, in this case) cannot be said to constitute a scale. Example 1 presents additional melodies with no scalar organization. Example 1b is the skeleton of the *Adonai malakh* mode, again showing how it cannot be analyzed in terms of "scale." Finally, in example 1c, we have a Gregorian model.

It cannot be overemphasized that the prayer modes are *not* scales. If, for the sake of convenience, the tones comprising a mode are listed in the shape of a scale, it ought to be done with great caution. The prayer modes do not always consist of stepwise intervals; they frequently contain skips. All prayer modes lend themselves to recitatives, which can follow the rhythm and sense of the text very closely. They, together with the *Missinai* tunes, the scriptural cantillation, and the seasonal motifs

Example 1

(the two latter to be discussed in later chapters) constitute what is generally called the *nusaḥ* of *minhag ashkenaz*. Every good cantor is familiar with both the expression and its entire musical contents. What is called *minhag ashkenaz* in this book, he will identify as "the old *nusaḥ*."[8]

The names of the prayer modes refer to texts in the Ashkenazic *siddur*, the traditional prayer book. Thus the *Adonai malakh* mode gets its name from the opening words of Psalm 93; the *Magen Abot*, from the first words of the prayer "Shield of the Fathers," which is part of the Friday evening liturgy; *Ahabah Rabah*, from the last benediction before the *Shema* of the morning prayer ("With Great Love hast Thou Loved Israel"). It is difficult to say anything definite about the history of those names. They appear here and there in popular Hebrew and Yiddish literature of the nineteenth century, especially in eastern Europe. There they are usually coupled with the words *ta'am* (taste, style) or *gust* (from the Italian *gusto*). Among German-speaking singers they are usually referred to as *Steiger*.[9] All the attempts at classifying the prayer modes are very recent and of little theoretical or historical value.[10]

The basic prayer modes can best be identified by their characteristic constituent motifs: incipits, cadencing motifs, linking motifs, and separating motifs. Example 2a is the *Adonai malakh* mode. This mode is mainly used for praising and thanksgiving prayers; the *tefillah* mode is only one of its many variants.

Example 2b, the *Magen Abot* mode, is the one most frequently employed in Western *minhag ashkenaz*. It usually appears in connection with narratives, didactic

Example 2

Incipits, cadencing, linking and separating motifs
a) of Adonai Malakh
b) of Magen Abot mode
(1)
(2)
c) of Ahabah Rabbah mode
d) of Seliḥah mode

prayers, or proclamations of faith. Thus the *Shema* of the High Holy Days belongs to this mode. It also forms part of the music for the prayers of Friday eve, especially the abbreviation of the Seven Benedictions [*m'ayn sheva*].

In the West the *Ahabah Rabah* mode, example 2c, is used where the text contains either a plea for God's mercy, or a supplication, or a remembrance of the dead. In eastern European tradition it is the dominant mode, used for all kinds of prayers. Among the *Ḥasidim* it is almost the only mode known.

Example 2d, the *Seliḥah mode*, is the most variegated mode in *minhag ashkenaz*. It is used for *seliḥot, bakashot, teḥinot* (penitential prayers), lamentations, *kinot*, and confession of sins. It is based on motifs of the chant of the Prophetic lesson, but it has no unique incipit or cadence. Most of its tunes might be said to be in natural (or "pure") minor.

Both the names and the formulas of the prayer modes are thus seen to be *a posteriori* constructions. What then were their functions, and what purpose did they serve? Here the answers of the practicing cantor and the analyzing researcher coincide; the prayer modes are the raw material, out of which endless, countless "limited" improvisations can be shaped. Indeed, the practice of limited improvisation—that is, improvisation whose boundaries are set by unwritten laws, reflecting centuries of practice, trial, and acceptance—was well-known in the tenth century. Yehuda ha-Levi, in his theological treatise "*Kuzari*," wrote as follows:

> No. 69. [The Kuzari asks] "Where is the superiority of the Hebrew language over all others? For truly, the others excel in poems, which are set in meter, and are therefore fit for musical composition?"
>
> No. 70. [The master replies] "It is quite established that melodies do not necessarily require metrical texts; one may sing a long or a short tune just as well to *Hodu Ladonai Ki Tob* as to *l'oṣeh nifla'ot* [verses of Psalm 118 with different numbers of syllables and stresses]. So much about metrical texts."[11]

With reference to the so-called *anshadiya* (metrical) tunes, the master said that the Jews "did not concern themselves with them because they considered other matters more useful and of higher value [namely, scriptural accents that regulate the proper intonation as well as the speed and the pauses of reading]."[12] And even as early as the tenth century Saadyah Gaon of Sura referred to the existence of modes that he traced back to the Temple: "With those that are written to a [lacuna in MS] tune it is the eighth and is [demanded by] beginning with the heading *lam'natze'aḥ al ha-sh'minit* [Psalm 12:1]. It is proven therewith that the orders of Levites had eight modes which they used in the Sanctuary."[13]

The hypothesis may be ventured that some of the modes could be dated as far back as the eighth century. However, such a hypothesis could be confirmed only if one could identify a mode that is common to both Ashkenazic and Sephardic tradition. Some Israeli scholar of this generation may yet succeed in tracing it. Even now, much is being learned about the interest of R. Yehudai Gaon in cantorial art and liturgical music.[14]

Improvisation

All ancient dicta aside, what are the confines of traditional improvisation in actual practice? This question touches upon the very essence of *minhag ashkenaz*, its melody types, its favorite ornamentation, even its ideal of melodic beauty. Moreover, and equally important, it involves the aims and conceptions of expressiveness of the Ashkenazic tradition.

A statistical comparison of many modal improvisations would yield empirical answers to this question. Short of such a mathematically reliable, although cumbersome, investigation, the examination of written or printed sources can be helpful. One observes that all improvisation upon given themes is based on the *tones fixés* (pivotal tones) in each mode. The variables are the frequency of their occurrence, the phrases that link them, and even the ethnic or regional preferences of vocal timbre and style of performance.

The close organic intertwining—indeed the inseparability of musical and liturgical traditions in *minhag ashkenaz*—may be demonstrated with one telling instance: in the *minhah* service of the Sabbath there is a special passage called the *kedusha de-sidra* (beginning with the words "*u-va le-tziyon go'el*" [a redeemer shall come to Zion]) and continuing with a number of scriptural verses. According to a Gaonic principle this *kedusha de-sidra* was to be sung to a melody used by students when reciting the *sidrah* (Torah lesson). Elsewhere, in a rarely observed decree, R. Saadyah Gaon had listed all those scriptural verses in which the community is expected to join the reader of the lesson. Among the verses listed are those quoted in the *kedusha de-sidra*.[15] This is probably related to the fact that in the Sabbath *minhah* of *minhag ashkenaz* the cantillation of the *Haftarah* (Prophetic lesson) dominates the chant of the entire service. If this conjecture is valid, it should apply also to passages from the liturgy of public fast days, which surround the nucleus Exodus 34:6–7, 32:11–14; 34:1–10. On those days, following Saadyah Gaon's prescribed list, Exodus 32:13 and 34:6 are chanted by the entire congregation. When we turn to the actual chant (example 3) we discover that it is a direct derivative from the cantillation of the Prophetic lesson. There is also an additional prayer for these fast days (example 4), inserted into the thirteenth benediction of the *Amidah*, which is chanted in the same mode as the Sabbath *minhah* service.

It would be incorrect to conclude from this argument that the original musical tradition has actually survived. If that were the case, the Sephardic and Ashkenazic

Example 3

Example 4

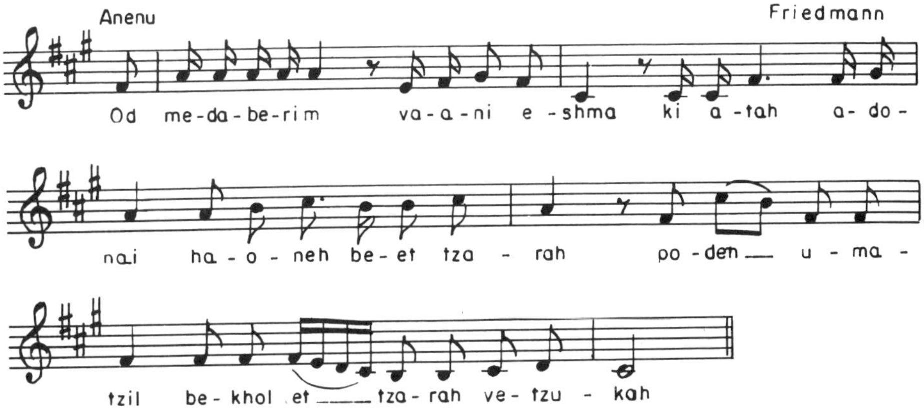

versions would resemble each other. Actually they differ widely. It is probably only the liturgical principle set down by Saadyah that is observed in both traditions but is realized in different forms.

Improvisation may produce operatic, recitative-like, lyrical, lachrymose, sentimental, majestic, or folksy renditions. These terms read like the list of "tones" or "Weisen" in the first act of *Die Meistersinger*, where David explains the so-called *Blumen* (ornaments and styles) to Walther.[16] Indeed, there is a fundamental and inherent similarity between these two lists: they are both based on the underlying doctrine of imitative (mimetic) musical expression, similar to that of the Baroque *Affektenlehre*, which attached a suitable musical formula to every mood. We may then describe the prayer modes as the carriers of "moods," "specific emotions," in *minhag ashkenaz*. Example 5 exemplifies and concretizes these rather abstract

Example 5

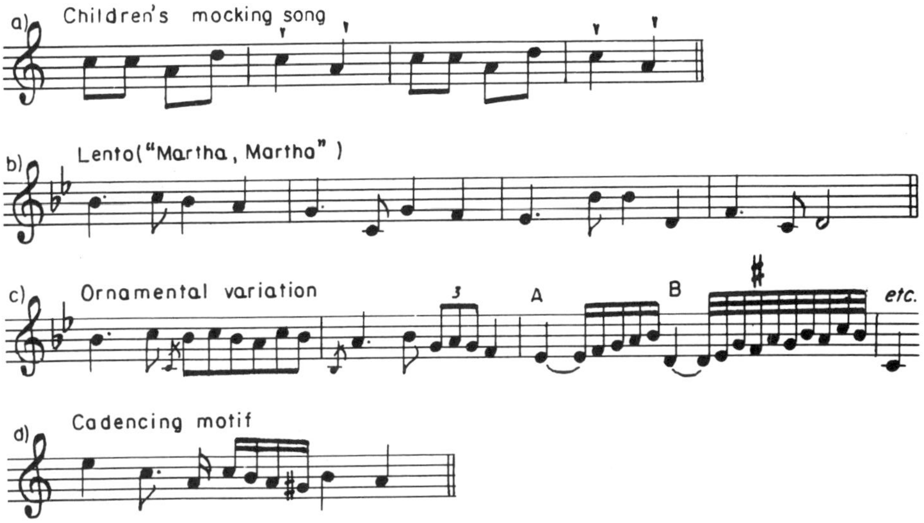

theories. Example 5a is the typical motif of a children's song, well known on three continents. It consists only of three tones, c, a, d, and no less than four intervals bring variety into the monotonous ditty. It cannot be located in any diatonic scale but may be viewed as a segment of the pentatonic (five-tone) scale. Its character is mocking and fresh, though its variability is meager. Its chief characteristic is the sharp rhythm and the restriction to three tones. As long as those remain recognizable, every variation will retain the basic mocking character of the tune.

A sentimental love song from Flotow's *Martha* (example 5b) is characterized by its wide intervals and its languid rhythm. A cantorial improvisation might run along the lines of example 5c. In the variations, the basic lines are dissolved in little ornaments, which normally make ample use of sequences. Another characteristic element is the turn to minor at the sign ϕ. The sentimental character has been preserved, but the melodic line has a strangely "fluffy" sound, as if two or three straight lines were replaced by a lot of little curved ornaments. It is this aspect that so attracts the cantors to a certain type of Italian opera, that of the Neapolitan school with its bombastic yet mellow melodies. They lend themselves well to this method of diminution. Aside from grace-note jumps, the wide intervals are retained at A and B to display the singer's pliability and elegance. The motif contains the descending minor triad and a cadential clause that was considered the equivalent of a sigh or a sob, in the *Affektenlehre* of the late seventeenth century. We can find it in the *seliḥah* mode (see above, example 2d).

Since a mode is supposed to express a special "mood," the trained hazan, even in our own time, pays attention to the specific and typical significance of each. The theological basis of this categorization of moods or emotions corresponds to the traditional rabbinic order of prayers. Yet there is a wide gulf between the postulates of traditional theory and regional practice. This is particularly obvious in the case of the *Ahabah Rabah* mode. In western Europe during the eighteenth century it had an exotic sound and was considered typical of the Polish and Russian tradition. Indeed, it was that exoticism that won the hearts of central European Jewry, and gained a sort of victory for the Polish hazanim.[17] At that time the mode was supposed to be the perfect expression of penitential contrition and deep lament—the theological ideal of a cantor's effect upon the worshipers. Today that mode is the most hackneyed of them all, and, what is worse, has almost totally lost its original association with penitence and supplication. Indeed, the *Ḥasidim* loved it so much that about 85 percent of their songs are in the *Ahabah Rabah* mode—even those with very gay or satiric texts.

It is instructive to observe how Salomon Sulzer regarded the *Ahabah Rabah* mode, and in what context he used it. He was one of the best transmitters and collectors and editors of *minhag ashkenaz*. Since he was not only indifferent but outright hostile to all hasidic elements,[18] he allowed the use of their favorite mode only where the texts (mainly penitential) specifically justified it. As the classic representative of *minhag ashkenaz* in the nineteenth century, Sulzer established its style, and as a result, one finds little influence of the *Ahabah Rabah* in most of the Ashkenazic compendia of the West. The situation is quite different in those compendia of the nineteenth century that appeared in Warsaw or Cracow, or even in Berlin, which

was a center of immigration from eastern Europe. In printed "Schools of Cantors" such as those by A. Friedmann (Berlin), B. Schorr (Lemberg), and A. Baer (Gothenberg-Berlin), the presence of *Ahabah Rabah* is considerable, whereas among the older western German school, such as Japhet (Frankfort) or Bamberger (Würzburg), it is very modest, if not altogether negligible. The situation changed rapidly after World War I, with the accelerated immigration from eastern Europe.

People not familiar with traditional Jewish music frequently remark about the elegiac or melancholy character of the music of *minhag ashkenaz*. What they generally have in mind are the *Magen Abot* or *Ahabah Rabah* modes. Indeed, the *Ahabah Rabah* had originally represented this mood, but the same does not hold true for the *Magen Abot* mode. The impression of melancholy stems from the identity of that mode with the so-called pure or natural minor, which in Western music usually expresses mourning or sorrowful sentiments. But this is not valid at all for the world of the Near and Middle East.

Provenance and Age

It is almost impossible to determine the origin of the prayer modes in *minhag ashkenaz* with certainty, in spite of some recent and significant discoveries. In the course of the last thirty years four ancient notated manuscripts of Hebrew music were discovered and dated in the twelfth century (see below, note 23). Judged at their face value, two of them, and perhaps a third, approximate the *Magen Abot* mode, or at least contain some of its key motifs. None of them bears any resemblance to the *Ahabah Rabah* mode. The counterparts of both those modes, however, are well known to the musicologist from Arabic, Turkish, Persian, and Armenian folklore. It therefore is possible to make only general statements on the development of these modes, without assigning any definite dates to their beginnings in the Jewish repertoire.

Treatises on rhetorics from the ancient world are replete with warnings against the recitation of one's speech in a monotone. A kind of singsong [*Sprechgesang*] was considered much more effective. In Christianity, according to one modern scholar (who bypassed the Jewish influence completely), it was found necessary to make the word resonate, since "the word was understood by the community as something sounded, not written. The musically fixed recitation gave birth in time to Western music, and the liturgical text became the gateway for music to enter the history of Christian thought and literature."

However, similar forces had been active in the body of Judaism long before they occurred in Christianity. Their result was scriptural cantillation. Yet they cannot have been operative in the chanting of prayers, since those were supposed to be improvised, at least in part. Perhaps other factors were important: it is well known to teachers of speech or singing that persons who speak haltingly, or even stammer, have no difficulty in chanting their texts quite fluently, once they have found fitting tunes. The same observation has been made with children. In view of this fact, a rather bold conjecture might be ventured, particularly in the light of

some superstitious notions that were current during the formative age of the synagogue prayers.

One encounters a startling concept of a prayer's "effect" in the Talmud. A passage from the Mishnah reads: "If one makes a mistake in the *tefillah* it is a bad sign for him, and if he is the reader of a congregation, it is a bad sign for them who have commissioned him.... It was related of R. Hanina ben Dosa that he used to pray for the sick and say, 'This one will die, this one will live.' They said to him: 'How do you know?' He replied, 'If my prayer is fluent in my mouth, I know that he is accepted, but if not, then I know that he has been rejected.... '" The Gemara (ca. two hundred years later) reads: "They said about R. Hanina, 'Whence come these words?' Rabbi Josua ben Levi replied, 'Scripture says, creating the fruits of his lips. I say, peace, peace, peace to the far and to the near, says the Lord, and I will heal him [Is. 57:19].'"[19] In his interpretation of the Prophetic verse, R. Josua took the liberty of construing a condition: "*If* the speech is forceful [fluent], then I shall heal him."

Pehaps the "messengers of the congregations" [*sh'lihey tzibbur*] wanted to assure themselves and those "who had commissioned them" of the fluency of their as yet unwritten prayers, which had to be memorized, in order to make them smooth in pronunciation and "more effective." Thus they might have invented melodic formulas to help them memorize the texts. These formulas eventually crystallized in prayer modes. We observe that the traditional names of the modes all relate to prayers that were already established during the first centuries, at a time when superstitions were not only uttered, but thought worthy of codification. It seems fair, then, to speculate that such beliefs furthered the growth of the prayer modes, the tissue that held together the body of the synagogue chant. In table IV, no. 4, are found the skeleton forms of the various modes.

The geographical area in which a mode is most popular usually suggests some tentative conclusions about its original carriers. The *Magen Abot* mode is perhaps best known of all Arabic modes or *Makamat*. It bears the designation *bayati* (homelike). We can trace it to the eighteenth century through the writings and observations of Guillaume Villoteau, the musical consultant of the French explorations of Egypt.[20] A. Z. Idelsohn has shown its regular occurrence in the seventeenth and eighteenth centuries, and I have been able to trace it to the early sixteenth century.[21] A genizah manuscript of the fifteenth century contains the mode, as was cogently proven by Bence Szabolcsi;[22] but prior to that document all traces disappear. Only one earlier fragment of notated Hebrew music was known. It belonged to the aforementioned manuscripts of the Cairo Genizah, and until very recently both the age and the provenance of those fragments were unknown.[23] Suddenly in 1964, two scholars, Dr. F. Golb of Chicago and Dr. A. Scheiber of Budapest, discovered, independently of each other, and during the very same week, the authorship of the musical fragment, or, as we may say today with a little more caution, the scribe of the fragment. Soon two more musical fragments turned up from the Cambridge collection of the Genizah, written by the same hand. The scribe (or author) of these oldest notated manuscripts of Hebrew music was a convert to Judaism, the Norman nobleman Jean [Giovanni] baron Drocos from Oppido in southern Italy. We

know his story from his own autobiography, of which the major part has come down to us in his own (Hebrew) script. He became a Jew under the spell of some mystic-mysterious dreams, in 1102, in open defiance of his background—he was brought up as a priest or even monk. He assumed the new name of Obadya ha-Ger (Abdias the proselyte). As his conversion to Judaism was, under the then existing laws, a mortal crime, he had to flee Europe. After some years of traveling in the major cities of the Near and Middle East (especially Aleppo, Damascus, Baghdad, and Cairo) he settled finally in Cairo, where he died after 1130.

These manuscripts were written in the so-called Beneventan notation, a form of medieval *neumes* developed by the monks of Benevento.[24] The longest and most interesting of the manuscripts contains a *piyut*, "*Al har horeb*," whose authorship is debated. It is strophic in form, and has a recurrent refrain—a quotation from Isaiah. Its melody is in a mode closely related to *Magen Abot*. The motif of incipit, characteristic of that mode, opens the simple melody; in the coda it moves to a melismatic close in the high register. It resists the normal classification by ecclesiastical scale (see table IV, no. 1). Actually, it is the oldest documented trace of the *Magen Abot* in the history of music. One cannot, however, assume that the mode made its first appearance at that date, as there are some early verbal descriptions that appear to refer to it. I am inclined to believe that the mode originated before the epoch of R. Yehudai Gaon—that is, it may antedate the eighth century. In the light of the most recent discoveries, it may even antedate Christianity.

Idelsohn dedicated a special study to the history and morphology of the *Magen Abot*, but he was, of course, unaware of either the twelfth- or the fifteenth-century genizah fragments. He had to content himself with rather unfounded conjectures. Quite different is the status of research concerning the *Ahabah Rabah* mode. Idelsohn's old conjecture has proved to be correct: this mode is basically alien to *minhag ashkenaz* and to the Western Sephardic tradition as well, having been introduced from Turkey via Russia and Poland to the cultural orbit of the Ashkenazic region. The theory was proposed about 1926; since then careful ethnographic and ethnomusicological studies have confirmed Idelsohn's opinion. He linked the mode to the racially (or linguistically) common origin of the Ugro-Altaic family of languages, which comprises the Hungarian, Estonian, Turkish, Finnish, Tartaric, and Mongol tongues. He attributed its occurrence in the Arabic and Persian family of *Makamat* to Turkish or Tartar importation, and assumed similar influences for the mode's importance in Armenian, Syrian, and Greek Orthodox Church chant.[25]

Such a generalization seems to function quite well, until we come upon one geographical and one historical stumbling block: neither the genuine Hungarian folk song, as analyzed and purified by Bartók and Kodály, nor the Estonian chants seem to contain the mode. The characteristic augmented second is entirely missing. Although both belong to the same family of languages as the Turkish, Hungary was for centuries exposed to Turkish rule and enforced acculturation. Yet there is little trace of the mode in the truly *rural* traditions of Hungarian folklore.[26] An even more important argument against Idelsohn's thesis was adduced by Curt Sachs, who drew attention to the "alien mode" that, in ancient Greece, the musician Olympos is said to have brought from Asia Minor, possibly Phrygia.[27] Whether

this "alien mode" was indeed the *makam hiğaz* is still controversial. As a matter of fact, the Indian and Persian art musicians are quite familiar with this mode. According to Sachs, three of ten groups of modern Indian *ragas* "belong to the so-called gypsy scale," which is yet another term for the expanded *Ahabah Rabah* mode.

Long before Idelsohn, a learned monk, Dom H. Gaisser, dedicated an entire essay to this mode, which he termed "chromatic oriental."[28] Since his time its occurrence in Persia, India, Mongolia, etc., has provided more and more evidence for the ancient Asian origin of the *Ahabah Rabah.* Some scholars have suggested that the ancient Greek "auletic" music (the *aulos* being a primitive Greek clarinet) contained the characteristic intervals of the mode. If that could be proven, then the *Ahabah Rabah* could be ascribed to the Pythagorean age, for Nelson Glueck, the late biblical archaeologist, discovered mouthpieces of *auloi* at his excavations in Aqaba. They seem to date from the fifth century B.C.E. However, the *Ahabah Rabah-Hiğaž* character of the *aulos* music has not been proven as yet.[29] Apparently neither Idelsohn's nor Sachs's theses or hypotheses are fully satisfactory, since they do not take into account all relevant facts. It is quite possible that the mode was introduced to the West more than once, and in different places, for example, Spain, Sicily, the Balkans, Ancient Greece, Armenia, Russia (almost certainly via the Black Sea), and North and East Africa.

The ubiquity of that mode is well documented. Yet in spite of Fétis, Idelsohn, Sachs, and other musicologists, the eastern European hazanim are still firmly (and wrongly) convinced that the *Ahabah Rabah* is principally theirs, and that all other appearances are borrowings from the world of Eastern Jewish chant.[30] This persistent belief is perhaps a product of the still existing "voluntary" ghettoes where many Jews live isolated from the world that surrounds them. The self-centered, self-reliant spirit prevailing in these establishments is inclined to disregard the thinking, building, and singing of other civilizations. The greater is their surprise, indeed their disappointment, when these hitherto secluded Jews discover that thoughts, customs, or melodies they had considered exclusively their own are age-old properties belonging to the civilizations of their Gentile environment.

The diffusion of the *Ahabah Rabah,* particularly its exorbitant popularity with the singers and their listeners, deserves a special study. It would have to deal with sociological and psychological [illegible], perhaps even with group narcissism, and thus falls outside the scope of this book. The intrusion of the mode in the Western world, not only in *minhag ashkenaz*, is a strange event in the history of melodies. A true parallel to it is the entrance of the very same mode into Byzantine chant after the fourteenth or fifteenth century. This can easily be verified by a comparison of Rebours's *Traité de Psaltique* with the older Byzantine material made accessible to us through later studies by Egon Wellesz and his friends and disciples.[31] During the seventeenth century, when the Cossacks' "civilization" came into contact with Eastern Jewry, the Jews began to love the *Ahabah Rabah* that they heard in the Cossack songs and dances; in due course they were pogromized and massacred by the Cossacks. It is ironic that they still love those very songs and dances and even today imitate them in—of all places—Israel. Yet the Jews are not the only ones who tried to "sing the songs of their rapers"; the Armenians did likewise,

only in their case it was the Turks whose musical taste they adopted, and they, too, had to pay for it dearly. No other folklore is closer to hasidic *niggunim* than the Armenian. The latter, however, is more introvert and tranquil, not as "motoric" as the *niggunim*, which are frequently used to accompany dancing. Example 6a is the Armenian and 6b the hasidic use of *Ahaba Rabah*.[32]

Example 6

Under these circumstances it is not easy to proffer a "first notation" of *Ahabah Rabah* in *minhag ashkenaz*. Since the mode came from eastern Europe, and the eastern hazanim learned the mysterious art of musical notation only late and hesitantly in the nineteenth century, we are constrained to guess. Russian Orthodox Church chant may have imported that mode from Byzantium. During the nineteenth century it was most popular in the Ukraine and in the provinces bordering the Black Sea, among Tartars and Georgians whose folklore contained the *Ahabah Rabah* mode. The Jews might have picked it up from any of those groups. It was unknown in *minhag ashkenaz* before the fifteenth century and belongs geographically to the Turko-Byzantine orbit. These considerations suggest the sixteenth century as the *terminus post quem* for the entrance of *Ahabah Rabah* in Russia, and the following century would probably mark the earliest use of that mode in the eastern European synagogue. From there the migrant cantors carried it to central Europe. This might have occurred under the impact of the *Sabbatai Zevi* mass movement, via Poland and Moravia.[33]

A Forgotten Mode

There is another mode, similar to the *Ahabah Rabah*, that has been preserved in remnants of tunes found in Gregorian chant, Middle Eastern synagogue song, and

chants of the Eastern churches. It was known and recognized in Greek sources of the second century of the common era, and referred to there as the *tropos spondeiakos*, or spondaic mode.[34] Not unlike the *Ahabah Rabah* mode, it was once considered (perhaps with better reason) a perfect expression of lofty and majestic religious sentiments. It falls outside the domain of *minhag ashkenaz* and will therefore not be discussed in detail. However, there is something to learn from the psalmodies that still exist in that ancient Hellenistic style. They contain strange cadencing formulas, called *differentiae* in Gregorian chant. Their function was to connect one mode with another, or, in other words, to modulate. This is, of course, the main function of all the cadencing motifs in the modes of *minhag ashkenaz*.

The modes may have undergone some changes, as we learn from the many manuscripts that have come down to us; and such changes depend on two variables: the regional tradition in which the writer-cantor originated, and the different elements of Western art music to which he was exposed. Other varieties of cantorial style appear in the hazan's technique of variation-improvisation, and in his preference for certain types of vocal ornaments, or what the Italians call his *embellimenti*.

Variants and Applications

The laudatory mode *Adonai malakh* appears in two variants: with and without the incipit on an ascending major triad. Of the two versions, the one containing the triad is, of course, more recent and betrays the influence of German folk song; a similar duplication obtains also in Gregorian chant. There the rising triad is conspicuous in the Germanic tradition of Gregorian chant that arose in the twelfth century, and thereafter in northern Germany. The Old and New Testament canticles, such as Exodus 15 and Deuteronomy 32, as well as the *Nunc dimittis*, *Magnificat*, and others, are normally sung in a fifth tone that approaches the *Adonai malakh* mode (example 7a). The *Adonai malakh* mode, seen in example 7b, begins

Example 7

similarly. Older versions correspond to the third tone. Example 7c is the opening of the celebrated *Magnificat tertii toni* that has inspired many composers and many compositions. The same incipit is found in many chants of *minhag ashkenaz*, for example, the *Akdamut* (see table VI, no. 1), or *BT* 408 (*Tefillah*), *BT* 592 (*berakhah* after the *Haftarah*), and others.

As a well-rounded tune the pattern appears in the late Gregorian Invitatorium (Psalm 95, *Venite exultemus Domino*). The very same psalm is chanted at *Kabbalat Shabbat* in the *Adonai malakh* mode. The mode has occasionally been identified with the scale of the eighth tone (G) but, as has been demonstrated earlier in this text, it has a leading tone below the finalis, which disqualifies it. Yet one may safely equate it with the fifth psalm tone of the Church.

Style and technique of *ḥazanut* stand and fall with the prayer modes. For it is the cantor's privilege of improvising within the framework of the modes that provides the necessary freedom of expression so desirable in worship. Most of the melody-skeletons of the prayer modes belong to the very "stock" of *ḥazanut*. They may be varied, but they cannot be replaced or omitted. The few fundamental modes were applied to clearly defined parts of the service ("sectional" prayer modes), or to specific holy days ("seasonal" motifs), or to the anticipatory chant before a *Missinai* tune.

Beyond these three or four modes, the *minhag ashkenaz* makes use of certain half-fixed melodic patterns, mainly for the High Holy Days. These patterns designate the prescribed sections of the service by their recurrent motifs or formulas. Liturgically speaking, Rosh Hashanah and Yom Kippur follow more or less the same order of fixed prayers (*tefillot keva*) but have different sets of *piyutim* inserted. Yom Kippur has one complete additional section, the concluding *neilah* service with its *piyutim*. While the fixed prayers, common to both holy days, are chanted in the same way, the *piyutim* are generally chanted according to certain *Missinai* tunes. Those texts of the fixed prayers that are not part of the *Missinai* repertoire are sung according to the sectional modes (see table III).

It is fairly easy to classify most of the cantorial styles of *minhag ashkenaz* along these lines, up to about 1860. After that the eastern European Jews developed a kind of cantorial virtuoso style of their own, responding, on the one hand, to the impetus of famous Western cantors, such as Sulzer, Naumbourg, Brod, and, on the other hand, to the anti-rabbinical influence of the *Haskalah*. They combined certain *arioso* motifs of the nineteenth-century Italian opera with Slavonic chants and dances; these elements were held together by the flexible medium of the prayer modes and thus a style without a sense of style came into being by mixing heterogeneous motifs indiscriminately and eclectically. Yet this hybrid virtuoso *ḥazanut* found not only well-beloved champions but an audience that consisted, originally, of genuine worshipers.[35]

Only much later, during the twentieth century, and under the corrosive influence of American-Jewish "resorts" with their "social directors," did it decline into a ludicrous phenomenon, as seen in the spa, the floor show, even the cantor and the supervisor of kosher food. Funeral and wedding parlors with their own cuisine and their own hazanim preserve the last remnants of the once glorious "golden virtuoso

ḥazanut" of Eastern Jewry in America. Its history would amount to an important survey of social and religious mores of American Jewry and has yet to be written; it will make highly interesting, if not always pleasant, reading. The admirers of this corrupt brand of *ḥazanut* are still numerous, and for them it is the only meaningful music. In Israel, however, which once was one of the centers of the virtuoso hazanim, the cult is dying out, in spite of daily radio performances of the old records. The style is gradually fading away there, after having made some weak inroads into popular music.

The prayer modes dominate and characterize entire sections of the liturgy. In many cases they are intertwined with nonmetrical motifs of the *Missinai* tunes, which (as we saw in chapter 3) broke away from their original contexts and pervaded many texts, creating free associations in the minds of the listeners, *if they are attentive.* Thus the evening service of the High Holy Days is dominated by the motif of the *Barekhu*, the morning [*shaḥarit*] service by a motif derived from the tune of *oḥila la'el*, the *musaf* service by motifs from the preceding *Kaddish* and by the "Great *Alenu*," *minhah* by the same motif as the morning service, and the closing [*Neilah*] service by a set of new motifs, anticipated by the *Neilah Kaddish*, a *Missinai* tune. Like leading motifs, these wandering and associative motifs hold the attention of the well-educated worshipers. In general, however, the prayer modes are older than the *Missinai* tunes; they are not as clearly settled in the major and minor tonalities.

Appendix: On the Question of Minnesongs and Related Synagogue Melodies

Both prayer modes and *Missinai* tunes—and even certain scriptural cantillations (to be discussed in detail in chapter 5)—seem to bear some relationship to the minnesongs of medieval Germany. Before proceeding to the consideration of the cantillations, therefore, we will digress briefly to examine that relationship. This question was raised after the discovery of a Jewish minnesinger, Suesskind of Trimberg. To what extent did the minnesong infiltrate German Jewish poetry and music? This problem has not been entirely solved to this day. Idelsohn touched upon the matter and identified tonalities and motifs employed by both the minnesingers and German hazanim, but he did not go into detailed investigation.[1] The following questions remain to be dealt with:

1. Was there direct or indirect contact between Jews and minnesingers? It is almost impossible to assume that the German Jews had borrowed their tunes directly from minnesingers. The generally haughty, if not hostile tone in which the Jews were treated in German poetry of the Middle Ages would indicate a decided disinclination on the part of the minnesingers to establish social relationships with the Jews. This would be less true of the vagrant singers, minstrels, jongleurs, and *Spielleute*, among whom there were a number of Jews. These might well have transmitted—with varying degrees of accuracy—songs they had learned from the knightly singers.

2. Is there any similarity of rhythm and meter between the Jewish and Gentile repertoires? There is a certain similarity between the tunes of the minnesingers and those of the German synagogue in their rhythm, which in both cases was neither metrical nor completely free. Some of the German tunes seem to belong to "rhythmic modes" borrowed from the *trouvères*, but by no means all of them. The syntactic accent together with the normal stress of the words dominate the minnesong. Many of the Hebrew prayers—not the *piyutim*—were rendered along similar lines, like "measured prose," wherein each musical phrase contained an approximately equal number of stresses. This treatment of the word in song is easily understood, if one regards it as a kind of free psalmody, whose strongest stress lies near the end of the verse or sentence. Yet even when one observes genuine metrical structures in minnesong, one should not forget that they were in general more primitive than the intricate and sophisticated Hebrew systems of prosody.

3. What was the place of melisma? The point in the German *Weisen* where melismas enter suggests the closest analogy to synagogue melodies. Ewald Jammers has shown in a carefully calculated statistical investigation that most melismas of the minnesong occur about three syllables before the end of an eight-syllable verse—in other words, three or four syllables before the cadence.[2] If we examine the place of melismatic accumulation in tunes based on the prayer modes, we find the following types: punctuating (or final) melisma (*BT* 555a); illustrative melisma

(*BT* 617); initial melisma (*Barekhu* of the Three Festivals, *BT* 560); emphasis-melisma (*BT* 855); and metrical melisma on the sixth syllable of eight (*BT* 560, 1029). In sum, the customary place of certain melismas in the prayer modes corresponds to the place in the minnesong where melisma is habitually inserted. One should remember, in all such comparisons, however, that plainchant influenced both the old Jewish style and the melopoiy of the minnesingers, who called them *Blumen* [*fioriture*].

4. Do the songs have a common tonality? Most of the *minhag ashkenaz* uses tonalities that were common to the whole of western Europe: the ecclesiastical modes and their variants. Many vague similarities can be found, but there is at least one case of conspicuous identity, that of the "Philipp's Tone" of Walther von der Vogelweide with the mode of the western Ashkenazic Torah cantillation. The cantillation moves in the major, contains some pentatonic elements, but ends on a finalis in the relative minor. Walther's "Philipp's Tone" follows the same scheme[3] (see table IV, no. 5*a*). Similarly, Walther's "Ottentone" contains an interesting parallel to the *Barekhu* of the eve of the High Holy Days (table IV, no. 5*b*).[4]

Whereas identities of tonality are far from cogent proof, what is significant is the concurrence of a number of characteristics, such as the pentatonic elements plus the major pattern, plus the finalis in the relative minor. Hence the comparisons refer not to individual melodies—in which case the similarities would be of minor significance—but to entire archetypes, to both tones and modes. This correspondence reveals much more than occasional identities. It indicates a genetic kinship.

5. Are there recurrent modes and motifs in common? Such recurrent motifs can be observed in four instances. The first is the *Bruder Veits Ton*, a pattern that will be encountered later and must have been the most popular melody line among the German Jews. It has many German contrafacts, among them "*Es wonet lib bei libe*" (*BAL*, no. 19). It will be discussed in detail in chapter 6, note 45. Second is the motif from the *Barekhu* of the High Holy Day eve, appearing in Walther's "Ottentone," mentioned above.[5] The ubiquitous third motif  is found in the *Sprueche* of Bruder Werner in the Jena manuscript (table IV, no. 6). As this motif permeates the entire *minhag ashkenaz* it must have come from more than one source. Finally, songs by the "Wilde Alexander" bear a marked resemblance to the cantillation of Lamentations. The former may be found in table IV, no. 7, and the latter in table Vd. See also the motif from a song by Oswald von Wolkenstein (table IV, no. 8).[6]

The analogies outnumber the differences in the examples cited. This fact enforces the assumption that tunes and forms of minnesong intruded frequently into the repertoire of the German synagogue. The favorite composers of the Jews seem to have been Walther von der Vogelweide, der Wilde Alexander, Oswald von Wolkenstein, and Wizlav von Ruegen. This selection testifies to the excellent musical taste of the Ashkenazim. If their preference for South German or Austrian minnesingers could mean anything, it might indicate that the Austrian-Bavarian Jews seemed to have more contact, however indirect, with the minnesingers than did the Jews of other regions.

5

Scriptural Cantillation

Your song revolving like the starry sky,	*Dein Lied ist drehend wie das Sterngewölbe,*
Start and ending always are the same,	*Anfang und Ende, immerfort dasselbe,*
And what is found in midst, it will proclaim	*Und was die Mitte bringt, ist offenbar*
That which remains in th'end, and first was there.	*Das, was zu Ende bleibt und Anfangs war.*

(Goethe)

Definitions and Functions

The people's institution of the Synagogue performed the divine service by way of the "sacred word" (scriptural lesson), in contrast to the hierarchical sanctuary of the Temple, which discharged its function by the "sacred deed" (sacrifice). These two forms of worship have dominated all monotheistic liturgies. It is immediately apparent that the scriptural reading holds the central position in the Synagogue's order of service. Although we know of hieroglyphic and cuneiform versions of sacred texts long before Mosaic Judaism stepped over the threshold of world history, there is no evidence that such texts were *publicly* and *regularly* read before a worshiping multitude. As the liturgy of the Temple did not provide for a continuous scriptural lesson, it was the Synagogue alone that established and fully organized this practice in all of its details.

Although the beginnings of public reading of Scripture are traditionally ascribed to Ezra and his time, there is no way to ascertain with exactness how far back the custom of chanting the sacred text goes. Moreover, the *locus classicus*, where this custom assumes the significance of a law, does not clearly describe the *musical* nature of the execution but only the theological importance of some kind of chant. It was pronounced by R. Shefatya in the name of R. Yohanan: "Who reads Scripture without melody and studies the Mishnah without chant, of him it is written: 'Wherefore I gave them statutes that were not good, and laws by which they will not live (Ez. 20:25).'"[1]

This was said well after C.E. 200, but the origin of the practice of chanting Scripture dates, by all accessible evidence, from pre-Christian times. A question is raised that is not merely semantic: is the singsong of a Mediterranean Jew who runs rapidly over a biblical text considered a chant of tones with definite pitches—a real

melody consisting of recognizable tones? It is quite possible to believe that cantillation was born out of *Sprechgesang* (*parlando*-recitation) and then stylized and elevated to a genuine musical phenomenon. When not carefully cultivated and guarded, it could easily relapse again into the singsong that is so closely related to market cries, or the theurgic murmuring of an esoteric shaman.[2] In other words, even assuming that R. Yohanan indeed referred to a musical practice of true singing, can it be said that cantillation originally and genetically consisted of definite tones that were heard as parts of musical tunes?

The question is not as abstruse as it may sound at first. Robert Lachmann, a fine scholar of Near Eastern music, a fieldworker with many years of experience, wrote more than thirty years ago: "Jewish, Christian and other forms of cantillation did not adapt themselves to scale systems from the urban sphere until a late stage in their development, or have not accepted them at all. . . . The influence of the hymn tunes and also of secular music, both of them conceived on the bases of instrumental scales, must have consolidated the cantillation step by step. Still there is sufficient evidence to show that the difference, with regard to scale, between cantillation and *melody proper* was keenly felt and difficult to eliminate. . . ."[3]

Of the three main traditions of Jewish liturgy, *minhag ashkenaz* was the first whose cantillation appeared in musical notation. It was more than one hundred years later that the Sephardic tradition was first notated. The discrepancies between the various notations of the Sephardic cantillation are easily explained, if one bears in mind the vague pitch of the Mediterranean *Sprechgesang*. Once more we must admit our indebtedness to Professor Lachmann's profound observations that "wherever cantillation has been subjected to a system of interval ratios, the system can be shown to have come from a musical sphere other than its own."[4] Later we shall find that this statement is applicable to every tradition.

The musical notation was made on the basis of the so-called Masoretic accents, which accompany every vocalized Hebrew scriptural text. At this juncture, let us set straight a number of widespread misunderstandings:

1. The Masoretic accents, called *ta'amei ha-mikra*, are *not* a kind of primitive musical notation. They were created by succeeding generations of grammarians in Babylonia and Palestine, and their evolution took several centuries. They provide an exact system of minute signs that govern the structure and punctuation of each biblical sentence. In a wider sense they represent the result of magnificent and punctilious philological examination of the scriptural text.

2. The cantillation of Scripture antedates the establishment of the *ta'amei ha-mikra* by at least nine centuries. The official link between cantillation and the Masoretic accents was provided by R. Natronai Gaon in about 850, in a rather legalistic decree, where he termed both cantillation and the *ta'amei ha-mikra* "traditions from Mt. Sinai," implying that the one system is as authentic as the other.[5] The text of this precept is found in the *Maḥzor Vitry* (ca. 1105).[6] In later centuries the sharp distinction between cantillation and the *ta'amei ha-mikra* gradually faded. Indeed Profiat Duran in his *ma'asei efod* ascribed the invention of the accents to Ezra "so that the love for reading would grow in the hearts of men, as a result of the sweetness of song which the accents bestow."[7]

3. There is evidence of the practice of cantillation in rabbinic literature, but it is couched in general terms only. No standard or method of execution of cantillation is defined.[8] The Talmud describes the practice of chironomy (mnemonic hand movements) and there is proof in other documents that such a practice existed. It was only later, when the chironomy was replaced by the Masoretic accents, that cantillation was organized and systematized.[9]

All groups of Jewry, however dispersed, accepted and absorbed the Tiberian system of Masoretic accents (ca. 900) as authentic; yet their systems of cantillation differ very much indeed. Idelsohn took great pains to prove, by many comparisons and often erroneous identification, that there was an *Urtradition* of all cantillation in Judaism—in vain, as we know today. Lachmann recognized this as early as 1938. He concluded: ". . . this accounts for the fact that the substance and even the number of the tunes vary from one community to another. Different Jewish groups in the Near East and in Europe have developed their common heritage each in its own manner, depending on particular historical and regional circumstances. There is, therefore, no other approach to Jewish cantillation as a whole than by studying it as different communities have preserved it."[10] Most recently the confluence in modern Israel, after many centuries of separation, of Jews from many parts of the earth, has shown that the old hypothesis of a primordial tradition of biblical cantillation, common to all groups of the Jewish diaspora, was a chimeric dream.

Although the origin of the tunes is vague, it is possible to document, to some degree, the beginnings of the *te'amim*. The biblical text was originally neither punctuated nor vocalized. The first intimation that signs or visual marks existed to facilitate correct public reading of the text appears in B. *Ned* 37b. There we read that Rab, suggesting a new interpretation of Nehemiah 8:8, understands the expression *pisukim* as "division of verses." Therefore the expression *pisuk ta'amim* must refer to a closer, more exact division of the verses, such as an internal caesura, the semi-cadence [*atnah*].[11]

However, the first reference to a concrete sign or mark comes somewhat later, in Exodus Rabba. par. 2, and it will be useful to recall this long-forgotten passage: "He said: 'Moshe moshe,' but you find [in the passage] 'Abraham, Abraham' that there is a *pesik*; also in 'Ya'akob, ya'akob' there is a *pesik*; in 'Shmuel, Shmuel' there is a *pesik*, but in the passage 'Moshe moshe' there is no *pesik*."[12] *Pesik* is the name of a separating accent, and the anonymous editor, commenting on Exodus 3:4, notes that in this passage the repetition of a name is not marked by the dividing sign that appears elsewhere, when a name is repeated. This sign (sometimes called "*pasek*") has also been found in the Proto-Palestinian Masorah of the sixth century.[13] Yet this accent has no musical function; it is used to separate similar letters, identical words, a duplication of the Divine Name, etc.—or to prevent a hiatus. It serves grammatical-phonetic ends.

Accents similar to those of the Tiberian Masorah[14] were long known to philologists and historians; it appears that various languages, such as Sanskrit, Greek, Armenian, Syrian, and even Latin, had developed signs to indicate the rise and fall of the reader's voice—signs organically linked to the punctuation of their respective sacred texts—in order to ensure proper declamation. These signs are named

ecphonetic accents, after the Byzantine word ἐκφώνησις, indicating the resonant reading of liturgical—and especially biblical—texts. The function of these accents was approximately the same as that of the Hebrew signs; even the shapes of the Byzantine accents resemble those of the Masoretes. It is clear that a give-and-take relationship existed between the two literatures, yet the details of this Greco-Jewish reciprocity are still controversial.[15] Seen in historical perspective, the *ta'amei ha-mikra* are a highly elaborate and philologically refined system of ecphonetic accents. Some of these systems, e.g., the Latin and the Byzantine, went the entire route from punctuation devices to exact *musical* notation; others, such as the Hebrew, the Syrian, the Armenian, or the Old Slavonic, stopped halfway before attaining clear musical identification and notation.

The reasons for this half measure are different in each case: in Judaism the principle of "*Al tosif*" ("do not add anything") and the fear of violating a tradition believed to be Mosaic would prevent any further innovation in the study of Scripture.[16] This fear was justified, since even the best musical system of notation could not guarantee an understanding of the syntactical structure of a sentence sufficient to preclude errors, misunderstandings, indeed, deliberate distortions. The Masorah itself was an interpretation of the text based upon punctuation that, in turn, relied on oral tradition. Since the discovery of the Dead Sea Scrolls we know that it was not faithful in every detail to the written text. It was the purpose of both cantillation and *ta' amei ha-mikra* to ensure the proper meaning of each sentence by visual and aural devices. We shall examine in detail cantillation and the scriptural accents as used in *minhag ashkenaz*.

The Musical Tradition of the Trop

Every effort to ascertain the actual style of cantillation in *minhag ashkenaz* must begin by studying the earliest terms used for it in the Hebrew literature of central and western Europe. In particular, we return to the question of whether the cantillation was a *Sprechgesang* close to elevated (oratorical) speech, or a musical chant with definable tones. The problem is not, as indicated above, an isolated Jewish phenomenon.[17] Saint Augustine himself takes a stand in this controversy: he reports that Athanasius had instructed his lector to chant in such modest modulations that the chant would be nearer to speech than to song.[18] And Augustine is in complete agreement with this stern discipline.

In R. Natronai's decision, which was authoritative for the medieval Ashkenazic region, the operative terms are *piskei te'amim* and *neginot ha-keriah*: "Even though punctuation marks [*piskei te'amim*] and melodies [*neginot ha-keriah*] of cantillations are '*Missinai*' [from Sinai] by way of oral tradition, they are enunciated without being indicated through marks in the scroll [during the synagogue service]."[19] Here a clear distinction is made between the accents and the cantillation itself. Another passage using specific terms affords some information: in the talmudic passage concerning the question of personal hygiene, the consensus is that the left hand should be used, and the reasons for that are given as follows: "Rabbi Naḥman, son of Isaac, said, 'Because one uses it [the right hand] to indicate the proper chant

[or the voice movement] of Scripture' and Rabbi Akiba said, 'One indicated with it [the right hand] the chant of Scripture.' Since R. Akiba antedated R. Naḥman by two full centuries, his authority outweighs all other opinions."[20] Rashi observes ad locum: "*Ta'amei ha-Torah* . . . these are the melodies of the accents [*ta'amei mikrah*] of the Torah, the Prophets, and the Hagiographa, next to the vowels . . . and one leads with his hand according to the direction of the cantillation [*ta'am ha-neginah*]. I have seen readers [do this] who come from the land of Israel."[21]

In both cases the word *ta'am* has a musical meaning; the expression that is used describes the proper rhetorical rise or fall of the voice. Other terms used for cantillation are *ne'imah* (cantilena) and even *rinah* (jubilation). Yet the most interesting explanation and terminology, authoritative for all of *minhag ashkenaz*, is found in Rashi's comment to B. *Kid.* 71a. This important passage has often been torn out of context, and not understood correctly:

> The text of the Gemarah first makes a statement about the chanting by the priests in the Temple while the elite of the priests "swallowed the divine Name." This is followed by an example, in the form of a reminiscence by R. Tarphon: "I ascended the dais after my mother's brother to bless [*le'dukan*] and inclined my ear to the High Priest and heard him swallowing the Name during the chanting of his brother priests."[22]

Rashi comments on this that while the elite priests "swallowed" the twelve-lettered Divine Name, the remaining priests uttered the four-lettered Name "as if they were in a hurry . . . in a melismatic (*florid*) chant [*ne'imat bisum*] called *trop*."[23] By whom was it called *trop*, and how did a practice of Temple days get the designation at the time of Rashi? Why is this accepted and authentic designation of scriptural cantillation in *minhag ashkenaz* connected by Rashi with the priestly mass chant of the Divine Name?[24]

The obscure comments of Rashi raise many questions: What has the pronunciation of the Divine Name to do with scriptural cantillation? Who calls a practice of the priests in the Temple (at Rashi's time) *trop*? There is mysterious silence in the literature about this passage, and even Idelsohn was strangely silent on this point. I explain this enigmatic remark fully in a special study ("*Trop* and *Tropus*," *HUCA*, Jubilee vol., Cincinnati, 1976) and shall limit myself here to a few remarks. In all Jewish traditions the priestly blessing, albeit a scriptural quotation, is chanted much more melismatically than normal cantillation. Indeed, one might call the chant of the *dukhan* a melismatic *tropus* of normal chant.

The operative word in Rashi's commentary occurs in R. Tarphon's anecdote. It is the term *dukhan*, which signified the recitation of the threefold priestly blessing in the Temple, the text of which is found in Numbers 6:24–26. Rashi simply could not imagine that such an important verse of Scripture would not have been cantillated in the Temple, as it was chanted in all the synagogues of his own time. Quite naively he transposed the custom of *minhag ashkenaz* back to the sanctuary of old.

The term "*trop*" is not found in Israel Levi's great dictionary, nor in that of Johannes Buxtorf, nor in Jastrow, nor, more astonishingly, in R. Nathan ben

Yehiel's *Arukh completum* (ed. Alexander B. Kohut), which antedates Rashi by a few years. Not even Samuel Krauss's big *Dictionary of Greek and Latin Loan Words in Talmud, Midrash and Targum*, or Avinery's *Hekhal Rashi* contains it. The word is derived from the poetic-musical term "*tropus*," a Latin word of the Middle Ages, not from the Greek "*tropos*," as has been suggested by Alfred Sendrey.[25] In the development of Western music the *tropus* played a great part. It was the musical paraphrase of an older Gregorian tune, or else a poetic paraphrase of an older text, often set syllabically to the old tune. The *tropi* originated in Rashi's time and even close to his French home town, during the tenth and eleventh centuries, in St. Martial, Limoges, etc.[26] This Latin prototype of "*trop*" would fit Rashi's use of the word exactly. Later the word was used exclusively for cantillation, especially in such popular books as the *Ma'aseh* book. Maharil speaks only about the *Stuben-trop*, to describe the singsong used for the loud memorizing of Torah and Mishnah in the *Stub* (schoolroom).

The gradual narrowing of the meaning of the word "*trop*" from what Rashi had in mind to its later popular usage must have taken place during the century following Rashi. At any rate, the term is limited to *minhag ashkenaz*, West and East, and is not known in the traditions of the other Jewish communities.

However the change of meaning occurred, there can be no doubt that Rashi, both in the excerpt above and in his comments to B. *Ber.* 61 and *Ber.* 62, refers to real tonal chant, not simply to *Sprechgesang*. That Torah cantillation was considered, somewhat later, to be an aesthetic experience is evident from the dictum of Elijah Levita (ca. 1468–1549): "The accents [and their melodies] are made also to teach the enjoyment of the Torah lesson, through the chant and the poem."[27] His younger contemporary, R. Samuel Archevolti, in his *Arugat ha-Bosem* (Venice, 1602), lamented the loss of the "original celestial melodies" of pristine cantillation, which was close to the "song of the angels" and promised the world-to-come to him who would always chant the Torah. Even the *Memor* books, those unforgettable documents of a hundred years of German Jewish martyrdom, often praised a man for his faithful chanting and "*leienen*" (cantillation) of the Torah. For example, R. Josua Abraham (Worms, 1639) is described as "the pious, the powerful, the singer . . . a faithful hazan and *ba'al keriah*" (i.e., singer of Scripture).

As a matter of fact, it was in *minhag ashkenaz* that cantillation was most exactly performed and most musically executed. And it was the *minhag ashkenaz* to which the Italian rabbis referred as "*sempre cantante*." Indeed it is here, in the chant of the Bible, heard at least three times a week, that the *minhag ashkenaz* surpasses all other Jewish traditions, both in melodic structure and variety. A comparison with musical recitations of other religious liturgies, such as the Byzantine *ekphonesis*, will certainly demonstrate the superiority of the Ashkenazic *trop* and of the Gregorian *oratio solemnis* to all other types of scriptural reading, East or West.[28]

Speculations on the archaic or original style of the Ashkenazic cantillation are as cheap as broken pennies, and no serious scholar has indulged in them. The practice of scriptural cantillation seems to have been generally known among Gentiles as well as among Jews. (Catholic clerics called it "*vox clamorosa Judaeorum*.") At the present time, the practice in *minhag ashkenaz* is applied to the five books

of Moses (Torah lesson), to the Haftarah (Prophetic lesson), to the books of Esther, Song of Songs, and Lamentations from the Hagiographa. In Western versions of *minhag ashkenaz* the books of Ruth and Kohelet (Ecclesiastes) are not regularly chanted. The mode of Job is used, although the book is not read publicly, and on rare occasions, a chapter of Proverbs is chanted. The Psalms are not chanted according to the Masoretic accents; in fact, the tradition of old psalmody is lost since the second generation of the sages of the Mishnah.[29] All psalmody of *minhag ashkenaz* is of relatively recent origin, with the exception of the chant for the *birkhot ha-shaḥar* (morning benedictions).

The distinction between psalmody and scriptural cantillation must be held clearly in mind. In general, psalmody consists of three, or at most four, motifs per verse, which function as either intonation, middle caesura, or cadential flourish, to which a coda is sometimes added in order to connect it with a different psalmody, or to a chant in a different mode. The structure of scriptural cantillation consists of a large and varying number of stereotyped phrases or formulas, depending on the accents pertaining to each verse. Even in the succession of the motifs, the difference between psalmody and cantillation is obvious: in the former, the order of the motifs is fixed and unvarying; in the latter, it is ever-changing, depending on the structure of the textual verse.

Tunes and Modes

Although the Ashkenazim follow a tradition of cantillation that is strongly acculturated to Western music *and its notation*, it is useful to remember that the cantillation represents a mixture of oral and written tradition. All notated music breaks melody down into a series of isolated and exact pitches; oral tradition, however, conceives cantillation purely as sound (not sharply defined pitches) in movement. Hence there are certain discrepancies between the notated tradition and its vivacious oral counterpart.[30]

There are two methods of categorizing and coordinating the cantillation: one is to trace the way from notation to chant (i.e., from theory to practice); the other is to trace every recurrent or stereotyped motif back to its notated and "standardized" accent or complex of accents. The second method can, of course, be undertaken only with the modern tools of tapes and other audio instruments. The two methods do not yield identical results, but only similar structures. Here we follow the first method, using the tabulation as given a hundred years ago by Abraham Baer in his *Ba'al Tefillah.* Wherever typical or repeated deviations have taken place, those will be noted. Only Pentateuch, Prophetic lesson, Lamentations, and Esther are discussed here; the tonality of each is examined and compared to that of other Jewish cantillations. Finally, the changes that have occurred since the first notation of Ashkenazic cantillation will be observed and statistically measured.

The cantillation was taught, at least in *minhag ashkenaz* from the time of the Middle Ages, in conjunction with the motifs of the Masoretic accents, arranged in a so-called *zarka* table—so named after the first accent, the *zarka.*[31] Rabbi Simon Zemaḥ Duran, the celebrated medieval apologist, attempted an explanation

of that old method of teaching the accents: "There arises a great melody and it is like a man who throws a thing after him, then has it returned to him, and one calls it therefore the *zarka* [pitcher, thrower] and after this melody will follow a pausa on three points [*segolta*], in order to show that his *pausa* is more important than the mark *zakef katan*, so that the mark of *zarka* that preceded it [the *segolta*] is more important than the mark *pashta* which, in turn, precedes the *zakef katan*."[32] This is no more than a didactic-mnemonic rule, not an explanation. Many more puns on the names of the accents follow it.[33]

The Middle Ages produced a good many such descriptions of the chant of the accents, but it was in the German humanist sphere that the first decisive step was taken to fix the oral tradition. It remains the merit of the great Reuchlin (1455–1522) to have prompted his fellow worker Boeschenstein to transcribe each accent of the Torah cantillation and to set the chant as a kind of *cantus firmus* in the tenor of a four-part arrangement.[34] This is further evidence that the German Jews chanted Scripture in a true melodic line, not just in singsong. It is not clear whether Boeschenstein was a renegade from Judaism; if he was, he accomplished more for the preservation of biblical tradition than many a pious exegete. It was his respectable ability to take musical dictation that resulted in that transcription. Reuchlin's comments on his own teachers and their theories are quite remarkable. One of those teachers, a certain Flavius Mithradates Romanus, was a decidedly shady character, a purely opportunistic convert to Catholicism and more than a bit of a charlatan.[35] Reuchlin well comprehended his dubious, basically low and greedy personality, and did not hesitate to refer to him in a distinctly ironic and caustic manner.[36] Yet he drafted Flavius's application of the Byzantine system of ecphonetic accents without any modification. This system operates with terms such as *tonoi*, *chronoi*, and *pathemata*, of which there is no trace in the tradition of Hebrew grammar. This concoction by Flavius Mithradates was taken over entirely by Idelsohn, who neither mentioned nor criticized his source.[37]

A whole group of German, French, Italian, and English humanists followed Reuchlin's examination of the niceties of Hebrew grammar. Most of them also published the notation of the Torah cantillation, with few differences, from Reuchlin's pioneering work. The Italian Ercole Bottrigari fixed the cantillation of the northern Italian Jews during the first third of the sixteenth century in his treatise *Trimerone* (manuscript in the library of Bologna). It deviates but little from Reuchlin's version.

The list of accents pertaining to the twenty-one prose books of the Bible is arranged in the conventional order, quoting the names of the single accents or their most frequent combinations. The names themselves are Aramaic and refer either to the function of the accent, for example, *atnahta* (rest, pause), or to its exterior shape, for example, *shalshelet* (chain, *catena*), or possibly to the position in the verse, for example, *kadma* (forward), used mostly at the beginning of a verse. The poetic books of the Bible are Job, Proverbs, and Psalms; they have their own system of accents, called *ta'amei emet* (*emet* being an acronym for the Hebrew titles *Iyob*, *mishlei*, *tehilim*). The technical literature on the *ta'amei ha-mikrah* is extensive, and it presupposes a precise knowledge of Hebrew grammar.[38]

A few grammatical rules are useful in studying the musical counterparts of these accents in *minhag ashkenaz*. The important accents are *disjunctives* [*mafsikim*], weak and strong. The strongest disjunctives are *sof pasuk* (end of a verse), *atnaḥta* (main caesura, pausa), *zakef katan* (strong comma), and *rebia* (weak comma). The "binding accents" are *conjunctive*, and are of musical significance only in connection with strong disjunctives, e.g., *munaḥ-zakef* or *merkha-sof pasuk*. In table V the motifs of the Torah cantillations are quoted according to the Western Ashkenazic tradition, which is at least two hundred years older and better preserved than that of Poland and Russia. The Lithuanian tradition is known only since the sixteenth century. Idelsohn, who generally favors the eastern European tradition, remarks: "The tune of the Pentateuch has often been mutilated past recognition in East Europe."[39]

Table V (after *HOM*, vol. 7) presents the motifs of (a) the Torah lesson, (b) the Prophetic lesson, (c) the Torah lesson as it is chanted on the High Holy Days,[40] (d) the chant of Lamentations, (e) the chant of Esther.

The Torah Lesson (Table Va)

Tonality. The tonality of Torah cantillation today is clearly in the major, with a few pentatonic elements such as *mahpakh-pashta* and *munaḥ-atnaḥta*. In Reuchlin's time these pentatonic elements occurred somewhat more frequently than they do today.[41] There is reason to believe that Torah cantillation had completely changed its original tonality long before Reuchlin's time, for there is evidence of similar changes in the "Germanic traditions" of Gregorian chant. It is instructive to compare German hymns before the middle of the fifteenth century with other popular tunes at about 1560. There too we find the change from archaic-sounding modal tunes to the new, lively major mode, which characterizes so many Lutheran hymns that were "taken from the street."[42] If one could assume a common *Urtradition* for all cantillations, as Idelsohn did, it would be fairly easy to explain the change in tonality; yet there is no evidence whatsoever of such an *Urtradition*. The alteration of the Torah cantillation may be the result of the ever-growing influence of Nordic, specifically Germanic, *secular* folk songs, which were quite familiar to the Ashkenazim, as evidenced in part by the previously mentioned Jew Wolfflein from Locham (ca. 1450),[43] or by the Jews' familiarity with many old German folk tunes, such as "*Herzog Ernst*" or "*Bettler-ton*" (to be discussed in chapter 6). To link the archaic elements in the cantillation of *minhag ashkenaz* with ancient Greek scales, as a contemporary compiler suggests, is sheer nonsense, posing as erudition.

Disjunctives and conjunctives in their musical importance. In other Jewish traditions, the conjunctives have practically no musical significance whatsoever, for example, in the chants of Djerba, or in the Torah cantillation of the Syrian Jews.[44] In *minhag ashkenaz*, however, the situation is different. Some conjunctives, when linked to disjunctives, constitute strong and musically characteristic motifs, including *mahpakh-pashta*, *munaḥ-atnaḥta*, and *merkha-tebir*. By themselves the motifs of the conjunctives are extremely flexible, and in the large tabulations of *ta'amei ha-mikrah*,

such as those given by Baer or by I. M. Japhet, each of the conjunctives is represented by at least three or four variant motifs, depending on the subsequent disjunctive.[45]

Cadential formulas. The Torah cantillation includes three final cadences: the close of a verse (example 1a); the close of a portion or *parasha* (1b); the close of an entire book (1c). The most interesting cadence is that of 1a,c, for it combines the basic motif of *sof pasuk* with a highly characteristic fall of a fourth to the *finalis* in minor, while the entire chant has been moving in the relative major. This falling fourth appears to be a motif borrowed from a late stratum of Gregorian recitation-tone, which, in turn, may have been influenced by secular German folk song or *Minnelieder*, as in example 2a. Not only did Wizlav of Rügen (d. 1325) frequently use this cadence, as Idelsohn noted, but it also appears in *Tageliedern*. In example 2b, Wizlav used it as melody for the "*senende claghe* (pining lament) of the unlearned. . . ."[46]

This motif has entered *minhag ashkenaz* on a broad front, and it is almost universally used as a closing phrase. No other Jewish group has a cadence even similar to it. The prevalence of the falling fourth and rising thirds in the Torah cantillation of *minhag ashkenaz* is one of the strongest components of its *Gestalt*. Pentatonic clauses are also characteristic. It is uncertain whether these pentatonic elements are the

Example 1

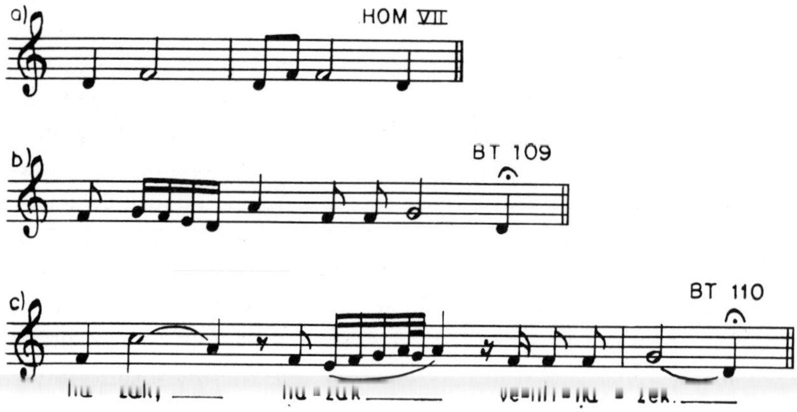

Example 2

archaic substrata of the tradition or whether they represent a later development. The older Boeschenstein-Reuchlin notation contains more pentatonic elements than Baer's transcription. In his profound *History of Melody*, Bence Szabolcsi observes: "Gregorian plainchant is the richest and most complete summary of ancient Mediterranean music. . . . In its pentatonic elements it seems to preserve an earlier stage of pentatonicism than appears in most known Jewish melodies, or in the entire *corpus* of extant Greek music. . . ."[47] This indicates the *archaic* character of pentatonic melodies. The musicologists Riemann, Hornbostel, and Lach explained the fact that pentatonicism was ubiquitous, by "assuming [it] to have occurred everywhere at a certain period. . . . Hence pentatonic remains presuppose a stage of evolution: a universal human tradition which survives in certain places and harks back to the same musical stone age."[48]

On the other hand the late Curt Sachs, one of the fathers of ethnomusicology, contents himself by reminding his readers that "our literature is full of answers [to this question]. But most of the opinions we hear are rash, contradictory, and worst of all, 'plausible,' that is, as the writer at his desk thinks it could have been."[49] For if this archaic pentatonicism was artless, so to speak, there is another species related to it born out of stylization; Szabolcsi is aware of this more recent kind: "The Gregorian form of pentatonicism, . . . although it is not apparently 'original' or 'primary,' it nevertheless reveals itself with far more classic simplicity in the pages of the Roman Gradual than in its sources in Oriental-Hebrew tune-types, as these are known today. In any case, it, too, is a form of pentatonicism which later creates its own mixed forms within its own sphere of influence. . . ."[50]

I am inclined to go a step further: it can be demonstrated that melodies that are chanted every day, or at least very frequently, are often smoothed out, or whittled down to such an extent that they skip one or two *pien-tones* (transitory tones in an oriental scale). I referred earlier to the Germanic "dialect of Gregorian chant"; once again similarities with *minhag ashkenaz* can be observed. Again I quote Curt Sachs: "The Germans and Scandinavians, unaccustomed to semitones, replaced them by their traditional thirds. In other words, the Northerners transformed the typical pattern of the first Church mode, D–F–A–B-flat–A, into the equally typical triple chain of thirds, D–F–A–C–A. Inversely, melodies sung in the fourteenth century, and probably many of older times, too, avoided the *sub-semitonium* or semitone below the tonic. . . ."[51] We need only examine two typical accent-motif combinations to understand the relevance of this observation. These are by turn diatonic and pentatonic variants. Examples 3a and c are older than b and d. This means that, just as in the German tradition of Gregorian chant, the older semitone was eliminated by elision and replaced by the third. The result sounds pentatonic to us today, but it is merely an elision, which occurs in all languages—even that of music.

Tempo and rhythm. All cantillation belongs to the category of free, prose-like rhythm. It is not bound to a fixed time unit; yet in practice it is regulated by the contents of the text, so that, for instance, the Ten Commandments are to be read solemnly and in strict articulation, requiring a longer time unit than the reading of the "table of the nations" (Gen. 10). The Torah cantillation of *minhag ashkenaz* does

Example 3

contain more metrical elements than do other Jewish traditions; a few accents are chanted almost in fixed time, for example, *mahpaḥ-pashta* or *kadma ve'azla* are sung in 6/8 time.

The Prophetic Lesson, or Haftarah Cantillation (Table Vb)

Tonality. One might describe the mode of the Prophetic lesson as "natural" or "pure" minor (identical with the Aeolian mode), but it would not be entirely correct. While the tonal range is identical with the scale of the hypodorian or second Church tone, the structure of Haftarah cantillation has a pattern of its own. Example 4 is a typical specimen. The tonal range of that pattern is seen in example 5. Here D

Example 4

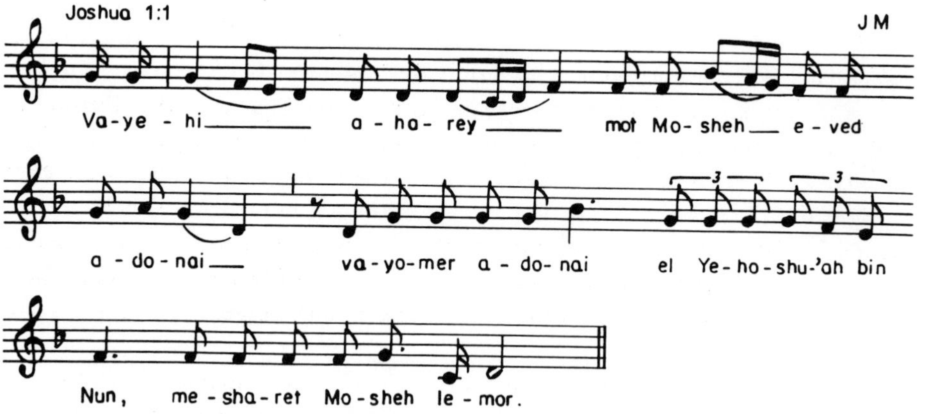

Example 5

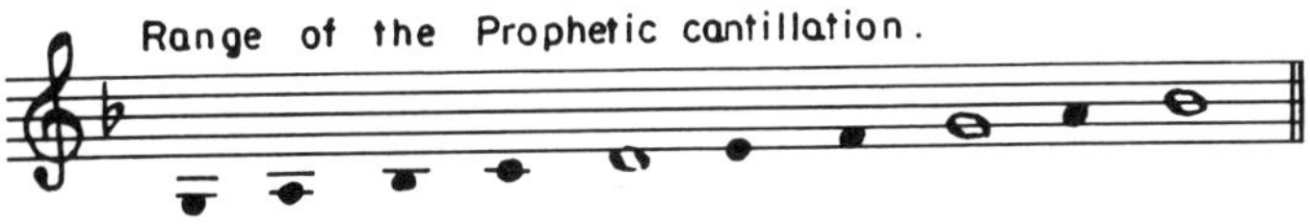

Example 6

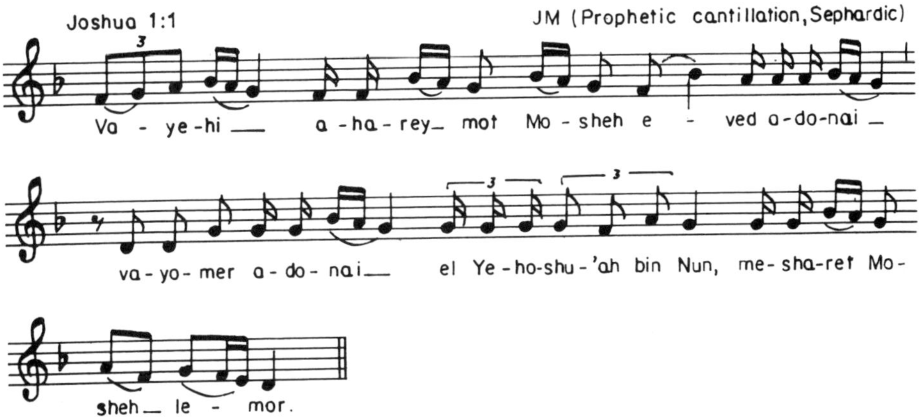

Example 7

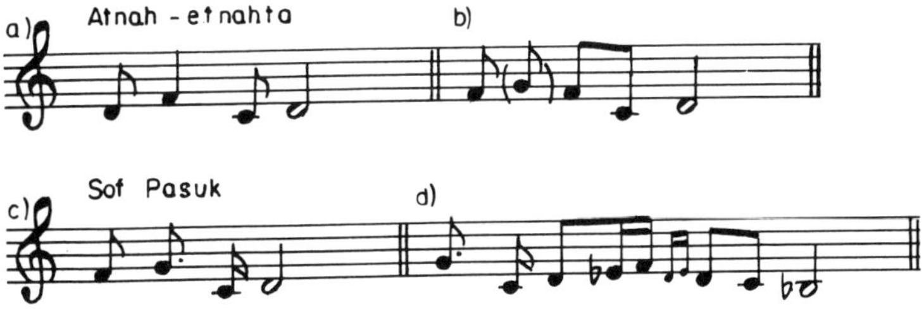

is the finalis, and G is the tenor. This is only one instance where there seems to be a common tradition for *minhag ashkenaz* and the oriental Sephardic rite. Example 6 is the oriental Sephardic rendition of the same verse. This moves in the same range, but is closer to the first Church tone (Dorian), not to the second, since it does not extend beneath the finalis D. This is, however, by no means final proof of the organic relationship between the two traditions. No pentatonic elements are noticeable in either tradition. There are also decisive differences, especially in the cadences, where the two types diverge both in motif structure and in tonal range.

Cadential formulas. The Prophetic cantillation of *minhag ashkenaz* includes only two half closes, the *munah-atnah* (example 7a) and the *merkha-atnah* (7b), which are

Message

For ______________________________

Date ____________________ Time ____________

From ______________________________

____

Phone No. ______________________________

☐ Telephoned ☐ Please Call

☐ Returned your call ☐ Will call again

By: ______________________________

very much alike; two full closes, *silluk-sof pasuk* at the end of each verse (7c) and a more extended *sof pasuk* at the end of a pericope (7d).

The conclusion of the Prophetic cantillation is often freely improvised to link it with the *berakhah* that follows the *Haftarah*, so that it modulates, as in example 7d, usually into the key of the lower third. None of these characteristics is found in the Sephardic tradition.

The fact remains that Prophetic cantillation was less sensitive, less labile, and more preserving of the entire line than of the individual small motif. Hence, in this chant, the smaller disjunctive accents and all conjunctives have no clearly invariable motifs but are very flexible and vary from region to region.

Torah Cantillation on the High Holy Days (Table Vc)

The cantillation of the Torah on the High Holy Days is rendered in a special mode —a unique characteristic of *minhag ashkenaz*. The origin of and reason for this Ashkenazic deviation are controversial. Leaving aside some purely fantastic speculations, two theories put forth by responsible scholars may be examined. The renowned historian Abraham Berliner, expanding upon a remark in Maharil, suggested: "The schoolchildren used a special cantillation for the recitation of Scripture in front of their teacher."[52] In this very mode, called *Stubentrop*, R. Jacob Levi (Maharil) chanted the scriptural pericopes of Rosh Hashanah and Yom Kippur. There are even reports of a special mode for Prophetic cantillation coming from the Rhineland.[53]

The second theory, proposed by Idelsohn, can be stated briefly: according to the *Zohar* (referring to Leviticus 16) the reading of that chapter on Yom Kippur, where the death of Aaron's children is narrated, should be accompanied by the weeping of the worshipers; and everyone who expresses his sorrow over this punishment may be sure his children will not die during his lifetime. Old Ashkenazic *maḥzorim* (e.g., Salonica 1550) contain a sign on this portion to indicate that it should be read in a tune different from the usual one, a tune more expressive of sadness and suffering. Idelsohn conjectures that the "search for such a tune led to the mode of Job which had no function in the Ashkenazic rite and suited these requirements. The Ashkenazim took this mode at first for the reading of the Pentateuch on the Day of Atonement; later they extended its use also to the days of Rosh ha-Shanah. . . ."[54]

To examine the problem more closely, we must first search for a notation of the *Stubentrop* and compare it with the penitential mode under scrutiny. Unfortunately, the oldest transcription (example 8) is found in a vicious anti-Jewish book, *The Ḥelek* (part of the tractate B. *Sanhedrin*) by the renegade Gerson of Halberstadt (d. 1627).[55]

Next we refer to the Job cantillation (example 9), forgotten in *minhag ashkenaz*, but sought out and perhaps identified among the oriental Sephardim, and presumably incorporated in later *minhag ashkenaz*.[56] We compare this with the *zarka* table (table Vc) and with the cantillation of the introductory prayers before the reading on *Rosh Hashanah* (example 10).[57] The long melisma at the end is a prototype of the full close. Finally, in example 11 we have the end of Genesis 22:19, according to the High Holy Day version of *minhag ashkenaz*.

Example 8

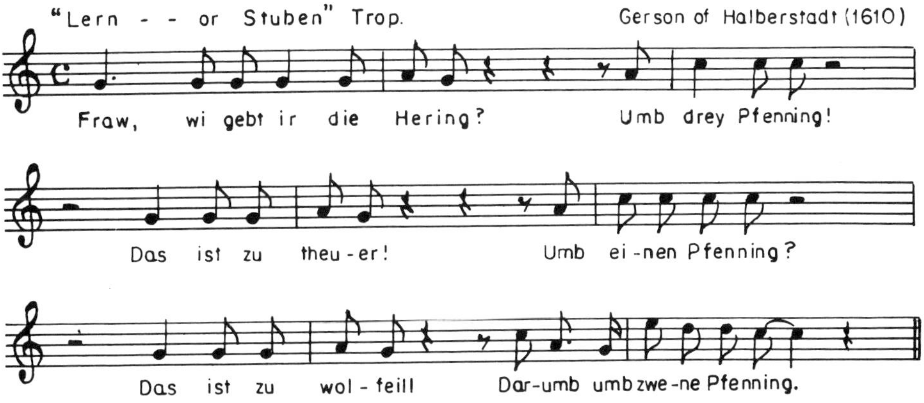

Example 9

Upon examining the four examples and table Vc, we must conclude that examples 10 and 11 are akin to each other as well as to the item in the table. Yet the Job cantillation shows little resemblance to the penitential Torah cantillation. This would certainly dispose of Idelsohn's conjecture. There is some relationship between the *Stubentrop* and the cantillation; the rising fourths and the mixolydian (not Lydian) mode with the B-flat are common and characteristic elements.

The Lamentation Mode (Table Vd)

Minhag ashkenaz carefully continues the tradition of chanting the Book of Lamen-

Example 10

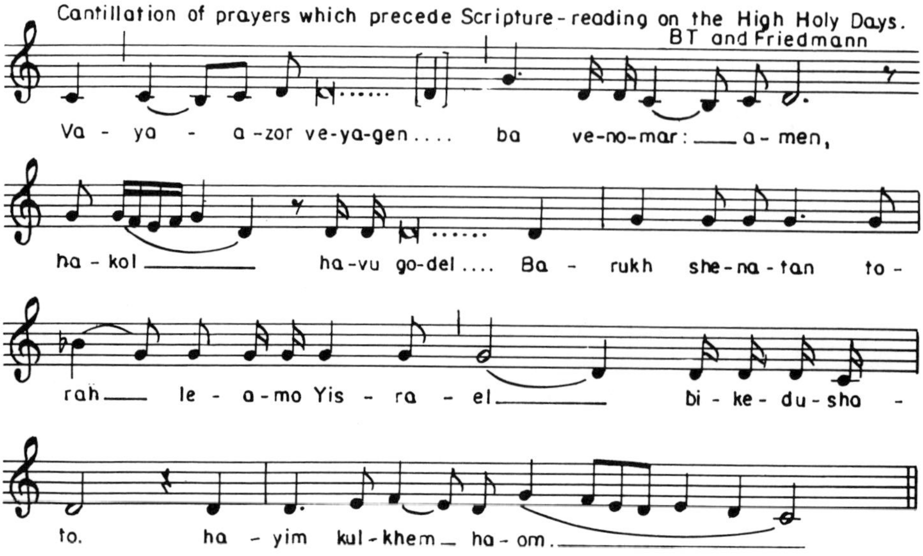

Example 11

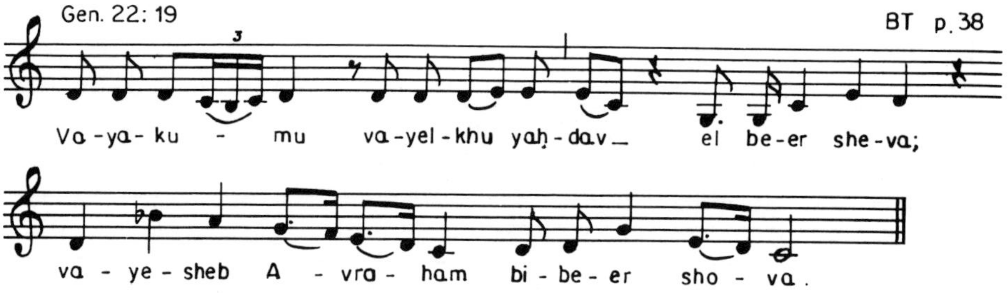

tations on the Ninth of Ab, the anniversary of the destruction of the Temple. Nowhere does the text of the Hebrew Bible approach as closely a kind of fixed meter as in Lamentations. The *kinah* (dirge) form, which occurs in some other biblical texts as well, may be described as consisting of two lines of three stresses each, followed by one line of two stresses or variations of this scheme. This is not a syllabic meter, but a rhythm of short phrases: *Eikháh yash'váh vadad / ha'ír rabáti am / hay'táh ke-almanah*. In addition, the book is cast in acrostical form, based on the Hebrew alphabet, a feature that was taken over in both the Greek and Latin translations where the Hebrew letter names are retained. Moreover, it is believed that the text of *Eikhah* was composed shortly after the destruction of the First Temple in 587 B.C.E. and underwent relatively few changes.[58]

The numerous regional chants of Lamentations have, in spite of their variety, so many elements in common that here the assumption of a common *Urtradition* seems to be justified. The verses are short and easy to memorize because of the

acrostical device. They are of tremendously dramatic impact and are often quoted in sayings and prayers. They might well have become folklore. The "How could you, oh God?" refrain permeates the book, truly masochistic self-accusations abound, hope is forsworn, desolation rampant. The beginning of the first chapter, in a modern English translation, casts the unaware reader (or better, listener) into desperation:

> How lone she sits;
> The city big with people widowed,
> Famed of nations
> Queen of countries
> And now enslaved.
>
> Weeping, she weeps in the night
> Her tears on her cheeks:
> She has no comforter of all her lovers,
> All her friends betrayed her—
> Became her enemies.[59]

The mode of Lamentations achieves its sharply profiled character through its cadential motifs, which are prominent in all variants. In *minhag ashkenaz* the mode has a highly characteristic contour, although its scale is identical with that of the *Haftarah*. Nobody will ever confuse the one with the other! This is a clear example of the thesis that the identification of a mode with a scale or tonality is purely superficial. It is like the passport description: eyes—brown, hair—brown, lips—red, no special marks, etc. What counts are the individual constituent motifs, especially those that indicate full or half cadences. In Lamentations, the two are almost completely identical, intensifying the feeling of monotony and hopeless despondency. These motifs occur in the chant of the weekday prayers during the "Three Weeks" of mourning before the Ninth of Ab, when the entire service is inundated with a flood of bitterness and grief. These cadential motifs are bracketed in example 12, the opening verses of Lamentations. This is certainly a heartbreaking melody.[60]

Example 12

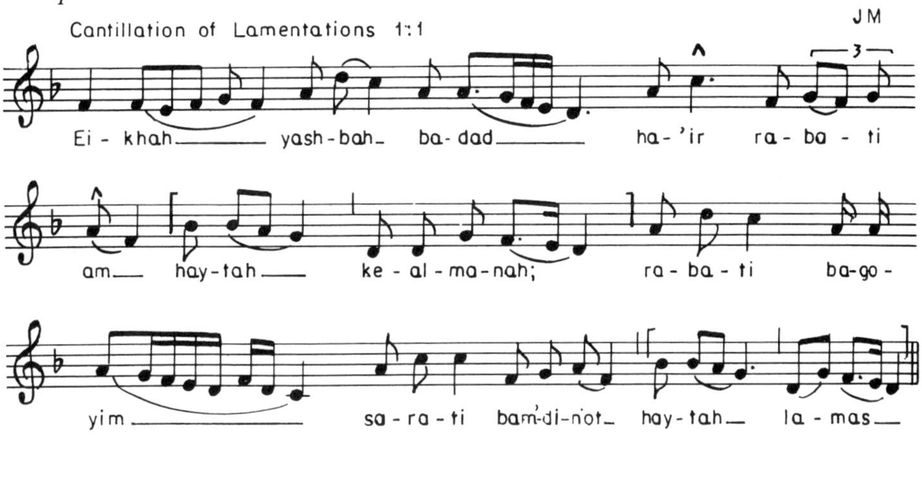

The tune is chanted perhaps sixty or seventy times in succession in a darkened synagogue, with the rabbi and cantor seated on the floor, occasionally interrupted by the wailing responses of the worshipers, who, on that evening more than on any other occasion, appear as mourners for Zion.

This cantillation closely approaches psalmody, because of the uniformity of the verse structure. Perhaps that is the reason that this mode of Lamentations was borrowed by the early Church, possibly during the first Christian centuries. Already the official *Ordines* of 700–730 contain the rubric of the reading of Lamentations during the *Triduum* (Maundy Thursday, Good Friday, Holy Saturday).[61]

In all Christian churches the Lamentations are heard during Holy Week. In some liturgies, such as the Roman, Georgian, Old-Gallican, and Greek, they belong to the catena of the twelve Old Testament lessons that can be traced back to the fourth century.[62] Among the most conspicuous elements of the Roman chant of Lamentations are the extended melismata with which the initial Hebrew letters are chanted. The reasons for this strange custom are listed in the old work on Roman liturgy, the *Rationale* by the bishop Durandus (d. 1296), and they are, as was usual in his time, both allegorical and deeply hostile to Judaism.[63] Example 13 presents some of the initial melismata that accompany the names of the Hebrew letters, and example 14 is a sample of the cantillation of the Persian Jews.

Example 13

Example 14

Example 15

Example 16

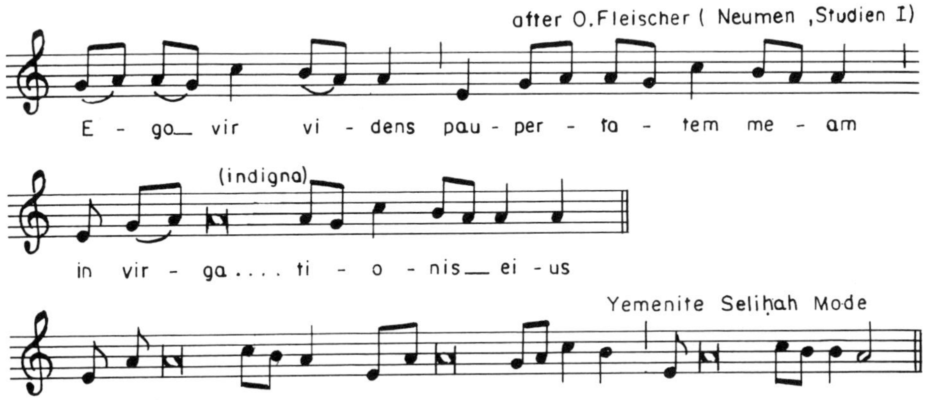

Returning to *minhag ashkenaz*, we find that the cantillation of *Eikhah* is more interesting than its Latin counterpart. Yet, when we compare the prayers of the Three Weeks and of the Ninth of Ab with the cantillation (example 15), we can notice immediately the old and deep relationship of the chants. It was Peter Wagner, the great Gregorian scholar, who called Idelsohn's attention to some parallels between Gregorian chant and ancient Yemenite tunes. The most impressive identity (example 16) was disclosed by Wagner.[64]

Cantillation of Esther (Table Ve)

Musical motifs of Lamentations are also read into the cantillation of the Book of Esther. This strange musical link between the "black fast" and the joyous day of triumph and jubilation merits a brief explanation. Since hardly a rabbinic source alludes to this linking, it should be stated, first, that this peculiarity is traditional only in *minhag ashkenaz*. None of the other communities utilizes this strange feature. Idelsohn suggests that the Ashkenazim, indeed, sing the book of Esther in a style more florid than that of any of the other communities, who follow the talmudic prescription to read it like a pamphlet [*ke-igeret*], fast and uninterrupted, for the congregation is "busy and troubled." Yet the Ashkenazim take their own good time with it. Purim, the day on which it is read, is a kind of carnival for them, one joyous day in a year of bitter weeks. Every reference to the Diaspora or Jerusalem is chanted in the mode of Lamentations, so that one would always remember—never forget—Jewish destiny, even while remembering the glorious past. Following are some of the verses treated in this way: "Who had been carried away with Yekonyah, King of Judah" (2:6); in the narration of Mordecai's anxiety, "He rent his clothes and put on sackcloth and ashes . . . and went out in the city wailing and crying bitterly" (4:1).

How does it happen that this use of leitmotifs was restricted to *minhag ashkenaz*? We remember that an even richer and more stringent application of leitmotifs appears in the *Missinai* tunes. In the first place, it seems that this literary-musical play with associations was a German specialty for in some of the German medieval folk epics literary leitmotifs do appear. Second, there is some explanation in the incredible, almost chauvinistic pride of the medieval Ashkenazim. In view of that pride, their inclination to paint every detail of the Book of Esther with loving care is quite plausible. The following paraphrase of Esther 1:2, taken from the Judeo-German translation, may indicate the "pan-Judaism" of the *minhag ashkenaz*:

> In days long gone by, there was great king Ahasuerus seated on his throne in his kingdom, whose capital was Shushan. You shall know, dear folks, that the throne "on which the king sat" had never belonged to him [Ahasuerus] nor to his parents; it was the throne that Hiram, King of Tyre, had made for King Solomon, together with other craftsmen in the service of King Solomon, and it was fashioned in the great wisdom of King Solomon, that the Holy One, Blessed be He, had granted him.[65]

Indeed, the commentary is full of references to the destruction of the Temple, and the contemporaneous popular book *Tzenah u-r'enah* (Go Out and See) contains the story of Esther, with some warning allusions to the Temple and its destruction. Hence it is understandable that the Ashkenazim were just as mindful of the Ninth of Ab in their festive chant as they were in their literary folklore.

The late Eduard Birnbaum, by far the most serious expert on all aspects of *minhag ashkenaz*, published an article entitled "Tradition of the Public Recitation of the *Megillah*."[66] There he quotes both the Targum and an old commentary on the prayer book *Ma'aglei Tzedek* (Pursuers of Righteousness), which provide the rabbinic basis of some specifically Ashkenazic customs on that occasion. Birnbaum

was describing the beginnings of *ḥazanut* in penetrating words: "The medieval cantor was entrusted with the task of indicating and distinguishing the application of clearly profiled melodies. Today one could call them 'traditional.'"[67] He explains why the benedictions before reading the Esther book contain no motifs of the cantillation but, strangely, quotations from the blessings that precede the sounding of the shofar on the New Year, and the blessings of the New Moon. He says it is because the shofar and the blessing of the New Moon are considered equivalent *mitzvot* (commandments), and in both the text "who has done wonders to our fathers" is quoted (cf. M. *Kid.* 1:7). He then gives a brief analysis of the cantillation of the Megillah and traces the customs of *minhag ashkenaz* pertinent to its recitation:

1. The congregation has responses to certain verses: in 2:4, 5:8,15; 8:16, 10:3 the Targum and the rabbinic exegesis see four promises of redemption, and this is the reason for general acclamation.[68]
2. The following verses are to be chanted like Lamentations: 1:7, for the vessels named in the verse are said to have been the sacred vessels of the Temple; 2:6, because of the association with the Temple; 3:15, "and the city of Shushan"; 4:16, because the text indicates, according to the Targum, the deep dissatisfaction, indeed desolation, of Esther because of her loneliness; 8:6, the words "*ki eikhakha,*" because *eikhakha* is bound to remind the worshiper of the first word of Lamentations, which is *eikhah.*
3. Verse 5:4 must be chanted in a special way, because four words contain the letters of the "ineffable Name," which must somehow be alluded to, according to cabalistic precepts.
4. Verse 7:9, together with the preceding words, contains the rare accents "*karnei para*" and "*yeraḥ ben yomo*" and should be chanted in broad lines, interrupted by the *Ausklopfen* (beating out) of Haman.[69]

Age and Continuity of the Biblical Cantillations

Having examined the main versions of cantillation in *minhag ashkenaz*, we return to some of the earlier questions pertaining to it. First we can try to ascertain how persistent the Ashkenazic tradition actually is. We can use the Torah cantillation as a prototype and compare the sixteenth-century Reuchlin-Boeschenstein transcription (table Vf) with that of Idelsohn, four centuries later. Of the twenty-four accents, sixteen are identifiable, if not fully identical; if we measure the deviation numerically, counting individual tones in each motif, the deviation amounts to 15 to 18 percent, certainly a sign of durability. There is, however, a fly in the ointment; the most important, also the most characteristic motif, musically speaking (the extended *sof pasuk*, which marks the full close of a paragraph), does not appear as such in Reuchlin. There we find only one cadence in the quietest possible form, as seen in example 17. This cadence is found in modern transcriptions also; but in Reuchlin the extensive *sof parashah* is missing altogether. What does this mean? Did Boeschenstein not hear it? Or was it not in existence at that time, and did it emerge only later? In subsequent transcriptions of Ashkenazic cantillation four different variants are to be found, in the writings of the following authors:

Example 17

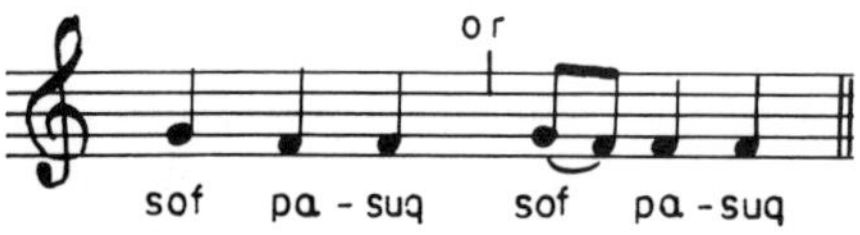

Example 18

Sebastian Muenster (ca. 1523), Alstedius, Pfeiffer, Guarin, Norzeni (ca. 1580–1630), Athanasius Kircher (ca. 1650), Gerbert, Ugolinus (ca. 1720–1760).

Most of these are copies of Reuchlin's or Muenster's tables with but slight deviations; Kircher and Gerbert, southern German priests and scholars, note wider intervals but do not deviate essentially from Reuchlin, nor do they contain an extended motif for *sof parashah*.

A remark in a manuscript of Ercole Bottrigari, a musical scholar of the sixteenth century, seems to shed light on the puzzling lack of any notation for this characteristic motif (example 18).[70] The pertinent passage (from a copy of the manuscript in my possession) reads as follows: [p. 22] *Siluc* over *sof pasuch*, che fin di chiusa o di verso s'interpreta non è stato da molti Grammatici, come afferma Elia Levita nel sopradetto suo libbro (titolato *Sefer Tob Tacham*) conosciuto; ma usato il poner due punti tra la una parola fine della chiusa, e l'altra principio della sequente. . . ." (*Siluk* or *sof pasuk*, meaning "end of clause or of verse," is not set by many grammarians, as Elijah Levita affirms in his book mentioned above, *Sefer Tub Ta'am*, but it is customary to put two dots between the word at the end of a sentence and the first word of the following.)

On page 24 of the manuscript we read further: "E finalmente è questo ultimo che e *Silicata* [*siluk*] et insieme *Sof pasuch*, il suo crederei che la sua composizione potesse essere tale che secondo il nostro costume qui vi pongo. . . . " (I can assume what is the musical movement of those accents. . . and finally that of the *Silicata*, the last accent, also called *Sof Pasuk*; I might believe that its composition is like what I write now, according to our custom.)

We surmise a misunderstanding here between the Gentile humanists who intended to transcribe the cantillation and their Jewish informants. The latter failed to chant the full close as they would have done at the end of a section, and certainly

at the end of the pericope. The humanists heard only the common *siluk* at the end of every verse. However, there is no accent written or printed indicating the *sof parashah.* It is interesting that the manuscript of Bottrigari gives an extended closing motif, although in his earlier musical tabulation he had cited the motif of example 19 for the *siluk.* Basing his conclusions on philological reasoning rather than on his actual experience, Bottrigari clearly differentiated between the end of a verse and the end of a paragraph. He helps us to realize that even what appears to be a glaring exception in the continuity of the tradition was not an actual one, but rather an error in transmission.

Example 19

The Relationship of Prayer Modes to Cantillation

Another question raised earlier concerned the relationship of the prayer modes to the cantillation. The statement is often repeated that the modes may be traced back to the Torah or Prophetic cantillations, and it does indeed have some validity, but it should be carefully qualified. In favor of the claim, there is the following evidence: the cadences of the prayer modes, especially in the case of the *Ahabah Rabah* and *Magen Abot,* are very similar to the *sof pasuk* of the Torah and Prophetic cantillations. Other motifs of cantillation such as *atnaḥ, zakef katan,* and *rebia* are also frequently recognizable in the melodies for weekday and Sabbath. The old *Stubentrop* and its extension in the cantillation of the High Holy Days has made vast inroads in the prayer chant of the entire penitential season, from the month of Elul to Yom Kippur. Also, the *eikhah* cantillation impregnates many prayers of the Three Weeks. But this is about the extent of the influence of cantillation on the prayer modes of *minhag ashkenaz.*

Other elements, other features, such as the *Missinai* tunes, are at least as characteristic of *minhag ashkenaz* as are the various cantillations. And we have not yet considered those formative elements of the "seasonal" leading motifs, which have colored large areas of the musical liturgy. These seasonal tunes are highly representative of *minhag ashkenaz* and were not developed by other Jewish communities. They were the important carriers of many German folk and church songs that entered the synagogue, often altered and distorted, in order to fit the totally different musical atmosphere of basic Jewish tradition. In the next chapter these melodies, as well as their German relatives, these most interesting components of *minhag ashkenaz* and its music, are discussed.

6

The *Piyutim* as Carriers of German Folk Song

To outrage you, who took it
not for granted?
Where else grows insult, as
was offered you?

An dir zu freveln, wem wars
nicht erlaubt?
Wo waechst die Schmach denn
die Dir nicht geschah?
(Richard Beer-Hoffmann)

The writings of Maharil ought to be understood not only as evidence of the consolidation of *minhag ashkenaz*, but also as a regulative instrument to maintain its stability. Prayer modes, *Missinai* tunes, and scriptural cantillation were considered by the German Jews authentic and integral elements of *minhag ashkenaz*. Its formative stage was, by and large, completed at the time of Maharil's death (1427). At that time the horrible massacre linked with the "Black Death," the organized murder of two thousand Jews in Strasbourg, the mass-suicide of six thousand Jews of Mayence and of untold more in the Rhineland and Bavaria, were still vivid in memory, although two new generations had emerged since. The majority of Rhenish and Western Jewry, horrified and terrorized by the new atrocities perpetrated by a greedy and murderous mob, had followed the repeated invitation of Polish kings and set out on a mass trek eastward. This flight was spurred by the ever stricter enforcement of the ghetto laws, which had been promulgated by Pope Innocent III at the fourth Lateran Council in 1215. The imposition of clothing requirements, the Yellow Badge,[1] the ghettos, the admission to fewer and fewer professions, and constant exploitation by the princes, the municipalities, and by every sort of blackmailer had made life for the German Jews intolerable.[2]

After five hundred years of settlement, the Jews were finally convinced that they, their lives, and their frequently promised privileges were merely instruments of the most unscrupulous exploitation by Gentiles, from the emperor down to the smallest burgomaster of a Swabian hamlet. The insecurity of the famous old communities had reached such insufferable dimensions that their Jews approached the status of outcasts [*Vogelfreien*] or proscribed outlaws. In the last decade of the fifteenth century the following expulsions took place, reneging upon duly sworn and dearly paid for letters of safe conduct and protection: 1492, from Mecklenburg; 1493, from Magdeburg; 1495, from Reutlingen; 1496, from Styria and Carinthia; 1499, from Nuremberg and Ulm; 1506, from Colmar and Noerdlingen, etc. All of this took place in addition to the cataclysm of the expulsion from Spain in 1492.

And so it continued, and as late as 1615 the Jews of Mayence, threatened by a furious mob, were forced to flee on the seventh day of Passover. The accusations of ritual murder or desecration of the Host, with their concomitant torture trials, did not cease. One case of such accusation even has a musical significance. In Chaucer's "Tale of the Prioress," he describes Little Hugh of Lincoln, wandering in fear of the Jews, singing over and over again the hymn "*Alma Redemptoris Mater*" (a hymn very popular at that time). The tale goes on to tell that he sang in vain, becoming victim to ritual murder by the Jews, but continuing to sing the "*Alma*" even after his throat was cut. This horror tale was the most infamous indictment of the Jews in England.[3]

Apropos of this musical reference, it should be noted that the motet *Cados, Cados* referred to earlier contains the opening strains of the "*Alma*" in one of its three voices (see chapter 2, note 42). The anonymous composer echoes the *Kedushah* with a rather scurrilous gibberish of Hebrew-sounding words.[4] This might have been naive imitation, or it might have been satiric parody. Of course, if the motet had been written by a Maranno, one might assume a symbolic significance for the Latin hymn. Yet it seems to have been composed by a German, for after the *Cados, Cados* the scrambled text continues, "*so si singhen*" and then relapses into the Hebrew gibberish. There can be no doubt that for those Jews who sympathized with Catholicism, the hymn "*Alma Redemptoris Mater*" must have had a special significance.

In spite of the never-ending chain of humiliations, the German Jews sensed the dawn of a new day, and it came, heralded by a deceptive aurora. A number of outstanding humanists in central Europe and Italy began to interest themselves in the Hebrew language and, subsequently, in the state of the Jewry of their day. They had acquired their knowledge of Hebrew from personal contact with learned Jews. One of the earliest representatives of the humanist movement was Johannes Reuchlin (see chapter 5). Others were Reuchlin's grandnephew Melanchthon, Martin Luther, Sebastian Muenster, Pico della Mirandola, Erasmus of Rotterdam—a galaxy of shining lights illuminating the intellectual life of the Renaissance. All of them had connections and intercourse with Jews, and although not all were sympathetic to them, they all offered plans for the improvement of Jewish existence.

It is well known that Martin Luther's earlier friendship for the Jews changed to vitriolic—indeed to murderous—hatred for them. Yet his former pro-Jewish utterances were not forgotten, nor were the honest and gentle words of the humanist and Hebraist Johannes Reuchlin.

To the elected leader of German Jewry [*Fuersprecher der gemeinen Judenschaft Befehlshaber und Regierer* = champion advocate, commander of all Jews of the German Nation], Joselmann of Rosheim (ca. 1478–1554), the humane words of Reuchlin and the new atmosphere of the Reformation were sufficiently encouraging to enable him to ward off the most vicious plans of Luther and his disciples.[5] He feared Luther, yet he was not intimidated by him, so that he publicly termed Luther's *Die Juden und ihre Lügen* a rough, inhuman book full of curses and slander. There the author demands the burning of all synagogues, destruction of all houses belonging to Jews, expulsion and proscription of all rabbis and scholars,

in short, the Nazi "*Endloesung*." Joselmann succeeded even in the restitution of the old and relatively helpful "*Judenregal*," belonging to the exclusively *imperial* jurisdiction. So forbidding a personality as Emperor Charles V was swayed by Joselmann and prevented further expulsions and deprivations of Jews.

The Seasonal Leitmotifs and Their Origin

The only place where the sorely afflicted Jews could freely pour out their hearts was, of course, the synagogue, with its prayers and songs. The texts of prayers had been fixed long before the Reformation, but the hazanim found expression appropriate for the fears, hopes, and expectations of their brethren in the two melody types: the seasonal and sectional leading motifs. With the introduction of these new melody types a development set in that is, in my opinion, prototypical for all of *minhag ashkenaz*. The *piyutim*, designed for specific feasts and holy days, brought new tunes into the service. Later, when the texts of these *piyutim* fell into oblivion, the hazanim, unwilling to part with their familiar melodies, imposed the metric tunes upon texts of fixed prayers [*tefillot keva*] in spite of the prose structure of those prayers. The preferred texts included the *mi khamokha*, the *hallel*, and the *kiddush*. In that way these melodies of old *piyutim* have been preserved until the present time. They now serve as the musical heralds of specific holidays—as seasonal motifs.

The second type, the sectional motifs, characterizes the main sections of the holiday's liturgy: morning service, *yotzer* section (after *Barekhu*), Torah service, and *musaf*. Each of these sections contained some *piyutim* of their own, especially in the service of the High Holy Days. Later, the melodies of those *piyutim* and their contrafacts were used as leading motifs, and signified entire sections. In the course of centuries these seasonal and sectional motifs crystallized to such an extent that every allusion to them was immediately understood and appreciated by the worshipers. These leading motifs are, next to the *Missinai* tunes, the musical features most characteristic of *minhag ashkenaz*.

Three examples (included in table VI) demonstrate concretely how the hope for a new status, a more orderly and secure future, affected the chant of the synagogue. One may perceive in each of them, respectively, sentiments dominant in the Jewish life at the time of the incipient Reformation: (1) strict adherence to their faith in all of its aspects (*Akdamut*); (2) hope for redemption (*Ma'oz Tzur*); (3) remembrance of Jerusalem (*Eli Tziyon*). All these texts are *piyutim* and do not belong to the category of *tefillot keva*. It is here that the alien element first intrudes, for there was no old musical tradition to go with the new texts. The cantors had to invent—or borrow—melodies suitable to these *metrical* poems; and they did find the fitting *metrical* tunes for them.

Akdamut (table VI, no. 1). The text is a didactic, rather dry Aramaic poem by Meir ben Isaac. The music is totally independent of the isosyllabic meter of the poem. In the table, *b*, *c*, and *d* are variants of the tune, and of these, *d* is a metrical version of this basically psalmodic tune. The tune itself serves as the leading motif

for the festival of Shabuoth, and is applied to the *kiddush*, the *hallel*, and the *mi khamokha*, all nonmetrical texts. Thus begins the forcing of meter on texts originally in free rhythm.

The motifs marked in the table as **I**, **II**, and **III** appear in all of the variants. The nuclear cell is doubtless the famous *Magnificat* of the third tone (*e*), which had sired many a theme of classical music, including the finale of the Jupiter Symphony of Mozart. Moreover, it was not the generally used tone of the *Magnificat* that so strongly impressed the German Jews, but its use in *secular German folk song*, transmitted in the specifically Germanized tradition of psalmody, as quoted by Peter Wagner (*Gregorianische Melodien*, p. 117 f.), after Codex Rosenthal 66. A significant similarity with the *Magnificat* and the Hebrew chant may be seen in the chorale *Jesaia dem Propheten* (*f*). It should be remembered that the original *piyut* did not employ a metrical tune but was sung as in *a* and *b*, using the chant of the *Magnificat*. Only gradually was the melody forced into the metrical straitjacket, and still later used for nonmetrical texts, as specific leitmotifs. For variations of the tune, see *HOM*, vol. 6, pp. 247, 255, 256, etc.[6]

Ma'oz Tzur (*table VI, no. 2*). The poem is by an Italian hymn writer named Mordecai, of the thirteenth century. The melody is definitely of German chorale character, consisting of three parts, each derived from a different source. The first phrase is identical with Luther's "*Nun freut euch liebe Christen gmein*" (*b*), which first appeared in Luther's own publication (Wittenberg, 1523). The tune appears again, with the text "*Freut euch, freut euch in dieser Zeit*" in Babst's *Gesangbuch* (1545), no. 27. An earlier print of this text, without music, bears the inscription: "to the tune of '*So weiss ich eins das mich erfreut, das pluemlein auf preyter heyde*' " (*c*).[7]

The second part bears a strong resemblance to "*Van Coninck Maximilian*" (*d*). Idelsohn attempted to identify this phrase with the *Bentzenauer* tone, but that is unjustified. That melody was the Fool's Tune or "*Narrenweise*" (example 1). The third phrase is literally identical with the popular song "*Ich weiss mir ein Meidlein huebsch und fein*," which has the refrain "*Be aware, trust her not, she's fooling you, she's fooling you*" [*Huet Du Dich, vertrau ihr nicht, sie narret Dich, sie narret Dich!*] (*e*). It became famous by Caspar Othmayr's setting (ca. 1560).

In *a* there are two motifs, A and B. For the first of these there appears to be no parallel in the entire repertory of German folk song of the sixteenth and seventeenth centuries. It is clearly related to the instrumental music of the late Baroque, where one may find parallels (example 2a).[8] The second would similarly be an anachronism in the sixteenth century. This is called a *Doppelschlag* (example 2b). It was very much in favor with the instrumentalists of late Baroque and early Rococo music (example 2c). Many such examples are listed in Robert Lach's monumental work, *Melopoiie*.[9]

The background of *Ma'oz Tzur* is still more complex. The first allusion to the tune—but by no means the complete melody—is found in Beer's manuscript (ca. 1760).[9a] There it is not identified in any way with Hanukkah, but rather with Shabuoth. Example 3 is a passage from the *hallel* of that festival. The first identification with the popular Hanukkah melody seems to have occurred in Braham and

Example 1

Example 2

Example 3

Nathan's song to Lord Byron's *Hebrew Melodies*, in particular in the song "On Jordan's Banks."[10] There is evidence that other melodies were sung to the text of *Ma'oz Tzur*: first, a melody of older vintage about which we hear only indirectly;[11]

and yet another, *f* in the second grouping of table VI, transmitted by the Venetian composer Benedetto Marcello.[12] Marcello cites the tune as "*Intonazione sopra ma'oz tzur.*" Today in Israel this noble tune is generally preferred to the Germanic one.

That melody seems to have become customary in German synagogues about 1750 or even a little earlier.[13] Yet the fact remains that meter and syllabic stress of the tune invariably go against the Hebrew accentuation. This would be unimportant if the Marcello tune had the same flaws; however, that version fits the Hebrew accents precisely. Moreover, there exists another poem for Hanukkah that, in turn, is much better suited to the Germanic tune than is the customary *Ma'oz Tzur.* It is the old *piyut, Sh'ney Zeytim* (Two Olive Branches), which used to be chanted on the Sabbath of Hanukkah. The meter of that *piyut* truly matches the metric structure of the Germanic tune.[14] Example 4 quotes the first stanza.

At this point I submit a conjecture that I cannot prove decisively: the original tune of *Ma'oz Tzur* in *minhag ashkenaz* was the one transmitted by Marcello, which fits the rhymes and stresses of the text exactly. At the same time the older *piyut, Sh'ney Zeytim* for the Sabbath of Hanukkah was sung to the Germanic tune. When, however, that *piyut* fell into oblivion, the cantors and congregations, unwilling to give up the popular tune, transferred this much more catchy air to the text of *Ma'oz Tzur.* In the United States, where even this text is not too familiar, the melody is maintained in an English paraphrase, "Rock of Ages." The cantors were not satisfied that the leitmotif would be heard only during the Sabbath of Hanukkah; they used the first few measures of the Germanic tune as a seasonal

Example 4

motif before and during the feast, imposing it upon regular (*keva*) prayers, such as *hallel* or *mi khamokha.*

Eli Tziyon (*table VI, no. 3*). During the Three Weeks (of mourning) between the seventeenth of Tammuz and the ninth of Ab, the old communities in Europe used to chant *seliḥot* and *kinot* (laments). The atmosphere of the "Black Fast," as the ninth of Ab was called, was anticipated by the musical leitmotif, to which the *piyut Eli Tziyon* was sung.[15] Its tune permeates not only the service of the fast day, but even the laudatory prayers of Sabbaths during the Three Weeks, when the tune is applied to *Lekha dodi* and *Adoṇ Olam*, as well as to the *tefillot* such as *mi khamokha* and *malkhutkha.*

Idelsohn has identified medieval Spain as the cradle of this old tune. He suggested that it was in all likelihood carried from there to central and eastern Europe by pilgrims, and that it was also picked up by Jewish singers.[16] I have found the oldest source of the tune in the famous Codex Calixtinus of Santiago. It is the Gregorian intonation of a hymn belonging to the liturgy of Saint James of Santiago de Compostela.[17] Example 5 is the Gregorian intonation, which contains the nuclear cell of the "*Eli Tziyon.*"

Example 5

The oldest of a number of German-Latin versions to the text "*Puer natus*" seems to be the tune of Heinrich von Loufenberg (Strasbourg, 1437) (see table VI, no. 3*b*).[18] Exactly one century later we encounter the chorale *Herr, nun heb den Wagen selb* (Strasbourg, Koepple, 1537) and another century later, *Lobe Zion deinen Herrn* (Cologne, 1638), which already uses the modern minor mode. The tune appears, in slight variations, in Spanish secular songs and, according to Idelsohn, also in Czech folk songs.[19] He is right in his conjecture that it was a pilgrim's song, for it is found among old English Christmas carols as "*Puer natus*" and is referred to as a pilgrim's song.[20] The melody occurs in the folk song of Spain, England, Germany, and Czechoslovakia as well as in *minhag ashkenaz.*[21] To the European Jews the tune sounded sad and despondent, and its strains seemed to express the mood of the fast in memory of the destruction of the Temple of Jerusalem.

The intrinsic proof of the Iberian origin of the tune lies in its structure; it belongs to the great family of *folias*, most popular dance form of Spanish-Portuguese music since the fifteenth century. Originally part of a fertility ritual, the *folia* became a dramatic dance in triple time, stylized by many composers, probably best known through Corelli's celebrated *folia* for the violin.[22] The typical and permanent element of the *folia* is, however, not its melodic line but its ground bass, which assumes the nature of a fixed progression, somewhat similar to—but freer than—

that of a passacaglia. The (implied) harmonic progressions of *Eli Tziyon* do not follow the strict ground bass exactly but show some minor deviations.

It is noteworthy that the derivates of the hymn in Christian tradition belong without exception to the Christmas season, and in some instances, as in Germany and England, are outright Christmas carols. The two feasts of the Apostle James are his "name day," 25 July (close to the ninth of Ab), and the date of the transfer of his relics to Compostela, 30 December (between Christmas and New Year's Day).[23] During the thirteenth century Compostela was an internationally famous place of pilgrimages,[24] visited by many thousands. As these pilgrims' songs were echoed in all the streets of Europe, the Jews had ample opportunity to hear them "*narrantes laudes Domini.*" There is an additional reason that the monastery in Compostela had some significance for Jewry. The aforementioned Codex Calixtinus contains a most interesting hymn, with a text that is a conglomeration of Latin, Greek, and Hebrew words and phrases, written at a time when knowledge of the Hebrew language was by no means as available as it became 300 years later. To give the reader an idea, a few verses are extracted from that hymn:

1a. Letabunda et cemcha [*simḥa*] gaudeat Yspania
2. In gloriosa Jacobi almi prefulgenti nizaha [*nitzaḥon*]
2a. Qui hole [*'olah*] celos haiom [*hayom*] in celesti
nichtar [*nikhtar*] gloria
3. Hic Jacobus Zebedei achin [*aḥiv*] meuorah [*meborakh*]
Johannes, supra jama [*yam*]
Galilee a salvatore nicra [nikra][25]

These three examples are typical of the process in which foreign tunes were borrowed for metrical *piyutim*, in which the *piyutim* themselves may or may not have fallen into oblivion, but the foreign material was preserved to serve as seasonal leitmotifs set to nonmetrical texts. These are not simple instances of acculturation, or of "passive assimilation," to use Hermann Cohen's terminology. They represent a continuing process of musical, and perhaps even ideological, adaptation of foreign material to a well-fixed traditional background. It is not easy to determine what forces were able to overcome the stern warnings against foreign tunes—warnings that had been heeded so faithfully two centuries earlier. A comprehensible explanation would require a greater familiarity with the inner state of central European Jewry than is available. Certainly, one factor was hope for a "new order," the *novus ordo seculorum* championed by the humanists, then the leading intelligentsia of Europe.

It was in such an atmosphere of hope that highly respected rabbis and scholars assisted those humanists of whose good will they felt assured. This is not the place to discuss in detail the psychological and sociological changes that took place during the sixteenth century. Desperation and hope, in alternation, were the inner forces that propagated first the adaptation of foreign tunes to the older *piyutim*, and later the retention of their melodic incipits as seasonal leitmotifs.

There are at least seventy-five instances of this process available from the sixteenth and early seventeenth century. It would serve no scientific purpose to examine each

of these with the minuteness of the above three instances. The following is merely a listing, from table VI, of a selected number of incipits together with the folk songs or the contrafacts from which they were originally borrowed.[26] The order of the listing is based on the order of the Jewish liturgical year, beginning with the High Holy Days.

Adon Olam for the High Holy Days (table VI, no. 4a). This poem was singled out by Maharil because of its "lovely and long drawn-out melody." The melody given here is only one of many variants of the once famous mocking song "*Das Papstaustreiben*" (Expelling the pope) (*b*). Some German variants are found in *BAL* 631; more interesting and of greater musical and literary importance is the incipit of Oswald von Wolkenstein's *Tagelied*, "*Wach auf mein Hort*" (*c*). In *minhag ashkenaz* the melody was originally sung to an old *piyut*, a fantasy of the mystic chant of the angels, preceding the *Kedushah*, namely *ha-aderet veha'emunah* (see example 2 in chapter 7).

When the rather bombastic *piyut* was forgotten, the tune was saved for the opening hymn of the morning service of the High Holy Days.[27]

A'apid Neser (*table VI, no. 5a*). This is a hymn by Eliezer Kallir. The melody is sung responsorially by the hazan and the congregation. The first half contains a motif that permeates a good deal of the *shaḥarit* service; it recalls an old song, "*Ich hört ein Sichlein rauschen* (*b*), but its lively half-march, half-dance rhythm is that of a *bergamasca*. This rhythm is encountered frequently in the literature (see below). The second half is a choir-refrain and is musically of a later date than the first half.

Yaḥbienu (*table VI, no. 6a*). This poem of the twelfth century, by Isaac ben Samuel, is sung to a melody almost identical to "*Ach Gott wem soll ichs klagen*" (*b*). In *BAL* it is quoted from a famous song collection by G. Foster (1519), who ascribed it to a master by the name of Gresinger.[28] The *pizmon, yashmi'enu . . . salaḥti* belongs to the same melody type.

Abinu malkenu (*table VI, no. 7a*). An ancient litany for the High Holy Days, the *Abinu malkenu* has opening lines by R. Akiba of the second century. Here the Western Ashkenazic tradition, from which the Eastern deviates considerably, will be discussed. In the form transmitted during the nineteenth century every verse is chanted by the hazan and then repeated by the choir or congregation. The many verses are divided into quatrains, in which the second, third, and fourth lines are modulating variations of the first line. The close tone-word relationship (usually an indication of great age) is obvious at first glance. Yet the melodic line is not homogeneous; lines 2 and 3 have different tonalities from those of lines 1 and 4. Line 2 seems to be a simple transposition of 1, but it does not cadence to the tonic. This Dorian cadence resembles the second line of a German song "*Wenn ich des Morgens fru aufste*" (*b*). Line 3 seems to have been taken out of the *Shabuoth* motif (table VI, 1*a*, third motif) and adjusted to the new words, while line 4 harks back to the same German folk song at the words "*Daz wir sie nicht verschrecken, wo lieb*

and lieb beinander leit" (*BAL* 204a). Very likely the first line antedated the others, adapted from the German song, which was popular and had more or less the same rhythm. Where did the first line originate? There is a famous old German tune, the *Bruder Veits Ton*, whose first line is almost identical with *Abinu malkenu.*

Example 6

Example 6 is its hypothetical incipit.[29] It is well known that the *Bruder Veits Ton* was extremely popular among the German Jews.[30] Our litany seems to have made use of its recitative-like structure and adopted it with only minor changes.

The second tune for the *Abinu malkenu* (*c*) is quoted from Idelsohn, and has been well known in *minhag ashkenaz* since the nineteenth century. It was composed by J. Drechsler,[31] probably at the suggestion of Sulzer, and reflects the influence of Beethoven very strongly.

There is yet a third tune, to the text *Abinu malkenu, kotvenu*, quoted in *BT* (no. 1136b), which is a melismatic version of the first line of *a* but is considerably later than the original version.

Ki hiney kaḥomer (*table VI, no. 8a*). This is an old *pizmon* in which man and his destiny are likened to clay in the potter's hand: for this grave, indeed threatening, thought the Ashkenazim used an old drinking song, "*Frisch auf, gut Gsell*" (*b*) (*BAL* 321). One is reminded of Professor Berliner's warning not to pay attention to the content of the German songs, "which do not in the least correspond to the Hebrew text." It was Emanuel Kirschner who first demonstrated the basic identity of the tunes.[32] In this instance we encounter a strict bar form, usual in both popular song and the songs of the Meistersinger. The Hebrew version has an *Abgesang* different from the German original, which uses motifs from the preceding *Stollen.* The Hebrew *Abgesang* is again one of the many *bergamasca*-like ditties that must have been very popular in the seventeenth and eighteenth centuries (example 7). (There will be more discussion of this use of the *bergamasca* later in this chapter.)

Example 7

Adirey ayumah (table VI, no. 9a). Eliezer Kallir based the text on the threefold exclamation "*Adonai melekh, adonai malakh, adonai yimlokh.*"[33] The melody of this refrain is an expansion of the motif for the end of a pericope in scriptural cantillation. The congregation interrupts the hazan three times in each stanza:

> *Hazan:* Mighty giants affirm strongly.
> *Congregation:* The Lord reigneth!
> *Hazan:* Creatures of lightning, loudly they bless.
> *Congregation:* The Lord has reigned!
> *Hazan:* Exalted powers powerfully affirm.
> *Congregation:* The Lord will reign!

The cantor sings his lines in an ornamental paraphrase of a once-popular folk song, "*All mein Gedenken, die ich han* [= *hab*]" (*b*) (*BAL* 127). This tune was so well known in the sixteenth century that even a century later composers used its theme for variations.[34] The technique of ornamentation to which the German tune was subjected in its Hebrew adaptation is typical of the way in which these foreign tunes were "adjusted" to the Jewish background. (This method will be examined later.)

Ledavid barukh (table VI, no. 10a). This is another example of the adaptation of the march-like *bergamasca* to a *piyut*. The *bergamasca* was a dance form that came from Italy (Bergamo) and spread throughout Europe. Shakespeare, for example, mentioned it several times as a dance that was fashionable in England. How the more or less secluded Jews of Germany and eastern Europe heard these dances and folk songs will be discussed later in this chapter. At this point, it will be useful to list those *piyutim* or other texts that were once chanted to somewhat diluted *bergamasca* tunes. In addition to *a*, the best known of these are *La-menatze'ah*, Psalm 67 (*BT* 715), *Adon Olam* for Passover (*BT* 776), *Netilat yadayim* for Passover (*BT* 777), *Omnam ken* (*b*) (*BT* 1319),[35] and *Eder va-hod* (*c*) (*BT* 1274).

Of the six pieces, *Ledavid barukh* and *La-menatze'ah* are used at the close of the Sabbath, *Adon Olam* and *Netilat yadayim* come from the morning services of Passover, and the last two are from the High Holy Days services. The first two are psalm texts, and are not metrical. *Netilat yadayim*, too, is nonmetrical. The remaining three texts are metrical poems, but they do not have the same metrical scheme. Apparently the *bergamasca* rhythm is forced upon the texts, be they metrical or nonmetrical. One of the main characteristics of *minhag ashkenaz* is its tendency to impose, indiscriminately, certain favorite melody patterns on all sorts of texts. And when these texts are forgotten, the main motifs of the tunes they were sung to are saved and used for prayers, either to serve particular liturgical occasions or to indicate them musically.

The use of the *bergamasca* was mentioned earlier in connection with the refrain of *Ki hiney kaḥomer* (table VI, no. 8*a*). That refrain suggests the song "London Bridge is Falling Down." The rhythm of this rogues' dance, as it appeared in the

commedia dell'arte, is a march rhythm of mixed quarter and eighth notes, often combined with a fixed ground bass, such as I-IV-V-I:

J. S. Bach quotes a stylized example of the dance in the second theme of the quodlibet, which appears as the last of his Goldberg Variations; it has been identified as the folk song "*Kraut und Rüben*" (*d*).[36]

Hodu la'donai (*table VI, no. 11a*). This is the festive Psalm 118, as sung on *Sukkoth* (Feast of Tabernacles). This psalm is the climax of the *hallel*, the group of psalms that marks each festival liturgy. Its refrain and the music to which it is sung were considered especially important because they established the mood, the general atmosphere of the holiday: bright and solemn at Passover, majestic at Shabuoth, dance-like and processional-like at Sukkoth, triumphant at Hanukkah, sober at the New Moon. Finally we have the *hallel* of Sukkoth and that of the "Feast of the Law" (Simhath Torah). Each of these assumes a style of its own from the ritual action connected with it. The *hodu* of the first days of Sukkoth accompanies the "shaking of the *lulav*" in the four directions of the compass. This "shaking," with its underlying fertility symbolism, has evoked special rhythms. There are two traditions of the chant: the older one, based on motifs of *Missinai* tunes, in particular those of the prayers for rain and dew, has the following rhythmic pattern,

which seems to imitate the body movements of the solemn shaking;[37] the second tune, not vocal but instrumental in origin, contains some of the clichés of German and Austrian dance music of the last third of the eighteenth century (*b*). It is in exuberant major, while the first tune remains in pure minor throughout.

The *hodu-anah* for Simhath Torah is chanted while the worshipers circle the altar seven times (the *hakafot*) and pray for success and divine help in the forthcoming year. Here we have two traditions that reflect their respective origins: the German and the Moravian.[38] Characteristically, the former (*c*) moves in march-like rhythm, whereas the latter is in slow triple measure (*d*). Yet both are derivatives of the nuclear motif seen in example 8. This is a little *piyut* that is recited at the end of the

Example 8

annual cycle of the Torah reading. Baer, the compiler, cautiously labeled it a "new tune," but in fact it goes back to the incipits of many old German folk songs, such as *BAL* 142 or 335, and especially 89. The strictly triadic line of the melody goes against the basic structure of traditional Jewish *melos*. The song "*Ach Muter gib mir keinen Mann*" (*e*) was included in the song collection of Isaac Wallich, the first Jewish collector of the Ashkenazic folklore.[39]

The chant of the *piyutim* for rain and dew (*tefillot geshem va-tal*) of the last day of Sukkoth and of Passover, respectively, belong to the category of *Missinai* tunes (see chapter 3). Yet integrated in that chant, almost buried in the various ornaments, is one element that detached itself from the *piyut* and became a seasonal leitmotif of Passover, or the Eighth Day of Sukkoth (*Sehemini atzeret*), in the chanting of the so-called *Tal-Geshem Kaddish* (example 9). It permeated entire sections of the chant

Example 9

for the Three Festivals. Idelsohn believed that this characteristic motif was gradually "welded together" from (alien) popular and traditional motifs.[40] So far as I have been able to trace this motif, it seems to come from the medieval Italian *ballata*; in a manuscript in the Vatican (Vaticana Rossi 215) a *ballata minima* of the late fourteenth century contains frequent occurrences of this motif, almost always as embellishment or transition. Yet Idelsohn may be justified in his assumption of a gradual growing together of the alien and the indigenous.

Akedah (*table VI, no. 12a*). The poetic paraphrase of Isaac's "binding" is one of the many insertions into the High Holy Day service.[41] The theme was treated frequently by medieval poets, and *minhag ashkenaz* has preserved the text of at least one poem; it was abbreviated, or omitted entirely, even from many nineteenth-century prayer books. Idelsohn likens this melody to a Christian hymn, "*Jesu, welche Qual hast du gelitten*,"[42] yet the parallels are not too convincing. A more probable parallel is an excerpt from scriptural cantillation (*b*) combined with the incipits of old German parting songs, a kind of *tonus lamentationis* such as "*Jetzt scheiden bringt mir schwer*" or "*Ach Lieb, was zeihst du mich?*" or "*Erlaube mir, feins Maedchen*" (*c*).[43]

Shofet kol ha-aretz (*table VI, no. 13a*). This is a *pizmon* by Solomon ibn Gabirol, a favorite *piyut* of the Sephardim, consisting of stanzas of six lines, three words per line, plus refrain. It is a part of the Ashkenazic Yom Kippur service and is examined here only because of its rather complex musical structure. Again we have a tune that is a potpourri of various melodic phrases popular in the sixteenth century. This is in a way the opposite of the frequent *Zersingen* of folk songs. Here a mosaic is

skillfully constructed so that it gives the impression of organic unity. It is easy, however, to realize that the tune consists of three lines, each corresponding to two lines of the text, plus refrain, chanted by the congregation. Line 1 is an ornamental paraphrase, the first line of the love song "*Mein Freud moecht sich wol meren*" (*b*). As often happened, the popular song was adapted for the Protestant Church very early (1524). The older secular tune first appeared in the *Lochamer Liederbuch* and was probably well known among German Jews. Line 2 also is related to both secular and religious songs. It is best known as "*Lobt Gott den Herrn ihr Heiden*" (Z4533). Line 3 is reminiscent of another love song, "*Jung Fräulein, soll ich mit euch gan,*" which is included in the Wallich collection. The refrain is a variant of line 2. The tune for *Shofet kol ha-aretz* is one of the *cantus firmi* used by Marcello. Today it is forgotten in Italy.

Kol mekadesh shevi'i (*table VI, no. 14a*). This is one of the oldest table songs (*zemirot*) of *minhag ashkenaz*. It appears as early as the *Maḥzor Vitry* (twelfth century).[44] There were a number of Christian religious songs among the older chants of *minhag ashkenaz*, yet it is hard to believe that the German Jews absorbed a song of the church that they knew as such. In all previous cases it was possible to find resemblances either to secular songs or to instrumental music. In this case it was claimed by Kirschner (followed uncritically and without acknowledgment by Idelsohn and later by Sendrey) that the basic secular melody to which it could be traced was the *Bruder Veits Ton*. Yet the identity of that song, as mentioned previously, was pure conjecture, based in turn on a speculation by Franz Boehme, the trustworthy compiler and editor of *BAL*. Boehme's identification of the *Bruder Veits Ton* has proved to be a mistake, however.[45]

Actually the tune of *Kol mekadesh shevi'i* combines three closely related songs (*BAL* 19, 20, 399a), but comes nearest to Adam Reisner's song quoted by Walther Lipphardt, a song called *Abendgesang* (*b*) with the words, "*O Daz ich kunt von Hertzen singen.*"It seems to be a variant of *BAL* 394, "*Lobt Gott ir frommen Christen*" (which Boehme again calls *Bruder Veits Ton*),[46] as well as "*Wolauf, ihr deutschen Christen*" (*c*). Kirschner also makes a comparison to a more recent hymn, "*Der Himmel jetzt frohlocken soll.*" More than a dozen old German songs have phrases similar to this simple Sabbath *zemirah*. This must not be understood in the sense that all eight were familiar to the Jews, but that the *mode*, the *incipit*, and some of the melodic phrases occurred in many contemporaneous songs. They were ubiquitous at the time—in the air.

She'eh ne'esar (*table VI, no. 15a*). This elegy for the fast day of the seventeenth of Tammuz was written by Solomon Ibn Gabirol in the same meter (called *Hazağ*) as the *Adon Olam*.[47] Its tune goes back to the once very popular song "*Wenn ich des morgens frue aufste*" (*b*) and the closely related "*Es wonet lieb bei liebe*" (*c*). The first two *Stollen* are almost identical; but as *Abgesang*, the Hebrew song, in allusion to the fast day, has the scriptural motif of the *sof pasuk* in the cantillation of Lamentations.[48] Example 10 illustrates very clearly how German songs were "Judaized" in the synagogue, just as Gregorian tunes were "Germanized" in the Lutheran Church. The Hebrew verb for "wailing" is clearly depicted in the melody.

Example 10

E. Kirschner, (Hebr. Poesien) IV 6
Va - ti - ba - kah
(and weep- ing was
ha - ir
the ci - - ty)

Zekhor Berit Abraham (table VI, no. 16a). This *pizmon* by Gershon ben Judah recalls, at least in its incipit, the song "*Ich reit einmal zu Braunschweig aus*" (*b*), which corresponds to a religious Protestant contrafact.

Adon Olam of Megillat Vinz (table VI, no. 17a). The Megillah itself is a long poem by Elhanan ben Abraham, of an incident in the history of the Jews of Frankfort. In 1614 one Vinzenz Fettmilch roused an angry mob to attack the Jews, forcing them to flee the city. In 1616, upon imperial edict, the Jews were escorted back to Frankfort in triumph, and Fettmilch was executed. To commemorate the occasion a Frankfort Purim was declared for the twentieth of Adar and observed each year with the reading of this Megillah, and the chanting of the *Adon Olam* to the Vinz tune, with instrumental accompaniment.[49] This seems to be the same as the Pavia tune (*b*).[50]

It is symptomatic of the fluctuating relations between Germans and Jews that the Hebraist J. C. Wagenseil (1633–1705), by no means a friend of the Jews, sponsored, or at least inspired hymns like the following one, which alludes to the *Megillat Vinz* and its tune:

Ein schön Lied, hübsch und bescheidlich	A nice song, lovely and modest
Fuer Weiber und fuer Meidlich	For women and maidens
Zu erkennen Gottes Kraft und macht,	To recognize God's force and power,
Wie der *Shomer Yisrael* hat bei uns gewacht.	In that He watched over us.
Darum tu *hashem letbarekh* loben	Therefore we praise Him, the blessed one
der uns hat geniedert und gehoben	Who has humiliated and uplifted us,
Vinz megilat soll man den *shir* heissen ueberall	Everywhere the song shall be called "*Megillat Vinz*"
Ist soviel als *megillas Antiochus* an der Zahl	Which equals in number the "*Megilat Antiochus,*"
ha'ich ein *niggun* drauf gebracht,	I set it according to a tune
als wie Pavia ist die Schlacht,	Like that of the battle of Pavia,
So sagt Elchonon ein Sohn Avrohom *Sal.*[51]	Thus says Elchonon ben Abraham of blessed memory.

(trans. E. W.)

The expression "humiliated and uplifted" in this hymn alludes to the expulsion and the subsequent triumphal return of the Jews. It is also a veiled quotation of a famous saying of the great Hillel.[52] The line "Which equals in number the *Megilat Antiochus*" indicates the numerical value of "*M*(e)*G*(i)*L*(a) *TV*(I)*NZ*" a cabalistic toying with the numerical value of Hebrew letters; the "Antiochus Scroll" was a popular description of the Maccabean revolt. Elchonon, son of Abraham, is the name of the chronicler mentioned above. The following is the first stanza of his epic song:

> I shall recount the powerful happenings
> And I shall speak of the great deeds of the Lord,
> Signs and wonders shall I report
> In praise, thanksgiving, and glory
> In the entire land and from county to county,
> To draw attention to His miracles.
> I shall exalt my Lord, the King—
> "And Abraham is your name forever and ever."[53]
>
> (trans. E. W.)

According to the text, there are stanzas of eight lines of eight to nine syllables, with three stresses per line. This corresponds with the Pavia tune cited in *BAL* 389 (*b*). There are two other Pavia tunes, but they consist of stanzas with either five or six lines (*BAL* 376, 397, 390), which could not fit the Hebrew text and its accentual stresses.[54] The German Jewish hymn quoted above, however, was a Christian hymn written by J. C. Wagenseil in order to win Frankfort's Jews for his missionary aims.[55]

The Method of Integrating Foreign Tunes

We have treated this last instance in some detail in order to demonstrate that the German Jews, ghetto or no ghetto, were very much au courant with regard to the current folk songs and dances. Aside from the *bergamasca*, *moresca*, *branle*, and the ubiquitous march, German song was absorbed to a remarkable extent during the sixteenth and seventeenth centuries. As suggested above, it was the false dawn of the new humanism, which beguiled German Jewry when the Middle Ages gave way to the Renaissance. They were under the illusion that they too might benefit from the new concept of man, and it took almost a century for them to grasp fully that they were tolerated only as long as they were needed. When the fair dream turned into a nightmare, the Ashkenazim had already squandered part of their inner strength, and had contaminated their organic and actively assimilating tradition with a heavy ballast of foreign contraband.

What was assimilated, and how was the foreign matter integrated? These two questions have thus far been ignored by all writers on Jewish music. Nearest to posing the question, if not answering it, was that constant pioneer Eduard Birnbaum, in his two *Liturgische Uebungen*. Those publications, however, were available to only a small number of German cantors before World War I.

The first question can be answered with a certain degree of accuracy: in the three special examples, and the subsequent fourteen in table VI, about twenty incipits of secular songs are adduced for comparison, as against eight religious intonations. This alone indicates the inclination of the German Jews for nonpolitical, nonchurchly sources. The very same tendency prevails in the Wallich collection (see note 43), in which all Christian references in the songs are carefully altered or eliminated. Thus the original text of "*Jesum das Laemmlein*" is edited as "*dem allmaechtigen Gott allein.*" We may therefore assume with a fair degree of certainty that the German Jews, more open-minded than before toward German tunes, had adopted a few of the catchier ones, carefully limiting themselves to nonpolitical, nonreligious, "neutral" texts. All of these secular tunes move in straight duple or in mixed duple-triple time, indicating the old Jewish inclination toward march-like rhythms.[56] This preference was evident from the numerous tunes in the meter of the *bergamasca* and the *moresca* mentioned above. The trend toward a somewhat vulgar type of song became stronger during the seventeenth and eighteenth centuries, presaging that approximation to the ill-mannered *Gassenhauer*, which was one of the reasons for the opposition of the rabbis, and which initiated the decline of Jewish musical tradition. More and more alien elements were adopted, without any adjustment or integration.

Almost all of the German or Polish tunes that were paraphrased by the Jews appeared in print in the sixteenth century. However, many of them antedate the printing of music and were known in handwritten form. It would be rash to assume that their integration into Jewish tradition occurred simultaneously with their first appearance. Assuredly that did not happen. The inclination toward the *bergamasca* and similar rough-stepping dances should lead us to doubt that this integration took place much earlier than the end of the sixteenth or the first third of the seventeenth century.

Turning now to the second question posed above, we seek to ascertain the precise way in which foreign tunes were assimilated into *minhag ashkenaz*. Two examples from table VI will help to clarify the process. First we observe *Adirey ayumah* (9*a*) and the German song that it resembles, "*All mein Gedenken*" (9*b*). While the Hebrew text has fewer syllables per line than the German, the melody of the verse is a full measure longer. This lengthening is obtained not only through ornamental devices, but from the actual insertion of the leading motif of the *tal-geshem Kaddish* (see example 9), which dominates the subsequent *musaf tefillah*. This borrowing of a familiar motif from the *Missinai* melody rendered the strange new tune familiar and associative to the listeners. Yet the German text counts six stresses per line, whereas the Hebrew verse has only five.

In another example from the table, "*Shofet kol ha-aretz*" (13*a*), we find a similar lengthening of the tune in the Hebrew song from four to five measures. The inserted measure is easily identified as the penultimate one in the Hebrew. The extension consists, again, of a borrowed old motif, this time from scriptural cantillation. There is little additional ornamentation, but a certain propensity to recitative-like intonation, approximating the *Sprechgesang* that was, of course, most familiar to Jewish worshipers.

The practice of "disguising" the foreign tunes under a heavy mantle of ornaments began in the sixteenth century; it reached its peak in the middle of the nineteenth century. Originally a device to camouflage Gentile tunes, it became more and more the pretext for cantors to show off their voices in coloratura arias. The intrusion of Italian opera manners in the Ashkenazic synagogue dates from the seventeenth century, and lasts, at least in the eastern European synagogue and its American derivatives, up to this very day (particularly in the old Orthodox synagogues of New York). Before the corrupting influence of Italian opera became dominant, the technique of cantorial ornamentation served as a formative stimulus toward the gradual "modernization" of the synagogal *melos*.

The favorite vocal ornaments of the old cantors were, in general, modest peri-heletic ornaments: trills, patterns of changing and neighboring notes, plus the dearly beloved chains of sequences, which in the older manuscripts are kept within moderate limits. The most conspicuous result of the ornamentation of foreign tunes is the decrease of the time units; if the half note was the general unit of Western music, during the Renaissance in the synagogue it became the quarter note, and then, in the eighteenth century, it became the eighth note. This must have lent a certain excitement, or restlessness, to the musical air of the synagogue. Gentile listeners referred to it, often maliciously, as the "*vox clamorosa Judaeorum*." The gradual opening of the synagogue's repertoire to European music created new tasks for the cantor. He had to become an expert in "ornamenting" or disguising foreign tunes and in adjusting them to the traditional background. This demanded some mastery of the technique of variation.

When the dynamism of the Renaissance began to ebb, the lovely dream of a new Jewish dignity faded away, and the dreary fight for survival was renewed. Freedom of movement was one of the first victims of the political developments that began in the seventeenth century. For the character of *minhag ashkenaz* this was of decisive importance. The Baroque age opened with a Jewry that was condemned to sit still when attacked, while its physical survival became a bargaining commodity for princes, cities, guilds, and court Jews.

Appendix: The Melodies of the Jews in the Popular Passion and Easter Plays[1]

All through the High Middle Ages and the Renaissance the Jews were caricatured in the popular Passion and Easter plays. They are represented sometimes as individuals, sometimes as personification of the Synagogue. Occasionally the personification of the Synagogue is a noble one, as in the famous sculpture in the Strasbourg cathedral. Otherwise it takes the form of a singing "*Judenschul*" (local synagogue) chanting a linguistic and musical gibberish—supposedly Hebrew songs—in the manner of the *Cados* motet, or the synagogue scene from the *Amfiparnasso* by Orazio Vecchi.

Of the handful of such plays, the Lucerne Easter play is probably the richest in "*Juden-Gesang.*" It contains no less than fourteen folios of such songs, some of them tragic, some of them scurrilous.[2] Example A1 is the author's transcription of three of them.

Example A1

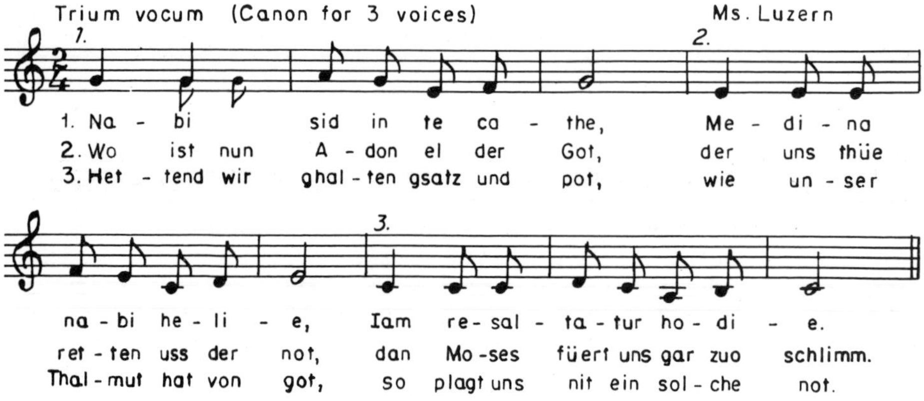

Translation: The Lord prophet in *te cathe* [?]
In the land of God's Prophet
Today dances joyously.
Where is now the Lord God (*Adon el*)
Who would rescue us from our hardship
For Moses leads us all too severely.
If we had obeyed the Law and its statutes
Which our Talmud had received from God,
Such a need would not plague us. Halleluja,
halleluja, halleluja, tetragrammaton Adonai.

Translation: [tentatively] Holy as in the beginning in the synagogue as He is.

Example A2 has a text in Latin hexameters (from the Palm Sunday graduale), and contains a translation of Psalm 118:25 plus "*Osanna in excelsis.*"

Example A2

Ms. Luzern
(Disticha)
de - - - cus pro - mi - sit O - san - na pi - um.
Is - ra - - el es tu rex da - vi - dis et
in - - cli - ta pro - les: no - mi - ne qui in do -
- - mi - ni rex be - ne - dic - - te ve - nis.
Ge - be - ne - dy - et sy der Her - - -
- - re Gott, der da kompt im na - men dess Her -
- - - ren bott. O - - - - - -
- - - - - san - - - - - - na
in der hö - - - - - he Gott

In M. Blakemore Evan's fine monographs, *The Passion Play of Lucerne*, the Jewish songs [*Judengesaenge*] are discussed and interpreted by Professor Gustave O. Arlt, who, not unjustly, calls the texts a "mixture of sense and nonsense." However, he is less than correct when he identifies a number of words as deriving from "current magic incantations."[3] He apparently did not recognize that they were almost all pure Hebrew words taken from the Hebrew Bible, for example: *Adonai*, *Heli* [= *Eli*], *Adonel* [= *adon el*], *Schemhamforas* [= *shem ha-m'forash* = the ineffable Name]. There is also the Greek word *tetragrammaton* [= YHWH = the ineffable Name].

Of the twenty-five "chants of the Jews" all but one or two are kept in clear major keys. Professor Arlt draws attention to some parallels in folios 2 and 8 with Protestant chorales. The more vivacious tunes smack strongly of children's songs, mocking and dancing ditties such as example A3. Only two short passages show some similarity with motifs of *minhag ashkenaz*, in folios 2 and 11–12. Folio 2 contains a three-part round that begins with the seasonal motif of the evening service of the High Holy Days (see chapter 3, examples 8a and b). In folio 11 there are two three-part canons (examples A4 and A5), written more clearly than the round in folio 2. They are not recognized as canons by Professor Arlt.

Two very interesting items occur in folios 11 and 12. These pieces, "*Messias, o hallae*" and "*Transit ad patres Lazarus*," both contain typical phrases from *Missinai* tunes, stylized in the manner of the late sixteenth century. All of the "Jews' tunes" are in straight, mostly duple meter. There are passages that sound slightly Jewish but are actually a musical gibberish, just as such words as "alla calla malla alla willa

Example A3

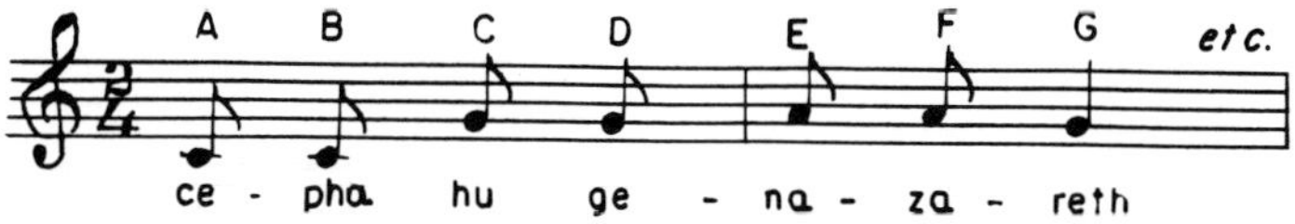

wigrui rui pfu pfu" are a linguistic gibberish, alleging to be a Hebrew sentence. This naive kind of imitation of the Hebrew sounds is quite different from the actual Hebrew and Greek words in the hymns of the Codex Calixtinus of Santiago de Compostela (see above, p. 93).

There remains only the question of who transmitted these expressions and bits of melody. Genuine Hebrew words such as *gamma hu* [= *kamokha, kamohu*] occur in so many Passion plays in so many locales and centuries that one cannot assume that they were transmitted by individuals. Rather, one must think in terms of widespread traditions, probably handed down by wandering musicians and *Baenkelsaenger*.[4] This conjecture of tradition by entire permanent groups of transmitters corresponds with the provenance of many Germanic elements in *minhag ashkenaz*.

In all of these texts, as well as in many of the pictures of the period, the Jew appears as a comic figure. There is no evidence of the slightest empathy with the

Example A4

Ms. Luzern

Solution of canon 2 on fol XI

Example A5

Ms.Luzern

Solution of canon 1 on fol. XI

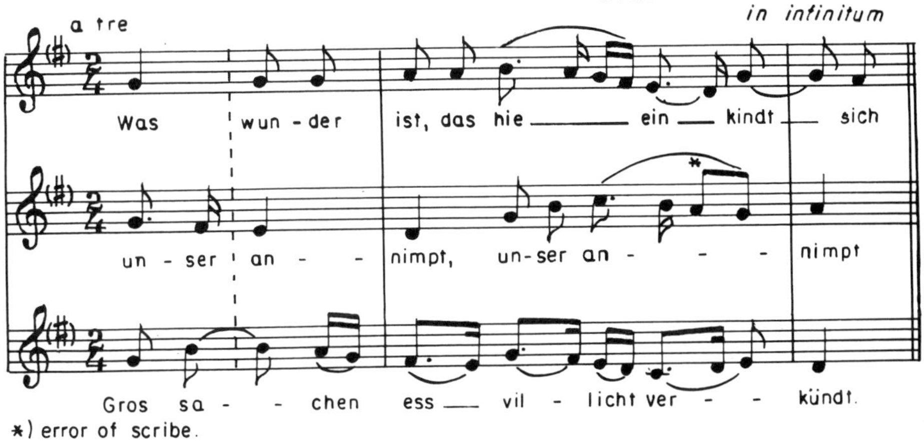

*) error of scribe.

Jews' tragic lot, nor of the faintest trace of Christian compassion in these folk plays. It is truly terrifying (perhaps less to the Jews, who have learned their lessôn in centuries of bitter experience, than to others) to observe that exactly the same merry and sneering laughter as that of the medieval jester or popular play accompanied the slaughter of millions of Jews in the Nazi popular press, notwithstanding the supposed "enlightenment" of more than two centuries. The same brand of humor was present in the old *Planctus Judaei* which was discussed and quoted in chapter 3.

7

The Synagogue of the Baroque

If all men of weak mind were equally haughty, and were ashamed of nothing and feared nothing, how could they still be kept together and within bounds? The mob is terrible, unless it is afraid. (Terret vulgus, nisi metuat.)

(Spinoza, *Ethics*)

The Intrinsic Conflict

How wide the world still was, in Europe of the seventeenth and eighteenth centuries, the era of the far-ranging Baroque! It encompassed simultaneously some of the crassest contrasts and antitheses. Spinoza had to witness the fraudulent Messianism of Sabbatai Zevi. Two protagonists of rationalist philosophy, Leibniz and Hume, were contemporaries of the Jewish mystic called the Baal Shem, founder of Hasidism. And two generations earlier, while the philosopher Pascal penned his lofty thoughts on God, good, and evil, hundreds of thousands of Jews were massacred by Ukranian Cossacks.

The mass murder was perpetrated at the end of the Thirty Years' War, which plunged most of Europe into misery, ruin, and devastation. Yet not long thereafter the greatest luxury, the highest artistic and sensuous refinements, could be admired in Versailles. Every one of two dozen German princelings felt he had to imitate this royally pompous style. Gold, silk, perfumes (but not clean water!) were the marks of the age. Under the genius of Newton, Leibniz, Huygens, and Pascal, mathematics began its brilliant rise and helped men to navigate the seas and chart the paths of the planets; yet at the very same time three Jews were burned in Berlin for having "purchased" a Christian child for magic or ritual purposes. Intellectual subtleties were admired while brutality was hardly concealed; the social graces were at their height while moral disgraces were public knowledge, though generally concealed.

At the very time when the plight of the Eastern Jews had reached the point of absolute hopelessness, a Jew—Jacob Bassevi Treuenberg of Prague (1662), born Jacob ben Samuel—became the first Jewish nobleman in the realm of the Hapsburg *Erblanden* (hereditary provinces).[1]

The Jewish Situation Before and After The Thirty Years' War

Central European Jewry was beset by external and internal dangers: free movement was threatened, the emperor's authority was weakened, Christian proselytism made inroads in its communities, and the intrusion of cabalistic prayers ruined the traditional unity of the Synagogue and alienated many worshipers.

The situation of the Jews in Germany proper was different from that of their brothers under direct Hapsburg rule in Bohemia, Moravia, Silesia, Upper and Lower Austria, Styria, Carinthia, the Tyrol, and parts of northern Italy. *Minhag ashkenaz* was then established in all of the German-speaking *Kronlaender*, but not in Hungary or occupied Italy. In the Hapsburg countries the Jews had to deal directly with the emperor or his closest relatives, who were governors of the hereditary lands. While the Jewish position was aggravated by the fanaticism of the Counterreformation, which most princes of the house of Hapsburg heartily endorsed, the Jews generally escaped the threat of expulsion.

In Germany proper, the Jews had to come to terms with their regional rulers; their middleman was often a court Jew. That his life was in constant peril is well known. Yet he was different from his brothers in that he was free to trade, to travel, and live very much as he liked. However, his amassed fortunes would only in rare cases be inherited by his children; more often than not, they were deprived of their rightful legacies.

Another danger, more subtle, became apparent: in those countries where the population was permitted to sympathize openly with the Reformation, strong missionary centers arose to proselytize the Jews. Normally these efforts did not achieve much success. However, when the missions began to include the services of learned Hebraists, a degree of friendliness developed between them and some Jews. The syndrome of anti-Papism, puritanism, and pietism seemed not wholly unacceptable. Men like Wagenseil and Osiander (father and son), thoroughly familiar with the Hebrew language and the customs of the Jews, devoted their lives to securing a mass conversion of European Jewry. In their wake, the pietists, who were close to the spirit of the Bible, appeared to be sympathetic to Jews, and prayed earnestly that they might "see the light."[2] Wagenseil persuaded a leading Protestant theologian, Jacob Spener, to champion the mission among the Jews. In the resulting prayers we encounter such passages as "May He grant us... wisdom and charity, so that we, for the sake of the *one Jew, Jesus*, may be of loving kindness toward all his brethren after the flesh...."[3]

A Jewish account describes the situation as follows: "The sufferings of the thirty years' war produced a state of pious devotion and engendered a sort of messianic pining, as such hopes constitute the comfort and blessings of the wretched ones.... What could be more natural, than such a mood in the turmoils of the time—and that it caused many to think of that point, where all messianic hopes were stored and surrounded by a splendid sacred halo—Biblical Judaism?"[4]

Threatened externally and internally, the central and eastern European Jews deemed any kind of escape desirable, whether physical or spiritual. A few doors,

and a vast region (the American continent) opened to them. Marranos and Portuguese Jews had found their way to America and had thrived there. Freedom of movement was the crucial condition, possible in the north and south, more difficult to achieve from the east. Only the central European Jews, especially those in small duchies, were immobile. Oddly enough, it was the footloose cantors, driven by hunger and insecurity, who found ways of wandering from place to place. Originally undertaken in flight from the murderous Cossack hordes, the cantors' migrations became adventures, after 1670, somewhat similar to those of wandering apprentices [*Gesellenreise*].

Thus, next to the much-envied *Hofjuden*, and the newly-arrived Marranos from Holland, who were looked upon rather askance, it was the traveling hazanim who, legally or not, enjoyed free movement. Together with their rabbinic antagonists, they constituted a sort of nomadic fraternity, who voluntarily and willingly renounced that highest aim of German Jewry: the eagerly desired *Staettigkeit* (security of settlement), which stood at the core of every privilege granted by the secular authorities. The large number of cantors fleeing westward heightened the competition for permanent positions. Some of their sharp practices, so offensive to the rabbis, were caused by the special dilemma of the hazanim; were they to be well-paid virtuosi, or starving saints?

Ḥazanut and Its Critics

The antagonism between the rabbi and the appointed hazan or cantor—not the lay precentor—goes back to the time when the hazan introduced and intoned the new *piyutim*, which most rabbis considered at best superfluous and at worst abominable. This occurred through the centuries from the eighth to the twelfth. Yet it was only during the sixteenth and seventeenth centuries that rabbinic criticism became truly vicious, though—it must be admitted—not without some good reason. The objections were directed against what the rabbis thought were the cantors' offenses and transgressions. Some are quoted in detail here, since they provide a representative picture of contemporary synagogue music, its performance practice, and the life in the German synagogue before the Emancipation.

Rabbi Samuel Archevolti (1515–1611), a poet and literary critic, differentiated between the two types of melody chanted in the synagogue. The first is dignified, suits the words of the prayer, and is expressive of its sentiments. The second is vulgar [*hamoni*] and is in no way reflective of the text, so that it is as distant from the first type as is East from West.[5]

Rabbi Yuspa Hahn (1568?–1637), by no means as erudite as Archevolti, repeated more or less the same arguments. He wanted to forbid the use of "foreign tunes" [*niggunim nekharim*] and opposed those sophists [*mit-hakmim*] who excused the practice with the claim that the true chant had been stolen from the Jews [*niggunim genuvim*].[6]

Rabbi Solomon ben Ephraim Lentschitz (near Prague, early seventeenth century) complained that Gentile "lords" sometimes capriciously appointed cantors and shofar-blowers. So long as the cantors did not possess a solid foundation in the

liturgy, they would pronounce the words incorrectly and misguide the boy-choristers in their charge. The *piyutim* which they sang were beyond their comprehension. . . . "Thus it can happen that ignorant men may learn the traditional tunes and usurp positions as cantors. . . ."[7]

Rabbi Menahem di Lonzano (1572–1619) in *Shtey Yadot* (Two Hands, Venice, 1615–1618) reported that few of the rabbis objected to the cantors who adapted [*mitḥabrim*] the songs and praises [*shirim ushebaḥot*] to tunes of Gentile origin. Yet the cantors were ignorant and obeyed no law. But nothing was more contemptible than the cantors who began a Hebrew song and then confused its text with similar-sounding words of a foreign language. Here Lonzano quoted a few rather amusing examples.[8]

Rabbi Benjamin Aron ben Abraham Salnik (1550–1619) warned that anyone who possessed a good voice and functioned in a synagogue should take great care not to sing "foreign tunes" [*niggunim nekharim*], for this constituted a sin [*aberah*].[9] They should not indulge in drawn-out vocalises [*me'arikhin niggunim*], for during this artful "spinning out" of melodies they could not be engrossed in their devotion [*kavanah*], and their only aim should be to please the listeners. He closed with the accusation: "Lengthening melodies causes the lengthening of our exile" [*arikhut ba-kolot hu arikhut hagalut*].[10]

Rabbi Joel Sirkes (1561–1640) of Cracow gave a formal ritual responsum (1596–1597) to the question of whether it is permitted to sing in the synagogue melodies which are also sung in the Christian churches. Sirkes argued that some of these melodies were originally Jewish, and proceeded to the heart of the question, the prohibition against imitating the customs of the Gentiles [*hukat ha-goyim*]. He quoted as precedent the decision of the rabbis against R. Judah the Prince, who objected to the use of the sword by Jews in punishing criminals, on grounds that it was Roman custom. To him the rabbis replied that the Jews had not learned the use of the sword from the Romans. Therefore, Sirkes argued, the *halakhah* was not with R. Judah. Similarly, the Jews did not learn these tunes from the Christians, but through the study of the art of music.[11]

Rabbi Jehudah Leib Zelichower (second half of the seventeenth century), in his *Shirey Yehudah (Songs of Judah)* (Amsterdam, 1697), spoke as *laudator temporis peracti* and objected to the many "foreign and strange songs" [*shirot nekharim vezarim*], which the old masters would not have tolerated, for most of them were borrowed from "the theaters." He then listed a great number of offenses and sins committed by the hazanim of his time. "They love long vocalises for *Kedushah, Barekhu, Kaddish* on Sabbath and holiday," so that it became impossible to maintain true devotion; they also indulged in idle chatter [*siḥa batalah*] during the service. Finally the author objected to the "helpers" of the hazan [*meshorerim*, etc.]. Either they raced through the texts or they drew out single syllables. "All this did not exist in the good old days."

Rabbi Solomon Lipschütz (1675–1758), in his *Te'udat Shelomo (Solomon's Testimony)* (Offenbach, 1715–1718), came to the defense of the hazanim, for he was convinced that no hazan could do justice to his office without knowledge of the art of music [*be-lo yediyat ha-musikah*], which, as he had learned from Moscato's

book *Nefutzot Yehudah*, belonged to the seven arts and sciences. He did criticize many bad habits of the cantors, and he seemed to be alluding to the great experiment of Salomone de' Rossi and his protector, R. Yehudah Leon da Modena: "Such singing is like prayer without true devotion [*be-lo kavanah*], and the singers in the synagogue find themselves at a crossroad [*al parashat derakhim*] and often do not know which is good, which is evil."[12] He appeared to be the first of the cantors who championed the introduction of art music in the face of the bitterly antagonistic rabbinate of his time.

Thereafter, it was mainly the question of the use of instruments in the synagogue, and the struggle of art music with the "traditional" that became the main concern of all rabbinical observations.[13]

Rabbi Yehudah Leib Puchowitzer, a "wandering Rabbi," in *Kevod ḥakhamim (Honor of the Wise)* (Venice, 1699–1700), took a rather positive attitude toward instrumental music in the synagogue. He used theological arguments with a cabalistic slant. For example, he argued that since the welcoming of the Sabbath [*Kabbalat Shabbat*] as a bride, a queen, a source of joy and rest was obviously instituted by divine inspiration, it would be senseless to forbid the expression of joy by musical instruments and singers, provided the Sabbath laws were not violated.[14] Here Idelsohn was undoubtedly correct when he ascribed the growing trend toward instrumental music to cabalistic ideas coming from Palestine, especially at the time of Sabbatai Zevi!

Rabbi Sabbatai Bass (1641–1718), author of *Siftey yeshenim (Lips of the Sleepers)* (Amsterdam, 1579–1580), claimed that instrumental music was a regular custom of the Meisl-Schul in Prague[15] and mentioned the use of an organ and stringed instruments [*ugab u-nebalim*] at the Friday evening service.

Rabbi Lippmann Yom-tob Heller (1579–1654) was a widely traveled rabbi. Of all the authorities quoted hitherto, he and his contemporary, R. Leon da Modena, were the most respected. He was a man of courage, but also of almost autocratic authority. This is evident in his "*ex-cathedra*" criticism of the hazanim, which had its roots not in questions of personal taste but in rabbinic doctrine. In his *Dibrey ḥamudot*, a commentary on R. Asher's exposition of the talmudic treatise *Berakhot*, he chastised the cantors for their arrogance and haughtiness. He explained a rather curious passage about R. Judah the Prince's strange behavior as precentor and said: "If the cantors put their hands on their cheeks while raising their voices, there is nothing wrong with that." This was an old custom already referred to in the Talmud. Rabbi Lippmann Heller would not permit any other gesture with the hands, especially putting them on the hips, usually considered a sign of arrogance. "They must be prevented from such deportment." Yawning or shaking their heads while singing (even today a favorite habit, especially of female singers) was disgraceful [*gnai hu*]. In general, he added, this misbehavior was found only in "these countries," meaning the countries of *minhag ashkenaz*, whereas elsewhere the cantors were content to sing, not to shout or make noise.[16]

In a quite different argument, sharply satiric in tone, the cantors and their helpers were blamed and accused on many counts. The anonymous pamphlet "*Sh'loshah tzo'akim ve'eynam me'anim*" (Three cry out but are not answered—the pun of the

title is untranslatable) originated during the second half of the seventeenth century, as Israel Adler has demonstrated convincingly.[17] This rhymed satire is the first bitter caricature of the cantor's practice of adding two "helpers," a *Bass* and a *Singer*, to his own voice. One of the first references to this new practice is found in a responsum of R. Yehudah Leon da Modena (1571–1648), the chief rabbinic authority on music up to the middle of the nineteenth century, when his liberal humanist attitude was replaced by the reactionary decisions of R. Moses Sofer-Schreiber (1763–1839). Rabbi Leon decried what he called the habit of Ashkenazic communities of permitting the "assistants to the hazan" to sing "an aria without rhyme or reason."[18]

In the pamphlet, the indictment of the "assistants" is more articulate and stringent: "merciless shouting, window breaking, crying, pressing their ears with their hands . . . and truly, their voices are pleasant to him who has no ears. Their boss is the hazan. . . . He stands in the middle. . . ."[19]

An accumulation of these objections forms a rather bitter section of another anonymous pamphlet full of scorn, "*Tokhekhah megulah*" (Open Reprimands), inserted in a rabbinic study by R. Hanokh Henich of Shaittach (in Styria) called *Reshit Bikkurim* (*The First Fruits*), in the last third of the seventeenth century.[20] There we encounter the following complaints: "They are often ignorant of rabbinic literature, and are unfamiliar with the prayer book. They often read too fast, and with bad articulation. They rest their elbows on the pulpit by putting their hands, which ought to be folded and at rest, on their jaws, temples, or throats. They introduce—into the most holy passages—some gibberish or incomprehensible words or syllables, such as da da da, la la, or they tear words apart. On the New Year or Day of Atonement, they ruin many prayers, especially *abot* or *alenu* or *ohila la'el* (see chapter 3). The cantors tarry with their singsong, while on the other hand they rush through the *piyut* that is part of these permanent prayers [*tefillot keva*] in such haste that no galloping rider could catch them. Moreover, they use quite an assortment of non-Jewish tunes, and make potpourris of many melodies at the memorial service and its *Kaddish* for the deceased, in order to entertain the listeners; in this way and by such behavior devotion becomes a mockery and subject to ridicule."[21]

Turning now to more commendatory reports, we add three interesting vignettes of the Prague synagogues. Next to Venice, the old community of Prague, some of its rabbis, and its hazanim and music lovers were the true champions of new style; they did not attain it, but it matured a hundred and fifty years after their time, with Salomon Sulzer and his confreres.

Rabbi Solomon Lipschütz, who was quoted earlier, gave a most enthusiastic picture of synagogue life in Prague at the beginning of the eighteenth century. There were new melodies to be heard on each holiday. Many hazanim came from outlying places, so as to learn from their Prague colleagues, and "they were not ashamed to do so" [*Lomdim mehem velo boshu*].[22] He lamented that those days were gone. "Each one wraps himself in the *talit* that is not his, and nobody wants to learn from his fellowman . . . and they are ignorant of the rules of music."

Generally praised as a celebrated hazan of Prague was a certain Yokele. Idelsohn has given detailed information about this Yokele (originally from Galicia).[23]

Glückel of Hameln (1646–1714) heard him in Metz and thought he had a phenomenal voice.[24] The traveler Abraham Levi heard him in Prague later than 1718, and praised him as famous in all of Europe. Levi also reported that the Prague synagogues made use of organ and cymbals, specifically "*klappen-zymbels*" (clavicymbals) and violins. "In particular, every Friday they determine with which music they shall receive the Sabbath, and not alone the songs of the so-called hymn of praise [*Lekha dodi*], but they also play very lovely pieces, after its conclusion, which takes perhaps one more hour, as the time is still early [before sundown, and the start of the Sabbath]."[25]

This report of a Jewish visitor, together with the other remarks on instrumental music in Prague's synagogue, may astonish us today by their calm, matter-of-fact tone. They contrast most favorably with the wild polemics on the question of instrumental music, particularly organ music in the synagogue, indulged in a century or more later by "liberals" and "conservatives" at many rabbinical conventions.[26]

A Gentile observer, the Frankfort chronicler J. J. Schudt, wrote in benevolent mockery about the instrumental music in pious Jewish Prague, and some of his remarks are quite entertaining today. In one of his passing observations he put his finger on the heart of the problem of all Jewish music: although God had commanded through Moses that there be a beautiful "musical harmony" for his service, only the ancient Jews paid attention to the command. It was perplexing to find music so little appreciated among the Jewry of his time, for "the Jewish *letzim* (clowns, vulgar musicians) are common music-makers [*gemeine Spielleute*] and mere beer fiddlers; and at the divine service no instrumental music whatever is heard, except in a few places such as Prague." (Wagenseil blamed the Jews for this poverty in more extreme terms: "You have no string music, although King David commanded it at God's behest.")

Schudt quoted details about the music in the Prague synagogues: "There are thirteen synagogues in Prague, of which the smallest is larger than the largest in Frankfort. In the Alt-Neu Schul they have an organ, which is very rare among Jews; it is played only on Friday eve shortly before the approach of the Sabbath, which is... welcomed as a *kallah* or bride in the song *lekha dodi likrat kallah*."[27]

In another passage we learn more about the organ builder and also its first player, a certain R. Meir Mahler. His name appears in the description of a Jewish parade in Prague on the occasion of the birth of a Hapsburg crown prince in 1706 (the archduke Leopold, who died in the same year).[28] An orchestra (of Jewish musicians) was hired, in addition to nineteen trumpeters, eight violinists, four tympanists, and "a new organ, made by R. Meir Mahler, which had cost more than four hundred florins...." A similar parade had taken place in 1678, where, among other instruments, three portative organs were employed.[29]

A minor satirical item may be added here, as it sheds light on the views of German Christians about cantorial singing and the adoption of German tunes. Johann Christian Wagenseil ended his less than philosemitic book *Sota* (on the Talmud) with some sneering words, in the form of an epitaph, on a cantor then well known and respected; it is here quoted in my translation from the Latin: "So that you

finally may have a good belly laugh, ye readers, I shall fill the rest of the page with a Jewish funeral lamentation upon the passing of a man who in our century shone—the Rabbi Lippmann, who served in the synagogue of Prague in the office of precentor." This elevated beginning is then followed by some trivial Judeo-German verses.[30]

At this point in the discussion, we pause to consider the growing loss of genuine traditional substance in *minhag ashkenaz*. It is necessary to define, or at least indicate, the point where the integrating powers of active assimilation failed and gave way to fashionable influences from the affluent outside world. Before the seventeenth century the majority of the tunes used in *minhag ashkenaz* were not felt as alien, but in later melodies one senses the strong endeavor on the part of the cantors to assimilate themselves to German or Italian art music. These attempts must have satisfied the congregations (although the rabbis protested), but to us the efforts that were made to compose art music without any musical education, even without knowledge of musical notation, do sound ludicrous indeed. We must judge them objectively today, and not yield to any sentimental impulse to justify them simply because they were products of the ghetto.

It added little to our understanding of the admittedly controversial style of Baroque synagogue music when Idelsohn termed it an "*ars nova*." That description is at once confusing and inapplicable. Nor did Cecil Roth's writings on the subject advance our perception to any great degree. To speak as he did of the intrinsic "drawbacks" of synagogue music and to make judgments from a frame of reference based on second- and third-hand sources can hardly add to the clarification of the subject.[31]

Undoubtedly new elements had entered the synagogue and its ritual. Was this just the "wind from the East"? Or was it caused by the limited cataclysm of the breakdown of the Sabbatean movement, or even the pseudo-security after the Thirty Years' War? Symptoms of the new era were well observed by the Jews; one such symptom was the liberalism of the humanists—so great that the Jewish astronomer and mathematician David Gans (1541–1613) could establish contact with the great Kepler, and still not forget his rabbinic training acquired under R. Moses Isserles, co-author of the *Shulhan Arukh*. On the other hand, Gans's younger contemporary, R. Lippmann Heller, was denounced by his Jewish enemies as a blasphemer of Christianity. In similar fashion, Spinoza was denounced by the elders of his own synagogue to the city government of Amsterdam. The inner coherence of the Jewish establishment displayed dangerous rifts. Through these, the ideas of the Gentile environment, turbulent and unfathomable, broke into the world of Ashkenazic Jewry. Among these new forces and ideas were also musical elements, especially from the Italian opera, and from the German and Austrian Baroque instrumental music.

Seventeenth-Century Sources

When appraising the Ashkenazic synagogue music of the seventeenth century, we must first take stock of those sources that are available in printed or written form.

Before 1730, the following items were, and, more important, still *are* accessible: the various notations of the "*trop*" and its Masoretic accents (see chapter 5); a few popular melodies for the domestic ritual of the Passover seder (see chapter 9); the synagogue compositions (art music) by Rossi, Carlo Grossi, Lidarti, and a few more commissioned by various Netherlandish, French, and Italian communities;[32] six tunes, out of eleven culled from *minhag ashkenaz* and Sephardic tradition, identified and printed in Gregorian notation as *Intonazione degli Ebrei Tedeschi* by Benedetto Marcello, with Hebrew text printed under the notes (see chapter 6, note 12).

To these must be added tunes that were written down or printed later—mainly during the nineteenth century—that had their origins in the seventeenth or early eighteenth century. To establish the dates of these, and to verify the conjectures, the following criteria will be applied: (1) tonality of major-minor versus (older) modality; (2) fixed metrical structure versus (older) free recitative; (3) triadic, bugle-like motifs versus (older) tetrachordal elements; (4) mixture of German with Hebrew words; (5) attempts to imitate instrumental effects; (6) use of older leading motifs; (7) excessive and non-organic ornaments.[33]

We shall investigate some of the tunes and forms that originated during the time span, roughly speaking, of the years 1590–1730 in the following order: Judeo-German contrafacts of German original tunes; Ashkenazic tunes notated by Marcello; the ritual of welcoming the Sabbath, and its tunes; tunes notated by R. Henle Kirchhan; Gentile caricatures of Hebrew melodies.

Contrafacts. Every student of folklore is familiar with this device, described in a previous chapter. Important for our quest are those examples of German folk tunes with secular texts that were later changed to newer religious poems of the Reformation and Counterreformation. Such *geistliche Kontrafakturen* (religious contrafacts) appear also in the Hebrew liturgy, as was well known to rabbis and cantors. They often wrote in their manuscripts of prayers, or *piyutim*, the incipit of another text, whose melody was to be used for their new piece. A classic example is the instruction given in the *Megillat Vinz* (see chapter 6), where the poet-hazan Elchanan says that this poem should be sung to the tune of *Pavia*, well known in German folk lore.

During the sixteenth century and even later, certain *piyutim* were furnished with similar instructions as to their melodies. An entire list of such Hebrew contrafacts was compiled from the collection of *piyutim* in the possession of the late Professor David Kaufmann of the Budapest Rabbinic Seminary. One must be grateful indeed to the diligent scholar Solomon Widder, who described the collection so appreciatively.[34]

Of the many contrafacts faithfully listed as *laḥanim (Weisen)* only a few of the best-known incipits cited are mentioned here: *Ana bekor'enu, Yishtabaḥ, Lo bikashti, al ne'eratz, le-da'agtekha.* Unfortunately, the original tunes of these texts are not known, so that we cannot today apply them to the newer *piyutim*. Only that of *Yishtabaḥ* has been more or less well preserved since the end of the eighteenth century.

The transplantation of melodies from one original Hebrew text to a later one appears, however, as only a small component of a much larger category of contrafacts. Indeed, there are several manuscripts in the Bodleian Library that contain religious poems consisting of German and Hebrew words in an apparently carelessly naive mixture, resulting in a strange jargon. A few examples may illustrate this close interlacing of two languages by virtue of song incipits:

To the tune of "*Halb schwarz, halb weiss*":

Ein Gesang will ich singen	A song I shall sing
Guten Wein will ich Schlingen,	Good wine I shall drink.
Azamera bazemer	
Ve-eshteh ḥemer.	

To the tune of "*Halb schwarz, halb weiss*":

Ich will Gott loben mit Gesang	I shall praise God with song
Die Freud soll gewaehren lang	May this joy last long.
Ahalel bir'nanah	
Besimḥat tovalnah.	

To the tune of the *Akedah*:

El maley raḥamim, derbarmiger Vater	God full of mercy, compassionate father
Derleis uns bald, dass mir wern patar galut	Redeem us soon from our exile.

To the tune of the *Akedah*:

Ach Gott, du lieber Herr	O, God, thou dearest Lord
Wie geht es in unseren galut schwer![35]	How hard is our exile.

The tunes notated by Marcello.[36] The following are numbered according to their position in Marcello's work:

2. "*Be-tzet Yisra'el*" (table VII, no. 2) is a *hallel* psalm. In Marcello, the text underlay is not exact. (Marcello indicated precise underlay in only two instances, where the tone word relationship corresponds exactly with the Sephardic accentuation.) The tune seems to be a thrice-embellished variation of a very simple motif, to which a cadence was added. Many similar pieces are found in Melchior Franck's dancing songs, which consist of three variations of a short theme, plus cadence. The tune quoted by Marcello seems to fit two verses of the psalm, and, as the *embellimenti* indicate, it is intended for the solo chant of the hazan. Its rhythm is of the *allemande* type, which suggests a German dance as its source.

4. *Ma'oz Tzur* (table VII, no. 4)[37] was referred to in chapter 6. Here we trace its style and origin. As was pointed out, this melody fits the meter of the *piyut* perfectly. Its tune is modal, vacillating between the hypophrygian and the Phrygian mode, and it has a solemn ring, far from the cheerful, almost vulgar German melody. Idelsohn mentions another *piyut* in the same meter, one composed by R. Abraham Samuel Bacharach (1575–1615) to fit the German tune.[38] The form

of the Marcello hymn is a *Bar* (a+a+b), most popular in the German *Meistersang* and the chorale, but rare in Italy. There are certain formal and motivic similarities to the Gregorian hymn "*Te Lucis*," which was sung in the streets on Corpus Christi day, so that the Jews may have heard it. The first several tones of this *Ma'oz Tzur* show some affinity with the incipit of the *Eli Tziyon* examined in the previous chapter.

6. *Hamabdil* (table VII, no. 6) is a merry piece, having some elements in common with no. 2, which abounds in repetitions of small motifs. Number 6 is somewhat more sophisticated, but it belongs to the type, among Marcello's Jewish themes, that Eitner has called "*baenkelsaengerisch bummelig*" (freely translated, "in the style of a dawdling small-beer singer").[39] And yet the original line of the piece was noble; it was ruined by too many and too cheap "diminutions," a specialty of the hazanim. In example 1, we juxtapose an interesting variant of that melodic line transmitted by Marcello with a German song that might have been its model.[40]

8. *Lekha dodi* (table VII, no. 8) is the hymn as sung by the German Jews in Venice. The melody is strange, indeed. It falls into two parts, of which the second begins to echo the first, but, in the variation, circumvents the sequence typical of the first part. This is clear evidence of *Zersingen* in often repeated oral tradition. Yet the influence of Western art music is undeniable, inasmuch as the first half

Example 1

ends on the dominant, and the second part leads back, rather clumsily, to the tonic. The incipit has, as the young Birnbaum recognized, a parallel in *BT*, no. 238, a *Lekha dodi* for the three weeks before the Ninth of Ab.[41] It is not easy to fit the text of the *Lekha dodi* to Marcello's tune; it can be done only if the initial phrase of each half is repeated. Idelsohn gives the version of the tune as it was sung in Venice in his time.[42] This is a little simpler than the original version, but it does not eliminate the irregularity that makes the Marcello version asymmetrical.

9. *Shofet kol ha-aretz* (table VII, no. 9) is a *pizmon* by Ibn Gabirol, a poem that plays a central role in the Sephardic New Year liturgy. It is quoted by Marcello, using a melody that has survived to this day. I have heard the tune in Breslau and in Tel Aviv; it is identical with *BT*, no. 1426, third tune. Idelsohn traces it unconvincingly, I think, to a Protestant hymn.[43] The tune was analyzed in the previous chapter.

10. The *Kaddish* (table VII, no. 10) is for the New Year's eve. Idelsohn is certainly correct in linking this cheerful tune (marked *presto*) to the traditional "*Schluss-Kaddish*" of the German cantors, which can be heard even today on Simhath Torah. Birnbaum thought it was the so-called "full *Kaddish*" [*Kaddish Shalem*], which cannot be proved, since Marcello did not insert the words under his notes. The parallel to the modern Italian variant of Marcello's tune is certainly obvious and convincing: the Italian version serves as the closing *Kaddish* after the *seliḥot* on the eve of the New Year.[44] It is kept in clear 4/4 time, whereas the Marcello tune seems to be in 4/2 with triplets. Yet, even in my earlier publication of 1937, I recognized the martial character of the tune, and made reference to it. Marcello has indicated the proper tempo here, quite boldly. He prescribed *presto*, and this for a *Kaddish* after *seliḥot*. Perhaps he sensed the merry character of the rondo finale, which, in this case, would bear out Birnbaum's conjecture that it was the concluding *Kaddish*. The true Baroque virtuoso-flourishes at the rhymes and cadences speak well for the arranger of the piece. It has the ternary form of the early Baroque dancing song, such as can be found in the works of Gastoldi, E. Reusner, M. Franck, S. T. Staden, and others.

In summing up this precious testimony of the German-Jewish sixteenth and seventeenth centuries, we note that Marcello has selected tunes that lend themselves easily to congregational singing or, at least, devotional response; some of his "German" tunes suggest fast military marches. Did the Jews of his time really prefer these martial strains? Scanning the various contrafact melodies, indicated in the many Prague handbills, the preferred tunes, as far as is ascertainable, were love songs, or company songs [*Gesellschafts Lieder*].[45] That most of them move in straight time and in march rhythm is undeniable. But they are not military, or even outright marches, except for the variants of the "*Pavia Ton*" and similar popular model tunes of the time.

Welcoming the Sabbath. The flight away from tradition and the adaptation of popular or instrumental tunes, which both cantors and congregations enjoyed, was perhaps caused by the intrusion of cabalistic prayers into the service, which only the adherents of the esoteric doctrine could comprehend. Quite obviously

the majority of worshipers were bored and eager for musical diversion. Of that cabalistic mirage that was launched and for a brief span sustained by the activities of the Pseudo-Messiah Sabbatai Zevi, only a few items have survived the radical housecleaning by the anti-cabalistic German rabbinate and its followers of the late eighteenth century. By far the most important remnant is the "Welcome of the Sabbath," the *Kabbalat Shabbat.* After initial resistance by German and Polish communities, it was generally, and often enthusiastically, accepted, and has since remained an integral part of the *siddur.*

The brief remarks here are based on an account by Abraham Berliner. Companies or fraternities that made it their custom to welcome the approaching Sabbath in formal and solemn manner were formed in Safed (Palestine) during the sixteenth century. They went into a garden, or a courtyard (there was no need to go out of the city), sang some psalms, preferably Psalms 95–98, then Psalm 29, and concluded with the poem *Lekha dodi*, consisting of seven stanzas written by Solomon Alkabetz. Later R. Isaac Luria, the "*Ari*," sanctioned this poem in preference to other similar *piyutim* because it corresponded best with his cabalistic concepts and inclinations. The acceptance of the poem into *minhag ashkenaz* was assured when it was recommended—together with other practices of welcoming the Sabbath—by R. Isaiah Horowitz in his magnum opus, *Sh'ney Luḥot ha-Berit* (the two tablets of the covenant). Horowitz, renowned among central European Jewry as the rabbi of Frankfort and Prague, had emigrated to Safed. Except for a few regional resistance centers, the European community soon accepted his recommendation.[46]

Even in some ultraconservative communities a compromise was established. The "Welcoming of the Sabbath" took place around the *bimah* (reading pulpit) and not before the Ark.[47]

Now we come upon a truly strange confluence of two disparate trends: the imitation of German tunes in a ritual with clearly cabalistic elements. What kind of music would fit this lovely, but strongly allusive text? True, the German Jews loved both the text and the whole ceremony of the *Kabbalat Shabbat*, but they never established a musical tradition for the *Lekha dodi.* Although they found a suitable psalmody for the preceding psalms, the text of the *piyut* was left to the musical invention of individual hazanim. The Birnbaum collection alone contains more than 800 melodies for the text, and many more are known. Many of these newly composed melodies reveal the influence of German instrumental music in bugle- or trumpet-like motifs characteristic of the tunes of the second half of the seventeenth century. Yet behind this musical fad lies a theological idea: the cabalists believed that trumpet calls were the fitting expression of *dveikut* (nearness to God).[48] Seen from the musical point of view, such simple triadic motifs were much more German than Jewish in character. This becomes apparent in example 2. This is a *pizmon* for the fast day, the tenth of Tebeth. The same trumpet blast also serves the fast of Esther, the day before Purim. There is another instance where the cabalistic preference for trumpet motifs suggests elements of instrumental pieces, perhaps German "intermedia." Example 3 is the prayer that serves as a bridge between the *Shema* and the *Tefillah: Al ha-rishonim.* This tune has been notated with bar lines, which are usually disregarded by the cantors in performance.

Example 2

Example 3

Measures 5, 6, and 7 transpose the same motif to the three steps of the tonic triad, thus preparing for the cadence. There follow eight regular measures, filled with resounding trumpet motifs, so that the first part resembles a stately dance and the last eight measures put one in mind of the "*basse-dance*," or "*Nachtanz*." The entire piece is essentially German Baroque, poorly conceived.

Example 4

Example 5

The collection of R. Henle Kirchhan. Such dance-like melodies were generally accepted in the synagogue. Others of similar nature may be found in the collection *Simhat ha-nefesh* (Joy of Souls) by R. Henle Kirchhan (Fürth, 1727), containing thirteen tunes on religious-ethical poems in Judeo-German (Yiddish).[49] Stylistically they are a mixture of synagogal melodies, like the one quoted in example 3, and German dance songs. Example 4 is a good representative of the collection.

Gentile parodies on Jewish song. Example 5 bears considerable resemblance to the "*Judentantz*" by Wolf Heckel (b. 1515), which is essentially a caricature.[50] From here to Hans Neusidler's vicious caricature of the "*Juden Tantz*" is only a small step. Yet from all these documents and testimonies one fact emerges: the German Jews, or their cantors, began to familiarize themselves with the art of reading and writing music. This was by no means as easy as it seems to us today. The most effective impediment was their mental inertia, which, for a long time,

prevented them from learning a new script and kept them reliant on their untrained musical memory. By the last third of the seventeenth century they had heard, if only through rumor and gossip, about the triumphs of Salomone de' Rossi and R. Leon da Modena in Venice. Also, they quite frequently heard their fellow musicians, the *klezmorim*, experiment with their instruments and play from written music.

Idelsohn, in his extensive description of the music of old Jewish communities, confined himself mainly to a history of *ḥazanut*. He himself was of eastern European background and was too subjective in his judgment of the music of the eastern European synagogue to evaluate it critically. Thus he praises the improvisation of Eastern hazanim in these rather extravagant words: "In this [kind of] improvisation . . . lay the chief power of the hazanim. Through it, they developed an admirable and distinctive art which surpasses the improvisation of even the Oriental singers, for they created a unique coloratura . . . of dazzling intricacy and brilliance, of soaring fantasy, of sharp-witted finesse. That type of coloratura is to be found in neither the greatest Arabic nor Turkish singers . . . nor in the best coloratura works of Italian music . . . which is too artificial and rather of instrumental than vocal character."[51]

However, we seek to gain an unbiased view of the tradition of music in *minhag ashkenaz*, and its development at a time when it was subjected to cabalistic trends as well as to the intrusion by German and Italian art music. It is necessary to consider the inner spirit and the image in which central European Jewry saw itself, rather than vocal techniques and the tricks of the cantors. In this respect the difference in status and security between the Jews in the Hapsburg *Erblanden* and those "at large" in German-speaking regions was highly significant and made a tremendous difference in their self-assessment. Under the Hapsburgs, they not only had a certain *Staettigkeit* but some of their brethren were made noblemen. This fact alone stirred admiration and certainly some envy among the rest of the German Jews. As usual in such cases, strict adherence to their fathers' faith was in inverse ratio to their social status.

Under such circumstances, certain breaches appeared in the otherwise impenetrable wall of spiritual Jewish homogeneity and self-defense. "It must have been a novel realization to Jews living during the Wars of Religion that they no longer were the most persecuted religious minority."[52] Moreover, it turned out that the cities were more prone to admit Jewish settlers than the rural environments—a complete reversal of the situation 150 years previously. Toward the end of the seventeenth century the Jews returned to Holland, Denmark, Prussia, and somewhat later to Saxony. In this climate of a devastated Germany, ravaged by the Wars of Religion, a "new tolerance" seemed to dawn; and it remains the unforgotten merit of the pietists to have set both example and pace toward a kind of "friendship" with a weary and anxiety-ridden Jewry.

Yet the communities were beset by the beginnings of a mass remigration of Jews from Poland and the Ukraine in consequence of the pogroms that had started in 1648. As usual, the cantors were in the vanguard of the refugees. Surprisingly, the German Jews took quickly to the somewhat "exotic" type of Polish *ḥazanut*.

Where there was strong resistance, separate congregations for the Jews from Poland were established. In the long run the "Polish style" became so popular in Germany that it served as a counterweight against the complete Germanization of *minhag ashkenaz*. Even 200 years later, Abraham Baer separated the two traditions in his *Ba'al Tefillah*, the first serious musical source and compendium of *minhag ashkenaz*, which has been quoted extensively above.[53]

From the east there came Polish hazanim, from the south, Italian singers. In their immediate environment the Jews heard hundreds of German songs and dances; yet in their synagogues they were subjected to incomprehensible or misunderstood cabalistic prayers.[54] In their hearts they desired good music—serious or entertaining—yet they were not permitted to attend a Christian concert. To what would they turn in their perplexity?

Appendix: Benedetto Marcello

The work that made Benedetto Marcello famous happens to be the very one that is of interest to the scholar of Jewish music. It bears a pompous, truly Baroque title—*Estro poetico-armonico (Poetic-Harmonic Inspiration)*—and was published between 1724 and 1726 in Venice, though most of its component pieces had been composed earlier. It extends to eight folio volumes. Marcello provided each tome with extensive prefaces in which he expressed some opinions—almost all of them obsolete—on the music of the Greeks and the Hebrews.

The following are a few passages from his prefaces that relate to the Jewish melodies in his work:

> In some instances...I have introduced recitatives, in order to afford the listeners...a suitable pleasure...also in order to approximate to a certain extent the practice, as one finds it in sacred scripture, especially with reference to precentors [*precentori*], characteristic of the Jewish people.... One will not deem it unsuitable that here several melodies of great age are adduced that belong to the chants heard in Jewish communities....

In the foreword to the second volume, the following remark appears:

> The ninth Psalm opens with the Sephardic intonation of *Le-David barukh* [in Hebrew letters], according to the very ancient and generally popular tune. In general, one does not find notated music among the Jews; they have transmitted the hymns, psalms...and other melodies by oral tradition....

Marcello briefly explained his use of the original melodies for his polyphonic choral compositions:

> In order to adjust to our [Italian] verses and meters, their [time] value had to be lengthened, and they [the tunes] had to be repeated several times. Yet nowhere and never was the original intonation altered in any way, although certain mannerisms are employed in Jewish chant, such as the *portamento di voce* and others. There are surely typical differences recognizable between the chants of the Spanish and the German Jews, according to the countries whence they came....

We learn that Marcello transcribed the original melodies "in a little more clearly arranged manner than the Jewish practice of his time"—in other words, he simplified the original melodies, adjusting them to his western European, time-bound taste. Although he claimed not to have altered anything essential, the musicologist is well aware of the inherent difficulties of a faithful transcription of native folk songs, not to speak of foreign ones. Nonetheless, systematic comparison has demonstrated that his transcriptions were, in general, faithful to the *substance* of the melodies, if not to the (ornamented) way in which they were probably sung. We must, therefore, recognize Marcello's efforts as a most respectable accomplishment.

8

Wind from the East

A certain scholar, when reading in the Pentateuch (Lev. 26:44), "Nevertheless, even when they are in the land of their enemies I shall not abhor them . . ." remarked bitterly: "What then has been left to Israel in the Galut *that has not been detested and abhorred? What has been left them? Only the Torah." For had that not been preserved for Israel, they would in no wise be different from the Gentiles.*

(H. N. Bialik, address at the inauguration of the Hebrew University, Jerusalem, 1925)

The Historical Conditions

In the past, Jewish historians generally assumed that the civilization of Polish and Russian Jews had its roots solely in German Jewry. In fact, most European Jews do have their origins there, but today we are aware of how much more complex the parentage of eastern European Jewry really is. It probably came about as the result of the confluence of Black Sea Jews—possibly refugees from Byzantium—moving westward and German Jews moving eastward. Remnants of Tartaric, Byzantine, and even older cultures were preserved by the Karaite sect. A beautiful manuscript of Karaite *zemirot* in the Tartaric language, written in Hebrew letters, in the Bibliothèque Nationale, Paris, contains rudimentary traces of Byzantine notation, probably of the fourteenth century. The few sources, however, are very scarce and scattered around the world, in the rare-book rooms of the great libraries. Nevertheless, there is no doubt that the ancient "*Sclavonia*" (Bohemia, Poland, and perhaps Podolia) was known in Hebrew literature as "Canaan" before the year 1200.[1]

These isolated hints indicate a possible Slavo-Byzantine element in the oldest songs and rites of the Russian Jews. Yet the complete dearth of musical or historical sources constrains us to abandon any attempt to speculate on the possible Byzantine or paleo-Slavonic elements in the musical tradition of Russo-Polish Jews. We pass directly to the High Middle Ages, which have left us in possession of good historical sources.

Three centuries had passed since the days of the Black Death, when many thousands of German Jews wandered to Poland as invited guests of friendly kings. The Jews had accomplished their adjustment *tel quel* to European conditions and mores. Their settlements had grown enormously; they had established an almost autonomous council of three, later of four, lands—Poland, Podolia, Lithuania, and Volhynia. Their talmudic academies had become famous among the Jews of the world, and even Christian contemporary chroniclers reported about the status of Polish Jewry during the seventeenth century, with a touch of envy and malice, to be sure:

> King Casimir's benefices and privileges lured an incredible mass of Jews to Poland, and there is no hamlet that did not swarm with Jews. . . . They had some lovely synagogues in Cracow, in Lemberg, and especially in Lublin . . . also many colleges and academies; in these the [talmudic and rabbinic] studies are advanced to the highest point, as was confirmed by R. Simon Luzzatto. . . . Hence German Jews go in hordes to Poland for their studies. . . . Likewise, if the German Jews want something exceptional [*was sonderliches haben wollen*], they get their rabbis and hazanim from Poland. Thus the notorious R. Naphtali Cohen, the arsonist of our Jews Street [in Frankfort], also from Poland, was called from Poznan to Frankfort, having been solemnly escorted by many fine carriages. . . .[2]

Yet, with all this intensity of rabbinic and talmudic studies, it must be said that their champions, diligent and often saintly scholars, were sometimes threshing chaff, for their efforts were frequently directed at hairsplitting and sterile exercises of the intellect, which they confused with constructive scholarship. Many of the best minds realized this, and quite frankly criticized the prevalent *pilpul* and *ḥilukim* (logical disputes). The rabbis did not seem to inhabit the same planet as the Western scholars; the names Copernicus, Kepler, Galileo, and Huygens would have meant nothing to them. The revolutionary discoveries of "natural philosophy," refuting the geocentric views of the Talmud, would have ruined their ideology. They were better off in their blissful ignorance—or so they seemed to think.[3]

In a curious passage, as erudite a scholar as R. Manasseh ben Israel, the friend of Rembrandt and the advocate of the Jews before Cromwell, derived the old Greek music theory, which he attributes to Pythagoras, from the prophet Ezekiel. The following is a paraphrase of his remarks. The knowledge of musical theory is generally attributed to Pythagoras. But in fact he only rediscovered its theorems after they had been forgotten for centuries. Yet there was a certain Alexander Polyhistor who learned the theory directly from the prophet Ezekiel. This man, in his inspired wisdom, had divined the secrets of many things. (Here it should be added that Alexander Polyhistor lived about eight centuries after Ezekiel.)

This was the roundabout way by which Manasseh gave his approval to Greek and Western music theory. Only by making the foreign ideas seem to derive from some biblical doctrine was it possible to introduce them into any Jewish system of thought. Without this "biblical passport" every idea that came from the Gentile world would have been considered heretical.[4] This total isolation resulted in an

unworldliness that left the rabbis and the organization of the Four-Land Synod helpless to defend eastern European Jewry when its physical survival was threatened.

In the middle of the seventeenth century Jewish life in Poland suffered a terrible collapse; a catastrophe of historic dimensions ruined forever the reputation of Poland as "the Jewish Paradise." In the Chmielnitzky massacres between 1648 and 1658 more than 100,000 Jews were slain. It is no accident that the cantors were in the vanguard of the fleeing masses, for even under normal conditions they were inclined to a nomadic way of life and were ready to change their habitat at the drop of a pin or the crack of a pistol. Not without reason did R. Selig Margolis berate these shiftless singers for leaving their communities in Poland and emigrating to Germany, even when there was no danger for them. In his opinion their behavior was "utterly selfish," because they were derelict in their duties and sought only greater security and higher salaries.[5]

When we turn to the singing style and content of the Eastern cantors, we become aware of the deep split between East and West. Since Polish cantors knew even less about musical notation than did their German confreres, we have no shred of written evidence for the earlier years and have to rely on written descriptions, or else on notations of the nineteenth century, which were designated as *minhag Polen*.

We begin with the literary evidence. The same R. Margolis who berated the cantors for deserting their congregations had to admit that the *good* cantors moved to tears many people who had not wept even at their parents' death, but who now cried in deep repentance and sorrow for their sins. But he qualified this apparent praise by saying, "Such ability is possessed by hazanim in our country [Poland] only, whereas in other countries they neither foster melody nor evoke emotion."[6]

Rabbi Solomon Luria (1510–1573), who was second only to Moses Isserles (1530–1572) as the greatest rabbinical authority of Poland, complained bitterly of the indifference of the congregations to the rabbis' recommendations of a hazan. "They insist that the hazan should remain accountable to them alone, free from the control of the rabbi. As a consequence, the piety of the Reader is subordinated to a pleasant voice and clear diction." All these nuisances he attributed to the fact that the congregations selected hazanim solely for their good voices. He insisted on observance of the regulations that prohibit a Jew from engaging a Gentile to work for him on the Sabbath, and that included playing music in or out of the synagogue.[7]

Another institution that became a subject of controversy was that of the hazan's two *behelfer* (assistants). The custom of adding to the solo voice of the regular hazan can be documented as far back as the middle of the sixteenth century but is certainly much older. It seems to have grown from yet older rabbinical safeguards concerning the propriety of the Torah reading. They held the opinion, "It is not very good that the hazan go up to the Ark all by himself."[8] It is understandable that the rabbis searched and found biblical precedents for three officiants in worship, while at the same time being careful to avoid trinitarian associations. The *Pesikta de R. Kahane*[9] speaks outright of three singers [*meshorerim*] analogous to the trio of Moses, Aaron, and Hur.

The triumvirate was praised by many, condemned by many. In Poland they were given the highly pejorative nickname "*keley ḥomos*" (instruments of violence, an inaccurate acronym for hazan, *meshorer*, and *Singer*).[10]

However, the two singers were under the thumb of the hazan. And whatever that gentleman's faults may have been, he was well versed in the prayer text and understood every shade of meaning in it. The hazanim insisted on musical conformity with the chant. The requisite responses of Amen had to agree with the *laḥan* (tune) of the antecedent benediction.[11] This kind of regulation undoubtedly engendered an intimate relationship between prayer and musical response. Out of it grew, in turn, the *seder ha-tefillah*, the musical structure of entire sections of the liturgy, each to be concluded by the cantor's *Kaddish*. Birnbaum, the profound student of Jewish liturgy and musical history, assumed that this development, perfected in Poland of the seventeenth century, made the engagement of the two assistants necessary.

Aside from rabbinic considerations, what was the musical function of the *meshorerim*, the *Bass*, and the *Singer* (low and high voices, respectively)? In the oldest manuscripts of the Birnbaum collection in Hebrew Union College in Cincinnati, which I have examined over a period of more than five years, the singers' prescribed function was merely to provide a change of timbre, and to provide a breathing spell for the cantor. Only in the later manuscripts do the three singers sometimes unite in a triad, usually poorly conceived. It is easy to see that no fair harmony could be established without the collaboration of instrumentalists, which took place only occasionally, in Prague. In Poland, the rabbis were much stricter and the *klezmorim* (street musicians) much poorer, and without any musical training. The main task of the *meshorerim* was to provide their master, the cantor, with new tunes; for just as the Jew expected freshly made soup on his table every Friday night, he demanded a good supply of new tunes for the Sabbath. Hence the better the musical memory, or the musical imagination of the *meshorer*, the more valuable was he for the cantor. Since neither the cantor nor his singers were able to read or write music, the new tunes were transmitted from mouth to ear, so to speak. Once a *meshorer* exhausted his supply of new tunes, he was as useless as an empty bottle and lost his job. He had to find another hazan as customer for his wares, until such time as he might establish himself as a cantor.[12]

For all the legalistic piety of the times, decorum was never particularly cherished in the eastern European synagogue. Certainly it was the cantor's last consideration. Frequently rival hazanim and their *meshorerim* came to blows right in the synagogue.[13]

We turn now to the musical evidence itself. In previous chapters the intrusion of German popular songs into *minhag ashkenaz* has been demonstrated. In the following pages some original sources of the Polish tradition are examined. This does not imply that the German and Polish Jews never created melodies of their own; the entire treasure of the prayer modes, of the *Missinai* tunes, of the psalmodies and cantillations speaks most eloquently for the musical creativity of the Jews. It comforted and entertained them even in the distress habitual in the Diaspora. On the other hand we must be aware that the Polish Jews, no less than the German Jews, were subjected to powerful cultural forces that encroached on their mores, thoughts, and songs.

The attraction of German folk song and dance for the cantors of *minhag ashkenaz* is well known, and several studies have estimated the quality and quantity of this alien material. No equivalent study of Polish or Russian elements in the Jewish tradition is known to me. The study by Idelsohn on a related theme is considered extensively later in this chapter. If there are any articles in Polish extant, they are inaccessible to me, but two very helpful Polish musicologists have assured me that until the middle of the nineteenth century nothing was written. It was only then that folklorists began to interest themselves to any extent at all in Polish *ḥazanut*. No earlier traces of its modes have come down to us.

Hence we must search for those components that gradually established the style of eastern European synagogue chant. A number of characteristic melodies of the Polish tradition will be compared with their counterparts in the Western ritual. The sources to be cited are *BT*; Idelsohn, *Music*; *HOM*, vols. 6 and 7; one manuscript in my possession by a hazan, Boruch Karliner (early nineteenth century); and Arno Nadel's transcription of Eastern chant for the domestic Sabbath ritual.[14]

First we shall examine two texts, each of which is sung to variants—Polish and German—of the same melody. In table VIIIA, no. 1*a* and *b*, we find a portion of the *Musaf Kedushah* of Yom Kippur. We have already seen the German version in chapter 3, example 14. Here it is presented in juxtaposition (as Baer gives it) with its Polish variant. They both derive in part from the *Missinai* tune of *ve-ha-kohanim* (see chapter 3, example 15). However, the Polish version develops only one motif, first presented ornamentally (in measures 1–3), later in simple manner (measures 8–10), and ending in a cadential phrase (measures 12–13). The German variant carries the first motif in measures 1–5; then in measures 7–10 there is introduced a second motif, which comes from *u-sh'menu karata li-sh'mekha*, the preamble of the High Holy Day *Kedushah*, as given in *BT* 1193a. A third motif follows (measures 10–12), which we have already come across in the *Barekhu* motif of Rosh Hashanah eve.

The Polish version consists of thirteen measures, the German, fourteen. Yet the former contains more tones in fewer measures; that is, it is more richly ornamented. Example 1 presents the ornaments of the Polish version. They may be part of the scale (diaheletic), the so-called *Schleifer*, or the typical "changing tone" formula:

The embellishments of the German variant are seen in example 2. These consist of either neighboring tones (measure 4) or of triadic elaborations of a tone (measure

Example 1

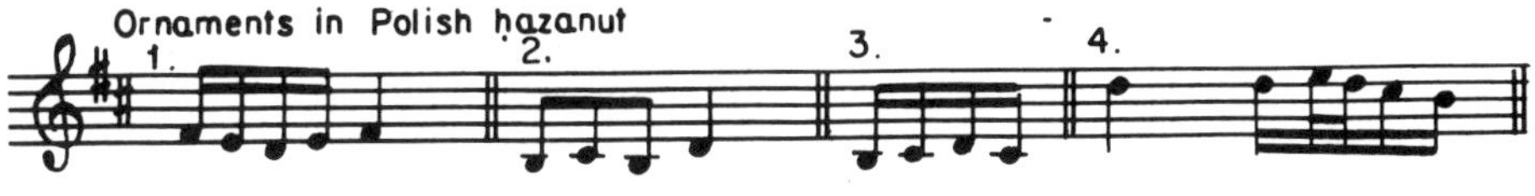

Example 2

5). The tonality is D major, with a slight bent toward its relative B minor in both versions.

Another example of Polish and German variants on the same text may be found in table VIIIA, no. *2a* and *b*. The text, *yareti*, is a *piyut* of the *shaḥarit Amidah* of *Rosh Hashanah*. The metrical tune is derived from the *Missinai* melody for *ohila la'el* (see chapter 3, example 13). Number *2a* consists of nine measures with fifty-nine tones, *2b* of ten measures with sixty-three notes. Again *2a* contains more notes per measure than *2b*. Both variants contain the same thematic material. Yet there are characteristic differences between them: the leading motif appears in *2a* in measure 3, in *2b* in measure 9, where it introduces the cadence. The meter of the text has not influenced the rhythmic flow in either variant. The tonalities, however, differ from one another. Number *2a* is in simple harmonic minor, except in measure 3, where it tends to Doric; *2b* is in natural minor and contains the Dorian element in measure 9.

We shall now examine one text with two German variants (table VIIIA, nos. *3a* and *b*), and one completely different Polish setting, *3c*. The text, *be-rosh ha-shanah*, is a section of the celebrated *u-netaneh tokef* from the High Holy Day service (see chapter 3 above). Here the essential difference lies in the tonality. Number *3c* uses the so-called gypsy scale, whereas *3a* and *b* consist of the various leading motifs of the *Missinai* tunes, especially those of *Kol Nidre* (see chapter 3, example 10). A synthesis of *3a* and *3b* has been accomplished in the lovely stylized composition by Salomon Sulzer on the same text. Apparently *3c* is not based on the old Ashkenazic tradition of the prayer, a phenomenon we shall observe frequently. This can also be noticed at the cadences: *3c* has a very simple one of a half-measure, whereas the two German versions prepare the cadence through leading motifs and end on the dominant. All evidence points to an earlier origin for the German versions.

Next we have two recitatives, one Polish and one German, set to a metrical *piyut*, *B'raḥ dodi*, which is an insertion into the Passover morning service (table VIIIA, nos. *4a* and *b*). The text, by the Roman poet Solomon ben Judah (who called himself The Babylonian in order to equate Rome with biblical Babylon), is a fervent plea for redemption, replete with allusions to the Song of Songs.[15] There is a strong resemblance, indeed a partial identity here, to the chant of *Al ha-rishonim* (*BT* 529) of the Sabbath *yotzer* service.

This melodic resemblance affords proof positive of the transmitters' profound comprehension of the prayers mentioned and, beyond that, of the stability and the expressive ethos of the guardians of *minhag ashkenaz*. Both the *Al ha-rishonim* and the *B'rah dodi* are parts of the *yotzer* section and belong to its climax, the *ge'ulah* (redemption). The Western Ashkenazim, under the spell of cabalist teachings,

introduced symbolic bugle and trumpet motifs into both prayers, whereas the Eastern branch just as habitually rendered it through the same recurrent motifs in the *Ahabah Rabah* mode. Since it was late in the sixteenth and in the first half of the seventeenth century that the German Jews were influenced by cabalistic interpretations of older prayers, we may set both the Eastern and Western variants at about 1650 or thereafter. The German version attests to the growing attraction of band music for the Jews. Standing music corps of the armies arose during the Thirty Years' War.[16] We hear of a *klezmer* who was baptized, and served in Wallenstein's camp.[17] This type of practice changed during the eighteenth century, when the German Jews, under the impact of great art music, turned increasingly to metrical melodies, whereas Polish Jewry, rigidly averse to any art music, remained under the influence of Slavonic (Polish, Ukrainian, Russian) folk songs and dances.

The final example for comparison is a prose text from Scripture, with its Eastern and Western settings. This verse, *ve'al yedey avodekha* (table VIIIA, nos. 5*a* and *b*), comes from the ancient *malkhuyot* section of the Rosh Hashanah service. That section is one of three (the other two being *zikhronot* and *shofarot*), which was incorporated into the New Year liturgy before the fall of the Second Temple.

The great age of these sections may explain in part why the three sets of ten scriptural verses are not chanted in cantillation in any of the three main liturgical traditions, Yemenite, Sephardic, or Ashkenazic. Another reason would be the difficulty of slipping quickly from one system of thought to another, since each section contains verses from Pentateuch, Prophets, and Hagiographa.[18]

Considering the central position of these prayers and the reverence accorded to their texts, it is puzzling to find that not even within the same tradition has one tune been prevalent. The simplest solution of the puzzle may be that in earlier times the rabbis themselves read these important prayers, before the cantors could usurp them; this solution becomes more acceptable if we consider that between the old *keva* texts of the three sections, later poetic pieces were inserted, and that these were left to the art of the hazanim. The examination and comparison of the two versions quoted in table VIIIA, no. 5, yield the following results.

The Karliner version approaches cantorial art music. It consists of fourteen measures and its tone-word relationship is comparable to that of a *recitativo accompagnato* with a strong *arioso* trend and many melismatic passages. The Baer version is the result of careful editing, as indicated by the frequent fermatas (always on the correct syllable) and the grammatically correct distribution of the stresses. Karliner's version does not have this advantage; more than once the musical stresses go against the grammar and syntax of the text (e.g., *avodekhó*, *melekh́*, *umibalódai*), and the word "*ve-ne'emar*" (as it is said) is repeated without reason. The German version is strictly syllabic, in my opinion as a result of Sulzer's reforms, which "trimmed" a good deal of melismatic fat from the traditional *ḥazanut*. The most important difference lies, however, in the treatment of tonality: Karliner vacillates between G minor, F major, and G major. His wavering, especially between the major and minor modes of the same key, speaks powerfully for western Slavonic influence.[19] In contrast to this flexibility, Baer's version remains strictly syllabic and in natural minor. Here we may observe the development of Polish and German tradition and taste during the late eighteenth and early nineteenth centuries.

To demonstrate that the Eastern tradition borrowed extensively from Polish melodic patterns, there now follows a number of such sources. Table VIIIA, no. *6a* presents the motif of *Kaddish* of Friday evening, as quoted by Baer and Idelsohn. It is a sequential motif. In *6c* is a tune for "another Paduano" (in "Polish gusto," by August Noermiger [1560–1613] from his *Tabulaturbuch* of 1598).[20] The similarity to the *Kaddish* motif is obvious. However, the melody is not necessarily Polish. This motif also occurs in older German folk songs.

In the table, nos. 7, 8, and 9 are Polish dances, of which many echoes survive in eastern European Jewish tunes, especially in those of the *ḥasidim*. Number 7 is a brief section of a "Polish *Dantz*" by Christian Demantius (1567–1643), from *Seventy-seven New Polish and German Dances with and without Words* (Nuremberg, 1601).[21] Numbers 8 and 9 are anonymous dance compositions taken from the excellent anthology *Music of the Polish Renaissance*.[22] There a great number of compositions can be found, most of which are of excellent quality and of a much higher standard than any synagogue music prior to the nineteenth century (except the compositions by Rossi and those collected by Adler in French and Italian communities). The volume is a bonanza of musical motifs that found their way into the synagogue tradition of the Polish Jews.

Finally, table VIIIA, nos. 10 and 11, are a Polish gigue and then a polonaise, which shall be compared with some synagogue melodies. Number 10 is the beginning of "A Good Polish Dance," a sort of fast gigue by Christoph Loeffelholz (1585).[23] Number 11 is the "Polonaise" by Johann Nicolaus Tischer, from *The Pleased Ear* [*Das vergnuegte Ohr*] (Nuremberg, 1680). Both of these selections contain motifs germane to hasidic *niggunim* and dances.

Other material for comparison is found in the tablatures by Jan of Lublin (fl. 1537–1548), J. B. Besard (1567–ca. 1625), G. L. Fuhrmann (1560–1618), J. Christianus (second half of the sixteenth century), V. Haussmann (1560–1614?), and Nicolaus of Cracow (fl. ca. 1520). All the composers mentioned seem to use Polish motifs as if they were slightly "exotic" ingredients. Only the two Poles, Jan of Lublin and Nicolaus of Cracow, both of whom were organists, wrote two valuable organ tablatures, in which one finds folkloristic motifs such as those in example 3.[24] These two motifs have been echoed often, usually in overornamented form, in the songs of the Polish Jews—again, especially in those of the *ḥasidim*. Some folk dances wandered over the European continent, e.g., the song "I pricked myself with a thorn," whose *double-entente* was widely enjoyed.[25]

Example 3

At this point we can begin to generalize about those traits that signify the Polish element in synagogal chant: (1) The favorite tonality (except for major) is natural or harmonic minor, or a mixture of natural minor and *Ahabah Rabah*. (2) Almost all the melodies quoted are subjected to sequential treatment. (3) Dotted rhythms occur frequently, especially in fast tempi. (4) In general, the melodies often move stepwise, and they are only occasionally based on triads. (5) The main ornaments are passing tones and changing tones. Rarely is a tune overburdened with ornaments or *embellimenti*. (6) One- or two-measure repetitions of the same motif are frequent, sometimes excessive. The essential differences between *minhag polen* and the Western *minhag ashkenaz* lie in the realm of tone-word relationship and in the tonalities preferred. The analyses and conclusions that follow are valid only up to about 1720, when Italian opera began to make serious inroads in both Eastern and Western *ḥazanut*, with different consequences.

The tone-word relation presents the most important difference in the two traditions. Eastern *ḥazanut* prefers syllabic, almost *parlando* passages, contrasted with *arioso* melodies replete with ornaments. The cantilenas, which are expanded by the use of sequences, use mainly simple but rich melismatic embellishments. The Western *minhag ashkenaz* reveals more attention to the meters of the texts than does *minhag polen*, where the hazan enjoys almost absolute freedom of improvisation. This ad lib element tempted the singers, who later introduced excessive coloraturas and created lengthy showpieces. These were always resented by the rabbis, who, for this reason, preferred Sephardic hazanim. The Western style, considerably more austere than the Eastern, shuns repetition of words, whereas the Eastern makes free use of it.

Another significant difference is in tonality. The Polish style uses a good deal of harmonic and Dorian minor, emphasizing the leading tone. The Jewish-Ukrainian style employs many chromatic deviations and utilizes a sort of gypsy scale.[26] Among the German Jews the tonality is much more often in major, or a church tone in contrast to the practice in eastern Europe. Of the minor modes, Western *minhag ashkenaz* uses mainly the natural, in which the leading tone—if it is used at all—is restricted to the final cadence.

Form and structure also differ in the two traditions. The Western *minhag ashkenaz* does not use much of the recitative-*arioso* juxtaposition. Instead of sequences it employs bugle-like motifs, borrowed from military bands, and hinting at cabalistic ideas. Consequently, it is full of triadic motifs, with the skips typical of them. The Eastern tradition avoids strictly closed forms (binary or ternary), unless they are needed for dancing songs; otherwise it tends toward the emotional rhapsodic.

Zemirot[27]

The utopian spirit of the Sabbataean movement stood in sharp contrast to the rationalist-legalistic mode of rabbinic thinking. The eastern European Jews were exposed to these antithetic concepts. The level of spiritual culture among eastern European Jewry was "chaotic" (S. Dubnow) or "demoralized" (Graetz). We have already seen some of the effects of the Sabbataean movement, which had aroused

false hopes and absurd dreams. The movement had caused wild excitement to the masses, which were already in a state of political and economic disintegration. And yet, out of this turmoil, from these masses torn between Sabbataean charlatans, genuine mystics, legalistic rabbis, and political imposters, surrounded by threatening pogroms, there sprang a set of songs of idyllic tranquillity, of escape from daily trouble and worry: the bouquet of table songs for Friday eve and Sabbath. The escape from worldly worries, ordained for the Sabbath, was not an attitude monopolized by the Sabbataeans; all messianic movements of Judaism contain a characteristic element of utopianism, from Jesus on to Moses Hess and Theodor Herzl. Even after the collapse of the Sabbataean movement there were literally scores of such pseudo-messiahs who excommunicated each other: impostors, naive souls, true mystics, etc. It is a shattering experience to fathom the lack of common sense of the masses of European Jewry panting and thirsting after a messiah. This total disregard of time and its changes—indeed, of most historical events—so typical of the pious orthodox Jew will help to explain some puzzling elements of the *zemirot*. For they are, from the musical point of view, unique in all folklore: their texts are not only independent of their tunes; the poems originated in various centuries from the ninth to the seventeenth. Their melodies, however, as we know them, all arose in one period, roughly between 1600 and 1850. The texts are expressions of homage to God, the giver of the Sabbath with its food and drink. They are table songs, cheerful, very pious, often mystically inclined, and in all kinds of meter and form. The melodies are plain, and do not pretend to any elegance.

Two traditions that go back to talmudic times were the generators of all *zemirot*. According to the first, the company of two angels on the eve of the Sabbath escort the Jew on his way home from the synagogue.[28] The *Zohar*—the great treasure of the cabalistic thought—expanded this idea, until all domestic activities of the Sabbath were supposed to be under angelic (or celestial) guardianship, especially the three ritually prescribed Sabbath meals. And according to the second tradition, the Sabbath is to be distinguished and solemnized by extraordinary food and drink.[29] In thus exalting the Sabbath over all ordinary days, the Jew is imitating the Lord himself, who had rested on the Sabbath from the labors of Creation. Most of the poetic thoughts that permeate the *zemirot* are based on, or derived from these main ideas. This explains the lack of good parallels in world literature; the only convincing ones are Anglo-Norman, usually Christmas carols like the following:

His house he fills with many a dish
Of meat and bread and also fish
    To grace the day;
May joy come from God above
To all those who Christmas love.
To English ale and Gascon wine.[30]

. . .

Another parallel would be in the verses by Alcuin, a contemporary of Charlemagne: "*Deus nostrae benedic convivia mensae*..." (God, bless the meals of our table, whatever

you have granted to your servants in your leniency; through you alone these gifts are blessed. Trans. E. W.).[31] No tune has come down to us for these lines.

In most of the *zemirot* the Sabbath is solemnized as the divine refuge from all sorrow and trouble. This hyperbole of all "normal" wishes led some cabalists to view the Sabbath meals as the earthly foretastes of the world-to-come—certainly a touching, yet infantile dream. An enthusiastic echo came from the West German Jews when their poet Heinrich Heine conjured up some of the dream's images, spiced with his inimitable irony: "Hör ich nicht den Jordan rauschen. . . ?" ("*Prinzessin Sabbath*"). Small wonder, then, that in torn, confused, demoralized Poland the *zemirot* were cherished greatly and sung regularly; many of their melodies were actually Polish. Since the tunes represent a type of clannish folk tradition, and not a genuine community tradition, they have no continuity beyond two or, at the most, three generations.[32] The texts are artful, their melodies simple and homey. They are not intended for the synagogue but for the intimate Sabbath meals of the family. This in itself explains the cardinal diversion from the usual synagogue chant. There is no hazan to introduce musical ornament; the tradition is carried not from master to disciple, but rather from father to son, so there is no "showing off" of vocal pyrotechnics. The pitch range of the *zemirot* is modest; there is no clear-cut musical form, and we frequently encounter a loose mixture of recitative and metrical melodies.

Table VIIIB includes seven *zemirot.* Six of them are Polish and one is German in provenance. They are all quoted from Arno Nadel's fine collection (Berlin, 1937). This is a small book that has unfortunately become very rare.

Kol Mekadesh Shevi'i (Who sanctifies the Seventh Day) (table VIIIB, no. 1), a poem replete with hidden or overt biblical allusions, is ascribed to Moses ben Kalonymos (tenth to eleventh century). We encountered it in chapter 5, set to an adaptation of an old German tune. The poem is isosyllabic (9–10 syllables per line), a fact that indicates its great age. The simple melody here consists of two parts: first a recitative-like proclamatory incipit reminiscent of the Talmud-study mode, followed by a modest metrical melody. The tune is strictly syllabic, without any embellishment, except in the last measure, where the cadence demands a slight melisma to parallel measure 4.

Yah ribon (Lord of all the world) (table VIIIB, no. 2) is a poem by the Palestinian mystic R. Israel Najara (sixteenth century). It is kept in Aramaic intentionally, since that is the language of the *Zohar* and contains many archaisms. Dr. Loewe (see n. 30) likens it, not without reason, to a Sapphic stanza, but it is rhymed, and the rhyming syllables of the first stanza [*ayya*] end every stanza thereafter. Actually, it is a trimeter, where anapests, jambs, and spondees interchange. The first stanza serves as refrain. The melody is full of verve and impetus, clearly in natural minor. The trend to the subdominant is quite obvious, as in most Judeo-Polish melodies. Nadel has slightly "normalized" the two cadences. The first (measure 7–8) is found in most variants in the Phrygian mode (F natural instead of F sharp); the second (measures 15–16) parallels measure 4 but ends in the tonic. Example 4 is a more usual variant for this cadence. This is a very popular melody. Its two parts are similar, but not identical; the second moves toward the relative major, but never reaches it. The tune is well balanced between syllabic and melismatic motifs.

Example 4

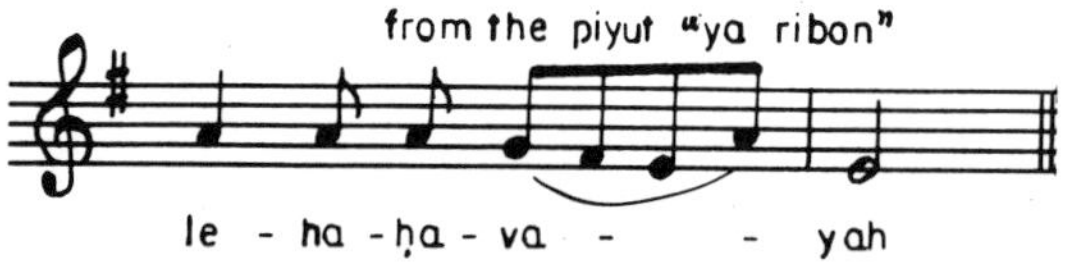

The second *Yah ribon* melody (table VIIIB, no. 3) is a rhythmic extravaganza, apparently of hasidic origin, as indicated by the inserted syllables la, la, ba, ba, etc. The loose form is interesting, and the bugle-like motif (measures 13–14) hints at German provenance. Hasidism and German style mixed often and well in Moravia during the eighteenth century. There, a last citadel of Sabbateanism had turned hasidic, but the hasidic glory did not last very long.

Tzur mi-shelo akhalnu (Bless the rock, our Lord, who fed us) (table VIIIB, no. 4) is a poem that does not refer directly to the Sabbath but is based on the three *berakhot* prescribed in the Torah. It must be very old, for it contains rhymes that are not yet pure, but only assonances or equal suffixes. It, too, is isosyllabic (7–5, 6–5 for the refrain, 6 for the lines). Leo Hirschfeld, the best authority on the literary aspects of the *zemirot*, dates it very early, possibly to the tannaitic period.[33] It may stem from a period antedating Arabic meter and rhyme, before the year 800. The melody is full of Polish-type sequences in minor, mostly syllabic and repetitious. The tunes of the refrain and of the bulk of the poem are very similar, hardly distinguishable. This speaks for non-hasidic origin, as do its double endings. The tonality is natural minor, somewhat inclined to the subdominant, and to the Phrygian mode. All these elements are indigenous to western Slavonic folk song.

Yom Zeh Mekhubad (This day is honored) (table VIIIB, no. 5) is a poem of eight-syllable lines with simple suffix rhymes by an otherwise unknown Israel ha-Ger, a name that indicates either a convert to Judaism or a "newcomer" from a land far away. The poem is hardly remarkable, but the tune is a great deal more interesting. The melody of the refrain recalls an old Czech dance, especially in measures 3 and 4. The tune of the strophe itself starts with a motif identical with a famous passage of the "*Hatikvah*," the Israeli national anthem. The melody of the words in that hymn [*od lo avdah tikvatenu*] is repeated three times, and the whole is concluded with a modal cadence. The motif in question occurs in the Sephardic tradition of the eighteenth century, but that was hardly known to the *meshorer* of this song. Idelsohn, in a comparison of *Yigdal*, the Sephardic *tal* (prayer for dew), the Polish *Pod Krakowiem*, Smetana's famous *Moldau* tune, and others, has shown that this is one of the many migrating melodies, a few of which have circumnavigated the globe.[34] In this case, the prevalence of music over text is just as obvious as in the hasidic *Yah ribon* described above. Acclamations such as *oi, veh, oi!* are inserted. The word *mi-kol* in the refrain is repeated three times to complete the melody. The entire piece, melodious and interesting as it appears, is a mosaic of folkloristic motifs, naively put together.[35]

Mah yafit (How lovely) (table VIIIB, no. 6) is easily the best-known *zemirah*, though its fame rests not with its beauty but with its tragic associations. This merry

tune was quite popular, not only among Jews; Polish landed gentry often forced "their" Jews, during drinking bouts and debaucheries, to play the buffoon for them, and the singing and mimicking of *Mah yafit* was an integral part of their drunken frolicking. It must be admitted that there were some Jews who sought to ingratiate themselves with the Gentile lords, and allowed themselves to be debased. To this day, the expression "*mah-yofis* Jew" carries the connotation of servile submission to any humiliation. It is a very bitter expression, yet it deserves to be remembered as a souvenir of the "gallant and chivalrous" Polish aristocracy as well as of the Jews without dignity.[36] Even Frederic Chopin, who had enjoyed the hospitality as well as the support of two famous Jewish clans (Meyerbeer and Mendelssohn) in Berlin, was quite frankly antisemitic in the absence of his Jewish friends. He wrote, "Poor Polish airs! You did not in the least suspect how you would be interlarded with *Majufes!* [The Judeo-Polish pronunciation]."[37]

The tune clearly recalls a German folk song, the hunting song "*Ein Jaeger aus Kurpfalz*," the melody of which goes back to the eighteenth century, and perhaps even further. The original melody underwent some changes as it traveled from the Rhineland to Poland, just as did the Jews, who emigrated from the Palatinate to Poland three and a half centuries earlier. This raises two questions: In what way did the tune change? And do the alterations say something about the music of Polish Jewry? A comparison with variant 1 (quoted after Idelsohn) shows that the Jewish melody consists of two basic motifs that are ordered in a primitive ternary form. The German tune consists of a main melody, the text of which changes in every stanza, and a bugle-motif refrain with the syllables "*trara, trara.*" This is basically a binary form that has the following structure:

A	B	
a (2 measures)	Refrain	d (2 measures)
b (2 measures)		e (2 measures)
a′ (2 measures)		a′ (2 measures)
Cadence	Cadence	c (2 measures)
c (2 measures)		

This is an almost artistic form, with variations and repetitions of basic motifs. The Jewish variant has the following structure:

a (2 measures)
a′ (2 measures)
b (2 measures)
c (2 measures)

This is a varied *Lied* form, typical of German folk songs. We find in variant 1 the primitive *Zersingen* of one of the constituent motifs, whereas variant 2 is a clearly German structure, which seems to demonstrate that German tunes lost their basic structure, but not their substance, when they were used and varied by the Polish Jews.

In table VIIIB, no. 7, we find a German setting of Psalm 126. This psalm traditionally introduces the Grace after meals on Sabbaths and festive days (on week-

days, Psalm 137 is chanted). Both customs seem to have originated at the time of the Mishnah.[38] The most popular Jewish and non-Jewish tunes were adapted to the psalm. Variants of the "*Hatikvah*" were sung by many, for almost eighty years, prior to the establishment of the State of Israel. Other catchy melodies were taken from operas or operettas. The example in this table is a typical march melody, such as the German Jews loved at the end of the seventeenth and all through the eighteenth century. In his transcription, Nadel took pains to have the musical stress put upon the grammatically correct syllables. Actually, neither the German nor the Polish Jews were at all meticulous about correct accentuation of their Hebrew prayers.

The structure of the first stanza is simple. It consists of the first three verses of the psalm, pressed into a metrical harness, decidedly against their natural prosody. This constraint causes some repetitions and shifts of accents:

a (4 measures)
b′ (4 measures)
c (4 measures)
c (4 measures)

This is a primitive binary form, with variations, and comes close to the old *Bar* of the minnesingers and meistersingers. The German-Jewish and the Polish-Jewish treatment of borrowed melodies differ in a number of ways, the most notable being the practice of *Zersingen*, for which the Eastern Jews had a decided flair. In the *Mužikališer Pinkas* (Vilna, 1927, p. 53) is quoted an eastern European setting of Psalm 126, which had been discovered previously in Aachen by Birnbaum. The tune was written in 1837 by cantor Joseph Gosowski, a Russian-born hazan. It is a typically Polish-hasidic counterpart of the German song (table VIIIB, no. 7). We shall return to this divergent attitude toward borrowed folk songs in the next chapter.

Other distinctions between *minhag polen* and *minhag ashkenaz* are in the realm of tone-word relation, tonality, ornamentation, and formal structure. To demonstrate the truly fundamental difference between the two *minhagim* it is necessary to define the area where it appears most conspicuous: in the tone-word relationship, that is, in the preference for metrical as against recitative style of the melodies. A comparison of forty melodies notated in *BT*, where both the German and the Polish variants are given, yields the statistical results (key: m = metrical, o = non-metrical) presented in the accompanying chart.

BT No.	Text	German Melody	Polish Melody	
441	o	m	o	*Sabbath*
445	o	m	o	
467	o	m	o	12 songs:
468	o	m	o	8 German versions metrical
470	o	o	o	12 Polish versions nonmetrical
474	o	m	o	3 metrical texts
503	m	o	o	
505	o	m	o	
506	o	o	o	
507	o	m	o	
634	m	m	o	
635	m	o	o	
773	m	m	o	*Festivals*
788	m	m	o	
814	o	m	m	7 songs:
840	m	m	m	7 German versions metrical
842	m	m	o	4 Polish versions nonmetrical
843	m	m	o	6 metrical texts
898	m	m	m	
961	o	o	o	*High Holy Days*
965	o	o	o	
975	o	m	o	21 songs:
978	o	o	m	9 German versions metrical
994/5	m	m	o	12 German versions nonmetrical
997	o	o	o	5 Polish versions metrical
998	o	m	o	16 Polish versions nonmetrical
1005	o	o	o	8 metrical texts
1020	o	o	m	
1021	o	o	o	
1024	m	o	o	
1058	m	o	o	
1098	m	m	o	
1115	o	o	o	
1116	o	o	o	
1155	o	m	m	
1184	m	o	o	
1189	m	m	m	
1190a	m	m	o	
1190d	m	m	m	
1198	o	m	o	

Careful interpretation of the statistical data indicates that the impression that out of forty tunes, twenty-four German metrical variants compare with only eight Polish metrical tunes is numerically correct but is also misleading. Although it is evident that there is a sharp difference between the attitude toward metrical organization displayed by the German Jews and the Polish Jews, this difference is by no means equally discernible in all tunes. It is most conspicuous in Sabbath chants, a little less so in festival tunes, and almost completely absent in the tunes of the High Holy Days. This disparity is easily understood: most of the High Holy

Day tunes are *Missinai* melodies that had come into being before the German Jews emigrated to Poland and Russia, and we are already aware that the *Missinai* tunes were very faithfully preserved.[39] On the three festivals some *Missinai* melodies are sung. None are used on the Sabbath or in the weekday services. It is this that accounts for the differing ratios.

Yet even this mildly statistical approach gives few positive data on the characteristics of eastern European Jewish songs. We shall therefore examine the question from two other angles: the changes within *one* melody during a period of 120–150 years, in Poland and Germany; and the intrusion of mazurka-like rhythms and other melody clauses typical of Slavic folk song.

A good test case for the changes within a melody is the semi-liturgical *zemirah*, *Eliyahu ha-nabi*, one of the most popular tunes for the afternoon of the Sabbath. This tune is certainly 150 years old and the earliest notation of it is found in a manuscript of the Brunswick-Tempel hymnbook in the Birnbaum collection, dated 1835.[40] This version is almost identical with the tune in Arno Nadel's book of *zemirot*. It will be compared with the tune in the manuscript of Levy of Esslingen mentioned in chapter 7. These are the *German* variants. Comparing them with three counterparts from the Vilna *Pinkas* of the turn of the century, one finds the two groups have only the incipit in common; in the German variants the incipit leads into a strictly metrical-periodical tune. In the Polish-Lithuanian versions the incipit leads into melodies that vacillate between syllabic exclamations and interspersed dancelike melismas.[41]

Similar examinations of, and comparisons with, other *zemirot* indicate that the eastern European versions are frequently just on the verge of shedding the musical meter altogether through their excessive *Zersingen*, principally in sequences. This predilection for sequential elaborations was undoubtedly that peccadillo of the Eastern hazanim that the rabbis called "prolonging the chants," and for which they censured them so harshly. And yet this liking for sequences seems to be characteristic of older Polish popular and even art music. The celebrated "Dead Man's Polonaise" by Oginsky (1765–1833) is a trustworthy testimony. Its sequential variations, which are still coarse, are seen in example 5. Even the embellishments do not obfuscate the initial 3/4 rhythm, with the pattern 
This is the rhythm of the *Eliyahu ha-nabi* tune, a genuine polonaise of the outgoing eighteenth century.[42] In the Vilna *Pinkas* one finds many examples of such polonaise-like rhythms, including nos. 11, 28, 122, 124, 131, 170, and 178. Polish dances of past centuries—and there are many scores extant—have two characteristic elements in common with the Jewish songs of the region: excessive extension of the incipit and a strong inclination to long sequential patterns. It was Chopin,

Example 5

with the sensitivity of genius, who refined and dissolved these patched-up sequences into filigree-like, melismatic tendrils.

The second, albeit more recent, element of eastern European Jewish folk song, mostly restricted to the secular sphere, is the intrusion of mazurka rhythms and motifs.[43] Its distinctive element is the stress of the second quarter in a 3/4 rhythm. The Vilna *Pinkas* contains quite a few of these mazurka-like tunes, especially in the *zemirot*.[44] This Slavonic element ought to be considered together with its concomitant tonality, which shifts between major and minor. Thus one may conclude that the Polish variants of Jewish tunes of *minhag ashkenaz* dissolve the metrical structure, extending the incipit. They incline, in their metrical tunes, to the typically Polish rhythms of polonaise and mazurka, with the insertion of sequential ornaments.

We must now turn to conclusions about Eastern versus Western music in the Ashkenazic tradition drawn by that most scholarly writer on the subject, Idelsohn, whose musical notations have served so extensively as source material for this book. First to be examined are certain statements in his one-volume history of Jewish music. On pp. 385 ff. he says the following about the German cantors: "Neither do the [German-Jewish] melodies show any Jewishness, for they are as a rule adopted from the German popular songs. . . . They have the marks of artistic endeavors of individuals." On the other hand "the folk-song of the Jews in the East-European countries took another course of development from that of the Jews in central Europe. It is distinguished by its genuine folk-character. Created out of the people, it remained anonymous. Neither can the time of the songs' creation be determined."

Taking these statements apart, item for item, we find a number of erroneous conceptions, which have exerted great influence on subsequent writers:

"The melodies of the German cantors show no Jewishness, . . . [being] adapted from German popular songs." We have seen in the previous pages that the same objection is valid (if it is indeed an objection) for Polish-Jewish melodies that are similarly adapted from Polish song.

"The folk-songs of eastern European Jews are distinguished by their genuine folk-character." What a tautology! All folk songs, not only Jewish ones, are distinguished by their genuine folk character.

"Created out of the people, . . . they remained anonymous." This sentence, more than any other in his entire literary output, shows that Idelsohn was a strict and uncritical adherent of Eastern *Haskalah* (enlightenment), and, like most of his contemporaries, he subscribed blindly to the folkloristic doctrine of the nationalist German romanticists. The idea that folk song is characterized by its anonymity, that it is "created out of the people," was one of the tendentious and naive conceptions of the successors to the great Herder, father of all folkloristic studies. It was known before the turn of the century that folk songs are creations of individuals, giving to the relationship between art music and folk music entirely new dimensions, of which Idelsohn was blissfully ignorant.

"Neither can the time of a song's creation be determined." Today the experienced ethnomusicologist is generally able to determine the age of any given melody of

European folklore within a margin of error of about thirty years. Considerable progress has been made in the methodology of folkloristic studies since Idelsohn wrote his essays. The method of comparing individual folk melodies of uncertain age and provenance has given way to the close examination of melodic archetypes and their development.[45]

In another article, Idelsohn makes more bold and dogmatic and unsubstantiated statements.[46] On the eastern European folk song he says: "Very few German musical elements can be traced in the folk tunes, while in the synagogue songs of these same people, many German elements have been retained. In the Slavic countries, the Jew instinctively swings towards his neighbor's oriental folksong [sic], so much more closely akin to his own song. The old melodies preserved indicate that the Jewish folktune has retained the same character from that date [ca. 1650] to the present." In his statistical breakup, Idelsohn distinguishes forty melodies based on biblical cantillations and prayer modes, three hundred based on natural minor, three hundred on harmonic minor, a small group based on the Phrygian octave species, fewer on the Dorian scale, two hundred or more on the *Ahabah Rabah* mode, twenty-five on Ukraine-Dorian (D–E–F–G-sharp–A–B–C) *without an octave*. Hence, he concludes, there is 12 percent in major, and about 88 percent in various modes, most of them in minor. "This fact [the relation 88:12] determines the Semitic-Oriental character of the East-European folksong of the Jews, for Semitic folksong is *mainly in minor*; whereas in the Slavic folksong, major and minor elements are about equal. . . . In the face of these facts," says Idelsohn, "we are prompted to accept the opinion that the preference of a scale is a *racial peculiarity*. . . ."

Here Idelsohn contradicts even himself. More than once he had denied the existence of "racial" traits in folk songs. Anthropologists and ethnomusicologists are still far from subscribing to such a theory, and it is senseless to speculate on it.

In addition, Idelsohn has often claimed the inherent similarity of eastern European Jewish songs with Arabic tunes, especially of Iraq and Syria.

In spite of these categorical and untenable declarations, Idelsohn's article is of considerable value. In the first place, it contains the case history of a popular song, which in itself is a rare event. The very same scholar, who holds the conviction that all folk song "is born and created out of the people," tells the following story about the song "*Havah Nagilah*": "This tune originated at the hasidic court of Sagadora, Bukowina,[47] and was brought to Jerusalem. In 1915 I wrote it down. In 1918, needing a popular tune for a performance of my mixed choir in Jerusalem, my choice fell upon this tune which I arranged in four parts and for which *I wrote the Hebrew text*. . . . The next day men and women were singing the song throughout Jerusalem. It quickly spread throughout the country, and thence throughout the Jewish world."

The same article contains the embryo of another Israeli popular tune. Idelsohn lists a number of Russo-Rumanian dancing songs of *hasidim* of his generation, including example 6. The tune obstinately repeats the incipit with many variants and turns out to be rather lengthy and turbulent. This, too, came to Palestine after

Example 6

Example 7

1932 (when Idelsohn's article was written), and was radically shortened and rearranged with a new Hebrew text, apparently by a good craftsman. The result was the popular song "*Hevenu Shalom Alekhem*," of whose *Vorlage* only one motif (example 7) remained intact, but this became the "generative" motif, or germinating cell. Idelsohn did not live to hear the song in its final version, the one into which it crystallized in 1937 or 1938.

Concluding the discussion about the difference between Polish and Western *minhag ashkenaz* beyond and apart from statistics and the details of morphological examinations, one is impressed by the different kinds of Gestalt and sonority in the two traditions. The rhapsodic lyricisms of a high coloratura tenor, interlarded with musical sobs (called *hoquetus* in medieval music), the repetitions of words and of syllables as cultivated in the Polish style stand in bold contrast to the more austere, metrically oriented, less lachrymose baritonal chant of the German tradition. This divergence pertains, however, only to the cantorial recitative and to some of the *piyutim*. For all practical purposes the pure Western Ashkenazic style is slowly fading away, yielding to a mixed tradition, in which the Polish element is considerably stronger. This is the situation now in the United States and also in Israel.

9

The Tunes of the *Haggadah*

This chapter considers the traditional Seder melodies up to the year 1914. This terminus was chosen because World War I and its aftermath caused so many and such consequential migrations of the Jewish masses that the hitherto stable oral tradition was decisively shaken, and in most cases completely contaminated. Elements originating in the hit song, the music hall, the various youth rallies intruded—and are still intruding—in increasing measure, into the old tradition. Up to that time, the tradition had been a strictly guarded musical legacy.

Before proceeding, we must distinguish between the general (common), the regional, and the family traditions, especially where musical notation was unavailable or unknown to the singers. As the recitation of the *Haggadah* takes place in the home, in the restricted circle of the family, the resulting particularism of its musical tradition has acted against the usual trend toward standardization or uniformity. This holds true especially for the time before *Haggadot* when music notes were printed.

When discussing the individual melodies, the criteria listed in previous chapters are applied. Four additional criteria are taken into account:

Similarity of structure, tonality, or motifs, to other Jewish melodies, whether or not they are part of the Seder ritual, can often give us a clue as to the provenance of a piece. Even more significantly, this is true of non-Jewish music from which many of the Jewish tunes are borrowed.

The same melody often appears in very different shapes and sounds; the variable elements are the timbre of the voice, the type of musical embellishment, the tempo, the relative emphasis, or neglect, of metrical accents, and other almost imponderable elements.[1]

Tonal range of melody is a clue to age: the smaller it is, the older, in general, is the melody.

In considering the tone-word relationship, a metrical text normally forces the melody into a commensurate rhythm, whereas a psalmodic form type is clearly recognizable by its parallelistic structure; the same holds true for a verse of scriptural cantillation.

First we shall divide the text of the *Haggadah* into categories, according to their rhythmic structure, as follows: (1) *simple*, often narrative prose; (2) *argumentative*, reasoning prose, of Mishnaic or Midrashic origin, such as *Mah Nishtanah* and *Amar Rabbi El'azar ben Azariah*; (3) psalmody, plain or ornate; (4) *psalmody* with refrain; (5) *poetic prayer* (oration) of the rabbinic period, such as the *birkhat ha-mazon*; (6) *semi-metrical prose*, such as *ha laḥma*, *The Ten Plagues*, and the benediction before

the second cup of wine; (7) *metrical poems* (*piyutim*), with or without rhyme, which make up the last part of the *Haggadah*, after the *hallel*.

Again we realize that metrical tunes are applied not only to metrical texts. The Ashkenazic tradition is unique among Jewish traditions in its strong penchant for metrical tunes, even when the text does not warrant such treatment. In particular, prayers familiar to all such as the *birkhat ha-mazon* or the *hallel* are almost always set to metrical tunes, which in many cases were borrowed from Gentile sources.

The selections belonging to category 1 (above) are all narratives; when they are not quotations from Scripture, they are simply recited upon one or two tones, sometimes closed by a little flourish. Where scriptural passages are to be emphasized, they have been cantillated, provided the celebrant was familiar with the chant. Two examples of this kind of recitation from the eighteenth century may be found in J. J. Schudt's *Memorabilia Judaica* (Frankfort, 1714–1717), one in Wagenseil's *Belehrung* (Königsberg, 1699), and one is notated in the autobiography of Isaak Lachmann (MS in Hebrew Union College, Cincinnati).

The texts of category 2, argumentative prose, have been chanted for the last three centuries in the study mode of Mishnah or Talmud, a mode that German Jews called *Stubentrop*. Its course is very simple, but of amazingly wide range, as seen in example 1. This tune, or its skeleton, cannot be older than 300, or at most 350 years, for in it the harmonic functions of the major scale are clearly pronounced. The *terminus a quo* is 1558, the year in which the major scale was "officially" postulated by Zarlino.[2]

Much older than such passages are the plain psalmodies of category 3. Most particularly the psalm "*Be-tzet yisra'el*" from the first part of the *hallel* (example 2a). That psalm was chanted in Poland, Bohemia, and Bavaria according to a

Example 1

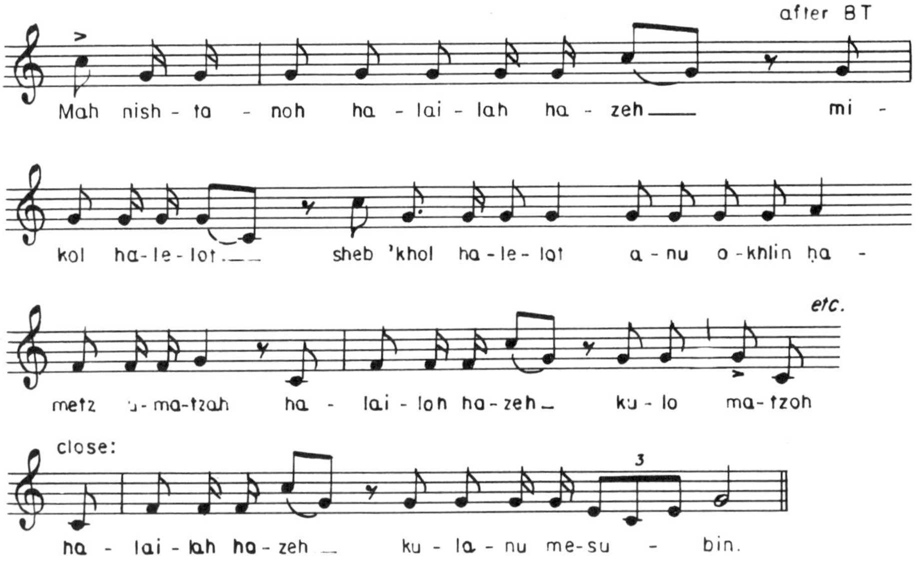

Example 2

strictly modal pattern that is almost identical with the *tonus peregrinus* of the Gregorian repertoire (to the same text) (example 2b). It is interesting that the *tonus* is itself of oriental origin, as indicated by both its name and its occurrence in the Near Eastern church.[3] Its double tenor (two different recitation tones) is considered rare in Gregorian chant but is commonplace in the Near East.

Elements of ornate psalmody occur in the *kiddush* (example 3a) or in the Moravian tradition of counting the ten plagues (example 3b). I heard this chant of the "plagues," which appears nowhere in print, from my own grandfather, who was born in 1840,

Example 3

and who heard it from his father. Its Moravian-Slovakian provenance was attested to me by my dear friend, the late Bence Szabolcsi of Budapest, who was probably the greatest expert on Jewish musical tradition of central Europe in our time. The nuclear motif of the "plagues" also occurs in an eastern European Jewish psalmody, the benediction on counting the *Omer* (example 4).

It is both interesting and disconcerting to observe how the best methodological categories can be invalidated in actual observation. We encounter, for example, one case which transcends all theoretical boundaries. Example 5 is the Moravian tradition of *ha laḥma*, semi-metrical, and presumably belonging to category 7,

Example 4

Example 5

containing certain psalmodic strains, and, what is more, a distinct similarity to the chants of both the "plagues" and the counting of the *Omer*. Most characteristic is the closing formula of *ha laḥma*, which is identical with that of the *Omer* blessing and the cadence of the west Ashkenazic Torah cantillation (example 5b).[3a]

Chant	Range	Tenor	Next Related Church Tone	Number of Tones Constituting Cadence	Finalis in Relation to Tenor
"plagues"	sixth or seventh	one (a)	*Tonus orationis*	six	(1) fourth below (2) fourth above
Omer	octave	one (a)	VII tone	five	second below
ha lahma	sixth	one (a)	oration	six	fourth below

The accompanying chart summarizes the comparison of closing formulas of three chants, the "plagues," *Omer* blessing, and *ha laḥma*. According to strictly musicological criteria, the chant of the "plagues" seems to be the oldest of the three; its range is very narrow, it has only one tenor, it comes closest to the *tonus*

Example 6

orationis, the number of tones constituting the cadence is five or six, the finalis is quite irregular—the fourth beneath the tenor or the fourth above it (example 6).

Variant 6 reminds us strongly of the Mozarabic tradition of the *Pater Noster*,[4] indicating that the chant is very old indeed. All three texts belong to the oldest part of the *Haggadah:* the listing of the plagues is a pre-tannaitic compilation, the benediction of the *Omer* is of tannaitic origin, and the formula of invitation, *ha laḥma*, couched in talmudic Aramaic, seems to belong to an equally old stratum.[5] It is also significant that before 1914 no metrical tunes had replaced these ancient formulas of prayer. Thus we may well assume that the tunes of these three pieces are the oldest of the Ashkenazic *Haggadah* ritual. The chant of the *ha laḥma* is closely related to the oldest types of orations; it also shows a distinct connection with the closing acclamation of the Seder, the passage "*le-shanah ha-ba'ah birushalayim*" and, even more noteworthy, with the characteristic cadence of the Three Festivals (example 7).

Example 7

A comparison of these chants with certain of the *birkhot ha-shahar* of the weekday service (the oldest of Ashkenazic chants) and with some orations and psalmodies of the oldest Gregorian and Byzantine repertoire (example 8) indicates a common source, probably the *tropos spondeiakos* referred to by Clement of Alexandria as the mode of Jewish psalmody in his time, and discussed above in chapter 4 (see also *Omer* blessing, above, example 4). The temptation is strong to consider the tonal skeleton of all these chants as pentatonic. Such an assumption, as I have shown elsewhere, is erroneous. Szabolcsi has given a convincing analysis of the problem and its inherent pitfalls in his profound study on the subject of the pentatonic system.[6]

Aside from the Halleluiahs that belong to the *hallel* psalms, and are chanted as part of the psalmody for those psalms, the *Haggadah* contains only one acclamation at the very end of the celebration: the group enthusiastically chants the prayer "Next year in Jerusalem" [*le-shanah ha-ba'ah birushalayim*]. This phrase parallels the conclusion of the *ha laḥma, ha-ba'ah beney ḥorin*. It has almost exactly the same musical shape (example 9) (cf. example 5b). Again we encounter, in the first phrase, that typical motif of the festival prayer chant (see example 7). In the third phrase there appears again the cadence formula of the Torah cantillation.

Example 8

a) Skeleton of Tropos Spondiakos.
Syriac 'Unita; in Sacred Bridge, p. 444
b)
gad-desh pa - gren v'naf-sha-tan vet-ra-ḥam 'a - leyn, 'a-leyn...
c) Antiphona "Postquam surrexit Dominus"
Mag - nus Do-mi-nus, et lau-da - bi - lis ni - - mis:
in ci - vitate Dei nostri, in mon-te san-cto e - jus.
d)
Dom, tztar-de - 'a, kin - nim, o - rov, de - ver, sh -
chin, bo - rod, ar - beh, ḥo - shekh, ma-kat be-kho - rot.
or
3
ma-kat be-kho - rot.

Example 9

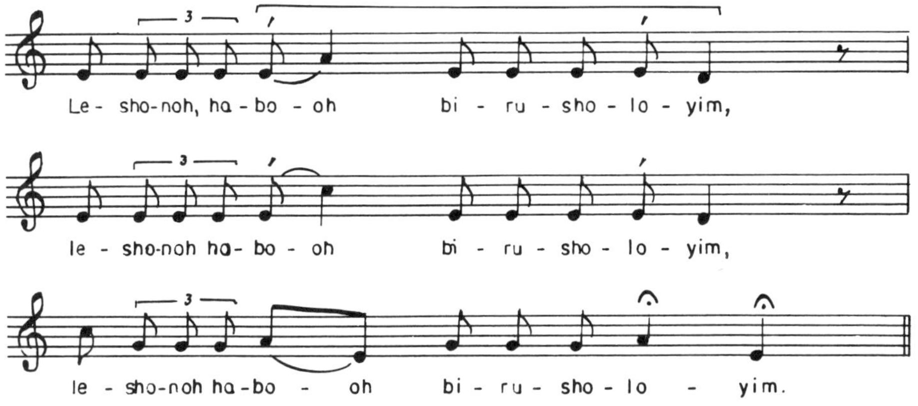
3
Le- sho-noh, ha-bo - oh bi - ru - sho - lo - yim,
le - sho-noh ha- bo - oh bi - ru - sho - lo - yim,
le - sho-noh ha-bo - oh bi - ru - sho - lo - yim.

Surely these identities are not accidental. We deal here with another set of wandering motifs, like those that played so decisive a part in forming the structure of the *Missinai* tunes (see above, chapter 3). While the constitutive motifs and their tonalities derive from a much earlier time, their grouping together and their recurrence in the oldest texts make us believe that these three melodies are contemporaries of the *Missinai* tunes.

Loosely related to them are the melodies of prayers such as the *kiddush*, *ve-hi she-amdah*, and similar pieces. They belong to the category of ornate psalmodies. The *kiddush*, which has come down to us in a more or less uniform tradition, is one of the many variants of the *Akdamut* (see table VI, no. 1, and comments in chapter 6). In chapter 6, the *Akdamut* was compared to the Gregorian *Magnificat* in the third tone. Like that ancient mode, the chant of the *kiddush* has a range of not more than a sixth, it has one tenor, and the constitutive formulas are clearly recognizable. It is impossible to say whether the mode originated with Jews or Christians. It is more than a thousand years old. The *kiddush*, in its present form, is, of course, more recent, but the venerable basic mode is clearly discernible in example 10.

Example 10

Inserted into the midst of these prayers, Midrashic arguments, and simple narrations is a sort of joyous litany, based on an ancient *Midrash*, the familiar *Dayenu*. Its literary motif was taken over by the early Roman, Byzantine, and Georgian churches as the raw material for the so-called *Improperia*. In that text, the crucified Jesus reminds the Jewish people of his benefits to them, substituting for the word *Dayenu* this phrase: "and what did you give me in return?" Probably the basic motifs were taken over by the Byzantine clergymen at the time of John Chrysostom, who followed the antisemitic line of Melito of Sardes (ca. 170).[7] The effect of these *Improperia*, chanted on Good Friday in churches bereft of light, is dramatic and strongly anti-Jewish.

The various melodies sung today to the *Dayenu* are very recent, hardly a hundred years old; some of them originated only during World War II. The oldest chant of *Dayenu* I have found is a primitive psalmody with the entire text, except for the refrain word, sung upon one tone of recitation, and the response intoned in two ways, as seen in example 11. The modes in example 11a are old hexachordal structures. In 11b a modern finalis is added, transforming the tonality to the minor. Obviously 11a is the older version. The mode is still familiar to many oriental Jews,

Example 11

but not set to this text. The first two *hallel* psalms mentioned above, the *ge'ulah* and the *berakhot* preceding the meal, close the first part of the Seder.

The musical atmosphere after the meal is a far cry from the archaic mood that prevailed at the beginning. Almost all melodies now are metrical, even if the texts are not, and the old paradox is proved again: the stricter the meter, the looser the line—a principle that is verified in every texted melody of a dance, be it a waltz or a can-can.

The text of the *birkhat ha-mazon* (grace after meals in the *Haggadah*) is the same as that after any other meal, with the exception of one or two insertions, which are variable according to the festival, Sabbath, or holy day on which it is recited. So, too, the melodies do not differ from those of other occasions. The text is not metrical but contains a good many rhymes and semi-metrical passages.[8] The Western Ashkenazim, always fond of metrical contrafacts to nonmetrical texts, included a number of choral responses and refrains in the simple recitation of the prayer. These insertions originate, without exception, in the secular German folk song of the late eighteenth and early nineteenth century. Example 12 lists the best-known motifs. With these melodies we find ourselves on the brink of vulgarity. In the Rhineland and in southwestern Germany these tunes were familiar as dancing songs.

The shift to a secular style in the music after the Seder meal becomes most noticeable in the second part of the *hallel*, particularly the verses *Hodu* and *Anah* from Psalm 118. Here the German *minhag ashkenaz* appears in different forms in the north and the south, both adaptations of German folk songs.

In the south the tunes for *Hodu* and *Anah* do not attain the rank of seasonal leitmotifs for all Ashkenazim, but it was widespread. Even the Jews of Provence, who had their own liturgical and musical tradition, seem to have used it.[9] Example 13 presents three variants, which, at first glance, do not seem to belong to the same melody type but, as seen here, one above another, reveal a strong relationship. Also, all three variants appear to be related to an old southern German-Catholic processional. The old processional, an Eastern song, was printed first in the Mayence *Gesangbuch* in 1628, but it is probably a half-century older than that.[10] Thus we see how a melodic pattern was varied between 1600 and 1860. When Loewenstamm's version was incorporated in the American Union *Haggadah*, it became popular in the United States. The cantorially embellished version by Judah Offenbach should not deceive us about the basic simplicity of the tune.

Example 12

Example 13

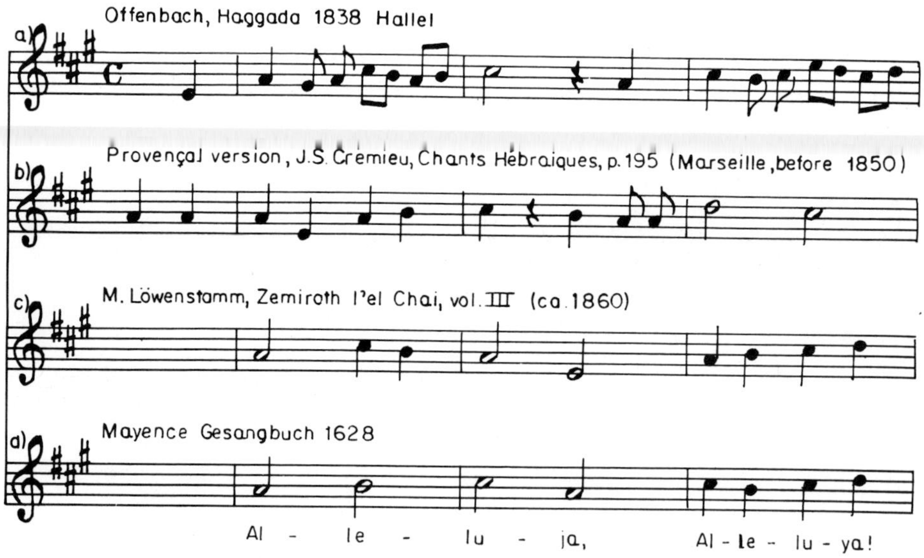

The northern melodic tradition for the *Hodu-Anah* is actually the older of the two. We discuss it second because it is clearly taken from the subsequent *piyut* of the Seder, *Adir Hu*. That tune was first published by Johann Stephanus Rittangel in Koenigsberg, in 1644, then by Gottfried Selig in *Der Jude*. It appeared again in 1769 with a Judeo-German text and has been printed hundreds of times since then. Example 14 presents the oldest notations extant of the *Adir Hu*.

Example 14

Example 15

Example 16

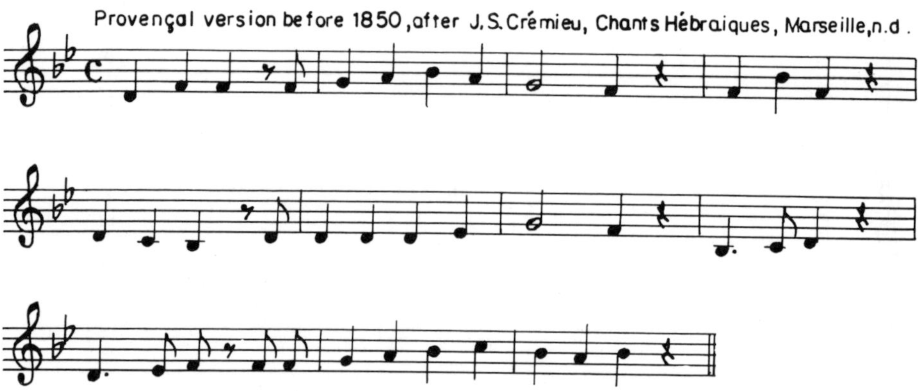

Example 15 is the same tune adapted for Psalm 118, for the *Hodu-Anah.* The melody was so popular that, like the Southern version, it was adopted (for *Adir Hu*) by the Provençal Jews in the version seen in example 16. Example 17 is the latest variant of both *Hodu* and *Adir Hu*, originally from northwest German tradition but now used by all Ashkenazic groups. Whereas no German song was taken over completely for these settings of *Adir Hu* and *Hodu-Anah*, certainly the motifs in example 18 from old forgotten German folk songs are close parallels.

Beginning with *Adir Hu*, the tunes which follow the *hallel* are all *piyutim* (except for *le-shanah ha-ba'ah*). Their strictly metrical shape and occasionally juvenile character are quite conspicuous. In the case of *Hodu-Anah* we distinguished between northern and southern tradition. We will now observe a similar difference between eastern and western customs. They contrast strongly, and hasidic elements become quite obvious in the eastern tradition. For *ḥasal sidur pesaḥ* two main types stand out. The German melody (example 19), composed by Judah Offenbach, smacks strongly of Haydn's early masses and choruses. The first eight measures are obviously meant for a precentor of sorts, while the second part corresponds to the stereotyped and customary close of the *Credo:* Amen, amen, amen, amen! The eastern melody is a twentieth-century contrafact on a Palestinian tune. It has a more archaic character; its range is only a sixth, and it has preserved its modal structure and some typically Hasidic ornaments (example 20).

Example 17

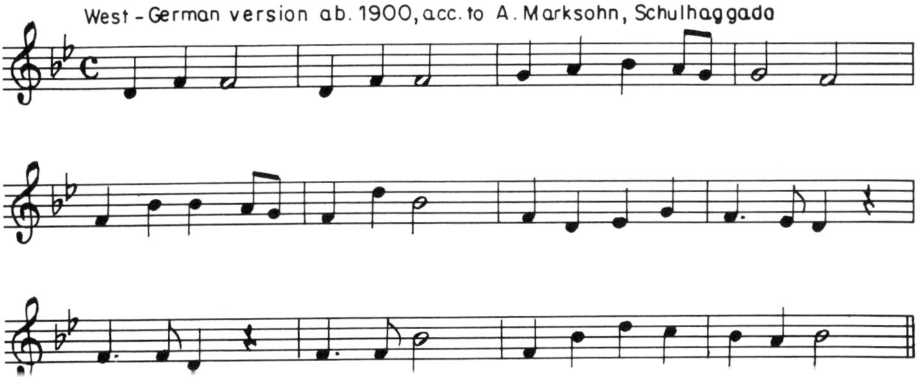

Example 18

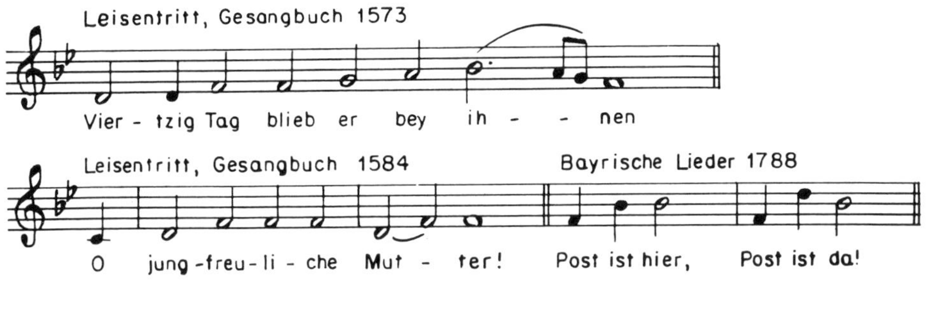

Example 19

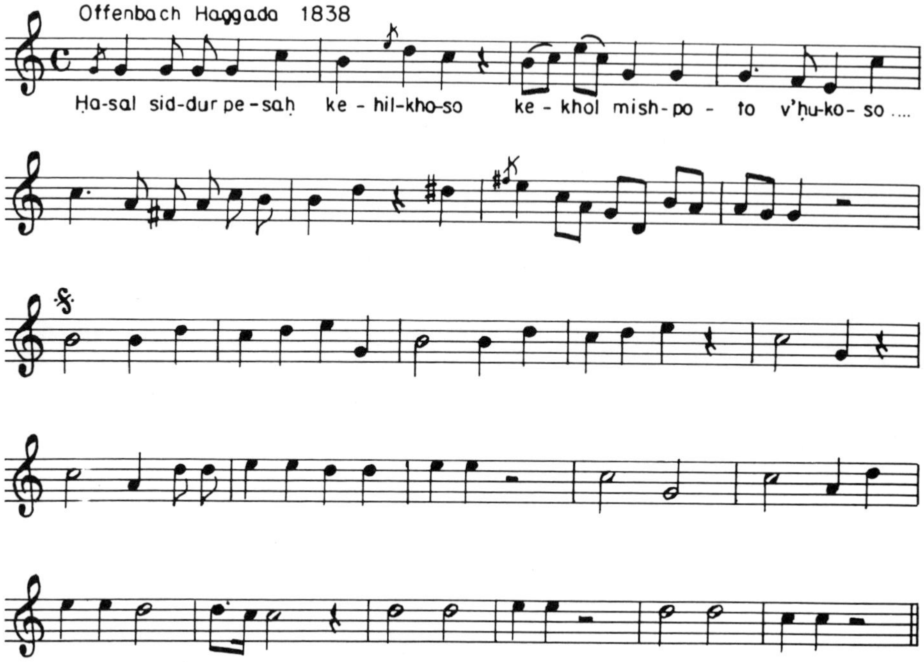
Offenbach Haggada 1838
Ḥa-sal sid-dur pe-saḥ ke - hil-kho-so ke - khol mish-po - to v'ḥu-ko- so ....

Example 20

East - European version (about 1920), in Haggadah, ed. L. Finkelstein, New York, 1942
Ḥa-sal si-dur pe-saḥ ke - hil - kho - so k'khol mish-po - to ve -
ken- niz- keh la' - so - so.
a)
le - sa - der_ o - so _

The twin poems *va-yehi ba-ḥatzi ha-lailah* and *va-amartem zebaḥ pesaḥ* are usually sung to the same tune. Both poems are part of the *kerobot* for the Passover feast day and have been incorporated into the *Haggadah.* Shalom Spiegel is convinced that from the beginning they were sung to the same tune. We cite a German and a Moravian melody (example 21). A third variant, of Provençal origin, is interesting because of its asymmetry (not quoted).

Example 21

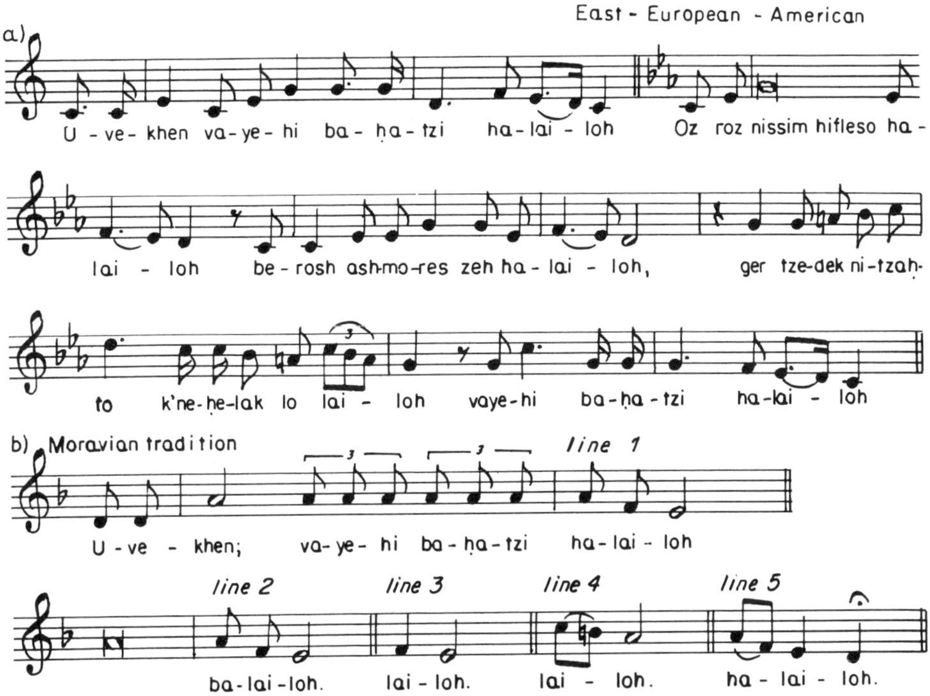

The first of these poems is by Yannai, and the second, *va-amartem*, by Kallir. Of the two melodic variants the first is of mixed German-Polish origin: the refrain is German, the rest, eastern European, set in a free psalmody. Each setting of the word "*lailah*" is made with care, appearing in either the dominant or the tonic. The second, Moravian, variant seems to be at least two hundred years old. It is rather primitive in structure, consisting only of a recitation tone, on which the bulk of the poem is spoken or chanted rapidly, and each verse is followed by one of five cadential formulas on the word "*lailah.*" The fact that major and minor dominants are used seems to establish some link with the first variant. These strict formulas confirm Spiegel's suggestion that the primitive rhyme was used by the poets to enable the company to join in the singing.

In the *ki lo na'eh* we again encounter Eastern and Western variants. The oldest version was first published by Rittangel (Koenigsberg, 1644) (example 22a). Its beginning is identical with the early Protestant hymn "*Kommt her zu mir, spricht Gottes Sohn,*" itself a contrafact of the contemporaneous "*Was wollen wir singen.*"[11]

Example 22

a) Rittangel, 1644
Ki lo no - eh, ki - lo ___ yo - eh
A - dir bim - lu - khoh bo - ḥur kah' - lo - khoh ge -
du - dav yo - me-ru lo, le - kho ___ u - le -
kho, le - kha ___ ki ___ le - kho, le - kho ___
af ___ le - kho a - do - noi ha - mam - lo - kho. ___
b) Der Lindenschmid-Ton, 1534, 1544 BAL. No. 375, 376.
Es ist nit lang, dass es ge - schach, dassman den Lind-schmid rei-ten
sah auf ei - nem ho - hen Ros - se.
etc.
c) Offenbach Haggada 1838
L'kho u- le-kho, l'kho ki le-kho, l'kho af le-kho, l'kho A-do-noi.
ha-mam-lo-kho, ki lo no - eh, ki lo yo - eh.

d) Moravian tradition, before 1850

This melody type became extremely popular under the name "*Lindenschmidt Ton*" at the end of the sixteenth century (example 22b). Both melody and text of this German Robin Hood ballad seem to have inspired the German Jews, possibly because the generous robber Lindenschmidt represented to them a champion of freedom.

Example 22c is the variant found in the Offenbach *Haggadah* of 1838. It has some motifs in common with the contemporaneous Moravian tradition (example 22d). They both show definite hasidic influence in their vivacious [*freilach*] polka-like rhythm and they share the motif of example 23. (This motif also appears in the eastern version of *ehad mi yode'a.*) In the Moravian version, a noteworthy feature is the constant change from major to minor and back, seen in the Eastern tunes in chapter 8, and, as we recall, familiar to the musician through the compositions of Dvořák, Smetana, and Schubert.

Example 23

A later Western tune (example 24) contains a number of German folk song motifs. Probably the oldest of them, from the fourteenth century, appears in *BAL*, p. 387. Similar elements occur in Adam Krieger's *Komm Galathea* (1676). In its present form the melody appears to have been patched together by a hazan without much imagination.

"*Eḥad mi yode'a*" is a text based on an old Catholic "riddle of numbers" song in Latin. Like the other songs, it appears in both Eastern and Western (example 25a)

Example 24

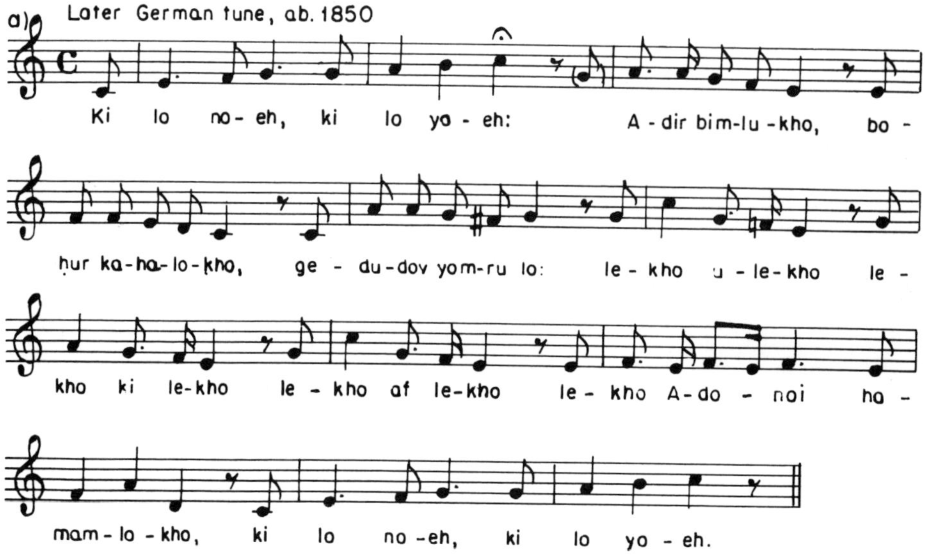

Example 25

Example 26

versions. The older Moravian tune (example 25b) resembles the Moravian *va-yehi ba-ḥatzi ha-lailah* in structure. It was a psalmodic kernel, to which four formulas are added for the first five stanzas. This is a cumulative song, and the accumulation of the formulas forms the refrain (example 26) in which the whole company is expected to join. If all thirteen stanzas are sung there emerges a primitive rondo: *R*1*R*2*R*3*R*4, etc., where *R* is the refrain, sung in reverse order. The motifs 4 and 3, in that order, yield a popular Slavonic song element, well known in Czech, Slovak, and western Polish folklore. Composers such as Dvořák, Smetana, and J. Suk used it frequently.

The last of these childlike *piyutim* is the famous *Ḥad Gadya.* The literary motifs of the old text occur in many remote and unrelated folk traditions.[12] There are at least three tunes sung by Ashkenazic Jews to this text. Example 27 is the best known.

There is another tune that I have seen nowhere in print. I heard it from my grandmother, while grandfather championed the version of example 27. My grandmother's tune (example 28) is much older and more interesting. It shows all the marks of a metrically changed cantillation—a rare form indeed. Even grandfather abandoned his own favorite (with its clear reminiscence of "*ein Maennlein steht im Walde*" in favor of the dignity of the older tune, when we sang the last stanza referring to "the Holy One, Blessed be He." Example 29 is a fragment of a Spanish tune, which is a distant relative of this second *Had Gadya.*[13] Its tonal skeleton can also be found in the tradition of the Provençal Jews.[14]

Example 27

Example 28

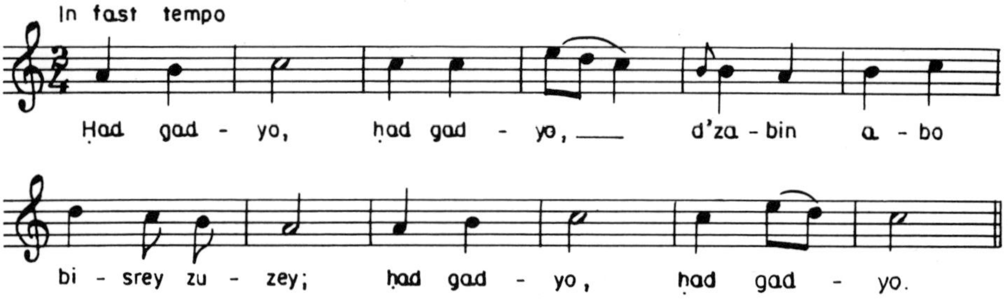

Example 29

Finally, we will compare two examples, one of the Moravian tradition prior to 1850 (example 30a) and one notated by the Jewish convert (30b)—one-time hazan of Prosnitz in Moravia—Friedrich Albert Christian. The tune appears in his book *Zevah Pesah* (Leipzig, 1677). Possibly the oldest kernel of all the old melodic versions of *Had Gadya* may be identified in the ancient "*In dulci jubilo*" (example 30c). But a much later version, composed or arranged by Offenbach for his *Haggadah* to German words, appears here in an English version (example 31).

For all the surface disparities of the Seder ritual music, there is a basic integration, even between the first part, preceding the meal, and the second, which follows it. Looking back over the material in this chapter, we will find three groups of texts that have musical motifs in common: (1) *Ha laḥma, Dam, tzefarde'a* (plagues), *Le'shanah ha-ba'ah*; (2) *Dayenu, ki lo na'eh, Eḥad mi yode'a, Va'yehi ba'ḥatzi ha-lailah, Ḥad Gadya*; (3) *Hodu-Anah, Adir Hu.*

Group 1 contains old texts exclusively, and, interestingly enough, only old melodies. Their inner relationship leads me to believe that this music belongs to the

Example 30

Example 31

oldest, best-integrated stratum. Group 2 is motley. It contains old psalmodic motifs, especially in the cadences, but also tunes of the sixteenth to nineteenth centuries. The cadencing motifs, some of which have a certain Slavonic flavor, may indicate the influence of slowly remigrating hazanim from Russia and Poland. It is this group that establishes a musical connection between the two parts of the *Haggadah*.

Group 3 displays no connection with the other groups. Musically it is almost entirely of German stock, and in some respects resembles the tunes of the German *birkhat ha-mazon*, which originated in the Rhineland and southern Germany between 1780 and 1830.

There is a principle common to most of the Seder tunes. The common motifs in group 1 and the refrains in group 2 are all intended to be sung in chorus by the whole company. Except for *Adir Hu* and its derivative in the *Hodu-Anah*, all of the music in the *Haggadah* is born out of the spirit of the word and its associations.

10

The Dawn of Emancipation

The price of progress in history
is paid by forfeiting human happiness.
(Sigmund Freud[1])

Decline of Western Jewry

Rarely in Jewish history were the signs of dissension as apparent as during the second half of the eighteenth century. That period of European civilization, acclaimed for a galaxy of important achievements and shining names in the arts, in philosophy, and even in statesmanship, was contemporaneous with an ugly and miserable decay in Western Jewry. The aftermath of the Sabbatean collapse was characterized by a craving for shallow pleasure, by the showy and often ludicrous conduct of wealthy Jews in public, notably in the spas. A serious examination of the deeper causes of this malaise would exceed the scope of this book, yet one of the many and complex causes may be suggested: the basic Jewish values had become dubious; the sense and purpose of the enormous sacrifices by individuals and communities in the past were now questioned. This moral crisis can be recognized by its external symptoms, although the crucial questions never came into the open. The loss of inner strength is palpable in the more and more repressive edicts of the leading rabbis. Their *teshubot* (responsa) reflect in mirror image the thoughts, wishes, and mores of the Jews during that period, especially when they dealt with questions of amusements and pastimes.

These severe measures did not deal with needs of the workday; they reveal the hedonism of the wealthy Jews, which was always sure to evoke the inevitable puritanical reaction of the rabbis. The rabbis were incapable of distinguishing between frivolous pastimes and truly artistic endeavors such as music. To them music was either a merrymaking noise at weddings, or a science of the Gentiles. The concept of art in the modern sense was totally foreign to them. They understood music as a set of more or less trivial skills, practiced by *klezmorim*, the folk musicians, or by *badḥanim*, the jesters and entertainers. For the rabbis, these skills were a world apart from the sphere of ritual and synagogue music.

All of this was true at the very time when Western art music was reaching its highest splendor. The fact is that the Jews of the time took relatively little notice of it. While Europe's music was being shaped by the great masters, Jewish secular music was represented only by those *klezmorim* and *badḥanim* so scorned by the rabbis. There remained the synagogue. Some distorted fragments of Haydn's

masterworks, of Mozart's melodies wafted into it, over the walls of the ghetto. This was, alas, at the expense of *minhag ashkenaz*.

During the years between 1660 and 1720, the musical tradition was waning, and the second half of the eighteenth century witnessed its worst decay. Its connection with folklore was dwindling, and the amount of Hebrew, Yiddish, or even German folk song used, stylized, or even abused was negligible compared to the overwhelming quantity of classical or operatic music absorbed and ridiculously parodied. This was true in synagogues from Alsace to Cracow, and from Padua to Copenhagen.

The situation can be described harshly as a decline, or recession, or it can be more charitably described as a loss of traditional substance replaced by the absorption of classical music. It can be interpreted as a natural consequence of the progressive acculturation of the Jewish community; it can be judged as a phenomenon of *absinkendes Kulturgut* from classical music, or it might be termed simply a budding parody of the Vienna classical style, undertaken with inadequate means and in poor taste. One might even consider it an attempt at popularizing serious music for the Jewish masses, in which the hazanim assumed, knowingly or unknowingly, the role of the transmitters and popularizers. None of these definitions takes into account one very basic fact: that Ashkenazic Jewry was not a socially homogeneous community. Indeed, if there had ever been real homogeneity, it no longer existed by the year 1700. At this time, Jewry was already divided into classes and was fully conscious of its stratification. Inasmuch as this stratification had a bearing on the development of *minhag ashkenaz*, we must observe the form it took.

There were at least four strata in the totality of European Jewry at the end of the eighteenth century:

1. Bankers, court Jews, and patricians. All privileged Jews belonged to this group. In Austria they were the *Toleranz-juden*, in Bohemia and Moravia, the *Familiants*, Jews who were privileged to marry whenever and whomever they chose; the high financiers of the various dynasties, the successors of the court Jews, and the native Jewish patricians. Most of them aspired to political liberation and the legalization of equal status with their neighbors. Many of them had already achieved social equality, and even admission to the nobility, through intermarriage. In this group, the *Familiants* were the weakest and poorest sector.

2. Scholars and rabbis. The dominant, frequently autocratic position of the rabbinate was reflected in the status of the individual rabbi, which was usually very high. This powerful position collapsed when the judicial power of the rabbi was abrogated in the course of the Emancipation. What remained was a kind of respect for the "spiritual leader" of the community, comparable to the respect due to the vicar or priest in the local Christian congregation. Since the rabbis foresaw such a loss of their power and prestige, they strongly opposed any step in the direction of Emancipation. A small minority of extreme liberals felt the impact of the French Revolution and were acquainted with the new philosophies of Kant and Moses Mendelssohn. They alone favored the deliverance from the ghetto, from its legal and intellectual confines.

3. Businessmen, artisans, and functionaries of the Jewish communities in the cities. All of these had high hopes for the Emancipation. When it finally came, they welcomed it, as though it were a Messianic era. Yet, together with the liberal intellectuals, they were the most disappointed and broken when the states that had promised full equality did not keep their pledges. Since they constituted the numerical majority of western and central European Jewry, their traumatic disappointment resulted in a decline, during the nineteenth century, of the radical reform movement. For it was that movement that had built upon the premises of a government-sponsored total equality. This proved to be a mirage, which began to disappear in 1820, and vanished altogether in Europe after 1930.

4. The *Landjuden*, or rural Jews. At the turn of the eighteenth century, these Jews of the small towns or rural districts constituted almost a quarter of the German, Austrian, and Alsatian Jewish population, which was affected by the emancipatory laws.[2] Always in the closest touch with the Gentile population, they neither entertained great hopes for the Emancipation nor were bitterly disappointed after its failure. There were no more fervent and faithful adherents of Orthodoxy than the rural Jews. With an incredible tenacity, they held fast to their old folkways, some of which they retained "for better or worse" until the years of the Holocaust. They opposed almost any change, large or small, especially those championed by the liberal and intellectual rabbis. This explains why their musical tradition, as notated so much later, in the middle of the nineteenth century, retained so many elements of the Baroque. This reinforces Bartók's and Kodály's theory of the shifty character of the urban versus the steadfastness of the rural tradition.[3]

The disparate trends within German-speaking Jewry were felt even before the French Revolution. In his fine essay "Songs and Singers of the Eighteenth Century,"[4] Idelsohn takes as his point of departure the Birnbaum collection of the Hebrew Union College Library (Cincinnati), the largest aggregation of written synagogue music of the period, reflecting all the varieties of style and performance practice. Surveying this material *de novo*, I reach conclusions somewhat different from Idelsohn's.

In order to present a well-rounded analysis of *minhag ashkenaz* during the second half of the eighteenth century, we shall undertake a detailed evaluation of oral tradition as practiced in the big cities by itinerant hazanim. This will be compared to the oral tradition of the small town synagogues, where sedentary lay cantors served for generations by hereditary privilege and custom. In these small sanctuaries the schoolteacher or sexton or even the ritual butcher served year-in, year-out, usually as honorary and unpaid functionaries. Their musical material was rarely fixed in written form, whereas the hazanim of the big cities left a considerable amount of their music, collected in hundreds of manuscripts. These form the majority of the material in the Birnbaum collection.

Taking into account the social stratification described above, I divide the material of the Birnbaum Collection into three parts, each reflecting a different set of influences, and each resulting in a different style: (1) manuscripts containing compositions of professional itinerant hazanim who served the large communities,

in such cities as Berlin, Prague, Leipzig, and Strasbourg;[5] (2) manuscript compendia from small rural communities of southern Germany and Austria, written by lay cantors or teachers for their own use (the best of these, though they originated in the first half of the nineteenth century, reflecting an oral tradition that is about 150 years older, and containing an abundance of Baroque elements); (3) the oral tradition of table songs and *zemirot*, which originated largely in the eighteenth or the beginning of the nineteenth century. Examples in the last category provide a classic case of the growing autonomy of music sung to Hebrew texts—the same tune serving a number of hymns indiscriminately. None of the old borrowed German or French tunes was left unaltered, so that none of the "original tunes" remained recognizable to the naive listener. In chapter 8 some of the Eastern *zemirot* were analyzed; later, we shall have occasion to discuss their Western counterparts. Most of them reflect the irresistible attraction of the newer German folk song for the southern German Jews, during and after the French Revolution. A little foretaste was offered the reader in the previous chapter on the tunes of the *Haggadah*.

The manuscripts of the large communities. At once we come upon a paradox. The oldest collections of synagogue songs, written by the migrating hazanim, are more neglectful of the basic musical tradition of *minhag ashkenaz* than are the later compendia. Stimulated by the intoxicating sounds of classical and operatic music, the Jewish singers adopted a peculiar Rococo style, full of the flourishes and frills that were so favored in the middle of the eighteenth century. Neglecting entirely the fluid recitative and the inherited prayer modes, they preferred fashionable ditties, imitating instrumental forms such as the minuet, rondo, polonaise, prelude, allegretto, indeed the very *galant* style of the Rococo, but without the accompaniment of the indispensable instruments. The loss of interest in the venerable Hebrew prayer texts was only a corollary of the Jewish accommodation to the Western hegemony of instrumental music. This neglect of the texts is manifest in the manuscripts themselves; only a few scribes took the pains to write the Hebrew words beneath the music. In most cases, the hazanim contented themselves with simple superscriptions such as "*Kaddish le-Musaf*," or "*Lekha dodi*," or simply "*tal*," leaving the task of "wording" the music to the performer or to the owner of the manuscript. This in itself shows the desire to forget the liturgical significance of the music and reveals the intention to have it performed *instrumentaliter*.

Instrumental music was prohibited in the synagogue, yet the attraction of instrumental music during the time of the Mannheim school and of the disciples of C. P. E. Bach and Haydn was so irresistible to the cantors that they surpassed each other in their imitation of orchestral effects in the synagogue. These efforts were of necessity crude and silly when performed by one soloist and two assistants, without any harmony. For them, the texts were nothing but pretexts upon which to hang their vocal paraphrases, and the individual word of the text became irrelevant and completely incomprehensible.

The texts selected to be performed were of hymnic, or laudation, character, such as *Lekha dodi*, Psalm 95, *Kaddish*, *El ha-hoda'ot*, *El Adon*, *Kedushah*, *mi khamokha*,

ashrei, and *anah* in the *hallel*. On the High Holy Days much stress was laid upon *mekhalkel ḥayim, ha-yom harat olam*, etc. Indeed, the increasing use of the same texts by all the cantor-composers of the eighteenth century is conspicuous and needs explanation.

In view of the great quantity of these compositions, one must remember that the synagogue had to replace concert and music hall, and the communities must have enjoyed these parodies of serious music, actually meant for instrumental ensembles. Perhaps they felt, even in these mutilated tunes, a breath, however slight, of great music. Since concerts and opera houses were not accessible to the Jews, they had to content themselves with these poor and purloined potpourris.

However, the true cause of this rather sudden decline in Jewish musical tradition lies deeper. For it stands to reason that the value of tradition first depreciated before its substance was debased. Many instances are known of hazanim, enticed by the high standards of Western art music, who escaped the confines of the ghettos. Seeing an opera, listening to an oratorio or a symphony must have been an unforgettable experience for a person who had never heard polyphonic music before. The rich harmonies of a choir and the wonderfully ordered texture of its contrapuntal lines, the conceptions of a systematic music theory must have persuaded these naive souls that the civilization that could produce music so much loftier than their own poorly sung tunes was more valuable than their own. If they returned to Judaism at all, they considered themselves "progressives" in introducing and badly imitating the style of music they had admired outside the ghetto. If they did not return, they persuaded their old friends, the durable hazanim (who hardly knew the rudiments of writing notes), to pour a few traditional drops into a barrel of diluted musical clichés from the popular or art music then in fashion. This, then, is the style of many of the manuscripts of the Birnbaum collection, of the (lost) Hanover compendium, and other "old" notations of the hazanim. Many of them were published by Idelsohn in *HOM*, vols. 6 and 7, and were amply discussed by him in books and articles.[6]

Rural communities. In the category of rural tradition, we have the writings of several modest men who endeavored to codify the old plain tradition in its supposed purity, without any artistic ambitions and adding no embellishments for chorus or organ. Their object was simply the preservation of an oral tradition, which they sifted and scrutinized to the best of their limited knowledge. In most cases they performed this work as a labor of love. For the purposes of this study, the following examples were examined: the manuscript of Leon Saenger (1781–1843), edited by Naumbourg in Munich in 1840, published in part in *HOM*, vol. 7 (this will be referred to henceforth as S-N); the manuscript of Maier Kohn (partly published in 1839, and later in *HOM*, vol. 7); a composition, "*Mekhalkel Ḥayim*," by Wolf Bass of Prosnitz, Moravia, written before 1775; and finally, possibly the best exemplar extant of the tradition of the *Landjuden*, a compendium in manuscript of four volumes, written by M(oses?) Levi in Esslingen between about 1850 and 1862. This manuscript contains the entire musical tradition of the High Holy Days as practiced in southwestern Germany in the mid-nineteenth century.

The older, and rather primitive compendia differ in two essential points from the Levi manuscript: they have no didactic purpose but serve as sketchbooks for the cantors or compilers themselves and they are far from complete. They cannot compare to the Levi manuscript in style-setting and integrating quality. The Levi manuscript quotes every word of every prayer with the music.

Levi anticipated by more than fifteen years the first printed musical *Kol-Bo* (compendium), Abraham Baer's well known *Ba'al Tefillah* (cited in many of the examples and tables in previous chapters as *BT*). The compiler was a humble teacher in a Jewish gradeschool in Esslingen, Wuerttemberg, Germany. He must have had a solid musical training, for his transcriptions are almost faultless. They show a fine sense for tradition and a constant attempt to give a clearly discernible, often elegant shape to the frequently amorphous traditional material. Levi also had a sound Jewish education, as we can see from his occasional references to talmudic treatises, or passages of the *Shulhan Arukh*. His manuscript has the additional merit of describing certain *minhagim* (practices) that are not otherwise known.[7]

The four stout oblong volumes of the Levi manuscript contain 892 music-staffed pages, covered with neat handwriting. Two of the volumes serve for worship on the two days of Rosh Hashanah, and two for Yom Kippur. The text of the prayers follows the text of Wolf Heidenheim's prayer book, or the old Roedelheim *Maḥzor*, strictly, including all *piyutim*, *seliḥot*, and *pizmonim* of the complete edition. Some of these poetic passages have fallen into oblivion, even in German Orthodoxy, for example, the *piyut*, *asher be-khol shanah na'ush* (between *Atah zokher* and *Ve-gam et no'aḥ* in the *musaf* section of the first day of Rosh Hashanah).

In general, the author makes a real effort, not always with success, to transmit the old chants in unadulterated, little-embellished style. From time to time he inserts a cadenza, in which he provides a more brilliant close to a piece. A conspicuous feature of the manuscript is its inclusion of almost wordless preambles to pivotal prayers such as *Barekhu* or the first sentence of the *Kedushah*. Such passages bear a close resemblance to the *entratas* of Baroque music. Two such *entratas* (examples 1 and 2) illustrate this feature. Examples like these, of which there are many, demonstrate that the hasidic *niggun*, sung upon a minimum of articulate words,

Example 1

Example 2

was not a unique form type in European Jewry. Neither can it be assumed that southwestern German Jews borrowed the *niggun* from the *Hasidim*, especially since these German-Jewish chants do not resemble hasidic tunes in any way.

Without trying to give a full analysis of Levi's manuscript, it is possible to convey its most important characteristics by comparing individual items with their equivalents in *BT*, the compendium that is generally considered authentic for *minhag ashkenaz*.

The first volume of the manuscript opens not with the evening service for Rosh Hashanah (which is contained in the Yom Kippur volume) but with the morning service. It starts with *Adon Olam*, to a tune that is clearly a variant of *BT* no. 995. The *barukh she-amar* is superior to Baer's version. This melody introduces the characteristic leitmotif seen in examples 3 and 4.

Example 3

Example 4

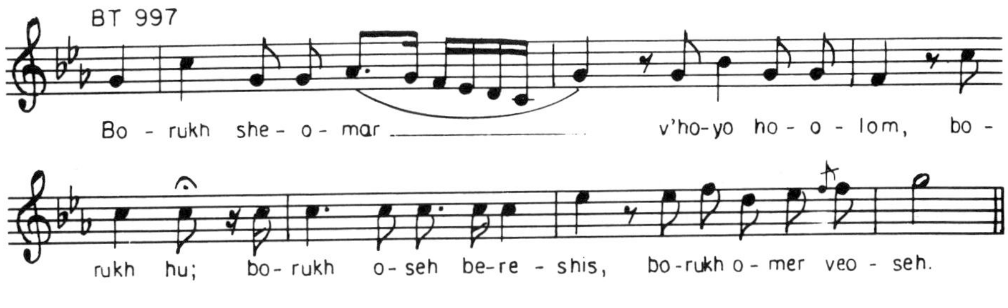

Levi links *ha-melekh* and the half-*Kaddish* by the same tune, which anticipates the *Barekhu.* It elaborates the tune, as quoted in example 1. Levi now introduces the main motif of the Rosh Hashanah *shaḥarit* with "*Barukh atah, Adonai, yotzer or*" (example 5). Baer quotes the same tune for *Yareiti.* Unlike Baer, Levi is inclined

Example 5

Levi, pp. 27/28
Bo - rukh a - toh a - do - noy e - lo -
he - nu me - lekh ho - o - lom yo - - - -
tzer or u - bo - rey ho-shekh, o - seh sho - lom

to divide many nonmetrical texts into stanzas to be sung to the tune of the first line. This is unquestionably a western German trait, influenced by the strophic structure of most German folk songs. On page 32 of the manuscript Levi gives us precious information about the traditional tune to which a continuation of *ha-me'ir la-aretz* is chanted. The text itself is interesting; it contains passages from the *yotzer* prayer of Rosh Hashanah, but also elements of the prayer as it appears when Rosh Hashanah falls on the Sabbath. An entire complex of the morning is chanted to what is referred to as the *niggun metim* (melody for the dead). Levi says, "From this passage on [*ma'asei bereshit*], the precentor chants the following in the *niggun metim*. This chant is used for *Yigdal* and *Adon olam* in the presence of dying persons."[8] This practice follows literally a Midrashic admonition that during the "Days of Judgment" (Rosh Hashanah and Yom Kippur) all Jews should think of themselves as on the verge of death. Examples 6 and 7 are two texts set by Levi to the *niggun metim*. Baer uses a variant of it for *Kulam ahubim* in example 8. For the subsequent *Amidah* Levi's melody agrees with Baer's, but Levi gives a simpler version. He deviates from the customary chant only at *zokhrenu*, where he slips into a paraphrase of a German military tune. At the *Kedushah* he returns to *BT* no. 1108 (example 9). However, at the close he introduces the long-spun phrase quoted in example 2. Only faint remnants of this are quoted by Baer in *BT* no. 1108. Yet Levi's version is very old and occurs in manuscripts of the early eighteenth century, as well as in the *Kedushah* parody, the motet "*Cados, Cados.*" (See chapter 6, n. 3.)

Example 6

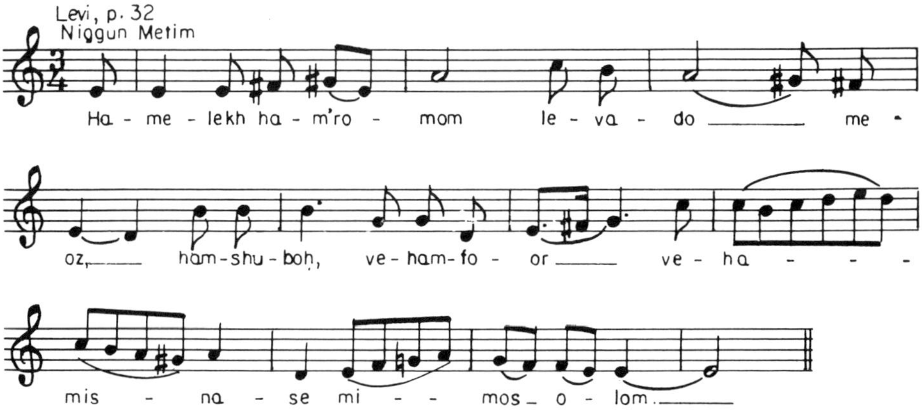

Example 7

Example 8

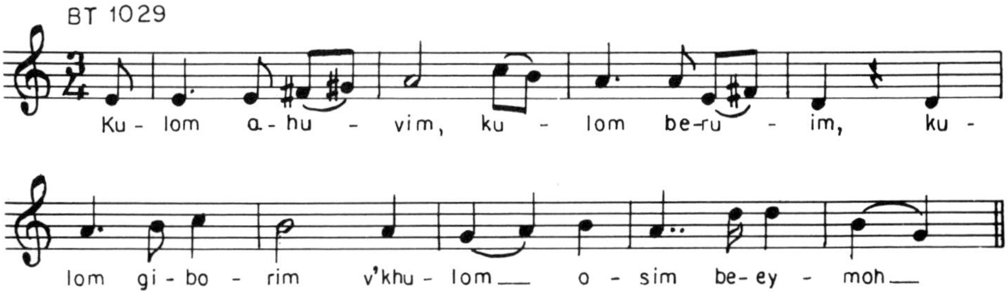

The prayers that follow, as far as *atah beḥartanu*, are linked by Levi by means of a common phrase and cadence. Here he is unlike Baer, who offers for this part of the service a variety of rather shapeless tunes that are hardly connected with each other. Example 10 presents the next passage, *u-bekhen ten paḥdekha*, in an archaic mode, which does not appear in *BT*. It is older and more authentic than Baer's version. The characteristic close (example 10a) is frequently elaborated upon by Levi, as in 10b. The entire repetition of the *Amidah* is based on this and similar

Example 9

Example 10

motifs, up to the priestly blessing, where Levi offers the Moravian tradition (example 11), which is also used for *va-timlokh*. For the *Abinu malkenu* (example 12) Levi gives a variant of *BT* no. 1135. His tune is better musically and also more suitable to the rhythm of the text. In stanzas 19–23 we encounter a version that may be found in Sulzer's *Shir Tziyon*, where credit for it is given to *Kapellmeister* Drechsler. Probably Drechsler merely arranged an old tune that Sulzer sang to him. This, again, is a piece of the Moravian tradition.

For Rosh Hashanah when it falls on the Sabbath, Levi adds a large number of special *piyutim*. Most of them are chanted in a variant of the old Ashkenazic *bergamasca* tune, *Ledavid barukh* quoted in table VI, no. 10*a*.

The *musaf* service is given in a most extensive and detailed version, which far exceeds Baer's presentation in richness and variety. In the following description only the most archaic pieces will be mentioned, and then only if they represent a deviation from *BT*.

Example 11

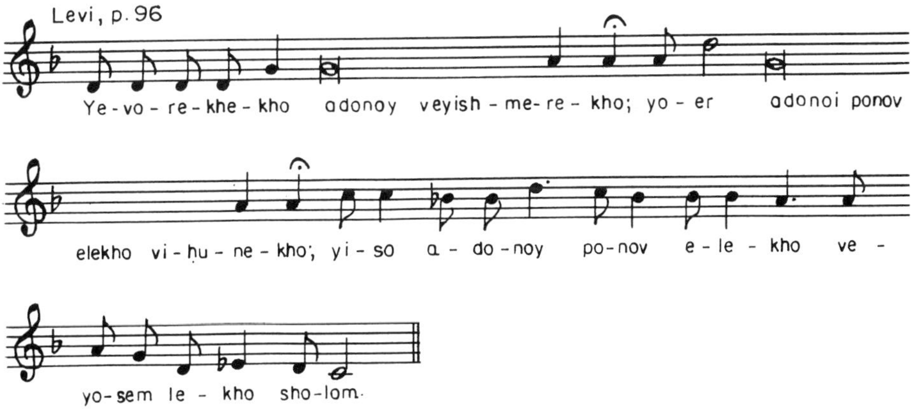

Example 12

The *Kaddish* of *musaf* in Levi's manuscript does not follow the generally popular version, but is actually a variant of *BT* no. 1164. Baer identifies the Levi tune as "German" and the better-known tune as "Polish" tradition. The German version given in the Levi manuscript shows a clear resemblance to the *neilah kaddish*, and is certainly much older than the Polish version. The *melekh elyon* opens with an *entrata*, very much in the hybrid instrumental style of eighteenth-century synagogue music described above. Each verse of the *piyut* is opened by another wordless *entrata*, which gave the hazan an opportunity to entertain his audience and to display his voice.

The *u-netaneh tokef* is presented in elaborate detail. Only two of the traditional motifs appear in Levi's version, on the words "*be-rosh ha-shanah yikatevun*" and "*ma'abir tzono*." The framework of the composition deviates in all other respects from the older tradition and may actually be an original composition by Levi himself. However, some passages are related to *BT* no. 1184,2. Most of the subsequent pieces parallel Baer to a great extent, up to *ha-boḥen ubodek*, where Levi introduces a tune called "*Polnisch*." This contains well-known hasidic elements. The *ve-ye'etayu*, on the other hand, is set to the tune of a *laendler*, a southern German dance of the early nineteenth century. Neither Baer nor any of the other compilers of German synagogue music offer any truly traditional melody for this text. We have to assume that the text was recited, not sung, in earlier centuries.

With the solemn *Alenu*, Levi returns to the old Ashkenazic tradition (cf. *BT* no. 1227, which is very similar, but more florid), into which he weaves a sort of

wordless *niggun* after the word "*kor'im.*" The old and very characteristic tune of *oḥilah la-el* is replaced by a theme that sounds like a poor imitation of Haydn's Concerto for Trumpet. Subsequent prayers are chanted in traditional psalmody, which is rather monotonous but is clearly based on the Torah cantillation of the Western Ashkenazim for the High Holy Days. The *zikhronot, malkhuyot*, and *shofarot* are rendered in similar manner, without any flourishes. *Ha-yom te-amtzenu* appears as a set of rather naive variations in the style of a German "*galant*" tune of the mid-eighteenth century. Example 13 presents the first two variations, quoted here as a curiosity.

Example 13

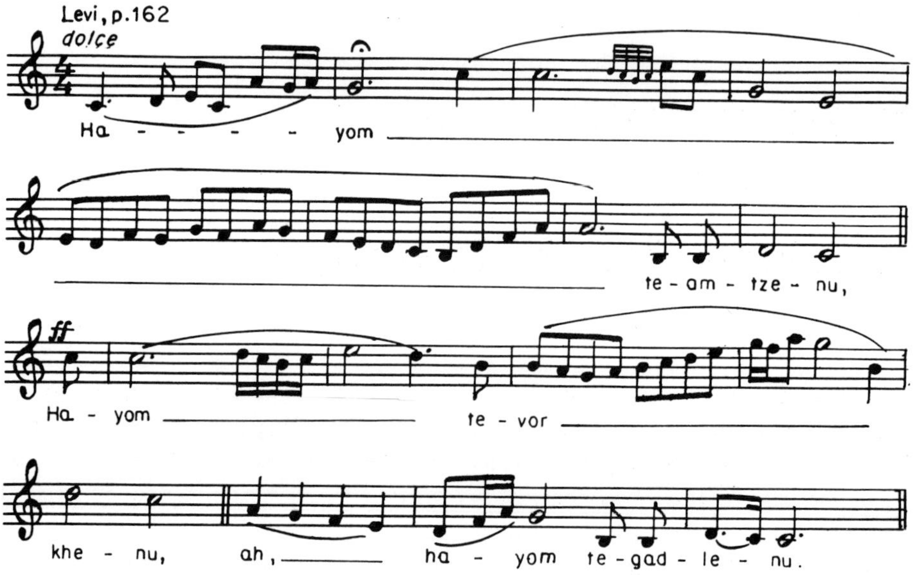

Some of the *piyutim* of the second day of Rosh Hashanah, such as *sagab holek* and *ḥarpek mishul ephraim*, are set in a curiously archaic pattern in pure Dorian and hypodorian modes. One may find parallels for these in the Provençal *minhag Carpentras*. It is not easy to explain these similarities; perhaps Jewish soldiers from Provence carried these tunes to southwestern Germany during the Napoleonic wars. But this is sheer conjecture.

A few words concerning the evening services of Rosh Hashanah and Yom Kippur conclude this brief description. The *Kol Nidre* is brief, kept in the strictest and simplest traditional lines without any ornaments. The *Barekhu* is introduced with great solemnity to the tune of the Three Festivals, which serves as an *entrata*; only then does the proper melody for the High Holy Days appear. The entire evening service is a rather archaic variant of the Western Ashkenazic tradition; it is made up of a high concentration of modal components. The *ya'aleh* follows an old pattern (cf. *BT* 1306) with which we are familiar through Lewandowski's fine stylization. The *seliḥot* that follow it lean toward a psalmodic style, ignore the

meter, and anticipate to a certain extent the melodic pattern of the *shaḥarit*. They are all in archaic modes with recurrent endings.

The *vidui* section is introduced by a psalmody, *anu azey panim* ("we have been insolent!") upon the archaic motif seen in example 14. The *anah tabo* and the *ashamnu*, both parts of the confessional of sins, curiously enough are presented in florid, almost operatic style, with an undeniably festive ring. The *al ḥet* section of the confessional is rendered as a set of variations on a secular German song, and its performance must have required more than half an hour. The closing *Adon olam* and *Yigdal* are sung to a Germanized variant of the tune called "Leoni" after the singer Leoni, whose real name was Jekel Singer, of Prague.

Example 14

Analyzing a massive and complex document like this Levi manuscript is somewhat like carrying on an archaeological excavation. One needs first to separate the layers, in chronological order; then one tries to reconstruct the original site, or, in the case of this document, to reconstruct from the corrupted material at hand the "ideal" shape of the tradition.

The methodology of this analysis cannot be discussed in detail but I must stress the fact that chronology alone cannot be properly used as the only standard for separating the layers of this manuscript. Other components, including the ethnic and the stylistic, complicate the picture and must be taken into account as well. The following example illustrates this point. There is a very considerable amount of plain psalmody contained in the manuscript. Yet this psalmody, as in all such sources, has undergone radical transformation, under the influence of both environmental factors such as southern German religious songs heard in the street, and of indigenous Judeo-German patterns such as the *Missinai* tunes from before 1500. Esslingen, the place whose musical traditions are codified by Levi, sheltered an old Jewish community, known before the time of Reuchlin; during the nineteenth century the dominant religion there was Lutheran (as it is today). Yet the psalmody in this manuscript is affected by the Catholic rather than the Protestant tradition, indicating that the Jewish psalmody of the manuscript antedates the Reformation. This conclusion is also confirmed by other criteria.

The analysis of the manuscript reveals three, possibly four chronological layers: the uppermost layer (the latest melodies) originated in southern Germany and the Rhineland; it contains a mixture of rearranged (i.e., extended and varied) German

and French folk songs, including a corrupted variant of the "*Marseillaise*," which had become familiar to all inhabitants of southern Germany through the armies of Napoleon and his Confederation of the Rhine. Another component of this layer is, once more, the reminiscence of German military band music, of which the Jews were so inordinately fond. Of course, to us, the imitation of an ensemble of trumpets, trombones, horns, and kettledrums by a single precentor seems ludicrous; but imagination, helped by memory, can be a powerful tool in music. The third, but sparsest component of the top layer consists of imitations or paraphrases of symphonic or operatic music of about the year 1800. It is especially noteworthy that no art music dated later than 1800 found its way into the manuscript of 1862. In previous centuries, in spite of all the laws of the ghetto and the enforced isolation of the Jews, cantors had been very much *au courant* with the immediate fashions of folk and art music of their environment. Why is this manuscript so far behind its own time? There are three possible explanations, which complement each other: (1) With Emancipation, the restrictions that had kept Jews out of the theaters and concert halls disappeared. Once the ban was lifted, the synagogue no longer was needed to serve as an ordinary music hall. (2) A corollary of this change was the growing concern with the decorum of the synagogue service, which, to a certain degree, prevented further intrusion of secular, especially operatic, music. (3) The young science of Judaism was deeply concerned with the preservation and purification of religious tradition; its adherents were able to recognize and identify their own contemporary secular music, and keep it out of the synagogue. But they were not sufficiently sophisticated to identify older music and could not recognize it as alien.

The next lower stratum in this chronology reflects the symbiosis between Jews and Germans during the era of the Renaissance and the Baroque. Through Idelsohn's studies,[9] much light has been shed upon this phenomenon. We have already demonstrated some of the most typical Baroque elements, such as *entrata*, cadenza, and a few of the dances fashionable in the late Renaissance. We shall now try to separate the clearly German elements from their Jewish elaborations and also to reconstruct the Judeo-German forms in their old purity. The Baroque elements stem mostly from Italian opera; the Renaissance passages, from dances, German, Italian or French.

The melodies as presented in the Levi manuscript deviate from their foreign sources in a number of respects. First, where the German *Vorlage* is strictly symmetrical, the Jewish version is usually extended and nonmetrical. This was not owing to any different or irregular number of syllables in the Hebrew text, for often the symmetry of the *Vorlage* could have been matched and maintained without much difficulty. The cause of this deviation must be sought in the Jewish fondness for *Zersingen*. To note a second difference, the Jewish tune is, in many cases, a modal version of what was originally in major. This seems to indicate that the Judeo-German versions originated during the twilight period between the prevalence of the ecclesiastical modes and the establishment of the new system of major and minor. This suggests the years between 1550 and 1620 as the time when the redaction of most of the foreign tunes took place. The most conspicuous diver-

gence between German *Vorlage* and Jewish variants is in the matter of musical ornaments. Whereas the original tunes contain ornaments mainly in the openings and cadences, the melodies of the Levi manuscript, except for the plain psalmodies, are indiscriminately scattered with embellishments. Even the cantorial imitations of trumpet melodies themselves contain many little embellishments, obviously added—usually with a heavy hand—to show off the cantors' vocal acrobatics. This trend toward vocal ornamentation is known to ethnomusicologists; it usually appears whenever folk songs are rendered in a formal public gathering.

Professor Hellmuth Christian Wolff has pointed out the interplay between Jewish-oriental elements and the fashion of improvisational singing during the European Baroque.[10] In his amply documented study, Wolff draws attention to certain types of cantorial improvisation, which he convincingly traces back to the seventeenth century.

The oldest layer of the manuscript material consists of psalmodies, semi-metrical paraphrases of *Missinai* tunes, and scriptural cantillation.

Numerous psalmodies are notated throughout the manuscript; in fact, more than 20 percent of the texts is rendered in psalmodic manner. These psalmodies do not conform to the customary conception: dichotomic structure of narrow range and fixed tone of recitation. To begin with, the texts, being post-biblical, are only partly parallelistic; the normal range of a hexachord, or even an octave, is frequently exceeded. And yet the fixed tone of recitation, the stereotype close, and the archaic mode are clearly discernible. Example 15 is one of the most frequent types. This represents a curious mixture of two antagonistic forces in ancient music: the logogenic and the pathogenic.[11] The logogenic (born out of the word) shows itself in the chiefly syllabic treatment of the text with its recurrent motif upon the rhyme "*-enu*"; the pathogenic (born out of emotion) enters with the solemn, rather dramatic cadence upon the words "*ha-yom la-adonenu.*" Technically speaking this piece is a psalmody with one tenor, with D as recitation tone, and G as finalis. Similar pieces occur quite often in the manuscript, always indicating great age; they are relatively uninfluenced by the music of the environment, ecclesiastical or secular.

Example 15

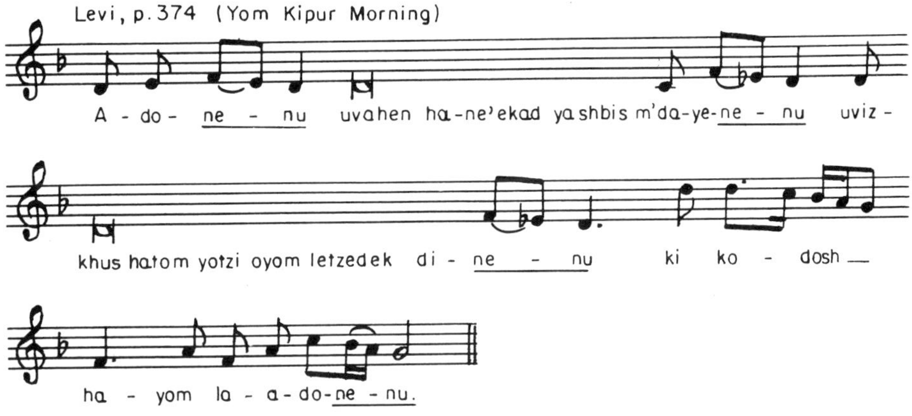

The *Missinai* tunes, too, have generally escaped contamination. In almost every case, the incipit, at least, is in agreement with the tradition of other western European regions.

The scriptural cantillation itself is not contained in these volumes; only where musical quotations from it appear are we able to judge the state of its tradition. It seems well preserved, on the whole, and still close to Reuchlin's and Muenster's notation of the cantillation practiced by southwestern German Jewry.

A fourth layer, which is different from the others, appears in the treatment of metrical and nonmetrical stanzas and litanies. It is here that we encounter those inklings of old military band tunes of the seventeenth and eighteenth centuries as well as obsolete street songs. Most of the melodies are strictly metrical, betraying their origins in the bands or in dance halls. The strict *piyutim* have their own metrical melodies. Some are a mixture of operatic with traditional elements. Others paraphrase German folk songs (such as "*Kapitän und Leutenant*" or "*Scheiden und Meiden*"), providing them with cantorial embellishments. Such style mixtures often sound downright funny to our ears, and it is this kind of hybrid musical practice that caused the chroniclers of the sixteenth and seventeenth centuries, such as Schudt and Michaelis, to characterize the Jewish singers and musicians as "*kahle Bierfiedler*" (clumsy beer-fiddlers). Yet it is amazing and touching, in the midst of the worst corruptions and distortions, to come upon a moment of genuine tradition, of pure *Gestalt*, noble, and essentially indestructible—what Goethe called "*gepraegte Form die lebendsich entwickelt*" (coined form in living development).

Table IX compares some examples from the rural tradition with their counterparts in the large city tradition. In all these cases the rural tradition is simpler, purer, less ornate than the neighboring southern German tradition of Munich. In no. 8, one of many examples from Berlin, one can see the complete lack of basic traditional lines in northern and middle Germany. (See the corresponding pieces of the Levi repertoire.)

After viewing so many examples of German influence, it is interesting to see how the rural Jewish communities were able to resist alien forces. Although the version of the Saenger-Naumbourg manuscript is dated earlier than the Levi manuscript, it is more ornate and less pure in style. Yet Levi Saenger, the Munich precentor, was no "virtuoso hazan." Born in 1781, in a small hamlet in Bavaria, he came as first cantor to the new synagogue in Munich in 1826, the same year in which Salomon Sulzer was appointed cantor in Vienna. "During his stay in Munich, S. Naumbourg, his disciple, was to notate the tradition of the south German synagogue,"[12] as represented by Saenger, and later by Maier Kohn. Much of that substance was later utilized by Naumbourg in his comprehensive *Zemirot Israel.*[13]

The oral tradition of table songs or zemirot. Some of the German-Jewish table songs have been discussed in previous chapters (see, in particular, the discussion of the *birkhat ha-mazon* after the Passover meal). Yet a few questions remain that cannot and should not be answered simply with the cry of that bugaboo, assimilation! Why did the northern German Jews develop their *zemirot* melodies almost fifty years after the southerners? Assuming that the table songs are affected by the

folk tunes of the immediate environment, why did the Vienna Jews of the nineteenth century show so much affinity to Moravian, not Polish, melodies? Is there a correlation between the socioeconomic status of the Jews and their preferences (or family tradition) for specific table songs?

According to Cantor L. Badrian, who gave the material to Cantor Albeck in Berlin (in 1907), the table song of example 16 was sung in the family of the children of the *hakham* Bernays (1792–1849) in Hamburg (manuscript in my possession). This is truly archaic in style, and no trace of either German folk song or Eastern *ḥazanut* is discernible in it. Yet there is a clear allusion to the response *seliḥah, akh ḥanun verahum lekhol pa'al*, of the High Holy Days.

Example 16

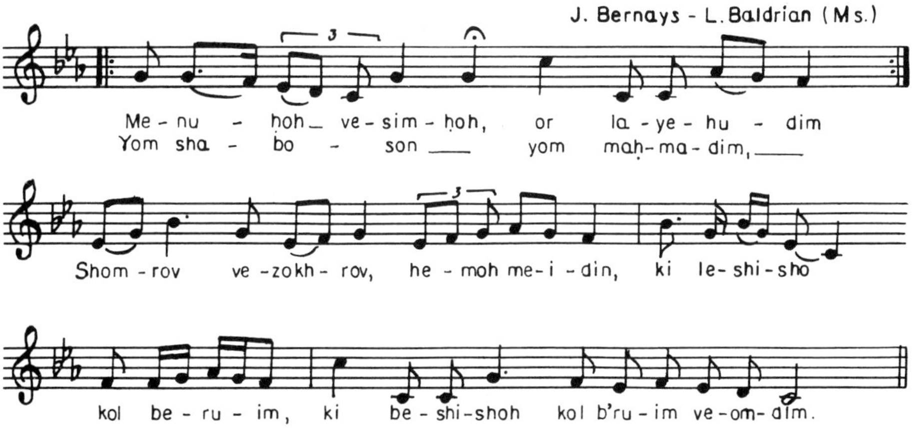
J. Bernays - L. Baldrian (Ms.)
Me - nu - ḥoh ve - sim - ḥoh, or la - ye - hu - dim
Yom sha - bo - son yom maḥ - ma - dim,
Shom - rov ve - zokh - rov, he - moh me - i - din, ki le - shi - sho
kol be - ru - im, ki be - shi - shoh kol b'ru - im ve - om - dim.

Habent sua fata cantilenae! The tune of example 17, to a *zemirah* text by Abraham ibn Ezra, *Tzam'ah nafshi*,[14] will sound vaguely familiar to many Americans. This tune was to find its way, with some variations, into the musical comedy *My Fair Lady*.

Example 17

E. Mayer
etc.
Tza - m'ah naf - shi le - e - lo - him le - el ḥai

The explanation of the Moravian strains in the *zemirot* of the Vienna Jews seems to lie in the demographic structure of Vienna Jewry in the nineteenth century. From 1848 on, immigration from Moravia brought an extraordinary enrichment to Jewish intellectual life in Vienna: Gustav Mahler, Sigmund Freud, Stefan Zweig, Hermann Broch, Adolf Jellinek, Moritz Steinschneider, Nehemya Bruell, and David Kaufmann are but a few of the most celebrated figures. The Moravian tunes

were preferred to the Polish ones, because they were musically much closer to the art music that the Vienna Jews revered at that time, the music of Mozart, Beethoven, and especially Schubert. Many themes from his *Lieder* were adapted to *zemirot*, and even to liturgical chant (with some alterations, of course!).[15]

The last question, concerning a possible correlation between the choice of certain types of table song and the socioeconomic situation, can be answered only with the help of reliable statistical data, which are not available at the present time.

A Question of Musical Taste

We turn our attention now specifically to the imitations of art music in both the West and the East. In the last third of the eighteenth century, standards of inverse ratio prevailed between the art music of central Europe and the contemporaneous synagogue chants of the large Jewish centers in the West. The loftier the heights reached in the music of the Gentiles, the more pitiful the Jewish attempts to imitate it—the gulf could not be bridged. In Idelsohn's study "Songs and Singers," he expressed his sincere belief that Eastern Jewry, being unaffected by the sharply declining tradition of western Jewry, was able to resist encroachments of Gentile art music more effectively than their Western brothers. Since the eastern European Jews were not able to write music, they left no documents of their musical style and this fact misled Idelsohn. The truth is that the Eastern Jews were in no way better equipped to withstand the intrusion of foreign tunes, so long as those tunes were carried and championed by persons or institutions of great authority. Example 18 is a *niggun* that imitates a French army march, borrowed by the *Hasidim* for use during Yom Kippur.

The authority in this case was none other than the leader of Habad Hasidism, Menahem M. Schneersohn. It is reprinted here from "A Thought for the Week," a leaflet of adaptations from the works of the "Alter Rebbe," edited by Y. M. Kagan.[16] The following is Kagan's description and explanation:

> This march is remarkable for its joyous, rhythmic character. It was played in 1812 by the armies of Napoleon when they crossed the Russian boundary near Prussia in their invasion of Russia. The "Alter Rebbe" [founder of *Chabad Hasidism*] had left his native town of Ladi when the armies of the enemy were approaching. He asked that the march be sung for him, and after a moment's contemplation, designated it as a song of victory. It is traditional that Lubavitcher Chassidim sing Napoleon's march at the conclusion of the *neilah* service on Yom Kippur, before the sounding of the shofar. The singing of this *niggun* symbolizes the victory of the Jewish people over "Satan" and the belief that their prayers have been accepted, and they are assured of a Happy New Year.

The musical text is as interesting as the explanation quoted in the footnotes. At first, one should assume that the Russian Jews welcomed Napoleon and his armies as their liberators. Most of them did, in fact. But not everybody shared this attitude: the Ladier Rebbe saw in the Revolution, in Napoleon's armies, and in the Eman-

Example 18

cipation enemies far worse than the Czar's suppression and murder of the Jews. Still there remains the paradox that the Alter Rebbe picked the *enemy's* march as a token of Israel's victory over Satan. As for the melody quoted, the skeleton of the tune is well known and can be traced to marches by the Gebauer brothers, *marches militaires* and similar pieces by François Gossec. The hasidic version has, however, changed the structure of the march, especially the first eight measures; thus the tune has lost its original elegance.

The original French song, "*Chant du Départ*," was written by Etienne Méhul to words by Marie Joseph Chenier, chief of the war department under Napoleon.[17] George Kastner, the best authority on martial music of the Napoleonic era, writes about it: "In order to strengthen the morale of his soldiers in the worst moments... and to inspire them to great deeds, Napoleon gave order to the musicians of various regiments to perform the hymn '*Veillons au salut de l'empire*,' the *Chanson du départ*."[18]

It was during the dawn of Emancipation that written compositions began gradually to replace the pure oral transmission. Yet it is impossible to determine any decade before about 1850 when the majority of Western hazanim really knew the art of notation. One must rather reckon in centuries: whereas many eastern European cantors did not master notation at all (until 1914), in Italy polyphonic notation in several clefs was known, indeed was the vehicle necessary and familiar to such master craftsmen as Salomone de' Rossi and R. Yehuda Leon da Modena (seventeenth century). Some Jewish communities in Italy and France took pains to heighten the splendor of their services by adding art music composed by Jews and Gentiles alike. This has been well documented in Israel Adler's *Musique Savante*. What is, to us, a mainstay of all music education—the ability to read and write music—was extremely rare among the cantors of the seventeenth century.

In both central and eastern Europe, the effect of the elementary knowledge of music theory and notation was to impair the untrained memory, together with the oral folk tradition that depended on it. The latter allows for numerous variants of a melody, whereas the transcription singles out and perpetuates one variant over all others, for better or for worse. The empirical law holds true: the richness of folk song of a given region stands in inverse ratio to the age and frequency of its notated transcription.[19]

The Jewish oral tradition was as sensitive to notation as any other folklore. Yet it is wrong to conclude that all *ḥazanut* was just folklore, as some have claimed. That would be to ignore all elements of sophistication, tone-word relationship, and musical stylization, which appeared at every stage in *minhag ashkenaz*.

In the eighteenth century, neither the rabbis nor the hazanim had any conception of the meaning of "folk song." Let us remember that the expression "*Volkslied*" was coined by Herder in the 1760s, and it took a long time for the word and the idea to penetrate the walls of the ghetto.[20] On the other hand, the Jewish singers and the rabbis knew perfectly well what was popular and what was considered traditional. The term "popular" meant "pleasing, attractive to the public." The term "traditional" meant "hallowed by literary and rabbinic testimony" (e.g., the *Missinai* tunes).

In former centuries the hazanim had been capable of assimilating foreign matter into the traditional substance of *minhag ashkenaz* (as was shown in chapters 6 and 7). Now, the hazanim of the big centers, in their incessant search for new entertainment for their listeners, were content to "popularize"—in other words, trivialize—classical music. It would be hard to be too severe in judging the chaotic condition of *minhag ashkenaz* at this time. From the point of view of musical taste, it was a time of clearly "*absinkendes Kulturgut.*" From the point of view of Jewish tradition, it was a period of rapid loss of sum and substance.

The indifference to the meaning of the prayers is demonstrated in the compendia of the itinerant cantors, not only by the absence of text underlay but also by the incredible repetition of texts selected for the purpose of composition. In Ahron Beer's notebook, for example, there are no less than fifty-two settings for *hit'orari* and *lekha dodi*, twenty-five for *malkhutekha*, sixteen for *hodu-anah*. It is impossible to quote here the many hybrid concoctions perpetrated in this period. The interested reader can examine the following items in *HOM*, vol. 6:

No. 150, a *Kaddish* for Passover by Moshe Pan, in which measures 1–4 allude to the leading motif from *Adir Hu, Hodu-Anah* (see chapter 9).

No. 202, *ha-melekh ha-meromam* by Margo, which contains elements of students' songs. Measures 5–8 are taken from "*Was kommt dort von der Hoeh.*"

No. 256, *Musaf kaddish* for Shabuoth, is a binary aria that includes the leading motif of Shabuoth in measures 11–12 (see table VI, no. 1*d*).

No. 300, *Lekha dodi* for the three weeks before the Ninth of Ab (by the cantor of Hanover),[21] contains a faithful reproduction of *Eli Tziyon* (see chapter 6) in measures 1–4, and thereafter varies it clumsily, in the *concertante* manner of Rococo instrumental music.

No. 332, *Melekh elyon* by Moshe Pan, has the superscription "*Tempo di Menuetto.*" It contains motifs that were later integrated into Haydn's celebrated *Kaiserlied*, "*Gott erhalte Franz der Kaiser.*"

No. 381b, *abinu malkenu*, could, without many alterations, fit into one of J. S. Bach's instrumental suites; how the text is to be set to this tune will always remain an enigma.

Although this sort of absurd eclecticism dominated the period, there were some rare exceptions to the general rule. A very few gifted melody-makers contributed some pieces full of expression and in fine taste, as seen in two examples taken from the Birnbaum collection. Example 19 is a *mekhalkel hayim* (ca. 1770) for the High Holy Days, by Wolf Bass of Prosnitz, in Moravia. Example 20, the end of a *Kaddish* for *musaf* of the High Holy Days, sounds like a foretaste of the Polish-Russian "virtuoso *ḥazanut*" of the nineteenth century, but it shows a far finer sense of tradition and good taste.

These two examples represent the best of the music of the Jewish communities in the large centers. As we have seen, the taste and quality were somewhat better in the small towns of Germany, Moravia, Bohemia, Austria, and northwestern Hungary. Nevertheless, such members of the Jewish bourgeoisie and intelligentsia as had an opportunity to hear or to play serious European music of the time had

Example 19

only contempt for this kind of synagogue music. They thought it degrading and shameful. It did much to alienate at least a generation from the music of the synagogue.

Example 20

Shalom FRIEDE (Amsterdam)
U - ve - ha - - - - - - - - - - - - yey
de - khol bes__ yis - ro - el, de - khol______ bet__ yis -
ra - - - el ______
Cantor
Bass
Singer
ba - a - go - loh__ us - viz - man__ ko - riv
ve - im-ru: ______ a - men.

11

The Emancipation in Germany and France

Who will not feel compassion's shudder,
when he sees
How our dehumanized mob torture Canaan's
people?
Do they not do it, because our princes
Forged them in irons much too heavy?
(F.G. Klopstock, "Ode to Emperor Joseph II")

For and Against Emancipation

The course of the Emancipation was not smooth. As we have seen, it raised hopes in the hearts of many—hopes that were cruelly disappointed. My late friend Isaiah Sonne used to say that the Western branch of Judaism in the nineteenth century bore triple fruit: the Reform movement, the science of Judaism, and political Zionism. This idea seemed heretical thirty years ago, but has gradually become acceptable, as one may discern in Arthur Hertzberg's excellent volume on the Zionist movement.[1]

Certainly one cannot understand the development of *minhag ashkenaz* during the nineteenth century without some awareness of the political events of the time and their consequences in the life of the Jewish community. The literary sources vary radically in their estimate of the effects of Emancipation. The subject was—and still is—highly controversial, and the reader might do well to consult a variety of the sources. This chapter only outlines the events that, directly or indirectly, made an impact on *minhag ashkenaz*.

In 1791 the French National Assembly promulgated a law by which the Jews were declared French citizens with equal rights. This law, "unparalleled since the days of the Roman Empire,"[2] was carried by the French legions under the great Napoleon's command to all the countries they occupied: Italy, the Low Countries, the German *Rheinbund*, central Germany, the Grand Duchy of Warsaw, and the cities of the Hansa. After a still more ambitious attempt at "normalizing" the Jewish situation, which entailed the convocation of a Grand Sanhedrin in Paris, Napoleon restricted his interests to problems of the conscription of Jewish-French youth in the army, and of mixed marriages.[3]

Germany and Austria did not immediately follow these principles. The Prussian Jews eventually achieved equality and emancipation under Chancellor von

Hardenberg in 1812. Austria was more tardy, because Austrian society moved very, very slowly and felt that Emperor Joseph's *Toleranz Edict* of 1782 had done just about enough for the Jews.

After Napoleon's defeat all emancipatory laws were repealed, and all states that had previously toadied to him quickly returned to the *status quo ante*, or at least tried to (i.e., all except the Netherlands, which continued to abide by the law of Emancipation). The new repression was contrived at the Vienna Congress in 1815 through a swindle so despicable that it badly damaged the credibility of the so-called Christian states before the world.[4]

Small wonder, then, that observant Jews—not only the Orthodox—expressed their disappointment in the entire concept of the Emancipation with ever-increasing bitterness. The Emancipation affected the various groups of German-speaking Jews in dissimilar ways. Rural Jewry had felt less of its benefits, and was consequently less disappointed, when the promises were not fulfilled. For them it was—and had always been—a matter of "business as usual," at least until 1848. The big centers, however, had seemed to benefit most: Frankfort, Hamburg, Vienna, Leipzig, Berlin, Breslau, Prague, Paris, and Amsterdam, as well as such westward-oriented communities of eastern Europe as Cracow, Posen, Lemberg, Warsaw, and later Budapest and Bucharest. The changes in the structure of the community, its functionaries, its liturgy and music, were most apparent in such pace-setting cities as Hamburg, Vienna, Paris, and Frankfort.

To begin, the Jewish communities became "Religious Societies." The ghetto was formally abolished. Communities lost their limited autonomy and their jurisdiction over all but strictly ritual matters; the rabbi ceased to be a judge and became both preacher and teacher. Salo Baron regards this emancipatory measure as "a necessity even more for the modern state than for Jewry; the Jews' medieval status was anachronistic and had to go. Left to themselves, the Jews might for long have clung to their corporate existence. For Emancipation meant losses as well as gains for Jewry."[5] Ismar Elbogen, on the other hand, felt that the Jewish generation of the Emancipation had little appreciation for the doctrines of the Talmud and the rabbis: "The splendour of the outside world attracted them; the Synagogue appeared to them dark and gloomy. This mood was not prevalent everywhere in Germany, but local variations notwithstanding, the general trend was identical."[6]

The variations depended on the social status of the Jews, which differed widely from country to country, from city to city. Some of the Jewish "intellectual plutocrats," such as the Itzigs, the Mendelssohns, the Beers in Berlin, and the Barons Arnstein, Eskeles, Wertheimstein in Vienna, attained some sort of social equality with the patricians and the nobility. In critical situations—as in the instance of riots—the entire mirage vanished.[7] A royal prince spat "hep, hep" at the ten-year-old Felix Mendelssohn during the "*Judensturm*" in 1819; Herr von Arnim was publicly whipped "*Unter den Linden*" by young Moritz Hitzig, whom he had insulted and to whom he refused satisfaction in a duel. As a matter of fact, some of the foremost German intellectuals were quite ready to concede social equality to the elite groups of German Jewry out of respect for the "spirit of Judaism" (Gottlob von Paulus), while denying them legal German citizenship.[8] And yet, even as

representative a traditionalist as R. Samson Raphael Hirsch, the father of Neo-Orthodoxy, spoke for the Emancipation, albeit in a prophetic strain that still sounds impressive today:

> I bless Emancipation, when I see how the excess of oppression drove Israel away from human intercourse.... I bless Emancipation, when I notice that no spiritual principle, even such as born of superstitious self-deception, stands in its way, but only passions degrading to humanity.... I bless it, if Israel does not regard Emancipation as the great goal of its task, but only as a new condition of its mission, and as a new trial, much severer than the trial of oppression; but I should grieve, if Israel understood itself so little ... that it would welcome Emancipation as the end of the *galut* and the highest goal of its historical mission....[9]

In France, conditions were different. The inner coherence of the French Jews was much weaker than that of their brethren in Germany, who had established an accepted standard and tradition, in spite of the centuries of oppression and humiliation. Neither customs nor theological doctrine, but the ritual was the first target of the French Reform leaders, spurred on by their friends in Germany. They objected mainly to the long prayers, primarily the *piyutim*, which were so unintelligible to the congregation that a spirit of genuine devotion could hardly be maintained.

At the time of the French Revolution, there were about 40,000 Jews under French rule. About three fourths of these Jews lived in Alsace and Lorraine, under medieval conditions. A small group of Sephardic Jews, wealthier and more enlightened than the Alsatians, lived in the southwest, mainly in Bordeaux and Bayonne. The Jews of the former papal possessions in Provence (Comtat-Venaissin) were united with France during the Revolution. Thus few of the French Jews were aware of the great intellectual upsurge of the Enlightenment and the political forces that were reshaping European society. After the Napoleonic enforcement of the emancipatory laws, the "Great Sanhedrin" of 1806–1807, the new economic opportunities, the unhindered access to the cities—with increased contact with Gentiles, and the resultant absorption of the majority culture—there emerged a generation of open-minded Jews.

The majority of French Jews affirmed the necessity for changes in the form of worship. Yet there was little agreement as to the means and the objects of change. The radical element urged the elimination of all *piyutim* from the liturgy, and the introduction of French hymns to be performed by a choir and supported by an organ. The moderate element attracted the great majority and ultimately prevailed after a long struggle against the unyielding Orthodoxy. They desired the omission of superfluous prayers, especially the *piyutim* that were no longer compatible with the sentiments and convictions of modern Jews. They demanded greater dignity in the service, curtailing hazanic excesses, introducing choir and organ, and shortening the ritual. By 1840 the basic issues in synagogue music were the relative status of rabbi and cantor, the revision of the chanted liturgy, the control of the cantor's performance, and the fusion of Sephardic and Ashkenazic ritual. These issues seem to have been resolved with comparative ease.

The larger German communities, however, were beset by internecine strife. Amazingly, these disputes were not concerned with questions of livelihood or individual welfare. The core of all the turmoil was, in fact, the problem of Jewish group identity, and so it remained until World War II. This problem had its effect on the service, on synagogue worship. Various experiments were undertaken, each representing a different response to the question of Jewish identity.

The most radical break with the past was made by aggressive Reform leaders. They arose in northwestern Germany, especially in Hamburg and Hanover, and scored their first tangible successes among the affluent and educated classes. For them, Judaism was a formal shell, with an ancient universalistic world religion at its core; but this core had become so encrusted with ancient, obsolete, and anachronistic ritual laws that it could no longer be comprehended without a thorough removal and dispatch of the crust. Judaism, in short, had one message for the world: ethical monotheism with a messianic aim. Hence the use of Hebrew was without meaning, the national aspirations of Judaism were unfounded, the differences of the various monotheistic religions were negligible and not to be stressed. Oddly enough, these radicals sought, and found, rabbinical authority to support most of their ideas and practices: two pamphlets designed for learned Jews, and written in Hebrew, argued on rabbinic grounds that most of these innovations were well justified by Jewish tradition. They were the *Or Nogah* (The Bright Light) by Eliezer Libermann (Dessau, 1818) and the truly erudite *Nogah ha-Tzedek* (Light of Justice) mainly by Rabbi Aron Chorin (Arad, Hungary, 1818). In fairness to the latter, it must be pointed out that Rabbi Chorin did not advocate reforms in cases where they were likely to upset the inner peace of the community. He enjoyed so high a reputation as a talmudist and modern educator that, together with I. Noah Mannheimer, he was considered a possible candidate for the Vienna rabbinate. As a result Chorin formally withdrew his most revolutionary suggestions, only to bring them up again in later years.[10]

The establishment of the *Neue Israelitische Tempel-Verein* (New Israelite Temple Society) in Hamburg in 1817 aroused all of German-speaking Jewry. The statutes of the society contained, among other principles, this portentous sentence: "In this service a German sermon and the singing of hymns, accompanied by organ, will be introduced."[11] Services were held only on Sabbaths and festivals, following the Protestant practice. Consequently, the first Hamburg prayer book contained only the liturgy for those days; somewhat later a supplement appeared with prayers for Purim and the Ninth of Ab. The texts were Hebrew and German, the hymns in German compiled by the preacher Eduard Kley, their music—again in strict Protestant style—written by Christians: Bethuel (the temple's first organist), A. G. Methfessel, I. A. G. Heinroth, the Jewish convert Ferdinand Hiller (friend of Felix Mendelssohn), and others. The organ was donated by Salomon Heine, uncle of the poet. The pronunciation of the Hebrew texts was Sephardic, not so much owing to the presence of the many genuine Sephardim in Hamburg (they were opposed to the temple), but because Kley considered it scientifically correct.[12] Scripture was read without cantillation, and the precentor, a Portuguese Jew, David Mendola, introduced Sephardic tunes for the Hebrew texts. Thus for a

while *minhag ashkenaz* was eclipsed by the Reform ebullience, but not for long! For in 1879 the newly appointed hazan, Moritz Henle, reintroduced scriptural cantillation. Later, as an old man, he restored the Ashkenazic pronunciation.[13]

All remnants of Portuguese glory vanished when Leon Kornitzer, last hazan of the temple, restored *minhag ashkenaz* to its fullest measure. The sum of the surviving innovations in the Hamburg Temple is made up of the following: the omission of most *piyutim* for Sabbath and festivals (only some for the High Holy Days were retained),[14] the German sermon, and the attention to decorum in the service (a hard-won achievement).[15] The most controversial, although by no means the most important innovations, were the German hymns and the organ. These had been introduced earlier in other groups, particularly by the radical Israel Jacobsohn in Seesen in 1808, during the French Occupation. While the Prussian government forbade all such experiments and forced the closure of the private synagogue of Jacob Herz Beer (father of the composer Giacomo Meyerbeer), the republican senate of the Free City of Hamburg granted its Jewish citizens full freedom of worship.

It cannot be claimed that the musicians and preachers of the early reform were tactful in their radicalism. Jacobsohn had borrowed the "theme song" of German Protestantism for his Jewish Songster, the chorale "*O Haupt voll Blut und Wunden*," which is the leading hymn of J. S. Bach's *Passion According to Saint Matthew*.[16] The innovations aroused both a storm of protest and a burst of enthusiastic acclaim. The issues that most incensed the antagonists were, in order of vehemence: instrumental music, especially the organ; the mixed choir of men and women; the German songs; the omission of prayers and *piyutim*. This was a most unfortunate list of priorities, and the consequences were deplorable. In the long run, and quite unnecessarily, the question of the organ became, for the Orthodox, the shibboleth of liberalism, however moderate.

The organ controversy has troubled the synagogue up to the present day, exclusively in *minhag ashkenaz*. The arguments pro and con fall into three categories: halakhic, aesthetic, and pragmatic. Both advocates and adversaries of the organ availed themselves of halakhic arguments. Against the organ: If the *magrepha* was indeed a forerunner of the organ, and used in the Temple, it is *ipso facto* forbidden, since it is forbidden to imitate any thing or instrument, any vessel or ritual of the Temple, in the synagogue. A variation of this argument was offered in favor of the organ: There was neither a water-organ nor a pneumatic organ in the Temple, and it is *not* forbidden to use a *non*-Temple instrument in the synagogue.[17] Other halakhic arguments for the organ were as follows: The Jerusalem sanctuary used an organ-like instrument, the *magrepha*, long before other cults did.[18] The Talmud does not mention the instrument, hence it is not among those that are forbidden. It is not even a "custom of the Gentiles" and the prohibition "Observe ye not their ways" is inapplicable; if we praise God, or ride a horse, etc., and the Gentiles do likewise, it is not imitating their customs, and is perfectly permissible. Maimonides allowed music (at a wine banquet, a wedding, etc.).[19]

The pamphlets mentioned above by Chorin and Libermann did not solve the problem.[20] One year later, in 1819, five Orthodox rabbis issued an emphatic

refutation under the title "*Eleh Dibrei ha-Berit*" (These are the Words of the Covenant) in Hamburg-Altona. By far the most lucid argumentation against the organ was put forth by Rabbi Moses Sofer, later the celebrated head of the Pressburg Yeshibah. He succeeded in making the following clear analysis. The organ, in general, is a Christian instrument; it must not be played on the Sabbath, and since the weekday must not be honored more than the Sabbath, it must not be played on weekdays either. It not only violates the commandment not to imitate Gentile customs, but in certain cases, comes close to the sin of idolatry. In refutation of the argument that proper praying is a joyful *mitzvah* and should be supported in every way, "Where do we find the idea that the joy of praying is a *mitzvah*? The contrary is true. It has been explained that the bulk of our prayers consists of pleas for pardon of our sins. How can we stand before the Almighty with instruments of joy and gladness, yet aware that we are sinners? . . . How can one come before the King of Kings to ask pardon with melodies of entertainment, with merry tunes? . . ."[21] Compared with this approach, that of the other authors of this Orthodox pamphlet appears dull, pedantic, and hairsplittingly casuistic.

Another argument against the organ is that by R. David Deutsch: "Rabbi Moshe Isserles (the *Rema*) writes, 'A hazan who sings melodies that belong to a non-Jewish ritual should be seriously warned to desist; if he does not obey, he is to be discharged.' Is the permanent installation of the exclusively Christian organ less harmful than the mere singing of a melody of a fleeting tune?"[22]

These are the most frequently quoted halakhic statements against the organ. They were often varied and sometimes confounded, for example, when not the organ itself but its player, Jew or Gentile, is placed at the center of the controversy.

General aesthetic reasons, too, were advanced both for and against the organ. Against the organ, the argument of the Orthodox was given weight by the alleged opposition against that instrument by such composers as Meyerbeer and Mendelssohn. They were said to have argued against its use in the Berlin Dome, the official Protestant cathedral of Prussia. Neither the allegation nor the argument holds water. Meyerbeer had no authority in the organization of the church music of the Dome.[23] Even Felix Mendelssohn, the *General Musik Direktor* of the Royal Dome, had to learn to his dismay that the clergy could overrule him in all musical questions.[24] The second aesthetic argument against the organ consisted of the erroneous statement that the organ was, and had always been, the ecclesiastical instrument par excellence. This argument is also untenable, since in Byzantium and in Eastern Christianity the organ was always considered a profane instrument and, for that reason, was banished from all worship.[25] Another opponent of the organ considered it a "purely Catholic" instrument, and claimed that the Protestant Church had inconsistently reintroduced it into their service. What would Bach have said to this turgid nonsense?[26] In sum, the halakhic arguments in favor of the organ and the aesthetic arguments against it are equally unconvincing.

One would assume that in the technical domain of pragmatic musical argument for and against the organ both parties would proceed with caution and would limit themselves to the authentic advice of recognized musicians. A vain hope! It is to be regretted that in all of their polemic they stooped to citing dubious authorities

in a questionable manner. For example, Heinrich Heine, a great poet but a man of poor judgment in music, claimed that "the tone of the organ sounded to the Lord like the squeaking of pigs." Dr. Max Grunwald of Vienna, author of the article in which this extremely offensive remark is quoted, speaks of a memorandum by Meyerbeer and Mendelssohn in the Berlin synagogues, dating from the year 1861.[27] Aside from the improbability that Mendelssohn would ever have collaborated in anything with Meyerbeer, we might mention that the famous grandson of Moses Mendelssohn had died in 1847!

By far the best argument for the organ in the synagogue was advanced by Sulzer in his *Denkschrift*,[28] where one reads, "To guide a congregation in singing, which all too often is disturbed by bad or anticipatory intonations, a powerful instrumental accompaniment is needed, which ought to be in the hand of a capable organist, who can steer the singing through all dissonances."

The Hamburg Jews, for their part, remained strangely silent about their correspondence with Felix Mendelssohn, who had, upon their request, composed a psalm for the Hamburg Temple, a fact usually suppressed by the Hamburg community. The following is a letter from the correspondence, which I have commented on elsewhere:[29]

Hamburg, 8 January 1844

Honored Sir!

Please accept the heartiest thanks of the directorship of the New Temple Society for your kind and prompt willingness to accede to its wishes. We shall greatly value even a partial fulfillment of those wishes on your part, and shall use with great pleasure whatever psalm compositions you send us that are adaptable to our Divine Service.

Let us especially suggest the Twenty-fourth, Eighty-fourth, and One hundredth Psalms, and of these, especially, we should greatly desire the composition of a master. Our new Temple building will be dedicated at Pentecost of this year, and the above-mentioned Psalms seem to be admirably suited to this occasion....

21 January 1844

The first two Psalms we named [24 and 84] should be treated as a cantata. If they are composed in a liberal translation, the translation of your blessed grandfather (of renowned memory!) should be the basis; however, we leave it entirely up to you, if you want to use a poetic version of these Psalms.... I must indicate the limitation that the accompaniment must be without *orchestra*, and for the organ alone....

Please accept (etc.)
Dr. Frankel
Direction [sic] of the Temple

Mendelssohn, however, chose Psalm 100, which he set for four-part mixed choir with small orchestra and *without organ*. The receipt of the work was gratefully

acknowledged on 12 April 1844. In a simplified version, without instrumental accompaniment, Psalm 100 was published by Bote and Bock in the anthology *Musica sacra* (Berlin, 1849). It also appears in this version in the collected works of Mendelssohn.

Thus we see, in sum, that neither the arguments for nor the arguments against the organ ever convinced a clear majority of the German-speaking Jews; in eastern Europe, the organ was very rare in the synagogue; it was not used in the Greek Orthodox Church. However, in the regions under Catholic jurisdiction, for example, in a Warsaw synagogue, an organ was used. Even in this regard, acculturation is discernible. As this is being written, the organ is hardly a problem to European Jewry, though it is still mildly controversial in England. In America the use of the organ is still spreading far and wide, and it can be found in all Reform and some Conservative synagogues, where it is correlated to the increasing practice of congregational singing.[30]

Another subject of controversy was the hymn. The German songs of the Reform synagogues followed the style of the Lutheran chorale quite indiscriminately, in both text and music. This entailed a cultural regression, for their models had been created during the sixteenth, seventeenth, and early eighteenth centuries, and served as congregational songs, not destined for art music. In liturgical art music, German Protestant composers used the chorale only as their starting point, or as leitmotifs. In cantatas, motets, psalms, etc., they went far beyond the simple hymn tunes. In the synagogue there was no inclination to follow this practice. The hymn, or "anthem" (as it is mistakenly called in the American Reform prayer books),[31] was never truly accepted, let alone integrated into true synagogue worship. Although it could be said of the organ that "it could at least be swallowed, if not totally digested" by many European communities, the old hymnals, while pets of some rabbis, are today just food for worms and scholars.[32]

These heated controversies about details of liturgical practice prevailed mainly in the German-speaking communities. To the West, problems of the liturgy appear to have been of a different character, even though the musical leadership there came from the East. During the eighteenth century, the route of wandering cantors usually began in the East, in Russia and Poland, moved via Cracow and Breslau toward Prague or Nuremberg-Fuerth, and thence westward toward the Rhine. Many reached the German banks of the Rhine. A few crossed over into France, mainly to Strasbourg or Metz. Among the two or three to reach Paris was the musical and religious maverick (or should one say chameleon?) Israel Lovy, alias Israel Glogau, alias Reb Yisroel Fuerth, alias Israel Mayence, alias Israel Strassbourg, etc., etc., who attained his aspirations in 1818, when he was appointed cantor of the Paris community. He endeavored to modernize the musical services by introducing a four-part "chorus," but his musical craftsmanship was not up to the task of arranging traditional tunes for a mixed chorus; thus he was forced to use his own shallow and trivial compositions. In 1832 he died, and all "reforming" attempts that he had sponsored died with him.[33] Yet Paris remained, from the Revolution on, the Eldorado of aspiring hazanim, although it was practically inaccessible to Russo-Polish immigrants.[34] After Napoleon, however,

the old sympathies of the *Rheinbund* for France were still alive and warm. Moreover, the sentiment was mutual, especially in the Jewish circles of France, which, by 1840, had achieved prestige and prosperity.

The French Reform

Munich, the capital of Bavaria and a former *Rheinbund* member, had begun to "modernize" its synagogue in 1826; in many respects it followed the pattern of Vienna. Its newly appointed cantor was Levi Saenger, who was an "old-timer" not only in age (1781–1843) but in background. (In chapter 10 a number of examples were cited from his manuscript edited by Naumbourg.) His musical knowledge was negligible, therefore it was decided to establish a choral society to adorn the worship service. As leader, a grade-school teacher of poor musical abilities and less musical education was appointed. This worthy man, Maier Kohn, was possessed by one ambition, to become chief cantor. He knew the traditional *minhag ashkenaz* quite well; one surmises this from the numerous surviving musical manuscripts written by him or his helpers.[35] One helper was Caspar Ett, father of modern Catholic church music in Germany; it was certainly wise of Kohn to call so eminent a musician to his aid. Since Ett knew next to nothing about *ḥazanut*, his arrangements in this sphere are weak (Idelsohn, who did not know about Ett's status, referred to him as "a certain musician Ett").[36] Among the active members of Maier Kohn's chorus was Samuel Naumbourg (1817–1880), scion of an old family of cantors and rabbis. He contributed one or two pieces to Kohn's collection, published in 1838, a collection that was completely eclipsed by Sulzer's *Schir Zion* of the same date. It must have been this unhappy coincidence and the comparison of the two works that caused the highly intelligent, well-educated, and vocally endowed Naumbourg to leave Munich. After the customary apprenticeship in Besançon as hazan, and in Strasbourg as choir director, he went to Paris, well provided with letters of introduction to the leading Jewish circles.

We know little about the standard of synagogue music in Paris before Naumbourg arrived there. It is not difficult, however, to assay the status of *minhag ashkenaz* in eastern France from the extant manuscripts and from personal experiences of the author during the last fifty years. It is possible to judge it by the music of the eastern French synagogues in Alsace, which has survived in several nineteenth-century manuscripts.[37] The following descriptions refer to arrangements found in those manuscripts by M. Halff: (1) *Zokhrenu* for the High Holy Days is a piece consisting of two parts, the first of which is a variant of the popular *Eyn kelohenu*, the second a mixture of an element of the "*Marseillaise*" with a traditional cadence of the High Holy Days. (2) A *piyut*, "*Kafram patz*," is from the liturgy of *Shabbat Shekalim*. This passage is part of a poetic insertion into the *yotzer* prayer, probably by the poet Eleazar Kallir. Today it is used in the strictly Orthodox ritual only. The tune is almost identical with the tradition as given in *BT* no. 650b. Considering the fact that this *piyut* occurs only once a year, and does not belong to the High Holy Days, the manuscript testifies to the faithfulness and resilience of *minhag ashkenaz*. (3) *Abodah* for Yom Kippur, *Vekhakh haya omer*, is an interesting variant of the ancient

Missinai tune, clearly influenced by the Moravian tradition. Since Moravian-Silesian cantors frequently lived and sang in Strasbourg (I knew two of them), one may observe in this instance how personal influence modified and varied local tradition. (4) An amusing item is the chorus-refrain of A. Rosenstok's *Lekha dodi*: it begins with a literal quotation from the students' song "*Hier sind wir versammelt zu loeblichem Thun, drum Bruederchen, ergo bibamus*" by Goethe. Another *Lekha dodi* by Halff could well be an aria of a French *opéra comique*.

This kind of hodgepodge, resembling others that we have already observed from the other side of the Rhine, has pretty much disappeared from Alsace. From my own observation of fifty-odd years, the musical condition of the Alsatian liturgy is almost exactly in the same stage as that of southern Germany before 1930, except that the arrangements of the tradition are by Naumbourg, rather than by Sulzer and Lewandowski. The old condition of chaos was finally overshadowed, if not fully eclipsed, by Samuel Naumbourg's lifework, the codification of a stylized *minhag ashkenaz*.

In Paris, the position of the official cantor had remained vacant since Israel Lovy's death in 1832. Naumbourg was well informed about the delicate and touchy conditions that beset the Central Consistory during the restoration, and he was fully aware of the dilemmas of its policy. He had established good connections to both synagogue and Consistory with the help of his protector, the composer Jacques Halévy, who was himself a cantor's son. Through Halévy he became acquainted with the Crémieux family and other leading personalities. Grasping the propitious opportunity, he addressed a memorandum to the government; in it he described the leaderless condition of the Paris synagogue, implying that it could become politically dangerous. Since he was a protege of Halévy and Crémieux, his memorandum was heeded by the ministry of religion and education. He was thereupon entrusted by the government with the reorganization of the worship service. Backed by important members of the Consistory, he subsequently attained the position of chief cantor in 1845.

It is not easy to comprehend the inner makeup of the Paris Jewish community during this period; part of it consisted of newcomers from Alsace and Germany, who were inclined toward Orthodoxy, or at least toward traditionalism. The other half, either of old Sephardic stock, or Provençal Jews coming from the papal enclave in the Comtat-Venaissin, were less observant, and looked down on the German-speaking Ashkenazic Jews with undisguised arrogance. They formed the upper social stratum and the Ashkenazim, who gradually outnumbered them, formed the lower. However, the new aristocracy, the barons de Rothschild and de Hirsch, belonged to this second group. They supported reforms, as long as the reforms remained moderate, which is to say insignificant in essence and confined to aesthetic improvements.

"Zeal for Reform Judaism was gone. The inner storm and stress which had driven the older generation upon the road to freedom no longer animated the younger people. Their efforts took a preponderantly esthetic direction. . . ."[38] These words describe aptly the situation in Paris in the middle of the nineteenth century. It is interesting to examine and compare the varying attitudes of the governments

toward the establishment of the "new-style" synagogues. In Hamburg the total indifference on the part of the Free City's senate guaranteed a certain amount of liberty, but at the same time it condoned—or at least permitted—a state of friction between the intransigent Orthodox and the radical reformers. This led to tension, which threatened momentarily to erupt into violence. In Munich, a paternalistic supervision facilitated a modicum of reform, while in Vienna, the metropolis of a supra-national empire, conditions were complicated by the government's all pervasive fear of liberals or democrats, who were regarded as potential revolutionaries. Hence strict supervision of all communal activities undertaken by the "tolerated" Jews was the order of the day, at least until 1848.

In Paris, the government of King Louis Philippe, the citizen-king, took great pains to keep the middle and upper bourgeoisie quiet and prosperous. The national leaders Guizot and Thiers, however, feared another revolution like that of 1830.[39] They regarded any organized religion, Christian or Jewish, as a stabilizing factor; therefore they aided and stimulated, while supervising, all religious institutions and activities.

It is to the credit of a great Jewish leader, Adolphe Crémieux, that he initiated the laws that ensured permanence and security to rabbis and cantors. His laws provided a sure social and economic standard for rabbis and the *sous-rabbins* or *ministres officiantes* (i.e., hazanim). The latter were officially recognized in 1823. It was again Crémieux who championed the cantors, by stressing the point that the hazan had the essential task of leading in prayer, which made him indispensable to Jews without authentic rabbinic knowledge. At that time the most experienced hazanim lived in Strasbourg and Metz; they were superior to all other French cantors and, understandably, aspired to the same status as that of the rabbis.

Yet their struggle was unwarranted. Just as the hazan had originally gained his function and status with the rise of *piyut*, so did he lose his rank when the *piyut* became outmoded, if not yet entirely outlawed. The issue of the *piyut* was placed on the agenda of the Conference of Chief Rabbis, which met in 1856. The Conference voted that the *piyutim* could be revised and declared that such a revision would be in the interest of Judaism. The details of the planned revision were left to a commission under the guidance of the Chief Rabbi of the Central Consistory. As a result, the number of *piyutim* was drastically reduced.

Another problem before the Conference was the regulation of the repertory and performance of the hazanim. Widely criticized for their ignorance and vanity, they were also reprimanded for their lack of Hebrew knowledge and their inability to comprehend the prayers they sang. To quote from the resolution of the Conference, "Their dancing and gesticulating while they sang profane melodies to the accompaniment of several assistants who rivaled them in volume was not in keeping with the dignity of worship." Finally the Conference adopted a set of principles; the following are the most important:

1. The Central Consistory will form, at Paris, a permanent commission charged with supervising synagogue music.
2. The commission will sponsor the composition . . . of a score [*Kol-Bo*,

or compendium] to be introduced in all of the synagogues of France. Traditional chants of both the Sephardic and Ashkenazic rites will be included.

3. The work adopted will be printed and furnished to those communities that want it, at a moderate price.

4. At each Consistory a commission will be formed in order to regulate the worship services, and to instruct the hazan in matters pertaining to his duties.

5. A month before each of the major festivals the commission will draft a program for the worship service and indicate those musical works that are to be sung. They will also control the Sabbath service.

6. In small communities the rabbi and the head of the administration will enforce the proper proceedings.

7. No new tune . . . may be introduced into the service without the prior permission of the local commission.

8. The hazanim are to avoid tunes with excessive repetition of words in the text and are to give preference to simple tunes in which their assistants can take part.

9. The synagogue administrators and the rabbis are to make sure that the hazan desists from reciting prayers "*de roulade*" and that he avoids all kinds of mannerisms that might prolong the service.

10. No one may be a hazan without knowing the Pentateuch, the early Prophets, the entire ritual, the basic grammatical elements of Hebrew, and especially the rules of proper reading. The certificate given to the hazan . . . must indicate that he has these qualifications.[40]

All these aspirations were realized for the first time with the official sponsorship of Naumbourg's comprehensive codification of *minhag ashkenaz*.

The heated controversy for and against Reform, which split most of the German communities, found only a weak echo in the Jewish public opinion of France. The organ question, which had so greatly excited the German Jews, failed to stimulate even one response among the French rabbis. They remained mute, a reaction that permits various contradictory interpretations. By 1845 the organ had been introduced in the temples of Nancy, Strasbourg, Lyon, Marseille, and Lille. The Sephardic communities were in the vanguard in the use of the organ. An Alsatian "liberal," Cerfberr de Medelsheim, writing in the middle of the nineteenth century, claimed that the Portuguese and Avignonese (Comtat-Venaissin) Jews were much more progressive in questions of religious observance than even the German Jews.

One of the main tasks of the Central Consistory in Paris was the creation of an equilibrium between the three rites used by French Jews: The "Alsacienne," or Ashkenazic, was used by two thirds of the Jewish population. For all practical purposes it was, and still is, identical with *minhag ashkenaz*. The second tradition was the Portuguese or Sephardic, originally centered in Bordeaux and Bayonne, later in Lyon. The colonial interests of nineteenth-century France strengthened the significance of the Sephardic element, since the North African Jews were reared in this rite. The growing immigration of Algerian, Moroccan, and other French-

speaking Jews during the twentieth century has swelled the Sephardic ranks so greatly that now they form by far the numerical majority of the Jewish population. Compared with these main traditions, the Provençal tradition is of minor importance and waning influence.

When Naumbourg was eventually charged with the reorganization of the service, he accomplished his task in an astonishingly short time. His collection of songs, the first—and probably the only—Jewish songbook actually commissioned by a government (1847), consisted of "*Chants liturgiques des Grand Fêtes*" and was later included in his *Zemiroth Yisrael, Chants religieux et populaires des Israélites* (3 vols., Paris, 1847–1864). The work, a compendium for the entire Jewish year, is set for cantor, male choir, and mixed choir, with and without organ accompaniment. It contains *ḥazanut*, stylized folk song, and even art music. The arrangements of the well-preserved tunes of *minhag ashkenaz* run the gamut from a primitive and simplified monody to the bombastic style of the "Grand Finale" of a French opera. One famous piece is typical: "*Min ha-metzar*" (Out of the Straits), a setting of Psalm 118 by Jacques Halévy, is included in the compendium, although that composition has little of a liturgical aura and is, rather, effective theater music.[41] However, Naumbourg did not allow total subservience to the musical fashion of Paris, to which not only Meyerbeer but even Richard Wagner had paid ample tribute. These operatic tastes were counterbalanced by two mutually antagonistic elements in Naumbourg's publications: the old South German *minhag ashkenaz* (of which Naumbourg remained a faithful transmitter and adherent); and the Renaissance, yet reformatory, art music of the long-forgotten Salomone de' Rossi, whose synagogue music he revived. Encouraged and subsidized by the Parisian baron Edmond de Rothschild, Naumbourg and the young Vincent d'Indy published de' Rossi's works for the first time in score, in 1877.[42] Thus three apparently incompatible trends are present in Naumbourg's collections: southern *minhag ashkenaz*, Parisian operatic music, and the strict, even austere *a cappella* style of de' Rossi. Yet not only to the autochthonous Jews of France and the widely spread Alliance Israélite Universelle but even to the Jews in France's fast-growing colonial empire—mainly to Judeo-Arabs accustomed to Sephardic tradition—Naumbourg's synagogue music assumed the status of a canon of musical tradition, at least until the turn of the century.

Naumbourg's treatment of *minhag ashkenaz* was generally inclined to simplify the old melodic lines indiscriminately, omitting many ornaments. He did this quite consciously, as can be seen in his essay included in the *Recueil*, called "*Etude historique sur la musique des Hebreux*." This essay is the second serious study on Jewish music and its history. The first, by Joseph Levin Saalschuetz, is easily superseded by it.[43]

Naumbourg's work, dedicated to the Paris Jewish community, sets out to identify the Hebrews as a Semitic people and lauds the Hebrew language as "*sonore, harmoneuse, facile à cadencer, tour à tour douce ou énergique*." Numerous passages demonstrate considerable knowledge of talmudic and rabbinic literature. In the chapter on the headings of the Psalms, he showed complete familiarity with the biblical scholarship of his time; the names of Gesenius, Ewald, Munk, and others, are

mentioned and their books are quoted. In connection with post-biblical—especially medieval—music, he ventured a number of comparisons of the ecclesiastical scales with traditional Jewish tunes, and he quoted some Gregorian tunes.[44] Some forty years later Idelsohn demonstrated the Jewish origin of those Gregorian chants.

Naumbourg's chapter on the harmony of the Greeks and Hebrews is untenable today. Also, the subsequent chapter on ancient Greek music is totally obsolete. However, his theory on the motifs of scriptural cantillation and its accents is based partly on Fétis's *Histoire Génerale de la Musique*, the best scientific work of its time. It is based also on his own sound philological interpretation. Only in a very few instances does his list of motifs deviate from his contemporary *minhag ashkenaz*. His remarks on the Ashkenazic tradition are particularly interesting. He made clear distinctions between *minhag ashkenaz* and the Sephardic and the Yemenite traditions, and even took cognizance of Karaite manuscripts, being fully aware of their historical significance.[45] He also referred to the first discoveries of the Babylonian Masorah and its accentuation, without fully comprehending the origin of these sources. He refuted gently, but decisively, the old Sephardic claim of its higher authenticity and greater age. "It is with the Ashkenazim that one still finds the precious rudiments of ancient Hebrew music. . . . The order established by Maharil is still in force and valid."[46] In mild criticism Naumbourg described the Polish style: ". . . they knew how to ingratiate themselves . . . among the communities, by their learned writings about their chant, although they did not possess the slightest notion of music theory or of art music. . . ."[47] "As for the recitatives, the hazan chanted them and surrounded them with a thousand ornaments. . . . In spite of these bizarreries, even incoherences, their chant often turned out to be remarkable, and aroused the admiration of the worshipers. This manner of singing no longer corresponds to the taste of our epoch, and one must wish that these bravura-airs will be silenced. . . ."[48]

At the end of his *Recueil*, Naumbourg added a few remarks of polemical nature, criticizing "some of my colleagues who have made a great and justified reputation from their liturgical compositions." He observed that all too often their synagogue music imitated music of "other religions," and he added, bravely and bluntly: "The Synagogue possesses, in its chants, a character *sui generis* that must be respected and preserved under all circumstances."[49] Indeed, he boldly advanced: "For the Catholic composer the liturgical text is nothing but a pretext," and he attacked the senseless repetition of words and syllables in the music of the Church, optimistically denying that this bad habit also infests synagogue chants: "With us, on the contrary, the multiple repetition of words is forbidden; oh, may our Israelite composers take for their models our traditional chants where not one word, not one syllable is repeated."[50] Naumbourg mentioned no names, but it is fairly obvious that he was aiming at Salomon Sulzer and the Vienna synagogue practice. Last, he criticized the organ, although he made use of it occasionally. In his opinion it was "useless" in the synagogue. The entire text of the *Recueil*, with its learned appendix on Salomone de' Rossi, bears eloquent testimony to Naumbourg's Jewish and musical knowledge, and his admirable achievements.

This erudition, together with his other lasting merits, were often publicly acknowledged. Most impressively, a year before his death, he was elected "officer of the Academie Française." He belongs in the roster of those men who saw beyond the petty struggles of the post-Emancipation years. He was able to erect a durable foundation for *minhag ashkenaz* in France, leaving a tradition that is still proudly alive.

12

The Model of Vienna and Its Impact on Eastern Europe

We must reshape our National music to serve the Lord.
(Salomon Sulzer)

At the end of the eighteenth century Vienna was still the capital of the old German Empire, and even after its demise in 1805 under Napoleon's sledgehammer strokes, it regained its position during and after the Vienna Congress in 1815. All through the nineteenth century it remained the cultural center of many nations. It is easy to understand why the treatment of the Jews there was closely watched by all the European powers. After the famous *Toleranzpatent* of Emperor Joseph II, Vienna, not entirely deservedly, achieved the reputation of a haven of relative security for the Jewish masses. "In the east of Europe, Vienna occupied the position that Paris occupied in the west. It was the center of science and art, of theater and music, of culture and refinement. In this life of the spirit the Jews took a considerable part, far greater than their relative numbers would lead one to expect."[1] This appraisal was valid for the middle of the nineteenth century, yet it was only in 1820 that the "tolerated" Jews of Vienna dared approach the Imperial government with a petition to be allowed to organize a community and a synagogue.

At that time there were 118 "tolerated" Jewish families in Vienna.[2] Their request was refused by the "good Kaiser Franz" in a personal note: "The increase and the expansion of the Jews must not be promoted in any way whatsoever, and their toleration must under no circumstances be extended to other provinces beyond those where it is presently admitted."[3]

Nonetheless, the negotiations between the Jews and the Austrian officials went on and reached some positive results in 1824. A number of pointed questions were posed by the authorities including such subjects as the language of prayer, choral songs in German, reading of Scripture, sermons, and especially the willingness of the "tolerated" Jews to "improve" their cult according to the will of His Majesty.[4] After settling some of these matters, mostly in the manner of the Hamburg Reform, the question of German congregational songs was left to a special committee, which was strongly disposed to introduce hymns and organ. A "first teacher of Religion" was to be appointed; this title, rather than the title "rabbi," was all that the Emperor and his police would permit. The driving spirit of all of these negotiations was

Michael Lazar Biedermann,[5] the new representative of the "tolerated Jews" who openly favored radical reform. It was quite in accord with his convictions that he signed a petition to the Emperor asking for a formal separation of the "improved" new worship from the "older" one, and for complete freedom of choice for every member of the community.[6] However, the appointed "teacher" Isaac Noah Mannheimer, a radical Reformist himself, modified his ideas and principles somewhat in order to gain the indispensable support of the less radical members of the incipient community.

There are some well-known names in the list of that first group of "tolerated" Jews. At the outset of the Emancipation, when the establishment of a community was of prime importance, the leading families were the Gomperz-Bettelheim clan, descendants of Rhenish and Hungarian families of rabbis and scholars, representing the intellectual elite of the old Vienna Jewry; the Königswarter family, *émigrés* from Bohemia, outstanding as bankers and philanthropists; the Heniksteins (originally Honigstein), baptized in the second generation (a scion of this family was the baron A. Von Henikstein, chief of staff in General Benedek's army, and the man chiefly responsible for the unfortunate battle of Königgraetz [1866]); and the family of Isaak Loew Hofmann, Edler von Hofmannsthal, a most influential and enterprising financier and merchant, who introduced the manufacture of silk to Austria, converted in the third generation. Most of these former *Toleranzjuden* intermarried and their descendants formed a singularly typical stratum of Vienna society.[7]

The first "first teacher of Religion" to be appointed was Isaac Noah Mannheimer. After his arrival in Vienna in 1825 he became "preacher" and then a kind of civil servant, entrusted with the office of registrar of the community. The official decree of his status contained the following significant passages: ". . . he must abide strictly by the statutes that are generally valid in the Imperial Royal states, and must not deviate from them in any way . . . nor permit any innovation or modification whatsoever. . . . He must, as a faithful Israelite, remain faithful to the conditions under which Government tolerates the Israelites; notably, he must remain faithful to the positive principles of Mosaism, and eschew most carefully any *tendency of a naturalistic religion*, especially in his lectures in the religious school or in the synagogue." The last passage was symptomatic of the mad fear with which the Vienna court recalled the revolutionary French deism, and its "religion of nature and reason."[8]

The constitution and its statutes, which characterized the Vienna Jewish community, survived the collapse of the Austrian monarchy. The following items from this constitution are the only ones concerned with the chanted prayers and their performance practice:

1. *Piyutim*. Only the following were retained: *tal* (prayer for dew, on Passover), *geshem* (prayer for rain, on the eighth day of Solemn Assembly), the *hoshanot*, prayers on Sukkoth and Simhath Torah, and most of the *piyutim* intercalated in the *musaf* service of the High Holy Days. The *Kol Nidre* was eliminated and reintroduced much later in a "reformed" version.[9] The entire *neilah* service of Yom Kippur,

however, was retained. Poems for special Sabbaths were omitted; of the "post-Mosaic" holidays, the following were retained: *Ma'oz Tzur* for Hanukkah, a few songs for the Ninth of Ab, and—since the weekday service was not altered or curtailed—all *seliḥot* before and during the Penitential season remained intact.[10]

2. Performance of prayer. Order, quiet, and "solemn stillness" were to be established during the service; special silence is mandatory for the silent *Amidah*, and even the *Amen* was not to be shouted. All intoning, aiding, or anticipating the cantor was strictly prohibited; also, all swaying and shaking was disallowed. The recitation of prayers before the congregation was a prerogative of the appointed cantor and was not to be done by anyone else, particularly strangers. The Priestly Blessing [*dukhan*] was retained for festivals and High Holy Days only, to be performed without chanting.[11] The "knocking" of Haman (on Purim) and of the willow for *Hoshanah* (on Hoshanah Rabah) were to be abolished. There was to be no "respect for special persons. . . . "[12]

3. The Cantor. "He is obliged to render [*vorzutragen*] the traditional Hebrew part of the service in a dignified manner that is faithful to its meaning and induces devotion. He must be perfectly familiar with the Hebrew language *and its correct pronunciation*, as well as with written and spoken German. He must be able to uphold the dignity of his office also in his private life . . . and must not pursue any other profession. . . . It is not permissible to emphasize some prayers at the expense of others, or to hurry on one day, while exerting a lot of energy, and spending a lot of time and art on another occasion that does not warrant special solemnity. Special tunes are to be designated for the Sabbath, and more solemn ones for the holy days and festivals. . . . The cantor is obliged to rehearse the pieces with his assistants [*Gehilfen*] and with the chorus. He also has to take care of the moral and religious life of the choristers, and is responsible for their deportment, which must be fitting to the dignity of the divine service. The assistants and choristers are under the cantor's jurisdiction. . . ."[13]

Most of these regulations appear trivial today, but in the years of their enactment they were thoroughly revolutionary. Yet they were not the only basis of the often praised "*Vienna ritus.*" Mannheimer's main merits rest chiefly with the compilation of the *Unity Prayer Book* (first edition, Vienna, 1840).[14] There he provided German translations to all Hebrew texts, eliminated most *piyutim* (as described above), and included a few German prayers, mainly in honor of the Emperor and his dynasty. A few German song texts were also included, and there were a few strict rules for the proper deportment of all worshipers. The prayer book unified the *Kultus-Gemeinde*, the strong institutional bulwark of Jewish unity. This institution was the legal representative of the Jewish community vis-à-vis the government and consisted, in turn, of a sort of miniature parliament, whose members were elected or appointed by the major parties. Since the *Kultus-Gemeinde* was entitled to levy taxes on the individual members, it did not depend on voluntary contributions. The government collected the taxes and guaranteed its major expenditures. The prayer book that Mannheimer edited under the aegis of the Vienna community was supported by the Austrian government and the Crown, which bestowed upon it

enormous authority. This was an event unheard of in former centuries.[15] In Vienna, the Mannheimer ritual became dominant. This great community could even afford to contain and support two disparate congregations, the Orthodox Polish group and the "Turkish" Temple, gathering place of the Sephardic-Levantine residents.

To complete the task of unification, a kind of songbook or hymnal was needed that would satisfy most groups, and thus create, at least for Vienna and the neighboring provinces, the inner Jewish unity it so urgently sought. In northern Germany, the ideological struggles and schisms threatened to destroy the last remnants of unity and Jewish identity in many communities where they were already undermined by the mass-conversions of halfhearted socialites and intellectuals. The type of songbook needed could not be provided by any simple musician or cantor. The hour demanded a statesmanlike, scholarly person. No committee or board could command the necessary authority. Moreover, the person would have to be agreeable to Mannheimer, as a congenial co-worker. It was the good fortune of *minhag ashkenaz* and, indeed, of the cause of Jewish unity that there was such a man, that he came to the fore, and that he achieved the lofty aims set for him by virtue of his charismatic and authoritative personality.

Salomon Sulzer

Salomon Sulzer was the man who dissuaded Mannheimer from using German hymns and who successfully opposed many radical reforms planned by Mannheimer.[16] And it was Sulzer's prophetic insight that inspired him to rejuvenate most of *minhag ashkenaz*, keeping the Jews of central Europe united, and immune to the siren song of Reform or neo-Orthodox ideologies.

The basic biographical data of this great man are easy to find. All Jewish references and many general musical references contain them. The following brief summary emphasizes facts of special pertinence to this study. He was born in Hohenems (close to the Swiss border) in 1804, and was trained as a boy by cantors who took him on their travels to southern Germany and Alsace. There he heard, and retained in his memory, the regional tradition. He was appointed cantor at the age of thirteen, in Hohenems, and studied theory and harmony at the music school of Karlsruhe. At the age of twenty-three he was formally appointed as cantor of the Vienna community. On 1 February 1826 the board of deputies petitioned the police to grant to Sulzer a temporary permit of residence; the request contained the passage that a definitive appointment would be made if Sulzer fulfilled the great expectations that his reputation promised. The formal appointment was granted by the government of Nieder-Oesterreich on 22 July 1827, and depended upon a *Schutzbrief* (letter of protection) for Sulzer, issued by Count Zichy-Ferraris on 15 March 1827. According to this document the Jew S. Sulzer was received as a member by the Jewish community of Carlburg (not Vienna!) in a Hungarian county; at the same time he was granted permission to marry Franziska Hirschfeld of Hohenems. The music for the temple's inauguration, however, a festive cantata, was not to be written by Sulzer but came from the pen of *Kapellmeister* Joseph Drechsler.

Salomon Sulzer (1804–1890), chief cantor of the Jewish Community of Vienna. Lithograph by G. Decker from a painting by J.M. Eigener (from *Schir Zion*, Wien: H. Engel, 1898–1976, 3 vols.). By courtesy of the Hebrew Union College-Jewish Institute of Religion Library, New York.

Sulzer, on his part, was astute enough to realize that he needed further instruction in composition. He studied assiduously with Ignaz von Seyfried, friend and disciple of Beethoven.

He became part of Viennese life, an intimate of artistic circles in that strange environment, vacillating between tranquillity and strife, attending secret meetings of democratic, revolutionary artists, poets, and musicians. Schubert was perhaps the most important influence in Sulzer's immediate circle of friends, which included Joseph Fischhof, a fine musician and fiery democrat, and also the composers Joseph Weigl and Franz Volkert. Beethoven and Schubert were still alive, but the time was approaching when their work would be all but forgotten in Vienna.[17]

Sulzer was the first personality since de' Rossi who combined in himself a thorough knowledge of Jewish tradition, a high musical erudition, and a full appreciation of classical music. And he estimated correctly the character of the Vienna Jewish community. Its members came from old and usually rich families, and their musical taste was conditioned by concerts and *soirées*, where the musical elite of composers, vocalists, and instrumentalists could be heard. They were familiar with some philosophy and with a good deal of classical literature. Many of them had read the works of Lessing, Schiller, and Goethe, or had seen performances of their plays at the famous Imperial Burgtheater.[18] To cope with such a community, Sulzer needed not only a thorough knowledge of the classics but also a close acquaintance with the musical fashions of the day: Bellini, Rossini, some distorted Mozart and Carl Maria von Weber, who dominated the opera, and even some "two-week celebrities." His musical guides were, without exception, master craftsmen, mostly music directors of churches or theaters or—as in the case of Drechsler—functionaries in both fields.[19]

Sulzer spoke for himself, but never more emphatically than when he stated his aims and tasks. The following is quoted from his *Denkschrift*, written at the age of seventy-two, on the occasion of his fiftieth anniversary as chief cantor of Vienna:

> I encountered chaos in Vienna also, and was unable to discover a leading principle in this maze of opposing opinions. Most important was the task of fighting the notion that saw a complete break with our past tradition as the best means for a reform of public worship, and which intended to disregard the ancient and venerable continuity of our liturgy. It was the intention of the misbegotten experiments of Hamburg and Berlin to reduce the entire service to a German song before and after the sermon. To abandon all tradition—this was the aim of a Reform that resembled the castor-oil plant of the prophet Jonah—"children born of the night, vanished in the night." Yet I was convinced from the very beginning that the "weeding out" of the liturgy could be effected only by way of a *restoration* that had to rest upon *historical foundations*, in order to recover the original nobility of form and substance. Thus one had to resume the given tradition and to restore it in a dignified and artistically correct manner. Old worshipers were to hear familiar and dear strains, young ones were to be made receptive to them, but the synagogue, . . . languishing far too long under the slavery of decayed and antiquated abuses, would celebrate its jubilee, and "in this year of jubilee shall return to its inheritance."[20]

> The Jewish liturgy must remain Jewish if it is to comply with the postulates of musical standards, and must not renounce its Jewish character if it is to enter into an alliance with the genius of art. It was now essential to "turn the hearts of the fathers to their children" (Malachi 4:5) and to warm the hearts of aspiring youths to the sentiments of their fathers.... First the pronunciation of the Hebrew language had to be standardized, and foremost the old national melodies and modes had to be rediscovered, collected, and arranged according to the rules of art [*nach den Gesetzen der Kunst zurecht gelegt werden*]. Yet new compositions were also indispensable, and here musical heroes such as Seyfried, Schubert, Fischhof, and others aided me. It is in dutiful gratitude that I keep their blessed memory in dear remembrance.[21] Although they abstained from any influence upon the purely liturgical element—the responsibility for that was exclusively mine—they contributed essentially to the adornment of synagogue chant, and by right, theirs is part of the success that the "Vienna Ritual" did achieve. My endeavors to mediate between past and future and to recover the tradition, in order to prepare the ground for future progress, was fully appreciated by the community. I count among the happiest memories of my life that moment when truth dawned in the great and noble soul of the blessed preacher Mannheimer, originally an adherent of radical reform, à la Berlin *Kulturverein*,[22] and he spontaneously confessed to me that my way was the only and uniquely right one that would lead to the desired aim. Our enterprise was visibly blessed by the Lord. It found favor with the most intelligent Jewish communities, recognition and emulation in all the world. The Vienna Ritual became a model and standard, our melodies were kindly received and recognized even beyond the ocean. The conviction was general that the pontificating [sic] priest and messenger of the community, fully conscious of the dignity of his status and of his roots in the national tradition of our songs, feels, composes, and sings....[23]

Later Sulzer stated: "The office, as such, demands from its incumbent above all strength of character and full consciousness of its lofty dignity...." Since genius is a gift of God, rarely conferred upon mortals, it might be desirable—so argued the aged Sulzer—"to separate the purely musical elements from all cantorial influence, and on the other hand, to keep the cantor free and immune from the creative pains of true artists."

He went on to advocate the introduction of the organ, which, in his earlier years, he had so successfully opposed. He added that the halakhic admissibility of the organ had been sufficiently demonstrated, and, stressing its Jewish origin (as *magrepha*), he repeated his motto that "each one shall return to his inheritance"—in this case the organ-*magrepha* should return to the synagogue. For Sulzer, purely musical reasons decided the question: "The organ alone is able to lead and to regulate congregational singing, to veil dissonances.... The organ frees the priestly office of the cantor from artistic bond, and protects him from a complacent pseudo-artistry.... It prevents him from relapsing into those hackneyed, trivial flourishes, which provincial hazanim employ *ad nauseam*, or else into that lachrymose virtuosity

of Polish cantors, which drives the younger generation, musically intelligent, out of the temple. . . ."

As for scriptural cantillation, Sulzer demanded only small modifications, so that it might be closer to the tone of emphatic speaking. He was opposed to calling unprepared laymen to the Torah, and took pride in the decorum of the temple. He was pleased with the prohibition of "anticipating the cantor," often practiced by all too zealous worshipers. Above all other goals and ideals, his most important aim was the unity of Judaism and its liturgy. He and Mannheimer set the pattern for Isaac M. Wise's "unity" prayer book, *Minhag America*.[24]

Sulzer's works comprise three volumes of compositions: *Schir Zion* 1 (1839), *Schir Zion* 2 (1865), and *Dudaim* (1850), plus some less important single pieces. The original editions are, strangely enough, not listed in the otherwise fairly reliable bibliography by Alfred Sendrey, and it is for this reason that I mention the major libraries where they may be found. This is the more necessary, as these excellent and magnificently produced volumes were replaced by cheap arrangements (the most popular by his son Joseph) or by bowdlerized editions and "popularizations" perpetrated by various—usually ignorant or unskilled—musicians or hazanim. In New York City the original editions are found in the New York Public Library (Jewish Division), and in the libraries of the Hebrew Union College-Jewish Institute of Religion and the Jewish Theological Seminary.[24a]

The difference in style between volume 1 and volume 2 of *Schir Zion* clearly indicates essential changes in Sulzer's approach to *minhag ashkenaz* and, notably, his painstaking revival of older traditions, both of Western and Eastern origin. Even a comparison of the forewords bespeaks the conspicuous modifications that had taken place in the composer's mind. In the first volume he stated: "I see it as my duty . . . to consider as far as possible the traditional tunes bequeathed to us, to cleanse their ancient and decorous character from the later accretions or tasteless embellishments, to restore their original purity, and to reconstruct them in accordance with the text and with the rules of harmony." Sulzer continued with the assertion that it was easier to achieve a stylized tradition for the High Holy Days and festivals than for the Sabbath service (particularly for Friday evening), for there was little authentic tradition accessible for the latter, and many "profane tunes" had been retained from former generations. Hence he was not loath to accept contributions from good Christian composers, some of which he might even have solicited, for example, Schubert's "*Tov le-Hodot*" (Psalm 92).[25] The preface of the second volume stressed the tradition originating in the time of Maharil, and also the inclusion of a good number of eastern Ashkenazic (Polish) elements. It mentioned a few pieces that he had provided with modest organ accompaniments. "The volume performs a mediatory mission between the past and the future." This, as we have seen, was a favorite idea of Sulzer's.

Most characteristic of the first volume are the numerous five- to eight-part *a cappella* settings. At first glance these appear to resemble Salomone de' Rossi's or Monteverdi's music. But Sulzer is firmly anchored in the style and tonality of the Vienna classics, and although he occasionally wrote contrapuntally, he retained for the most part a well-balanced homophonic diction. His cantorial recitatives are

quite impressive, without many embellishments, and traditional in a noble—one is tempted to say classical—style, with impeccable taste.[26]

As he himself observed, he could follow the lines of genuine tradition more easily on festivals, and notably on the High Holy Days, than on Friday evening or even Sabbath morning. This fact is well known to anyone at all familiar with Jewish liturgical music. Contrary to Idelsohn's statement, the *minhag ashkenaz* has only three traditional themes for Friday evening: *Kabbalat Shabbat* (not more than 500 years at the most), the *Adonai malakh* (Psalm 93), and the quotations from Genesis 2:1–3 (*va-yekhulu*) and Exodus 31:16–17 (*ve-shomeru*), which are chanted in the *Magen Abot* mode. The rest does not correspond to any particular tradition; this is easily proved by comparing three or four cantorial compendia of the nineteenth century, where the melodies for Friday evening differ considerably from one another.

On the other hand, the noble setting of many sections of the High Holy Day service, such as *u-netaneh tokef* on Rosh Hashanah, and *ya'aleh*, or *alenu* on the eve of Yom Kippur (to name only the most celebrated), have set a standard of liturgical music in *minhag ashkenaz* that has not been surpassed to this day.

In the second volume, issued twenty-seven years later, Sulzer abandoned his original intention of introducing *a cappella* art music to the synagogue. He now realized that this aspiration was not realistic. This kind of art music had reached its zenith during the seventeenth century and could not be revived in a city that was the spiritual and actual home of Schubert, Bruckner, of the Austrian church composers, and, indeed, of Johann Strauss—father and son. The *genius loci* is discernible in Sulzer's music with both its noble and its "folksy" elements. Had not Schubert, Beethoven, and even Mozart occasionally spoken the native musical dialect, and, in so doing, lifted it to the high level of their art?[27] Some of the tunes in this collection came from far away places, yet they had already been chanted early in the century, and several are found in manuscripts in the Birnbaum collection.[28] The modal flavor is more stressed in the second volume than in the first. In the "new edition" Sulzer's son Joseph unfortunately and unskillfully reduced many of these old tunes to major and minor. Every change for purposes of practicability or facility exacts a price; in this case it is dullness, with which the son imbued his father's noble lines.

The great choral structures recede in the second volume, and the hazan comes more into his own than before. A few recitatives are accompanied by organ; the finest composition is the priestly benediction for the festivals. We recall, in the list of the Vienna regulations quoted above, that the priestly benediction was to be spoken, not sung. The reason for that was the disorder created by the active participation of the *kohanim* (Priests; now frequently uneducated laymen) in the *dukhan*. Sulzer found a way of retaining the venerable custom by reducing the singing to the solo of the hazan, with a two-tone response for the congregation, led firmly by the organ. The composition breathes a high and quiet solemnity. In the best of his "free" choral compositions, Sulzer's *melos* is influenced by the elegant lines of Schubert's *Lieder*. Thus many of them have become widely popular in all kinds of congregations, and his *Kedushah* responses, or *Hodo al eretz*, or *Adon Olam* are sung today in most Orthodox services rather than in liberal ones.[29]

However, it was not only his compositions that opened to Sulzer the hearts of thousands, perhaps of millions, of his fellow Jews on both sides of the Atlantic. His magnificent voice, his imposing, indeed majestic figure, his innate dignity reminded many of his listeners of Shakespeare's verse: "Grace seated on his brow, a combination and a form indeed, where every god did seem to set his seal"; yet this does not completely account for the charisma that emanated from him. Even Franz Liszt, certainly no friend of Jews, was forced to admit: "Only once we witnessed what a really Judaic art could be, as the Israelites would have poured out their suppressed passions and sentiments, and revealed the glow of their fire in the noble art forms of their Asiatic Genius, in its full majesty and fantasy and dreams.... In Vienna we heard the famous...Sulzer, who served in the capacity of precentor in the synagogue.... For moments we could penetrate into his real soul and recognize the secret doctrines of the fathers.... Seldom were we so deeply moved by emotion as on that evening, so shaken that our soul was entirely seized by meditation and given to participation in the service...."[30]

The causes of this great appeal were not simply of an aesthetic nature, but lay deeper. What surrounded Sulzer with dignity and loftiness was what he himself was inclined to describe as "the Grace of God."[31] Expressed in less mystical terms: "The millennial ethos of the nation that had produced prophets, priests, and eternal laws deeply antipathetic to most peoples, because of the Law's inhibitions of the barbaric *Id*, had for once united itself with the beautiful, and had found musical expression."[32]

Even as severe and occasionally biased a judge of Sulzer as the Lithuanian Idelsohn, who during his life was never able to take an objective and critical view of the chant of eastern European Jewry, was obliged to write about the great hazan: "He was surely inspired, full of enthusiasm for Jewish ideas—at least the Prophetic ideas. A sacred fire burned in his heart, the light and warmth of which inflamed all his hearers...."[33]

There was another reason for Sulzer's enormous popularity, a reason forgotten by this generation, but vividly recalled by his contemporaries. In the Revolution of 1848, in spite of his forty-four years, forgetful of his official position, of his family, of his own danger, Sulzer fought at the barricades as a fiery democrat. He was captured and sentenced to a long prison term. Because of his wide renown, he was soon pardoned. The details of this incident are hard to ascertain.[34] In an official book on the Revolution, Sulzer's name is not mentioned. Yet there is no question that he did take part actively in it, for there are newspaper articles of the time mentioning his name and that of his friend Fischhof, also that of his admirer, the music critic Alfred Becher, who was shot under martial law in November 1848.[35]

Sulzer was convinced that the Jewish liturgical composer ought to be measured by the same critical yardstick as the best church composer, and he was ready and willing to be judged accordingly. Companion of Schubert,[36] disciple of Seyfried, colleague of Drechsler and of many professors of the Vienna conservatory, Sulzer was an archenemy of the intellectual ghetto, and, what is more, of the voluntary isolation of many Jewish artists who were afraid of open competition with their Gentile confreres. He loved to cite one proverb: "He who cannot swim should drown!" Yet he was by no means always as secure and lofty as he liked to appear.

Two letters of the wordly Sulzer will illustrate this. The first, addressed to Baron Vesque von Puettlingen, director of the *Gesellschaft der Musikfreunde*, Vienna, was written in 1846. After a formal apology for his own dissatisfaction with his performance of a song by Vesque because of the "abominable heat," he continued: "...I was so fatigued that I feared not to be able to finish 'The Omnipotence' [*Die Allmacht*, a poem by the archbishop von Pyrker, music by Schubert, and a favorite piece of the Viennese, as well as of Sulzer]. Having executed this *Lied* that I know so well by summoning my last resources and by a major effort, I could not hope to attain the full plaudits of the public with your song, let alone your own approval. Please forgive me...I shall be at your service at any and all times."

And an even more revealing document is the following excerpt from a letter addressed to the famous (and feared) Viennese music critic Eduard Hanslick. It was written shortly after the publication of the second volume of *Schir Zion* (1865) and represents what was called in Vienna "a bid for fair weather." After expressing his gratitude for the recognition and praise that he had received from Hanslick as singer and cantor, Sulzer's letter (dated 28 November 1865) continues: "As the hart pants for the wells of living water, so my soul longs for the quickening word... from your lips. The strange [Hebrew] text, as well as the highly original notions characteristic of our religion, may somewhat complicate a sober judgment. Nonetheless, your truly kindhearted welcome to my work...is sufficient guarantee to me that you will overcome all impediments, and reach a conclusion that will amply compensate me for my lengthy toils and efforts. It will surely illumine the rest of my days.... Yours, etc."[37]

Hanslick was not a man who could be easily swayed by empty flattery (as Wagner had learned to his displeasure), and what he wrote was assured of a worldwide echo. Sulzer did not pen his letter in vain. The leading daily paper of Vienna, then an internationally known newspaper, the *Neue Freie Presse*, contained an extensive article by Hanslick on Sulzer and his work. Only the most significant passages are quoted here:[38]

> [Alluding to the fiftieth anniversary of Sulzer's cantorial debut] ... one may claim that at present all of Vienna is interested in "old Sulzer"...although his art serves only genuine worship, and worship of a minority's religion at that.... He is one of the most popular figures of Vienna. Who does not know him, that remarkable highly characteristic head, surrounded by long gray locks, with the large, round, fiery eyes, and the energetic broad mouth of commanding authority, above the hawk's nose that completes the inventory of oriental physiognomy.... Even today no foreign musician leaves Vienna without having listened to the celebrated cantor.... His performance, from the slightest breath to the most powerful torrent of tones, combines the charm of the exotic with the persuasiveness of a glowing faith...fiery tones—perhaps even a little too much flame.... It was the sharpest possible contrast to the monotonous repetition of ritual formulas.... A contrite sob and enthusiastic soaring to God...intensely spurred by the thought of representing the whole community, nay the whole house of Israel, with the faith and truth of every tone. Years ago Sulzer had had a wonderfully supplementary and elucidative

> counterpart in the late preacher Mannheimer. Old Mannheimer preached the way Sulzer sang. The same command of the substance, the same strange and yet enthralling passion that carried all listeners with him.... It was the most glowing and enrapturing pulpit-oratory of my life, here in words, there in tones....[39] Sulzer's *Schir Zion*, second volume, lies open before me. I am totally incapable of judging about earlier synagogue songs and their reforms by Sulzer. I have no right to judge these. Yet all the experts testify that it was Sulzer who restored order, dignity, and lofty aesthetic form in the musical liturgy of Judaism, that he had rescued it from a desolate state of amorphous and capricious negligence.... The second volume is incomparably superior to the first, which seemed indebted to the Haydn-Mozart style...at any rate, German. The chants of the second part have not only more liturgical character, but they bear—and this is very important indeed—more distinctly, the stamp of genuine Jewish-oriental music.... Indeed, the characteristic elements of oriental-Jewish music are nowhere lacking in this second volume. It is true, the notes must be brought to life in that national rendition.... Yet even the notes themselves carry these typical marks; we find them especially in the recitatives, which, if chanted by a master like Sulzer, assume the nature of inspired improvisation.... Thus we may recognize in *Schir Zion*, though it represents modern synagogue music, a strongly national tendency....

In these pages, we are more concerned with *minhag ashkenaz* and its history and essence than with the personality of one cantor, however eminent. Hence the task of critically evaluating Sulzer's work from the point of view of *minhag ashkenaz* must not be shirked, even if he is correctly called the "father of modern synagogue music." However, only criticism by serious modern scholars and musicians—they must be both!—can engage our earnest attention. We already know how he was idolized by his contemporaries. The glowing epitaph on his tombstone reflected that veneration.[40] Yet not too long after his death in 1890, the first serious critic raised his voice: a Russian cantor, well read and not without comprehension of the basic problems. He was Pinhas Minkowski from Odessa (1859–1924, died in Boston), an older contemporary and serious rival of Idelsohn. His pamphlet on "Sulzerism" was the first to chide Sulzer, because of his tendency toward assimilation—that is, because of the non-Jewish character of his compositions and arrangements. To a certain extent he was justified.[41]

Significantly enough, the serious critics of Sulzer's treatment of *minhag ashkenaz* were all of eastern European background and bias; after Minkowski, we find Idelsohn and Abraham W. Binder. Idelsohn judged as a scholar; Binder, as a practical musician of the synagogue. Of the two, Idelsohn shows much deeper insight. In the light of Hanslick's review quoted above, Idelsohn's remarks are particularly relevant: "Sulzer's music affords but another proof of the general phenomenon which we may observe in regard to the identifying of the music of a foreign people. Music, the originality of which has so dwindled that it would not be recognized as their own even by its own people, is yet by another people considered foreign.... For example, the Oriental pieces by Rimsky-Korsakov, the Oriental parts...of *Samson and Delilah* by Saint-Saëns, would hardly be

recognized by Orientals as their own music. . . . The Jew considered these creations non-Jewish, while the Christians felt it foreign to them, and therefore counted it Jewish. . . ."[42]

Yet, strictly speaking, this is no valid argument, as long as there is no concrete answer to the eternally silly question of "what is Jewish in music?" And only concrete arguments can be taken seriously. Idelsohn claimed that "Sulzer's complete ignorance of the elements, types, and forms of Jewish music led him to imitate imitations instead of drawing directly from the source."[43] What elements, what forms, has Idelsohn in mind? And from what (uncorrupted) source should Sulzer have drawn? From the totally corrupt eastern European *ḥazanut* of his day? Idelsohn alleged also that "He did not understand the Semitic-Oriental character of the Jew—despite the conviction of gentiles that he was the embodiment and symbol of the ancient Hebrews." In concrete terms, he did not subscribe to the theory or practice of *fixed modes* in his recitatives; even less willing was he to anticipate Idelsohn's highly debatable ideas on the harmonization of traditional modes.[44] True, he employed a harmonic style that was close to Schubert's idiom; yet, as he himself explained, he had to make oriental melodies palatable to a community conditioned in its musical taste to the mainstream of Western music, and in Vienna, to boot! Each of his traditional tunes is easily recognizable, and that procrustean bed into which A. W. Binder claims he forced *minhag ashkenaz* distorts the basic melodies far less than the critics would have us believe.

The fundamental dilemma remained incomprehensible to Idelsohn, Binder, Rosowsky, Freed, and many new composers of the synagogue. A mode is a purely *melodic* structure; it is in no way compatible, let alone identical, with a *harmonic* construction. Where it sometimes occurs that a modal pattern is harmonized "in style," it is owing to the merit and talent of an individual composer, to a "lucky inspiration," such as we sometimes find in the music of Bartók or Janaček.

Binder wrote an essay in observance of the seventy-fifth anniversary of Sulzer's death, in which he concludes, "He [Sulzer] evidently did not object to the Protestant style, for he included in his *Schir Zion* the works of Seyfried, Schubert, and Fischhoff [sic], who were non-Jews."[45] As it happens, Seyfried and Schubert were devout Catholics, Fischhof, a leading member of the Vienna *Kultus-Gemeinde*, a renowned musician, a faithful and observant Jew. As a general answer to the critics it must be stated that, coming as they did from eastern Europe or the United States, they had no conception of the meaning of *Kultus-Gemeinde* as one of the strongest bulwarks of Judaism. Also, they truly and sincerely believed that national music forms itself collectively as if by some kind of parthenogenesis.

The sophisticated critic is fully aware that no composer can, so to speak, jump over his own shadow. Would any of them minimize Mozart for not having invented the supple harmonies of Wagner? At the bottom of all Sulzer criticism lies the naïveté of historical thought that was, and still is, characteristic of the Jew who was brought up in the *shtetl*, or in its American counterparts.[46]

Sulzer taught many hundreds of hazanim, thus extending his personal influence to practically all communities of *minhag ashkenaz*. Of his many contacts with eastern European *ḥazanut*, perhaps the tragicomic story of his encounter with the

"Vilnaer Balhabeissl" is symbolic. ("Vilnaer Balhabeissl" is a nickname for Joel David Levinsohn [1816–1850].)

This young man, possessed of a magnificent lyrical tenor with a fabulous "pearly coloratura," was idolized wherever he appeared as hazan in eastern Europe, notably in Vilna and Warsaw. He studied with the composer Moniuszko for a while, and became somewhat familiar with the mainstream of classical music. It was then that he grew aware of the narrow confines of Eastern *ḥazanut*. Until that time he had lived in a "fantastic realm of self-glorification" (Idelsohn), not to say megalomania. Moniuszko suggested to his financially independent disciple that he make an extended trip to western Europe. In Warsaw he fell in love with a Polish lady singer, and fled to Vienna, where he meant to "teach that fellow Sulzer what's what in *ḥazanut*" (Birnbaum). Sulzer received him cordially, and hospitably; yet listening to the celebrated cantor proved catastrophic for the young man. "[His] fantasy was shattered as he listened to the powerful, artistic and overwhelming singing of Sulzer. He felt that his own voice and singing were only those of a child in comparison with those of a hero."[47] As his love for the forbidden Gentile woman grew in his heart, he became a penitent, but under the double impact of the two traumatic shocks his mental health was seriously impaired, and he ended his days in an asylum in Warsaw, still a young man, in 1850.[48]

Behind this romantic tragedy lies the tremendous superiority of quality and formative power of Western musical education and tradition, of which the Easterners, satisfied with their own products, and without the opportunity of comparison, were blissfully unaware. When this ignorance was breached, admiration, envy, hatred, and grudging emulation ensued; and even the best of the highly talented Eastern writers, singers, and composers had to experience a period of "contemptuous admiration" for Sulzer before they regained a sober and reasoned judgment.[49]

Aside from Sulzer's personal appearance and mannerisms, which induced slavish imitation beyond all bounds of good sense and good taste, his legacy to the synagogue—not only to its music—has been far-reaching and his example decisive. The standards of decorum, originally mocked, the aura of dignity that has surrounded the worship service since his time, and last, but not least, the baritone timbre of his voice—these were the three paragon innovations he established, in addition to the new musical repertoire. Previously, a sweet flexible tenor voice had been the ideal of cantorial sonority. After Sulzer, it was a high baritone of mellow quality, typical of the German oratorio of the nineteenth century, that most appealed to German Jews.

In two realms his long-lasting influence was eventually overcome by subsequent cantors and synagogue composers: in their novel treatment of *minhag ashkenaz* as ethnic folklore, and in aiming at its artistic transfiguration inside the synagogue and out. In individual cases, Sulzer's contemporaries and followers could emancipate themselves from his towering influence by cultivating special spheres of *minhag ashkenaz*. To their efforts in the latter part of the nineteenth century the last chapter is dedicated.

13

The Age of Dispersion

The espousal of chauvinism under the flag of national art is another symptom of the declining standards of both esthetics and ethics in the era of materialism.

(Albert Schweitzer, 1922)

The Haskalah

The ferment within Ashkenazic Jewry brought on by the Emancipation had as one of its most significant consequences the deep division of Western Jewry into many factions. This was not necessarily a catastrophe; it was incontrovertible evidence of the vitality with which Judaism entered the modern age. Without this inner dissension there would probably be no state of Israel today. Undoubtedly, the dominant movement of the first half of the nineteenth century was the *Haskalah* (enlightenment). It began with Moses Mendelssohn in the West, and the East followed suit hesitantly, with a time-lag of almost two generations. Western *Haskalah* effected advances in three areas: religion, the "Science of Judaism" [*Wissenschaft des Judentums*], and internal community politics. The situation in eastern Europe was more complex. *Haskalah* at first opposed the tyrannical Orthodoxy and some of the hasidic groups. Later, social issues made themselves felt as well, and against the constant oppression by the Russian government the new Jewish nationalism, mixed with elements of *Haskalah*, became the catalytic agent that dissolved the hitherto antagonistic groups and their vested interests in the furnace of a fiery will to survive as a nation. This new nationalism, born out of disappointment and desperation, was, at the end of the nineteenth century, the most influential factor in eastern European Jewish thought. The last achievement of this nationalist *Haskalah* was its merger with the worldwide Zionist movement aided by such lofty spirits as Ahad Ha-am and Haim Naḥman Bialik.

Aside from the advocacy of a few prophetic minds such as Moses Hess, and perhaps the two great scholars Moritz Steinschneider and S. D. Luzzatto, no defense of the Jewish *nation* as such was undertaken in the West; its true spirit, growing in stature and pathos with every new publication, emerged in eastern Europe. The relation of the *maskilim* (adherents of *Haskalah*) toward the three established mass movements of Eastern Jewry was, to say the least, ambivalent: originally they championed liberalism and reform, later, disappointed by the mass conversions

initiated by assimilationist reform, they turned against the "Berliner *Haskalah*" and its representatives in the East.[1] They sympathized with Orthodoxy as a positive and defensive force, and even flirted with hasidic groups because of their intrinsic interest in all aspects of Jewish folklore.

Thus the *Haskalah* polarized the western and eastern communities, with far-reaching effects in every area. In the West, the principal struggle was between the neo-Orthodox and the liberals, revolving around the question of the validity of rabbinic (not biblical) law. In all other respects, the western *Haskalah* led either to assimilation and baptism or to the science of Judaism, with its deep penetration into all matters concerning the Jewish civilization, poetry and music. This meant study—historic, aesthetic, scientific—with some reflection of Hegelian thought.

Eastern *Haskalah* aspired to national unity. It caused cleavages, however, by raising the conflict between intellectualism and emotionalism. On the intellectual side there was antagonism between rabbinic legalism and philosophy (represented by Nahum Sokolow, Ahad Ha-am, etc.). On the emotional side, the conflict was between neo-Hasidism together with nationalism and the secular folklorists, such as Jacob Klatzkin and Haim Naḥman Bialik.

In music, these trends were reflected in a concern with art music and the hope of creating an art music for the synagogue. There was some interest in creating an art music based on *minhag ashkenaz* even earlier, but most early attempts fell into oblivion. Only two documents have survived from the end of the eighteenth century and the beginning of the nineteenth. The first of these is "Hebrew Melodies," poems by Lord Byron, set to music by John Braham (born Abraham)[2] and Isaac Nathan, published in London in 1815. This music does not presume to be written for the synagogue, but it was clearly art music based on *minhag ashkenaz*. The composers were fully aware of the synagogal origin and function of their melodies, as their preface indicates:

> The "Hebrew Melodies" are a Selection from the favourite Airs which are still sung in the religious ceremonies of the Jews. Some of these have, in common with all their Sacred Airs, been preserved by ceremony and tradition alone, without the assistance of written characters. Their age and originality, therefore, must be left to conjecture. But the latitude given to the taste and genius of their performers has been the means of engrafting on the original Melodies a certain wildness and pathos, which have at length become the chief characteristics of the Sacred Songs of the Jews. . . . Of the Poetry it is necessary to speak, in order thus publicly to acknowledge the kindness with which Lord Byron has condescended to furnish the most valuable part of the Work. . . .

The second half of this preface reminds one of J. G. Herder's essay on Hebrew poetry, especially the passage about the "wildness and pathos" of the original melodies. This speaks well for Nathan's erudition. For it was apparently Isaac Nathan (1791–1864) who was on friendly terms with Byron. He wrote a good part of the music, and attached to it the name of Braham, a celebrated personality who might attract the public.

"On Jordan's banks" from "Hebrew Melodies."

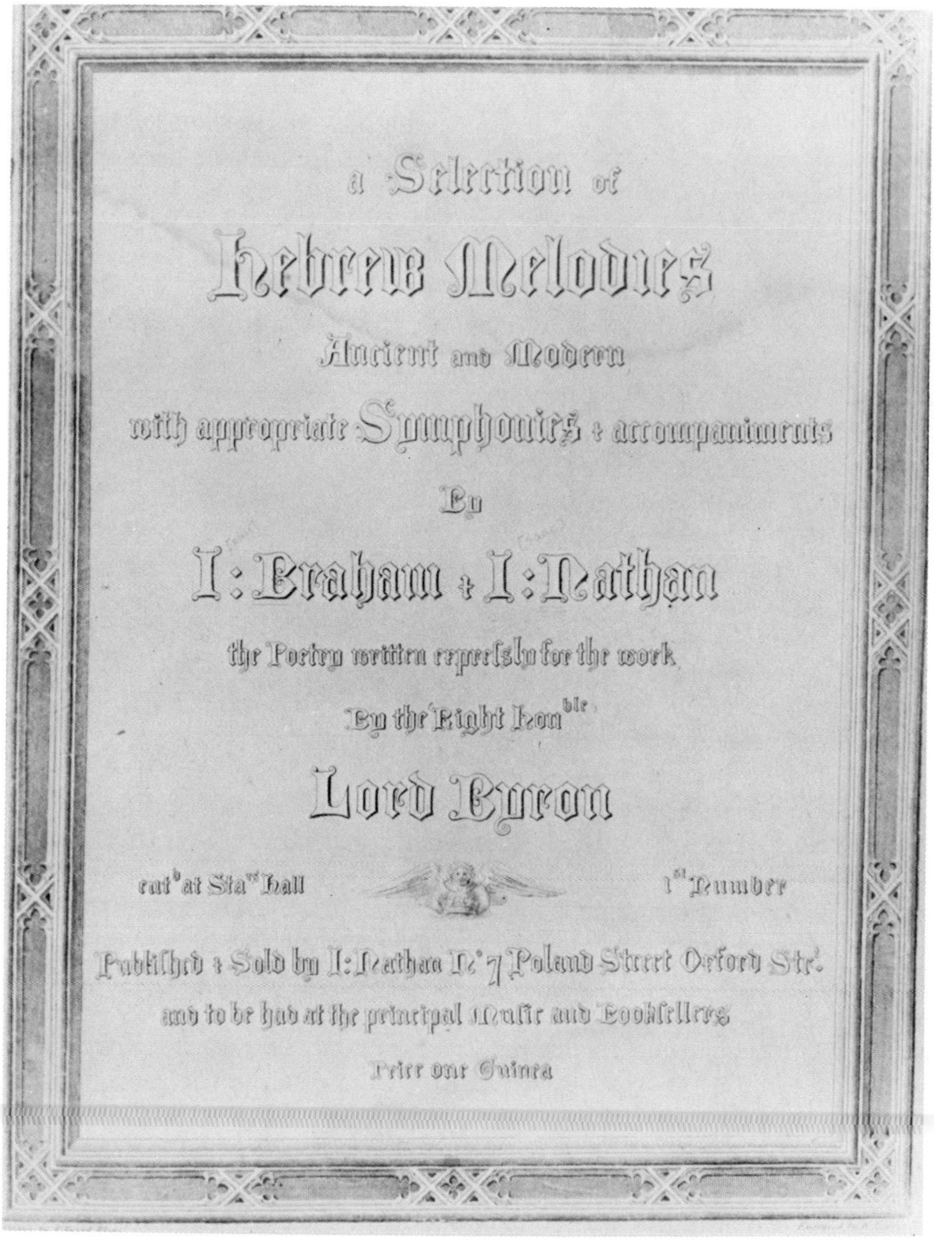

a Selection of

Hebrew Melodies

Ancient and Modern

with appropriate Symphonies & accompaniments

By

I: Braham & I: Nathan

the Poetry written expressly for the work

By the Right Honble

Lord Byron

entd at Stars Hall 1st Number

Published & Sold by I: Nathan No 7 Poland Street Oxford Strt

and to be had at the principal Music and Booksellers

Price one Guinea

Title page from Lord Byron's "Hebrew Melodies" set to music by John Braham and Isaac Nathan, London, 1815.

The poem "The Harp the Monarch-Minstrel Swept" is set to an almost literal arrangement of the melody to the *piyut Ya'aleh taḥanunen* (May our Supplications Rise) from the service for the eve of Yom Kippur. Other poems were set to the tunes of *Ma'oz tzur*, *Lekha dodi*, *Kaddish* after the lesson, *Yigdal* for Sukkoth, and the Passover priestly blessing. Here we reproduce the beginning of *Ma'oz Tzur*.

Francis L. Cohen, the music editor of *The Jewish Encyclopedia*, claims that four of the six tunes of *minhag ashkenaz* were of non-Jewish origin; he does not identify the tunes, except for the *ya'aleh*, for which he claims a foreign source without naming it.[3] Although this is not impossible, Cohen gives no proof, and neither Birnbaum nor Idelsohn has ever seconded his doubts.[4] *Grove's Dictionary of Music* (third and fourth editions) takes a more benevolent view of Braham and Nathan. The latter was instructor of the history of music to none less than George IV, who, although not a paragon of virtue, was a capable musician and did a great deal for the recognition of the Viennese masters in England. If Nathan guided George's musical taste, his influence was surely beneficial.[5]

The second document, an unpublished manuscript, is a copy of Karl J. Christian Fasch's hitherto unknown choral composition upon the Hebrew text *Ha-nerot halalu* (These Lights), a prayer for the evenings of Hanukkah. The manuscript belongs to the Birnbaum collection, and has been performed and recorded under my direction in the album *Israel Sings*. The accompanying text to that album notes only that a Jewish disciple of Fasch had arranged Fasch's melody and set it to the Hebrew prayer. That is not quite correct: all that can be definitively stated about the manuscript is that the original composition came from Jews connected with the Berlin Singakademie, of which Fasch was the first director, and that the line of the soprano was written by Fasch.[6] We do not know whether it was written specifically for the Hebrew text, but it seems possible, because the tone-word relationship is very natural. The Singakademie had included a number of Jewish members before 1800, especially from the Itzig family, and later from the Mendelssohn family.[7] Fasch also wrote a group of *Mendelssohniana*, settings of texts by Moses Mendelssohn, or of translations by him, and *Davidiana*, settings of Psalm verses in Luther's translation. It is quite possible that the manuscript in the Birnbaum collection is a copy of one of the *Mendelssohniana*, originally set to the Thirtieth Psalm, "for the dedication of the house." Perhaps some musical *maskil* in Berlin who was close to the Singakademie, and who loved the composition, put the Hanukkah text in as a substitute for the psalm "*Le-Hanukat ha-bayit*."[8]

In both documents one may recognize a factor—but only one of many—that caused the transition from purely functional liturgical music to Jewish or Hebrew art music: the example set by the environment. In northern Germany the models were the Berlin-school disciples of Johann Sebastian Bach and the orthodox Lutheran church music, with its dominant *chorale* form. In the south, the models were the Vienna masters, foremost among them Haydn, Mozart, and Schubert, who united all trends in Catholic Church music. It was the great accomplishment of Sulzer that he did not become merely an imitator of those immortals, but was able to revivify the synagogal folklore of *minhag ashkenaz*. In Paris, Naumbourg chose to stylize the same material in the manner of French grand opera.

All of this reflects the influence of *Haskalah* on the music of the synagogue. In Berlin it was the second generation that took an interest in transforming the chant into art music, and that was a vital force in determining its development. Members of the older generation had attended the Reform synagogue that Jacob Herz Beer established in his own home. First one Ahron Beer, then a "cantor without a voice" named Asher Lion were engaged as cantors.[9] Of the younger generation, such fiery orators as Leopold Zunz and Eduard Israel Kley preached at the synagogue. But after two active years, following a denunciation by Orthodox fanatics, the Prussian government closed this synagogue in 1817. Yet because the other synagogues were badly in need of repair, the Beer synagogue was designated by the government as temporary sanctuary. Upon the demand of the Orthodox party, the government issued a decree to the effect "that the religious services of the Jews should be held . . . only according to the customary ritual, without the least innovation in the language or the ceremonial, the prayers and songs, entirely in accordance with ancient custom" (9 December 1823).[10]

Idelsohn justly calls Asher Lion a "champion of the rococo style" of the eighteenth century—a time when cantors enjoyed ample freedom to "modernize" the tradition with popular ditties and operatic airs. Engaged to serve as hazan in the Orthodox Heidereutherstrasse synagogue, Lion returned to his old habits as if nothing had happened. He hired a *Bass* and a *Singer* to support his dwindling voice. The *Singer* was a young boy from Wreschen (west Prussia) whose name was Louis Lewandowski. By that time (1835 or 1836) word had reached Berlin that Sulzer had most successfully reformed, improved, and strengthened the "Jewishness" of the liturgical music in Vienna. Lion was not a man to favor innovations unless they were backed by rich bankers! It was for reasons of self-preservation that he had abandoned his earlier sympathies with the *maskilim*. He resisted the influence of Sulzer, but in vain. The breakthrough to the Vienna forms is told charmingly by Lewandowski himself.[11]

Louis Lewandowski

Louis Lewandowski (1821–1894) came to Berlin at the age of twelve, after his mother's untimely death, with a number of letters of recommendation, but with little money. His father was one of those indomitable small-town lay cantors who did more for the preservation of *minhag ashkenaz* than many a virtuoso hazan. As a *Singerl* in the so-called choir of cantor Lion, he met a number of influential people, among them the Hebraist Solomon Plessner, who was a frequent visitor in the house of Alexander Mendelssohn (first cousin of Felix). Although alienated from Judaism, Mendelssohn had maintained his relations with a good many of his learned Jewish friends, all of whom were *maskilim*. Like most members of his family, he was an active philanthropist. Plessner introduced young Lewandowski to him, and he helped the boy win permission to take the examination for entrance to the Royal Academy of Arts. Lewandowski passed the difficult examination and became the first Jewish student of the Academy. At that time Felix Mendelssohn was approaching the acme of his fame. Small wonder that the ambitious boy hoped to

emulate him. Among his teachers were the mediocre Rugenhagen, director of the Singakademie and rival of Mendelssohn,[12] and the great contrapuntist Eduard Grell. It was this man from whom Lewandowski learned his fine and neat technique of choral composition.

In 1838 the young *maskil* and cantor Hirsch Weintraub came to Berlin with his choral ensemble and gave several synagogue concerts, which he spiced with choral arrangements of Rossini overtures. The main pieces, however, were compositions and arrangements by Sulzer, sung from as yet unpublished copies of *Schir Zion*.[13] Weintraub also rendered a few excellent cantorial improvisations. Many years later, Lewandowski remembered the profound impression made upon him by Weintraub's ensemble and the artistic Hebrew songs. It was the first time he had heard "Jewish music" in the classical forms, in choral settings that he knew so well from his studies at the Academy.

In 1840 the cantor Lion had to capitulate to the demand for musical reforms. Hard pressed, he obtained a copy of Sulzer's work. Poor Lion! The score was written in four different clefs. He could read only one. His *Bass* of the time was an old man named Kaspar. Lewandowski described him thus: "It is said that he growled so furiously because his wife whipped him regularly." Kaspar could not read music but held his own by occasionally imitating a phrase in his lowest register, "so that the listeners might hear and fear." Lion tried to train his singers to read, and had them read all the parts as if they were in the treble clef. Obviously, that did not work! After a number of miserable rehearsals, Lion's authority was in grave danger, and in his need, he remembered his former *Singerl* who was now studying music at the Academy. He invited Lewandowski to a confidential interview and implored him to solve the riddle of the score. Wisely, Lewandowski transcribed all the parts in the treble clef, so that old Lion could read and control the singers' parts. Later, Lion "allowed" Lewandowski to "help him" with the training of the singers. Although now Lewandowski was attached to the "Old Synagogue," his companions were all young Reformists. His rabbi was Michael Sachs, a moderate Reformist from Prague, a personality of poetical, philosophical, and musical aptitude, and a profound scholar to boot. Lion's advancing age demanded his replacement by a younger cantor, and a very talented man was found and engaged. He was Abraham Jacob Lichtenstein, from Stettin (1806–1880). He was an experienced hazan with a lovely voice, an excellent melodist, and had studied in Stettin with Karl Loewe, a musician of fine taste.[14]

Lewandowski was required to make choral arrangements for Lichtenstein. He now stood at the crossroads of his life. He had to choose between devoting all of his efforts to the "ennoblement" of synagogue music and aspiring for the laurels of a symphonic composer. An apocryphal yet credible anecdote has it that the young man complained to his teacher Grell about the heavy burden he carried as choir director and arranger for the synagogue. This deprived him of the time necessary for writing larger works of chamber or symphonic music. Grell is said to have replied, "My dear L., please abandon your hope to become another Mendelssohn. You are not of Mendelssohn's calibre. Rather bend your best efforts to the improvement of your people's liturgical music [*Geistliche Musik*]!"[15]

Lewandowski wisely heeded the advice. He remained at the Old Synagogue with Lichtenstein until 1866, when both of them accepted a call to the New Synagogue (Oranienburgerstrasse), a large Reform temple with an organ and a service compiled by Abraham Geiger. (In 1855 Lewandowski and Lichtenstein had been sent to Vienna for six months to study with Sulzer, so authoritative was Sulzer's status by that time, even in Berlin!) Now that Lewandowski had a mixed choir and an organ at his disposal, many former restrictions were removed and he was able to compose at will.[16]

His main works are *Kol Rinnah*, recitatives for the cantor and two-part choral pieces for congregational singing, published in 1871, and *Todah ve-Zimrah*, services for the entire liturgical year for cantor, four-part choir, and organ, in two volumes, published between 1876 and 1882. It should be recalled that Sulzer had published the large second part of his *Schir Zion* in 1865. It was a long time before Lewandowski dared to compete with the "Old Man of Vienna."

The accomplishments of Sulzer and Lewandowski interest us not so much as independent compositions but rather as examples of their style of arrangement and, to a lesser degree, as examples of comprehension and interpretation of important liturgical texts. Here we shall compare briefly the treatment of the main forms—recitative, response with choir, and choral arrangement of *Missinai* tunes—by the two masters.

Recitative. Sulzer was a cantor's cantor. Nothing in the liturgy, orthodox or liberal, was unfamiliar to him. His recitatives avoided repetition of words, and they were carefully suited to the proper phrasing and accentuation of the Hebrew text. They shunned coloraturas except for special solemn occasions and they were deeply rooted in the Hebrew tradition. Lewandowski was never a cantor. His knowledge of Hebrew remained elementary, and his phrasing and accentuation were not impeccable. For example, in his very popular *u-netaneh tokef* he gave the following: "*U-ve-shófor gódol yitóka ve-kol demómoh dákkoh* (rest) *yíshomá*." Sulzer accentuated and phrased the passage correctly. Lewandowski's recitative style originated directly in the German oratorio of the Berlin school. Sulzer preferred, whenever possible, to be terse and simple, avoiding what he regarded as "senseless" melismata. To illustrate the difference between the two, examples 1 and 2 are their respective settings of the *Shema* of the High Holy Days. These are obviously two very different treatments of the same melody. Sulzer phrased strictly according to syllable, avoided all ornaments, and used seventeen tones; Lewandowski, adding ornaments in the second and sixth measures, used thirty-two tones, almost twice as many as Sulzer. Moreover, he permitted himself a coloratura on *Adonai*, contrary to all traditional practice.

Response with choir. In the instances where the raw material is taken from *minhag ashkenaz*, the same comparison is valid as in the case of the recitatives. Sulzer was correct, simple, terse; Lewandowski was ornate, inclined to repeat words, incorrect in his accentuation, and occasionally bombastic. Where there was no traditional source from which either composer could draw, Sulzer used a line that is indebted

Example 1

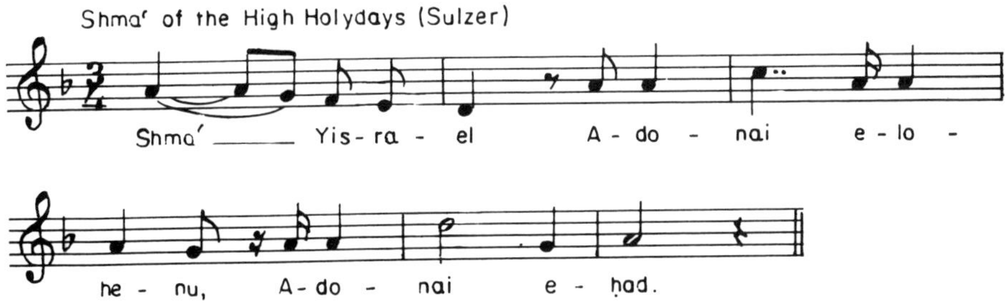
Shma' of the High Holydays (Sulzer)
Shma' Yis - ra - el A - do - nai e - lo -
he - nu, A - do - nai e - ḥad.

Example 2

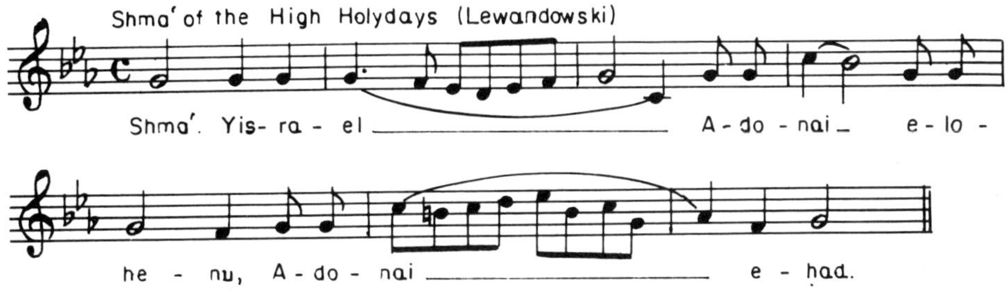
Shma' of the High Holydays (Lewandowski)
Shma'. Yis - ra - el A - do - nai e - lo -
he - nu, A - do - nai e - ḥad.

to Mozart and Schubert, with a general preference for triple time over duple. Lewandowski seemed, rather, to be influenced by the Mendelssohnian choir lied. Lewandowski handled the choir with greater skill, while Sulzer wrote a better line for the cantor. A good example is the melodic and choral treatment in the settings of *Lekha dodi* by each of them (Lewandowski's in D major, Sulzer's no. 1 in F). In both compositions, the refrains are intended for congregational singing, and both tunes have become very popular. Lewandowski's tune is considered "German," Sulzer's tune, "classic."

Adaptation of Missinai tunes. Here even the raw material that the two men used was not always identical. It was not simply a question of authenticity. After comparing Lichtenstein's manuscripts with Lewandowski's printed music, Idelsohn wrote, "For twenty-five years Lewandowski worked on Lichtenstein's *chazzanuth*, until the material acquired a new form—the form bestowed by Lewandowski's genius. And in publishing that *chazzanuth* . . . Lewandowski did not mention even the name of Lichtenstein, apparently believing that this music was or had become his. Only by means of Lichtenstein's own manuscripts do we recognize the origin."[17] Lichtenstein had transmitted and championed the eastern versions, whereas Sulzer preferred the western.

While working on the Birnbaum collection, I examined the beautifully calligraphed melodies of Lichtenstein and found them to be identical with the melodic line of Lewandowski's choral and organ arrangements. Also, I found them to be

purer, and finer, than Lewandowski's arrangements. The details of the great prayers of the High Holy Days are more effectively represented in Lewandowski's arrangements, especially in the intensely lyrical passages. Sulzer is less lyrical, more dramatic, and more intent upon the liturgical atmosphere of the entire service. Lewandowski kept his music free from Protestant elements, especially from calamitous chorale structures. Sulzer did not keep his pieces as pure from Catholic encroachments.

Lewandowski burned too much incense at the altar of his adored Mendelssohn. Sometimes an entire piece is a paraphrase of a Mendelssohn composition. A case in point is "*Enosh ka-ḥatzir yamav*," which so closely resembles the first duet from Mendelssohn's *Elijah*, "Zion Spreads her Hands." In addition, there are innumerable "Mendelssohn reminiscences" throughout his music, as in the famous "*Zakharti Lakh*" (I Remember Thee).

To sum up the characteristics of the two great champions of *minhag ashkenaz*: Sulzer was a classicist by nature, a traditionalist by education, Reformist by temperament, singing priest, born leader, *grand seigneur*, and pioneer. Lewandowski was a romantic by nature, conservative by inclination, musician-composer, patriotic Prussian, choirmaster par excellence, a faithful subordinate. Sulzer was a charismatic leader, Lewandowski a highly talented follower.

Hirsch Weintraub

We turn back now to Hirsch Weintraub (1811–1882), whose appearance in Berlin made such a strong impact on the young Lewandowski. He was a less eclectic composer than Lewandowski, having drawn exclusively on eastern tradition for use in his imaginative songs. He was the prodigal son of the celebrated hazan Kashtan (redheaded) Weintraub from Dubno, in Russia. Father and son were confirmed *maskilim*. The son traveled with a choir ensemble, and with his violin, and was for a time a glorified *klezmer*, until he settled down most respectably as cantor in Koenigsberg, where he soon gained wide recognition.

Weintraub published a selection of his synagogal compositions, in which *minhag ashkenaz* is so thinly diluted as to be hardly discernible. These "modern" compositions constitute the first part of his compendium. The second part, smaller but finer, consists of a number of examples of traditional *ḥazanut* in eastern style, which either he or his father had sung and written. Some of them are harmonized plainly, but they are of much higher value than the first part, representing a truly stylized eastern tradition. In addition to these, there are hundreds of unpublished manuscripts by Weintraub in the Birnbaum collection, some of enchanting loveliness and melodic richness; if they were cleansed of their ornamental ballast, they would rise and soar. In Weintraub one can detect the influence of Sulzer, both good and bad. The "modern" compositions are poor imitations of Sulzer's choruses. The fine *ḥazanut* emulates Sulzer's noble recitatives and adds the warm eastern flavor to them. These pieces deserve publication.

Weintraub left a biography of his father Solomon Kashtan (published in 1875), which gives a sharply contoured picture of life and mores among Polish-Russian

hazanim in the first third of the nineteenth century.[18] It is valuable in that it explains the inner reasons for the success of *Haskalah*, and the split between the *Hasidim* and their opponents, the *mitnagdim*. It also exposes the incredible arrogance of the hasidic *rebbes*. One episode illustrates this point: the young *Singerl* (Kashtan), while traveling with the Mohilever hazan, had once allowed himself to mock the singing of the son of the revered hasidic *rebbe* of Shipetovke. The offended father, a "wonder-*rebbe*," threatened to destroy Kashtan's voice and thereby his existence. On the very next day, young Kashtan felt his voice fade away and remembered the *rebbe*'s threat. Six weeks passed, and still the lad could not sing. He implored the Mohilever hazan to take him back to Shipetovke, where he might apologize to the *rebbe*, and entreat him to restore his voice. The *rebbe* did listen to the craven pleas of the boy and "gave him back his voice." Kashtan never forgot this experience, especially since it repeated itself some years later under the following aggravating circumstances.

> Once there came to the city [of Dubno, where Kashtan was a permanent hazan] one of the lesser hasidic *rebbes*, and my father [Kashtan], though in his youth he had journeyed to the old hasidic *rebbes* . . . and was well beloved by them, could not kowtow to the new hasidic rabbi . . . and his attachment to Hasidism had cooled somewhat. In Dubno, one of my father's warmest friends was the rabbi Hayim, the son of Reb Hillel, of an exalted family in Israel, a great scholar of the Torah, rich, wise, and clever. To this outstanding man my father said, "Let us go to the new *rebbe* who has come here and welcome him," and they went. When they came they inquired as to his health. And the *rebbe* said to my father, "It is two weeks since I arrived here, why didn't you come sooner? Don't you know it is within my power to take away your voice?" My father answered, "I fear not, neither am I afraid before you, for if the *rebbe* is a God-fearing man and truly pure, then he will not do such a thing as to take away the *parnoseh* [livelihood] from a man, from his wife and children, and if this is not so [that he is a true man of God], then he surely can do nothing." He arose and went away with his friend, Reb Hayim.[19]

These and similar occurrences freed an entire generation of pious and intelligent people from the tyranny of the *rebbes*. Yet the time came when these faithful Jews became suspicious of the *Haskalah*, for they were increasingly aware that the path of the German *Haskalah* led most often to assimilation and baptism, and they felt that they must find other ways of coping with the threats of Russian oppression and persecution. It was then that the *maskilim* led the way to the new Jewish nationalism; the "year of decision" was 1881, when all over "Holy Russia" waves of pogroms and massacres killed, plundered, raped, and humiliated the Jews. Russian composers and cantors who contributed to the eastern *minhag ashkenaz* were exposed to these persecutions; they followed a course that led from the older *Haskalah* with its Mendelssohnian optimism to the grim new nationalism and, in one instance, to the shining new hope of incipient political Zionism.

The Russian Composers

Only two generations of Russian Jewish composers are relevant to our discussion, covering the years from 1850 to 1920. The most important figures were Boruch Schorr (1823–1904), Eliezer Gerovitch (1844–1913), David Nowakowski (1841–1921), and Pinhas Minkowsky (1859–1924).

Boruch Schorr was a Galician (born in Lemberg), who learned his trade as *Singerl* in Odessa. He officiated for five years in New York, but he felt that his services were not appreciated and yielded to urgent pleas by his friends to return to Lemberg, where he served for many years until his death. His compositions are contained in his *Services for the High Holy Days*. Being a *maskil*, however observant, he could not escape Sulzer's dominating influence in the harmonization and shaping of the traditional melodies. In his last years he composed some nationalist songs.

Eliezer Gerovitch was by far the most original and the best-trained cantor-composer in the field of eastern *minhag ashkenaz*. He studied harmony and counterpoint at the St. Petersburg Conservatory. His splendid tenor voice secured for him the appointment of the much-coveted post as chief cantor of St. Petersburg. Yet the harsh climate there was so detrimental to his health and his voice that he preferred the less glamorous, but healthier position as cantor in Rostow-on-the-Don, where he remained until his death. Gerovitch published two fine volumes: *Shirei Tefillah*, for Sabbath, the Three Festivals, and the High Holy Days, and, many years later, *Shirei Zimra* for Yom Kippur and the New Year. His arrangements demonstrate his solid training, but his originality lies mainly in the strange affinity between the melodic substance of *minhag ashkenaz* and the Russo-Byzantine elements that he stressed in many of his works. In his best efforts he reminds one of Mussorgsky's strength and originality, without ever attaining that master's stature. He made use of traditional melodies as *cantus firmi*, a technique never heard before in the synagogue. This was indicative of the trend toward art music, engendered by his contrapuntal flair. The Russian musicians recognized his talents, and the authorities of the Pravoslav Orthodox Church in Rostow frequently visited his services.

David Nowakowski, although better known than Gerovitch, was a decidedly weaker composer, and his relation to *minhag ashkenaz* was unquestionably more tenuous. As Idelsohn rightly observes, Nowakowski's music is the "most Europeanized" synagogue music of the East.[20] I have seen many of his unpublished compositions, which are at present in New York, in a private collection. During his lifetime he published only two small services, one for Friday evening and one for *Neilah* of Yom Kippur. His indebtedness to Mendelssohn's and Brahms's oratorio style is quite obvious, but his lengthy, often fugal choruses and responses render his compositions unfit for actual liturgical use. His contribution is less valuable than that of the previously mentioned cantor-composers.

The last of this quartet of leading composers was a disciple of Nowakowski, Pinhas Minkowsky. He was not the most creative of the four, but surely the most eloquent. A gifted *maskil*, he was born into a family of distinguished ancestry. (His mother was a descendant of Rabbi Lippmann Heller.) After a good number of years devoted to talmudic and musical studies, he served as cantor in Kishinev,

Odessa, Vilna, and in New York, at Adat Yeshurun, then the largest and richest Orthodox synagogue. After five successful years he returned to serve as chief hazan of the Great (Brody) Synagogue of Odessa in 1889. There he worked in close association with Nowakowski, who was its music director. They installed an organ and a women's chorus, and their association, which lasted until 1918, was happy and fruitful. In 1919 Minkowsky returned to America and died in Boston in 1924.

Here we are concerned mainly with his literary output, for his compositions did not have any influence, except in Odessa, and are not of lasting merit. Minkowsky was a respectable popularizer rather than a musical scholar. His articles in *Ha-Shiloah*, *Reshumot*, *Ha-tekufa*, and other magazines, contain interesting details, each of which, however, must be checked carefully. But he was a man of courage, of convictions (sometimes changing), of literary merit, and a friend of Bialik, Tchernichovsky, Ravnitzky, and a host of other *maskilim* of Odessa. In his autobiography, Minkowsky writes, "We did not drag church music, or lemonade music with Italianate virtuoso cadenzas into the synagogue, as they do in American Reform and orthodox congregations, that are 'deformed'! We installed an organ, a women's choir, and we reworked the old *nusḥa'ot* in such a manner that the Jews used to say, 'When one wishes to hear a Jewish Reform service, one must go to the Brody temple.'"[21]

Having been a personal student of Sulzer, he wrote a pamphlet against "Sulzerism," but in later years, when writing the history of *ḥazanut* (in Yiddish), he concluded with a two-page tribute to the "great old man, Sulzer." Sulzer, he said, "had laid the cornerstone to the true art . . . of *ḥazanut* . . . and just as the first Solomon is immortal through his Song of Songs, of the poetic word, so will the later Solomon be immortal by his 'Song of Songs' in tones of music." Minkowsky's scholarly suggestions—at least those that were of merit—were consolidated independently of him by a much more profound scholar. And with Eduard Birnbaum we return to the German *Haskalah*.

Eduard Birnbaum

This introvert scholar and cantor, favorite disciple of Sulzer, and executor of his will,[22] was the scion of a distinguished family in Cracow, where he was born in 1855. Combining general and talmudic studies in true *Haskalah* fashion, he drew deep from the fount of Sulzer's experience. He continued his musical studies at his first position in Magdeburg with A. G. Ritter, the Dom organist and theoretician, and showed his early interest in the history of Jewish music.[23] His first publications, some promising essays, appeared in 1880. Hirsch Weintraub chose young Birnbaum as his successor when he retired from his position in Koenigsberg. He recognized the young man's potential; moreover, both men came from the East, but were West-oriented *maskilim* as well as traditionalists. Birnbaum's publications brought him into contact with many well-known personalities in Jewish cultural life and music: Ismar Elbogen, David Kaufmann, Adolf Jellinek, Rabbi Moritz Guedemann, Alexander Marx, Romain Rolland, Hugo Riemann, Guido Adler, Hermann Kretzschmar, Joseph Joachim, and many others. He was possibly the only

cantor in history who was considered and treated as a peer by rabbis and scholars, for he was not only a musically erudite man, but an accomplished rabbinic scholar with a phenomenally wide knowledge of medieval Hebrew literature. This erudition was a solid basis for over fifty learned essays on Jewish music. To help his memory, he made a detailed alphabetical index of every important Hebrew book he had studied. A good many of those old handwritten indices are in the library of Hebrew Union College. He was fond of indexing and cataloguing; thus, over many years of study and toil, he assembled an alphabetical card-catalogue of every tune, for every prayer used in *minhag ashkenaz*, indicating the incipit of the text, of the tune, the first print or the oldest manuscript of the item. This treasure of *minhag ashkenaz* consists of about 10,000 cards. It, too, is in the College library.[24]

One highly interesting item consists of handwritten marginal notes by Birnbaum in a copy of I. M. Japhet's book on the accents of scripture, *More ha-Kore; die Accente der Heiligen Schrift* (Frankfort, 1896). He fully appreciated Japhet's solid introduction to the accents, but he justly contrasted it to the pseudo-folk songs, in the worst German *kitsch* style, that appeared under Japhet's name in the songbook of the ultra-Orthodox synagogue of Frankfort, where he was the chief cantor for many years.[25] A tentative bibliography of Birnbaum's publications is found in *HUCA* 18 (1944).

Minhag Ashkenaz in the United States

The last phase in the development of *minhag ashkenaz* occurred in the United States. In the second half of the nineteenth century the Jewish population in the United States consolidated to such a degree that two dominant parties, Orthodox and Reform, began to reshape their liturgy and its music. The earlier immigrants (excluding the Spanish and Sephardic Jews, who took no part in *minhag ashkenaz*) were from western Europe. Before the 1850s, and before Isaac M. Wise championed the Reform movement, the old Orthodox communities employed cantors, but most of them were only part-time functionaries, and musical illiterates, as can be read in Alois Kaiser's autobiography, and in Rabbi Isaac Wise's *Reminiscences*. It was somewhat later that a group of these hazanim formed an organization, part professional, part social, sometimes dominated by pretty questionable characters. Yet men belonged to it who were as eminent in their profession as Isaac Rice, A. Ansell of Baltimore, Samuel Welch of New York, Morris Goldstein of Cincinnati, and Osias Hochglueck of New York and Philadelphia. These men were not Americanized. They were poorly paid, and it was understandable that when the opportunity arose, many of them left their old congregations to join the new and affluent Reform temples.

Thus the conditions of the American hazan were different from those of their colleagues in the "old country." Hazanim had preceded the rabbis to this country by many years, since a cantor was indispensable for the organization of regular services, whereas a rabbi was not. Also, western Ashkenazim preceded the immigration of eastern Jews by about fifty years. That gave the western Jews a chance to prosper while the later immigrants were still new and unsettled. The "Germans"

brought their wealth and prestige into the Reform institutions, whereas the eastern immigrants, with their poverty and their large numbers, generally supported Orthodoxy. The Conservative movement began to function significantly only after World War I, when, for all practical purposes, the guardianship of *minhag ashkenaz* came under its wing. Scientific study in this field, however, remained—as it had been in Germany with Zunz and Birnbaum—the domain of Reform and liberal scholars.

The split between radical Reform and traditional Orthodoxy came when the second generation of German immigrants reached maturity. Since most of the western Jews had come to America via Hamburg, they had been strongly impressed and influenced by the new Reform temple of that city. It served as a model for the first Reform synagogue in Charleston, South Carolina, established in 1843. Most Reform communities followed the northern German pattern, with Protestant-sounding hymns, organ, huge deletions from the prayer book, and other Reform innovations. The farsighted Isaac M. Wise, statesman of American Reform, tried to stem this tide, and introduced Sulzer's and Lewandowski's music as a check, but without much success. Unlike Mannheimer and Sulzer, Wise was unable to avert the intrusion of sterile doctrinal disputes, which led to a clean schism between Orthodox and Reform, as it had in Germany. His attempt at a united liturgy, like Mannheimer's *Unity Prayer Book*, bore the proud name *Minhag America*. But this statesmanlike and conciliatory proposition was rebuffed by his rabbinical colleagues in 1885 at the Pittsburgh convention of the Central Conference of American Rabbis. The northern German rabbis won, and Rabbi Wise lost the fight for unity. From that day on, the very survival of *minhag ashkenaz* hung in the balance, until the mass immigration of Polish-Russian Jews in the 1890s gave it a new lease on life.

In his *Reminiscences*, Rabbi Wise wrote, "In those times, the average American congregation's '*parnass*' (president) was an autocrat. He was president, *shamash* (sexton), hazan, rabbi. He ruled the quick and the dead. He was the Law and the revelation, the lord and the glory, the majesty and the spiritual guardian of the congregation. He suffered no rival, all were subject to him. This was an inheritance from olden times, brought to these shores from the small European congregations" (p. 53).

An enthusiastic disciple and lifelong friend of Sulzer, Rabbi Wise "had a keen sense of the central importance of music in worship. He wished to modernize the musical tradition of the synagogue. . . ." In Albany he himself trained the choir of the synagogue, in spite of rather ridiculous difficulties. "The choir was a thorn in the side of some of the obscurantists and reactionaries, for there were women in it. . . ."[26]

Today, more than four generations after the beginning of the American Reform movement, it is easy to see that it deviates in many essential points from its German parentage. Yet every emancipation breeds slavery of its own making. The radical ideology of the Reform, assimilationist in character, won out over Rabbi Wise's statesmanship, and insisted upon the Protestant hymn as the dominant form of choral and even congregational singing. Thus it had become a slave of its German

parentage. This was defensible, as the relationship of the Reform movement with German culture remained unbroken. Some of these bonds remained unbroken after the First, even after the Second World War, with its murderous holocaust: members of the Reform movement continued to sing some of their killers' songs, exactly as had their eastern brothers after the massacres of 1648.[26a] This was hardly compatible with the ideas of the New World. It was even less compatible with the practice of *minhag ashkenaz*. The Jews were never at home with the square and symmetrical melody typical of the Lutheran church. Yet they were constrained by the proliferation of Reform hymnals, first those brought from Germany, and later those published in the United States. The following is a partial listing:

I. Jacobson, *Religiöse Lieder* (Cassel, 1810–1816)
H. Goldberg and I. Freudenthal, *Gesaenge fuer Synagogen* (Braunschweig, 1833)
G. Rosenstein et al., *Gesangbuch des Hamburger Tempel-Vereins* (Hamburg, 1845)
Penina Moise, ed., *Charleston Collection of Hymns* (Charleston, S.C., 1846)
Isaac M. Wise, *Hymns, Psalms and Prayers* (Cincinnati, 1868)
O. Löb, *Israelitische Tempel Gesaenge* (Chicago, 1876)
Isaac Moses, *Hymnal* (New York, 1894), in many editions
Henry Gideon, *New Jewish Hymnal* (New York, 1910)
Central Conference of American Rabbis, *Union Hymnal* (New York, 1st ed., 1892, 2d ed; 1897, newly revised ed., 1914, 3d ed., revised and enlarged, 1932)
Central Conference, *Union Songster* (New York, 1960)
Harry Coopersmith, *Songs of My People* (Chicago, 1937)

The most recent collections of hymns relinquish the Protestant hymn type more and more. Its place is taken by a strange mixture of Israeli and American popular tunes. A few interesting songs have emerged.

The long-neglected tradition began to return to American Reform, strengthened by the younger generation of trained cantors. For what was possible in Europe, i.e., the introduction of a certain type of ritual by an *entire community* as decided by its *Kultus-Gemeinde*, was prohibited in the United States because of the strict separation of Church and State as postulated in the Constitution. Thus every congregation is autonomous and its leadership is responsible only to its (voluntary) members. It is this lay leadership that, together with the rabbi and the (lay) chairman of the ritual committee, decides on all synagogue music, its type, performers, and performance. Hence a local tradition is in America almost identical with a *personal* tradition, linked to *this* rabbi, *that* cantor, *that* chairman, *that* organist, etc. To some degree, the fact (*mirabile dictu*) that *minhag ashkenaz* did not disappear altogether rests on the work of a number of cantor-composers who bridged the worst years, and fixed at least a part of it in creditable arrangements. Among them was Alois Kaiser (1840–1908) of Baltimore, a personal disciple of Sulzer, who brought both Sulzer's music and his own adaptations of that music (under various titles) to America. Along with William Sparger, he contributed to *A Collection of the Principal Melodies of the Synagogue*, a splendid souvenir of the Jewish Women's Congress held in Chicago in 1892. This is a most respectable survey of *minhag ashkenaz*, as seen through the eyes of a disciple of Sulzer. The editors closed by pleading with the Jewish women

of America to "preserve carefully its [*minhag ashkenaz*] characteristics and originality," but in fact they really only promoted the hymn form. Since Baltimore was one of the main ports of entry for immigrants at that time, Kaiser's influence remained strong, even after his death.

Max Graumann, in his *Musical Service for the New Year and the Day of Atonement* (New York, 1937), and Morris Goldstein, in his *Evening Service for New Year and the Day of Atonement* (Cincinnati, n.d.), transmitted *minhag ashkenaz* for the moderate Reform service. They too established lasting local traditions, which are still alive in New York and Cincinnati. In the same category of "local transmitters" is Edward Stark (1863–1918) of San Francisco, whose father was a student and fellow countryman of Sulzer; in his service for the High Holy Days he stylized the European *minhag ashkenaz* so as to make it acceptable to American worshipers. His works were widely acclaimed. Another "Americanizer" was Sigmund Schlesinger (1835–1906), who appeared as the main representative of *minhag ashkenaz* in the South. There his synagogue music was still popular as late as ten years ago. It is an eclectic hodgepodge of mutilated *minhag ashkenaz* mixed with Italian opera, German "beer songs," and a good deal of "Kosher Schmaltz!"

On the other hand, the representatives of eastern *minhag ashkenaz* who came to America did not show better taste. They were mostly "virtuoso hazanim" who traveled the length and breadth of America, giving "synagogue recitals," which usually provided them with a comfortable income. One cannot, of course, speak of genuine liturgical music in these cases, since every prayer, every passage, was chanted to impress the listeners (not worshipers) by the brilliance of their voices and by their vocal acrobatics. This pernicious abuse of the tradition became exceedingly popular among the Orthodox immigrants from eastern Europe. The vocal flourishes reminded them of their old *shtetl* and its *schul*. For this nostalgic indulgence, they had to pay good money, of course. At the turn of the century, such hazanim were only beginning to appear in the United States, for prospective audiences were not yet sufficiently prosperous to support them. The serious eastern cantors such as Minkowsky and Zavel Kwartin made only passing impact on large audiences.[27]

Today, in a historical perspective, both extremes—the radical Reform, with its hymns and its neglect of tradition, and the virtuoso hazanim, with their abuse of tradition—seem to move nearer to each other; both indicate the fading of basic tradition and accommodation to the wishes of the communities. And again there recurs a certain pattern in the history of synagogue music: if the laymen revolt against rabbinical tyranny, they will find rabbis to lead them toward assimilation, thereby eliminating musical tradition and its carrier, the cantor. Conversely, if the people adhere obediently to the whims of the rabbis, no innovations are permitted, and the hazan is permitted only new trills, but no new music. The embellishments eventually crowd out the basic tradition, and what remain are just weeds smothering the noble plants. Between these extremes the science of Judaism had to find its narrow, untrodden path. Its moderate liberalism had saved *minhag ashkenaz*, among many other Jewish values threatened after the Emancipation, for it had encouraged men like Sulzer, Birnbaum, Idelsohn, and many more. To this

day the serious literature on Jewish music, the serious new music of the Synagogue, was and is produced by adherents of that moderate group.[28]

The musical expression of this spirit began to flourish in the twentieth century. Three masterpieces of synagogal art music were created in the first part of the century, by three great composers: Arnold Schoenberg's "*Kol Nidre*," Ernest Bloch's "*Avodat ha-Kodesh*," and Darius Milhaud's "*Service Sacré*."[29] However, the first of these is not strictly liturgical, the second is not based on actual tradition, and the third does not purport to employ *minhag ashkenaz* but is based on *minhag Carpentras*, the rite of Provençal Jewry.

There are inherent problems posed by these three works, as well, which beset all attempts to create art music specifically for the synagogue. A basic conflict exists between the functions of synagogue chant and the concept of an autonomous art music. It is true that a parallel conflict, in the case of the church, was resolved by the great composers of the Catholic Church. They were concerned, however, with a purely passive congregation. In Jewish practice, worshipers are required—and prefer—to participate actively in the ritual. They cannot be expected to participate in sophisticated and difficult choral works. Thus it would seem that no "proper" synagogue service is compatible with "proper" art music, traditional or otherwise. This is one of the dilemmas remaining in the twentieth century that has not yet been resolved.

Popular Song as Carriers of Minhag Ashkenaz

Before completing this assessment of the development of *minhag ashkenaz* we must recognize that much of its substance reaches us indirectly, through its incorporation into the music of other forms. *Klezmorim* (folk musicians) and *badḥanim* (entertainers) who functioned both in Europe and in America introduced many a passage of synagogue chant—not always with due reverence!—into their routines. And the Yiddish theater, with its popular operettas, was an indirect transmitter of *minhag ashkenaz*. The Yiddish operetta reached its peak with the works of Abraham Goldfaden. He was born in Volhynia in 1840, and went through the phases of thought typical of an intelligent Russian Jew: talmudic studies, *Haskalah*, slight assimilation, strong Jewish nationalism. When regular performances of his theatrical troupe were systematically proscribed by the Czarist government, he emigrated to America after the "years of decision" (1881–1883). He died in New York in 1908. In his operettas—mostly historical romances—Goldfaden used a good many tunes of the eastern synagogue, in order to touch the hearts of his public. Idelsohn has listed these tunes, which include, next to *minhag ashkenaz*, elements of French, Italian, and German opera and Ukrainian folk songs.[30]

Such faithful endeavor paid good dividends after a time. The Yiddish theater flourished in New York, and its impulses reached the synagogue. Many a recent synagogue melody in the United States can be traced back to the Yiddish theater, if not via Goldfaden then via Eliakum Zunser (1840–1913), the last Yiddish minstrel in the United States.

Even more decisive was the contribution of the *letzim*, *klezmorim*, and *badḥanim*, both in Europe and America. This group reached its European peak with Jacques Offenbach, the ingenious composer, son of Isaac Juda Eberst (Judah Offenbach) from Cologne. The father was originally a *klezmer* who elevated himself to the status of a cantor. He was a well-read man of solid Jewish erudition; we had occasion to discuss his Passover *Haggadah* in chapter 9. In the case of Jacques Offenbach, we have the rare privilege to observe "*aufsteigendes Kulturgut*" (ascending culture) by tracing the rather trivial synagogue ditties that he borrowed and ennobled in his operettas and operas. Whereas "descending culture" from art music down to street and hit songs is quite frequent, the opposite phenomenon is rather rare.

Strange how close to the sublime lies the ridiculous in Offenbach's inventions; in this respect he resembles Heine and the young Mahler. In his case, however, no *Weltschmerz* tarnished his humor, and the old standby of the *letzim*, the *Galgenhumor* of the outlaw, is discernible only in his letters, not in his art.

Late in his life Offenbach's perpetual grin covered a hidden tear, but the world hardly noticed it; and it would be an error to drag him into kinship with the buffoon's "*Ridi, Pagliaccio!*" Offenbach possessed the sovereign artist's mastery of objectifying his personal emotions; not a trace of self-pity is detectable in the last act of the *Tales of Hoffman*, although the master was well aware of his approaching end. "I do not want to be pitied or to be acclaimed," wrote Offenbach a few months before he died, leaving *Tales of Hoffman* not quite finished. Offenbach belongs to the "resurgents" of musical history, and in this respect he is in illustrious company: Heinrich Schütz, Claudio Monteverdi, Johann Sebastian Bach, Anton Bruckner—to name only the most celebrated.

The German Jews never forgot or forgave his double apostasy from Germany and Judaism, and the "frivolity" of his libretti. Except for the postmortem enthusiasm for the *Tales of Hoffman*, they followed the lead of Richard Wagner who, in a pamphlet against France during the war of 1870 and 1871, had viciously attacked Offenbach. One may read in a magazine as representative of German bourgeoisie as the *Gartenlaube* the following lines:

> He [young Offenbach] sang in the Paris synagogue, along with his father, for three months. There he chanted the praise of Jehovah, of the archangels, of the patriarchs, of the major and minor prophets, and certainly did not dream that he would once, in the dim future, instead of reciting the sacred awe of Mt. Sinai set to music the dissolute mess of Mt. Olympus.[31]

Who wrote these sarcastic lines? Mr. L. Kalisch, the Jewish playwright of farces, under the title: "The Talented Dissipation of the Theater." On the other hand, Nietzsche considered Offenbach a genius of music "who did not have to carry German ballast."

Minhag Ashkenaz in Nineteenth-Century Art Music

A voice still heard . . . indeed, one may still perceive it, even outside the Synagogue; in the concert halls of the world, music-lovers will hear for a long time echoes of *minhag ashkenaz*. In this last section, we shall briefly note some elements of *minhag ashkenaz* in the art music of nineteenth-century composers up to the death of Gustav Mahler, the greatest composer of German-speaking Jewry. To prevent misunderstanding and to avoid the "loose talk" that abounds in this area, the criteria that guide the following discussion must be defined: (1) melodic substance originating in *minhag ashkenaz* (not common to it and folk song); (2) ornament and rhythm typical of *minhag ashkenaz;* (3) extra-musical spiritual message based on Jewish thought.

I do not wish to be misunderstood: in no way do I mean to reclaim such art-music compositions for the realm of "Jewish Music." Nothing could be farther from my intention. When Brahms wrote *Hungarian Dances*, Scharwenka, *Polish Dances*, when Mendelssohn called the finale of his *Italian Symphony* a tarantella, nobody claimed Brahms for Hungarian music, Scharwenka for Polish music, or Mendelssohn for Italian music. Also, the reader will have grasped by this time my own skeptical attitude toward the postulates and claims of nationalistic art music. In almost all of the cases to be cited, the composer was quite unaware of the sphere of *minhag ashkenaz* in whose neighborhood he had come. Notwithstanding these mental reservations, there does exist one passage in Mendelssohn's *Elijah* that unmistakably reveals the influence of a High Holy Day tune.[32] Of the numerous Jewish composers after him, we shall consider only those who are internationally known and have made use of *minhag ashkenaz* in their music. In the interval important to us—between the Emancipation and the First World War—only a few great composers produced works that occasionally contained faint memories of *minhag ashkenaz*. Aside from the case of Jacques Offenbach, briefly mentioned earlier but deserving closer study, we should remember Gustav Mahler, Arnold Schoenberg, and Ernest Bloch. The almost forgotten Anton Rubinstein also deserves mention, for, although born Christian, he must have studied the chant of the Synagogue diligently. In his songs and in his opera *The Maccabbees* he made ample use of motifs from *minhag ashkenaz*.

When we turn to Gustav Mahler, the greatest composer of Ashkenazic stock, we must remind ourselves that we are concerned here exclusively with the possible evidence in his music of the influence of *minhag ashkenaz*. All further extensions of that question, however closely related to it, exceed our scope. The evidence occurs in three areas:

1. Melodic substance. The third movement of the Third Symphony starts with a theme that Mahler borrowed from his own song, "*Kuckuck hat sich zu Tode gefallen.*" The first seven measures are almost literally identical with a *freilach* (gay dance) of hasidic origin. The rhythmic structure is likewise closely related to hasidic dances (which in turn often imitate Russian and Rumanian dancing tunes). Mahler's rhythm 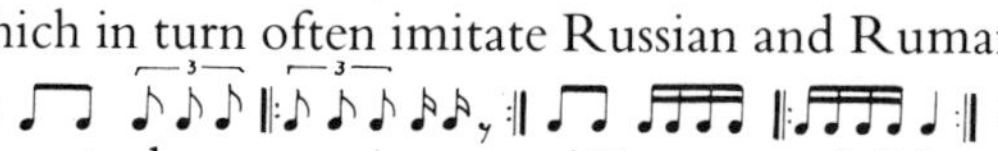 etc., is asymmetric, and this deviation rarely occurs in central European folklore.

2. Open recitative as against closed forms. Mahler emancipated himself from the closed forms that were the Vienna ideal in his *Lied von der Erde* and in some movements of his Ninth and Tenth Symphonies. In the last movement of the *Lied von der Erde* and in the first and fourth movements of the Tenth Symphony, we observe the new recitative-like form type. With it began a weakening of the conventional western tonalities. This open, word-bound type of melodic recitative, as well as many of the ornaments, comes close to the cantorial technique of variation and ornamentation.

3. The Prophetic message of many of Mahler's symphonies are so well known that they need no special mention. They were correctly compared with prophetic outbursts.

The late Theodore Adorno, whose book about Mahler and whose oration on Mahler's centenary contain most penetrating insights, reached the following conclusion: "Sometimes . . . not only in the recitative . . . Mahler's music approaches the gestures of speech so closely, that it sounds as if it were about to speak. . . . Extreme resemblance to language is part of Mahler's symbiosis of song with symphony. . . . The complexion of his music precludes a synthesis free from deviations. . . . Mahler's deviations are closely related to manners of speaking: his wrought and forced idiosyncrasies convulse as if in the jargon."[33]

All these observations hold true also of certain types of cantorial paraphrases of *minhag ashkenaz*. We can see how forces that produced some of the characteristic elements of *minhag ashkenaz* were also active in a person who was quite alienated from Judaism and its music. A non-Jewish author, Heinrich Berl, tried to disentangle these questions in some articles in *Der Jude*, and in his book, *Das Judentum in der Musik*.[34] The late Arno Nadel replied to him quite correctly, saying that there was only one authentic source of Jewish music, the folklore of the synagogal chant. The more important question of the inner relationship between *minhag ashkenaz* and Mahler's music is still unanswered, and will remain so.

Epilogue

We have accompanied the course of *minhag ashkenaz* to the outbreak of World War I, when the veneer of human civilization that once covered the earth began growing thinner. What has remained of *minhag ashkenaz*, and what happened to it after the series of cataclysms that started in 1914? The answer to this question would require a new book and a fresh view.

Surveying and summarizing a millennium of Jewish song contained in *minhag ashkenaz* we behold a strange spectacle: in the history of a people condemned to wanderings across half the globe, the liturgical tradition was never breached in a thousand years. To be sure, it was modified. Many texts and many songs were forgotten, and newer ones replaced them. In Europe, the folk song of German civilization, with which many Jews felt so strong an affinity, certainly helped to mold their sacred songs. We shall not try to verify or refute the idea of a "fundamental similarity of thought and behavior between Germans and Jews," as suggested by some Judeo-German wishful thinkers. Yet, undoubtedly, a millennial symbiosis has left many lasting impressions and deep scars in the two peoples concerned.

Seen in its logical totality, the tradition of Ashkenazic Jews presents three aspects: the purely textual, which remains outside the scope of this book, the musical, and the socio-theological. The musical aspect is characterized by the dialectical forces of western tonalities and Jewish modes, of western closed forms versus Jewish recitatives, of western polyphony versus Jewish monophony.

Viewed from a wider angle of historical perspective that encompasses many centuries, the totality of *minhag ashkenaz* presents some strange propensities: its attitude to tradition is Janus-faced, it contains cycles of neglect through intrusions of alien elements (German or Polish), alternating with trends toward strict conservatism, which all too often bear the earmarks of willful regression. Parallel trends are discernible in the sociological cycles of the rabbi-layman relationship, in the theological typology of the Orthodoxy-Reform dialectics, in the New Left-Zionism dissension.

If this side of *minhag ashkenaz* proves the old truism that each musical style reflects all the forces active in its time, another aspect of *minhag ashkenaz* contradicts all aesthetic commonplaces: according to a generally observable rule, periods of expressive music alternate with others of more formalistic nature. Such an oscillation is entirely lacking in *minhag ashkenaz*; there expression rules supreme and has virtually subdued all formative forces. It is this absolute reign of the expressive forces in Jewish liturgical music that has paralyzed the more creative impulses to

absolute music among the European Jews. Small wonder, indeed, that immediately after the Emancipation both hazan and *klezmer* turned to the concert hall, inundating the field of secular music like turbulent waters long dammed up and now free to tumble down. Even today opera exercises a strong attraction for the hazan, as does the concert hall for the instrumentalist. This is characteristic of the ashkenazic civilization, for the oriental hazan never experienced the opera's attraction, and the instrumentalist has a relatively low status in the Near East.

Leaving aside purely musical considerations, I am tempted to venture a longer view, a vision in historical depth. Not so much in its motif structure or tonality, or in cantillating tradition, can we trace the fundamental unity of all Jewish liturgical music, but in the attitude toward new elements, to personal inventions, and to the relative evaluation of its own forms. The general attitude one encounters during this millennium reminds me of the three styles in oration, as described by Aristotle and his disciples: the *topoi*, the *eristics*, and the comprehensive *rhetorics*. The *topoi*—the "noble platitudes" (after Cicero)—correspond to those ideal patterns that constitute the *basic* substance of Jewish musical tradition; the *eristics* correspond to the "argumentative" style, well known to the hazanim, who derived it from talmudic *pilpul*. They called a melody of the *eristic* type a "*sebarah*" (argument, hypothesis); and the main purpose of *ḥazanut*, a thousand times emphasized, was to arouse contrition and penitence, preferably by persuasion through the emotions. New inventions are not really needed in such a system of esthetics. According to Bruno Snell, in early Greek literature the poet prayed to the Muse for inspiration and originality, and it was only later, in the Hellenistic period, that the author took credit himself for these talents.[1] So also in the musical tradition of Judaism. Originality, per se, is of no great value; the *topos* dominates almost everything and has the integrating power of *active assimilation*.

Principles such as *topoi* and *eristics* do no doubt occur in many patterns of civilization, but the connection with the "persuasive" rhetoric is indeed singularly important in *minhag ashkenaz*. With all these structural and conceptual components the course of *minhag ashkenaz* remained dependent upon the political fate of the Ashkenazim. This dependence was one of the main reasons that *minhag ashkenaz* never attained full autonomy in its musical style, always fluctuating between certain predetermined limits.

Our first question, that of continuity of tradition, is affirmed once more: Jewish thinking and singing have been obsessed by two eternal *topoi*—God's transcendence and the Messianic Age—and by one *eristic*, unaltered through prosperity and Holocaust—Israel and the Nations.

Tables

Table I

I

2

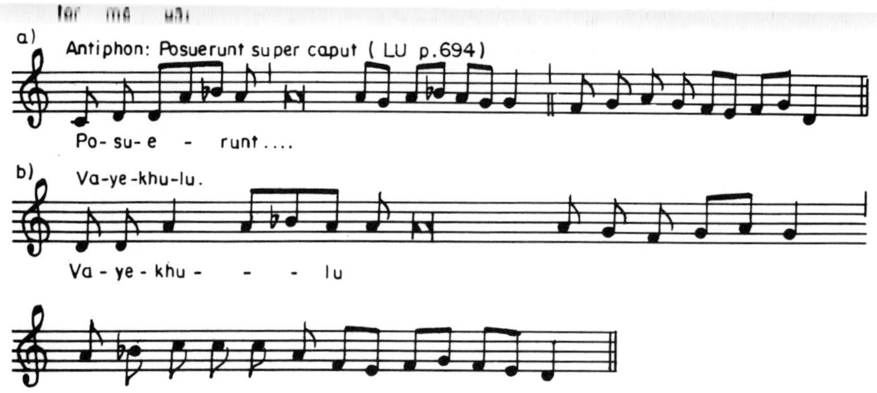

3

Ms. B. Badrian Sr. Zokhrenu

Zokh - - re - - nu, zokh - - re - - nu, zokh -
re - nu le - ḥa yim, me - lekh ḥo - fetz ba - ḥa - yim
etc.

4

a) HOM VII, 13

Ba - rukh a - tah a - do - nai . . . . ba - sha - lom.

b) LU p. 877, Antiphon Accipite

Ac - ci - - - pi - - - - - te ___ spi - ri - tum sanc - tum
. . . . pec - ca - ta

c) BT 47b. Emet sha'atah hu Adonai

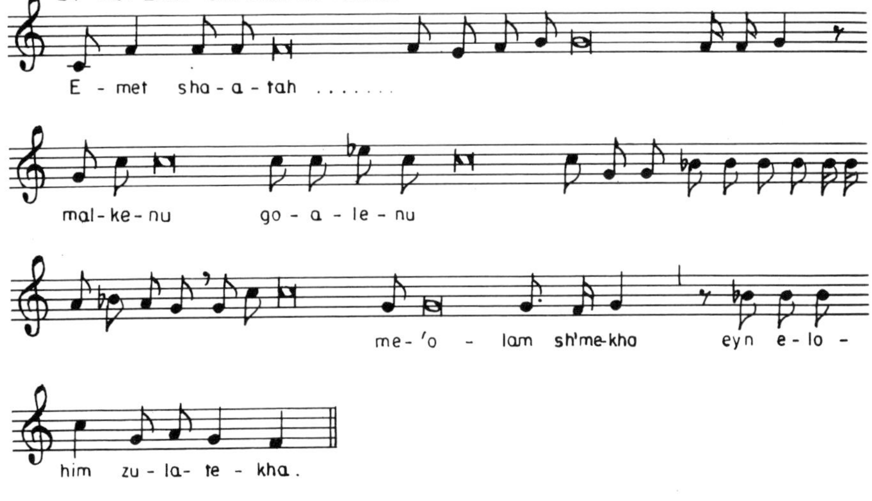
E - met sha - a - tah . . . .
mal - ke - nu go - a - le - nu
me - 'o - lam sh'me - kha eyn e - lo -
him zu - la - te - kha.

Table II

I
a) Antiphon "Adstiterunt reges", Good Friday, Matins. (LU p. 665)
Ad-sti-té-runt re-ges ter-rae .... in u - num,
ad-ver-sus Do-mi-num et ad-ver-sus Chri-stum e - jus.
b) (Tones)
2
a) Yotzer (L. Saenger, Munich, written by Naumbourg. (HOM VII, part II, No. 83)
Ba-rukh a- ta ...... o - lam
yo- tzer or ......
...... u-bo - rey ḥo - sheḥ.
b) (Tones)
3
HOM VII, No. 23
Ba-rukh a-tah a-do-nai, ha-el ha - ka - dosh.
4
Ve-ha-ko-ha - nim etc.
k' she-ha - yu ...... m' fo-rash.
5
a) Consolo 206, 207 Sephardic chant for Hoshanah Rabah. (transposed)
A - na El na etc.

b) Lamentations, music of the accents, final clauses. HOM VII 288

T'li-sha K'ta-nah mer' - kha, tif - ḥa, — ger-sha-yim, ——
dar - ga, — mer - kha sof pa-suq

6 a) From the Kaddish, morning of Rosh Ha-shanah, Sephardic, Consolo 206, 207 (transposed)

Ve- yish - ta - bah, ve - yit - pa - ar —— ve - yit - ro - mam — ve -
etc.
yit - na - sey, — ve - yit - ha - dar, ve - yit - ale — ve - yit - ha - 'lal

b) From the Kaddish, morning of Rosh Ha-shanah, Ashkenazic, HOM 188 c

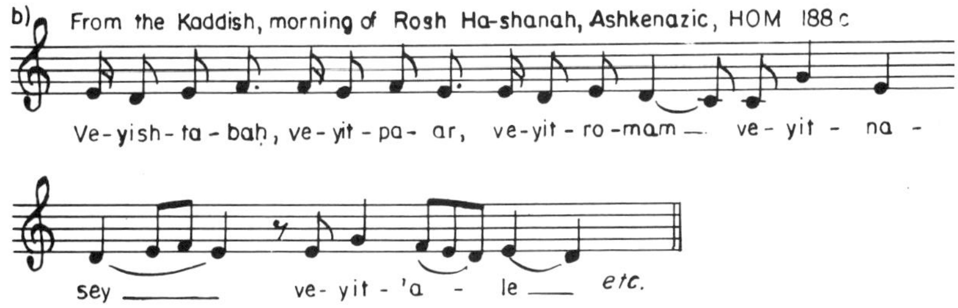
Ve-yish - ta - baḥ, ve - yit - pa - ar, ve-yit - ro - mam — ve - yit - na -
sey —— ve- yit - 'a - le —— etc.

7 a) Barukh Asher baḥar, Roman. Piatelli A 22

Ba-rukh a - tah a - do-nai, e - lo - he - nu me - lekh ha - 'o - lam ....
ha - ne - e - ma - rim be - e - met. —

b) Nishmat, Roman. Piatelli A 14

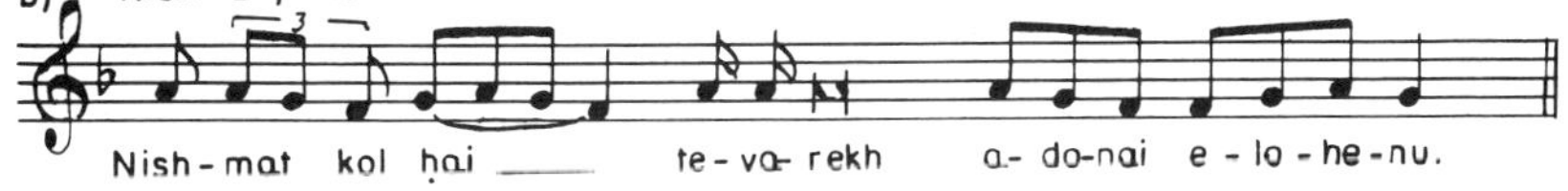
Nish - mat kol ḥai —— te - va- rekh a - do-nai e - lo - he - nu.

c) Psalm tones. HOM I, IV, VII. Sacred Bridge, pp. 488, 490, 491

8 a) Piatelli A 3

le - kha — do - di — lik - rat — ka - lah pe - nay — sha -

bat _ ne - ka - be - lah. le - kha do - di ___ lik -
rat _ ka - lah, pe - ney sha - bat ne - ka - be - lah.
b)
mas - kil ___ mikh - tam _ shi - ru _ re - yim, li kh'vod _ ish
tov
etc.
c)
etc.
d) Haydn, Andante, Surprise symphony.

9

a) H. Neusidler, Der Juden Tantz, DTÖ, vol. 37, p. 58
etc.

10

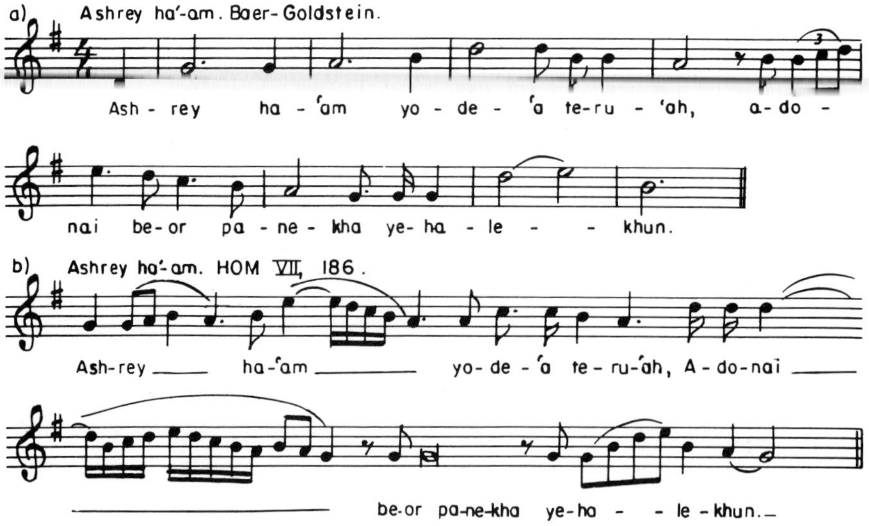
a) Ashrey ha'-am. Baer-Goldstein.
Ash - rey ha - ʿam yo - de - ʿa te - ru - ʿah, a - do -
nai be - or pa - ne - kha ye - ha - le - - khun.
b) Ashrey ha'-am. HOM VII, 186.
Ash - rey ___ ha - ʿam ___ yo - de - ʿa te - ru - ʿah, A - do - nai ___
be - or pa - ne - kha ye - ha - - le - khun. _

II

a) BT. 102
Ga - de - lu la - a - do - nai — i - ti etc.
b) On fast days. BT. 65
po - deh u - ma - tzil be - khol et tza - rah ve - tzu - - kah.
c) Kaddish, Sabbath minhah. BT 699
da - a mi ran be' ol - ma ve - i - me - ru a - men.
d) BT. 205
3
Va - to - mer tzi - yon —
e) cf.
se - laḥ — la - nu
f) Adon 'Olam (Seliḥah mode) BT 241
A - zai me - lekh she - mo nik - ra.
g) Va - tim - lokh (M. Levi Ms.)
ya - a - lo - zu . . . . be - ri - nah ya - gi - lu.

Table III

IIIA. Sectional Motifs

I

2

3

4
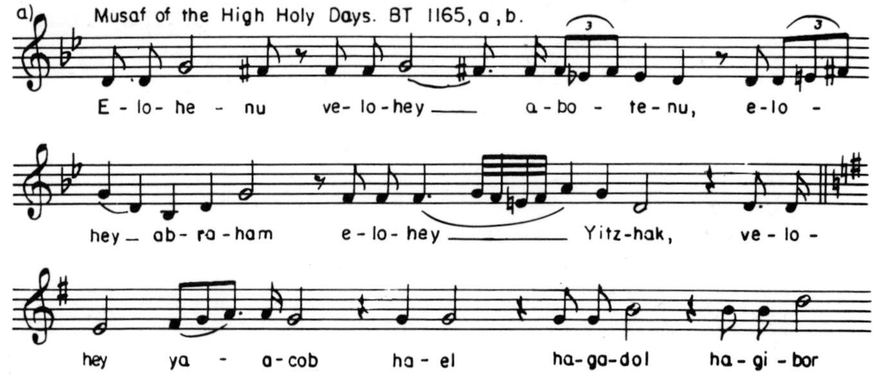

ve-ha-no-ra el 'el-yon, go-mel ha-sadim to-
bim ve-ko-ney ha-kol ve-zo-kher ḥas-dey a-bot
u-me-vi go-el li-b'ney be-ne-hem.
b)
e-lo-he-nu ve-lo-hey a-bo-te-nu, e-lo
hey A-bra-ham, e-lo-hey
yitz-hak ve-lo-hey ya-a-cob ha-
el go-mel ḥa-sa-dim to-bim ve-ko-
ney ha-kol ve-zo-kher ḥas-dey a-bot u-me-
vi go-el li-b'ney be-ne-hem.
etc.

Tal and Geshem Kaddish. after BT 834 and 835a.

5

yit-ba-rakh ve-yish-ta
bakh ve-yit-pa-ar ve-yit-ro-mam ve-yit-na-sey ve-
yit-ha-dar ve-yit-'a-le ve-yit-ha-lal she-

IIIB. Linking and Leading Motifs

a) BT 1100

I

b) BT 1011

c) BT 1158

d) BT 1303 (transposed)

2

a) Invocation of the Thirteen Attributes. BT 1140

b) Seliḥah, mode of the Thirteen Attributes. BT 1309

3

a) Leading motif from Kol Nidrey. HOM VII, 207. M. Kohn

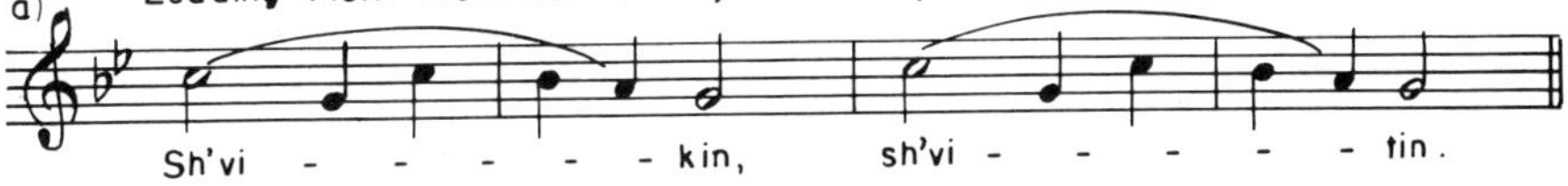

b) BT 1357

c) BT 1471

lah ——— na, me - ḥal ——— na ḥa - mol — na, ra -
ḥem - na, ka - per ——— na ke - bosh ——————— ḥet ———
— va - ʿa - - von.

Table IV

The oldest Hebrew notated songs. Obadiah the Proselyte (Ovadyah ha-Ger)
Transcribed by H. Avenary.

I

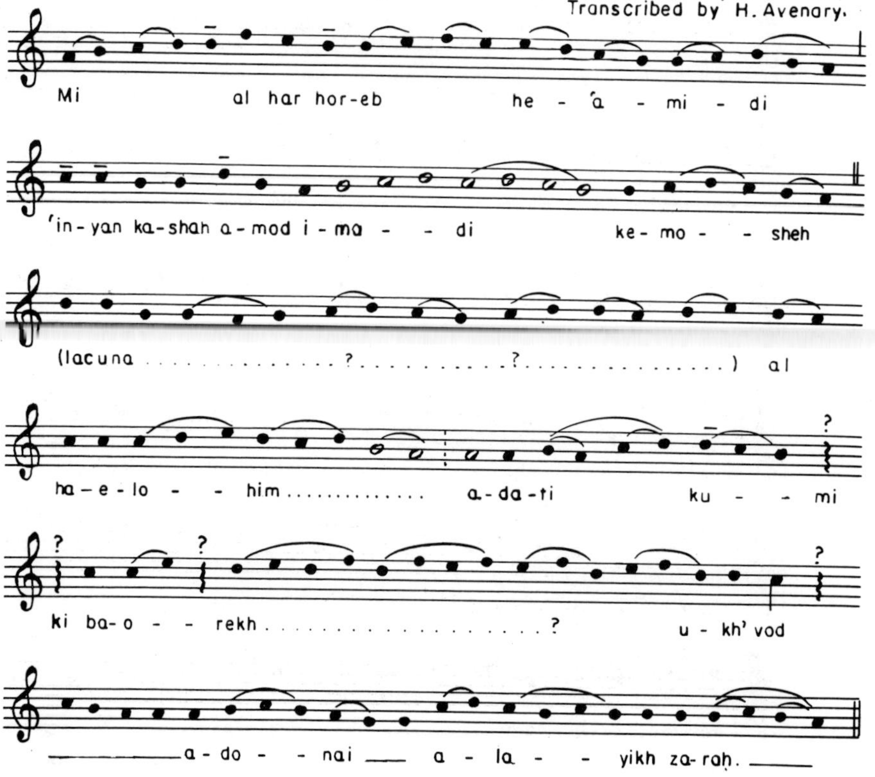
Mi al har hor-eb he - ʿa - mi - di
ʿin-yan ka-shah a-mod i - ma - - di ke- mo - - sheh
(lacuna . . . . ? . . . . ? . . . .) al
ha – e - lo - - him . . . . a - da - ti ku - - mi
ki ba- o - - rekh . . . . ? u - kh' vod
———— a - do - - nai —— a - la - - yikh za- raḥ. ———

2

Ve - e - - da - mah . . . . , ve - e - - da - -
mah . . . . . . a - da - ber ___ ba - - she - ʿa - -
- - rim, ________ u - mah ___ o - mar,
u - mah ___ o - mar u - ma _ ʾa - an ___
(♭) (♭)
la - me - de - - ni ________ .

3

Ba - rukh _ ha - ge - ber _ a - sher yiv - taḥ ba - ʾdo - nai,
Jer. 17:7
ve - ha - yah ___ a - do - nai miv - ta - - ḥo.
Be - taḥ _ el a - do - - nai _ be - khol li - be - - kha,
Prov. 3:5
ve - el bi - nat - kha ________ al ti - sha - - én.
Be - khol de - ra - khe - - kha da - - ʿe - - hu,
Prov. 3:6
ve - hu ye - ya - sher ___ or - - - ḥo - te - - kha.
Ash - rey _ a - dam ________ ma - tza ḥo - - khmah,

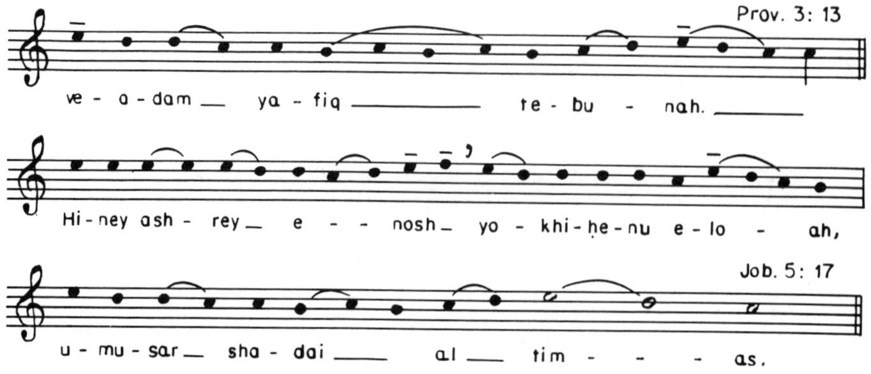
Prov. 3: 13
ve - a - dam __ ya - fiq ________ te - bu - nah. ______
Hi - ney ash - rey __ e - - nosh __ yo - khi - ḥe - nu e - lo - ah,
Job. 5: 17
u - mu - sar __ sha - dai _____ al ___ tim - - - - as.

4

Skeleton of the Modes
The Magen Abot mode. (F = final tone, CF = co-final)
F
CF
Skeleton
Cadence
subtonal
The Adonai Malakh mode.
CF
F
Skeleton
The Ahabah Rabah mode.
F
(♯)
Skeleton
Cadence
The Seliḥah mode.
CF
Skeleton
F

5

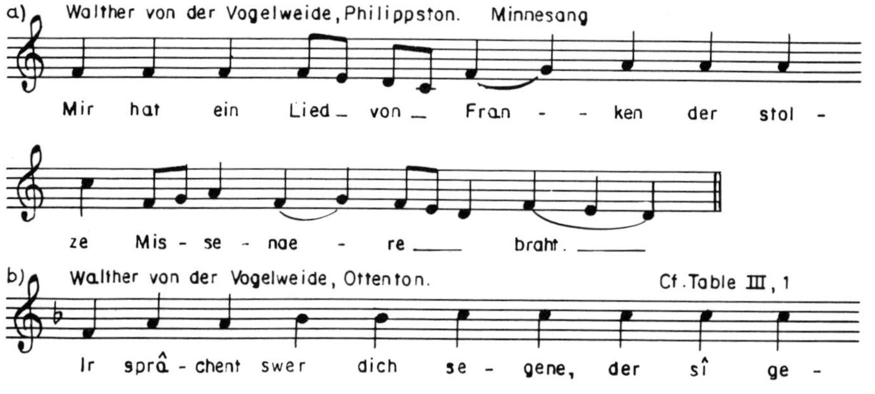
a) Walther von der Vogelweide, Philippston. Minnesang
Mir hat ein Lied __ von __ Fran - - ken der stol -
ze Mis - se - nae - re ___ braht. _____
b) Walther von der Vogelweide, Ottenton. Cf. Table III, 1
Ir sprâ - chent swer dich se - gene, der sî ge -

se - gnet, swer dir fluo - che sî ver - fluochet!

6

Bruder Werner
Un - recht ge - wyn - nen gût, des wolt ich
mich vil gar er - we - gen; mich duch - te daz
were all - ez wol ge - tan.

7

Der Wilde Alexander.
Cf. Mode of Lamentations, Table V.
O - wê daz nach lie - be gut Leit so man ez
tri - be

8

Oswald von Wolkenstein.
Der Herbst mit sues- sen Trau - ben mir mein Hau - ben

Table V

a)
Torah (Pentateuch) HOM VII
Zarka
segol
munah
munah
revia
mah'pakh
pashta
zakef katon
zakef gadol
merkha
tifka
etnahta
pozer
telisha ketanah
telisha gedolah
kadma ve'azla
azla geresh
gershayim
darga
tevir
yetiv
pesik
sof pasuk
shalshelet
merkha
tifha ..... sof pasuk

b)
Haftarah (Prophets)
Zarka
segol
munah
revia
mah'pakh
pashta
zakef katon
zakef gadol

c) Torah (for the High Holy Days)

d) Eykhah (Lamentations)

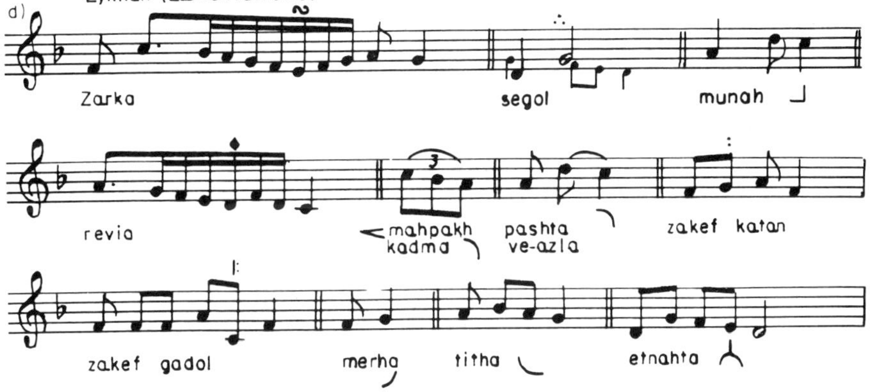

f) The Pentateuch motifs according to Boeschenstein in Reuchlin's De Accentibus, Hanau, 1518.

etnahta
sof pasuk
telisha ketanah
kadma
azla
pazer, karney farah
telisha gedolah
gershayim
merkha kefulah
geresh
shalshelet
yerahben yoma
mehurbal
ga'aya
makel
samiḥ
meteg
yetiv
pesik
legarme

Table VI

Akdamut and its variants.
Idelsohn, Music, p. 156
I
a)
I
II
III
Ak - da - mut mi - lin v'sha-ra-yut shu-ta, av - la sha-kil-na har man ur'- shu - ta
b)
"Akdamut" J. E.
c)
I
Baer, BT 736
II
III
d)
M. Levi, Compendium
I
III
II
III
e)
Magnificat III Toni LU 215
I
II
III
f)
Eisleben Ges. Buch 1598, Nr. 67
(. . . .)
I
Je - sa - je — dem Pro-phe-ten das ge-schah, auf ei - nem ho - hen Thron
III
in hel - lem Glantz sind mit den an-dern sie flo-gen frei,
g)
LU p.1868 4. Sunday Advent
Ro - ra - te coe - li de su - per . . . .
a)
Ma'oz Tzur
2
A
BT

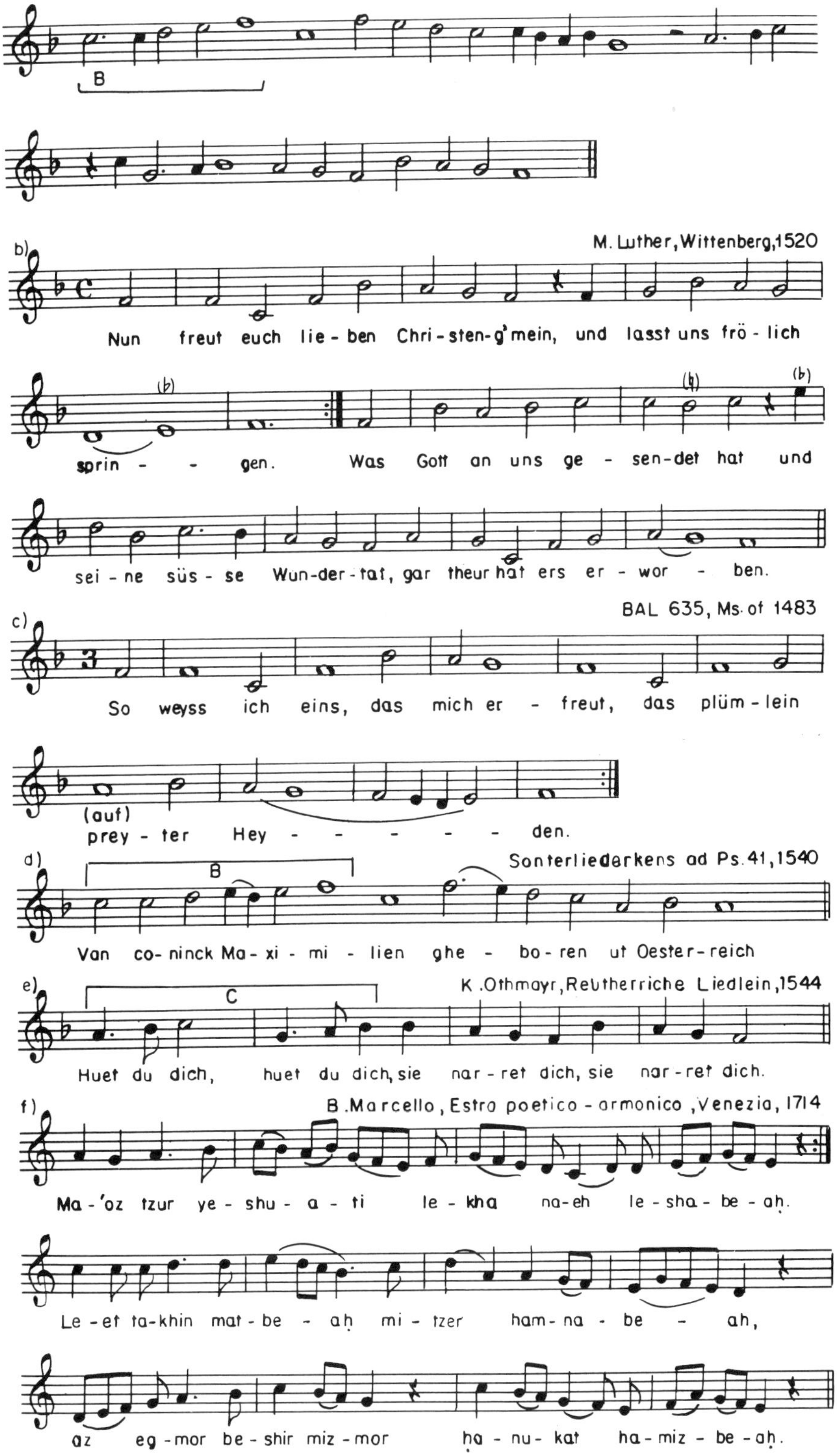
B
b)
M. Luther, Wittenberg, 1520
Nun freut euch lie - ben Chri - sten - g'mein, und lasst uns frö - lich
(♭)
(♮)
(♭)
sprin - - gen. Was Gott an uns ge - sen - det hat und
sei - ne süs - se Wun - der - tat, gar theur hat ers er - wor - ben.
c)
BAL 635, Ms. of 1483
So weyss ich eins, das mich er - freut, das plüm - lein
(auf)
prey - ter Hey - - - - - - den.
d)
Sonterliedarkens ad Ps. 41, 1540
B
Van co - ninck Ma - xi - mi - lien ghe - bo - ren ut Oester - reich
e)
K. Othmayr, Reutherriche Liedlein, 1544
C
Huet du dich, huet du dich, sie nar - ret dich, sie nar - ret dich.
f)
B. Marcello, Estro poetico - armonico, Venezia, 1714
Ma - 'oz tzur ye - shu - a - ti le - kha na - eh le - sha - be - aḥ.
Le - et ta - khin mat - be - aḥ mi - tzer ham - na - be - aḥ,
az eg - mor be - shir miz - mor ḥa - nu - kat ha - miz - be - aḥ.

3

a) Eli Tziyon.
BT 213
E - li tzi - yon v - a - re - ha ke - mo i -
shah be - tzi - re - ha, ve - khiv - tu - lah ha -
gu - rat sak 'alay ba - al ne - u - re - ha.
b)
Pu - er na - tus in Beth - le - hem, ein
Kint ge - born zu Beth - le - hem, un - de gau -
det Je - ru - sa - lem, Al - le - lu - ia, al -
K. Meister, Kathol. Kirchenlied Nr. 31
le - - - - lu - ia.
BT 206
Te - ka - ne le - tzi - yon qi - náh ge - do - lah ve -

4

a)
BT 995
A - don 'o - lam a - sher ma - lakh be - te - rem kol ye - tzir niv - ra
b) Papstaustreiben
BAL 631
c) Tagelied.
Oswald v. Wolkenstein. VLJ 332
Wach auf, mein Hort, es leucht dort her von

O - ri - ent der lich - te Tag.
a) A'apid nezer BT 1099
5
b) BAL 179
Ich hört ein sich-lein rau - schen, wol rau-schen durch das Korn.
a) Yahbi'enu BT 1479 (transposed)
6
Yah-bi- e - nu tzel ya - do ta - ḥat kan-fey ha-she-khi - nah
b)
Ach Gott, wem soll ichs kla - gen das heim - lich lei - den
BAL 208
mein, sol ich von ihr mich schei - den
a) Abinu Malkenu BT 1136
7
2
A - bi - nu mal-ke - nu, ḥa - ta - nu le - fa - ne - kha, A -
3
bi - nu mal- ke - nu, en la - nu me-lekh e - la a - tah, A -
3
4
bi - nu mal-ke - nu a - sey i - ma - nu le - ma - an she-me - kha, A -
bi - nu- mal-ke-nu, ḥa - desh 'a - le- nu sha-nah to - - vah.
b) BAL 204 a
So kumt mein Lieb und beit mir ein gu - ten Mor - - gen.
c) J. Drechsler, before 1832
A - bi - nu mal- ke-nu khat - ve-nu b' - se - fer ha - yim to - bim.

8

a) Ki Hiney Kahomer
BT 1321
Ki hi - ney ka - ho - mer be - yad ha - yo - tzer.
b)
Frisch auf gut gsel lass um-mer gahn Tu - mel dich guts wein - lein.

9

a) Adirey ayumah
Cantor
BT 1102
A - di - rey a - yu - - - - mah ya - a -
L
di - - ru ve - kol.
Choir
A - do - nai me - lekh!
Cantor
Be - ru - ey ba - - rak ye - va -
L
- - re - khu be - kol.
Choir
A - do - nai ma - lakh!
Cantor
Gi - bo - rey go - vah, yag - bi - ru be - kol.
Choir
A - do - nai yim - lokh!
b) All mein Gedenken
BAL 127
All mein Ge - den - ken die ich han, die sind bei dir, Du
solt an mich ge - den - ken, het ich al - ler wunsch ge - walt, von
dir wolt ich nicht wen - - - - - ken.
c) Kaddish before "tal" prayer
BT 834

d) Kaddish of Musaf, Rosh ha-Shana
BT 1164

10

a) The Bergamasca
Le-David Barukh
BT 713
Le-Da-vid ba-rukh a-do-nai tzu-ri
ha-me-la-med ya-day ba-krav
b) Omnam ken
M. Kohn, HOM VII, 315a
Om-nam ken ye-tzer— so-khen
c) Eder vahod
BT 1274
E-der va-hod e-ten be-tziv-yon
she-va e-e-rokh be-niv ve-ni-ga-yon.
d) J. S. Bach "Kraut und Rüben" (Goldberg variations, no. 30)
etc.
Kraut und Rü-ben ha-ben mich ver-trie-ben.

11

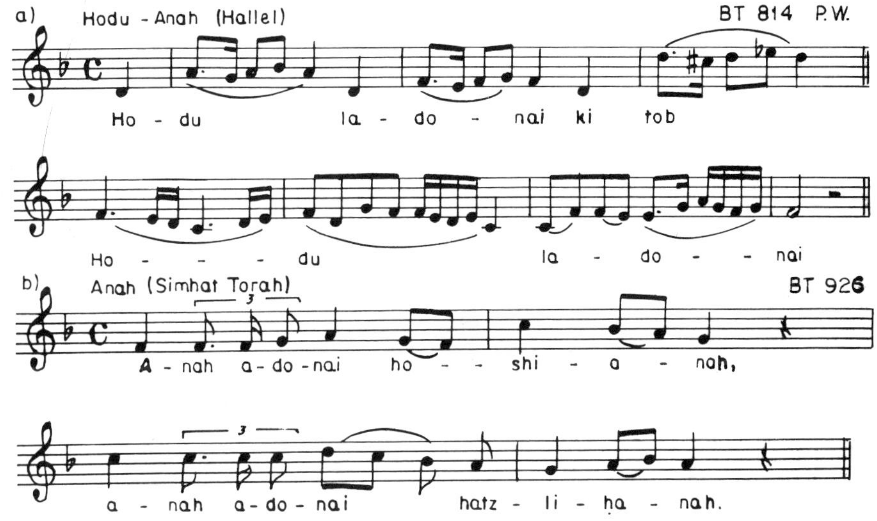
a) Hodu-Anah (Hallel)
BT 814 P.W.
Ho-du la-do-nai ki tob
Ho-du la-do-nai
b) Anah (Simhat Torah)
BT 926
A-nah a-do-nai ho-shi-a-nah,
a-nah a-do-nai hatz-li-ḥa-nah.

c)
Anah (Simhat Torah) Moravian tradition
A - nah a - do - nai ho - shi - a - nah!
A - nah a - do - nai hatz - li - ḥa - nah.

d)
Ach Mutter
BAL 39
Ach Mut- ter gib mir kei - nen Mann, ich
leb nit lan - ger denn ein jar.

12

a)
Akedah (Tumat tzuram)
BT 1320
3
Tu - mat tzu-ram ve-ḥas - dam, tiz - kor le-ni-ney mal - a - dam.

b)
Mu - naḥ re - vi - - a

c)
Erlaube mir, feins Mädchen.
VLJ 250
Er- lau - be sie zu bre - chen, es ist die höch-ste Zeit

13

a)
Shofet kol ha-aretz
BT 1426 (third tune)
Sho - fet kol ha - a - - - - retz ve - a -

b)
Mein Freud
BAL 128
Mein Freud wolt sich wol mê - ren, wolt Glück mein hel - fer sayn

14

a)
Kol me-Kadesh Shvi'i. Mode of Bruder Veit's Ton.
E. Kirschner VIa)
Kol me - ka-desh she-vi - i ka - ra - ui lo sho - mer sha - bat ka -
dat me-ha - le - lo.

b) Abendgesang — Adam Reissner

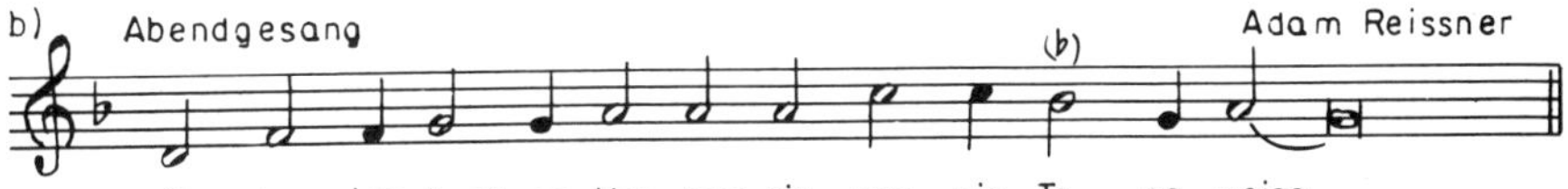

c) Wol auff — BAL 399a (transposed)

15 a) Elegy for the fast-day of 17th of Tammuz. — E. Kirschner VI a.

b) Wenn ich des morgens fru auf ste — Transmitted by H. Isaac, VI J421

c) Es wohnet Lieb bei Liebe. (Schmeltzl Quodlibet 1544, no. 6) — BAL. 19

16 a) Zekhor Berit Avraham. — BT 1475

b) Te Bruinskije staet — BAL 429 = Z4525

17

a) Adon Olam.
The Vinz Tune
HOM VII 346 a
A - don o-lam a - sher ma-lak be - te - rem kol — ye -
tzir niv- ra, le - at na - a - sah
b) The Pavia Tone, applied to Megillat Vinz.
BAL 389
Ein schön Lied, hübsch und be-scheid-lich für Wei - ber und für Maid-lich.

Table VII

The Ashkenazic Tunes Transmitted by B. Marcello

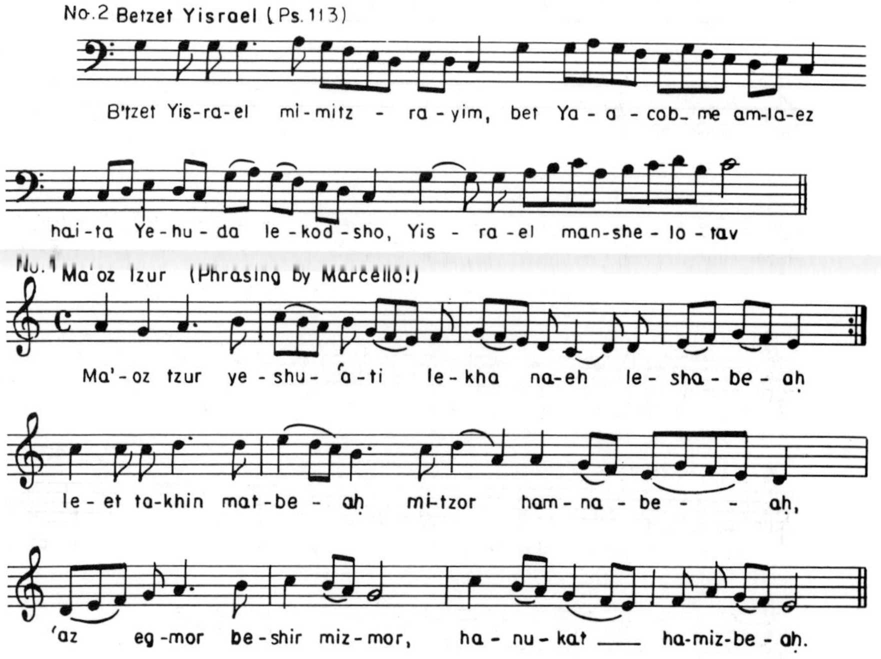
No. 2 Betzet Yisrael (Ps. 113)
B'tzet Yis-ra-el mi-mitz - ra-yim, bet Ya - a - cob — me am-la-ez
hai-ta Ye-hu-da le-kod-sho, Yis - ra-el man-she - lo - tav
No. 1 Ma'oz Izur (Phrasing by Marcello!)
Ma'-oz tzur ye - shu- 'a-ti le-kha na-eh le- sha-be- aḥ
le-et ta-khin mat-be - aḥ mi-tzor ham-na - be - - aḥ,
'az eg-mor be-shir miz-mor, ha - nu - kat —— ha-miz-be - aḥ.

No. 6 Hamabdil

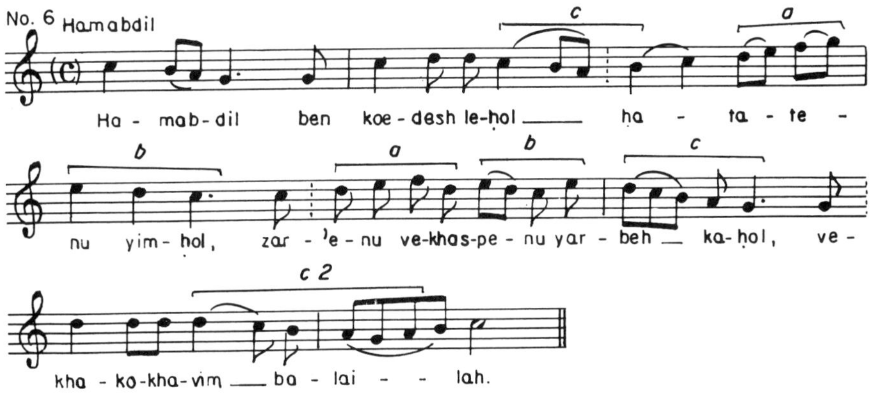

No. 8 Lekha Dodi

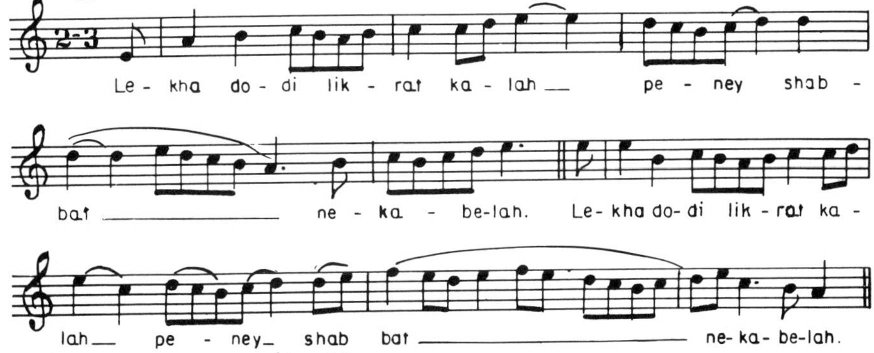

No. 9 Shofet Kol Ha-aretz (Adagio)

No. 10 Kaddish for the eve of New Year (Presto)

Table VIIIA

a) Polish
BT 1206
I
E - ḥad hu e-lo - he - nu hu a-
- bi - nu hu - mal - ke - nu hu mo - shi - e - nu ve -
hu yash - mi - e - nu be-ra - ḥa mav she - nit le - ey - ney kol
ḥai li - h' - yot ıa - khem le - lo him
b) German
E ıad hu e - lo - he - nu hu - a - bi - nu hu
mal - ke - nu hu mo - shi - e - nu ve -

-hu yash-mi-e - nu b'ra-ḥa-mav__ she - nit le-ey-
ney__ kol__ ḥai______ li-h'-yot la-khem le-lo-him.

2

Yareti
a) Polish
BT 1058
Ya-re-ti bit-tzo-ti si-aḥ le-has-kil, ku-mi__ le-ḥa-
lot,__ pe-ney no-ra ve-do-ḥil,______ ve-ka-ta-ne-ti ma-as la-
khen as-kil t'bu-nah ha-tzar-ti ve-ekh o-ḥil
b) German
Ya-re-ti bit-tzo-ti si-aḥ le-has-kil______ ku-
mi le-ḥa-lot__ pe-ney no-ra ve-do-ḥil,______ ve-ka-
ta-ne-ti ma-as la-khen as-kil t'bu-nah ha-tzar-ti ve-ekh o-ḥil

3

Be-Rosh ha-Shanah
a) German
BT 1188
b) German
Be-rosh__ ha-sha-nah__
______ yi-ka-te-vun
c) Polish
Be-rosh ha-sha-nah yi-ka-te-vun

4

a) B'raḥ Dodi
Polish
BT 788a
Be - raḥ do - di ad she-teḥ - patz a - ha - bat __ ke-lu - le - nu
Shuv ___ le - ra - ḥem ki _ hi - lu - nu ma - le -
khey ya-van har'-sha - ah, sho - ve - nu to - la - le - nu
b) German
BT 788 b
Be - raḥ ___ do - di ___ ad she - taḥ -
patz a - ha - bat ke - lu - - le - - nu Shuv ___ le -
ra - ḥem ki - hi - lu - nu ma - le - khey ___ ya - -
van har'-sha-ah, sho - ve - - nu to - la - le - - nu

5

a) Ve -'al Yedey
B. Karliner (transposed)
Ve - 'al ___ ye - dey a - va - de - kha
ha - - ne - vi - im ka - tuv le - mor
Ko a - mar a - do - nai me - lekh yis - ra - el ve - go - a - lo,
a - do - nai ___ tze - va - - ot: a - ni ri - shon va - a -
ni ___ aḥ' - ron, u - mi - ba - la - dai ___ en ___ e - lo -

him, ve - ne - e - mar, ve - ne - - - e - mar.
b)
BT 1233
Ve- al ye - dey a - va - de- kha ha - ne-vi - im ka- tuv le -
mor Ko ___ a - mar a - do - nai
me - lekh yis - ra - el ve - go - a - lo, a - do - nai tze - va -
oth: a - ni ri - shon va - a - ni a - ha - ron, u - mi - ba - l'a - dai en e - lo -
him, ve - ne - - e - mar
6
a)
BT 406
b)
HOM VI p.10
Ba - a - ga - lah u - viz-man ka - - - riv
c) Ein andrer Paduano
Aug. Noermiger
7
Polnischer Art Tantz
Chr. Demantius
8
Polish Dance
Anonymous

9 Polish Dance — Anonymous

10 Ein gutter polnischer Danncz — Christof Loeffelholtz, 1585

11 Das Vergnügte Ohr, Polonaise. — Joh. Nicolaus Tischer

VIII B. Zemirot

I

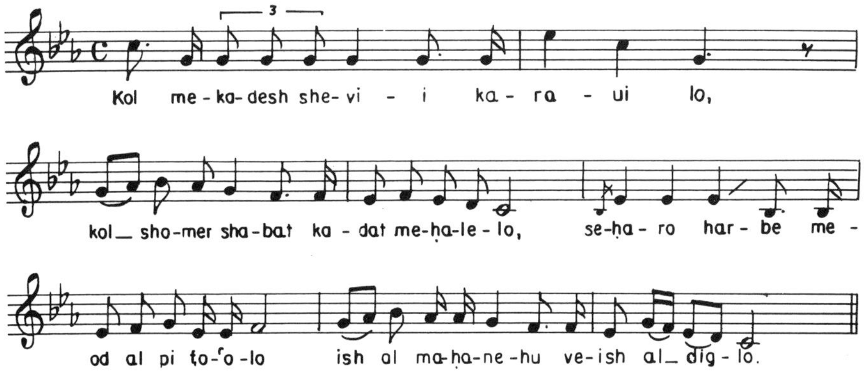

2

3

a tempo
f quasi tromba
ant hu mal - ka me- lekh-mal-kha-ya (la la la etc.
pp dolce
ppp
f
- - - - - - - - - - - - la) ant hu mal - ka
me- lekh mal - kha - ya. O - vad ge- vur - tekh ve -
etc.
tim - ha - ya (la la la la la la la la la..... she -
far ka-da-mai le - ha-ḥa - va - - ya.

4

Refrain
Tzur mi-she-lo a-khal - nu bar-khu e-mu-nai, sa -
1.
va - nu ve-ho-tar-nu kid'-var a-do-nai
2.
Verse
kid'-var a-do-nai. Ḥa - san et 'o - la-mo ro -
e - nu a-bi-nu, a-khal-nu et laḥ-mo ve -
livelier
ye-no sha-ti - nu al ken no-deh lish-mo u-ne-
ḥa-le-lo be-fi-nu a - mar - nu ve-a-ni-nu ein

Refrain
ka - dosh ka - do - nai. ___ Tzur mi - she-lo etc.

5

Refrain
Yom ___ zeh me - khu - bad ___ mi - kol _ mi - kol _
mi - kol _ ya - mim, - ki ___ bo ___ sha - bat ___
Verse
tzur o - la - mim. She - shet ya - mim ta - a - seh me - lekh -
te - kha, ve - yom ha - sh'vi - i le - lo - he - kha sha - bat lo ta - a - seh
rit.
bo ___ me - la - kha eh veh oy! Ki khol 'a - sah she - shet ya - mim.
Refrain
a tempo
or
etc.
Yom ___ zeh me - khu - bad ___ me - khu - bad ___

6

Mah ya - fit u - mah na - amt a - ha - bah be - ta - a - nu - gim,
at sha - bat, at sha - bat me - sos _ nu - gim, le -
kha ba - sar, le - kha ba - sar ve - gam _ da - gim ne -
kho - nim, ne - kho - nim mib' - od ___ yom.
Me - e - rev ad, e - rev lev _ ḥa - dim, be -

vo i - tekh, be - vo i - tekh et___ do - dim,___
gil___ ve - sa - son la - ye - hu - - dim lim -
tzo,___ lim - tzo ___ fid - yom.

7

After A. Nadel
Shir___ ha - ma - a - lot be - shub___ a - do - nai___ et
shi - bat tzi - yon ha - yi - nu ke - hol - mim; az___ yi - ma - le se -
hok___ pi - nu___ ul - sho - ne - nu ri - - nah.
Az___ yom - ru ba - go - yim hig - dil a - do - nai
la - 'a - sot 'im e - leh, hig - dil a - do - nai___
con espressione
- yi - nu,___ ha - yi - nu se - me - ḥim.

8

Goslovski - Birnbaum
Shir ha - ma' - los, b'shub a - do - noi
es___ shi - vas tzi - yon, ho - yi - nu ke - ḥol - mim.

Oz _ yom - ru va - - go - yim_ hig-dil a - do- noi
la - a-sos im - ey - leh_ hig-dil a - do-noi la-a-sos i - ma - nu, ho -
Solo dolce
yi - nu s'mey- ḥim. Shu - voh a - do - - noi
es she-vi-she-nu,_ ka - a - fi - kim ba - ne - - - - gev, ha -
zor' - im be - dim' - oh b'ri - noh yik - tzo - ru,
ho - lokh ye - lekh u - vo - khoh ___ no - seh me - shekh ha - zo - rah
bo yo - vo ve - ri - noh, vo yo - vo ve - ri - noh,
1.
vo yo - vo ve - ri - noh,___ no - seh a - lu - mo - sov.
2.
rall.
no - seh a - lu - mo - sov.

Table IX

I

2
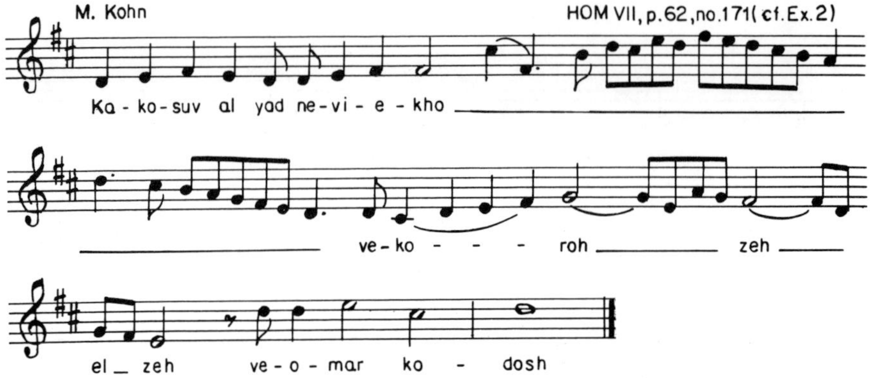

3

4

v'ho - yoh ho - o - lom,
bo - rukh hu, bo - rukh o - sey ve - re - shis

5

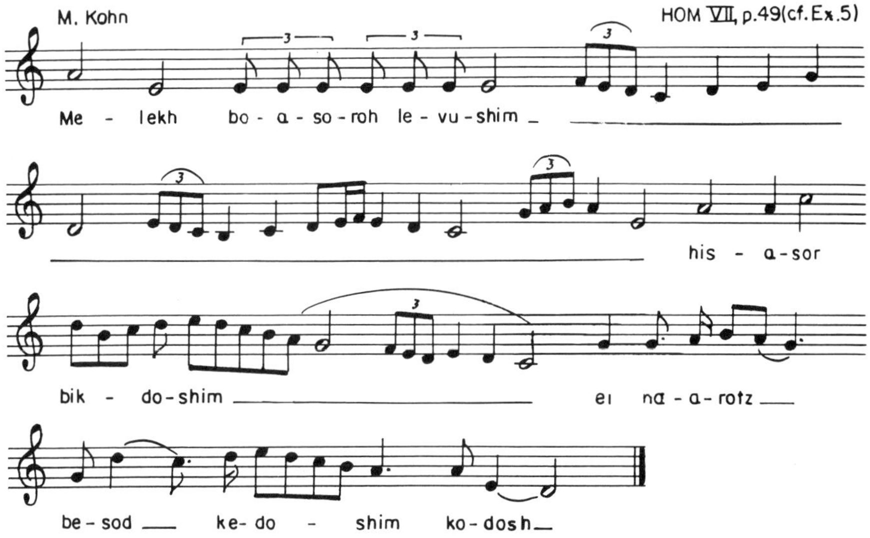
M. Kohn
HOM VII, p.49(cf. Ex.5)
Me - lekh bo - a - so - roh le - vu - shim
his - a - sor
bik - do - shim el na - a - rotz
be - sod ke - do - shim ko - dosh

6

S-N, no. 135
(cf. Ex. 6)
Yo - tzer me - sho - ra - sim va - a - sher me - shor - sov ku -
lom o - me - dim be - rum 'o - lom u - mash -
mi - im be - yir' - oh ya - ḥad b'kol div -
rey e - lo - him ḥa - yim u - me - lekh 'o - lom.
etc.

7 M. Kohn HOM VII, p.55,152 (cf.Ex.7)

Te - mu-khim be - de - shen seh a - ke - dah
te - - - sher a - sher bo nif - - ko - doh.

8 A. Beer (Adirey ayumoh) Adagio HOM VI, no 337

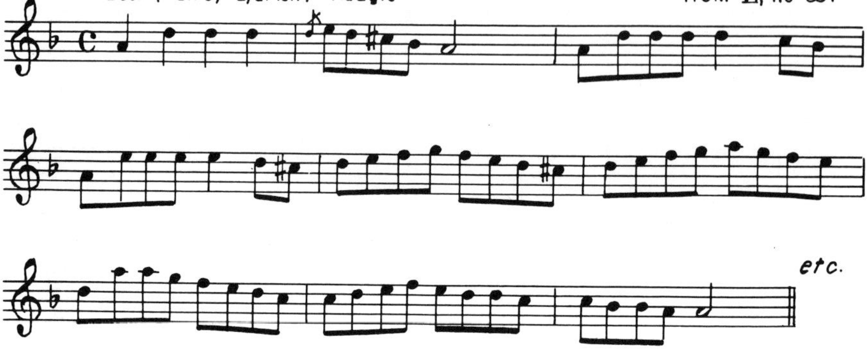
etc.

Notes

Chapter 1

1. Hirsch Jacob Zimmels, *Ashkenazim and Sephardim* (London, 1956), pp. 5 ff. See also Ephraim Urbach's article on this topic in the *Hebrew Encyclopedia.*
2. Goldschmidt, *Mah'zor.*
3. Zimmels, op. cit., p. 7.
4. Rashi to B. *Ta'anit,* 10a: "In our practice we follow the customs of the Babylonian Jews."
5. Obadiah 5:20. See Rashi, Ibn Ezra, ReDaK (abbreviation for **R. Da**vid **K**imchi) *ad locum* in *Eben Boḥan,* p. 53, No. 865–66.
6. Hermann Vogelstein-Rieger, *Geschichte der Juden in Rom* (Berlin, 1896), p. 179.
7. Baron, IV, p. 4.
8. Abraham ben Nathan Ha-Yarhi (thirteenth century), *Ha-Manhig* (Berlin, 1860), 43a, 30b, and passim (ordered according to paragraphs).
9. Ibid. See also *Menorat Ha-Ma'or,* ed. Hyman G. Enelow (New York, 1930), 2:13; Mordecai Jaffa, *Lebush* (Prague, 1622–1624), nos. 133 and 619.
10. Zunz, *Ritus,* pp. 21, 36.
11. Origines, "*De oratione*" (comment on 1 Tim. 2:1), in *Die Griechischen christlichen Schriftsteller* (Leipzig, 1899–1943), 3:297–403.
12. After George Foote Moore, *Judaism* (Cambridge, Mass., 1936, 1948), where the sources are given.
13. B. *Ber.* 34a.
14. Zunz, *Poesie,* pp. 115 ff.
15. See chapter 2 of *Sefer Hasidim,* ed. Aaron Freimann (Frankfort, 1924). In the early eighteenth century the opposition to the secularization of the liturgy was still quite articulate.
16. See Zunz, *Ritus.* On the European continent, the boundaries of *minhag ashkenaz* coincide with the historic frontiers of the German language and its dialects. Even when Yiddish has not been the vernacular for more than a century, as in Belgium, Holland, or Hungary, *minhag ashkenaz* prevails.
17. There are faint traces of *minhag ashkenaz* in the independent Provençal rite of the Comtat-Venaissin. These are probably remnants of Ashkenazic immigration into that area.
18. The well-known musicologist Hans Joachim Moser, rabidly anti-Jewish, made the naive and blissfully ignorant statement: "Merkwuerdigerweise habe ich in einem Gespraech mit dem grossen Alt-Testamentler Hermann Gunkel erfahren, dass schon der althebraeische Psalter diese Erscheinungen (Pausa, Flexionsakzente, etc.) kannte, und habe ihm fuer seinen Kommentar einige Musikbeispiele zusammenstellen koennen" ("Remarkably, I learned in a conversation with the great Old Testament scholar Hermann Gunkel that these phenomena had already occurred in the old Hebrew Psalter, and was

able to put together a few musical examples for his commentary") (*Musik in Zeit und Raum* [Berlin, 1960], p. 289).

19. Anton Baumstark, *Nocturna laus* (Muenster, 1957), pp. 39, 102.

20. *WSB*, pp. 129, 137. See also Edith Gerson-Kiwi, "*Justus ut Palma*," *Festschrift Bruno Staeblein*, ed. Martin Ruhnke (Kassel and Basel, 1967), pp. 64 ff.

21. On the psalm tones, the *Octoechos*, and their Jewish background, see *WSB*, pp. 373 ff.

22. Eric Werner, "Musical Aspects of the Dead Sea Scrolls," *Musical Quarterly* 43 (1957): 21 ff.

23. David Friedlaender, friend of Moses Mendelssohn, called their songs "sheer *arias di bravura*," echoing many previous rabbinic criticisms. See below, chapters 7 and 8.

24. *WSB*, pp. 171 f., 500 ff.; Edith Gerson-Kiwi, "*Der Sinn des Sinnlosen*," *Festschrift Walter Wiora* (Kassel and Basel, 1962; New York, 1967), pp. 520–521; Idelsohn, *Music*, pp. 418–419.

25. *WSB*, pp. 167–189.

26. Idelsohn, *Music*, p. 148.

27. See, for example, R. Dov Baer of Lubavich in his *Kuntres ha-hit-pa'alut*, published by Samuel of the house of Levi (Koenigsberg, 1847?); see also Solomon Geshuri, *Ha-niggun ba-hasidut* (Jerusalem, 1955–1959).

28. Julius Wellhausen, *Reste arabischen Heidentums im Alten Testament* (Berlin, 1887), p. 110; Enno Littman, "*Der Beduinentriller li, li*," *Wellhausen Festschrift* (Leipzig, 1915); *WSB*, p. 311, no. 119.

29. Hanoch Avenary, "The Cantorial Fantasy," *Yuval, Studies of the Jewish Research Center*, vol. 1, ed. Israel Adler (Jerusalem, 1968).

30. Goldschmidt, *Mah'zor*, p. 21.

31. Ibid., p. 19.

32. See Louis Finkelstein, "*La Kedouscha et les bénédictions du Schma*," *Révue des Études Juives* (Paris, 1932), pp. 3 ff.

33. Goldschmidt, *Mah'zor*, p. 24.

34. Such a monograph appeared as this book was in preparation. It is mainly limited to the cantor's social status, but is well documented; see Leo Landman, *The Cantor* (New York, 1972).

35. M. *Megillah* 24.

36. B. *Ber.* 34.

37. M. *Rosh Hashanah*, near the end.

38. See Wagner, *Gregorianische Melodien*, 1:20, 29–30.

39. The main exponents of this theory are Paul Kahle (*The Cairo Geniza* [London, 1952]), and Jacob Mann ("Changes of the Divine Service under Religious Persecutions," *HUCA* 4 [1927]: 289–291). Recently a number of objections to this theory have been advanced; one is by Joseph Heinemann (*Ha-tefillah bi-t'kufat ha-tanna-im* [Tel Aviv, 1964]), and earlier by Alexander Marmorstein ("Judaism and Christianity in the Middle of the Third Century," *HUCA* 10 [1935]); also by Chaim Schirmann ("Angelology in Synagogal Poetry," *JQR* 40 [1951]). We do not enter into this debate as it demands of the reader a considerable mastery of talmudic and rabbinic sources.

40. See *WSB*, pp. 179, 237–238; Othmar Wessely, "*Die Musikanschauung des Abtes Pambo*," *Sitzungsberichte der Oesterr. Akad. der Wissenschaften, Phil. Hist. Klasse*, no. 2 (Vienna, 1952–1953). See also *Patrologia Orientalis*, ed. Frederic Nau (Paris, 1908–1909), vol. 8, Introduction.

41. Ginzberg, 2:507 ff.

42. M. *Ber.*, 1:4.

43. Ginzberg, 2:516.
44. Samau'al al-Maghribi, named Al-Marabi, *Ifham al-Yahud: The Silencing of the Jew*, trans. Moshe Perlman (New York, 1970). See also Elbogen, pp. 283–284.
45. Zunz, *Ritus*, p. 164.
46. Ginzberg, 2:623.
47. Zunz, *Poesie*, p. 6.
48. Ginzberg, 2:509 (trans. R. S. Schwarzschild).
49. *Sefer ha-Eshkol*, ed. Hirsch Filipowski (Warsaw, 1876), p. 135; also, "Natan ha-Babli," in Adolf Neubauer, *Medieval Jewish Chronicles* (Oxford, 1887), 3:83–88. "Rav Tzemah wrote, 'Close to us are the hazanim, and the first hazanim received the tradition from the master Rab Yehudai, and it is said that the tradition was in their hands (from other hazanim) and he had it from his teacher as far back as Raba [third century] until the first four hazanim received that tradition from the master from far far back. . . .'" It is now established that the great rabbi occasionally acted as hazan; and it is known today that it was he who introduced the chanting of *Kol Nidre* into the synagogue in Sura (see chapter 3).
50. In Eric Werner, "The Doxology in Synagogue and Church," *HUCA* 19 (1945–1946): 303 ff., some sources are given. Yehudai's disciple Ben Baboi, however, took a much more rigid attitude inasmuch as he prohibited any *piyutic* insertion in the first three benedictions of the *Amidah*. See also Ginzberg, 2:511, 514–515.
51. Bernhard Ziemlich, *Mah'zor Nuernberg* (Berlin, 1886), pp. 67 ff.
52. Zunz, *Gottesdienstliche Vortraege* (Berlin, 1832), p. 427 n. The decision of R. Meir is explained there, and parallel passages are quoted. The more intricate decisions are found in *Tashbetz* no. 245; *Mah'zor Ma'aglei Tzedek* (Venice, 1568), fol. 22; and in *Hibburey Likkuttim* (Venice, 1715), fol. 4.
53. *Or Zarua* 1:113.

Chapter 2

1. A useful but not complete list of all Jewish notated music before 1800 was undertaken by Hanoch Avenary-Loewenstein in his study "Manginot ha-Yehudim . . ." in *Kiryat Sefer* 19 (Jerusalem, 1942–1943), pp. 259–266. Since then about twenty-five additional old sources have come to my attention; some of them will be referred to in subsequent chapters.
2. On the development of *siddur* and *mahzor* see Elbogen; also, Abraham Z. Idelsohn, *Jewish Liturgy* (New York, 1932), pp. 56 ff.
3. Mishnah and Gemara *Ber.* 29b.
4. *WSB*, pp. 313–324; Horace M. Kallen, *Judaism at Bay* (New York, 1932); Mordecai M. Kaplan, *Judaism in Transition* (New York, 1936).
5. Profiat Duran, *Ma'asey Ephod*, ed. Kohn (Vienna, 1865), pp. 20–21. In his preface he considers music the "eighth way" to obey the will of God; yet he dislikes metrical songs [*shirim*], considering them no better than lightmindedness [*letzanut*] (p. 5). He distinguishes between the tradition of Spain [*minhag sefarad*], the tradition of Germany [*minhag ashkenaz*] and that of France [*minhag tzarfat*].
6. Henrike Hartman, *Die Musik der sumerischen Kultur* (Frankfort, 1960), pp. 120–140; W. Stauder, "Sumerisch-babylonische Musik," *MGG*.
7. Roland de Vaux, O.S.D. *Ancient Israel: Its Life and Institutions*, trans. John McHugh (London, 1961–1962), pp. 60–61; also, Otto Eissfeldt, *The Old Testament* (New York, 1966), pp. 94, 133.

8. As late as 1819 R. Moses Sofer preferred, for theological reasons, the unorganized unison singing of the praying and shouting congregation to any harmony or choral arrangement (in his letter "*Eleh dibrey ha-b'rit*," Altona, 1818–1819).
9. The hostility against "foreign" tunes appears first in B. *Hagigah* 15b, where R. Elisha ben Abuya's apostasy is traced to the influence of "Greek tunes in his mouth." But here, as later, in Yehudah Ha-Levi's or Maimonides's strictures against Arabic poetry or music, the rabbinic opposition was directed against the immoral effects of such tunes. In medieval Europe it was aroused by outspoken hatred of the pogromizing Christians.
10. *Sefer Hasidim*, ed. Freimann (Frankfort, 1924), p. 85. See also pp. 106, 207, 332, and 400, to mention only the most significant passages.
11. Most of the old sources on angelic concerts are written in Hebrew, Aramaic, or corrupt Greek and have never been translated into a modern language. They belong to the lore of gnostic or cabalistic doctrine. A few titles will suffice: *Pirkey heḥalot*, ed. Adolf Jellinek (Leipzig, 1853–1877); *The Third Book of Enoch*, ed. Hugo Odeberg (Cambridge, 1928); *Sefer ha-Yetzirah*, ed. Lazarus Goldschmidt (Frankfort, 1894). The most influential source of Christian angelology was (pseudo) Dionysus Areopatiga (sixth century). The ideal concept of harmonious unison in all celestial hymns, based on the formula "*una voce dicentes*" [*b'kol eḥad ne'imah aḥat*], permeates the entire Jewish, and thence the Christian imagination. See *WSB*, chapter 10; also, Ambrosius, "*Enarrationes in duodecim Psalmos*," Psalm 1:1 (in *PL XIV*, 921 f.). The angelic unison remained the aesthetic-theological ideal of the Neoplatonists and the early cabalists, until the Western nations found pleasure in, and justification for, polyphony.
12. Some ultrapietists in eastern Europe objected to "set" melodies as late as the eighteenth century. Idelsohn uses through all of his publications a misleading terminology: instead of "set" melodies he speaks of "rhythmical" tunes, and by "rhythmical tunes" he means "metrical" ones; he uses the term "melody" only for metrical inventions. Indeed, he actually speaks of "unrhythmical" music (*Music*, p. 126).
13. Walter Salmen, *Das Lochamer Liederbuch* (Leipzig, 1951). In this essay the author minimizes the part of the Jews, especially of Wolfflein of Locham, in the writing of the excellent manuscript.
14. Cf. H. Avenary, "Genizah Fragments of Hebrew Hymns and Prayers Set to Music," *Journal of Jewish Studies* 16 (1966): 87–104.
15. Consolo, *Libro*; Piatelli, *Canti*. About the link between Italian and Ashkenazic talmudists, see Vogelstein-Rieger, *Die Juden in Rom* (Leipzig, 1896), pp. 179–180.
16. On the doctrine of *ethos* in general, see the article "Ethos" in *MGG*; the article is one-sided, as it refers only to Greece or the Hellenistic culture. For a wider horizon, see Werner-Sonne, "The Philosophy and Theory of Music in Judaeo-Arabic Literature," *HUCA* 16, 17 (1942–1943), and Curt Sachs, *Rise of Music in the Ancient World* (New York, 1943). See also Hermann Abert, *Die Lehre vom Ethos* (Leipzig, 1899), and Walter Vetter, *Antike Musik* (Munich, 1935).
17. Curt Sachs, *History of Musical Instruments* (New York, 1941); more recently, see the article "*Juedische Musik*," in *MGG*.
18. Eric Werner, "Musical Aspects of the Dead Sea Scrolls," *Musical Quarterly* 43 (1957).
19. *WSB*, pp. 315–320.
20. See note 9 above.
21. A critical study on the rabbinic (not biblical or scholarly) attitude to music in the synagogue is greatly needed. Neither Idelsohn nor his older contemporaries Minkowsky and Birnbaum had the temerity to reveal the perennial intolerance of the rabbinic mind toward every artistic aspiration. Almost all serious hazanim with scholarly interests

suffered from rabbinic contempt, yet none dared to oppose it openly. Perhaps one can gauge the extent of rabbinical opposition to hazanic efforts by the dictum found in the ethical will of R. Moshe Sofer, *Tzeva'at Moshe* (Vienna, 1863): "The face of the man who changes anything in the synagogue ought to be defaced!"

"כל משנה בית הכנסת פניו ישונה"

22. Paul Levy, "*Geschichte des Begriffes Volkslied,*" *Acta Germanica* 7, no. 3 (Berlin, 1911); Walter Wiora, "*Herders Ideen zur Geschichte der Musik,*" *Im Geiste Herders* (Kitzingen, 1953).

23. All available versions of these psalmodies show the same non-scalar structure of a melodic recitation on three or four tones, which are by no means always contiguous. See especially Edith Gerson-Kiwi, "Religious Chant, A Pan-Asiatic Conception of Music," *Journal of the International Folk Music Council* 13 (London, 1961); idem, "*Justus ut Palma,*" *Festschrift Bruno Staeblein*, ed. Martin Ruhnke (Kassel and Basel, 1967). These ancient formulas, common to Ashkenazic and Sephardic traditions, decidedly refute Oliver Strunk's tortuous theories, expressed in his article "Byzantine Psalmody and its Possible Connection with Hebrew Cantillation," *Bulletin of the American Musicological Society*, nos. 11–13 (1948): 19–21.

24. The best study on the subject is still Otto Gombosi, "*Studien zur Tonartenlehre des fruehen Mittelalters,*" *Acta Musicologica* 10 (1938); 11 (1939).

25. This specific peculiarity of the *Adonai malakh* mode was well known before the turn of the nineteenth century, yet none of the many writers on Jewish music—not even Isaak Lachmann, in *Der Juedische Kantor* (Bromberg, 1890) or in *Oesterr.-Ungarische Kantorenzeitung* (Vienna, 1888)—had the insight to deviate from the then accepted "scientifically" approved concept of the mode-scales.

26. Higinio Anglès, "*La Musique juive dans l'Espagne médiévale,*" *Yuval, Studies of the Jewish Music Research Center* 1, ed. Israel Adler (Jerusalem, 1968), pp. 53 ff.

27. See Albert Wolff, "*Fahrende Leute bei den Juden,*" *Mitteilungen zur Juedische Volkskunde* 27, no. 3 (1908). Important are Eduard Birnbaum's rich bibliographical additions to the essay, pp. 90 ff; see also the article "*Juedische Musik*" in *MGG*.

28. Cf. Arthur Spanier, "*Der Spruchdichter Suesskind,*" *Jahrbuch fuer jued. Geschichte und Literatur* 31 (Berlin, 1938); R. Strauss, "Was Suesskint von Trimperg a Jew?" *Jewish Social Studies* 10 (New York, 1948).

29. Walter Salmen, *Das Lochamer Liederbuch* (Leipzig, 1951).

30. Werner Danckert, *Das Volkslied im Abendland*, 2d ed. (Berlin, 1962), p. 74. See also note 27 above and Birnbaum's additions.

31. My transcription of the motet is contained in my essay "Hebrew Music," *Anthology of Music*, ed. Fellerer (New York, 1961), p. 19.

32. A passage in Robert Lach's monumental work, *Studien zur ornamentalen Melopoiie* (Leipzig, 1913), pp. 288–289, testifies to this scholar's deep insight into the mutation of Hebrew Ur-motifs in Gregorian transmission: "Waehrend in der Urzeit des abendlaendischen Kirchengesanges . . . diese altorientalische Melopoiie mit ihrem Tongeschnoerkel und ihrer ueberwuchernden Koloratur in strotzender Lebensfuelle in Bluete stand, laesst sich, je aelter die gregorianische Kunst wird, um so mehr ein Erstarren, ein Versteinern der anfange so leichtfluessigen Tonwellen bemerken; dickfluessig, schwerfaellig gleich erkaltender Lava stroemt der melodische Fluss dahin. . . . "

33. *HOM*, vol. 7, chapter 3.

34. Ibid., p. xix; cf. Consolo, *Libro*.

35. See Idelsohn's comparisons as suggested in his "Parallels between Old French and Old Jewish Songs," *Acta Musicologica*, vol. 5 (1932).

36. Table II, no. 5b, contains the final clauses of the mode of Lamentations, *minhag ashkenaz*. This is one of the oldest Ashkenazic traditions, still close to the Gregorian version of Lamentations. Cf. *WSB*, pp. 342, 362, 476.

37. *Weisen* exist in both metrical and nonmetrical versions; for like modes, they are indifferent to any rhythmic organization imposed upon them. Yet the contrafact *texts*, when adjusted to an older tune, had to have the same meter as the model. Abraham ibn Ezra referred to this matter in his *Tzaḥot* (1145, first printed edition, 1546), 7b:

והחרוזים שיש להם טעם ונגינות צחות באורם להיות משקל כל חרוז וחרוז שוה....

(The lines that have rhythm and melody must be alike in meter, line for line.) Cf. Zunz, *Poesie*, p. 116, where a few more testimonies are quoted.

38. Gerbert, *Scriptores Musicae sacrae* 2, p. 25 (Guido of Arezzo).

39. For more about the *Spielleute*, their adversaries, and their importance for folk song, see Walter Wiora, *Europaeische Volksmusik und Abendlaendische Tonkunst* (Kassel, 1957), pp. 88, 101–102, where a good bibliography is also to be found.

40. Paul Nettl, *Alte juedische Spielleute und Musiker* (Prague, 1923), pp. 37–39, where some sources are listed.

41. The law, as pronounced in the *Sefer Hasidim*, ed. Freimann (Frankfort, 1924), p. 332, no. 1348, also p. 84, no. 262 f., prohibited using the songs of monks, or singing, in their presence, songs of the Jewish repertoire. In daily life such rules were disregarded countless times, as most cantors neither knew nor cared about the origin of their tunes, always excepting scriptural cantillation and *Missinai* tunes.

42. See *Monumenta Judaica* 2 (Cologne, 1963–1964), p. 195, n. 120. About "*Alma Redemptoris Mater*" in the motet *Cados, Cados* see Eric Werner, "The Oldest Sources of Synagogue Music," *Proceedings of the American Academy for Jewish Research* 16 (1947). A modification and rectification of my original assumption was necessitated by Professor Dragan Plamenac's profound monograph, "A Reconstruction of the French Chansonnier in the Biblioteca Columbina, Seville," *Musical Quarterly* 37 (October 1951); 38 (January 1952).

43.

לא תסיג גבול רעך אשר גבולו. p. 84 #817 ספר החסידים. ראשונים. שהתקינו
הניגונים: שלא יאמר ניגון של תורה לנביאים וכתובים ושל נביאים לתורה ולכתובים,
וכו' שהוא מתוקן שהכל הלכה למשה מסיני, שנאמר 'יעננו בקולי' (Ex. 19:19)

44. *Sefer Ḥasidim*, ed. Freimann (Frankfort, 1924), no. 302.

45. Ibid., p. 84, no. 262 ff. with special stress on the *Shema* in case of a *Kiddush ha-shem* (sanctification of the name, a euphemism for martyrdom).

46. Cf. *Maḥ'zor Ma'agley Tzedek* (Venice, 1568), fol. 22. Also see *Sefer Ḥasidim*, op cit., no. 256. Also, *Menorat ha-Ma'or*, ed. Hyman G. Enelow (New York, 1930), 2:13.

47. For a splendid example of *Zersingen* and variations of a song in twelve versions, see Alexander von Sydow, *Das Lied* (Goettingen, 1962), pp. 449–450; for melismatic style see Robert Lach, *Studien zur ornamentalen Melopoiie* (Leipzig, 1913), pp. 68, 84, 242 ff.

48. Similarly, Hebrew medieval poets frequently closed their poems with a scriptural quotation to confer upon them both authenticity and weightiness.

Chapter 3

1. There are many accounts and documents of the period. See especially: *Monumenta*

Judaica (Cologne, 1963), 2:61; Simon Dubnow, *A History of the Jewish People* (New York, 1925–1930), 4:340; 5:172 ff., 303 ff.; Julius Aronius, *Regesten zur Geschichte der Juden in Deutschland* (Berlin, 1889–1902), esp. pp. 112, 173, 244, 472–474, etc.; *Germania Judaica*, vol. 31; Ismar Elbogen, *Geschichte der Juden in Deutschland* (Berlin, 1935), p. 55 f.

2. A relatively small number emigrated to Italy, where they formed a group of flourishing communities called APAM (Asti, Fossano, Moncalvo).

3. For a discussion of the theological and emotional effects of the persecution, see Hermann Cohen's sublime ideas on the pride of persecution in his *Religion des Judentums* (Leipzig, 1919), pp. 284, 305, 325, 331, 424, and passim.

4. *Sefer Ḥasidim*, ed. Freimann (Frankfort, 1924), p. 207, no. 817. Also Goldschmidt, *Mah'zor*.

5. B. *Ber.*, 62a.

6. Abraham Berliner, "Maharil," from *Aus Dem Leben der deutschen Juden im Mittelalter* (Berlin, 1900).

7. Maharil, *Hilkhot Yom Kippur*, 47b.

8. Mordecai Jaffa, *Ha-Lebush* (Prague, 1622–1624).

9. Herz Treves, *Siddur* (Thiengen-am-Rhein, 1560).

10. Ephraim ben Jacob, *Memor Books and Kinoth*, most recent edition by Joshua Haberman (Jerusalem, 1970).

11. *Maḥzor Vitry*, ed. Simon Halevi Hurwitz (Nuremberg, 1923).

12. The litanies of the High Holy Days and their psalm verses are sung to archaic tunes. See *WSB*, pp. 172–182.

12a. The Hebrew was the model after which the papal acclamation was shaped: Christus vincit, Christus regnat, Christus imperat.

13. A. Z. Idelsohn, "Songs and Singers of the Eighteenth Century," *HUCA*, Jubilee vol. (1925): 399.

14. Even this statement is true only relative to the other main forms of *minhag ashkenaz* such as the prayer modes, the melismatic chant, and scriptural cantillation. The form structure of the *Missinai* tunes will be discussed later in this chapter.

15. In his last studies, Idelsohn abandoned this naive approach and recognized the existence of "wandering melodies," even though he reluctantly admitted that he could not identify the primary sources. See his comparative examples of the *Yigdal* tune, table 28 in *Music*, pp. 222 ff.

16. Idelsohn claims (in *HOM* vol. 7, p. xxxiv) to have quoted the melody from Hugo Riemann, *Handbuch der Musikgeschichte* (Leipzig, 1921–1922), vol. 1, pt. 2, p. 27. The quotation there, however, is the correct Gregorian reading without Idelsohn's "adjustments."

17. This is a simplification. Actually the last two categories are often contemporaneous and overlap. Also, the third category is dependent on local custom. Thus, for example, the *birkhat ha-mazon* (grace after meals) is a nonmetrical text; yet in West Germany, southern Germany, Austria, western Czechoslovakia, Alsace-Lorraine, and parts of North America, it is invariably chanted metrically to relatively recent melodies. This will be discussed further in chapter 9.

18. The considerable musical interests of Burgundian Jewry may be gauged from Philip de Vitry's plea to R. Levi ben Gerson (Gersonides) to provide him with a mathematical basis for his *Ars Nova* notation. Gersonides complied with his wish in a treatise, *De numeris harmonicis*. See Werner, "The Mathematical Basis of the *Ars Nova*," *Journal of the American Musicological Society* 9 (1956): 128 ff.

19. Goldschmidt (*Mah'zor*) denies any organic link of the *Kol Nidre* with the theology

of Yom Kippur and suspects it was originally a popular custom, perhaps of a superstitious nature. He seems to be unfamiliar with the role of Yehudai Gaon in introducing the *Kol Nidre* in his synagogue in Sura (cf. Ginzberg, p. 120). The custom of reciting *Kol Nidre* on the eve of Yom Kippur received its halakhic sanction for *minhag ashkenaz* through R. Meir, the son-in-law of Rashi, and it was R. Tam who demanded that the formula for the absolution of vows be stated three times.

20. Johanna Spector has investigated the possibility of the melody's reconstruction in her doctoral thesis dealing with the original text and tune of the *Kol Nidre* (text of thesis in typescript in the Hebrew Union College Library, Cincinnati).

21. Maharil, *Hilkhot Yom Kippur*, p. 88 f. It seems to have been this rule that allowed apostates to attend, unseen, the prayers on the eve of Yom Kippur. The text, more a legalistic formula than a prayer, exists in several variants. The main difference between them is that some speak of the cancellation of past vows, and others, of vows to be made. Although their formula referred exclusively to vows made by men to God (not by man to man), it has cast suspicion for centuries on oaths sworn by Jews. For some centuries a special oath, the oath *more Judaico*, invalidating the *Kol Nidre*, was instituted by the Gentile courts.

22. Mordecai Jaffa, *Ha-Lebush* (Prague, 1622–1624), no. 619.

23. According to Idelsohn (*HOM*, vol. 7, p. xxxv), the first notation of the melody was by Ahron Beer of Berlin (about 1765).

24. Friedrich Gennrich, *Formenlehre des mittelalterlichen Liedes* (Halle, 1932), pp. 194–195.

25. The earliest versions vindicate Arnold Schoenberg's unerring instinct, which led him to abandon the generally popular *appoggiatura* (suspension) between the third and fourth tones of the melody. In his *Kol Nidre* for baritone, orchestra, and chorus—a monumentalization of the melody worthy of a Beethoven—the suspension is conspicously absent.

26. See table IIIB, no. 3.

27. Maharil, *Hilkhot Yom Kippur*.

צ׳ב–צ׳ד: בניגון אתיתי לחנך עד גמירא ש״צ אומר אדרת יקר כול בניגון אאפיד נזר, וכו׳....

28. Ibid.

29. Judah David Eisenstein, "*Kaddish*" in *JE*, vol. 7.

30. Goldschmidt, *Mah'zor*, preface.

31. Menahem Zulay, "References to *u-netanneh tokef* in Ms. British Museum G5557 Fols. 57b–68b," *HUCA*, Jubilee vol. 2 (1925): 425 f.

32. For a detailed and extensive examination of the poem see Werner, "Hebrew and Oriental Christian Metrical Hymns," *HUCA* Anniversary Edition, vol. 23, part II (1950–1951): 425 ff. I repeat here merely that its meter is isosyllabic and that the basis of the *piyut* is a Greek-Byzantine poem on the *parousia* (reappearance) of Christ, written by the convert Jew Romanus of Constantinople. Moreover, the literary and theological motifs of the Hebrew poem resemble the famous Latin sequence of the requiem "*Dies irae*" (which originated two centuries later).

33. It was Professor Egon Wellesz, the pioneer in the field of Byzantine music, who followed the example Idelsohn had set in his article "*Maqamen.*" He proved convincingly that similar methods prevailed in the composition of Byzantine chants. See Wellesz, *Eastern Elements in Western Chant* (Oxford, 1947), pp. 88 ff.; see also Wellesz, *Byzantine Music* (2d ed., Oxford, 1961), pp. 326 ff. It would be an error to believe that this method of permutating a number of more or less fixed motifs is restricted to the Orient. It can

be shown that Franz Joseph Haydn and other composers occasionally used similar methods of shifting entire complexes of themes, although on a higher artistic level, in double and triple counterpoints. See Leopold Nowak, "*Das Finale von Haydns Symphonie in E flat,*" *Veroeffentlichungen der Haydn-Gesellschaft* (Cologne, 1969).

34. The latest alteration was made by Ashkenazic Jews, actually in response to pressures by Christian governments, when one passage was claimed to contain an oblique reference to Jesus. The text contains a series of essential doctrines of Judaism, or alludes to them, and the Byzantine authorities quite understandably demanded that Jewish converts repudiate it explicitly. See Elbogen, pp. 80 ff.; also J. Kaufman Kohler, "*Alenu,*" in *JE*, vol. 1; also James Parkes, *The Conflict of the Church and the Synagogue* (London, 1934), app. 3.

35. From the letter of R. Barukh ben David, an eyewitness, in *Emek Ha-Bakhah*, ed. Meir Wiener (Leipzig, 1858), pp. 31, 172.

36. The following reliable sources are available: Adolf Neubauer-Morris Stern, "Blois" in *Hebraeische Berichte ueber die Judenverfolgung* (Berlin, 1892); Stern, *Quellen zur Geschichte der Juden* (Berlin, 1892), 2:58–78; Henri Gross, *Gallia Judaica* (Paris, 1897), p. 117; Siegmund Salfield, *Martyrologium* (Berlin, 1898), pp. 16 f.; 101 ff.; *Emek Ha-Bakhah*, ed. Meir Wiener (Leipzig, 1858), pp. 28–31. See also Abraham Berliner "Maharil" op. cit., n. 6; Scipion du Pleix, *Histoire Generale de France* (Paris, n.d.), 2:152; Zunz, *Poesie*, p. 24.

37. Helen Wagenaar-Nolthenius, "*Der Planctus Judei und der Gesang juedischer Maertyrer in Blois,*" *Mélanges à René Crozet* (Poitiers, 1966), p. 881. I am convinced that in manuscripts of that time additional evidence could be discovered.

Chapter 4

1. About medieval European folk song, see the excellent work by Werner Danckert, *Das Europaische Volkslied*, 2d ed. (Bonn, 1970).

2. Few of these terms lend themselves to precise definition, yet each of them can be circumscribed and explained intelligently.

3. Samuel Naumbourg, *Recueil de chants religieux* (Paris, 1874). See also chapter 11.

4. Even in some modern textbooks written by reliable scholars one still encounters this obsolete interpretation of the modes, simply continuing the ideas of Riemann, Fétis, Gevaert, Combarieu, etc.

5. Amedée Gastoué, *Les Origines du chant Roman* (Paris, 1907); also Wagner, *Gregorianische Melodien.*

6. Idelsohn, "*Maqamen.*"

7. For example, Donald Jay Grout, *A History of Western Music* (New York, 1960), pp. 51–52.

8. The term "*nusaḥ*" (Hebrew), beloved by the old-time cantors, does not exactly denote musical tradition. In the big talmudic dictionaries the word is either missing altogether or is interpreted as "formula, copy, recipe." In Isaac Lampronti's *Paḥad Yitzḥak* it is interpreted as a kind of repeated formula or copy, certainly not a flattering description of a cantor's repertoire! Idelsohn avoided it whenever he could; the only learned hazan to use it was Isaak Lachmann in most of this articles in *Der Juedische Kantor* (Bromberg). It is regrettable to find the term in the new *Encyclopedia Judaica.*

9. The etymology of the apparently German *Steiger* is by no means clear. If we could comprehend the original significance of that expression, it might explain how the hazanim understood or applied the prayer modes and their constituent motifs. The Indo-European

root is apparently *stigh*, to step (Greek, *steichein*, to walk or to climb); the word "*Steiger*" in middle-high German stands for the "climber of steps or stairs," or else the "*Steg-reif*," which stands for improvised performance. Sulzer seems to have been aware of this meaning, because he frequently speaks—and not admiringly—of the "*Stegreif* performance" of the old-time hazanim (in his *Denkschrift* [Vienna, 1876]). This might indicate that the Judeo-German *Steiger* originally and elliptically stands for the "stirrups" [*Stegreif*], not for a particularly characteristic motif, but for any performance without "dismounting from the stirrups." Perhaps one might also understand this expression as the borrowing of western European terminology by the cantors, who, not yet secure in the "new art" of notation, compensated for this lack with the help of mnemonic devices, of which the "characteristic scale" (or *Stieg*) was one.

10. All the old errors in this subject are repeated by the musical experts of the new *Encyclopedia Judaica*.

11. My translation is based on the Arabic text together with the Hebrew translation by Ibn Tibbon and by A. Zifroni (Jerusalem, 1967), pp. 124–125. For special help in the interpretation of this difficult passage I am indebted to my late friend Isaiah Sonne.

12. *Das Buch Al-Chazari* (Arabic), ed. Hartwig-Hirschfeld (Leipzig, 1887). Also, *Das Buch Kusari* (German and Hebrew), ed. David Cassel, 2d. ed. (Leipzig, 1869).

13. Hanoch Avenary, "Saadya's Psalm Preface," *HUCA* 39 (1968): 152–153; also in other editions of Saadyah's writings; see *WSB*, p. 379; also, Eric Werner and Isaiah Sonne, "Theory and Philosophy of Music in Judaeo-Arabic Literature," *HUCA* 16 (1941): 295–296. Today the entire question of the age of modes is obsolete; for the deciphering of Akkadian tablets leaves no doubt that the Babylonians, as well as the ancient Near East, used musical modes.

14. See above, chapter 3, n. 19; also, *WSB*, p. 379, and Eduard Birnbaum, "*Ueber die Verdienste der Gaonen um die juedische Liturgie*," *Israelitische Wochenschrift*, no. 4 (1903). See also *Sefer ha-Eshkol*, ed. Benjamin H. Auerbach (Halberstadt, 1869), chapter 1, 24, p. 55, which quotes Rav Tzemaḥ, who traced hazanic tradition back to Yehudai, saying that he, in turn, had received it from previous hazanim who had learned it from Raba of the third century. Yehudai's advice as to the form of a chanted *berakhah* was perhaps normative and helped to determine the form and style of synagogue chant: "A *berakhah* before and after a prayer should be chanted in the same mode; the prayer itself should be of a different, but not completely opposite mode" (see *Geonica*, ed. L. Ginzberg [New York, 1909], p. 41). This suggestion refers to the frequently observable ternary form of prayer: (a) *Berakhah* before the prayer proper (e.g., the *Shema*); (b) the prayer itself, chanted or spoken; (c) the closing or sealing *berakhah* (*ḥatimah*).

15. *Teshubot ha-Ge'onim*, ed. Harkavy (Berlin, 1887), no. 308, Hebrew text, p. 310. See also Rashi, in *Likkute ha-pardes* (Polna, 1813), p. 9, and *Geonica* (op. cit.), where one reads:

בטעמן שהתינוקות קורין לפני רבן

16. Richard Wagner, *Die Meistersinger*, act 1, scene 3.

17. "This mode has captivated entire regions, so that one identified synagogue chant with *Ahavah-Rabah*" (Idelsohn, *HOM*, vol. 7, p. xxvi).

18. Salomon Sulzer's hostility to Hasidism and all hasidic elements in music dates from the year 1848, when the rioting Hasidim poisoned his close friend Rabbi Abraham ha-Cohen in Lemberg. The rabbi and one of his sons died. The murderers were captured and, after due trial, were sentenced to death and hanged.

19. *Ber.* 34b, Mishnah and Gemara.

משנה:
המתפלל וטעה סימן רע לו ואם שליח צבור הוא, סימן רע לשולחיו, מפני שלוחו של אדם כמותו. אמרו עליו על ר" חנינא בן דוסא, שהיה מתפלל על החולים, ואמר: זה חי וזה מת, אמר לו, מנין אתה יודע? אמר להם אם שגורה תפלתי בפי, יודע אני שהוא מקובל, ואם לאו, יודע אני שהוא מטורף.

גמרא:
אמרו עליו על ר' חנינא ב" דוסא וכו": מנא הני מילי? אמר ר' יהושע בן לוי דאמר קרא. "בורא ניב שפתים שלום שלום לרחוק ולקרוב אמ' ה' ורפותיו".

20. Guillaume Villoteau, *Receuil de tous les mémoires sur la musique des Egyptiens et des Orientaux* (Paris, 1846), 2:467 ff. (Sur les Juifs).
21. Werner, "Preliminary Notes for a Comparative Study on Catholic and Jewish Musical Punctuation," *HUCA* 15 (1940).
22. Bence Szabolcsi, "A Jewish Music Document of the Middle Ages; The Most Ancient Biblical Melody," *Semitic Studies in Memory of Immanuel Löw*, ed. Alexander Scheiber (Budapest, 1947).
23. For a full account of the discovery, identification, and interpretation of the genizah fragments see Israel Adler, "Synagogue Chants of the Twelfth Century," in *Ariel, A Quarterly Review of the Arts and Sciences in Israel*, no. 15 (Jerusalem, Summer 1966).
24. Some important details in the notation used by Obadyah are still controversial, especially the Hebrew clef that he used, and its significance. A fairly good bibliography on the subject is found in Hanoch Avenary, "Genizah Fragments of Hebrew Hymns and Prayers set to Music," in *Journal of Jewish Studies* 16, nos. 3 and 4 (London, 1966): 87–104.
25. Cf. Egon Wellesz, *A History of Byzantine Music*, 2d ed. (Oxford, 1961), pp. 315, 415 IV, *echos plagios* (third line).
26. Bela Bartók, *Serbo-Croatian Folk Songs* (New York, 1951); also, *Die Volksmusik der Magyaren* (Budapest, 1935), and *Hungarian Folk Music* (Oxford, 1931). See also Zoltán Kodály, *Folk Music of Hungary* (Budapest, 1960); and E. Wellesz, "*Der serbische Octoechos*," *Zeitschrift fuer Musikwissenschaft* 2 (1919).
27. Curt Sachs (*The Rise of Music in the Ancient World* [New York, 1943]) opposes Riemann's hypothesis that Olympos was the carrier of the "new mode" (pp. 208, 256, 282). He shows it to be an integral part of Arabic and Indian folklore (pp. 177, 179, 214). Hans Hickmann, who in his *Orientalische Musik* (Leiden and Cologne, 1970) sums up his rich studies in the field, relies almost exclusively on Henry George Farmer, as some Jewish scholars do on Idelsohn. Those two excellent scholars were pioneers, but not infallible sources in the fields of Arabic and Jewish music.
28. *WSB*, pp. 445, 458, no. 61; see also *HOM*, vol. 1, Introduction.
29. Batya Bayer, *The Material Relics of Music in Ancient Palestine and its Environs* (Tel Aviv, 1963). Dr. Bayer informs me that a revised edition is forthcoming.
30. I once provided an old Armenian church song with Yiddish words and had it sung at a cantors' convention; the assembly was completely enchanted by this "typically Jewish melody," and was prepared to introduce it into the synagogue. When I showed them the true source of the melody, they were surprised and angry. A week later the episode was forgotten, and they went back to their old conviction of the essential Jewishness of the *Ahabah Rabah* mode. That conviction is on a par with the belief that the German language is a dialect of Yiddish!

31. Jean Baptiste Rebours, *Traité de Psaltique* (Paris, 1907); E. Wellesz, *Eastern Elements in Western Chant* (Oxford, 1947), pp. 1, 2; also, Dom Hugo Gaisser, "*L'Origine et la vrai nature du mode dit 'chromatique-orientale,'*" *Mémoires du Congrès Internationale d'histoire de la musique*, ed. Jules L. Combarieu (Paris, 1901). Most Byzantinists do not take cognizance of the intrusion of the so-called gypsy scale into their territory. They prefer to ignore it. This is especially true of Maria Stoehr, in her article "Byzantinische Musik" in *MGG*.

32. After Leonzio Dayan, *Les Hymnes de L'Église Armenienne*, vol. 5 (Venice, 1957), p. 362.

33. Gershom Scholem, *Major Trends in Jewish Mysticism* (New York, 1946), pp. 303–305. The first "rabbinic reformer," R. Aaron Chorin, was perhaps one of the last adherents of Sabbateanism. For more concerning this, see chapter 10.

34. Probably because of its use for libations and other similar purposes.

35. The memories of those virtuoso hazanim still exert a strong psychological attraction on those who once heard them. This attraction is associative to performance, as that of the Missinai tunes is to musical content.

Appendix to Chapter 4

1. Idelsohn's remarks are limited mainly to the comparison of tonalities. Cf. *Music* pp. 147, 175; also *HOM*, vol. 7, Introduction.

2. Ewald Jammers, *Ausgewaehlte Melodien des Minnesangs* (Tuebingen, 1963), pp. 38–41, 53–57.

3. Ibid., pp. 153–154.

4. Ibid., pp. 156–157.

5. Ibid., no. 29, p. 157 f.

6. Ibid., nos. 29, 64, 79 (especially Wizlaw von Rügen, and Oswald von Wolkenstein, pp. 206–207.

Chapter 5

1. B. *Meg.* 32a.

"הקורא בלא נעימה ושונה בלא זמרה עליו הכתוב אומר: וגם אני נתתי להם חקים לא טובים ומשפטים לא יחיו בהם"

2. Lachmann, "*Musiksysteme.*"

3. Robert Lachmann, *Jewish Cantillation and Song in the Isle of Djerba* (Jerusalem, 1940), pp. 8 ff. These revolutionary remarks have been overlooked by almost all writers on Jewish music.

4. Ibid., p. 10.

5. See also Rashi to B. *Ber.* 62a and to B. *Ned.* 37a.

6. *Maḥzor Vitry*, ed. Abraham Berliner (Berlin, 1889), p. 91. There is a later edition of the *Maḥzor*, which is superior textually but harder to use.

7. Profiat Duran, *Ma'asei Ephod*, ed. S. Friedlander and Jacob Kohn (Vienna, 1865), p. 40.

8. For example, B. *Ber.* 6a

Tos. *Parah* 4:7

במקום רנה שם תאה תפילה – שאין תא של תורה אלא בלילה

Exod. Raba 47:5

זמר כל יום;

9. Cf. B. *Ber.* 62a with *Dikdukei Ha-Te'amim*, ed. Wolf Baer and Hermann L. Strack (Leipzig, 1879), p. 18. Also, Joseph Dérenbourg, *Manuel du Lecteur* (Paris, 1921, new ed.), p. 204.

10. Lachmann, *Musiksysteme*, p. 16.

11. Cf. B. *Meg.* 3a with *Ber. Raba* par. 36. Morris Jastrow was not well advised to translate *pisuk te'amim* as punctuating marks or accents.

12. *Shemot Raba*, par. 11.

ויומר משה משה, אתה מוצא באברהם אברהם יש בו פסיק, אבל משה משה אין בו פסיק.

13. Hans Bauer and Pontus Leander, *Historische Grammatik der Hebraischen Sprache* (Leipzig, 1922), pp. 156–160.

14. The existence of the Proto-Palestinian school of Masoretes (sixth to seventh centuries) is well documented today; see especially Paul Kahle, *Masoreten des Ostens* (Berlin and Leipzig, 1913); idem, *Schweich Lectures*, 2d ed. (London, 1959).

15. Carsten Høeg, *La Notation ecphonétique* (Copenhagen, 1937); see also *WSB*, pp. 410 ff., where a bibliography on the subject will be found.

16. It was only due to the profound work *Masoret ha-masoret* by Elijah Levita, in 1538, that the scholars—not the rabbis, even less the Jewish public—had to abandon the idea that the accents were Mosaic in origin. For a long time, Levita was considered a heretic.

17. See Solange Corbin, "*Musica speculativa et cantus pratique*," *Cahiers de civilization médiévale* (Poitiers, 1962), p. 5.

18. Augustine, *Confessions* IX, 33: "Tam modico flexu vocis faciebat sonare lectorem psalmi, ut pronuncianti vicinior esset quam canenti."

19. Natronai's decision may be found in *Maḥazor Vitry*, ed. Abraham Berliner (Berlin, 1889), p. 91.

אף על פי שנתנו פסקי טעמים ונגינות המקריאה מסיני במסרת על פה נאמרו ולא בסימני נקידה בספר....

20. B. *Ber.* 62a.

טעמי תורה: נגינות טעמי מקרא של תורה, נביאים וכתובים בין בניקוד... מוליך ידו לפי טעם הנגינה. ראיתי בקוראים הבאים מארץ ישראל....

21. Rashi, ad locum.

בראשונה שם בן 12 אותיות היו מוסרין אותו לכל אדם; משרבו הפריצים היו מוסרין אותו לצנועים שבכהונה והצנועים שבכהונה מבליעין אותו בנעימות אחיהם הכהנים. תניא א' ר' טרפון "פעם אחת עליתי אחר אחי אמי לדוכן והטיתי אזני אצל כהן גדול, ושמעתי להבליע שם בנעימת אחיו הכהנים".

22. B. *Kidd.* 71a.

מבליעים אותו: אותן שלא היו בקיאין בו ומדריכין בשם בן ארבע אותיות כשהיו מושרין (שיר) את קולם בנעימה היו אלו ממהרים להבליע את השם בן 12 (י'ב) ולא היה נשמע לרבים מקול נעימות חבריהם בנעימת ביסום קול שקורין "טרוף".

23. Rashi, ad locum.
See A. Darmsteter-David S. Blondheim, *Les Glosses Françaises dans les Commentaires talmudiques de Rashi* (Paris, 1929), p. 143, no. 1035, where a number of variants of the word "*trop*" are listed, among them *trumpa* (= *trumba* = *tromba*, perhaps signifying the accent *shofar mehupakh*), *timbre*, *tinpar*, etc.

24. These questions are not dealt with in the literature on cantillation. Idelsohn does not even refer to the problem.

25. Alfred Sendrey, *Music of the Jews of the Diaspora* (New York, 1971). See the correct, if cautious discussion of the subject in Elbogen, pp. 503–504.

26. See Benno Staeblein, "Tropus," *MGG*. It is noteworthy that the excellent Eduard Birnbaum came very close to the correct interpretation in a note in *Allgemeine Zeitung des Judentums* (Berlin, 1891), p. 264. In this sense the *piyut El Adon* is a textual trope of *El Barukh*.

27. Elijah Levita, *Sefer Tub Ta'am* (Venice, 1538), chapter 2. The principal interest of the *ta'amei ha-mikra* for the musicologist is their musical significance. The grammarians Ibn Hayyuj and Ibn Balaam (eleventh century) divide the accents into three groups, of which only one had musically definable properties, while the others seemed to serve purely phonetic and punctuating-interpretive functions. In my article "The Doxology in Synagogue and Church" in *HUCA* 19 (1945): 330, 331, I tried to draw the attention of scholars to this problem; it seemed to have been in vain, as may be seen from the recent prolegomenon by Aharon Dothan to the reprint of William Wickes's books on the Masoretic accents (New York, 1968–1969), Wilhelm Bacher had already made available the sources necessary for such an investigation in his *Sh'loshah Sifrei Dikduk me-R. Yehudah Hayyuj* (Budapest, 1876–1877).

28. See Curt Sachs, *The Rise of Music in the Ancient World* (New York, 1943), pp. 82 ff.; idem, *Wellsprings*, where many examples of liturgical recitation are listed.

29. See my remarks on this difficult question in "The Origin of Psalmody," *HUCA* 25 (1954).

30. The cantillation of *minhag ashkenaz* does not lend itself to ethnomusicological field-work. It would be pointless to compare the cantillation of any given twenty singers. Some would have been trained only orally; some, more stringently, according to schoolbooks that contain the usual "standardized" formulas of the cantillation. The comparative approach was used by Solomon Rosowsky in his *Cantillation of the Bible—The Five Books of Moses* (New York, 1957), in which he used the Lithuanian chant as paradigm. See my review in *Jewish Quarterly Review* 49 (1959): 287–288.

31. The oldest such table known to me was written into the cover of a copy (found in the library of Hebrew Union College, Cincinnati) of a Hebrew grammar by R. David Kimchi (known as ReDaK) printed about 1500.

32. Rabbi Simon Duran, *Magen Abot* (Leghorn, 1785), pp. 55, 56.

33. There are yet other explanations in R. Abraham di Balmes, *Miknei Abram*, part 2 (Venice, 1523), where he maintains an allegoric-didactic tone. For further rabbinic descriptions of the *ta'amei ha-mikra* see Idelsohn, *Toledot ha-neginah ha-ivrit* (Berlin, 1924–1925), pp. 102–107.

34. Johannes Reuchlin, *De Accentibus et orthographia linguae Hebraicae* (Hagenau, 1518), 3:70–83. Johannes Boeschenstein's sketches and transcriptions are still available in the Bavarian State Library in Munich; the text is written in a curious *Judendeutsch*.

35. He was probably identical with the equally shady Sicilian Raimondo de Moncada. Other evidence indicates that he was the son of R. Nissim Ibn al Fraadj, that he was converted, became professor of Hebrew at Cologne University, and was promoted to the rank of Cardinal by Pope Leo X (see *Monumenta Judaica* [Cologne, 1963–1964], 1:164).

36. See Werner, "Two Obscure Sources of Reuchlin's *De Accentibus*," *Historia Judaica* 16 (1954): 39 ff. Some of my conjectures in that article are, however, obsolete.

37. Idelsohn must have been strongly impressed by the table of the Byzantine interpretation of the accents as transmitted by Mithradates and printed by Reuchlin, who admitted

"*sese non intellexisse*" (that he had not understood it at all). Idelsohn used it without explanation in both *Music* and *Toledot ha-neginah* (op. cit.). In neither book does it make sense. In neither case does Idelsohn cite his sources.

38. The most important works are still those by Baer-Strack and Wickes, cited above, and the bibliography by Otto Eissfeldt, *Introduction to the Old Testament* (Oxford, 1965).

39. *HOM*, vol. 7, p. xxi. In *minhag ashkenaz* this is a distinctive chant.

40. The German Jews took the musical tradition of scriptural cantillation very seriously; this can be seen from the stern warning not to mix the various cantillation modes, as pronounced in the *Sefer Hasidim*, ed. Freimann (Frankfort, 1924), p. 207.

41. See Loewenstein-Avenary, "*Eine pentatonishe Bibelweise in der deutschen Synagogue*," *Zeitschrift fuer Musikwissenschaft* 12 (1930): 513 ff.

42. Wagner, *Gregorianische Melodien*, vol. 3, pp. 100, 525; also *HOM*, vol. 7, pp. xv ff.

43. Loewenstein-Avenary, "*Philologisches zum Lochamer Liederbuch*," in *Zeitschrift fuer Musikwissenschaft* 14 (1931): 317 ff.; also Walter Salmen, *Das Lochamer Liederbuch* (Leipzig, 1951), which must be read with caution.

44. Lachmann, "Musiksysteme," p. 42.

45. *BT*, pp. 30 ff.; see also Israel Meyer Japhet, *Moreh ha-Korei* (Frankfort, 1896), in German.

46. *Jenaer Liederhandschrift*, ed. Eduard Bernoulli and Franz Saran (Leipzig, 1901), 2:45.

47. Bence Szabolcsi, *A History of Melody* (New York, 1945), pp. 32 ff.

48. Ibid., pp. 216–217.

49. Sachs, *Wellsprings*, p. 153.

50. Szabolcsi, op. cit., p. 220.

51. Sachs, *Wellsprings*, pp. 154–155.

52. Abraham Berliner, *Aus dem Leben der deutschen Juden im Mittelalter*, 2d ed. (Berlin, 1900), p. 53.

53. Cf. Maharil, *Hilkhot Yom Kippur*.

מנגן הקריאה דשחרית ודמנחה (p. י'ב).
יום כפור, כלמידת הנערי' שקו' "שטובן טרוף" (Stuben-Trop) קורין ערין
שבאחרי כמעשה ארץ מצריים וכו'... שהיה אמור הפטרה בניגון בני־ריינוס (Rhine)

54. Idelsohn, *Music*, pp. 57 ff.

55. This rare book published in Helmstedt in 1610 contains a plethora of interesting details of the life of German Jewry.

56. After Idelsohn, *Music*, p. 59.

57. After *BT* and A. Friedmann, *Der Synagogale Gesang* (Berlin, 1904), pp. 59 ff.

58. According to Otto Eissfeldt, *Introduction to the Old Testament* (Oxford, 1965), pp. 95 ff.

59. After Chaim Raphael, *The Walls of Jerusalem* (New York, 1968), p. 89.

60. This mode, with its two tenors (epicenters), is closely related to the *tonus peregrinus* of the Roman church. See *WSB*, p. 130, no. 30, etc.

61. The further back one traces the Christian sources, the more pronounced are the elements of its Jewish legacy, in the texts, rubrics, and ecclesiastical customs of Holy Week. But how deeply rooted a hatred of everything Jewish emanates from them. The late Cardinal Bea, initiator of the last council's resolution about the Jews, understood this very well indeed. The entire complex of the Christian liturgy before Easter warrants the closest historic-philological scrutiny by Jewish scholars. On the *Ordines*, see *Hebdomada Sancta*, vol. 2 (Rome, 1957).

62. See Alfred Rahlfs, "*Die Alt-testamentlichen Lesungen der griechischen Kirche*," *Nachrich-*

ten der Koenigliche Gesellschaft der Wissenschaft von Goettingen, Phil. hist. Klasse (1915–1916), where the main sources are listed.

63. Durandus, *Rationale divinorum officiorum*... (Venice, 1519), pp. 100–102.

64. Wagner, *Gregorianische Melodien*, vol. 3, pp. 239 ff. In his review of Idelsohn's *Chants of the Yemenite Jews* Wagner drew attention to these and other parallels.

65. Translated by E. W. after Max Gruenbaum, *Juedisch-Deutsche Chrestomathie* (Leipzig, 1882), p. 204.

66. Eduard Birnbaum, "*Musikalische Traditionen bei Vorlesung der Megillah,*" *AZJ*, nos. 12, 13, 15; pp. 136, 151, 177.

67. Ibid., p. 136.

68. Alluding to the triumphal antiphony on the shore of the Red Sea, in B. *Sota* 36a.

69. An author of the sixteenth century, the Jewish convert Antonius Margarita, opponent of Josel of Rosheim, suggests in his book *Der gantz juedische glaub* (Leipzig, 1531), G III, 4, that the "knocking" of Haman is based upon the Christian custom on Good Friday, whenever the name of Judas Iscariot was mentioned in church.

70. A copy of this unpublished manuscript, *Trimerone*, was given to me by the late Professor Isaak Heinemann, who had inherited it from his maternal grandfather Japhet in Frankfort. The original manuscript, written in 1599, is found in the library of the Liceo Musicale of Bologna.

Chapter 6

1. The ingenious inventor of the Yellow Badge, as well as the champion of the most severe legislation against the Jews, was the celebrated philosopher and theologian Cardinal Nicolaus Cusanus. See J. Uebiger, "*Kardinal Nicolaus Cusanus,*" *Historische Jahrbucher der Goerres-Gesellschaft* (Cologne, 1887), 8:638 ff.

2. A German writer on Jewry, certainly no friend of the Jews, had to admit: "Doch ist wol niemals, weil Juden in der Welt gelebt, ihnen ein Haerteres Saeculum als das XIV gewesen, dass zu verwunderm, wie noch ein einziger Jude in Deutschland beysolcher grausamer massacre koennen ueberleben" (J. J. Schudt, *Frankfurter Merkwerdigkeiten* [Frankfort, 1714]). (There has never, while Jews have lived in the world, been a more horrendous century than the fourteenth, so that one can only be amazed that a single Jew in Germany managed to survive such terrible massacres.)

3. "As I have seyd, thrughout the Juerie/ This litel child, as he cam to and fro,/ ful murly than wolde hy synge and crie/ O *Alma redemptoris* everemo/... This cursed Jew hym hente, and heeld hym faste,/ And kitte his throte, and in a pit hym caste./... "My throte is kut unto my nekke boon,"/ Seyde this child. ... Yet may I synge *O Alma* loude and cleere."

It might be noted here that in the Cathedral of Lincoln, at the shrine of Little Saint Hugh, there is now a plaque containing a recantation of the blood accusation and a prayer for forgiveness for the terrible massacre that followed it.

4. This type of benevolent parody of Hebrew prayers was not at all rare during the Renaissance. The classic example occurs in Orazio Vecchi's *L'Amfiparnasso*. See also appendix to this chapter.

5. Selma Stern, *Josel von Rosheim* (Stuttgart, 1959); also M. Maurer, "*Martin Butzer und die Judenfrage in Hessen,*" *Zeitschrift des Vereins fuer hessische Geschichte* 64 (Darmstadt-Kassel, 1953): 39 f.

6. Of a cast similar to that of the *Akdamut* is the ancient *piyut*, "*Az shesh me'ot*," glorifying the 613 *mitzvot* of the Torah. This *piyut*, too, is recited in the *musaf* of Shabuoth, at the end of the *azharot* (warnings). The text is believed to antedate the eighth century. The melody bears, unmistakably, a motif of the *Abodah* of Yom Kippur (cf. *BT* no. 851). This is, to a certain extent, an expansion of the allusive style of the *Missinai* tunes. Birnbaum conjectures that this allusion goes back to the *halakhot gedolot* of R. Yehudai Gaon, the "father of *hazanut*." He quotes Michael Sachs's remark concerning the age of the text:

והסיום 'אז שש מאות' כי הוא מסידורי הגאונים החתימה המורגלת והיותר קדמונית אשר השתמשו בה בתחלה, ומפני זה היא מונחת במקום כבודה כנחלת אבות מורשה מימי קדם . . .

"And the ending, *az shesh me'ot*, is from the *siddur* of the Geonim. It is the regular closing, and is the earliest that was used at first. Therefore, it occupies an honored place as an inheritance of the fathers from ancient times" (*Kovetz ma'asey yedey ge'onim* [Berlin, 1856], p. 99). However, the tune cannot possibly be as old, since it is in a completely Western minor, and can hardly antedate the late fourteenth or early fifteenth century. See ex. 11.

Example 11

7. It is by no means impossible that Luther, who liked "*den Leuten aufs Maul zu schauen*," and who frequently picked up street songs in order to "baptize them in the church," made use of the secular tune "*So weiss ich eins. . . .*" This conjecture, or at least the identification of the melody of "*So weiss ich eins. . .*" with "*Freut euch, freut euch*," was made by Franz Magnus Boehme. Though generally accepted, this conjecture has not been conclusively proven.

8. See J. S. Bach's Goldberg Variations, no. 22; also his Suite in F Major for harpsichord, in the *Bourrée*, with the repeated introduction  to the cadence.

There are many similar instances in Bach's cantatas and, in more ornamented form, the formula can be found in Mozart's *Zauberflöte*. Even young Beethoven used it, e.g., in the Trio, Opus 1, No. 3, slow movement, third variation.
9. Robert Lach, *Beitraege zu einer Geschichte der ornamentalen Melopoiie* (Vienna, 1912–1913), pp. 420, 427, 447 ff., with many examples and ample bibliography.
9a. The manuscript of Ahron Beer of the eighteenth century is one of the earliest compendia of *minhag ashkenaz* (Birnbaum Collection, H.U.C., Cincinnati).
10. John Braham and Isaac Nathan, *A Selection of Hebrew Melodies* (London, 1815). "The poetry was written expressly for the work by Lord Byron."
11. David Kaufmann, *Ha-osif* (Warsaw, 1875), p. 298.

בניגון מעוז צור, זאת יסדתי על ארבע גלויות ועל חנוכה שנת ר' י'

(ר' בענדיט ברוך אורויילר ז'ל) אומר

(The late R. Bendit Uhrweiler said: "I arranged this according to the tune of *Ma'oz Tzur*, for the *four g'luyot* [?] and for Hanukkah.") This might be a poem by Barukh bar Sheshet! Idelsohn (*HOM*, vol. 7, p. xlii) wrongly assumes that the statement by R. Bendit Uhrweiler affords proof of the melody's antiquity.
12. The humanist composer Benedetto Marcello composed musical settings of Italian paraphrases of the first fifty psalms, for chorus and orchestra, entitled *Estro poetico armonico*. In the course of the fifty, he used no less than eleven synagogue tunes as *cantus firmi*, citing them, together with their Hebrew texts, and identifying them as coming from either Ashkenazic (Tedeschi) Jews or Sephardic (Spagnuoli) Jews. This tune, identified as of the Tedeschi, is no longer known in Italy.
13. The singing of *Ma'oz Tzur* was left to the domestic celebration of kindling the Hanukkah lights. See B. *Shabbat* 21b; see also *Diney Hanukah be-Tefillat Yisrael* (ed. Mecklenburg), *Minhag Poland* (Lissa [?], 1863), pp. 203–204. It was only after the seventeenth century that the hymn was sung in the synagogue.
14. On the meter of "*Sh'ney Zeytim*" see Zunz, *Poesie*, p. 216. There is some controversy about the authorship of the poem. Zunz (in *Ritus*) and Israel Davidson (in his *Thesaurus of Medieval Jewish Poetry* [New York, reprint of 1968–1969]) attribute it to Solomon ibn Gabirol. Samuel David Luzzatto (in the *Mahzor B'ney Roma* [Leghorn, 1856], 2:21) attributes it to Solomon of Carcassonne. Idelsohn in *Jewish Liturgy and its Development* (New York, 1932), p. 319, rightly observed that the *piyut* is sung to "a variation of the tune for '*Ma'oz Tzur*' (German version)." He quotes such a variation in *HOM*, vol. 7, no. 323, without mentioning his source. The Birnbaum collection in the library of Hebrew Union College contains a number of such variations. The full text of the poem may be found in Seligmann Baer, *Avodat Yisrael* (Roedelheim, 1868), p. 633. How closely the Germanic tune fits the "*Sh'ney Zeytim*" can be seen by comparing the rhyme on "-iru" with the melodic contour.
15. It should be noted that the poem *Eli Tziyon* is the very last of the *kinot* section.
16. Idelsohn, *Music*, p. 171.
17. Wagner, *Jacobusliturgie*, p. 64. The copy of the manuscript in the Hispanic Society in New York, which I consulted, has an initial tone E.
18. The tune originated at Santiago de Compostela, and it seems plausible that the monk Heinrich von Laufenberg set his new text to the old tune after visiting there.

19. Idelsohn, *Music*, table 26, no. 7.
20. The oldest version of "*Puer Natus*" is in the Hereford Breviary (1515, for Epiphany), with a number of variants in the text. Translations appear as "A Babe is Born in Bethlehem" or "The Child is Born in Bethlehem."
21. Peter Wagner, in *Jacobusliturgie*, rightly emphasizes, "These songs once sounded in the mouths of many thousands of pilgrims from all European countries in praise of God and His apostle."
22. See Otto Gombosi, "*Folia*," *MGG*.
23. Wagner (*Jacobusliturgie*) cites the *Codex Calixtinus* as source for two possible dates for the Jacobus celebration in Compostela: VII *Kalendis Augusti* (*Passio S. Jacobi*) and *Kalendis Januarii* (*Translacio et electio eiusdem colitur*).
24. The text of the first *Invitatorium* states in its opening hymn:

Armeni, Gregi, Apuli,
Angli, Galli, Daci Frisi,
Cunctae gentes, linguae, tribus
Illyc pergunt muneribus.

25. Wagner, *Jacobusliturgie*, p. 66. The Hebrew words are:

שמחה, נצחון, עולה,
היום, נכתר, אחיו,
מברך, ימה, נקרא

26. The pioneer studies in this field were done by Eduard Birnbaum, Emanuel Kirschner, and Idelsohn. Their researches and my own have been used uncritically, unacknowledged, and with many "copyist's errors" by subsequent writers. The reader is advised to read chapters on borrowings from alien sources with some skepticism. To give but one example: Alfred Sendrey, in "writing out" Idelsohn, confused a Spanish with a Czech folk song, for both were printed on the same page in Idelsohn (*Music*, p. 173).
27. In the manuscript compendium of M. Levi of Esslingen (Birnbaum Collection, H.U.C., Cincinnati) this melody was still used for the older *piyut*.
28. See Kirschner, *Poesien-Singweisen*.
29. Until 1967 the melody of the *Bruder Veits Ton* existed only as a conjecture of German folklorists. It had never been fully identified. See below, note 45.
30. Mentioned in Berliner, *Aus dem Leben der deutschen Juden im Mittelalter*, 2d ed. (Berlin, 1900); also by Kirschner and Idelsohn.
31. Cf. *HOM*, vol. 7, no. 179, ii.
32. Kirschner, *Poesien-Singweisen*, pp. 3–5
33. About this acclamation and its Christian counterpart "*Christus regnat*," etc., see *WSB*, p. 272, no. 39, and pp. 523–524.
34. Cf. Heinrich Albert, "*Trefflich hoch*," *Volkslieder fuer die Jugend* (Berlin, 1931), no. 502.
35. The *pizmon*, *Omnam ken*, an alphabetical acrostic with the refrain "*salaḥti*" ("I have pardoned") to be sung by the congregation, is one of the rare compositions by an English Jew, the poet and martyr R. Yom Tob of York, killed in 1189.
36. See Erich Valentin, "*Bergamasca*," *MGG*. See also Paul Nettl, "*Die Bergamasca*," *Zeitschrift fuer Musikwissenschaft*, vol. 5 (Leipzig, 1923–1924). For Bach's theme and the original text, see Philip Spitta, *Bach* (English ed., New York and London, 1951), 3:175.
37. This so-called *Schuettel-hodu* (from the "shaking" of the *lulav* as it is sung) is similar to a fantasy for lute by Valentin Greff Backfark, a German-Polish composer of the sixteenth century. The similarity lies in both its rhythmic and intervallic patterns. See his lute book in *Denkmaeler der Tonkunst Oesterreich*, ed. Guido Adler, vol. 23, 2 (Vienna, 1911–1912).

38. Compare the *hakafot* in Sulzer's *Schir Zion*, vol. 2, with *BT* 926 (in this book, table VI, no. 11*b*), or Hirsch Weintraub's choral paraphrase in *Shirey Beth Adonai* (Koenigsberg, 1859).

39. In the middle of the sixteenth century a certain Eisik Wallich, leader and parnas of the community of Worms, made a collection of German songs, which he wrote down in Hebrew letters. Many of the songs (written without music) were the most popular of his time. This collection is now part of the Oppenheim assembly of such documents in the Bodleian Library, Oxford. See Friedrich Rosenberg, "*Eine Sammlung deutscher Volkslieder in hebraeischen Lettern,*" *Zeitschrift fuer die Geschichte der Juden in Deutschland* 2 (1888–1889): 232–296; 3 (1889–1890): 18–50. See also Moritz Steinschneider's famous catalogue of Hebrew manuscripts in the Bodleian Library. Most of the German songs examined for this study are found in the Wallich collection.

40. *HOM*, vol. 7, pp. xxxvi-xxxvii.

41. Maharil, *Hilkhot Rosh ha-Shanah.*

42. Wilhelm Baeumker, *Das Katholische deutsche Kirchenlied*, vol. 4, no. 19 (Freiburg, 1911).

43. These songs come from the old centers of German Jewry, Cologne and Mayence, and were published before 1520. They were very popular, and were often arranged by composers. See Albert, *Volksliederbuch für die Jugend*, nos. 340, 341.

44. This melody was notated by Kirschner in *Poesien-Singweisen.*

45. Dr. Walther Lipphardt, by a lucky find, discovered a manuscript with the *Bruder Veits Ton*, in the version of a half-forgotten collector of folk songs, Adam Reissner, former secretary of the Landsknecht captain Georg von Frundsberg. Lipphardt published the song in *Jahrbuch fuer Liturgik und Hymnologie*, vol. 10 (Kassel, 1965–1966). I reproduce it here (example 12) with his kind permission. It not only resembles the version formerly

Example 12

(To note 45)
after Dr. Lipphardt
Gott grüss dich, Bru - der Vei - te!
Hörst du kein neu Ge - schrei? Zu Rom ist um -
ge - fal - len die Braut von Ba - by - lon, sie
sass in ho - hen eh - ren dar - zu in ho - hem prayss,
ir stul ist ir zer - schmol - zen er war ge - baut of eiss.

identified as the *Ton*, but its strains are echoed in the tunes of many *piyutim* of *minhag ashkenaz*. There is obviously no religious significance to this example. It was a mocking song by the Swiss soldiers against the *Landsknechte*, referring to their battles, and printed in 1515. The great scholar of German folk song, Rochus von Liliencron, was correct in identifying the *Bruder Veits Ton* with a song that came out in Ott's *Gute Newe Liedlein* (Nuremberg, 1544). See *Festschrift fuer Walter Wiora*, eds. Ludwig Finscher and Christoph Mahling (Kassel, Basel, and New York, 1967), pp. 286 ff. (Translation of the text of *Bruder Veit:* God greet you, brother Veit, haven't you heard the new rumor?/ In Rome the Bride of Babylon has fallen/ her honor was high, as was her price,/ Her throne has melted, it was built on ice.)

46. Boehme, in *BAL*, pp. 494 ff., explains on three closely printed pages the rather intricate controversy, which, though obsolete today, contains many interesting details.

47. *HOM*, vol. 7, p. 295.

48. Kirschner, *Poesie-Singweisen*. Most recently Hanoch Avenary's edition of this tune is a fair example of Israeli musical scholarship. See his *Hebrew Hymn Tunes* (Tel Aviv, 1971), p. 28. Yet nobody has noted that Boeschenstein, Reuchlin's collaborator, wrote a poem in the tone of our song, "woelt Ihr mich merken eben?" between 1512 and 1514.

49. Johann Jacob Schudt, *Juedische Merkwuerdigkeiten* (Frankfort, 1714).

50. *HOM*, vol. 7, 346b and p. xliv. See also Elbogen-Sterling, *Geschichte der Juden in Deutschland* (Frankfort, 1966), pp. 113–114.

51. The text is quoted from S. Riemer's study, *Philosemitismus im deutschen evangelischen Kirchenlied des Barock* (Stuttgart, 1963), pp. 70–71.

52. השפלתי זו הגבהתי, והגבהתי זו השפלתי: (שמות ר)

(Leviticus Rabba, Parsha 1).

53.

אמלל גבורות ואדברה מעשי ה' הגדולים, אותות ומופתים אספרה שבח והודי
והילולים בכל מדינה ומדינה ופלך על נפלאותיו להער, ארוממך אלהי המלך.
ואברהם שמך לעולם ועד.

מגילת עפה

(in *Megilat Afah*, ed. Rosenlicht [Cracow, 1879]).

54. Rabbi Joseph Hahn-Noerdlingen, *Yosef Ometz* (Frankfort, 1713), no. 953.

55. Johann Christian Wagenseil, *Belehrung der Juedisch-teutschen Schreibart* (Koenigsberg, 1699), p. 119. About the *Pavia Ton* see Rochus von Liliencron, *Die Deutschen historischen Volkslieder* (Berlin and Stuttgart, 1884), 3:425–426, no. 372, where the *Pavia Ton* is ascribed to Hans von Wuerzburg.

56. *The Jewish Encyclopedia*, Kirschner, and Idelsohn traced some of the tunes of *piyutim* back to Christian church songs. A critical examination shows that those church songs were contrafacts of older secular songs that the Jews picked up, generally avoiding ecclesiastical material. Dr. Alfred Sendrey seems to believe in the direct borrowing of ecclesiastic tunes. He assumes that the Sephardim made use of the famous tune "*L'homme armé*." His erring (but undisclosed) source is the *JE* article "Music of the Synagogue," by F. L. Cohen. The same holds true for Sendrey's claim that Heinrich Isaac's "*Innsbruck, ich muss dich lassen*" was used by German Jews. This "discovery," too, can be found in *JE*, vol. 9, p. 130.

Appendix to Chapter 6

1. I am indebted to Mr. Paul Hess of the Zentralbibliothek of Lucerne, for making this material available to me.

2. Of the ample literature on the subject only two books will be cited, since they, in turn, contain rich bibliographies: Ernst August Schuler, *Die Musik der Osterfeiern und Passionen des Mittelalters* (Kassel and Basel, 1951); and M. Blakemore Evans, *The Passion Play of Lucerne* (New York and London, 1943).
3. Evans, op. cit., pp. 6 ff.
4. *Baenkelsaenger* is one who sings while seated on a little bench. That is, he is a vagrant singer. Some of the parallel Hebrew-sounding gibberish is found in Schuler's book (op. cit.), pp. 367, 370–372.

Chapter 7

1. L. S. Porta, "*Chronik der Familie Loewenstein Porta,*" *Juedische Familien-Forschung* (Berlin, 1924–1931), 1:12–15; also Baron, p. 336, no. 18. The family may be related to the Disraelis, as Cecil Roth surmises in "*Ursprung der Familie Bassevi,*" *Juedische Familien-Forschung* (1927–1928), 4:58–60.
2. Moritz Guedemann, *Juedische im Christentum des Reformationszeitalters* (Vienna, 1870). To give but one example: Luther was born in Eisleben, and a Protestant scholar interpreted its Latin name Islebia as meaning in Hebrew "*Ish-leb-jah*" (a man after the heart of the Lord).
3. Siegmund Riemer, *Philosemitismus im deutschen evangelischen Kirchenlied* (Stuttgart, 1963), pp. 26 ff. A number of Christian hymns appeared in Hebrew translation as a sign of good will on the part of the "Boehmisch-Maehrischen Brueder.
4. Ibid., p. 71.
5. Rabbi Samuel Archevolti, *Arugat ha-Bosem* (Venice, 1602), fol. 110. The pertinent passage is also quoted in Israel Adler's fine work, *Pratique*, p. 256. Adler conjectures (p. 47) that the term "*meshubaḥ*" corresponds to *musica reservata*, especially the reference to the Temple Levites. I am not convinced that the term means anything more than exquisite, or excellent. There can be no question, however, that the term "*shir hamoni*" equals *musica volgare*.
6. The text here is after Adler, *Pratique*, p. 245. Full text in Hahn-Noerdlingen, *Yosef Ometz* (op. cit.), 1st ed., 1627, fol. 77a, and no. 889, fol. 110b.
7. M. Guedemann, *Quellenschriften* (Berlin, 1891), p. 85, *amudei shesh.*
8. Text in Adler, *Pratique*, p. 244, also p. 15.
9. Ibid., p. 15.
10. Quoted by R. J. Juspa after R. Schäftel Horowitz, in Adler, *Musique*, p. 245.
11. Rabbi Joel Sirkes, *She'elot u-teshubot bebatey kenesiot she-me-zamrim bahem be-vet tefilatam*, etc. (Frankfort, 1696–1697). The interpretation here is based in part on Solomon Freehof's *Treasury of Responsa* (Philadelphia, 1963), pp. 157 ff.
12. Adler, *Pratique*, pp. 250 ff.
13. Idelsohn, *Music*, pp. 162, 201, etc. Others have followed this categorization, to the confusion of general musicologists not familiar with Idelsohn's solipsistic terminology.
14. Adler, *Pratique*, pp. 244 ff.
15. Ibid., p. 29.
16. The tone of the text is blunt and of autocratic sternness. In the great modern editions of the Babylonian Talmud the work by R. Lippmann Heller is found as commentary to Rabbenu Asher's exposition of *Berakot* no. 122; otherwise in R. Asher's work it is found as *me'adney melekh* and *dibrey ḥamudot.*
17. Adler, *Pratique*, p. 16, note 35.

18. Rabbi Leon da Modena, in his responsum, included in the first edition of Salomone de' Rossi's *Shirim asher lishlomo* (Venice, 1622). The text may also be found in the collection of Modena's responsa, *Zikney Yehudah* (Jerusalem, 1955–1956), no. 6.
19. Adler, *Pratique*, p. 248.
20. After the text in M. Guedemann's *Quellenschriften* (Berlin, 1884), pp. 300 ff.
21. My rather free translation replaces the singular with "they" and omits some remarks that can be understood only by readers familiar with the fine points of Hebrew liturgy.
22. See Idelsohn's biographical study, "*Ha-ḥazanim bi-kehillot mefursamot,*" in *Reshumot* (Tel Aviv, 1927 and 1930), 5:343, 361.
23. Idelsohn, "Songs and Singers," pp. 407–408.
24. Alfred Feilchenfeld, *Denkwuerdigkeiten def Glueckel von Hameln* (Berlin, 1913), pp. 297–302. There was evidently a panic in the synagogue, whose cause remains obscure. But the celebrated cantor Yokel behaved strangely. In the midst of the tumult he left the synagogue, went home and abandoned his pulpit to an underling, while he remained quietly in his apartment. Not much later (1715), a handbill was printed in Frankfort entitled "*Ein neu Klaglied auf dem ma'aseh ha-gadol*" [sic] deploring the catastrophe of Metz. It starts with the words, "*Esa* [I will lift up], *Ich will aufheben mein Stimm mit Schreien und Klagen*." (In Steinschneider, no. 3645.)
25. Adler, *Pratique*, p. 252. For a full description of Levi's travels, see *Israelitische Letterbode*, ed. M. (?) Roest (Amsterdam, 1884). See also Isaac Rivkind, *Klezmorim* (New York, 1960 [Hebrew]), which is a review of the book *Ha-Klezmorim* by Joachim Stutchewsky (Tel Aviv, 1958).

For evidence of the extent of instrumental music in the synagogues of Prague, see epitaphs from the old cemeteries in Leopold and Moriz Popper, *Die Inschriften der alten Prager Judenfriedhöfe* (Braunschweig, 1893), 1:24. We read there of at least four harpists named Harfner, and at least three violinists named Fiedler. The following are a few selected epitaphs: "David, son of the precentor R. Jacob, a case-maker (*Futeralmacher*), David was both an instrumentalist and vocal musician, also well trained in the science of music; there was no other like him in our generation, hence his death was a great sorrow to us. . . ." "Here reposes the 'vessel of Manna' [man of great piety and charity], the dear Abraham Klezmer, son of the respected Hirsch Kubin, may he rest in peace. He, too, belonged to the pledged fraternity of singers and musicians who ever sanctified the 'reception of the Sabbath.'" (The "fraternity" referred to in this epitaph may have been one of the sodalities attached to the synagogue, like the fraternities of an Italian church, such as the Scuola S. Rocco in Venice.) Some of the groups were of cabalistic nature and intent. One of them was known as the *Shomrim la-boker* (Watchers of the Dawn). See Adler, *Pratique*, pp. 95–100.

Frequently mentioned in the old cemetery epitaphs are *Klapzymbels* and *Klappzimmerer*, both words corruptions of *clavicymbalist*, a familiar kind of Jewish musician. The oldest of them was buried in 1639; several of them belonged to the families Ulma, Mendl, Teinsch, Jacob Bendavid, etc. On the entire subject of old *klezmorim* see Isaac Rivkind, *Klezmorim* (New York, 1960), which is written in Hebrew.

As controversial as were the players of instruments and of the organ in the synagogue on Friday eve, so beloved and honored by the rabbis, were the singing fraternities, particularly those "singers of the *Barukh she-amar*," a morning prayer that was often drawn out to an hour's length. On the singing of *Barukh she-amar* see Idelsohn "*He-hazanim . . .*" in *Reshumot* (Tel Aviv, 1927 and 1930), 5:356. In the *Or Zarua*, R. Isaac of Vienna tells

the following tale: "I have known a Jew from Worms called R. Bunem [Bonhomme]; he was an old undertaker, and I heard the following tale from him as true." Rabbi Isaac goes on to tell that the sexton [*shamash*] once rose and found at the door of the synagogue a living corpse with a crown of grass and sprigs on his head; he was afraid, and took him for a spook; then he remembered, and asked: 'Did I not bury you yesterday?' 'Yes,' said the mysterious visitor. 'Did you reach eternity?' 'Yes.' 'In what condition were you?' 'I was fine!' 'How did you, a simple man, attain such a privilege?' 'Well, it was only thanks to my enthusiastic daily singing of *Barukh she-amar* in the synagogue, that I was carried to the garden of Eden.'"

For more about the days when the chant of *Barukh she-amar* was most desirable, see *Maḥzor Me'agley Tzedek* (Venice, 1568), introduction.

26. More about this question in chapter 12. I am convinced that the emotionalism and the uninhibited polemics on this question have two principal causes: the absence of a supreme rabbinical court to decide *ex cathedra* on the *aggiornamento* of *halakhah*; and the ignorance of some of the rabbis, who hopelessly confused most of the arguments.

27. J. J. Schudt, *Juedische Merkwuerdigkeiten* (see chapter 6, n. 49), sixth book, chapter 34, p. 366.

28. J. J. Schudt, *Juedisches Frankfurter und Prager Freudenfest* (Frankfort, 1716).

29. As prelude to the public discussion over the organ in the synagogue, the Hebrew periodical *Bikkurei ha-ittim* (Vienna, 1823), 4:257 ff., recalled the story of Meir Mahler, the builder of Prague's first organ in a synagogue; this was based on the old Judeo-German "*Naje Zaytung un juedischer Oyfzug*" (Prague, 1716).

30. Wagenseil, *Sota* (Altdorff, 1674), p. 83.

31. Cecil Roth, *Jews in the Renaissance* (Philadelphia, 1959), p. 292. In this book the intellectual interests in Jewry outside of Italy are hardly touched upon by the author, as if the Renaissance had affected only the Italian Jews.

32. An almost complete list of these works with fine musical illustrations is given in Adler, *Pratique*, vol. 1.

33. Some of these criteria have been listed by Hanoch Avenary (H. Loewenstein) in *Kiryat Sefer* (Jerusalem, 1943), 19:266 ff.

34. Solomon Widder, I. Loew Memorial Volume, ed. Alexander Scheiber (Budapest, 1947), pp. 15, 74, 96 ff.

35. The examples quoted the incipits of German-Hebrew songs upon melodies popular at the time. By no means do all contrafacts go back to German tunes; a number refer to liturgical melodies, such as the *Akedah*, or songs by local musicians, such as R. Salomo Kristall, or the tunes of hazanim. These incipits are found in Steinschneider, nos. 3652–3707. Many more pieces like these are included in the celebrated Oppenheimer collection in the Bodleian Library.

36. The text here is extracted from my article, the first extensive and critical study on the Marcello work, and its Hebrew melodies (*MGWJ*, 1937). Idelsohn had repeatedly drawn attention to this source in *Music* (pp. 167, 171, 202) and *HOM* (vol. 6, appendix) and in his study on the German Jews in Italy (*HUCA*, 11, 1936). Yet he never examined them critically. In preparing this book, I found a brief, solid article on the tunes of Marcello by the young Eduard Birnbaum, under the misleading title "*Briefe aus Koenigsberg*" in *Der juedische Kantor* (Bromberg, 1883), pp. 348 ff. This article should be added to my tentative bibliography of Birnbaum's writings in *HUCA* 18 (1944). Birnbaum's article also contains the first resolute defense against one of the worst plagiarizers in the field, F. L. Cohen, later the musical editor of the *Jewish Encyclopedia*.

37. The learned Nikolaus Forkel committed two blunders when he referred to these tunes in his *Geschichte der Musik* (Leipzig, 1801), as if the texts were translations of the psalter, in particular assuming that no. 4, *Ma'oz Tzur*, was identical with Psalm 16.
38. According to the responsum *ḥavot ya'ir*, no. 288, where a stanza of the poem is quoted. The last line fits neither the Italian nor the German tune; however, something of a case might be made for the Italian tune. See Idelsohn, "Traditional Songs," p. 576.
39. See Rudolf Eitner, in *Monatshefte fuer Musikgeschichte* (Leipzig and Berlin, 1891), no. 11. He, too, blames Marcello, who "had composed the Psalm itself in exactly the same happy-go-lucky manner as was the *habitus* of his *cantus firmus* [the Hebrew tune]." Truly Guedemann was right in saying, "Hazanut is Baroque in itself."
40. Cf. *BAL*, no. 105, first found in G. Forster, *Frische Teutsche Liedlein* (1549), vol. 3, no. 6. There are some religious contrafacts of this secular *Lied*. It may be a parody upon Wolkenstein's *Tagelied*, "*Wach auff, mein hort, es leucht daher*." This may be debatable, but Idelsohn's conjecture, which links the tune of Marcello to a much more recent Protestant hymn, is untenable.
41. Eduard Birnbaum ("*Briefe aus Koenigsberg*," op. cit., p. 349) traces the tune to a Polish folk song. The comparison is not, however, at all convincing—the less so, as the Polish melody was first printed in 1875 and never appeared either before or after that date.
42. Idelsohn, "Traditional Songs," p. 589.
43. *HOM*, vol. 7, introduction, p. xli.
44. Idelsohn, "Traditional Songs," p. 589.
45. Steinschneider, *Catalogue of the Bodleian Library Hebrew Manuscripts*, nos. 3625 ss.
46. A. Berliner, *Randbemerkungen zum taeglichen Gebetbuch* (Berlin, 1909). The tendency of this outstanding study is both strictly Orthodox and anti-cabalistic.
47. Ibid., p. 44. The author points out the cabalistic origin of the singing of *Shalom alekhem* and of *Eshet Ḥayil* as parts of the domestic ritual on Friday evening.
48. Personal communication of the late A. J. Heschel; see also Adler, *Pratique*, pp. 97–115.
49. The melodies are all reproduced in *HOM*, vol. 6, pp. 232–234.
50. After Paul Nettl's transcription in his interesting book, *Alte juedische Spielleute* (Prague, 1923), p. 41.
51. Idelsohn, *Music*, p. 183.
52. Baron, vol. 14, p. 292.
53. Baer also lists some Portuguese tunes.
54. The Polish hazanim considered their coloratura arias as the proper counterparts to *pilpul* (talmudic sophistry), and transferred a talmudic expression to their art: they called their extended melismata and the forms they developed from them a "*sebarah*" (hypothesis, argument).

Chapter 8

1. See *Ha-Asif* IV, ed. Nahum Sokoloff (Warsaw, 1886), pp. 4, 16 (Ibrahim ibn Jakub). See also Julius Aronius, *Regesten zur Geschichte der Juden im Deutschen Reiche* (Leipzig and Berlin, 1887–1903), pp. 130–131; and Roman Jakobson and Morris Halle, "The Term *Canaan* in Medieval Literature," *Festschrift Max Weinreich* (London and The Hague, 1964), pp. 147 ff.

2. J. J. Schudt, *Juedische Merkwuerdigkeiten* (Frankfort, 1714), pp. 284 ff. In his description of the "Sabbath Fever" the author takes pains to describe the singers and musicians as half-deaf, one-eyed, meanwhile hypocritically deploring the loss of the lofty Levitical art music of the Temple. The entire passage is an observer's indictment of the rabbinical tyranny that suppressed any serious music in the ghetto.

3. I have seen a manuscript in the Hebrew National Library in Jerusalem, written by a learned rabbi of Verona in the 1820s. This treatise on musical theory was based on ideas of the eleventh and twelfth centuries in the Neo-Pythagorean spirit. For the author, the entire development of music theory, including Zarlino, Huygens, Mersenne, Rameau, and C. P. E. Bach, had passed unnoticed.

4. Manasseh ben Israel, *Nishmat hayyim* III.

ואמנם מתיחסת האמונה הזאת לפיתאגורס להיות שהוא חדשה מאחר שנתעלמה ונסתרה כמה מהשנים ולא להיותו הראשון שפרסמה וגם הוא לדעת אליכסנדר פוליסטור (Polyhistor) למדה ושמעה מיחזקאל הנביא אשר הי' רבו, כי החכמה המפוארה שהיתה לו והסודות הנפלאות אשר בין צורותיו וציוריו העלים מאין באו לו, האם רוח ה' נוצצה בו?

I am deeply indebted to my good friend Dr. Philip Birnbaum, who afforded me this important interpretation of Jewish medieval thinking.

5. Selig Margolis, *Hiburey Likutim* (Venice, 1715), fols. 4–5.

6. Ibid.

7. Solomon Luria, *Yam shel Shelomo*, Hullin nos. 1–49. Quoted after Meyer S. Lew, *The Jews of Poland* (London, 1944), p. 157.

8. *Soferim* 14:14 אינו מן המובחר שיעמוד חזן יחידי

Parallel to this passage from *Pirkey de Rab Eliezer*, chapter 44,

מכאן אתה למדת ששליח צבור אסור להתפלל, אם אין שנים עומדין אצלו וכו'

9. *Pesikta de R. Kahane*, ed. Solomon Buber, 1st ed. (Lemberg, 1868)

מכאן לשלושה שצריכין לירד לפני התיבה שליח צבור.

For the dedication of a new Torah scroll guest cantors and *meshorerim* were frequently invited. For weddings four *meshorerim* were usually used, and ten boys sang the seven benedictions for the newly wedded couple during the week after the wedding (Paul Christian Kirchner, *Juedisches Ceremonial* [Frankfort, 1720]).

10. Idelsohn, *Music*, p. 207.

11. A manuscript of a hazan of the early eighteenth century (in my possession) refers to *Deuteronomy Rabba*. ופיו אם דמוע

Also, Birnbaum, *Liturgische Uebungen* (Berlin, 1912), 2:7.

12. This sociologically significant *ménage* has not been sufficiently examined to permit definite conclusions about its influence on musical tradition. In general it appears that it did more harm than good; but this belongs to a history of *ḥazanut*, not of *minhag ashkenaz*.

13. Rabbi Jacob Emden, *Megillat Sefer*, ed. Kahane (Warsaw, 1896), pp. 27–29.

14. Arno Nadel, *Zemirot Shabbat. Die Haueslichen Sabbatgesaenge* (Berlin, 1937). The following pages in this text are of technical interest only. The reader may wish to skip them and proceed directly to the latter portion of the chapter, dealing with the *zemirot*.

15. Hermann Vogelstein, *Geschichte der Juden in Rom* (Berlin, 1896), pp. 181–184.

16. Hermann L. Eichborn, "*Studien zur Geschichte der Militaer-Musik*," *Monatshefte fuer Musikgeschichte* 14 (Leipzig and Berlin, 1892): 93 ff.

17. Meyer S. Lew, *The Jews of Poland* (London, 1944), p. 126, no. 47.
18. Elbogen points out that as late as the year 140 the Tannaites were not agreed on the selection of biblical verses for the three sections. This would indicate that the synagogal liturgy was at that time still in *statu nascendi*.
19. This is, by the way, the same trait of major-minor tonality that is characteristic of Schubert, Smetana, Dvořák, Mahler, and other Austrian-Bohemian or Polish composers of the nineteenth century.
20. Wilhelm Merian, *Der Tanz in den deutschen Tabulaturbuechern* (Leipzig, 1927), pp. 240 ff.
21. The original title is *77 auserlesene polnischer und deutscher art taenze* (Nuremberg, 1601). The passage quoted in table VIII is found in the edition by Huchler (Wilhelmshaven, 1964).
22. Jozef M. Chominsky and Zofia Lissa, *Music of the Polish Renaissance* (Warsaw, 1955).
23. Christoph Loeffelholz, *Tabulaturbuch* (1572–1619); our example from Merian, op. cit., p. 187, no. 16.
24. See the valuable study by Alicia Simon, *Deutsche Einfluesse in der polnischen Musik bis zur Zeit der Klassiker* (Zurich, 1927); also Hieronym Feicht, "*Baroque, Polen*," in *MGG*. Of the considerable literature on old tablatures for lute or organ, we mention here only: Karl Geiringer, "*Vorgeschichte und Geschichte der europaeischen Laute*," *Zeitschrift fuer Musikwissenschaft* 10 (1927–1928): 560; also the rich material in Oscar Chilesotti, "*Un catalogue international des sources de la musique pour le luth*" (Paris, 1957–1959), where some bibliographies are given.
25. The "*goût polonais*" became so popular in France that the great Rameau wrote a slightly parodistical stylization of it in the "Indes Galantes," of which the Polish air became quite famous.
26. See comments on *Ahabah Rabah* above in chapter 4.
27. The associative power of music has been recognized and hailed ever since Aristoxenos, the disciple of Aristotle. The thesis was most drastically expressed in an epigram by Karl Kraus, a contemporary of Freud and Mahler, in these words: "What is the 'Ninth' of Beethoven compared to a street-song, played on a hurdy-gurdy and on a memory?"
28. B. *Shabbat*, 119b.
29. B. *Shabbat*, 118b.
30. See Loewe, *Minstrelsy*. This is a charming book, and in its terminal essay on the literary parallels to the *zemirot* it shows considerable erudition. But it is marred by two blemishes: the melodies given are neither "traditional" nor are they interesting from the musical point of view. Nor does the author's effort to "conform" the old Hebrew texts to Anglo-Saxon or Norman poetry make much sense, whereas his Latin parallels are most interesting. A number of Byzantine and German parallels could easily be added.
31. The angelology is absent from this piece, as in the verses of Prudentius that are adduced as parallels by Dr. Loewe (ibid., pp. 126. 128).
32. "Every family has its own tunes, and every family deems its own tunes better than any others. . . . Tunes, even in the best of families, get a little out of hand sometimes . . ." (Loewe, *Minstrelsy*, pp. 6–7). Charmingly put, indeed! This is another example of *Zersingen*.
33. Leo Hirschfeld, *Die Haueslichen Sabbathsgesaenge* (Mayence, n.d.), p. 27; and Loewe, *Minstrelsy*, pp. 75 ff.
34. Idelsohn, *Music*, pp. 222–225; also *HOM*, vol. 4, *Hatikvah* table. The first, and still quite valuable study on migrating tunes was written by Wilhelm Tappert, and appeared as *Musikalische Studien* (Berlin, 1868).

35. In this instance the surprisingly harsh judgment of Chaim Harris (*Toledot haneginah be-Yisrael* [New York, 1950], p. 346) is justified: "Many of the songs at the courts of hasidic rebbes were cheap, unoriginal, and not genuine folksongs. . . . "
36. For the story of the *mah yafit*, see Loewe, *Minstrelsy*, p. 47, note in German (apparently to spare the feelings of English Jewry that is so easily shocked!); also Chaim Harris (op. cit., p. 356), who finds more forceful words for the story of that song, and the loss of dignity, sometimes incurred willingly by the Jews.
37. Friedrich Niecks, *Frederic Chopin* (New York and London, 1888), p. 183.
38. B. *Sota* 10a; B. *Ber.* 48b; Jer. *Ber.* VII, 2. The singing of psalms was also supposed to prevent indecent language at the table.

שבזמננו זה שרגילין הרבה לנבל פיהם במשתה היין

as in Hahn-Noerdlingen, *Yosef Ometz* (Frankfort, 1713), no. 133.
39. The *Missinai* tunes were called "*Scarbove*" in east Europe, an expression whose etymology is controversial.
40. It is that version which Idelsohn included as no. 1 in table 32 of *Music*.
41. The *zemirot* as notated in the *Vilnaer Mušikališer Pinkas* (Yiddish), ed. Bernstein (Vilna, 1927), especially nos. 11–125, are a bonanza for the serious student of folklore; all stages of popular song are represented there.
42. F. M. Boehme, *Geschichte des Tanzes in Deutschland* (Leipzig, 1886). See also "*Polonaise*" in *MGG*, and Lucjan Kamienski, "*Entwicklung der Polonaise bis Beethoven*," *Kongressbericht* of the Beethoven Centennial (Vienna, 1927), pp. 66–70.
43. Boehme, op. cit., especially the dances by Valentin Haussmann and Christian Demantius, nos. 136, 175.
44. *Vilnaer Pinkas*, op. cit., nos. 58, 76–80, 93, 116, etc.
45. Landmarks in these new approaches are *The Wellsprings of Music* by Curt Sachs (The Hague, 1962), Bence Szabolcsi's fine book, *A History of Melody* (Budapest and New York, 1965), and the German books by Alexander von Sydow (*Das Lied* [Goettingen, 1962]), Walter Wiora (*Das echte Volkslied* [Heidelberg, 1950]), and Werner Danckert (*Das Europaische Volkslied*, 2d ed. [Bonn, 1970]) on folk songs.
46. A. Z. Idelsohn, "Musical Characteristics of East-European Folksong," *Musical Quarterly* 23 (New York, 1923–1924): 634 ff. Here Idelsohn considers Slavic folk song "oriental," for which claim there is no tenable reason whatever. He also refrains from stating what *is* the character of the Jewish folk song of about 1650, at the same time minimizing or totally neglecting the natural alterations that occur in every folk song older than a generation.
47. Apparently in 1908, as we are told by former adherents of that court, or by persons who claim to have heard that tune at that time.

Chapter 9

1. Once again I must warn the reader of the old Herder-inspired theories about folk song, expressed by Idelsohn, as quoted in chapter 8, and echoed in Jewish writings by Steinthal, Marek, Rosowky, and others. They constitute the tacitly accepted axioms of most "nationalistic art." The controversy arising out of the application of similar theses to American folklore originated about eighty years ago with the publication of the Child Ballads, and the subsequent battle of "communalists" and "anti-communalists." The first scholar who opposed the excessive estimation of everything "folkish" was Wilhelm Tappert, in his *Musikalische Studien* (Berlin, 1868), pp. 36, 39.

2. Gioseffo Zarlino, *Instituzioni harmoniche* (Venice, 1558).
3. *WSB*, pp. 466 ff.
3a. An examination of the rhythmic structure of the *Ha lahma* shows that the first phrase has three stresses, the subsequent ones have four; this change permeates the whole text.
4. Wagner, *Gregorianische Melodien*, vol. 3, pp. 57 ff.; also Higinio Anglès, *La Musica Medieval en Toledo* (Muenster, 1938).
5. On the age of *ha laḥma* see Zunz, *Gottesdienstliche Vortraege*, Hebrew revised ed. by Hanoch Albeck (Jerusalem, 1953), p. 61. Before Albeck, the same conclusion was reached by Maurice Liber, in his fine critique of the literary style of the piece, "*Le Seder de la Diaspora*" in *REJ* 81 (1925): 217. He believed that this public invitation originated before the destruction of the Temple, but was modified and added to afterward. On the other hand, E. D. Goldschmidt contends that the text is Talmudic, or even post-Talmudic (*Hagadah shel Pesah ve-toldoteha* [Jerusalem, 1960], pp. 7–9).
6. Bence Szabolcsi, *Bausteine zu einer Geschichte der Melodie* (Budapest, 1959), pp. 236 ff.
7. In the Byzantine liturgy it is the hymn "*Hote to Stauro*"; cf. *Georgian Kanonarion*, ed. Kikelidze (Tiflis, 1912). Correctly, the *Improperia* number fifteen verses, like the *Dayenu*, to match the numerical value of the letters "*yod*" and "*heh*" (the deity). See my study "*Zur Textgeschichte der Improperia,*" *Festschrift Benno Staeblein* (Erlangen, 1965). Also "Melito of Sardes," *HUCA* 37 (1966).
8. See the excellent studies on rhymes in old prayers by Jefim Schirmann in *JQR* 39 (1948–1949).
9. Jules Salomon and Mardochée Crémieu, *Chants Hebraiques* (Marseilles, n.d.).
10. Karl Severin Meister, *Das deutsche Kirchenlied* (Freiburg-im-Breisgau, 1869), no. 329.
11. In *BAL*, nos. 375 and 376, and p. 463. The editor concludes: "The strophic structure of five lines—we call it the *Lindenschmid-Ton*—dominates the folksong from the thirteenth to the seventeenth centuries." About its antecedents see W. Tappert, *Musikalische Studien* (Berlin, 1868), pp. 58 ff.
12. It seems the Grimm brothers were the first ones to be aware of this literary wandering motif, used in the so-called "*Lambertus-Lied.*"
13. Felipe Pedrell, *Cancionero musical popular español* (Barcelona, 1921), 2:97.
14. Salomon and Crémieu, op. cit., p. 200, no. 28.

Chapter 10

1. Sigmund Freud, *Das Unbehagen in der Kultur* (Vienna, 1913; revised ed. 1922).
2. There is no clear sociological census available of the population of central European Jewry between 1800 and 1845. Such a breakdown would be hard to establish. The former Polish Jews of Galicia as well as the Jews of Hungary were not fully affected by the new laws. The French Jews were not a homogeneous group in 1800. Except for the Jewish communities in the papal province of the Comtat-Venaissin, all Jews had been excluded from the kingdom of France from the fourteenth century to the revolution.
3. Zoltán Kodály, *Folk Music of Hungary* (Budapest, 1960), pp. 8 f., 14 ff. The distinction between rural and urban song had already been postulated by the Grimm brothers. In Bela Bartók's painstaking studies on folk songs this distinction plays a decisive role.
4. Abraham Z. Idelsohn, "Songs and Singers of the Eighteenth Century," *HUCA*, Jubilee vol. (1925).
5. Ibid., p. 423; see also p. 407: "Inasmuch as the art [of classical variation] demanded

professional singers to devote themselves to it, it excluded laymen entirely. Hence the traditional occupancy of the position of the precentor by rabbis and prominent men was. . .impossible."

6. In "Songs and Singers," introduction to *HOM*, vol. 7; in *Music*, pp. 287 ff.; also in Eric Werner, "The Birnbaum Collection," *HUCA* 18 (1943).

7. One of these *minhagim* is carried out on the eve of Yom Kippur. The benediction over the *talit* (prayer shawl) is recited by all fathers of families, according to their age. This procedure must have taken fifteen minutes at least, even in a small congregation like that of the author. My friend Dr. Hermann Blumenthal informs me that this custom was still observed in his home town, a small village in the neighborhood of Marburg, Germany.

8. I am indebted to my esteemed friend, the late Rabbi Hugo Hahn of New York City, who, as a young man, heard this tune (in Germany) in the houses of mourners, and who confirmed in every detail the statements made by Levi.

9. Idelsohn, "Songs and Singers," see also *Music*, chapter 8.

10. Hellmuth Christian Wolff, "*Orientalische Einfluesse in den Improvisationen des 16. und 17. Jahrhunderts*," *Congress Book of the International Musicological Society* (Kassel, London, and New York, 1960), pp. 308–315.

11. This fine and elucidating distinction was first introduced by Curt Sachs in his *Commonwealth of Art* (New York, 1951).

12. Cf. *HOM*, vol. 7, introduction, p. vi. Aside from Samuel Naumbourg's own reminiscences, Idelsohn relies here mainly on the reports of Emanuel Kirschner, the deserving last cantor of the Munich community.

13. A major part of the Saenger-Naumbourg manuscripts, formerly owned by Emanuel Kirschner, was bequeathed to the library by Dr. A. Kirschner, son of the cantor. It now forms part of the Birnbaum Collection (H.U.C., Cincinnati).

14. Eugene Mayer, "A German-Jewish Miscellany," *Leo Baeck Yearbook* (London, 1958), pp. 208 ff.

15. Ibid., p. 208. Sulzer's personal friendship with Franz Schubert helps to explain that composer's influence on Sulzer's music. More on this in chapter 12.

16. Published by *Vaad le-hafotzas sichos* (Brooklyn, N.Y., 1 August 1969).

17. Jouvin-Gillet, *Marches et chansons des soldats de France* (Paris-Strasbourg, 1919).

18. George Kastner, *Les Chants de l'armée Française* (Paris, 1855), p. 53.

19. Charles Seeger, "Prescriptive and Descriptive Music Writing," *Musical Quarterly* 44 (New York, 1958–1959): 184–195.

20. Idelsohn, "Songs and Singers," p. 399.

21. The "Cantor of Hanover" was Judah Elias, "*Musicus and Vorsaenger*." The first serious report on this lost manuscript, the *Hanover Compendium*, was written by Arno Nadel in English and German, and appeared in the now rare *Musica Hebraica* (Jerusalem, 1938), 1:28–31. The precious manuscript was owned by Nadel, who was killed in Auschwitz. His description was possibly over-enthusiastic, since the music examples quoted are in no way better than those of Ahron Beer, and others of the Birnbaum Collection. The Hebrew colophon of the manuscript has the curious text:

זה הבודק שייך להאלוף והמרומם ראש לכל המשוררים יהודה בן המנוח
אליהו זצ״ל חזן ונאמן דק׳ק הנובר, נכתב לסדר ולפרט וישבתם לבטח בארצכם.

Nadel gives these data: "The collection is dated 1744, and contains 302 neatly written, textless, but titled melodies.... The numerous tunes are mainly settings of *kadeshim*, *hodu's*, *ana's*, *malchutkha's*, etc...."

Chapter 11

1. Arthur Hertzberg, *The Zionist Idea* (New York, 1959), pp. 120, 123. Close to Isaiah Sonne's ideas, actually anticipating them, is Salo Baron's thought-provoking study, "Ghetto and Emancipation" in the *Menorah Journal* (New York, June 1928).
2. After Ismar Elbogen, *A Century of Jewish Life* (Philadelphia, 1944), p. XXVI.
3. Hertzberg (op. cit., p. 22) is inclined to consider the convocation of the Paris Sanhedrin a kind of bombastic farce, and its background a "comic opera setting." He might think differently if he knew what the well-meaning Christians and progressive German liberal-minded intelligentsia wrote about it. They saw it as the prelude to the solution of the Jewish question. See, for example, Johann Peter Hebel, in his popular *Schatzkaestlein* (published in innumerable editions; first ed. Stuttgart-Tuebingen, 1811). See also the correspondence of the Humboldt brothers.
4. About the trick and the deception, see Elbogen, *A Century of Jewish Life* (Philadelphia, 1944), p. XXXI.
5. Baron, "Ghetto and Emancipation," *Menorah Journal* (New York, June 1928): 10.
6. Cf. Elbogen, *A Century of Jewish Life* (Philadelphia, 1944), p. XXXV.
7. See Werner, *Mendelssohn*, pp. 524 ff. See also Hilde Spiel, *Fanny Arnstein* (Berlin, 1962).
8. This problem is masterfully expounded by Selma Tauebler-Stern in her essay "*Der literarische Kampf um die Emanzipation*" in *HUCA* 2 (1950): 171–197.
9. In Nahum N. Glatzer, *The Dynamics of Emancipation* (Boston, 1965), pp. 35–39.
10. Gershom Scholem adduces strong arguments for his thesis that Chorin was a late (and latent) adherent of Sabbateanism, and that the Hamburg champions of radical Reform were also descendants of Sabbatean parents or grandparents. See *Major Trends in Jewish Mysticism* (New York, 1946), pp. 304, 419; notes 36, 38.
11. Elbogen, p. 402.
12. *Festschrift zum 100-jaehringen Bestehen des Israelitischen Tempels in Hamburg* (Hamburg, 1918), pp. 68–70.
13. Idelsohn, *Music*, p. 240.
14. Elbogen, p. 403. Many of the old prayers were recited in German, and the translations left many questions open.
15. There are many jokes and anecdotes, mostly of eastern European provenance, which take pains to ridicule the decorum of the German synagogues, not necessarily of only the liberal ones. All these stories make a virtue out of disorder, and have a strong bias, suggesting sour grapes.
16. The hymn is no. 160 in Eduard Kley's *Israelitisches Gesangbuch*, 1st ed. (Hamburg, 1818).
17. *Oraḥ Ḥayim* 560, no. 3, and *Tur Oraḥ Ḥayim*, ibid. ad locum.
18. Cf. B. *Arakhin* 10b; M. *Tamid* 3:8. Many conjectures were ventured concerning this enigmatic instrument. Two suggestions seem to come near the truth: the *magrepha* was a primitive steam-siren of small dimensions; or else it was a noise-instrument to terrorize enemies, human or superhuman, or even to scare the worshipers in the Temple (see Joseph Yasser, "The *Magrepha* of the Herodian Temple," *Journal of the American Musicological Association* 13 [New York, 1960]: 24–42).
19. Cf. S. Jona, "Abraham J. S. Graziani," *REJ* 4 (1881): 115. For the extensive halakhic elucidation of the text I am indebted to my friend Dr. Philip Birnbaum, who has frequently and willingly loaned me a helping hand in similar instances.
20. Chorin retracted many of his views publicly but remained a confirmed Reformist at the bottom of his heart. A detailed account of Chorin's attitude may be found in Jakob

Petuchowski's *Prayerbook Reform in Europe* (New York, 1968), pp. 93 ff. Eliezer Libermann, however, was a more questionable character; according to Graetz, he was later converted to Catholicism. See, however, Petuchowski, op. cit., pp. 86 ff.

21. Moses Sofer, in *Eleh dibrey ha-berit* (Altona, 1819), pp. 58–60. Aside from the halakhic aspects, which lie outside our scope, the weakness of R. Sofer's arguments lies in his inability to understand that music can express sorrow, just as well as joy. For him music was a merrymaker, and nothing else. Yet this well-read scholar was a contemporary (1768–1839) of Beethoven and other world-famous composers. This in itself indicates the total intellectual and spiritual isolation in which he and most Jews still lived.

22. David Deutsch, *Die Orgel in der Synagogue* (Sohrau, 1863), p. 42 (quoted after Abraham Berliner, *Zur Lehr und Wehr* [Berlin, 1904], p. 53).

23. Berliner, op. cit., p. 38. Actually there were two small organs built for the professional chorus. In checking the original correspondence of Meyerbeer, I found that he had been misrepresented, for he referred not to the Dome, but to his father's synagogue. Mendelssohn has been similarly misrepresented. See Ludwig August Frankl, "*Die Orgel in der Synagoge*," *Der Juedische Cantor* (Bromberg, 1870), no. 26.

24. Werner, *Mendelssohn*, p. 392 f.

25. Egon Wellesz, in his definitive work, *A History of Byzantine Music*, 2d ed. (Oxford, 1961), pp. 105 ff. Also, see Willy Apel and Friedrich W. Riedel "*Orgelmusik*," *MGG*.

26. The Orthodox Calvinist churches had originally rejected the organ and all instrumental music.

27. Max Grunwald, "*Der Kampf um die Orgel*," *Oesterreichische Wochenschrift*, 14 March 1919, p. 164; 21 March 1919, p. 175. The same author seems to confuse J. Weber, author of the witty *Democritus*, with Carl Maria von Weber, the composer. To cap all the anachronisms in Grunwald's writings we find the following outrageous nonsense: "As A. B. Marx said about G. Mahler's performance of a Beethoven quartet by the entire string section: 'an outpouring of the heart—in military fashion, by whole regiments.'" A. B. Marx, contemporary and fellow renegade of Heine, died in 1866 when Mahler was exactly six years old!

28. Salomon Sulzer, *Denkschrift*, p. 11.

29. Werner, *Mendelssohn*, p. 216–217. The entire correspondence from the Hamburg side is found in the "Green Books," vols. 15 and 16 (Bodleian Library, Oxford). In *Music* (p. 247), Idelsohn erroneously states that Mendelssohn later declined to write the psalm.

30. When the question arose, I was able to dissuade the late Nelson Glueck, former president of the Hebrew Union College, from installing an organ at the College synagogue, which is attached to its School of Biblical Archaeology in Jerusalem. For in Israel, the organ is *the* instrument of Lutheran and other Western churches.

31. The expression "anthem" is a corruption of the Latin *antiphona*, which requires the quotation of a psalm-verse and "Anthymn."

32. The Birnbaum collection contains about two dozen handwritten hymnbooks of German synagogues, all in "mint" condition 140 to 150 years after they were written, a sure sign that they were rarely put to use.

33. Idelsohn praises him far more than was merited by his accomplishments (*Music*, p. 229). His compositions in the Birnbaum collection are mostly poor attempts at harmonizing traditional tunes.

34. It was not only the French Consistoire who discouraged the Polish or Russian Jews, the French government acted likewise, mainly for political reasons, especially after the 1830 revolution and the revolts of the same year in Poland. The first years of Chopin in Paris tell that tale.

35. A number of these arrangements are preserved in the Birnbaum collection. Idelsohn published some of them in *HOM*, vol. 6.
36. Idelsohn, *Music*, p. 262.
37. This discussion is based in part on Morton Rosenthal, "History and Stylistic Development of Synagogue Music in France," rabbinical thesis, Jewish Institute of Religion (New York, 1960).
38. Elbogen, *A Century of Jewish Life* (Philadelphia, 1944), p. 97.
39. Heine wrote about this era: "Everything is as quiet as a winter night after a new fall of snow, but in the silence you hear continually, dripping, dripping, the profits of the capitalists, as they steadily increase. You can actually hear them piling up, the riches of the rich. Sometimes there is the smothered sob of poverty, and often, too, a scraping sound, like that of a knife being sharpened."
40. The official text is in *Archives Israélites* 17 (Paris, 1855–1856), pp. 308–310.
41. According to Idelsohn (*Music*, p. 512, n. 14), Naumbourg arranged a song of Meyerbeer, "*Kindergebet*," for the synagogue, to accompany the text of *u-benuḥo yomar* for the Sabbath. His later statement that Meyerbeer had written no music for the synagogue has been refuted by the identification of a packet of his autographs deposited in the Berlin State Library, which contained some liturgical compositions. This collection of manuscripts—required to remain closed until 1935, then inaccessible in the Hitler era—had disappeared completely by the end of World War II.
42. The original editions of de' Rossi's music consisted only of part books. Since all these parts were dispersed all over Europe, Naumbourg did not succeed in finding all of them, at least not all of the Hebrew compositions. Three are lacking in his edition: Psalm 111 for eight voices; Psalm 121 for five voices; and Leviticus 23:4 for three voices. These pieces were edited by this writer in a critical edition and published by the Sacred Music Press (New York, 1953).
43. Joseph L. Saalschuetz, *Geschichte und Wuerdigung der Musik bei den Hebraeern* (Berlin, 1829).
44. Samuel Naumbourg, *Recueil* (Paris, 1874), pp. XVII ff.
45. Ibid., p. XXXIII.
46. Ibid., p. XXXVI.
47. Ibid., p. XXXVII.
48. Ibid.
49. Ibid., p. XXXIX.
50. Ibid., p. XL.

Chapter 12

1. Elbogen, *A Century of Jewish Life* (Philadelphia, 1944), p. 169.
2. Gerson Wolf, *Geschichte der Israelitischen Cultus-Gemeinde Wien* (Vienna, 1861), p. 83.
3. Siegmund (?) Husserl, *Gruendungsgeschichte, des Wiener Stadt-Tempels* (Vienna, 1906), p. 83.
4. Ibid., p. 92.
5. Biedermann was born Michael ben Eleazer in Pressburg in 1769, the son of a peddler. He became an engraver whose work was praised by the Vienna court, and in 1792 he became a "tolerated" Jew of Vienna. After 1810 he served as a kind of "representative" of the Jewish community vis-à-vis the court.
6. Fortunately this was not permitted.

7. Many of these patricians have pompous tombs in the Waehring or in the Central Cemetery of Vienna. Since the present Jewish community of Vienna is not able to finance the maintenance of these graves, most of them are a shambles. The non-Jewish descendants of the former Jewish notables refuse to bear the cost of maintenance.
8. Husserl, op. cit., p. 132.
9. Wolf, op. cit., p. 82.
10. Ibid., p. 27.
11. Ibid. Sulzer changed this, as described later in this chapter.
12. Mannheimer insisted upon this rule, being a confirmed democrat. Yet upon the demand of the "tolerated," the following paragraph was added: "The tolerated have priority in renting their pews before the officials of the *Gemeinde*." The government, of course, protected the "tolerated" Jews.
13. Wolf, op. cit., pp. 37–39.
14. Rabbi Isaac M. Wise's celebrated prayer book *Minhag America* was fashioned after the Mannheimer model, and Wise expected it to be acceptable to all Jewish groups of America. But the clique around Rabbi David Einhorn resisted this valiant and farsighted effort, thus transplanting the political split between northern Germany and Austria to American Jewry and creating a permanent schism.
15. Mannheimer knew the volatile tempers and opinions of his fellow Jews too well not to ensure some stability for the statutes just agreed upon: "According to a biblical model (Nehemiah 10) he called together all deputies, representatives, chairmen and members of the community (on 20 April 1829) in the Temple. There the statutes were read to them by the actuary," and they had to sign them, man for man. Mannheimer himself was fully aware of the novelty of the measure, and referred in his diary to the biblical pattern. See Moses Rosenmann, *Isak Noa Mannheimer* (Vienna, 1922), pp. 66 ff.
16. Ibid., pp. 66, 67, 68, notes.
17. Once there were many legends and anecdotes current about the first years of Sulzer in Vienna. I made a special trip to Vienna in 1970 to examine the correspondence of the community with Sulzer, which, according to the historians, reposes in the archives of the *Kultus-Gemeinde* of Vienna. The trip was undertaken in vain, however, for the entire corpus of the archives of the Vienna Jewish community had been "loaned" to the National Archives in Jerusalem, and not even copies of the documents existed. Any explanation of the purpose of this removal of official documents was categorically refused to me by Mr. Wilhelm Krell, then executive director of the community's office. Its president, Dr. Anton Pick, likewise refused to disclose the purpose of the transaction as well as the expected date of return of the documents. As far as Jerusalem is concerned, it should be mentioned that Dr. Daniel Cohen, director of the Israel Archives, Jerusalem, promised to inform me about the Vienna documents, but has failed to do so, in spite of my repeated requests. Neither did he respond to the Leo Baeck Institute in New York, which also asked Dr. Cohen for certain information.
18. This can be concluded from a careful reading of Mannheimer's sermons. He often cited classic German poetry without mentioning his sources, and he could apparently count upon his audience's full recognition and comprehension.
19. Joseph Drechsler, born in 1782 in German Bohemia, died in 1852 in Vienna. He studied theology, then law, then composition. He was music director at St. Stephan's Cathedral and Kapellmeister for the Leopoldstaedter Theater, as well as a friend of the playwright Ferdinand Raimund.
20. Leviticus 25:13. This was, appropriately enough, the motto of Sulzer's *Denkschrift* at the fiftieth anniversary of his Viennese cantorate.

21. See *Denkschrift*, p. 8. Joseph Fischhof was perhaps Sulzer's most intimate musical friend. He was an excellent pianist, pedagogue, a collector of manuscripts by Bach and Beethoven, and an enthusiastic democrat, as well as a faithful Jew. His strong personality overcame most of the hindrances in the career of a Jewish artist before 1848. Eventually he became professor at the Vienna Conservatory, and he died in 1853. The second volume of Sulzer's *Schir Zion* is dedicated to his memory.

22. Sulzer was not thinking of the *Kulturverein* of Zunz, or similar organizations, but of the synagogue in the house of Jacob Herz Beer and similar radical experiments.

23. *Denkschrift*, pp. 9 ff. Sulzer demanded official recognition of the *priestly* dignity of the cantorial office, which had never been granted anywhere. The great pride that came close to that of a king, or a prophet, as a person elevated by "the grace of God" permeates all Sulzer's writings. This attitude, born out of the respect for his office, is sometimes misunderstood for excessive vanity.

24. See James Heller, *Isaac M. Wise* (New York, 1965). About the Pittsburg Platform, pp. 458–467; about the relations of Mannheimer and Sulzer with Wise, pp. 75, 158–159; on the prayer book *Minhag America*, pp. 302 ff.; about the German doctrinaires, Einhorn et al., pp. 297 ff. On page 298 Wise's supreme goal is quoted: "We must have union, at any risk and at any sacrifice, principles excepted." Alas! He did not attain this goal for many complex reasons, some that affect American Jewry to this day.

24a. It is with great pride that the author announces the publication of Sulzer's works in a critical edition in the August 1976 *Denkmäler der Tonkunst in Österreich*.

25. Idelsohn is mistaken in his claim that Sulzer did not give full credit to the Gentile composers who contributed to his *Schir Zion*. Not only are they carefully listed on the last page of volume 1, but they are mentioned in his preface to volume 2, and in his *Denkschrift*.

26. Some criticisms of Sulzer's style are justified indeed; as he sometimes sinned against the spirit of Jewish liturgy, so did Haydn, Mozart, Beethoven (to name only the greatest) sin against that of the Mass. Yet, while their critics maintain a respectful tone, every scribbler feels entitled to castigate Sulzer, even after hearing some of the most outrageous *ḥazanut* by "virtuoso cantors."

27. Alfred Sendrey, one of the above-mentioned critics, points to the resemblance of Sulzer's "*ha-yom te'amtzenu*" to a popular hit song of the nineteenth century, "*Auf der gruenen Wiese.*" Actually, the Hebrew composition was written not by Sulzer but by Franz J. Volkert, a Gentile contributor. Moreover, the theme to which Sendrey alludes is a popular motif of the eighteenth century, well known through G. Sarti's use of it, as quoted in Mozart's *Don Giovanni* (finale of act 2).

28. Jakob Schoenberg, "*Alte Elemente in Sulzer's 'Schir Zion,'*" *Gemeinde-Blatt Nuernberg* (Nuremberg, Hanukkah, 1925), and Arno Nadel, "*Sulzer und die ostjuedische Tradition,*" *Bnai-Brith Blaetter* (Vienna, 1924).

29. The incipit of *Hodo al eretz* resembles the slow movement of Beethoven's Archduke Trio, Opus 97, a theme that also inspired Cesar Franck's "*Panis Angelicus.*" In its primitive form the theme belongs to the category of "wandering tunes," and can be found in Haydn's Symphony No. 82 (last movement), in Handel, and in a number of student songs.

30. Franz Liszt, "*Les Israelites,*" *Des Bohemiens et leur musique en Hongrie* (Paris, 1859), pp. 46 ff.

31. Sulzer, quite naturally, was fully aware of the impression that he made on his contemporaries. But he was convinced that "it has pleased Divine Providence to bestow upon just me those gifts that made a regeneration . . . possible" (*Denkschrift*, p. 4).

32. These words referred to Gustav Mahler. Søren Kierkegaard, *Entweder-Oder*, trans.

Charles Schrempf (Wiesbaden, 1955). Though Sulzer and Mahler were extremely distant from one another in their lives, temperaments, intentions, and convictions, there is a decided affinity between the two musical prototypes of Austrian Jewry in artistic purity, epitomized by Arnold Schoenberg.

33. Idelsohn, *Music*, p. 253.

34. I have been informed by the Vienna municipality that most of the *Acts* of the Imperial Tribunal dealing with the captured revolutionaries were burned in 1849 and on other occasions, such as the burning of the Palace of Justice in 1927.

35. In W. D. Dunder's *Denkschrift ueber die Wiener Oktober Revolution* (Vienna, 1849), where a list of the sentenced revolutionaries is found (pp. 903–908), the name of Sulzer is missing. Perhaps there is some truth to the legend that a member of the Imperial family (possibly the mother of the Emperor) had a weakness for the imposing singer and saved him.

36. Some of the documents related to the friendship of Schubert and Sulzer are found in Alfred Einstein, *Franz Schubert* (New York, 1951). I made some of the letters available to the author. Others are still in my possession.

37. For his kindness in drawing my attention to these letters, and for making them available to me, I am deeply indebted to Professor Dr. Friedrich Racek, chief librarian of the Vienna City Library. His faithful help has compensated me for the uncooperative attitude of the Vienna *Kultus-Gemeinde*.

38. Eduard Hanslick, "Salomon Sulzer," *Die Neue Freie Presse*, no. 551 (Vienna, 1866).

39. It was his loyalty to his beloved Mannheimer that involved Sulzer in a serious disagreement with the succeeding rabbi, Adolf Jellinek. He got into a hot dispute with the younger rabbi (in the hall of the temple), because he felt that the memory of Mannheimer's close collaboration with him was being slighted, perhaps not without intention. At any rate, he was suspended from office (in 1865) for three months. The storm that broke out in the inner circles was carefully hushed up, and after a few weeks, Sulzer was quietly reinstituted in his office. See *AZJ*, 3 and 10 October 1865, pp. 620, 635.

40. The Hebrew text of the epitaph reads as follows:

ציון קבורת נעים זמירות ישראל משורר שלמה בן יוסף זולצער הלוי ש'צ
לכבוד ולתפארת עדת ווינא. משנת......אז ישיר שיר ציון במקהלות ראש
למנצחים בנגינות. שירותיו ישוררו בכל קהילות. יצא להאיר....וקולותיו
יחדלון כ'ה' טבת ת'ר'ן זכרונו לברכה לעד.

Trans.: "Zion buried the sweet singer of Israel, the chief cantor Salomon ben Joseph Sulzer, the Levite, the messenger of our prayers, who sang to the honor and glory of the community of Vienna from the year 1826. . . . There he sang the Song of Zion, in lofty choirs, he, the chief of all the conductors of music. [The German text here has *Meistersaenger*.] His songs will be sung in Israel's communities; wherever he went, he brought light . . . his voice faded on the twenty-fifth of Tebet . . . may his memory be a blessing forever."

This epitaph was probably written by the same Jellinek with whom Sulzer had clashed in the past. In his eulogy Jellinek used similar expressions of loving admiration: "*Dein liederreicher Mund ist nun verstummt*. . ." (Thy mouth, so rich with song, has now been silenced).

41. Pinhas Minkowski, "*Der Sulzerismus und die moderne synagogale Liturgie*," *Oesterr.-Ungarische Kantorenzeitung* 25 (Vienna, 17 February-6 October 1905).

42. Idelsohn, *Music*, p. 254 f. Idelsohn's observations about Sulzer have a peculiar quality.

Almost every criticism is immediately qualified, while every word of praise is soon toned down. One reaches the conclusion that Idelsohn's attitude to Sulzer was deeply ambivalent; emotionally he disliked him, while intellectually and musically he respected him as "a genius."

43. Ibid., p. 258.

44. Ibid., pp. 180–181. Idelsohn, the author of the epoch-making study *Makamen*, was not aware of the fundamental incompatibility of a scalar-modal melodic line with a harmonic foundation, that is, contrived out of a "scale-model" and its harmonic functions. He sought to construct such "modal harmonies," not realizing that in doing so he forced his melodies into a procrustean bed much more restricting than the Western harmonies that Sulzer used. Nonetheless, Idelsohn conceded: "Sulzer's harmony expresses depth and exaltation. In it he voices his Jewishness only through his inclination toward interrupted cadences..." (p. 481).

45. Abraham W. Binder, *Studies in Jewish Music*, ed. Irene Heskes (New York, 1971), p. 287. His other critical remarks are no more correct.

46. This syndrome of naïveté and cockiness in argumentative dialectics is characteristic also of some Israeli writers on the history of music.

47. The story of the Balhabeissel is told here after Idelsohn, *Music*, pp. 300 ff. The report of Birnbaum is given in his biography of Sulzer in the *Israelitische Wochenschrift* (Vienna, 1904); the article by Isaak Lachmann quoted from *Der Juedische Cantor* (Bromberg, 1892), pp. 75 ff., and some reminiscences by N. H. Steinschneider in *Talpiyot* (Berditchev, 1895).

48. The musical example by the Balhabeissel, as given by Idelsohn in his *Manual of Musical Illustrations* (Cincinnati, 1926), is far from impressive. It could be characterized as dull, childish, and monotonous.

49. Some of my friends from eastern Europe, among them notable cantors, have confirmed to me this peculiar "love-hate" toward Sulzer. I mention here only the late lamented Arno Nadel and Leb Glantz, and my friend Cantor Israel Alter.

Chapter 13

1. Cf. Arthur Hertzberg, *The Zionist Idea* (New York, 1959), pp. 154 ff.

2. John Braham, the son of the hazan Abraham Singer, was, in his time (1777–1856), a most renowned opera and concert singer. He was adopted by Meir Leoni, composer of the *Yigdal* named for him. He appeared as both hazan and theatrical singer from his youth. For a number of years he was closely allied with the Storaces, brother and sister, both excellent musicians. Nancy Storace, beloved of Mozart and the superb first Susanna in *Figaro*, sang together with Braham before the Empress Josephine. What a constellation of personalities! From modest Leoni, to Storace, to Lord Byron, to Josephine Bonaparte! Later Braham composed some operettas and made a fortune, which he later lost by ruinous enterprises. This man deserves a detailed biography. He was the first great hazan to move back and forth between the synagogue and the theater, hovering between riches and poverty. See the article on Braham in *MGG* (Suppl.) and *Grove's Dictionary of Music*, 3rd ed. (New York, 1946).

3. Francis Lyon Cohen, "Isaac Nathan" in *JE*, vol. 9. It is true that the arrangement of the traditional tunes in the Byron songs leaves a good deal to be desired in craftsmanship, especially in the rather childishly set basses. But the style of English "domestic chamber music" was of exactly the same caliber and compositorial skill.

4. Eduard Birnbaum, "*Ueber Lord Byron's Hebraeische Gesaenge,*" in *Der Juedische Cantor* (Bromberg, 1886), pp. 46 ff.
5. Some highly interesting observations on the Byron-Nathan collaboration are found in Israel Abrahams, *Bypaths in Hebraic Bookland* (Philadelphia, 1943), pp. 207–218.
6. Martin Blumner, *Geschichte der Singakademie zu Berlin* (Berlin, 1891), pp. 14, 16. In the appendix a rather incomplete list of the supporting families is added. More about this in Werner, *Mendelssohn*, pp. 99 ff., 227 f.
7. This limits the time of the arrangement to about 1795–1830, for after that no Jewish family was admitted to the Singakademie.
8. In northern Germany the custom was to sing *Ha-nerot halalu* in place of Psalm 30.
9. David Friedländer, one of the older *maskilim*, and a disciple of Moses Mendelssohn, usually scoffed, and not without reason, at the *minhag ashkenaz* as performed and mutilated by these two hazanim.
10. A. Freimann, "Berlin," in *JE*, vol. 3, p. 75.
11. The following narrative is based on two articles by Lewandowski, "Hirsch Weintraub" in *Der Juedische Cantor* (Bromberg, 1882), p. 18, and "Two Cantors of Old-Berlin" in the same journal (1886); also Aaron Friedmann, "*Lebensbilder beruehmter Kantoren*" in *Der Synagogale Gesang* (Berlin, 1904), 1:84 ff.; and Idelsohn, *Music*, pp. 270 ff.
12. Werner, *Mendelssohn*, pp. 100, 193, 227 f.
13. Of the first volume of *Schir Zion* more than two dozen copies, nicely calligraphed, could be purchased in Vienna; some of them were used as early as 1832 in Copenhagen, Brunswick, and other places. Some of these are now in the Birnbaum collection.
14. This was the same Abraham Jacob Lichtenstein from whom Max Bruch heard the *Kol Nidre*, discussed in chapter 3 above, and later in this chapter. Part of a letter from Bruch about the *Kol Nidre* is quoted in Idelsohn, *Music* (p. 513).
15. I heard this story, which I could not verify elsewhere, when I was studying at the Berlin Hochschule fuer Musik, from Professor Ismar Elbogen, who, in turn, had heard it from Hermann Cohen, the son-in-law of Lewandowski.
16. Idelsohn erroneously attributed Lewandowski's "creative period" to his association with the organ synagogue in 1864. In fact, Lewandowski was an adversary of the organ in the synagogue. See Abraham Berliner, *Zur Lehr und Wehr* (Berlin, 1904), p. 10. Idelsohn contradicted himself in stating (*Music*, p. 282) that Lewandowski "gave to the organ a specific role." On page 283 he blandly remarked, "Lewandowski ... composed ... without putting into the organ any artistic part of the composition ... the organ was simply a support to the voices of the choir."
17. Idelsohn, *Music*, p. 276.
18. Weintraub, *Ha-Maggid* (Lyck, 1875–1876), pp. 121 ff.
19. This is quoted in part from Dr. N. Entin's unpublished essay on the influence of the *Haskalah* on synagogue music. (Manuscript in the possession of the Library of the Hebrew Union College-Jewish Institute of Religion, New York.)
20. Idelsohn, *Music*, p. 306.
21. Pinhas Minkowski, *Die Geschichte fun Chasonus* (New York, 1923–1924), p. 87 (Yiddish).
22. The legal proceedings connected with the probation of Sulzer's will vanished mysteriously in 1902 or 1903. (*Verlassenschafts-Zahl* D 202/1890, *Bezirks-Gericht Innere Stadt*, is missing.) Birnbaum, Sulzer's favorite disciple and executor of his will, seems to have had an inkling of the motives behind this disappearance. I am indebted to the Municipal Library of Vienna for this and other information concerning Sulzer.

23. There is no full biography or complete bibliography of this important scholar. In the *Birnbaum Memorial Volume*, ed. Aaron Friedmann (Berlin, 1922), there is a biographical sketch, and a tentative bibliography can be found in an extensive essay by this writer on the Birnbaum collection (*HUCA* 18, 1944).

24. In spite of all my efforts, I was not able to persuade any foundation or institute for the preservation of Jewish culture to publish this precious document. While worthless patchwork on Jewish music compiled by copyists is printed, this complete catalogue lies untouched and unstudied, buried as in a genizah.

25. Idelsohn (*Music*, p. 284) shows little sympathy for Japhet in his correct observation: "We may even come to the conclusion that his [Japhet's] style was similar to that of the ultra-Reform of Germany." The only difference was that the Reform copied the Protestant chorale, while Japhet was content with the style of Frankfort's sentimental *Rhein-Lieder* in the style of Abt or Silcher, of which his synagogue compositions are faithful copies.

26. J. Heller, *Isaac M. Wise* (New York, 1965), pp. 134, 165. The prohibition against women's singing in the company of men goes back to the talmudic dictum *kol be-ishah ervah*, the voice of woman is a *pudendum*. This ancient conception of the female voice as an instrument of seduction was incompatible with the ideas of American reform. See Wise, *Reminiscences*, p. 53. Rabbi Wise's reaction was natural. He was fully aware of the position of the synagogue's music between artistic chant and stylized folkloristic tradition. For enlightening me on this matter, I am deeply indebted to my late beloved friend Rabbi James G. Heller, who, in his masterful biography of Rabbi Wise, has offered the most authentic history of the early Reform movement in America.

26a. One example—a badge of shame and thoughtlessness—of the so-called tradition of the Reform movement may suffice: the mass singing of "*Ein kelohenu*," a German soldiers' march. No rabbi, no scholar, has been able to overcome this testimony of American-Jewish indifference and lack of taste. But if Reform sins in this way, the Conservative and Orthodox movements sin another: they have eliminated from their rituals the noble style of Sulzer, based on Beethoven and Schubert, and of Gerovitch, based on authentic folklore and on Mussorgsky, in favor of theatrical trash such as "Fiddler on the Roof" and *niggunim* culled from Israeli nightclubs.

27. As recently as 1952, a Yiddish writer, Israel Rabinovitch, had nothing but praise for the virtuoso hazanim who destroyed our basic tradition, at the same time as he expressed his contempt for serious students in unmistakable terms. See I. Rabinovitch, *Of Jewish Music* (Montreal, 1951–1952). Indeed, the most recent scholarly publication on Jewish music, the serious and thorough essay in the new *Encyclopaedia Judaica*, written by its music oracle, Hanoch Avenary, fails to distinguish, in false impartiality, between good and bad music. Although the author admits that these hazanim often violate halakhic principles, that in their style "there is no rule of adhering to one plan or another," and presumes that this disorder "is exactly as the ancient *nusah* demands," he carefully refrains, in the name of objectivity, from comprehending this barbarism that sails under the flag of Jewish piety, the lapse of values as a typical form of cultural regression, parallel to the "New Ghetto," justifying Theodor Herzl's fears. Still worse, Dr. Avenary frequently "adorns himself with other scholar's plumes."

28. It is a corollary of this situation that modern musical services of the synagogue, written by Israeli composers, cannot be performed in an Israeli synagogue, because of the prohibitions of an intransigent and tyrannical rabbinate. Some of Israel's music critics are followers of the anti-musical rabbis, among them Mr. Y. Boehm of the *Jerusalem Post*.

29. All three compositions were written in America. The Bloch and Milhaud works were commissioned by Temple Emanu-El in San Francisco. The *Kol Nidre* by Schoenberg is a votive composition celebrating his return to Judaism, and was written for R. Jacob Sonderling in Los Angeles. See Werner, "Schoenberg's *Kol Nidre*," *Musical Quarterly* 44 (New York, 1958): 242 ff.

30. Idelsohn, *Music*, pp. 452 ff.

31. *Die Gartenlaube* (Leipzig, 1872).

32. See Werner, *Mendelssohn*, p. 471 f.

33. Theodore Adorno, *Mahler* (Frankfort, 1960). This is the most penetrating synopsis of the master and his work.

34. Heinrich Berl, *Das Judentum in der Musik* (Stuttgart, 1926). Arno Nadel's reply appears in *Der Jude* (Berlin, 1926–1927).

Epilogue

1. Bruno Snell, *Dichtung und Gesellschaft* (Hamburg, 1965), p. 127.

Glossary of Foreign Terms

Ab (Hebr.-Aram.). The eleventh month of the Jewish year, except in leap year when it is the twelfth. The ninth day of Ab [*Tisha b'Ab*] is the anniversary of the destruction of the Temple.

Abgesang (Germ. "closing song"). Old designation of a constituent part of the medieval *Bar* form, which consists of two *Stollen* and the *Abgesang* (A-A-B, where B stands for *Abgesang*).

abodah (Hebr. "service"). Generally, a divine worship or liturgy; in particular, the recitation of the service of the Temple on the day of Yom Kippur, as described in its *musaf* service.

abodah zarah (Hebr. "strange worship"). The classical term for any form of idolatry or paganism.

abot (Hebr. "fathers"). The first benediction of the *Amidah*, recalling the patriarchs and God's recognition of their merits.

Adonaí malakh (Hebr. "the Lord has ruled"). The opening words of Psalm 93, also the name of the musical mode to which it is chanted traditionally.

Ahabah Rabah (Hebr. "Great Love"). The opening words of a benediction preceding the *Shema*; also the name of the musical mode to which it is chanted.

Akedah (Hebr. "the binding"). The sacrifice of Isaac; thereafter the many prayers alluding to it.

Amidah (Hebr. "stand"). The prayer of eighteen [nineteen] benedictions, which is recited while standing.

Anshadíya (Arab. "metrical or dancing song"). The medieval Arabic term for certain secular songs of popular character.

atnah (Aram. "rest, pause"). The second strongest disjunctive accent of the Masoretic punctuation, comparable to a semicolon or caesura.

Ba'al keriah (Hebr. "master of reading"). The lector of Scripture, an office often filled by the hazan, or by a learned layman of the congregation.

Bá'al Tefillah (Hebr. "master of the prayer"). The designation of the elected (not appointed) honorary precentor.

badḥan (Hebr. "joker"). A merrymaker or clown at joyful gatherings, especially weddings; comparable to the medieval *joculator* and the so-called social director in Jewish-American resorts.

bakashah (Hebr. "petition"). A type of penitential prayer, closely related to *seliḥah*.

Barekhú (Hebr. "praise ye!"). The opening word of the call to worship, with which all important services start.

berakháh (Hebr. "benediction"). The general expression of praise, blessing, or salutation. (Pl., *Berakhot*, frequently refers to a tractate of the Babylonian Talmud, and abbreviated as B. *Ber.*)

birkhát ha-mazón (Hebr. "benediction of food"). The grace after meals.

cénto (Lat., Ital.). A "farcing" of individual scriptural verses from different books and chapters of the Bible.

debaráh (Hebr. perhaps "verbalization"). A *piyut* recited before or after the scriptural lesson, based on the pericope of the day.

din (Hebr. "law, verdict"). A law or ordinance without reference to its provenance or date.

dráydel (Yidd. "top"). A child's toy used on Hanukkah to symbolize the whims of fortune.

dúdáim (Hebr. "mandragora"). The Biblical name of the mandrake root, supposed to be strongly aphrodisiac.

dukhań (Hebr. "priestly privilege of blessing the congregation"). In particular, the practice of blessing by the *kohanim* (descendants of the Aaronide dynasty).

eikháh (Hebr. "how!"). The first word of the book of Lamentations, which serves as the Hebrew title for the book. The Lamentations are recited on the Ninth of Ab.

enyana (Syr. "response"). A type of Aramaean literature and chant, essentially a response between a precentor and the congregation.

Galút (Hebr. "dispersion"). The term for Israel's exile.

Gaoń (Hebr. "leader," corresp. with Lat. *princeps*). Title of a person of central rabbinic authority with strong legal powers; later, an honorary title like "excellency."

Gássenhaúer (Germ.). The old designation of a vulgar street song.

geburót (Hebr. "powers, great actions"). The second benediction of the *Amidah*, which ascribes all powers to God.

Gemará (Hebr.-Aram. "completion"). The sum total of talmudic discussions on the text and contents of the Mishnah and related matters.

Gemátria (corruption of Gr. *Geometria*). The practice of expressing every Hebrew word or name in terms of its numerical value, obtained by adding up the numerical values of their constituent letters. G plays a major role in the cabalistic interpretation of Scripture.

genizáh (Hebr. "hiding place"). Burial chamber of old and torn Hebrew manuscripts that could not be destroyed because they contained the divine name. The most famous genizah was discovered by professors Taylor and Schechter in old Cairo at the turn of the century.

géshem (Hebr. "rain"). The prayer for rain that is recited in solemn manner on the eighth day of Sukkoth, when the normal rain begins in the Near East.

gust (Yiddish, loan word from Ital. *gusto*). A musical formula of intonation, perhaps comparable to a recurrent melodic pattern.

habdaláh (Hebr. "separation, distinction"). The highly symbolic ceremony at the end of the Sabbath or a feast, to distinguish it from the ordinary weekday.

Haggadáh (Hebr. "narration, tale"). The generic term for any non-legalistic text of rabbinic literature. In particular it refers to the ritual narration of the Exodus rendered at the domestic celebration on the eve of Passover [Hebr. *seder*].

hakafót (Hebr. "circuits"). The ritual march of the worshipers carrying the scrolls of the Torah around the altar on the festival of Simhath Torah.

halakháh (Hebr. "course, way of going"). The collective term for all post-biblical laws and legal opinions and discussions pertaining to them.

hallél (Hebr. "praise"). The collective name of Psalms 113 through 118, which are chanted on many festive occasions throughout the year.

haskaláh (from Hebr. *sekhel*, "reason"). The period of Jewish enlightenment beginning with Moses Mendelssohn and reaching, especially in eastern Europe, to the end of

the nineteenth century. It may be considered the beginning of the "modern age" for European Jewry.

Hatikváh (Hebr. "hope"). The Zionist anthem with text by N. Imber. Since the establishment of the state of Israel, it has become the national anthem.

hoda'ah (Hebr. "recognition, thanks"). The general term for all thanksgiving prayers.

Hoshanáh Rabah (Hebr. "Great Hoshana"). The name of the sixth day of Sukkoth, on which many of the *Hoshanot* are chanted.

Hoshánot (Hebr. pl. of *hoshana*, "save now"). The collective term for those prayers of the Sukkoth festival that close with the refrain *hoshana* (save now).

ḥakham (Hebr. "wise"). Title of rabbinic authority.

Ḥanukkah (Hebr. "dedication"). The feast of the rededication of the Temple, after the Maccabean victory at the end of the third century B.C.E.

Ḥasidism (from Hebr. *hasid*, "pious"). A designation of Jewish sects, which occurred at least three times in history, each time with a different meaning: (1) during the second commonwealth; (2) in the Rhineland during the High Middle Ages; (3) in eastern Europe, after the seventeenth and during the eighteenth century. This latest movement is still alive and active. Originally it was conceived as a revolt against rabbinic legalism.

ḥatimáh (Hebr. "seal"). The formal end of a prayer or its closing *berakhah*, which seals it.

ḥazan (Hebr.-Aram.). The appointed and paid precentor of the synagogue. Originally an elevated sexton, the hazan achieved the office of precentor or cantor during the seventh and eighth centuries, when he appeared as poet, singer, and arranger of *piyutim* (see *piyut*).

Ḥazanut. A type of vocal improvisation practiced by hazanim. Its frequently highly ornamented style, tonality, and motif structure vary regionally.

Júdenregál (Germ. "imperial jurisdiction over the Jews"). A most important legal instrument that, in theory, regulated the legal status of German Jews vis-à-vis the emperor and his electors.

Kabbalat Shabbat (Hebr. "Welcome of the Sabbath"). The first part of the Friday eve liturgy, consisting of psalms and *piyutim*.

Kaddish (Aram. "sanctifying"). A very old prayer, dating back to early Christian times, perhaps antedating Christianity. It may best be described as the Great Doxology of Judaism. The liturgy contains five types, of which the best known are the mourner's *Kaddish*, recited during the year of mourning and the half-*Kaddish*, which serves as an emphatic conclusion to each major section of the liturgy. None of these texts contains any reference to death.

Kavód (Hebr. "weight, honor, glory"). A term that has both a secular and theological significance. In its theological use, the *Kevod Adonai* may be paraphrased as "glory of the Lord," comparable to the Greek *doxa*.

kavvanah (Hebr. "direction, orientation"). The general term for intensity and concentration in prayer.

Kedushah (Hebr. "sanctification"). The expanded preamble to the third benediction of the *Amidah*. It is based upon a poetic juxtaposition of Is. 6:3 and Ez. 20:25, to which an alleluiatic verse is usually added. The *Sanctus* or *Ter-Sanctus* of the Christian mass is a shorter version of the *Kedushah*. There are still five variants of the text of the *Kedushah* in liturgical use.

kiddush (Hebr. "consecration"). The ritual blessing of wine.

kináh (Hebr. "dirge"). The generic name for all laments and dirges. They play a large part in ritual, literature, and music of the Near East from oldest times.

laḥan (Arab.-Hebr. "type of melody"). The medieval designation of a melody type, not quite a mode, more typical than an individual melody. It comes nearest to a melody pattern.

lais (Old French). Probably, like *Leis*, an abbreviation of *Kyrie Eleison* of the Catholic mass. Later, a poetic form used by the troubadours and *trouvères*.

Leich (Middle-High Germ.). A poetic form that was popular in minnesong.

letzim (Hebr. "mockers, clowns, vagrant musicians"). A contemptuous designation of the Jewish vagrant musicians.

luláb (Hebr.). The festive bouquet that is ritually used during the Sukkoth festival, consisting of palm branches, myrtle, willow, and citrus fruit [*ethrog*].

Ma'aseh book. A collection of medieval stories and legends in early Judeo-German.

mafsíq (Hebr. "punctuating, ending"). Any strong disjunctive Masoretic accent.

maftir (from Hebr. *haftarah*, "dismissal"). The closing section of the Torah lesson; also the name given to the lay reader who is called up for the reading of that section, and then proceeds to read the Prophetic portion.

maḥzor (Hebr. "cycle"). The prayer-book containing the annual cycle of prayers for festivals, High Holy Days, and fast days. (Not for weekdays and the Sabbath.)

Makam (Arab. "place, standing place"). Any established pattern in Arabic poetry and music.

malkhuyót, zikhronót, shofarót (Hebr. "kingdoms, remembrances, *shofar* sounds"). The three central prayers of the New Year liturgy, consisting of scriptural *centos*, referring to the topics alluded to in the titles: God's kingdom, God's promises and faithfulness to them, God as supreme judge on the Day of Judgment.

Masorah (Hebr. "tradition"). The intensive grammatical, phonetic, and textual arrangement of the Hebrew Bible; it occupied many generations of Hebrew scholars from the fifth to the tenth centuries. The Masoretic text of the Bible is the generally accepted one.

maskil (from Hebr. *Haskalah*). One who participated in the *Haskalah* movement (see above); a Jew educated in the secular disciplines, generally a rationalist and frequently nonobservant.

meshorér (Hebr. "singer, poet"). The old designation for a vocal soloist, not necessarily of sacred music. Later it became the name of a paid chorister in the synagogue, or a member of a choral ensemble.

midrash (Hebr.). All post-biblical, rabbinical, and medieval explanations of the Bible, especially those of legendary or sententious exegesis.

minhag (Hebr. "custom"). A normative tradition in all its aspects (liturgy, pronunciation, customs, folklore, clothing, mores, etc.).

minḥah (Hebr. "gift"). Originally the name of a sacrifice in the Temple offered during the afternoon. In the Synagogue, the afternoon prayer.

Mishnah (Aram. "second law"). The six sections of the oral tradition of Jewish Law, as compiled under the aegis of R. Judah the Prince (ca. C.E. 200). The Mishnah forms the nucleus of all further discussions and expoundings of rabbinic literature (see "Gemara," "Talmud").

Missinai tunes ("Tunes from Mt. Sinai"). The collective designation of some of the oldest and most solemn melodies of the Ashkenazic synagogue; today, used only on the High Holy Days and the Three Festivals.

Mitzvah (Hebr. "commandment, privilege"). From its literal meaning of commandment, to the later significance of an ethically commendable act, the word traveled a long path characteristic of the development of Jewish ethics.

negináh (Hebr.). Melody.

nigguń (Hebr.). Melody, especially wordless tunes of the Hasidim.

Omer (Hebr.). The "counting" of the 49 days between Passover and Pentecost.

piyuť (Hebr. "poem"). A religious poem, with meter and sometimes rhyme, inserted into the fixed liturgy.

rébbe (Yiddish). The usual title of a hasidic rabbi.

Rosh Hashanáh (Hebr. "New Year"). The feast of the New Year, which occurs in September or early October.

sebaráh (Hebr. "argument, interpretation"). A talmudic term for a type of logical or deductive process of thought.

Séder ha-tefilláh (Hebr. "order of the prayer"). The prescribed and traditional framework of the liturgy for any specific day of the Jewish year.

Séfer (Hebr. "book"). In the narrower sense, a handwritten scroll of the Pentateuch (*Torah*).

seliḥáh (Hebr. "pardon"). A category of penitential prayers for God's forgiveness and mercy.

Shabuoť (Hebr. "weeks"). The festival celebrating the gift of the Torah at Mt. Sinai. Its name derives from its date, exactly seven weeks after Passover (a pentacontade).

shaḥarit (Hebr. "dawn, morning"). The morning prayer, mandatory for the observant Jew.

shébaḥ (Hebr. "praise"). The general term for all laudatory prayers.

she'eláh (Hebr. "question"). The formal statement of a controversial legal matter, coupled with the request for an authoritative rabbinical reply or legal opinion.

Shemá (Hebr. "hear!"). The first word of the Jewish profession of faith, *Shema Yisrael*, Hear, O Israel (Deut. 6:5). In rabbinic literature the term "*Shema*" stands for the prayers that surround the *Shema* as well.

shir (Hebr. "song, poem"). Corresponds to the Latin *carmen*, signifying both a poem and its chant. The scriptural *shirim* are the Canticles such as Moses' song at the Red Sea (Ex. 15) or the Song of Deborah (Judges 5), etc.

Shomeŕ Yisraél (Hebr. "guardian of Israel"). A *piyut* that begins with these words.

sidduŕ (Hebr. "ordered matter"). The traditional prayer book for weekdays and Sabbaths in contrast to *maḥzor*, the prayer book for festivals and High Holy Days.

sidrá (Aram. "portion, order"). Another name for the scriptural lesson, especially the lesson from the Pentateuch.

Siḥáh Bataláh (Hebr. "inane conversation"). The contemptuous rabbinic term for idle chatter during worship.

Sota (Aram. "adultery"). The title of a tractate of the Talmud.

Steíger (Yiddish). A loose and imprecise term in the professional language of hazanim, indicating a mode of prayer or its intonation.

Stollen (Germ.). A sort of rhymed couplet in medieval German poetry, usually indicating two lines or verses in a *Bar*.

tá'am (Hebr. "taste, reason, style, sign"). A term used in Hebrew grammar for any Masoretic accent, as in *ta'amei ha-mikra*.

ta'ameí ha-mikrá (Hebr. "signs of Scripture"). The usual name of the Masoretic accents of Hebrew Scripture.

Tágelied (Germ. "song of the day"). In medieval poetry, the farewell song of the knight when he must part with his lady at the dawn of day [Ital. *Alba*].

taḥanuń (Hebr. "for mercy"). The general term for all supplicatory prayers.

tal (Hebr. "dew"). The prayer for dew that is recited in solemn manner on Passover; thereafter, a short sentence is said in every service until Sukkoth (see *geshem*).

Talmud (Hebr. "study"). There are two forms: the Babylonian (abbr. B.) and the Palestinian or Jerusalemite (abbr. J. or Y.) texts. It consists of the Mishnah, the Gemara referring to it, and various commentaries and supercommentaries, which are compiled in large folio sets in stereotype fashion.

tefillah́ (Hebr. "prayer," pl. *tefillot*). The most general term for the spoken, written, or chanted liturgical (i.e., set and accepted) prayer. In a more particular sense, it refers to the *Amidah*.

tefillot́ kéva (Hebr. "fixed prayers"). The oldest obligatory prayers of Jewish worship. *Kaddish, Kedushah, Amidah, Shema, Barekhu*, and most of the *Shaharit* service belong to them, as opposed to the *piyutim*.

teshubah́ (Hebr. "reply, responsum"). The generic name for a rabbinic decision of a controversial question, or the answer to a *she'elah* (see above). Many *teshubot* have attained legal authority.

trop (from Lat. "*tropus*"). The western Ashkenazic name for scriptural cantillation; sometimes erroneously applied to the accents that indicate the course of the cantillation.

vidúi (Hebr. "Confession"). The collective and anonymous confession of sins of the individual as well as of the community.

Vógelfrei (Germ. "free as a bird"). The old legal term for outlaws.

Vórlage (Germ. "model, original version"). In the narrower sense the pristine form of a text or melody, from which all later versions are derived.

Yeshivah́ (Hebr.-Aram. "session, academy"). A rabbinic academy, wherein the Talmud and later rabbinical sources are the main course of study.

Yishtabáḥ (Hebr. "exalted!"). The opening word of an old prayer; thereafter, the name of the mode in which the prayer is traditionally chanted.

Yoḿ Kippuŕ (Hebr. "Day of Atonement"). The highest holy day of Judaism, a fast day, yet also the "Sabbath of Sabbaths," a day of collective repentance for all Jews.

yotzeŕ (Hebr. "creator"). A section of the daily morning service.

zemirot́ (from Hebr. *zemer*, "song"). The domestic Sabbath songs, chanted in the home by the family on Friday evenings, and on the Sabbath before and after meals.

Zohár ("splendor"). The title of the fundamental book of the *Cabala*. In its present form it originated in Spain during the thirteenth century.

Contents of Music Tables

Table VII. Ashkenazic Tunes Transmitted by B. Marcello

Table VIIIA

Table VIIIB. *Zemirot*

Table IX

Incipits of Tunes Quoted

Index of Names

General Index

5955638R0

Made in the USA
Lexington, KY
01 July 2010